Knowledge–Based Intelligent System Advancements:
Systemic and Cybernetic Approaches

Jerzy Jozefczyk
Wroclaw University of Technology, Poland

Donat Orski
Wroclaw University of Technology, Poland

INFORMATION SCIENCE REFERENCE

Hershey · New York

Director of Editorial Content:	Kristin Klinger
Director of Book Publications:	Julia Mosemann
Acquisitions Editor:	Lindsay Johnston
Development Editor:	Mike Killian
Publishing Assistant:	Casey Conapitski & Milan Vracarich Jr.
Typesetter:	Mike Brehm
Production Editor:	Jamie Snavely
Cover Design:	Lisa Tosheff

Published in the United States of America by
Information Science Reference (an imprint of IGI Global)
701 E. Chocolate Avenue
Hershey PA 17033
Tel: 717-533-8845
Fax: 717-533-8661
E-mail: cust@igi-global.com
Web site: http://www.igi-global.com

Library of Congress Cataloging-in-Publication Data

Knowledge-based intelligent system advancements : systemic and cybernetic approaches / Jerzy Jozefczyk and Donat Orski, editors.   p. cm.
  Includes bibliographical references and index. Summary: "This book presents selected new AI-based ideas and methods for analysis and decision making in intelligent information systems derived using systemic and cybernetic approaches"--Provided by publisher.   ISBN 978-1-61692-811-7 (hardcover) -- ISBN 978-1-61692-813-1 (ebook) 1. Expert systems (Computer science) I. Jozefczyk, Jerzy, 1956- II. Orski, Donat, 1971-
  QA76.76.E95K555445 2011
  006.3'3--dc22

British Cataloguing in Publication Data
A Cataloguing in Publication record for this book is available from the British Library.

All work contributed to this book is new, previously-unpublished material. The views expressed in this book are those of the authors, but not necessarily of the publisher.

Table of Contents

Section 1
Modeling

Section 2
Analysis

Section 3
Decision Making

Detailed Table of Contents

Section 1
Modeling

Systems are considered where not only knowledge but also information and measurement data are processed. The aspect of creating their models is highlighted. General tools and methods are used, in particular: estimation and identification. To cope with uncertainties, which are widely considered, stochastic and fuzzy sets based approaches are proposed.

Chapter 1

> *B. John Oommen, Carleton University, Canada & University of Agder, Norway*
> *Luis Rueda, University of Windsor, Canada*

A novel approach for modeling of time-varying systems is considered. More specifically, the estimation of the parameters of probability distributions is dealt with. A new method for on-line estimation is proposed and its convergence is proved. The applicability of the method to pattern recognition and data compression is examined.

Chapter 2

> *Pavel Kucera, Brno University of Technology, Czech Republic*

The problem of reliable measurements is addressed. Triple Modular Redundancy system based on analogue measurement channels is considered. The reliability models of different elements of the system are determined using the Markov processes, and their values are analytically calculated.

Complex systems identification problems are presented, i.e. identification with the use of limited measurement possibilities as well as global and multi-stage identification. The usefulness of the two-stage identification is shown for a specific biomedical system dealing with the rehabilitation of patients with muscle impairment relies.

A new framework for handling uncertain symbolic and numeric temporal information is presented. To manage the uncertainty, two models are employed based on probabilistic extensions of Temporal Constraint Satisfaction Problem framework and Interval Algebra approach.

A particular modeling problem is discussed. Namely, investigations concern a contour reconstruction via the curves interpolation with prospective applications to object recognition and image processing. The method of Hurwitz-Radon Matrices is proposed, its properties are explained, and the usefulness for object recognition is justified.

Chapter 6

Another concept of modeling with application to complex systems is proposed. The Takagi-Sugeno fuzzy model turned out convenient and useful for describing of a class of non-linear dynamical systems. Two real-word examples for the fault diagnosis as well as results of simulation illustrate the advantage of the proposed model.

Section 2
Analysis

General tools, both analytical and simulation, for analysis of economic, production, control, computer systems are applied. The systems of different nature are described using knowledge discovered from data, given by experts or created on the basis of scientific rules. Various cases of AI-based approaches are employed for analysis of knowledge-based systems, e.g.: learning, clustering, linguistic summaries, agent-based modeling, heuristic optimization methods.

Chapter 7

Tadeusz Baczko, Polish Academy of Sciences, Poland
Janusz Kacprzyk, Polish Academy of Sciences, Poland
Sławomir Zadrożny, Warsaw School of Information Technology, Poland

Non-standard data analysis technique is proposed which can support national innovation systems. Such a technique provides results of the data gathering in a form suitable for the important analysis goals. For this purpose, the linguistic summaries of data are shown to be promising data analysis tool.

Chapter 8

Aleksander Moczala, University of Bielsko-Biala, Poland

The problem of knowledge exchange in an inter-enterprise cooperation process design is presented, which aims at the increase of the innovation. An analysis of the cooperation process of enterprises and the usage of knowledge as the base for modeling and management make it possible to solve the problem and to elaborate new information systems for the cooperation aided production.

Chapter 9

Eleonora Riva Sanseverino, DIEET Università di Palermo, Italy
Gaetano Zizzo, DIEET Università di Palermo, Italy
Giuseppe Fileccia Scimemi, DISEG Università di Palermo, Italy

A case study consisting in an analysis of power dispatch in a power distribution system is investigated. Optimal dispatches are determined by means of original Genetic Algorithm and Ant Colony Optimization algorithms. The case study is preceded by the general introduction to multi-objective optimization and to the corresponding selected solution tools.

The concept of so called binding neuron with feedback is described as well as its statistical properties are analyzed. Such a neuron uses as one of its inputs the feedback and delayed output impulse. The binding neuron model can mimic the operating manner of a biological neuron.

A knowledge-based intelligent control system for a mobile robot is presented. The on-line learning, based on experts' demonstrations is applied. Real–world experiments showed the advantage of the proposed control system in comparison with the approach based on evolutionary algorithms.

Diverse clustering techniques are used to personalize an e–learning educational system according to individual students' needs. The clustering techniques are analyzed in detail. The considerations are illustrated by experiments conducted for different sets of real-world and simulation data of students' learning styles.

Different issues of industry competitiveness are investigated, using an agent-based model: redundancy in terms of organizational knowledge, comparison of the effects of environmental shock as well as opportunism perturbations. The results are discussed with respect to industry profitability and knowledge efficiency.

Section 3
Decision Making

Methodological and practical aspects of control problems, being constantly inherent issues of cybernetics, are mainly addressed. Their modern and up-to-date versions, namely, multivariable fuzzy control, adaptive control, and adaptive control combined with learning are discussed, the first two in comprehensive surveys. Real-world applications of knowledge-based intelligent systems for diagnosis and for control in one biomedical and in two technical systems, respectively are presented.

Chapter 14

Pedro Albertos, Universidad Politécnica de Valencia, Spain
Antonio Sala, Universidad Politécnica de Valencia, Spain
Mercedes Ramírez, Universidad de Oriente, Cuba

A survey of fuzzy control in multivariable cases, presenting both heuristic and the function-approximation approaches is given. A discussion on their main characteristics as well as a recapitulation of their crucial advantages and drawbacks are provided.

Chapter 15

Keith J. Burnham, Coventry University, UK
Ivan Zajic, Coventry University, UK
Jens G. Linden, Coventry University, UK

A concise technical overview of the most important developments in self-tuning control (STC) is presented. Based on the experiences of the authors in the industrial application of STC, extensions of the standard linear model-based approaches to encompass a class of bilinear model-based schemes, is proposed.

Chapter 16

Tadeusz Banek, Lublin University of Technology, Poland
Edward Kozłowski, Lublin University of Technology, Poland

A control problem of stochastic systems is considered where parameters in the systems' model are uncertain and are modeled by probability distributions. The trade-off between learning of systems' parameters values and optimization of the objective function is investigated. Resulting concept of an active learning is presented and then used for the determination of the optimal control algorithm.

Amine Chohra, Paris-East University, France
Nadia Kanaoui, Paris-East University, France
Véronique Amarger, Paris-East University, France
Kurosh Madani, Paris-East University, France

A concise overview of some methodological aspects of hybrid intelligent diagnosis systems for a large
variety of biomedical and technical applications is presented. Then, the biomedical case study is described dealing with Auditory Brainstem Response testing and designing.

Zenon Zwierzewicz, Szczecin Maritime University, Poland

The investigations are concerned with a specific adaptive ship control in the case of substantially limited knowledge of the ship's model. Two control problems, i.e. the ship course-keeping and the ship
path-following are considered as well as two solution methods are used as the base for the determination of control algorithms.

Sergiu Zaporojan, Technical University of Moldova, Republic of Moldova
Constantin Plotnic, Technical University of Moldova, Republic of Moldova
Igor Calmicov, Technical University of Moldova, Republic of Moldova
Vladimir Larin, Microfir Tehnologii Industriale Ltd, Republic of Moldova

The proposal of a knowledge-based intelligent system for a microwire casting process is presented, and
partial results are described. The most important elements of the system enable data acquisition from
the process and fuzzy control to stabilize the process' conditions based on operator's rules and on a
mathematical model of a molten drop.

Foreword

Norbert Wiener launched the idea of cybernetics, first at the Macy conferences in the early forties, then, in 1948, with his famous book *Cybernetics or Control and Communication in the Animal and the Machine* which contained also a chapter on societies. Ludwig von Bertalanffy's general theory of systems, which made its first appearance in German, under the name of *allgemeinen Systemlehre,* in the forties, became widely known in the fifties and mainly in 1968 with his *General System Theory,* later *general systems theory*, expressions which were often misunderstood, the adjective "general" having to do with "theory" and not with "system(s)". Less mathematically founded than Wiener's work or the theory of dynamical systems, it contains original and interesting views often inspired by biology. Concurrently, in parallel with cybernetics and systems, occurred the wide development of *informatics* and *artificial intelligence*.

Wiener was quite aware of the imprecision or uncertainty which affects every measurement and all types of knowledge. He was an infant prodigy, as his father wished him to be, and at the age of ten, he wrote a *Theory of Ignorance*, a very fundamental subject since ignorance is much more widespread than knowledge, always rare and uncertain. That is why his cybernetics gives a large place to probabilities, statistics and information, particularly when it deals with signals. Had he lived some years more, he would certainly have appreciated Lotfi Zadeh's concept of *fuzzy sets*.

This book, devoted to cybernetic and systemic approaches to knowledge-based intelligent systems, is founded mainly on communications at the *14th International Congress of Cybernetics and Systems* of the World Organisation of Systems and Cybernetics (Wroclaw 2008) completed by other contributions, on the same subjects, by renowned scientists. The nineteen chapters have been written sixty years after the publication of *Cybernetics* and forty years after that of *General System Theory*. During this period of about half a century, cybernetics and systems have evolved. It is interesting to observe in which directions they seem to move now, at least in the field of knowledge-based intelligent systems.

The most striking trait of these chapters is that, if knowledge, even when it is a mere measurement, the gathering of data or pattern recognition, is generally the main subject of interest, it is never considered as an absolute entity but only as a relative and limited item which is not given but which must be obtained, or learned, with more or less difficulty, not forgetting also the diagnosis of faults. So probabilistic thinking or fuzzy logic are very often present to take into account the uncertainty not only about signals entering a system but also concerning its very structure. But, knowledge is not uniquely concerned, resulting actions play also their part with fuzzy control or more generally decision making.

These observations seem to show a coherent general evolution towards what we could call the study of "cybernetic systems", not only robots but more generally systems, from artificial devices to conscious beings, able, metaphorically or not, to perceive, decide and act. This study is a generalisation of mere epistemology to what we may call *epistemo-praxiology,* a synthesis of knowledge and action to which cyberneticians and systemists contributed, even unconsciously, more than many philosophers.

Robert Vallée
Professeur émérite à l'Université Paris-Nord
President of the World Organisation of Systems and Cybernetics

Robert Vallée *was born in Poitiers, France, from parents professors. After graduating (1946) from "Ecole polytechnique" (Paris) and getting a doctorate in mathematics under the direction of André Lichnerowicz (Université de Paris), he taught in several universities : Ecole polytechnique, Université Paris I, Université Paris-Nord (Professor emeritus, 1987). He had many contacts with Norbert Wiener, mainly in 1954, while participating to the Foreign Students Summer Project of MIT. He devoted his researches mainly to cybernetics and systems science and published many articles on these subjects. After founding the "Cercle d'Études Cybernétiques" (1950) under the aegis of Louis de Broglie, he introduced the notion of "observation operator" in a series of notes to the "Académie des Sciences" and later the concept of "inverse transfer of structures" (1974). In 1995, he published "Cognition et système. Essai d'épistémo-praxéologie". One of his main interests is duration ("internal time" of a dynamical system, 1996). He assumed many other activities: member of the council of societies such as Société Mathématique de France, French Association for the Systems Sciences (AFSCET, Président d'honneur, 2009), World Organisation of Systems and Cybernetics (Director-General then President, 2003) ; member of the editorial board of journals such as Kybernetes, Revue Internationale de Systémique (Rédacteur en chef) , Cybernetics and Human Knowing. His action and researches deserved him awards and medals in particular the Norbert Wiener Memorial Gold Medal (1990) and doctorate honoris causa of Universitatea din Petrosani (Romania, 1999).*

Preface

Since the first part of the twentieth century, cybernetics and systems research have been developed as scientific disciplines. Investigations, launched in the area of cybernetics, previously dealt with control and information processing. In a more narrow sense, they consisted in the consideration of analogies of the control and the information processing between life beings and systems of different nature, e.g. technical, economic, social as well as of activities requiring traditionally understood intelligence. Nowadays, a notion 'cybernetics' is used more and more rarely, but the corresponding research is continued and developed, e.g. in the framework of artificial intelligence, intelligent computing, control theory. The cybernetics as an interdisciplinary scientific and research discipline is strongly connected with systems studies dealing, among others, with methodological and applied problems of analysis and decision making (synthesis) for systems of different nature. From many known systems theories, only mathematical systems and their applications are addressed in this book. Other aspects of systems-based research are not considered.

Systems research in the area distinguished provides scientists from different disciplines with useful tools for solving analysis and decision making problems. On the other hand, the development of computer science technology enables researchers and practitioners to computerize and to automate more and more effectively such man's activities as reasoning, understanding, learning, perception. It leads to the advancement of intelligent systems which now are intensively developed and investigated as a vital scientific discipline. It seems that nowadays knowledge – understood, roughly speaking, as facts, principles and the ability of reasoning on their basis – is an indispensable element of any intelligent system.

Taking into account mentioned methodological tools developed in systems research, it is interesting and useful to apply them also for intelligent systems. In particular, these tools concern modeling and identification of systems, analysis and simulation of systems as well as decision making for systems of different nature, e.g. control, diagnosis, pattern recognition, clustering.

The following well recognized general topics are represented in chapters collected and presented in this volume: complex systems, control theory and engineering, cybernetics and economy, fuzzy systems, information and communication systems, systems modeling, control, management and decision making. Particular specific investigations presented in any chapter refer to one or more system-based tools. On the other hand, knowledge, information or data are used in different aspects as well as existing artificial intelligence-based facets are highlighted in the problems considered.

A considerable part of the book is based on original presentations delivered during the 14th International Congress of Cybernetics and Systems of World Organisation of Systems and Cybernetics (WOSC) which was held in Wroclaw, Poland in September 2008. These chapters encompass updated and substantially extended results of previously conducted studies as well as of fruitful discussions during the Congress.

Other chapters, brought by known researchers, joined this group and make it possible to have as the result a valuable collection of works pertaining not only to important methodological issues on intelligent systems but also to applications in medical, economic, and technical systems. From all submissions, nineteen most adequate chapters have been selected and included into this book. The chapters have been divided into three sections, namely: Modeling, Analysis and Decision Making.

The **first section** comprises six chapters in which systems are considered where not only knowledge but also information and measurement data are processed. The aspect of creating their models is highlighted. General tools and methods are used, in particular: estimation and identification. To cope with uncertainties, which are considered, stochastic and fuzzy sets based approaches are proposed.

The **first chapter** by B. J. Oommen and L. Rueda aims to consider modeling of time-varying systems using knowledge-based and intelligent approaches. Authors concentrate on using new estimation methods which are based on the principles of stochastic learning and are referred to as the Stochastic Learning Weak Estimators (SLWE). The chapter reports conclusive results that demonstarte the superiority of the SLWE methods in two applications: pattern recognition (PR) and data compression. The application in PR involves artificial data and real-life news reports from the Canadian Broadcasting Corporation (CBC). For data compression, the underlying distribution of the files being compressed is modeled as being non-stationary. The advantage of the SLWE in both these cases is demonstrated.

P. Kucera presents in the **second chapter** an applicable reliability model of the TMR (Triple Modular Redundancy) system, based on analogue measurement channels, which has been still missing unlike the model of the standard TMR system based on digital channels. The description of analogue measurement channel's structure is followed by the presentation of the reliability model of the wiring system. The standard TMR model is presented and its reliability model is also given. An analogue TMR measurement channel system is introduced and its reliability model based on Markov processes is presented. Then the reliability model of the communication channel is described. The analytical calculation of model's reliability and the presentation of a simple numerical example complete the chapter.

The **third chapter** by K. Brzostowski, J. Drapała and J. Świątek focuses on selected parametric problems of a complex systems identification. Problems of the identification with limited measurement possibilities as well as global and multi-stage identification are explained in detail. The usefulness of the two-stage identification is shown for a specific biomedical system dealing with the rehabilitation of patients with muscle impairment relies. To manage this problem, an adaptive decision making system based on the two-stage identification is applied with an additional knowledge given by a physician. The fuzzy and neuro-fuzzy approaches are employed for knowledge representation. The pattern recognition algorithm as well as the learning procedure supplement the decision making system. The results of simulation experiments using real-world data complete the chapter.

In the **fourth chapter** by M. Mouhoub and J. Liu, a new framework for handling uncertain symbolic and numeric temporal information is presented. To manage the uncertainty, two models are employed based on probabilistic extensions of Temporal Constraint Satisfaction Problem (TCSP) framework and Interval Algebra (IA) approach. In a probabilistic CSP, each constraint is given a probability of its existence. In the consequence, there is more than one CSP to solve unlike the traditional CSP. A branch and bound algorithm along with a constraint propagation are proposed to determine the solution (model) of the highest probability. An experimental study conducted on randomly generated temporal problems demonstrates the efficiency in time of the algorithm. The considerations are supplemented by several examples illustrating main topics.

Foundations of computer vision, image processing and machine vision, the important topics of knowledge-based intelligent sytems are addressed by D. Jakóbczak in the **fifth chapter**. The classical problem in these areas is that of determining an object via characteristic features. The important feature of the object is its contour. The accurate reconstruction of contour points leads to the possibility to compare the unknown object with models of specified objects. The chapter deals with a new method of contour reconstruction via the curves interpolation. First, the contour points of the object to be recognized are computed. Then, one compares models of known objects, given by the sets of contour points, with co-ordinates of interpolated points of an unknown object. The contour points reconstruction and the curve interpolation is possible using a new method of Hurwitz-Radon Matrices.

M. Pokorný and P. Fojtík consider in the **sixth chapter** fuzzy modeling of non-linear dynamic systems applicable for the fault diagnosis. Takagi-Sugeno fuzzy model is used with the decomposition of the non-linear dynamic system into the number of linear sub-models, so that it is possible to overcome difficulties in conventional methods for dealing with nonlinearity. A linear residual generator formed by Kalman filters which are designed for each linear subsystem is then proposed to create diagnostic signals (residuals). Since the task is formulated on a statistical basis, the diagnosis uses a generalized likelihood ratio test. Two real-world examples are presented to demonstrate the applicability of the approach proposed.

General, both analytical and simulation, tools for analysis of economic, production, control or computer systems are discussed in the **second section**. The systems of different nature are described using knowledge discovered from data, given by experts or created on the basis of scientific rules. Various cases of AI-based approaches are employed for the analysis of knowledge-based systems, e.g.: learning, clustering, linguistic summaries, agent-based modeling, heuristic optimization.

Baczko, Kacprzyk and Zadrożny report in the **seventh chapter** a successful attempt to apply the AI based knowledge discovery from data for the innovativeness evaluation of enterprises, being a crucial aspect for the development of a national economy. Proper functioning of a national innovation system requires a lot of information to be gathered and then analysed. In this chapter the pioneering system for the evaluation based on integrated indicators constructed for individual enterprises in Poland is described. An evaluation methodology has been developed, incorporating both quantitative and qualitative characteristics of the enterprises. The linguistic summaries of data are shown to be a promising data analysis tool. These summaries make it possible to grasp the essence of the collected data and communicate it in an intuitive, natural language like form.

The problem of knowledge exchange in the inter-enterprise cooperation process design is presented in the **eighth chapter** by A. Moczala. The development of an innovative character of an enterprise requires facilitating of initialization, creation, and extension of cooperative links among enterprises. The collaborative design process gathers enterprises which have to achieve a common objective with respect to a new product, i.e. the innovation by knowledge sharing. The development of methods and algorithms of knowledge exchange in such a cooperation enables the elaboration of computer aided systems for the production cooperation which is outlined. The analysis of the cooperation process among enterprises is also shown.

A case study comprising an analysis of power dispatch in a power distribution system is investigated by E. R. Sanseverino, G. Zizzo and G. F. Scimemi in the **ninth chapter**. The problem is formulated for small connected distribution sub-systems called 'microgrids'. To evaluate costs, power losses and voltage deviations in the system, the corresponding multi-objective optimization problem is stated with knowledge about the complex system in the form of mathematical models. The authors use two heuristics to solve the problem, i.e.: their own version of non-dominated Genetic Algorithm, originally determined earlier, and Ant Colony Optimization algorithm being the novel proposition. The case study and its analysis are preceded by a general introduction to multi-objective optimization and to the corresponding selected solution tools.

The analysis of binding neuron output firing statistics is considered by A. Vidybida and K. Kravchuk in the **tenth chapter**. Such a neuron uses as one of its inputs the feedback and delayed output impulse which allows to mimic the operating manner of a biological neuron. The neuron is driven externally by the Poisson stream. The influence of the feedback, which conveys every output impulse to the input with time delay, on the statistics of neuron's output spikes is considered. The distributions found for the case of instantaneous feedback include jumps and derivative discontinuities and differ essentially from those obtained for BN without feedback. The statistics of a neuron with delayed feedback has remarkable peculiarities as compared to the case without delay. It is concluded that delayed feedback presence can radically alter the neuronal output firing statistics.

G. Narvydas, V. Raudonis and R. Simutis provide us in the **eleventh chapter** with the practical application of a knowledge-based intelligent control system for a mobile robot. The main idea of the chapter is to show that, while creating intelligent control systems for autonomous mobile robots, it is the most important to transfer as much as possible human knowledge and human expert-operator skills into the intelligent control system. The successful transfer ensures good results. One of the most advanced techniques in robotics is an autonomous mobile robot on-line learning from the experts' demonstrations, which is briefly described in this chapter. The results of experiments are also presented in which a mobile robot Khepera II is used.

An intelligent e-learning system tailored to different students' needs is described by D. Zakrzewska in the **twelfth chapter**. The individual requirements of learners may depend on their characteristic traits such as dominant learning styles. Finding groups of students with similar preferences can help when systems are being adjusted for individual requirements. The performance of personalized educational systems is dependant upon the number and the quality of student clusters obtained. The application of clustering techniques for grouping students according to their learning style preferences is considered. Such groups are evaluated by disparate validation criteria and the usage of different validation techniques is discussed. Experiments were conducted for different sets of real-world and artificially generated data of students' learning styles.

The role of efficiency for firms' competitiveness in the context of an agent-based modeling and a knowledge redundancy is discussed by L. Biggiero in the **thirteenth chapter**. Through an agent-based model of industry competitiveness based on suppliers' quality, the chapter tests four groups of hypotheses. It innovates current literature in two ways: firstly, it considers redundancy in terms of organizational knowledge. Secondly, it compares the effects of two forms of perturbations: environmental shock and opportunism. The results show that these two forms impact differently on industry profitability, and that knowledge redundancy can compensate the effects of environmental shocks but not of opportunism. Moreover, it demonstrates that, as agents exchange more information, knowledge efficiency declines.

Methodological and practical aspects of control problems, being constantly inherent issues of cybernetics, are mainly addressed in the **third section**. Their modern and up-to-date versions, namely, multivariable fuzzy control, adaptive control, and adaptive control combined with learning are discussed, the first two in comprehensive surveys. Real-world applications of knowledge-based intelligent systems for diagnosis and for control in one biomedical and in two technical systems, respectively are presented.

P. Albertos, A. Sala and M. Ramírez describe in the **fourteenth chapter** the state of the art of fuzzy-logic control with application to multi-input/multi-output systems. The basic steps in designing of such control systems are given. Two approaches of the fuzzy control are presented. The idea of the first, heuristic approach consists in compiling a set of rules provided by human experts in order to control a complex plant. The application of the second, function-approximation approach to modeling and control is then introduced together with the description of some universal approximation ideas and the popular Takagi-Sugeno approach to modeling of non-linear systems, including fuzzy polynomial ones. The summarization of main advantages and drawbacks of both approaches complete the chapter.

The **fifteenth chapter** by K. J. Burnham, I. Zajic and J. G. Linden starts also with the review of crucial developments in self-tuning control (STC). The notion of two coupled sub-algorithms forming the basis of STC together with enhancements to produce adaptive on-line procedures are discussed. The techniques covered include optimal minimum variance, sub-optimal pole-placement and long range model-based predictive control. Based on the experiences of the authors in the industrial application of STC, extensions of the standard linear model-based approaches to encompass a class of bilinear model-based schemes, are proposed. Some on-going developments and future research directions in STC for bilinear systems are highlighted. These include the requirements for combined algorithms for control and fault diagnosis and the need for models of differing complexities.

The idea of adaptive control is considered also by T. Banek and E. Kozłowski in the **sixteenth chapter**. It is used for the determination of an optimal control algorithm for the case where the knowledge representation of the uncertain system's parameters is given in the form of probability distributions. A general approach to self-learning based on ideas of adaptive control is presented to cope with the uncertainty. The trade-off between learning of systems' parameters values and optimization of the objective function is investigated. The conditions of optimality for the general stochastic adaptive control problem along with the resulting algorithm are presented. By using analytical results and numerical simulations, it is shown how control actions depend on a priori knowledge about a system.

A fault diagnosis and its application to diagnostic decision-making systems are dealt with by A. Chohra, N. Kanaoui, V. Amarger and K. Madani in the **seventeenth chapter**. A reader is provided with a short overview of some methodological aspects of hybrid intelligent diagnosis systems for a large variety of biomedical and technical applications. Firstly, main diagnosis tasks for such applications are presented. Then, the description of fault diagnosis systems is followed by the presentation of the design procedure of hybrid intelligent diagnosis systems. Then, the suggested approach is developed for a computer aided diagnosis in the biomedical system. Auditory Brainstem Response test is investigated, and the corresponding prototype design and experimental results are presented.

The practical oriented considerations are again comprised in the **eighteenth chapter** by Z. Zwierzewicz, which are concerned with a problem of adaptive ship control in the case of limited knowledge of the ship's model. Two tasks of ship control are considered: the ship course-keeping and the path-following. Two different approaches to the control synthesis problem are proposed. The first one is based on adaptive feedback linearization technique, while the second one refers to the backstepping method where the tuning of unknown parameters is also taken into account. It has been demonstrated that the thereby determined controllers enable on-line learning of unknown model characteristics, having at the same time the performance comparable to the one obtained for the case of fully known model parameters.

In the last, **nineteenth chapter** by S. Zaporojan, C. Plotnic, I. Calmicov and V. Larin a real-world application-based decision-making problem is addressed. Preliminary results of an applied research project concerning the development of an intelligent plant for microwire casting are given. To maintain the important characteristics of the casting process, the knowledge-based decision-making system is proposed which consists of a sub-system of data acquisition from the process and a fuzzy-logic controller based on the knowledge representation given by a human operator and a mathematical model of a molten drop's shape. A hardware implementation of the decision-making system considered, in particular of the control system, is also proposed.

Each chapter of this book is self contained. We are convinced that the book as a whole and any of its part can be useful for researchers and students in the field of knowledge-based systems and intelligent systems of different nature, in particular in the area of computer, information and control systems.

Jerzy Jozefczyk
Wroclaw University of Technology, Poland

Donat Orski
Wroclaw University of Technology, Poland

December 2009

Acknowledgment

The Editors wish to acknowledge the contributions of all Authors who elaborated and presented in their chapters valuable scientific and research results. We are also indebted to all reviewers for their competence, professionalism and diligence demonstrated during the review process. They have made a significant contribution to the final version of this book. Thanks are also due to all members of IGI Global team involved in the preparation of this book for their consistent support.

Jerzy Jozefczyk
Wroclaw University of Technology, Poland

Donat Orski
Wroclaw University of Technology, Poland

Section 1
Modeling

Chapter 1
Stochastic Learning-Based Weak Estimation and its Applications

B. John Oommen
Carleton University, Canada & University of Agder, Norway

Luis Rueda
University of Windsor, Canada

ABSTRACT

Although the field of Artificial Intelligence (AI) has been researched for more than five decades, researchers, scientists and practitioners are constantly seeking superior methods that are applicable for increasingly difficult problems. In this chapter, our aim is to consider knowledge-based novel and intelligent cybernetic approaches for problems in which the environment (or medium) is time-varying. While problems of this sort can be approached from various perspectives, including those that appropriately model the time-varying nature of the environment, in this chapter, we shall concentrate on using new estimation or "training" methods. The new methods that we propose are based on the principles of stochastic learning, and are referred to as the Stochastic Learning Weak Estimators (SLWE). An empirical analysis on synthetic data shows the advantages of the scheme for non-stationary distributions, which is where we claim to advance the state-of-the-art. We also examine how these new methods can be applicable to learning and intelligent systems, and to Pattern Recognition (PR). The chapter briefly reports conclusive results that demonstrate the superiority of the SLWE in two applications, namely in PR and data compression. The application in PR involves artificial data and real-life news reports from the Canadian Broadcasting Corporation (CBC). We also demonstrate its applicabilty in data compression, where the underlying distribution of the files being compressed is, again, modeled as being non-stationary. The superiority of the SLWE in both these cases is demonstrated.

DOI: 10.4018/978-1-61692-811-7.ch001

INTRODUCTION

Artificial Intelligence (AI) is the sub-field of computer science that deals with the intelligent behaviour of machines. Researchers who work in AI attempt to create intelligent machines or design algorithms that will help the machine make intelligent decisions. Although the field of AI has matured over the last five decades, researchers, scientists and practitioners are expanding their horizons by seeking superior methods, namely for those applicable for increasingly difficult problems. In this chapter, our aim is to consider knowledge-based novel and intelligent cybernetic approaches for problems in which the environment (or medium) is time-varying. To achieve this, in the larger context of this book, our chapter deals with enhancing AI by techniques generally used within the overall field of "Cybernetics".

The Webster's dictionary defines "Cybernetics" as "the science of communication and control theory that is concerned especially with the comparative study of automatic control systems (as the nervous system, the brain and mechanical-electrical communication systems)". The word "Cybernetics" itself has its etymological origins in the Greek root *kybernan* meaning "to steer" or "to govern". Typically, as explained in the *Encyclopaedia Britannica*, "Cybernetics is associated with models in which a monitor compares what is happening to a system at various sampling times with some standard of what should be happening, and a controller adjusts the system's behaviour accordingly". Modern cybernetics is an interdisciplinary field, which philosophically encompasses an ensemble of areas including neuroscience, computer science, cognition, control systems and electrical networks. In this context, we mention that a fundamental tool used in cybernetics is the so-called Learning Automaton (LA). The aim of this chapter is to show how we can use LA-based estimation methods to investigate, model and solve

problems which are inherently difficult because they are, as mentioned, time-varying.

What is a "Learning Automaton"? What is "Learning" all about? How are LA related to the general field of "Cybernetics"? The linguistic meaning of "automaton" is "a self-operating machine or a mechanism that responds to a sequence of instructions in a certain way, so as to achieve a certain goal. The automaton either responds to a pre-determined set of rules, or adapts to the environmental dynamics in which it operates. The latter types of automata are pertinent to tools used in this chapter, and are termed as "adaptive automata". The term "learning" in Psychology means the act of acquiring knowledge and modifying one's behavior based on the experience gained. Thus, in our case, the adaptive automata we study in this chapter, adapts to the responses from the Environment through a series of interactions with it. It then attempts to learn the best action from a set of possible actions that are offered to it by the random Environment in which it operates. The Automaton, thus, acts as a decision maker to arrive at the best action.

Every statistical problem involves a fundamental issue, namely that of estimation. Since the problem involves random variables, decisions or predictions related to the problem are in some way dependent on the practitioner obtaining reliable estimates on the parameters that characterize the underlying random variable. These estimates are computed from the observations of the random variable itself. Thus, if a problem can be modeled using a random variable which is normally (Gaussian) distributed, the underlying statistical problem involves estimating the mean and the variance. Put in a nut-shell, *in this chapter, we shall review a new family of estimation methods that are based on the primitive cybernetic tool, the LA. Further, we shall demonstrate that these estimates are powerful when the medium or environment is non-stationary.* We shall also demonstrate its applicability in two real-life application domains.

BACKGROUND

The theory of estimation has been studied for hundreds of years (Bickel & Doksum, 2000 ; Casella & Berger, 2001 ; Jones, Garthwaite, & Jolliffe, 2002). Besides, the learning (training) phase of a statistical PR system is, indeed, based on estimation theory (Duda, Hart, & Stork, 2000, Ch.3; Theodoridis & Koutroumbas, 2006, pp. 28-34; Herbrich, 2001, pp.107; Webb, 2002, pp. 40-76). Estimation methods generally fall into various categories, including the Maximum Likelihood Estimates (MLE) and the Bayesian family of estimates (Bickel & Doksum, 2000, Ch.2; Casella & Berger, 2001, pp. 315-325; Duda, Hart & Stork, 2000, Ch.3; Theodoridis & Koutroumbas, 2006, pp. 28-34).

The MLE and Bayesian estimates are well-known for having good computational and statistical properties. However, the fundamental premise for assessing the quality of estimates is based on the assumption that the parameter being estimated does not change with time. In other words, the distribution is assumed to be *stationary*. Thus, it is generally assumed that there is an underlying parameter θ, *which does not change with time*, and as the number of samples increases, we would like the estimate $\hat{\theta}$ to converge to θ with probability one, or in a mean square sense.

Consider, however, the scenario when the parameter θ changes with time. Thus, for example, let us suppose that the Bernoulli trials leading to the binomially distributed random variable were done in a time-varying manner, where the parameter "switched" periodically (or gradually changed) to, possibly, a new random value. As opposed to the traditional MLE and Bayesian estimators, in this case, our new estimators can be shown to converge to the true value fairly quickly, and just as quickly *"unlearn"* what they have learned so as to adapt to the new, "switched" environment. As we shall see presently, the analytic results proven in this chapter, for the accuracy of convergence

and the rate of convergence, are also empirically valid for the case when the data possesses a high level of non-stationarity.

Traditional Methods for Non-Stationary Environments

The traditional strategy to deal with non-stationary environments has been one of using a *sliding window* (Jang, 2000). The problem with such a "sliding window" scheme for estimation is that the width of the window is crucial. If the width is too "small", the estimates are necessarily poor. On the other hand, if the window is "large", the estimates *prior* to the change of the parameters influence the new estimates significantly. Also, the observations during the entire sliding window must be retained and updated during the entire process. Thus, if the window concerns the observations of the most recent 50 time units, these observations are used in obtaining the current estimate. But when the next sample is observed, the least recent observation must be deleted, and the current observation must take its place. Although a comparison of our new estimation strategy with some of the other "non-sliding-window" approaches is currently under way, it is appropriate to mention that we have shown that if one attempts to *detect* the point where the parameter has switched, the accuracy of the detection using these newly-reported estimators is superior to the detection using a window-based methodology.

Apart from the sliding window approach, many other methods have been proposed, which deal with the problem of detecting change points during estimation (Krishnaiah & Miao, 1988), including the Bayesian method for point detection in stochastic processes (Ray & Tsay, 2002), and the sequential change-point detection and estimation method (based on approximations from large samples and the null hypothesis) (Gombay, 2003). Another method has been recently proposed in (Baron & Grannot, 2003), which deals with the problem of detecting early and frequent changes in the parameters of the distributions. An approach that is related to our work is that of estimating the log-normal multivariate distribution in non-stationary environments (Ho, Stapleton, & Subrahmanyam, 1995). In all brevity, we state that these methods are quite different from the scheme that we propose. First of all, unlike the work of (Ray & Tsay, 2002), our method does not require the assumption of any prior distributions for the parameters. Our method is also different from the work of (Gombay, 2003), because it does not infer the change in the parameter by invoking a hypothesis testing strategy. Neither does our method implicitly assume the large sample approximations of the index used to infer the change, (which in their case is the score vector). Finally, this work is quite distinct from the techniques proposed in (Krishnaiah & Miao, 1988) because it does not invoke any likelihood ratio tests or cusum tests. More importantly, the main and fundamental difference that our method has over all the other reported schemes is the fact that our updating scheme is not additive, but *multiplicative*. Based on the actual event that has occurred at any particular time instant, our estimation procedure multiplies the current estimate of the parameter with a multiplying constant, and thus this multiplication operation is *random*.

Rationale for the Chapter and its Contributions

There are a few problems that we have recently encountered, where strong estimators pose a real-life concern. One scenario occurs in pattern classification involving moving scenes. The same situation is also encountered when one attempts the adaptive encoding of files which are interspersed with text, formulae, images and tables. Similarly, if we are dealing with adaptive data structures, the structure changes based on the information about the underlying data distribution, which is given by the estimator. Thus, if the estimator used is "strong" (i.e., it converges w. p. 1), it is unlikely

that the learned data structure will change from a structure that it has converged to. Indeed, we can conclusively demonstrate that it is sub-optimal to work with strong estimators in such application domains, i.e., when the data is truly *non-stationary*.

In this chapter, we shall present the "weak" estimators, referred to as the Stochastic Learning Weak Estimators (SLWE), which are developed by using the principles of stochastic learning and LA. In this context, we mention that we use the term "weak" convergence when the random variable converges with regard to the first and second moments. We do believe that in the case of the random variables currently under consideration, they also converge with regard to *all* their moments, but this is currently unproven.

In essence, the estimate is updated at each time instant based on the value of the current sample. However, as alluded to earlier, this updating is not achieved using an *additive* updating rule, but rather by a *multiplicative* rule, akin to the family of linear action-probability updating schemes (Narendra & Thathachar, 1989; Norris, 1999). The formal results that we have obtained for the binomial distribution are quite encouraging. To render the explanation simple, let us assume that the learning updating rule has a user-defined coefficient, λ. We show that our new estimator converges weakly, and that this convergence is *independent of the value of* λ. Amazingly enough, the speed of the latter only depends on the same parameter, λ, which turns out to be the *only* non-unity eigenvalue of the underlying stochastic matrix that determines the time-dependence of the estimates. Additionally, the variance of the estimate is also controlled by the *same* coefficient, λ. Similar results are true for the multinomial case, except that the equations transform from being of a scalar type to be of a vector type. Additional details of the methods discussed in this chapter can be found in (Oommen & Rueda, 2006; Rueda & Oommen, 2006). The use of a non-linear updating rule for obtaining weak estimators, applicable for data compression, is also briefly alluded to.

Weak Estimators for Binomial Distributions

Through out this chapter we assume that we are estimating the parameters of a binomial/multinomial distribution. The binomial distribution is characterized by two parameters, namely, the *number* of Bernoulli trials, and the parameter characterizing *each* Bernoulli trial. In this regard, we assume that the number of observations is the number of trials. The aim is, thus, to estimate the *Bernoulli* parameter for each trial, which is achieved here by using stochastic learning methods.

Let X be a binomially distributed random variable, which takes on the value of either '1' or '2', where we depart from the traditional notation of the random variable taking values of '0' and '1', so that the notation is consistent when we consider the multinomial case. We assume that X obeys the distribution S, where $S = [s_1, s_2]^T$. In other words,

$$\begin{aligned} X &= \text{'1' with probability } s_1 \\ &= \text{'2' with probability } s_2, \end{aligned}$$

where,

$$s_1 + s_2 = 1.$$

Let $x(n)$ be a concrete realization of X at time 'n'. The intention of the exercise is to estimate S, i.e., s_i for $i = 1, 2$. We achieve this by maintaining a running estimate $P(n) = [p_1(n), p_2(n)]^T$ of S, where $p_i(n)$ is the estimate of s_i at time 'n', for $i = 1, 2$.

Consider a user-defined parameter, λ, which can vary between 0 and 1 (i.e., $0 < \lambda < 1$), meaning that a value close to 0 implies a slower con-

vergence, while a value close to 1 implicates a more rapid convergence. A t ypical value of λ that works very well for many practical applications is very close to 1 (e.g., 0.99). Then, the value of $p_1(n)$ is updated as per the following simple rule:

$$p_1(n+1) = \begin{cases} \lambda p_1(n) & \text{if } x(n) = 2, \\ 1 - \lambda p_2(n) & \text{if } x(n) = 1. \end{cases}$$

$$(1)$$

where $p_2(n+1) = 1 - p_1(n+1)$. The reader will observe that this rule is analogous to the cybernetic primitive LA, the L_{RI} updating scheme. Also, in the interest of simplicity, we omit the index n, whenever there is no confusion, and thus, in such cases, we use P and $P(n)$ interchangeably.

We shall show that the mean of P, obtained as per as per (1), converges exactly to S.

Theorem 1: *Let X be a binomially distributed random variable, and $P(n)$ be the estimate of S at time 'n'. Then, $E[P(\infty)] = S$.*

Proof. Based on the updating scheme specified by (1), the conditional expected value of $p_1(n+1)$ given P can be seen to be:

$$E[p_1(n+1) \mid P] = \lambda s_2 p_1 + s_1 - \lambda s_1 + \lambda s_1 p_1$$

$$(2)$$

$$= (1 - \lambda)s_1 + \lambda p_1(s_1 + s_2) \tag{3}$$

$$= (1 - \lambda)s_1 + \lambda p_1. \tag{4}$$

Taking expectations a second time, we can write (4) as:

$$E[p_1(n+1)] = (1 - \lambda)s_1 + \lambda E[p_1(n)]. \tag{5}$$

As $n \to \infty$, $E[p_1(n)]$ converges to a limit because the coefficient of the linear difference equation is λ, with $0 < \lambda < 1$. Futhermore, if it converges to $E\left[p_1(\infty)\right]$, we can solve for $E\left[p_1(\infty)\right]$ from (5), and thus:

$$E[p_1(\infty)](1 - \lambda) = (1 - \lambda)s_1, \qquad (6)$$

implying that $E\left[p_1(\infty)\right] = s_1$. Similarly, $E\left[p_2(\infty)\right] = s_2$, and the result follows. ▪

The next results which we shall prove indicates that $E\left[P(n+1)\right]$ is related to $E\left[P(n)\right]$ by means of a stochastic matrix. We derive the explicit stochastic dependence, and allude to the resultant properties by virtue of the stochastic nature of the matrix. This leads us to two results, namely that of the mean of the limiting distribution of the vector $P(n)$, and that which concerns its rate of convergence. It turns out that while the former is independent of the learning parameter, λ, the latter is determined *only* by λ. The reader will observe that the results we have derived are asymptotic. In other words, the mean of $P(n)$ is shown to converge exactly to the mean of S. The implications of the "asymptotic" nature of the results will be clarified presently.

Theorem 2:*If the components of $P(n+1)$ are obtained from the components of $P(n)$ as per (1), $E\left[P(n+1)\right] = \mathbf{M}^T E\left[P(n)\right]$, where $\mathbf{M}$ is a stochastic matrix. Thus, the limiting value of the expectation of $P(.)$ converges to S, and the rate of convergence of P to S is fully determined by λ.*

Proof. Consider (5). Since $p_1 + p_2 = 1$, we can write:

$$E\left[p_1(n+1) \mid P\right] = (1 - \lambda)s_1(p_1 + p_2) + \lambda E\left[p_1(n)\right] \qquad (7)$$

$$E\left[p_2(n+1) \mid P\right] = (1 - \lambda)s_2(p_1 + p_2) + \lambda E\left[p_2(n)\right]. \qquad (8)$$

Substituting the above equalities, simplifying and taking expectations again leads to the following vectorial form:

$$E\left[P(n+1)\right] = \mathbf{M}^T E\left[P(n)\right], \qquad (9)$$

where

$$\mathbf{M} = \begin{bmatrix} (1 - \lambda)s_1 + \lambda & (1 - \lambda)s_2 \\ (1 - \lambda)s_1 & (1 - \lambda)s_2 + \lambda \end{bmatrix}$$
$$= (1 - \lambda)\begin{bmatrix} s_1 & s_2 \\ s_1 & s_2 \end{bmatrix} + \lambda \mathbf{I}, \qquad (10)$$

is a stochastic matrix. Since, as $n \to \infty$, both $E\left[P(n+1)\right]$ and $E\left[P(n)\right]$ converge to $E\left[P(\infty)\right]$, it follows that:

$$E\left[P(\infty)\right] = \mathbf{M}^T E\left[P(\infty)\right]. \qquad (11)$$

Using (10), we now show that:

$$E\left[P(\infty)\right] = S, \qquad (12)$$

as follows:

$$E\left[p_1(\infty)\right] = (1 - \lambda)s_1 \left\{ E\left[p_1(\infty)\right] + E\left[p_2(\infty)\right] \right\} + \lambda E\left[p_1(\infty)\right] \qquad (13)$$

$$= (1 - \lambda)s_1 + \lambda E\left[p_1(\infty)\right] \qquad (14)$$

$$\Rightarrow E\left[p_1(\infty)\right](1 - \lambda) = s_1(1 - \lambda). \qquad (15)$$

which implies that

$$E\left[p_1(\infty)\right] = s_1.$$

An exact parallel argument leads to the result that

$$E\left[p_2(\infty)\right] = s_2,$$

whence the first result of the theorem is proven. Observing that $\left(\mathbf{M} - \lambda\mathbf{I}\right)$ has the common factor $(1 - \lambda)$, it follows that the convergence of P to S, which is determined by the eigenvalues of is $\mathbf{M}$, is *fully determined* by λ. The theorem thus follows.

From the analysis given above, we can derive the explicit expression for the asymptotic variance of the SLWE. We show that a small value of λ leads to fast convergence and a large variance. As opposed to this, a large value of λ implies slow convergence and a small variance.

Theorem 3: *Let X* be a binomially distributed random variable governed by the distribution S, and $P(n)$ be the estimate of S at time 'n' obtained by (1). *Then, the algebraic expression for the variance of* $P(\infty)$ *is fully determined by* λ.

Proof. Using the same notation as above, the square of p_1 at time '$n + 1$' is given by:

$$p_1^2(n + 1) = \lambda^2 p_1^2 \qquad w.p.\, s_2 \tag{16}$$

$$= 1 - 2\lambda(1 - p_1) + \lambda^2(1 - p_1)^2 \qquad w.p.\, s_1 \tag{17}$$

$$= 1 - 2\lambda + 2\lambda p_1 + \lambda^2(1 - 2p_1 + p_1^2) \tag{18}$$

$$= 1 - 2\lambda + 2\lambda p_1 + \lambda^2 - 2\lambda^2 p_1 + \lambda^2 p_1^2. \tag{19}$$

Using (1), we can write $E\left[p_1^2(n+1) \mid P(n) = P\right]$ as:

$$E\left[p_1^2(n+1) \mid P(n) = P\right] = $$
$$\lambda^2 p_1^2 s_2 + (1 - 2\lambda + \lambda^2)s_1 + 2\lambda(1 - \lambda)p_1 s_1 + \lambda^2 p_1^2 s_1 \tag{20}$$

$$= \lambda^2 p_1^2 + 2\lambda(1 - \lambda)p_1 s_1 + (1 - \lambda)^2 s_1. \tag{21}$$

From (21), we observe that as

$$n \to \infty,$$

both

$$E\left[p_1^2(n)\right]$$

and

$$E\left[p_1^2(n + 1)\right]$$

converge to

$$E\left[p_1^2(\infty)\right].$$

Thus, by gathering terms involving

$$E\left[p_1^2(n)\right], \tag{21}$$

can be written as:

$$E\left[p_1^2(\infty)\right](1 - \lambda^2) = $$
$$2\lambda(1 - \lambda)E\left[p_1(\infty)\right]s_1 + (1 - \lambda)^2 s_1, \tag{22}$$

which can also be expressed as:

$$E\left[p_1^2(\infty)\right](1 + \lambda) = 2\lambda E\left[p_1(\infty)\right]s_1 + (1 - \lambda)s_1 \tag{23}$$

$$= 2\lambda s_1^2 + (1 - \lambda)s_1, \tag{24}$$

where the last equalities hold since $E\left[p_1(\infty)\right] = s_1$. Thus, we have:

$$E\left[p_1^2(\infty)\right] = \frac{2\lambda s_1^2 + (1 - \lambda)s_1}{1 + \lambda}. \tag{25}$$

We finally compute the variance of $p_1(\infty)$ as below:

$$Var[p_1(\infty)] = E[p_1^2(\infty)] - E[p_1(\infty)]^2 \tag{26}$$

$$= \frac{(1 - \lambda)s_1 s_2}{1 + \lambda}, \tag{27}$$

since $s_2 = 1 - s_1$, and the theorem is thus proved.

When $\lambda \to 1$, the variance tends to zero, implying mean square convergence. The *maximum* value of the variance is attained when $\lambda = 0$, and the *minimum* value of the variance is achieved when $\lambda = 1$.

Our result seems to be contradictory to our initial goal. When we motivated our problem, we were working with the notion that the environment was non-stationary. However, the results we have derived are asymptotic, and thus, are valid only as $n \to \infty$. While this could prove to be a handicap, realistically, and for all practical purposes, the convergence takes place after a relatively small value of *n*. As we will see later, in practice, choosing a value of λ in the interval [0.9, 0.99] gives quite good results. Thus, if λ is even as "small" as 0.9, after 50 iterations, the variation from the asymptotic value will be of the order of 10^{-50}, because λ also determines the rate of convergence, and this occurs in a geometric manner (Narendra & Thathachar, 1989). In other words, even if the environment switches its Bernoulli parameter after 50 steps, the SLWE will be able to track this change. Observe too that we do not need to introduce or consider the use of a "sliding window".

Weak Estimators for Multinomial Distributions

In this section, we shall consider the problem of estimating the parameters of a multinomial distribution, which is a generalization of the binomial case introduced earlier. The multinomial distribution is characterized by two parameters, namely, the *number* of trials, and a probability *vector* which determines the probability of a specific event (from a pre-specified set of events) occurring. In this regard, we assume that the number of observations is the number of trials. Thus, we encounter the problem of estimating the latter probability *vector* associated with the set of possible outcomes or trials.

Let *X* be a multinomially distributed random variable, which takes on the values from the set $\{`1`,...,`r`\}$. We assume that *X* is governed by the distribution $S = [s_1,...,s_r]^T$ as follows: $X = `i`$ with probability s_i, where $\sum_{i=1}^{r} s_i = 1$.

Also, let $x(n)$ be a concrete realization of *X* at time '*n*'. The intention of the exercise is to estimate *S*, i.e., s_i for $i = 1,...,r$. We achieve this by maintaining a running estimate $P(n) = [p_1(n),...,p_r(n)]^T$ of *S*, where $p_i(n)$ is the estimate of s_i at time '*n*', for $i = 1,...,r$, where as in the binomial case, the vector $P(n) = [p_1(n), p_2(n),...,p_r(n)]^T$ refers to the estimate of $S = [s_1, s_2,...,s_r]^T$ at time '*n*', and we omit the reference to time '*n*' in $P(n)$ whenever there is no confusion. Then, analogous to the binomial case, the value of $p_i(n)$ is updated as per the following simple rule (the rules for other values of $p_j(n), j \neq i$, are similar):

$$p_i(n + 1) = p_i + (1 - \lambda)\sum_{j \neq i} p_j \text{ when } x(n) = i \tag{28}$$

$$= \lambda p_i \qquad \text{when } x(n) \neq i. \qquad (29)$$

The reader will observe that this rule is analogous to the cybernetic primitive LA, the *multi-action L_{RI}* updating scheme.

We now derive the explicit form of the dependence of $E[P(n+1)]$ on $E[P(n)]$, and the consequences of this dependence. The results which we shall now show are that, as in the binomial case, this dependence is by means of a stochastic matrix. We first derive this explicit dependence, which, in turn, leads to the resulting properties by virtue of the ergodic nature of the Markov matrix. As before, this leads us to two results, namely to that of the limiting solution of the expected vector of the chain, and to conclusions concerning the rate of convergence of the chain. It turns out that both of these, in the very worst case, could only be dependent on the learning parameter λ. However, to our advantage, while the former is *independent* of the learning parameter, λ, the latter is *only* determined by a linear function of λ.

Theorem 4: *Let the parameter S of the multinomial distribution be estimated by P(n) at time 'n'* obtained by (28) *and* (29). *Then,* $E[P(\infty)] = S$.

Proof. First of all, we can rewrite the rule given in (28) and (29) as follows:

$$p_i(n+1) = p_i + (1-\lambda)(1-p_i) \ w.p. \ s_i \qquad (30)$$

$$= \lambda p_i \qquad w.p. \sum_{j \neq i} s_j. \qquad (31)$$

Thus, the expected value of $p_i(n+1)$ given the estimated probabilities at time 'n', P, is:

$$E[p_i(n+1) \mid P]$$
$$= p_i s_i + (1 - \lambda - p_i + \lambda p_i)s_i + \lambda p_i(1 - s_i) \qquad (32)$$

$$= p_i s_i + s_i - \lambda s_i - p_i s_i + \lambda p_i s_i + \lambda p_i - \lambda p_i s_i \qquad (33)$$

$$= (1 - \lambda)s_i + \lambda p_i. \qquad (34)$$

Taking expectations a second time, we have:

$$E[p_i(n+1)] = (1-\lambda)s_i + \lambda E[p_i(n)]. \qquad (35)$$

As $n \rightarrow \infty$, both $E[p_i(n+1)]$ and $E[p_i(n)]$ converge because the multiplying factor of the resultant linear difference equation is λ, which is both positive and strictly less than unity. Further, if it converges to a quantity $E[p_i(\infty)]$, we can write:

$$E[p_i(\infty)](1-\lambda) = (1-\lambda)s_i \qquad (36)$$

$$\Rightarrow E[p_i(\infty)] = s_i. \qquad (37)$$

The result follows since (37) is valid for every component p_i of P. ∎

We now derive the explicit dependence of $E[P(n+1)]$ on $E[P(n)]$ and the consequences.

Theorem 5: *Let the parameter S of the multinomial distribution be estimated at time 'n' by P(n) obtained by* (28) *and* (29). *Then,* $E[P(n+1)] = \mathbf{M}^T E[P(n)]$, *in which every off-diagonal term of the stochastic matrix,* $\mathbf{M}$, *has the same multiplicative factor,* $(1-\lambda)$. *Furthermore, the final solution of this vector difference equation is independent of* λ.

Proof. From (34), we can write the conditional expected probability, $E[p_1(n+1) \mid P]$ as follows:

$$E[p_1(n+1) \mid P] = (1-\lambda)s_1 \sum_{j=1}^{r} p_j + \lambda p_1. \qquad (38)$$

9

Similarly, for all other conditional expectations of $p_i(n+1)$, we have:

$$E\left[p_i(n+1) \mid P\right] = (1-\lambda)s_i \sum_{j=1}^{r} p_j + \lambda p_i. \quad (39)$$

Organizing the terms of (39) in a vectorial manner for all $i = 1,\ldots,r$, it follows that $E\left[P(n+1)\right] = \mathbf{M}^T E\left[P(n)\right]$, where the stochastic matrix, $\mathbf{M}$, is:

$$\mathbf{M} = \begin{bmatrix} (1-\lambda)s_1 + \lambda & (1-\lambda)s_2 & \cdots & (1-\lambda)s_r \\ (1-\lambda)s_1 & (1-\lambda)s_2 + \lambda & \cdots & (1-\lambda)s_r \\ \vdots & \vdots & \ddots & \vdots \\ (1-\lambda)s_1 & (1-\lambda)s_2 & \cdots & (1-\lambda)s_r + \lambda \end{bmatrix}. \quad (40)$$

The limiting solution for $E\left[P(n)\right]$ exists, since $\mathbf{M}$ has one eigenvalue, which is unity, and all the other eigenvalues of $\mathbf{M}$ are strictly less than unity. The limiting value is obtained by solving the following vectorial difference equation, and taking the limit as n is increased to infinity.

$$E\left[P(\infty)\right] = \mathbf{M}^T E\left[P(\infty)\right]. \quad (41)$$

We can write (40) as follows:

$$\mathbf{M} = (1-\lambda)\left[S \mid S \mid \cdots \mid S\right]^T + \lambda \mathbf{I}, \quad (42)$$

and hence every element of $(\mathbf{M} - \lambda \mathbf{I})$ has a common multiplicative factor of $(1-\lambda)$ (as does every off-diagonal element of $\mathbf{M}$ itself). Combining (41) and (42), we can write:

$$E\left[P(\infty)\right] = (1-\lambda)\left[S \mid S \mid \cdots \mid S\right]^T E\left[P(\infty)\right] + \lambda \mathbf{I} E\left[P(\infty)\right]. \quad (43)$$

which, on simplification, leads to the result that:

$$E\left[P(\infty)\right] = S, \quad (44)$$

which can be verified for all $i = 1,\ldots,r$ as follows:

$$E\left[p_i(\infty)\right] = (1-\lambda)s_i \sum_{j=1}^{r} E\left[p_j(\infty)\right] + \lambda E\left[p_i(\infty)\right] \quad (45)$$

$$= (1-\lambda)s_i + \lambda E\left[p_i(\infty)\right] \quad (46)$$

$$\Rightarrow E\left[p_i(\infty)\right](1-\lambda) = (1-\lambda)s_i, \quad (47)$$

implying that $E\left[p_i(\infty)\right] = s_i$, and proving the theorem.

The convergence and eigenvalue properties of $\mathbf{M}$ follow.

Theorem 6: *Let the parameter S of the multinomial distribution be estimated at time 'n' by P(n) obtained by (28) and (29). Then, all the non-unity eigenvalues of $\mathbf{M}$ are exactly λ, and thus the rate of convergence of P is fully determined by λ.*

Proof. To analyze the rate of convergence of the vector difference equation, we first find the eigenvalues of $\mathbf{M}$, namely $\xi_1, \xi_2, \ldots, \xi_r$. To begin with, observe that $\mathbf{M}$ can be decomposed as follows:

$$\mathbf{M} = \Phi \Lambda \Phi^{-1}, \quad (48)$$

where:

$$\Phi = \begin{bmatrix} 1 \\ 1 \\ 1 \\ 1 \\ \vdots \\ 1 \end{bmatrix} \begin{bmatrix} -\dfrac{s_2}{s_1} \\ 1 \\ 0 \\ 0 \\ \vdots \\ 0 \end{bmatrix} \begin{bmatrix} -\dfrac{s_3}{s_1} \\ 0 \\ 1 \\ 0 \\ \vdots \\ 0 \end{bmatrix} \cdots \begin{bmatrix} -\dfrac{s_r}{s_1} \\ 0 \\ 0 \\ 1 \\ \vdots \\ 1 \end{bmatrix}, \quad (49)$$

contains the eigenvectors of $\mathbf{M}$. The computation of the inverse of Φ is far from trivial. However, by a rather simple algebraic "trick" it is easy to verify that if the Identity matrix is subtracted from the inverse of Φ, we get the following simplified form:

$$\Phi^{-1} - \mathbf{I} = \begin{bmatrix} s_1 - 1 & s_2 & \cdots & s_r \\ -s_1 & -s_2 & \cdots & -s_r \\ \vdots & \vdots & \ddots & \vdots \\ -s_1 & -s_2 & \cdots & -s_r \end{bmatrix}. \quad (50)$$

Upon studying (48), we see that $\Lambda = diag(1, \lambda, \lambda, \ldots, \lambda)$, which contains the eigenvalues of $\mathbf{M}$. Thus, $\xi_1 = 1$, and $\xi_i = \lambda$ for $i = 2, \ldots, r$.

Indeed, all of these assertions can be easily verified for $i = 1$ as follows:

$$\mathbf{M} \begin{bmatrix} 1 \\ \vdots \\ 1 \end{bmatrix} = \begin{bmatrix} (1-\lambda)(s_1 + \ldots + s_r) + \lambda \\ \vdots \\ (1-\lambda)(s_1 + \ldots + s_r) + \lambda \end{bmatrix} = 1 \begin{bmatrix} 1 \\ \vdots \\ 1 \end{bmatrix}. \quad (51)$$

Similarly, they can be easily verified for $i = 2, \ldots, r$ as below:

$$\mathbf{M} \begin{bmatrix} -\dfrac{s_i}{s_1} \\ 0 \\ \vdots \\ 0 \\ 1_i \\ 0 \\ \vdots \\ 0 \end{bmatrix} = \begin{bmatrix} -\dfrac{[(1-\lambda)s_1 + \lambda]s_i}{s_1} + (1-\lambda)s_i \\ 0 \\ \vdots \\ 0 \\ -\dfrac{(1-\lambda)s_1 s_i}{s_1} + (1-\lambda)s_i + \lambda \\ 0 \\ \vdots \\ 0 \end{bmatrix} = \lambda \begin{bmatrix} -\dfrac{s_i}{s_1} \\ 0 \\ \vdots \\ 0 \\ 1_i \\ 0 \\ \vdots \\ 0 \end{bmatrix}, \quad (52)$$

where 1_i represents the presence of unity at position i.

Consequently, the rate of convergence of the matrix determining the vector difference equation is *fully* determined by the second largest eigenvalue, which is λ, since λ is an eigenvalue of multiplicity $r - 1$. The result follows.

A small value of λ leads to fast convergence and a large variance. On the contrary, a large value of λ leads to slow convergence and a small variance. Although the results we have derived are asymptotic, and thus, are valid only as $n \to \infty$, realistically, and for all practical purposes, the convergence takes place after a relatively small value of n. As in the binomial case, if λ is even as "small" as 0.9, after 50 iterations, the variation from the asymptotic value will be of the order of 10^{-50}, because λ also determines the rate of convergence, which again, occurs in a geometric manner (Narendra & Thathachar, 1989). In other words, even if the environment switches its multinomial probability vector after 50 steps, the SLWE will be able to track this change. Our experimental results demonstrate this fast convergence.

To conclude this section, we observe that the computational complexity of the SLWE is linear on the sample size. If we assume that the sample size is n (size of the input), then the worst-case time complexity of the SLWE for estimating parameters in the binomial case is $O(n)$. For multinomial random variables, the worst-case time complexity of the SLWE is given by $O(rn)$, where r is the size of S. Note that the complexity for the binomial case is a particular case of that of the multinomial scenario, where $r = 2$ is a constant. For both cases, the space complexity is linear in the size of S, i.e. $O(r)$.

Experimental Verification on Synthetic Data

In this section, we present the results of our simulations on synthetic data. To assess the efficiency of the SLWE, we have estimated the parameters for binomial and multinomial random variables using randomly generated values for λ. We have also estimated the parameters of these random variables by following the traditional MLE with a sliding window, whose size is also selected randomly.

Binomial Random Variables

The estimation of the parameters for binomial random variables has been extensively tested for numerous distributions. In the interest of brevity, we merely cite one specific example. Also, to make the comparison meaningful, we have followed the MLE computation using the identical data stream. In each case, the estimation algorithms were presented with random occurrences of the variables for $n = 400$ time instances. In the case of the SLWE, the true underlying value of s_1 was obtained randomly for the first step, and modified after every 50 steps using values drawn from a uniformly distributed random variable in [0, 1].

In order to demonstrate the superiority of the SLWE over the MLE that uses a sliding window (MLEW) on an ensemble of experiments, we report the respective averages and the confidence intervals. The same experiment was repeated 1,000 times, and the ensemble average at every time step was recorded. Clearly, the variations of the estimates in this setting would be much smoother. However, to perform a fair evaluation, the value of λ for the SLWE and the size of the window were randomly generated from uniform distributions in [0.55, 0.95] and [20, 80] respectively. It is well-known in LA schemes that choosing a value of λ close to 1 (for the binomial case, we have empirically found that $\lambda \approx 0.9$) gives quite good results. The plots of the estimated probability of 1, p_1 for the SLWE and the MLEW for four cases are shown in Figures 1 (a), (b), (c) and (d), where the values of λ are 0.817318, 0.59153, 0.9234 and 0.770685, and the sizes of the windows are 32, 48, 45 and 66 respectively. In the figures, the 99% confidence intervals for

the averages of the estimates obtained from the SLWE are also plotted (the diamond-shaped symbols). Observe that the MLE follows s_1 *exactly* in the first window, but it is thereafter severely handicapped in tracking the variations. The weakness of the MLEW is accentuated in the cases in which the size of the window is larger, e.g. 66. In contrast, the SLWE adjusts to the changes much more quickly, as expected, in a geometric manner. Regarding the confidence interval, even though it is substantially high, e.g. 99%, in most of the cases, the true probabilities fall inside the interval. The results we report here are typical.

Multinomial Random Variables

We have also performed simulations for multinomial random variables, where the parameters were estimated by following the SLWE and the MLEW. We considered a multinomial random variable, X, which can take any of four different values, namely '1', '2', '3' or '4', whose probability change (randomly) every 50 steps. As in the binomial case, we ran the estimators for 400 steps, repeated this 1,000 times, and then took the ensemble average. For each experiment, we computed $\| P - S \|$, the *Euclidean distance* between P and S, as this was a measure of how good our estimate, P, was of S.

The plots of the latter distance obtained from the SLWE and the MLEW are depicted in Figures 2 (a) and (b), where the values of λ are 0.957609 and 0.986232, and the sizes of the windows are 63 and 43 respectively. The values for λ and the window size were obtained randomly from a uniform distribution in [0.9, 0.99] and [20, 80] respectively. Note that we have chosen a range for λ whose end points are both close to 1 (even closer than those of the binomial case) -- this is in accordance with the suggested values for multi-action LA schemes, and has been corroborated by our empirical results. The reason for using the

Figure 1. Plot of the expected value of $p_1(n)$, at time 'n', which was estimated by using the SLWE and the MLEW. (a) $\lambda = 0.817318$ and window size = 32; (b) $\lambda = 0.59153$ and window size = 48; (c) $\lambda = 0.9234$ and window size = 45; (d) $\lambda = 0.770685$ and window size = 66.

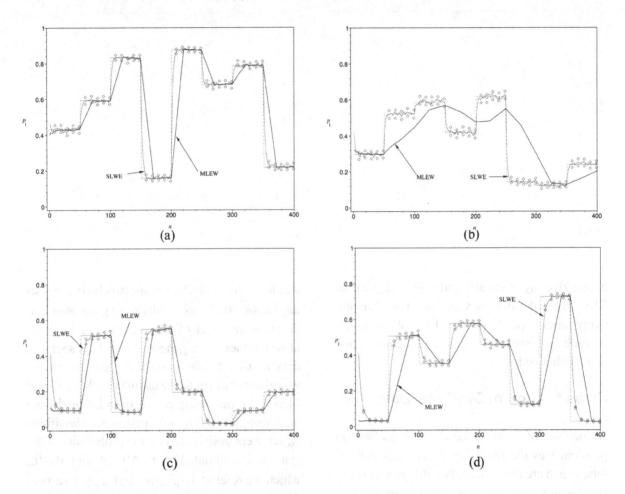

(a)

(b)

(c)

(d)

same interval for the sliding window is because the user generally has no clue about which window size is optimal depending on the different input values. From the two figures, we observe that the errors for the MLEW and the SLWE converge to zero relatively quickly. However, this behavior is not present in successive epochs. We notice that the MLEW is capable of tracking the changes of the parameters when the size of the window is small, or at least smaller than the intervals of constant probabilities. The MLEW, however, is not able to track the changes properly when the window size is relatively large. Since neither the

magnitude nor the frequency of the changes is known *a priori*, this scenario demonstrates the weakness of the MLEW, and its dependence on the knowledge of the input parameters. Again, such observations are typical.

APPLICATION DOMAIN I: PATTERN RECOGNITION

The power of the SLWE was also demonstrated in two pattern recognition experiments in which the classification was achieved on non-stationary

Figure 2. Plot of the Euclidean norm of $P - S$ (or Euclidean distance between P and S), for both the SLWE and the MLEW: (a) $\lambda = 0.957609$ and size of window = 63; (b) $\lambda = 0.986232$ and size of window = 43

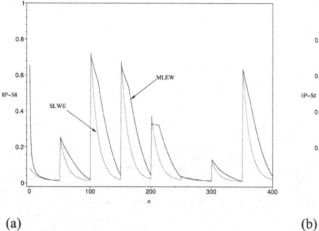

(a)

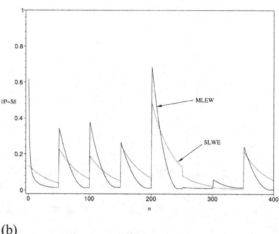

(b)

data derived synthetically and from real-life data files obtained from the Canadian Broadcasting Corporation's (CBC's) news files. We now describe both these experiments and the respective results obtained.

Classification of Synthetic Data

In the case of synthetic data, the classification problem was the following. Given a stream of bits, which are drawn from two different sources (or classes), say, S_1 and S_2, the aim of the classification exercise was to *identify* the source which each symbol belonged to. To train the classifier, we first generated blocks of bits using two binomial distributions (20 blocks for each source), where the probability of 0 for each distribution was s_{11} and s_{12} respectively. For the results that we report, (other settings yielding similar results are not reported here) the specific values of s_{11} and s_{12} were randomly set to be $s_{11} = 0.18$ and $s_{12} = 0.76$, which were assumed unknown to the classifier. These data blocks were then utilized to compute MLE estimates of s_{11} and s_{12}, which

we shall call s'_{11} and s'_{12} respectively. In the testing phase, 40 blocks of bits were generated randomly from either of the sources, and the order in which they were generated was kept secret to the classifier. Furthermore, the size of the blocks was also unknown to the estimators, MLEW and SLWE. In the testing phase, each bit read from the testing set was classified using two classifiers, which were designed using the probability of the symbol '0' estimated by the MLEW and SLWE, which we refer to as $p_{M1}(n)$ and $p_{S1}(n)$ respectively. The classification rule was based on a linear classifier, and the bit was assigned to the class that minimized the Euclidean distance between the estimated probability of 0, and the "learned" probability of 0 (for the two sources) obtained during the training. Thus, based on the MLWE classifier, the nth bit read from the test set was assigned to class S_1, if (ties were resolved arbitrarily):

$$(p_{1M} - s'_{11}) < (p_{1M} - s'_{12}),$$

and assigned to class S_2 otherwise. The classification rule based on the SLWE was analogous, except that it used p_{1S} instead of p_{1M}.

The two classifiers were tested for different scenarios. For the SLWE, the value of λ was arbitrarily set to 0.9. In the first set of experiments, the classifiers were tested for blocks of different sizes, $b = 50,100,...,500$. For each value of b, an ensemble of 100 experiments was performed. The MLEW used a window of size w, which was centered around b, and was computed as the nearest integer of a randomly generated value obtained from a uniform distribution $U[b/2,3b/2]$. In effect, we gave the MLEW the advantage of having some *a priori* knowledge of the block size. The results obtained are shown in Table 1, from which we see that classification using the SLWE was uniformly superior to classification using the MLEW, and in many cases yielded more than 20% accuracy than the latter. The accuracy of the classifier increased with the block size as is clear from Figure 3.

In the second set of experiments, we tested both classifiers, the MLEW and SLWE, when the block size was fixed to be $b = 50$. The window size of the MLEW, w, was again randomly generated from $U[b/2, 3b/2]$, thus giving the MLE the advantage of having some *a priori* knowledge of the block size.

The SLWE again used a conservative value of $\lambda = 0.9$. In this case, we conducted an ensemble of 100 simulations, and in each case, we computed the classification accuracy of the first k bits in each block. The results are shown in Table 2. Again, the consistnt superiority of the SLWE over the MLEW can be observed. For example, when $k = 45$, the MLEW yielded an accuracy of only 73.77%, while the corresponding accuracy of the SLWE was 92.48%. From the plot shown in Figure 4, we again observe the increase in accuracy with k.

In the final set of experiments, we tested both classifiers, the MLEW and SLWE, when the *block*

Table 1. The results obtained from testing linear classifiers, which used the MLEW and SLWE respectively. In this case, the blocks were generated of sizes $b = 50,100,...,500$, and the window size w used for the MLEW was randomly generated from U[b / 2, 3b / 2]. The SLWE used a value of $\lambda = 0.9$. The results were obtained from an ensemble of 100 simulations, and the accuracy was computed using all the bits in the block.

b	MLEW	SLWE
50	76.37	93.20
100	75.32	96.36
150	73.99	97.39
200	74.63	97.95
250	74.91	98.38
300	74.50	98.56
350	75.05	98.76
400	74.86	98.88
450	75.68	98.97
500	75.55	99.02

size was made random (as opposed to being fixed as in the previous cases). This was, in one sense, the most difficult setting, because there was no fixed "periodicity" for the switching from one "environment" to the second, and vice versa. This *block size* was thus randomly generated from $U[w/2, 3w/2]$, where w was the width used by the MLEW. Observe again that this implicitly assumed that the MLE had some (albeit, more marginal than in the previous cases) advantage of having some *a priori* knowledge of the system's behaviour, but the SLWE used the same conservative value of $\lambda = 0.9$. Again, we conducted an ensemble of 100 simulations, and in each case, we computed the classification accuracy of the first k bits in each block. The results are shown in Table 3. As in the above two cases, the SLWE was uniformly superior to the MLEW. For example, when $b = 20$, the MLEW yielded a recognition accuracy of only 53.09%, but the corre-

Figure 3. Plot of the accuracies of the MLEW and SLWE classifiers for different block sizes. The settings of the experiments are as described in Table 1

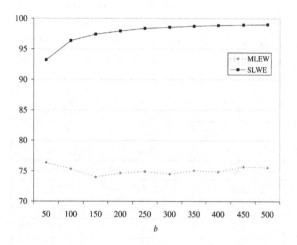

Table 2. The results obtained from testing linear classifiers, which used the MLEW and SLWE respectively. In this case, the blocks were generated of size b = 50, and the window size w used for the MLEW was randomly generated from U[b / 2, 3b / 2]. The SLWE used a value of $\lambda = 0.9$. The results were obtained from an ensemble of 100 simulations, and the accuracy was computed using the first k bits in each block.

k	MLEW	SLWE
5	50.76	56.46
10	51.31	70.00
15	53.15	78.65
20	56.03	83.66
25	59.47	86.78
30	63.19	88.90
35	67.03	90.42
40	70.65	91.57
45	73.77	92.48
50	76.37	93.20

sponding accuracy of the SLWE was 83.79%. From the plot shown in Figure 4, we again observe the increase in accuracy with *k* for the case of the SLWE, but the increase in the case of the MLEW is far less marked.

Results on Real-life Classification

In this section, we present the results of classification obtained from real-life data. The problem can be described as follows. We are given a stream of news items from different sources, and the aim of the PR exercise is to detect the source that the news come from. For example, consider the scenario when a TV channel broadcasts live video, or a channel that releases news in the form of text, for example, on the internet. The problem of detecting the source of the news item from a live channel has been studied by various researchers (in the interest of brevity, we merely cite one reference (Santo, Percannella, Sansone, & Vento, 2004)) with the ultimate aim being that of extracting *shots* for the videos and using them to classify the video into any of the pre-defined classes. Processing images is extremely time-consuming, which makes real

time processing almost infeasible. Thus, to render the problem tractable, we consider the scenario in which the news items arrive in the form of text blocks, which are extracted from the closed-captioning text embedded in the video streams. A classification problem of this type is similar to that of classifying files posted, for example, on the internet.

To demonstrate the power of our SLWE over the MLE in such problems, we first downloaded news files from the Canadian Broadcasting Corporation (CBC), which were from either of two different sources (the classes): *business* or *sports*, obtained from the CBC web-site (www.cbc.ca), between September 24 and October 2, 2004, and can be made available upon request. To select the files randomly, we drew 20 files (without replacement) from the original dataset, composing the training dataset. The remaining files were assigned to the testing dataset. With regard to the parameters, for the SLWE we randomly selected a

Figure 4. Plot of the accuracies of the MLEW and SLWE classifiers for different values of k. The settings of the experiments are as described in: (a) Table 2, and (b) Table 3

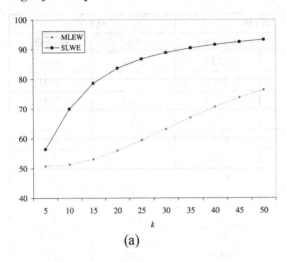

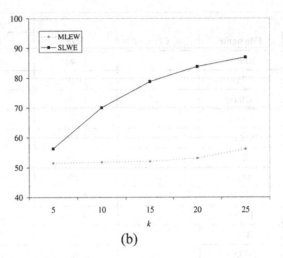

(a)   (b)

Table 3. The results obtained from testing linear classifiers, which used the MLEW and SLWE respectively. In this case, the blocks were generated of a random width b uniform in U[w / 2, 3w / 2], where w was the window size used by the MLEW. The SLWE used a value of $\lambda = 0.9$. The results were obtained from an ensemble of 100 simulations, and the accuracy was computed using the first k bits in each block.

b	MLEW	SLWE
5	51.53	56.33
10	51.79	70.05
15	52.06	78.79
20	53.09	83.79
25	56.17	86.88

value of λ uniformly from the range $[0.99, 0.999]$, and for the case of the MLEW, the window size was uniformly distributed in [50, 150]. In our particular experiments, the value for λ was 0.9927, and the value for the size of the window was 80, where the latter was obtained by rounding the resulting random value to the nearest integer. The results of the classification are shown in Table 4, where we list the name of the files that

were selected (randomly) from the *testing* set. The results reported here are only for the cases when the classification problem is meaningful. In a *few* cases, the bit pattern did not even yield a 50% (random choice) recognition accuracy. We did not report these results because, clearly, classification using these "features" and utilizing such a classifier is meaningless. But we have reported all the cases when the MLEW gave an accuracy which was less than 50%, but for which the SLWE yielded an accuracy which was greater than 50%. The superiority of the SLWE over the MLEW is clearly seen from the table - for example, in the case of the file *s5.txt*, the MLEW yielded a classification accuracy of 72.99%, while the corresponding accuracy for the SLWE was 93.43%. Indeed, *in every single case*, the SLWE yielded a classification accuracy better than the corresponding accuracy obtained by the MLEW. In order to corroborate the results, we "switched" the training and testing datasets, and re-ran the experiments. We observed that the accuracy obtained is similar to that of the original training and testing datasets (approximately 70.3% for the SLWE, and 59.6% for the MLEW).

We conclude this section by observing the following. First, a much better accuracy can be

Table 4. Empirical results obtained by classification of CBC files into Sports (S) and Business (B) items using the MLEW and SLWE.

File name	Class	Size	MLEW		SLWE	
			Hits	Accuracy	Hits	Accuracy
S19.txt	S	1,981	1,136	57.34	1,568	79.15
S7.txt	S	763	379	49.67	458	60.03
S20.txt	S	1,435	901	62.79	1,111	77.42
S5.txt	S	1,629	1,189	72.99	1,522	93.43
S10.txt	S	1,129	915	81.05	1,051	93.09
S8.txt	S	790	435	55.06	673	85.19
B8.txt	B	5,206	3,304	63.47	3,374	64.81
S17.txt	S	1,277	794	62.18	972	76.12
B3.txt	B	3,469	2,389	68.87	2,716	78.29
B1.txt	B	3,328	2,122	63.76	2,337	70.22
B18.txt	B	1,905	1,220	64.04	1,388	72.86
B4.txt	B	1,377	956	69.43	1,061	77.05
B14.txt	B	1,360	853	62.72	1,037	76.25
B10.txt	B	3,997	2,080	52.04	2,073	51.86
B15.txt	B	2,114	1,182	55.91	1,396	66.04
B11.txt	B	2,202	1,399	63.53	1,669	75.79
B2.txt	B	3,436	2,402	69.91	2,882	83.88
S15.txt	S	1,640	836	50.98	1,087	66.28
S4.txt	S	2,923	1,720	58.84	2,244	76.77
S2.txt	S	3,016	1,524	50.53	1,866	61.87
B19.txt	B	2,718	1,588	58.43	1,745	64.20
S14.txt	S	2,194	1,319	60.12	1,458	66.45
B9.txt	B	3,536	2,167	61.28	2,588	73.19
S3.txt	S	3,159	1,413	44.73	1,622	51.35
S13.txt	S	2,848	1,567	55.02	1,670	58.64
S12.txt	S	1,874	894	47.71	1,032	55.07
S9.txt	S	3,592	1,642	45.71	1,971	54.87

obtained using similar features if a more powerful classifier (for example, a higher order classifier) is utilized instead of the simple linear classifier that we have invoked. Second, the average size of each file tested was 313 words. Noting that a television speaker of a news program speaks at an average rate of 150 words per minute, we see that the SLWE can detect the source in approximately *two* minutes.

APPLICATION DOMAIN I: DATA COMPRESSION

The second application problem that we consider to demonstrate the power of the SLWE involves data compression, and can be described as follows. We are given an input sequence, $X = x(1)...x(M)$, where each input symbol, $x(i)$, is drawn from a source alphabet, $S = \{s_i, ..., s_m\}$, where $m \geq 2$

, and whose probabilities are $P = [p_1, \ldots, p_m]^T$. The encoding process is rendered by transforming X into an output sequence, $Y = y(1) \ldots y(R)$, where each output symbol, y(i), is drawn from a code alphabet, $A = \{a_1, \ldots, a_r\}$. The intent of the exercise is to determine an encoding scheme that minimizes the size of Y, in such a way that X is completely recovered by the decompression process. The encoding process is rendered adaptive, and thus, the data is encoded by performing a single pass. This is carried out by assuming that $P = [p_1, \ldots, p_m]^T$ is unknown, as opposed to the static coding algorithms which require two passes -- the first to learn the probabilities, and the second to accomplish the encoding. Adaptive coding is the best choice in many applications that require on-line compression such as in communication networks, internet applications, e-mail, ftp, e-commerce, video streaming, and digital television.

A crucial problem that has received little attention in the literature is that of compressing data, which "simultaneously" comes from different sources, or perhaps, possesses different stochastic characteristics. Examples of data that exhibit this kind of behavior can be found in real-life data files, including text files containing tables, figures, and Object Linking and Embedding (OLE), postscript files containing text, equations, and figures, Windows executable files, dynamic link libraries, and font format files. A few efforts have been made to develop techniques that utilize higher-order statistical models for stationary distributions. The most well-known adaptive coding technique is Huffman's algorithm and its enhancements (Gallager, 1978; Knuth, 1985). Other important adaptive encoding methods include *arithmetic coding* (Hankerson, Harris, & Johnson, 1998), *interval coding* and *recency rank encoding* (Hankerson, Harris, & Johnson, 1998 ; Muramatsu, 2002). In (Rueda & Oommen, 2002), the authors introduced greedy adaptive Fano coding algorithms for binary code (and *r*-ary) alphabets. Adaptive

coding approaches that use higher-order statistical models, and other structural models, include *dictionary techniques* (LZ and its enhancements) (Weinberger & Ordentlich, 2002), *prediction with partial matching* (PPM) and its enhancements (Jacquet, Szpankowski, & Apostol, 2002). Other static coding methods which are worth mentioning include *block sorting compression* (Effros, Visweswariah, Kulkarni, & Verdú, 2002), and *grammar based compression* (GBC) (Kieffer & Yang, 2000).

On the other hand, little work has been done to enhance the probability updating phase, so that the updates obtained yield better estimates of the true probabilities of the data coming from potentially *time-varying* sources and probability distributions. One of the reported approaches consists of periodically multiplying each counter by a positive real number less than unity (Gallager, 1978). Another approach, suggests that the probabilities of occurrence should be real numbers to represent the frequency counters (Cormack & Horspool, 1984). These authors proposed an exponential incrementing of the counters by choosing a multiplication factor $\alpha > 1$, suggesting a value of α slightly greater than unity, e.g. $\alpha = 1.01$. A third method utilizes a window as a circular buffer, in which the last t symbols encoded are stored (Bell, Cleary, & Witten, 1990). All these approaches lack from a sound theoretical basis, and hence are limited to produce *only marginal* improvements in compressing time-varying source data.

A Generic Estimate-Based Adaptive Fano Coding Scheme

We shall first show how we can implement the adaptive Fano method using an "arbitrary" *generic* estimation process. Consider first, the implementation of the encoding procedure for the greedy adaptive version for Fano coding, which is shown in Algorithm Greedy_Adaptive_Fano_Encoding. At each time step, a list that contains the source alphabet symbols, $S(n) = \{s_1(n),...,s_m(n)\}$, is maintained.

```
Algorithm Greedy_Adaptive_Fano_
Encoding
Input: The source alphabet, S.
       The input sequence, X.
Output: The output sequence, Y.
Method:
   S(1)←S
   for i←1 to m do // Initialize
   probabilities of occurrence
      P̂_i ← 1/m
   endfor
   j←1
   for n←1 to M do // For every
   symbol of the source sequence
      t←1; b←m; p ← ∑_{i=1}^{m} P̂_i
      while b>t do
         y(j)←Partition(S(n), P̂(n),
         A, x(n), t, b, p)
         j←j+1
      endwhile
      UpdateProbabilities(S(n),
      P̂(n), x(n))
   endfor
end Algorithm Greedy_Adaptive_
Fano_Encoding
```

The starting list, $S(1)$, is S itself, and contains the source symbols in a canonical order. The occurrences for all symbols are initially set to equal probabilities for all sysmbols. Every symbol in the input sequence is read from first to last, in a sequential manner and processed one at a time. At time 'n', $x(n)$ is encoded by invoking the partitioning procedure, which returns the corresponding output code alphabet symbol, and that code alphabet symbol, $y(j)$, is sent to the output. A separate counter, j, is maintained to keep track of the output symbols, since a variable-length, prefix encoding scheme is produced. Once the partitioned list (bounded by b and t) contains a

single symbol, it means that the input symbol has been encoded, and the probabilities are updated by invoking the UpdateProbabilities procedure, discussed below. Details regarding the implementation of the partitioning procedure can be found in (Rueda, 2002; Rueda & Oommen, 2004). In this chapter, we consider the binary code alphabet instantiation, i.e. $A = \{0,1\}$. The extension of the Fano coding algorithm to multi-symbol code alphabets can be found in (Rueda, 2002).

The decoding procedure is similar to the encoding. To maintain the entire process consistent, the probabilities of the symbols are updated using the same procedure as that of the encoder (i.e., at time '1', all symbols are considered equally likely). The decoding procedure is detailed in Algorithm Greedy_Adaptive_Fano_Decoding.

```
Algorithm Greedy_Adaptive_Fano_
Decoding
Input: The encoded sequence, Y.
       The source alphabet, S.
Output: The source sequence, X.
Method:
   S(1)←S
   for i←1 to m do// Initialize
   probabilities of occurrence
      P̂_i ← 1/m
   endfor
   n←1; t←1; b←m; p ← ∑_{i=1}^{m} P̂_i
   for j←1 to R do
      Partition(S(n), P̂(n), A,
      y(j), t, b, p)
      if t=b then
         x(n)←s_t(n)
         UpdateProbabilities
         (S(n), P̂(n), x(n))
         n←n+1; t←1; b←m;
         p ← ∑_{i=1}^{m} P̂_i
      endif
   endfor
```

```
end Algorithm Greedy_Adaptive_
Fano_Decoding
```

The procedure that updates the probabilities is similar to that invoked by the encoder, thus rendering the two processes synchronized. For every symbol read from the encoded sequence, at time 'j', the Partition procedure is invoked, which keeps narrowing the partitioned sublist, until it contains a single symbol (when $t = b$). At this stage, the original source symbol is identified (the one at position t), which is sent to the output. Then, the UpdateProbabilities prodedure is invoked to maintain the same list as that of the encoder at every single step.

A few important properties have to be taken into account when implementing the encoding and decoding algorithms. First, the encoder and the decoder must use the same labeling scheme. Second, they both have to start with the same initial probabilities. Third, they must both use the same probability updating procedure, which is discussed presently. Finally, the encoder uses $\hat{P}(n)$ to encode $x(n)$, which, obviously, is known to the decoder too.

Using the SLWE to Update Symbol Probabilities

The reader will observe that in the last sub-section, we assumed that the algorithm had access to an estimation process, which we assumed to be generic. In this sub-section, we discuss how we use the SLWE to update the probabilities of the symbols while the encoding takes place. We use two variants of the SLWE, namely the model based on the linear reward-inaction (L_{RI}) and nonlinear reward-inaction (N_{RI}) learning automata schemes (Narendra & Thathachar, 1989). Assuming that the nth symbol from the input is unknown, our method encodes the symbol using the estimates for the probabilities at time $n-1$, $\hat{P}(n-1)$, and updates the probabilities using the SLWE.

The scheme that utilizes a linear scheme implements the estimation procedure discussed earlier. That is, the probabilities of the symbols for the next encoding step are updated as per (1). The procedure for updating the probabilities at time 'n', which is invoked by the encoding and decoding algorithms, is implemented in Algorithm Probability_Updating shown below. The probabilities of the symbols at time 'n' are maintained in a vector, $\hat{P}(n)$, which is updated in the algorithm.

```
Algorithm Probability_Updating
Input: The source alphabet,
       probabilities and input
       symbol at time 'n',
       S(n), P̂(n) and x(n).
Output: The updated probabili-
       ties, P̂(n+1).
Method:
   procedure UpdateProbabilities
   (var S(n), P̂(n): list, x(n):
   symbol)
       iₓ← index of x(n) in S(n)
       for j←1 to m do
         if iₓ=j then
```
$$\hat{p}_j(n+1) \leftarrow \hat{p}_j + (1-\lambda)\sum_{k\neq j}\hat{p}_k$$
```
         else
```
$$\hat{p}_j(n+1) \leftarrow \lambda\hat{p}_j$$
```
         endif
       endfor
   endprocedure
end Algorithm Probability_Updating
```

The algorithm for updating the probabilities by using a nonlinear SLWE scheme is similar to the linear case, except that the updating rule of Algorithm **Probability_Updating** is substituted for the following:

$$\hat{p}_1(n+1) = \hat{p}_1 + \sum_{j \neq 1} \hat{p}_j - \theta_j(\hat{P}) \qquad (53)$$

when $x(n) = s_1$

$$= \theta_1(\hat{P}) \qquad (54)$$

when $x(n) \neq s_1$

where $\theta_j(\hat{P})$ is a *nonlinear* function of $\hat{p}_1, \ldots, \hat{p}_m$. In our implementation, we use the function $\theta_j(\hat{P}) = (\hat{p}_j)^\kappa$, where k is a positive real number. In practice, k is typically chosen to be near 2.0. This substitution is trivial and is omitted to avoid repetition.

An SLWE-Based Adaptive Entropy Coding Scheme

The results discussed above explained how the SLWE can be incorporated to yield schemes which are (soon shown to be) more efficient than those that estimate using a traditional MLE scheme. They, albeit, "sit on top of" a suboptimal compression method, in this case the Fano coding method. However, with little imagination, this strategy can be easily generalized for any compression method, where the estimation is achieved using the SLWE and not a traditional estimator. Indeed, we now demonstrate that even better results can be obtained if the Fano coding method is substituted by an *entropy-based* method, such as *arithmetic coding*. To make the model simpler, we assume that the symbol at time 'n', say s_i, is encoded using a number of bits determined by its information amount, $-\log_2 \hat{p}_i(n)$, which, in essence, assumes that all symbols in X occur independently of each other. Under this assumption, the entire input sequence, X, can be encoded using

$$\left\lceil -\log_2 \prod_{n=1}^{M} \hat{p}(x(n)) \right\rceil = \left\lceil -\sum_{n=1}^{M} \log_2 \hat{p}(x(n)) \right\rceil$$

bits.

The formal algorithm to achieve this is straightforward—it merely involves substituting the estimation phase of the entropy-based compression with the SLWE. It is, thus, omitted here. The corresponding encoding schemes using those entropy based methods for the traditional adaptive encoding, and the encoding that use linear and nonlinear estimation schemes are referred to as *Traditional Estimator Adaptive Entropy-based (TEAH), Linear-SLWE Estimator Adaptive Entropy-based (LEAH)* and *Nonlinear-SLWE Estimator Adaptive Entropy-based (NEAH)* respectively, which is to be contrasted to the *Linear-SLWE Estimator Adaptive Fano (LEAF)* and *Nonlinear-SLWE Estimator Adaptive Fano (NEAF)* methods defined for the Fano scheme. Note that by "traditional" we mean that the entropy-based encoding algorithm receives as input, at each step, the estimates obtained from the *traditional* MLE. In other words, a frequency counter is maintained for each symbol, which is increased by unity when that symbol occurs in the input, where the frequency counters are initialized to unity. This initialization aims to avoid the *zero-frequency* problem (Bell, Cleary & Witten, 1990).

Experimental Results

To demonstrate the power of our encoding schemes, we have conducted some experiments on various real-life files taken from different sources. The set of files that we have chosen include Microsoft Word documents containing tables, figures, and OLE objects, postscript files containing text, equations, and figures, Windows executable files, dynamic link libraries, and font format files. The list of the files and their descriptions are given in Table 5.

In our experiments, we have implemented the traditional estimator adaptive Fano (TEAF) coding algorithm as proposed in (Rueda, 2002). We

Table 5. List of the files and their descriptions, which were used in our experiments

File name	Description
agentsvr.exe	Microsoft Agent Server program, version 2.00.0.3422, taken from a Windows 2000 platform.
ariali.ttf	Arial Italic font file from Windows 2000, version 2.76.
authinst.doc	Microsoft Word document that contains instructions to authors preparing manuscripts submitted to Lecture Notes in Computer Science (LNCS) for Springer-Verlag.
expaper.doc	Microsoft Word document that contains a template of a typical paper to be submitted to a Conference.
fanocode.ps	Postscript format of the conference version paper of (Rueda & Oommen, 2004), presented at the IEEE Systems, Man and Cybernetics, held in Tucson, AZ, USA, 2001.
faxocm.dll	Fax setup dynamic link library for Windows 2000, version 5.0.2148.1.
grantapp.doc	Microsoft Word document that contains the application form to a SHARCnet fellowship grant.
lncsinst.doc	Microsoft Word document that contains the instructions for submitting camera-ready papers to LNCS.
oplclass.ps	Postscript format file of a paper on pattern classification, published in IEEE Trans. on Pattern Analysis and Machine Intelligence, February, 2002.
timesbi.ttf	Times New Roman Bold Italic font file from Windows 2000, version 2.76.
twain.dll	A dynamic link library file from Windows 2000, version 1.7.0.0, which implements the Twain Image Acquisition Driver.
vcmd.exe	A Windows 2000 executable file, version 4.0.4.3405, which processes voice/speech commands.

have also implemented the adaptive Fano coding approaches introduced above using the linear and nonlinear schemes, which we have called *Linear-SLWE Estimator Adaptive Fano (LEAF)* and *Nonlinear-SLWE Estimator Adaptive Fano (NEAF)* respectively. For the LEAF we set the value of λ to be 0.999, and for the NEAF the value of k was set to be 2.0. The experimental results obtained from the simulations on the files described above are shown in Table 6.

The first and second columns contain the names of the files and their original sizes. The subsequent columns contain the results for the three coding methods tested, grouped in two columns each; the first column contains the size (in bytes) of the compressed file, and the second column contains the compression ratio, calculated as $\rho = \left(1 - \ell_Y / l_X\right) 100$, where l_X is the length of the input file, and ℓ_Y is the length of the compressed file. The last row shows the *total* for each column representing the file sizes, and the *weighted average* for the columns containing the compression ratios.

The results from the table show that the LEAF and the NEAF compress approximately 8% and 9% (respectively) more than the traditional adaptive Fano coding, TEAF. The best results for the LEAF have been obtained in compressing Postscript and Word document files. We also observe that the NEAF achieves much better compression ratios than the TEAF in word document files, and in file ariali.ttf.

The experimental results for the entropy-based adaptive coding methods are shown in Table 7. The results show that, if enhanced by using the linear and nonlinear SLWE schemes, a gain of nearly 9% and 10% (respectively) is obtained with respect to the traditional entropy-based encoding scheme. As can be expected, we observe that the entropy-based encoding methods achieve more efficient compression than the Fano coding. We also notice that the LEAH and the NEAH achieve the best results for word documents, dynamic link libraries, and Postscript files. As opposed to this, it can be seen that the NEAH works slightly less efficiently in executable files. This behavior indeed demonstrates that encoding methods which are enhanced with SLWE schemes work much

Table 6. Compression ratio and compressed file sizes for the traditional adaptive Fano coding scheme, the LEAF and NEAF coding schemes on real-life data files.

File name	Orig. size(bytes)	TEAF		LEAF		NEAF	
		l_y (bytes)	ρ (%)	l_y (bytes)	ρ (%)	l_y (bytes)	ρ (%)
agentsvr.exe	242,448	191,922	20.84	179,533	25.95	182,418	24.76
ariali.ttf	200,684	173,210	13.69	157,356	21.59	153,102	23.71
authinst.doc	630,784	203,365	67.76	158,642	74.85	149,370	76.32
expaper.doc	62,976	43,712	30.59	37,949	39.74	36,463	42.10
fanocode.ps	165,149	108,206	34.48	94,085	43.03	98,363	40.44
faxocm.dll	77,584	49,793	35.82	42,958	44.63	43,183	44.34
grantapp.doc	126,976	81,849	35.54	66,980	47.25	68,770	45.84
lncsinst.doc	104,448	86,713	16.98	74,994	28.20	76,320	26.93
oplclass.ps	167,772	110,998	33.84	93,097	44.51	96,251	42.63
timesbi.ttf	233,892	203,463	13.01	186,318	20.34	181,968	22.20
twain.dll	94,784	80,102	15.49	71,998	24.04	72,690	23.31
vcmd.exe	362,256	298,426	17.62	263,722	27.20	271,547	25.04
Avg./Total	2,469,753	1,631,758	33.93	1,445,534	41.47	1,430,445	42.08

better for data which shows a substantially *high degree of non-stationarity*. This is the case for the Word documents used in the testing, which contain fragments of text, followed by a table or a figure, followed by text again, and so on. A similar scenario occurs in the postscript files used in the testing, which contain text, figures, tables and mathematical equations. These two types of files are the ones in which the learning schemes achieve superior compression ratio.

FUTURE RESEARCH DIRECTIONS

Throughout this chapter, we have utilized the principles of learning as achieved by the families of Variable Structure Stochastic Automata (VSSA) (Lakshmivarahan, 1981; Lakshmivarahan & Thathachar, 1973; Narendra & Thathachar, 1989; Thathachar & Oommen, 1979). In particular, the

learning we have achieved is obtained as a consequence of invoking algorithms related to families of linear schemes, such as the L_{RI} scheme, although the applicability of a non-linear scheme has also been demonstrated (without a formal analysis) for data compression. The analysis is also akin to that of *these* learning automata algorithms. This involves, first, determining the updating equations, and then taking the conditional expectation of the quantity analyzed. The condition disappears when the expectation operator is invoked a second time, leading to a difference equation for the specified quantity, which equation is later explicitly solved. We have opted to use these families of VSSA in the design of our SLWE, because it turns out that the analysis is considerably simplified and (in our opinion) fairly elegant.

We would like to mention that this chapter leads to various "open problems". A lot of work has been done in the last decades which involve

Table 7. Experimental results obtained after testing the entropy-based coding utilizing the traditional probability updating method, the LEAH and NEAH learning schemes on real-life data files.

File name	Orig. size (bytes)	TEAH		LEAH		NEAH	
		l_y (bytes)	ρ (%)	l_y (bytes)	ρ (%)	l_y (bytes)	ρ (%)
agentsvr.exe	242,448	190,249	21.43	178,054	26.56	180,260	25.65
Ariali.ttf	200,684	171,966	14.31	156,373	22.08	151,516	24.50
authinst.doc	630,784	201,094	68.12	132,149	79.05	113,289	82.04
expaper.doc	62,976	43,082	31.59	36,778	41.60	34,989	44.44
fanocode.ps	165,149	107,264	35.05	93,177	43.58	97,520	40.95
faxocm.dll	77,584	48,195	37.88	40,716	47.52	40,569	47.71
grantapp.doc	126,976	78,268	38.36	64,669	49.07	65,761	48.21
lncsinst.doc	104,448	85,261	18.37	73,375	29.75	74,283	28.88
oplclass.ps	167,772	109,874	34.51	92,023	45.15	94,724	43.54
timesbi.ttf	233,892	202,013	13.63	185,102	20.86	180,167	22.97
Twain.dll	94,784	79,401	16.23	71,249	24.83	71,638	24.42
Vcmd.exe	362,256	296,507	18.15	261,404	27.84	268,287	25.94
Avg./Total	2,469,753	1,613,173	34.68	1,385,069	43.92	1,373,004	44.41

the so-called families of Discretized LA, and the families of Pursuit and Estimator algorithms. Discretized LA were pioneered by (Thathachar & Oommen, 1979) and since then, all the families of continuous VSSA have found their counterparts in the corresponding discretized versions (Oommen, 1986; Oommen & Christensen, 1988). The design of SLWE using discretized VSSA is open.

The Pursuit and Estimator algorithms were first pioneered by Thathachar, Sastry and their colleagues (Rajaraman & Sastry, 1996; Thathachar & Sastry, 1985, 1986). These involve specifically utilizing running estimates of the penalty probabilities of the actions in enhancing the stochastic learning. These automata were later discretized (Lanctot & Oommen, 1992; Oommen & Lanctot, 1990) and currently, extremely fast continuous and discretized pursuit and estimator LA have been designed (Oommen & Agache, 2001; Papadimitriou, 1994b, 1994a). The question of designing SLWE

using Pursuit and Estimator updating schemes is also open. We believe, however, that even if such estimator-based SLWEs are designed, the analysis of their properties will not be trivial.

To conclude this section, we highlight other possible directions for future research. First of all, although successful applications of the scheme to adaptive data compression have been presented, the problems involving establishing a standard benchmark that contains files with non-stationary source data, and the evaluation of the different estimation methods on compressing those files are open, and are currently being studied. In this context, the use of the SLWE in enhancing *entropy-based* encoding methods, such as *arithmetic coding* is still unexplored. The use of *higher-order* models coupled with these encoding methods would also imply substantial improvements in compression efficiency – another interesting problem to investigate.

Secondly, applications of the SLWE to other statistical PR problems such as the inference of hidden Markov models are currently being pursued. Another problem that is being investigated is that of deriving SL-based weak estimators for other distributions, such as the Gaussian, exponential, gamma, and Poisson. Some initial results in this direction are currently available.

CONCLUSION

Although the field of AI has been researched for more than five decades, researchers, scientists and practitioners are constantly seeking superior methods that are applicable for increasingly difficult problems. In this chapter, we have considered knowledge-based novel and intelligent cybernetic approaches for problems in which the environment (or medium) is time-varying. More specifically, we have considered the problem of estimating the parameters of a distribution from its observations. Unlike traditional estimators that possess *strong* convergence properties, we have argued that there is a need for estimators that do not possess such strong convergence properties.

Motivated by real-life applications, we formally presented an estimation method based on the principles of stochastic learning, which yields the estimates of the parameters of both binomial and multinomial distributions, where the convergence of the estimate is "weak". In each case, the mean of the asymptotic distribution has been derived, and various results concerning the rate of convergence and limiting variances have also been derived.

Experimental results for both binomial and multinomial random variables demonstrate the power of the scheme for non-stationary distributions. We have also presented the results for pattern classification and for adaptively encoding data files drawn from non-stationary sources. These results demonstrate the superiority of the SLWE over the MLE.

REFERENCES

Baron, M., & Grannot, N. (2003). Consistent estimation of early and frequent change points. In *Foundation of statistical inference*. Heidelberg, Germany: Springer.

Bell, T., Cleary, J., & Witten, I. (1990). Text compression. In Bickel, P., & Doksum, K. (Eds.), *Mathematical statistics: Basic ideas and selected topics* (2nd ed., *Vol. I*). Upper Saddle River, NJ: Prentice Hall.

Casella, G., & Berger, R. (2001). *Statistical inference* (2nd ed.). Pacific Grove, CA: Brooks/ Cole Pub. Co.

Cormack, G., & Horspool, R. (1984). Algorithms for Adaptive Huffman Codes. *Information Processing Letters*, 169–165.

Duda, R., Hart, P., & Stork, D. (2000). *Pattern Classification* (2nd ed.). New York: John Wiley and Sons, Inc.

Effros, M., Visweswariah, K., Kulkarni, S., & Verdú, S. (2002). Universal Lossless Source Coding With the Burrows Wheeler Transform. *IEEE Transactions on Information Theory*, 48(5), 1061–1081. doi:10.1109/18.995542

Gallager, R. (1978). Variations on a Theme by Huffman. *IEEE Transactions on Information Theory*, 24(6), 668–674. doi:10.1109/TIT.1978.1055959

Gombay, E. (2003). Sequential Change-point Detection and Estimation. *Sequential Analysis*, 22, 203–222. doi:10.1081/SQA-120025028

Hankerson, D., Harris, G., & Jr, P. J. (1998). *Introduction to information theory and data compression*. Boca Raton, FL: CRC Press.

Herbrich, R. (2001). *Learning Kernel Classifiers: Theory and Algorithms*. Cambridge, MA: MIT Press.

Ho, T., Stapleton, R., & Subrahmanyam, M. (1995). Multivariate Binomial Approximations for Asset Prices with Non-stationary Variance and Covariance Characteristics. *Review of Financial Studies, 8*(4), 1125–1152. doi:10.1093/rfs/8.4.1125

Jacquet, P., Szpankowski, W., & Apostol, I. (2002). A Universal Predictor Based on Stochastic Learning-based Weak Estimation of Multinomial Random Variables and Its Applications to Pattern Matching. *IEEE Transactions on Information Theory, 48*(6), 1462–1472. doi:10.1109/TIT.2002.1003834

Jang, Y. M. (2000). Estimation and Prediction-Based Connection Admission Control in Broadband Satellite Systems. *ETRI Journal, 22*(4), 40–50. doi:10.4218/etrij.00.0100.0405

Jones, B., Garthwaite, P., & Jolliffe, I. (2002). *Statistical Inference* (2nd ed.). Oxford, UK: Oxford University Press.

Kieffer, J. C., & Yang, E. (2000). Grammar-Based Codes: A New Class of Universal Lossless Source Codes. *IEEE Transactions on Information Theory, 46*(3), 737–754. doi:10.1109/18.841160

Knuth, D. (1985). Dynamic Huffman Coding. *Journal of Algorithms, 6,* 163–180. doi:10.1016/0196-6774(85)90036-7

Krishnaiah, P., & Miao, B. (1988). Review about estimation of change points. In *Handbook of Statistics* (Vol. 7, pp. 375–402). Amsterdam: Elsevier.

Lakshmivarahan, S. (1981). *Learning Algorithms Theory and Applications*. New York: Springer-Verlag.

Lakshmivarahan, S., & Thathachar, M. A. L. (1973). Absolutely Expedient Algorithms for Stochastic Automata. *IEEE Transactions on Systems, Man, and Cybernetics, SMC-3,* 281–286.

Lanctot, J. K., & Oommen, B. J. (1992). Discretized Estimator Learning Automata. *IEEE Transactions on Systems, Man, and Cybernetics, 22*(6), 1473–1483. doi:10.1109/21.199471

Muramatsu, J. (2002). On the Performance of Recency Rank and Block Sorting Universal Lossless Data Compression Algorithms. *IEEE Transactions on Information Theory, 48*(9), 2621–2625. doi:10.1109/TIT.2002.801477

Narendra, K., & Thathachar, M. (1989). *Learning Automata. An Introduction*. Upper Saddle River, NJ: Prentice Hall.

Norris, J. (1999). *Markov chains*. New York: Springer.

Oommen, B. (1986). Absorbing and Ergodic Discretized Two-Action Learning Automata. *IEEE Transactions on Systems, Man, and Cybernetics, SMC-16,* 282–296.

Oommen, B., & Agache, M. (2001). Continuous and Discretized Pursuit Learning Stochastic Learning-based Weak Estimation of Multinomial Random Variables and Its Applications to Pattern Schemes: Various Algorithms and Their Comparison. *IEEE Trans. on Systems, Man and Cybernetics, SMC-31(B),* 277-287.

Oommen, B., & Christensen, J. R. P. (1988). Epsilon-Optimal Discretized Reward-Penalty Learning Automata. *IEEE Transactions on Systems, Man, and Cybernetics, SMC-18,* 451–458. doi:10.1109/21.7494

Oommen, B., & Lanctot, J. K. (1990). Discretized Pursuit Learning Automata. *IEEE Transactions on Systems, Man, and Cybernetics, 20*(4), 931–938. doi:10.1109/21.105092

Oommen, B., & Rueda, L. (2004). A New Family of Weak Estimators for Training in Non-stationary Distributions. In *Proceedings of the Joint IAPR International Workshops SSPR 2004 and SPR 2004* (pp. 644-652). Lisbon, Portugal.

Oommen, B. J., & Rueda, L. (2006). Stochastic Learning-based Weak Estimation of Multinomial Random Variables and Its Applications to Non-stationary Environments. *Pattern Recognition, 39*, 328–341. doi:10.1016/j.patcog.2005.09.007

Papadimitriou, G. I. (1994a). Hierarchical Discretized Pursuit Nonlinear Learning Automata with Rapid Convergence and High Accuracy. *IEEE Transactions on Knowledge and Data Engineering, 6*, 654–659. doi:10.1109/69.298184

Papadimitriou, G. I. (1994b). A New Approach to the Design of Reinforcement Schemes for Learning Automata: Stochastic Estimator Learning Algorithms. *IEEE Transactions on Knowledge and Data Engineering, 6*, 649–654. doi:10.1109/69.298183

Rajaraman, K., & Sastry, P. S. (1996). Finite Time Analysis of the Pursuit Algorithm for Learning Automata. *IEEE Transactions on Systems, Man, and Cybernetics, 26*(4), 590–598. doi:10.1109/3477.517033

Ray, B., & Tsay, R. (2002). Bayesian Methods for Change-point Detection in Long-range Dependent Processes. *Journal of Time Series Analysis, 23*(6), 687–705. doi:10.1111/1467-9892.00286

Rueda, L. (2002). *Advances in Data Compression and Pattern Recognition*. (PhD Thesis), School of Computer Science, Carleton University, Ottawa. Canada.

Rueda, L., & Oommen, B. J. (2002, March). Greedy Adaptive Fano Coding. In *Proceedings of the 2002 IEEE Aerospace Conference*. BigSky, MT, USA. Track 10.0407.

Rueda, L., & Oommen, B. J. (2004). A Nearly Optimal Fano-Based Coding Algorithm. *Information Processing & Management, 40*(2), 257–268. doi:10.1016/S0306-4573(03)00007-4

Rueda, L., & Oommen, B. J. (2006). Stochastic Automata-based Estimators fro Adaptively Compressing Files with Nonstationary Distributions. *IEEE Transactions on Systems, Man, and Cybernetics, 36*(5), 1196–1200. doi:10.1109/TSMCB.2006.872256

Santo, M. D., Percannella, G., Sansone, C., & Vento, M. (2004). A multi-expert approach for shot classification in news videos. In *Image analysis and recognition, LNCS* (Vol. 3211, pp. 564-571). Amsterdan: Elsevier.

Thathachar, M. A. L., & Oommen, B. J. (1979). Discretized Reward-Inaction Learning Automata. *Journal of Cybernetics and Information Sciences*, 24-29.

Thathachar, M. A. L., & Sastry, P. (1985). A Class of Rapidly Converging Algorithms for Learning Automata. *IEEE Transactions on Systems, Man, and Cybernetics, SMC-15*, 168–175.

Thathachar, M. A. L., & Sastry, P. (1986, December). Estimator Algorithms for Learning Automata. In *Proc. of the platinum jubilee conference on systems and signal processing*. Bangalore, India.

Theodoridis, S., & Koutroumbas, K. (2006). *Pattern Recognition* (3rd ed.). Elsevier Academic Press.

Webb, A. (2002). *Statistical Pattern Recognition* (2nd ed.). New York: John Wiley & Sons. doi:10.1002/0470854774

Weinberger, M. J., & Ordentlich, E. (2002). On Delayed Prediction of Individual Sequences. *IEEE Transactions on Information Theory, 48*(7), 1959–1976. doi:10.1109/TIT.2002.1013136

KEY TERMS AND DEFINITIONS

Parameter Estimation: A process by which, given a know parametric form of a probability density function, the underlying parameters are learned from a set of finite, or possibly infinite, samples.

Non-Stationary Data: A source of data in which the distribution (or its parameters) change with time.

Learning Automata: A finite state machine that interacts with an environment and a teacher, and takes actions based on information provided by these two.

Pattern Classification: A field of machine intelligence that consists of making a decision involving some risk and based on pre-defined categories or patterns.

Data Compression: A field of information and data management that aims to change the representation of the data so as to minimize the size of the new representation with the aim of recovering as much information as possible when decompressing.

Adaptive Coding: A field of data compression that involves representing input data in such a way that the rules for encoding that data change over time.

Text Classification: A field of pattern classification that aims to classify data composed of symbols representing text, and by extracting the appropriate features.

Chapter 2
On Analogue TMR System

Pavel Kucera
Brno University of Technology, Czech Republic

ABSTRACT

This chapter presents a reliability model of the TMR (Triple Modular Redundancy) system based on analogue measurement channels. While reliability modelling of the standard TMR system (based on digital channels) has been well described in many previous publications, an applicable reliability solution for analogue measurement channels is still missing. First, the structure of analogue measurement channel is described in this chapter. Then, the reliability model of the wiring system is introduced. Next, the standard TMR model is presented and its reliability model is mentioned. An analogue TMR measurement channel system is introduced and its reliability model based on Markov processes is presented. Then the reliability model of the communication channel is described. Finally, the reliability of this model is analytically calculated and the solution is applied to an example.

INTRODUCTION

There are many methods on how to improve reliability of the system. One of the common methods is a concept of redundancy. Redundancy is simply the addition of information beyond what is needed for standard system operation. This information can be a physical value or electric signal, hardware element or subsystem, an application or software module. The concept of redundancy is based on

Murphy's idea: "If anything can go wrong, it will". That means that there is no such thing as a never-failing system, because systems are designed and created by humans. Redundancy can improve our chance to ensure standard operation of the system for a long time.

The concept of redundancy is very often managed by a technique of fault masking. Fault masking is simply preventing faults (electric shorts, endless loop, electromagnetic interference, etc.) from introducing errors (incorrect values) within a system. Commonly used techniques for masking

DOI: 10.4018/978-1-61692-811-7.ch002

Figure 1. Analogue measurement of a TMR channel.

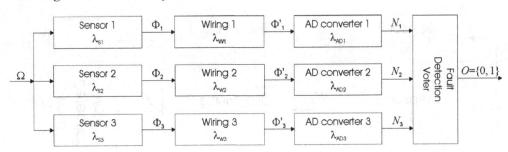

an error of a discrete signal are usually based on the TMR (Triple Modular Redundancy) system. The advantage of the TMR system is that it can easy solve the problem of what the correct output of the redundant structure should be and how to ensure that the faulty element does not produce an error within a system. For instance, if there are 3 discrete sensors in the measurement channel then the TMR simply chooses a majority signal from these sensors. One faulty sensor does not produce an incorrect value within a system.

The TMR system is a complex system. It consists of several sub-systems; each has its own reliability parameter. A common way how to describe reliability of the single element or sub-systems is to use the failure rate value (common symbol is λ and the unit is h^{-1}) or Mean Time Between Failure (the short is MTBF and the unit is h). If the exponential failure law is considered for the element, then the failure rate of the element is reciprocal for the MTBF (Johnson, 1976). Because of uniformity, only failure rate λ and reliability R are used as reliability parameters in this chapter.

If the analogue measurement channel is considered in Figure 1, then 3 sensors measuring the same physical value are within the TMR system (Sensor 1, 2 and 3). A sensor usually has a reliability parameter defined by a manufacturer (λ_s). However, each sensor in Figure 1 is connected by a medium (this chapter only considers metallic wiring) and this medium also has a reliability value (λ_w). How can the failure rate of this medium be declared and how does it influence the reliability

parameter of the entire TMR system? It cannot be defined by the manufacturer of the sensor because it heavily depends on the concrete situation, i.e. where the sensor is installed, what the environment is, what the quality of this medium is, etc. A continuous signal from the analogue sensor must be converted from the analogue value into its discrete version. This discrete value is often represented by a number in the computer memory. This transformation is done by the Analogue-to-Digital converter (ADC). The ADC also has some reliability value, usually declared by the manufacturer.

The modern control system, where the key control elements are redundant, usually relies on an industrial communication bus (fieldbus), like Profibus, AS-Interface, DeviceNet, EtherCat, etc. An industrial bus significantly improves reliability of the medium λ_w and it also enables the implementation of the ADC directly into the sensor. Such structure with a communication bus is shown in Figure 2. Modern sensors are equipped by a microcontroller (intelligent sensors), which brings many advantages in the area of diagnostic features of the sensor. It is easier for the TMR system to decide, what measurement channel is faulty and if the sensor is connected to the superior system by a fieldbus. Reliability of the single sensor then includes the reliability of the physical value sensor, microcontroller, ADC, and firmware. Modern approaches, like formal methods, ensure that this kind of sensor can be developed with a lower

Figure 2. Analogue measurement TMR channel with industrial bus.

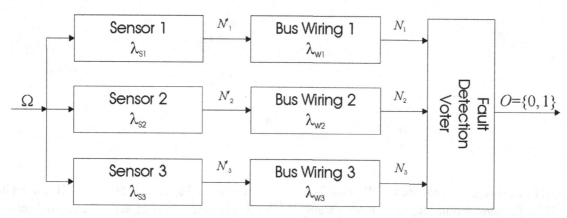

failure rate compared to the sensors considered in Figure 1 (Kucera, 2002).

Finally, the key element in the TMR system, the voter, is also an application specific element. It can be a hardware module, software module, or a combination of both. In this chapter it is strictly considered that the voter is a software implemented solution in a microcontroller. Evaluating the reliability of the software-implemented voter is not an easy task and it is out of the scope of this chapter. Modern approaches reveal the possibility of utilization of formal methods, temporal logic, timed automata, etc. into the area of software application design with the aim to improve reliability parameters of the modern systems (Kucera, 2004), (Penczek 2006).

Current systems, where fault-tolerant behaviour is required, usually rely on some kind of independent protection mechanism. This protection mechanism is responsible for safety behaviour of the entire system (for instance, shutting down the system) in the case that the system works with incorrect value(s). If this protection mechanism is based on the measurement of critical physical values in the technology (temperature, pressure, vibration, etc.), then this measurement is a crucial element in the entire protection mechanism. Critical physical values are usually not measured

by analogue sensors, because the protection mechanism is influenced only by their minimal and maximal limits, i.e. if the physical value is above or below some safety level. For example, the speed of the turbine is measured by a speed indicator. A protection mechanism must cut off the turbine if its speed is higher than the safety level. Speed of the turbine is an analogue value measured by a sensor and it is represented as a number in the meaningful range, for instance <0; 15 000> min^{-1}. Input into the protection mechanism is not an analogue speed value but the discrete (Boolean) value that indicates if the speed is above the safety level or not (true/false, 0/1, etc.). If these discrete and analogue values are combined and evaluated by a fault-detection mechanism, then the reliability of the entire protection mechanism can be significantly improved.

The price of the analogue sensors of a physical value is not a decisive aspect for the control system and analogue sensors are commonly used in protection mechanisms. There is a possibility to implement a fault-detection feature into the TMR system and to improve the reliability parameter of the TMR system itself. The question is how to model and how to evaluate this reliability parameter. This chapter would like to suggest the solution to this problem.

BACKGROUND

The concept of redundancy by the TMR system is focused in the central element - in the voter; if the voter fails, the complete system fails. This chapter only considers TMR systems with a single voter, implemented by a software module. Implementation of the standard TMR system based on digital measurement channels and a single voter has been well-known for many years; the reader can find comprehensive information including reliability modelling for a discrete TMR system in (Johnson, 1976); however, an easily applicable analytical solution for a discrete value, which is measured by analogue measurement channels and evaluated by a computer (i.e. by a software), is still missing. Furthermore, the reliability modelling of the transmission medium (analogue, discrete, or serial) for the physical values is also missing.

Moving implementation of the voter from the hardware into the software brings a question about the reliability of such a solution. Recent work reveals the possibilities of software-implemented hardware. For instance G. Saha in (Saha, G. K. 2006) presents a software implemented self-checking technique that is capable of detecting hardware-transient faults in a processor's registers. It allows the TMR's decision mechanism (voter) to move from its hardware implementation into the software implementation. In this software implementation, another technique must be used to achieve fault-tolerant behaviour of the voter. Software fault tolerance has been introduced in many previous publications, including error detection, monitoring mechanisms, and error recovery. Brian Randell and Xu Jie introduced the evolution of the recovery block concept for achieving the fault tolerance in the software in (Lyu, 1995). Laura Pullum describes an effective technique for an N-version programming operation considering both fault-free and failure scenarios in software in (Pullum, 2001). The time redundancy approach, which is capable of detecting permanent faults that occur during the executions of two or more task

replicas, is a powerful tool significantly improving reliability of the voter in the TMR system. An expression for estimating the probability of detecting data errors generated by permanent faults with time redundant execution can be found in (Aidemark, 2003). Another approach is based on idea: how to evaluate the reliability of the application running in the Programmable Logic Controller (PLC). PLCs are commonly used as key elements in the redundant structures and the reliability of the software running in PLC can be evaluated by a method of error modelling (Kucera, 2004). Completely different approaches are based on formal methods. Formal methods significantly decrease software design error as well as running errors. Using different modelling and verification techniques (temporal logic, timed automata, time Petri nets, etc.) in the area of software design is possible and it will be the basic concept of the application design in the future (Kucera, 2002).

Evaluation of the reliability of the system described in this chapter is based on a Markov modelling technique, which has been introduced in 1906 by A. A. Markov; comprehensive information can be found in (Meyn, 1993). Reliability of the communication channel is based on the author's Ph.D. thesis (Kucera, 2003) and the US Military handbook (MIL-HDBK-217, 1995).

TMR SYSTEM WITH ANALOGUE CHANNELS

A TMR system with analogue channels is a system where a physical analogue value is measured, but only its discrete representation (TRUE/FALSE) is important for further processing (for example, for a protection mechanism). This is a common task in the area of fault tolerant systems or fail-stop/safe systems. For example, in a turbine protection system where the speed is measured by three incremental sensors, only a speed above the critical one is important. Other values that are lower than this critical speed are not considered by this protection mechanism. A TMR system with analogue channels represents a situation that is shown in Figure 1 or 2.

The physical value Ω (voltage, temperature, pressure, etc.) is transformed in the triple sensors with the failure rate λ_{si}, to its electrical representation $\Phi_I \subseteq R$. An electrical signal then flows through the transmission channel with the failure rate λ_{wi}, to the ADC with the failure rate λ_{ADi}. The original electrical signal Φ is influenced by the transmission channel, thus the transfer function (mapping function) f has an impact on the original signal, $f: \Phi \rightarrow \Phi'$, where $\Phi' \subseteq R$. The ADC transforms the influenced electric signal Φ' into its integer representation N by the gain function $g: \Phi' \rightarrow N$, where $N \subseteq Z$. Finally, the Fault Detection Voter (FDV) transforms sets of integer values $N_{1,2,3}$ from Figure 1 or 2, into the binary set $O = \{0,1\}$. If the industrial bus and intelligent sensor are used (Figure 2), than the transform functions f and g are hidden in the sensor and they are not accessible to the designer of the system. However, many diagnostic functions are available in intelligent sensors and unknown transfer functions f and g are not crucial. The communication bus (Bus Wiring) in Figure 2 transforms integer representation N' from the intelligent sensor into the value N. It represents not only the original integer value, but also the diagnostic information from the intelligent sensor.

The Fault Detection Voter ensures the opening of the switch for the faulty channel - Figure 6. This is significantly different from the standard TMR system in which the faulty module influences the voting mechanism in the presence of a fault in the measurement channel. The Markov model of this system is shown in Figure 7. While reliability parameters (failure rate) of the sensors and ADC are usually known from the specification of the manufacturer, reliability parameters of the wiring and entire system in Figure 1 or 2 must be determined in a different way.

Reliability Modelling of the Wiring

Wiring is a block that represents the transmission channel between the sensor and the ADC in Figure 1. It also represents the situation where the ADC is a part of the sensor and the transmission channel is a serial communication bus – Figure 2. If the system in Figure 1 or 2 is considered, then the number of wires in the system is:

$$W = 3 \cdot n \quad [-], \tag{1}$$

where n is the number of necessary wires for the connection of the single sensor. Parameter n depends on the output of the sensor. It can be a current loop, differential voltage channel, RS485; in all these examples, $n=2$. However, if the sensor is connected to the communication bus by more wires (CAN, RS232, I2C, etc.), parameter n is equal to 3 or it can be even greater. The failure rate of such a wiring system is equal to:

$$\lambda_w = \lambda_0 \left[M\pi_m + W \int \pi_e(l)dl \right] \quad [h^{-1}], \tag{2}$$

where:

λ_0 is a basic failure rate of the single connection: $\lambda_0 = 10^{-7}$ h^{-1},

M   is the total number of connected elements to the wiring,

π_m is a mechanical coefficient of the quality of the connection,

W   is above defined number of wires from equation (1),

π_e is a coefficient of electrical coupling.

The mechanical coefficient of the quality of the connection π_m, is calculated as:

Figure 3. Typical waveforms of the electrical coefficient

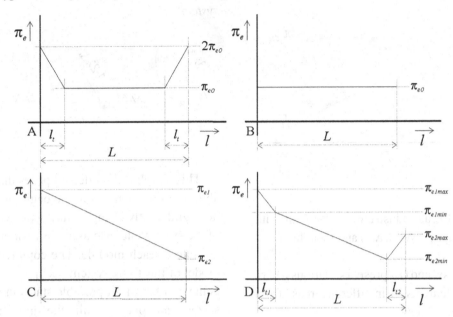

$$\pi_m = \pi_j \pi_v \ [-], \qquad (3)$$

where:

π_j is a junction coefficient:

    $\pi_j = 1.0$ for a soldered connection,

    $\pi_j = 1.5$ for a plug-in connection,

    $\pi_j = 2.0$ for a screw connection,

π_v is a coefficient of vibration:

    $\pi_v = 0.0$ for an environment with no vibrations,

    $\pi_v = 1.0$ for stationary industrial mounts (switch-boards, static facilities ...),

    $\pi_v = 2.0$ for non-stationary industrial mounts.

The coefficient of electrical coupling π_e $[m^{-1}]$ determines electromagnetic influences of the environment (EMI). Typical waveforms of this coefficient for two elements on the bus ($M=2$) with mutual distance L are shown in Figure 3.

Waveforms A and B represent situations, where both control elements are in the same area - from the EMI point of view. Waveform A determines a situation where the wire connection has a shield-ing. In this case, the electrical coefficient π_e has a constant value π_{e0} in the interval $l \in (l_t, L - l_t)$ due to the fact that the EMI has the same effect on the shielded part of the wire connection. The non-shielded part of the wire connection in the interval $l \in <0, l_t> \cup <L - l_t, L>$ is called the terminal length (l_t) and the electrical coefficient typically starts at the value $2\pi_{e0}$ at the zero distance from the control element and falls down to the value π_{e0} after terminal length l_t and vice versa for the other control element. Terminal boards are usu-ally the weak spots of the bus systems because they are usually not shielded in the industrial environment and waveform A reflects these weak-nesses. On the other hand, waveform B is typical for non-shielded bus subsystems; therefore, the electrical coefficient has a constant value π_{e0} in the entire interval $l \in (0, L)$. Typical values of this coefficient are:

$\pi_{e0} = 0.1 \ m^{-1}$ for a laboratory or industrial environ-ment with none or minimal EMI,

$\pi_{e0} = 0.3 \ m^{-1}$ for an industrial environment with low EMI (low-power drives and switches),

Figure 4. General electrical coefficient.

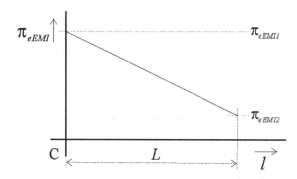

$\pi_{e0} = 0.5\ m^{-1}$ for an industrial environment with high EMI (high-power drives and switches).

Waveforms C and D represent situations where both control elements are in different areas - from the EMI point of view.

Formally, waveform D is the Cartesian product between waveform *A* and the general electrical coefficient π_{eEMI} in Figure 4, thus:

$$\Pi_e(C) \cong \Pi_e(A) \times \Pi_{eEMI} . \tag{4}$$

RELIABILITY MODELLING OF THE TMR SYSTEM

The TMR system is a special example of the *M*-of-*N* system. TMR is a configuration where *M*=2 and *N*=3, e.g. 2 of the 3 modules (2-of-3 system) must work for the majority voting mechanism to function properly. This system is used in the area of fault-tolerant systems as a typical fault masking system. In many cases, all three modules are identical not only from the reliability point of view, but also from their implementation.

The reliability *R* of this system can easily be calculated with the use of the Markov model. A simplified Markov model of the TMR system (all three modules are identical from the reliability point of view) is shown in the following Figure 5 (Johnson, 1976).

Figure 5. Simplified Markov model of the TMR system

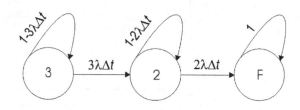

This simplified model supposes that the reliability of the voter is 1 at the beginning and it is not significantly changed during the working life of the system and also assumes an identical failure rate of each module. The complete Markov model of the TMR system occupies 2^3 states - it is the number of all possible states in which the system can appear - while the simplified model considers only three Markov virtual states {3, 2, F}. State 3 represents the situation in which all three modules in the TMR system are functioning correctly. State 2 is the state in which two modules are working correctly and one module is not functional. State F is the state in which two (or all three) modules have failed. For example, the probability of transition from state 3 to state 2 depends on the probability that any of the three modules may fail: $p=3\lambda(\Delta t)$ and the probability that the system remains in state 3 is: $p=1 - 3\lambda(\Delta t)$. The reliability of the TMR system is the probability of being in either state 3 or 2, where the system works correctly:

$$R_{TMR}\left(t\right) = 3e^{-2\lambda t} - 2e^{-3\lambda t} = 3R(t)^2 - 2R(t)^3$$
$$[\text{-}], \tag{5}$$

where $R(t)$ is the reliability of the single module at time t.

The voter is the key element in every TMR system. It is responsible for the correct interpretation of the input signals. In case of binary classified values (inputs) $I_{1,2,3}=\{0, 1\}$, the voter simply calculates the following Boolean equation:

Figure 6. Fault Detection Voter.

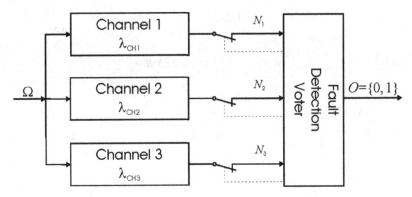

$$O = I_1 \wedge I_2 \vee I_1 \wedge I_3 \vee I_2 \wedge I_3. \qquad (6)$$

Analogue TMR System

An analogue TMR system has three analogue inputs (voltage, current, etc.). These inputs are usually represented by numbers stored in a computer's memory. These numbers are results of Analog/Digital conversions of the original analogue signals with the resolution of 8, 10, 12 bits or more.

The Markov model of the analogue TMR system is identical to its discrete counterpart as well as the reliability that the system works correctly - equation (5). The difference lies in the voter itself. It cannot simply decide what analogue signals have majority at one moment using Boolean equation (6). Analogue voters use a different approach called the mid-value selection. This method chooses a value that lies between the remaining two values. Software implementations are usually based on either sorting these three signals and choosing the middle one or simple *if-else* statements.

Current voters are usually based on microcontrollers with high reliability and computational power. They are able not only to select a mid-value signal in real-time processing, but also to compute fault analysis with the aim to decide which measurement channel is faulty and to change an original 2 to 3 system to a 1 to 3 system, i.e. per-

fectly parallel system. It significantly improves the reliability of the original TMR system; however, the challenging question here is how to evaluate this improvement.

RELIABILITY MODELLING OF THE FDV

The schematic diagram of the Fault Detection Voter (FDV) from Figure 1 or 2 is shown in Figure 6. The FDV enables to open the switch for the successfully recognized faulty channel and this is significantly different from the standard TMR system in which the faulty module influences the voting mechanism. The Markov model of this system is shown in Figure 7 (Kucera, 2006).

Failure rate of the i-th channel in Figure 1 is calculated as:

$$\lambda_{CHi} = \lambda_{Si} + \lambda_{Wi} + \lambda_{ADi} \ [h^{-1}], \qquad (7a)$$

where λ_{Si}, λ_{Wi}, and λ_{ADi} are failure rates of the sensor, ADC, and transfer medium. Failure rate of the i-th channel in Figure 2 is calculated as:

$$\lambda_{CHi} = \lambda_{Si} + \lambda_{Wi} [h^{-1}], \qquad (7b)$$

Figure 7. Markov model of the Fault Detection Voter.

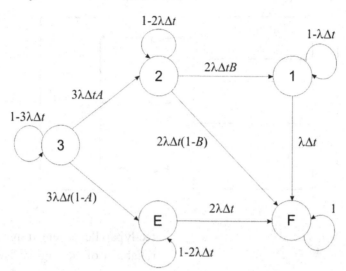

where λ_{Si}, λ_{Wi} are failure rates of the sensor and communication bus. For simplicity, it is assumed the failure rates of the channels are identical, i.e.:

$$\lambda_{CH1} = \lambda_{CH2} = \lambda_{CH3} = \lambda \ [h^{-1}]. \tag{8}$$

The system is assumed to begin in the fault free state, which is labelled as state 3 at time $t=0$; all three channels operate correctly. The system remains in this state as long as a failure of some channel does not occur. The probability of being in the same state 3 at the end of the period Δt is calculated as $1-3\Delta t$, where $3\Delta t$ is the probability of leaving state 3 during Δt time period. The probability of exiting state 3 depends on the ability of the voter to recognize the faulty channel. The probability that the failure channel will be correctly handled, while the system is in state 3, is denoted as A. If the failure channel is not correctly handled, it is with the probability $3\lambda\Delta t(1-A)$, then the system enters the state E - Error state; two channels operate correctly and one does not and it is not obvious which one it is. It is the same situation as state 2 in Figure 5 for a standard TMR system - where a faulty channel is masked. The next failure, with

the probability $2\lambda\Delta t$, moves the system into state F (Failure state), where the FDV fails.

If the first failed channel is handled correctly, then the system enters state 2 (two channels operate correctly and they are known) and the system remains, with the probability $1-2\lambda\Delta t$, in this state until another failure of any channel occurs. If a second failure occurs, the FDV recognizes the faulty channel with the probability $2\lambda\Delta tB$ and the system enters state 1 (one channel operates correctly and it is known which one), where it remains until a failure of this channel occurs. If a failure of this module occurs, the system enters state F – the FDV fails.

If the second failure is not correctly handled, the probability is $2\lambda\Delta t(1-B)$, then the system enters the failure state F immediately. The probability that the failure channel will be handled correctly, while the system is in state 2, is denoted as B.

Reliability Analysis of the FDV

The complete set of discrete-time equations for the Markov model of the system in Figure 7 can be written as equation (9):

$$\begin{bmatrix} p_3(t+\Delta t) \\ p_2(t+\Delta t) \\ p_1(t+\Delta t) \\ p_E(t+\Delta t) \\ p_F(t+\Delta t) \end{bmatrix} = \begin{bmatrix} 1-3\lambda\Delta t & 0 & 0 & 0 & 0 \\ 3\lambda\Delta t A & 1-2\lambda\Delta t & 0 & 0 & 0 \\ 0 & 2\lambda\Delta t B & 1-\lambda\Delta t & 0 & 0 \\ 3\lambda\Delta t(1-A) & 0 & 0 & 1-2\lambda\Delta t & 0 \\ 0 & 2\lambda\Delta t(1-B) & \lambda\Delta t & 2\lambda\Delta t & 1 \end{bmatrix} \cdot \begin{bmatrix} p_3(t) \\ p_2(t) \\ p_1(t) \\ p_E(t) \\ p_F(t) \end{bmatrix}$$

$$(9)$$

where $p(t)$ is the probability the system is being in the state 3, 2, 1, E or F. If the considered time limit is $\Delta t \rightarrow 0$, then this set of equations can be written as a set of differential equations (10):

$$\frac{dp_3(t)}{dt} = -3\lambda p_3(t)$$

$$\frac{dp_2(t)}{dt} = 3\lambda A p_3(t) - 2\lambda p_2(t)$$

$$\frac{dp_1(t)}{dt} = 2\lambda B p_2(t) - \lambda p_1(t)$$

$$\frac{dp_E(t)}{dt} = 3\lambda p_3(t) - 3\lambda A p_3(t) - 2\lambda p_E(t)$$

$$\frac{dp_F(t)}{dt} = 2\lambda p_2(t) - 2\lambda B p_2(t) + \lambda p_1(t) + 2\lambda p_E(t)$$

$$(10)$$

Initial conditions of the set of differential equations (10) are based on the fact that the system in Figure 7 starts in the perfect state 3 at time $t=0$; thus $p_3(0)=1$, $p_2(0)=0$, $p_1(0)=0$, $p_E(0)=0$, $p_F(0)=0$. The simultaneous differential equations (10) can be solved using the Laplace transform or another approach. The solution for the state value p_F is the probability that the system in Figure 7 is in state F:

$$p_F(t) = 1 + (2-3AB)e^{-3\lambda t} + (6AB-3)e^{-2\lambda t} - 3ABe^{-\lambda t}$$

$$(11)$$

where:

λ is a failure rate of a single measurement channel (8),

A   is the probability that the failure channel will be correctly handled if the system in Figure 7 is in state 3,

B   is the probability that the failure channel will be correctly handled if the system in Figure 7 is in state 2.

If the constant failure rate and the exponential failure law are considered in the system, then the probability that the FDV system is in state F is from equation (11):

$$p_F = 1 + (2-3AB)R^3 + (6AB-3)R^2 - 3ABR$$

$$(12)$$

where $R=e^{-\lambda t}$ (exponential failure law), λ is a failure rate of the single measurement channel, and A and B are instances of the probability that the first (second) failure of the channel is handled correctly. The probability that the FDV system operates correctly is then from equation (12):

$$R_{FDV} = 1 - p_F = (3AB-2)R^3 + (3-6AB)R^2 + 3ABR$$

$$(13)$$

Fault Detection Parameters

It is very important is to determine coefficients A and B. There are many ways of how to decide which channels failed at time t. A method based either on collection of possible failures or a method based on the physical correctness of the signal will be introduced.

The first method simply assumes that all detectable errors and all possible errors that can occur in the system in Figure 7 are known. If the system is in state 2, then the faulty module will be recognized correctly with the probability B and will not be recognized correctly with the probability $1-B$. The coefficient B is then equal to:

$$B = \frac{\sum \text{detectable errors}}{\sum \text{all errors}}.$$

$$(14)$$

The detectable error in the measurement channel depends on the fault detection algorithm in the voter. If this algorithm statically checks whether the values are in defined ranges, then it is easy

Figure 8. Physical correctness of the signal approach.

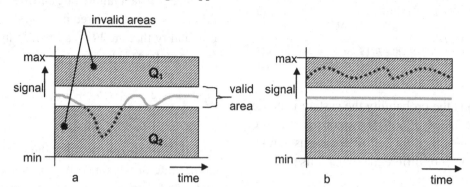

to detect the failure channel and to disconnect it. This approach is the second method that is based on the physical correctness of the signal. The principle is shown in Figure 8a (Kucera, 2008).

Physical correctness means that not all values of the signal are physically possible. For instance, the current loop 4-20 mA ensures that signals below 4 mA are in the invalid range and such a measurement channel will easily be recognized and removed from the TMR by a FDV - Figure 8a. The solid line represents a situation where the signal is inside the valid area and the dashed line represents a situation where it is not. Ranges of areas Q_1 and Q_2 depend on the real situation. Sometimes, area Q_1 is equal to zero or to the maximum possible value. In other cases, area Q_2 is equal to zero; for instance the speed of a turbine could be within the range of 0 to 40 000 revs/min. The incremental sensor, however, is able to detect a speed within the range of 0 to 100 000 revs/min. Then the range of area Q_2 is zero and the range of area Q_1 is 60 000 revs/min.

The probability that the faulty channel will be recognized using this technique is equal to:

$$B = \frac{Q_1 + Q_2}{max - min},$$ (15)

where *max* is a maximum value from a sensor and *min* is a minimum value from a sensor represented as a number *N* in Figure 1 or 2.

This technique has limitations. Practical experience shows that a signal can be faulty but in the valid range. This is shown in Figure 8b, where the real signal is out of the valid range (dashed line), while the value from the measurement channel is trapped in the valid range because there is an error in the measurement channel (sensor, wiring, AD converter, etc.). In this case, equation (15) fails and coefficient *B* is wrongly calculated.

If the system in Figure 7 is in state 3, there is an advantage that at least two modules are working correctly and the probability that the faulty channel will be recognized can be easily calculated from the probability B, equations (14) or (15). Behaviour of the system from Figure 7, which is in state 3, is the same as the behaviour of the system from Figure 5. The only difference is that the $\lambda \Delta t$ value of the single element is now the probability that the faulty channel will be recognised correctly; and it determines parameter B. Parameter B is, in fact, reliability of the decision-making mechanism; thus, it can be derived from equation (5) that parameter A is equal to:

$$A = 3B^2 - 2B^3.$$ (16)

EXAMPLE

Let us consider a simple fault detection software algorithm that checks triple temperature measurement channels Ω in the range of <20; 1200> °C. Checking is based on simple decision, if the value from the sensor is in the valid range or if it is not (Figure 8a). In the easiest way, it can be done by simple *if-then* statements in higher programming language. *If* the value from the measurement channel is outside the valid range, *then* remove this faulty channel from the decision mechanism. Information about temperature is transformed in the sensor with the input range <0; 1500> °C into the electric signal Φ <4; 20> mA. The electric signal is transferred via physical medium into the signal Φ' and this signal is converted in the 12-bit ADC into the integer number N by the following gain function:

$$g = \frac{4095}{20}, \tag{17}$$

where $N=g\Phi'$ is in the range <0; 4095> and Φ' is in the range <0; 20> mA. Table 1 shows possible errors and the capability of the FDV to detect them.

Table 1 does not cover all possible errors as they always depend on implementation details of the channel.

In our example, if the wire loop is disconnected (high impedance problem – row 5 in Table 1), then any temperature converted by the sensor into its electrical representation is detected by the ADC as 0 mA and the output integer N is zero (or close to zero). If the gain function (17) is considered, then it is an easily detectable error because FDV simply checks every channel for conditions: *if* $N_i < LOW_1$, then mark i_{th} channel as faulty, where N_i is an integer number returned by the i_{th} channel and LOW_1 is the lowest possible value of this number. Level LOW_1 is determined by a conversion result lower than 4 mA, i.e. LOW_1 = 819. LOW_2 and $HIGH_2$ represent a situation where temperature is outside its physical range of <20; 1200> °C, thus $LOW_2=863$ and $HIGH_2=3440$. Not all errors are easy to detect. For instance, if the output signal from the faulty

sensor is trapped inside the valid range (Figure 8b), the above mentioned *if-then* condition or another range condition will not work. This kind of error is not detectable that way and the time-varying algorithm must be used. Such an algorithm can increase the number of detectable errors and parameter B from the equation (14) can be increased. If Table 1 is considered, then the lowest probability that the faulty channel will be recognized without consideration of the actual state of the Markov model in Figure 8 is from equation (14):

$$B = \frac{8}{9} = 0.\bar{8}. \tag{18}$$

Thus, if the system is in state 2 and the decision which channel is faulty must be made, this decision will succeed with a probability of $0.\bar{8}$. If the system is in state 3, the probability A is higher due to the TMR effect described in equation (16):

$$A = 3B^2 - 2B^3 = 0.966. \tag{19}$$

Figure 9 shows curves of reliability in the standard TMR system from equation (5) - line R_TMR. It also shows a system with the Fault Detection Voter from equation (13) - line R_FDV. The coefficient AB is taken from the above example, i.e. $AB=0.857$. It is evident that the FDV system has a higher reliability than a single channel even if the reliability of the single channel is lower than 0.5, where the TMR system has lower reliability then a single measurement channel (i.e. redundancy does not produce a better result than a single element in the system). Using simple *if-then* statements in the voter can increase the reliability of the entire TMR system based on an analogue measurement channel. For instance, if the reliability of the single channel is 0.8, then the reliability of the standard TMR system is 0.896 and the reliability of the TMR system with the

Table 1. Possible errors in the measurement channel.

No.	Error	Detect.	Remark
1	Sensor error - power loss	TRUE	$N<LOW_1$
2	Sensor error - impossible temperature	TRUE	$N>HIGH_2$ or $N<LOW_2$
3	Sensor error - temperature stuck in the range	FALSE	Time-varying problem
4	Wiring error - wire loop short circuit	TRUE	$N<LOW_1$
5	Wiring error - wire loop high impedance	TRUE	$N<LOW$
6	Wiring error - power loss	TRUE	$N<LOW_1$
7	AD error - conversion out of range	TRUE	$N>HIGH_2$ or $N<LOW_2$
8	AD error - power loss	TRUE	$N<LOW_1$
9	AD error - input signal out of range	TRUE	$N>HIGH_2$ or $N<LOW_2$

fault detection voter with the parameters described in this example is 0.978. This is a better result, approximately by 10%.

FUTURE RESEARCH DIRECTIONS

The presented FDV for an analogue measurement TMR channel is an easy to use method for determining reliability parameters of such a system. A method was also suggested of how to determine reliability parameters of the wiring. The problem is how to determine a reliability parameter of the voter itself. As was mentioned in the background section of this chapter, there are many techniques that are applicable for the software tolerance aspects of the voter such as error detection, monitoring mechanisms, error recovery, recovery blocks, time redundancy, data and design diversity, N-version programming, acceptance voting, and many others. These methods help make software implementation fault-tolerant; however,

the crucial question is how to determine reliability parameters: failure rate λ and reliability R.

Software reliability models are used to describe the evolution of the software debugging process and to measure the quality of the software. Two types of software reliability exist: dynamic models and static models. Dynamic models follow the changes of the software throughout the entire testing period. Static models usually measure the quality of the software by taking one snapshot. This snapshot is taken either at the beginning of the debugging process to assist managers in planning or at the validation phase. Software reliability is defined to be the probability of failure-free operation of a computer program in a specific environment for a specified period of time. For instance, Yu in (Yu, 1988) supposes that the defect model of the software product is a function:

$$D = f(M, ED, T, other), \qquad (20)$$

where:

D   is the number of defects to be found in a certain time period,

M   is a static program metric - such as lines of code, volume, etc.,

ED   is the defect found in the earlier stages of testing,

T   is the testing time in CPU time, calendar time, etc.,

other stands for additional parameters such as the programmer's skills, programming language, task complexity, etc.

Usually, a static model assumes that some variable(s) influences the number of errors placed in the software and that the influence may be described via regression analysis between the errors found in a software project and the variables that supposedly influence the errors.

Future work will be focused on function (20) for the purpose of the software-implemented

Figure 9. Comparison of a TMR system and FDV with AB=0.857.

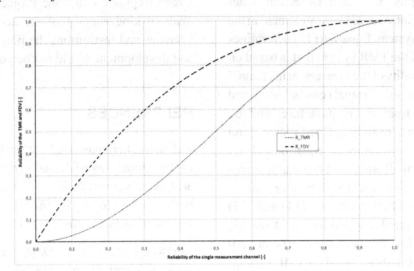

Fault Detection Voter with the aim to determine the reliability parameter of the entire analogue measurement channel in Figure 1 or 2.

As was mentioned in the introduction, modern development techniques are based on formal methods. The author's recent research reveals the possibility of automatic implementation of the formally described algorithm into target hardware (Kucera, 2009). The formally described Fault Detection Voter can be mathematically proved and future development tools enable either automatic or semi-automatic implementation of the FDV algorithm into the target hardware without human intervention. It decreases the failure rate of the software part of the voter and increases the reliability of the entire TMR system. Future work will be also focused on the area of formal specification of the FDV algorithm with the aim to simplify its verification, implementation, and testing.

CONCLUSION

There are many applications where correct behaviour of the control system is a decisive problem not only because of safety features (power plants, chemical processes, transportation, etc.), but also for the availability of the system and the cost of the final product. Modern control algorithms running either in embedded systems or in centralised control stations rely on the system's redundancy. Redundancy is often managed by the concept of TMR. It is easy to calculate reliability of this redundant structure if the failure rates or reliabilities of the used components are known (from equation 5). Also, the voter, as the key element in the TMR concept, performs relatively simple work. It either performs mid-value selection from the continuous signals or calculates Booleans equation (6) for discrete signals. Today, control systems often work with continuous signals because the price of the analogue sensors is decreasing and they can be easily connected to the control element by an industrial bus. The presence of the continuous signals in the voter intuitively increases reliability of the TMR systems because even a simple *if-then* decision algorithm can decide which measurement channel is faulty and this channel will be removed from the voting mechanism (Figure 7). Original 2-of-3 systems can degrade to 1-of-3 system (i.e. perfectly parallel redundancy) without cut-off of the technology. The challenging question is how to evaluate this improvement.

In this chapter, the Fault Detection Voter (FDV) has been introduced as a key element in the standard TMR system. Equation (13) determines the reliability of the TMR system that is based on this FDV. Reliability of the measurement channel (based on a continuous signal) can be calculated by parameters from the manufacturer and by equations (7a) or (7b) and (2). Coefficients A and B can be determined either by equation (14) (if the ratio between all errors and detectable errors is known) or by equation (15) if the more robust approach is used. Both equations (14) and (15) only provide a rough approximation of reality; however, even low levels of the coefficient AB bring a better result then a standard TMR system. For instance, if the FDV algorithm is able to detect 8 possible problems in the measurement channel from 9 possibilities, then for the reliability of the single channel $R=0.8$, our system produces about a 10% better result then the standard TMR system. Furthermore, this detection is nothing complicated. It is based on easy-to-prove *if-then* statements described in Table 1.

If the reliability of the standard TMR system from equation (5) and TMR system with a Fault Detection Voter from equation (13) is compared, then the TMR system with the FDV is better for any value of the coefficient $AB \in (0, 1>$. In the best case, where $AB=1$, i.e. ability of the FDV to recognise a faulty channel is 100%, the system behaviour is like a 1-of-3 system (i.e. perfect parallel system) and in the worst case, where $AB=0$, the system behaviour is like a standard 2-of-3 (i.e. TMR) system.

ACKNOWLEDGMENT

This research has been supported in part by the Ministry of Education, Youth, and Sports of the Czech Republic under the Project 1M0567 (Centre for Applied Cybernetics) and by the Research Intent MSM0021630529 (Intelligent systems in automation) and by the Grant Agency of the Czech Republic under the Project GA1890030. Without kind support of the above-mentioned agencies and institutions the presented research and development would not be possible.

REFERENCES

Aidemark, J., Folkesson, P., & Karlsson, J. (2003). On the probability of detecting data errors generated by permanent faults using time redundancy. In *Proceedings of the 9th IEEE International On-Line Testing Symposium*, IOLTS'03, pp. 68-74.

Johnson, B. W. (1976). *Design and Analysis of Fault-Tolerant Digital Systems*. Boston, MA: Addison-Wesley Longman Publishing Co., Inc.

Kucera, P. (2003). *Formal methods in industrial communication*. Unpublished Ph.D. thesis, Brno University of Technology, Czech Republic. Retrieved from http://taceo.eu

Kucera, P., & Honzik, P. (2009). Automation of Real-Time Embedded System Design. *Proceedings on The 13th World Multi-Conference on Systemics, Cybernetics and Informatics: WMSCI 2009*. [Orlando, FL.]. *Intern.Inst. of Informatics and Systemics., I,* 237–242.

Kucera, P., Honzik, P., Hyncica, O., & Fojtik, P. (2008). On Analogue TMR System. In *14th International Congress of Cybernetics and Systems of WOSC Proceedings*. Poland, Wroclaw: Oficyna Wydawnicza Politechniki Wroclawskiej, p. 501-510

Kucera, P., & Hyncica, O. (2006). Reliability model of TMR system with fault detection. *Proceedings of IFAC WORKSHOP on Programmable Devices and Embedded Systems PDeS2006*. Brno: VUT v Brne, p. 468-472

Kucera, P., & Zezulka, F. (2004). *Software reliability model for PLC. Proceedings on the 8th World Multi-conference SCI'04. Intern. Inst. of Informatics and Systemics* (pp. 349–352). Orlando: Nagib Callaos.

Kucera, P., Zezulka, F., Sveda, M., & Vrba, R. (2002). Executable specifications for Process Automation and Microelectronics. *IEEE TC-ECBS and IFIP WG10.1 Joint Workshop on Formal Specifications of Computer-Based Systems.* Lund, University of Stirling, p. 91-98.

Lyu, R. M. (Ed.). (1995). *Software fault tolerance.* Chichester, UK: John Wiley & Sons, Inc.

Meyn, S. P., & Tweedie, R. L. (1993). *Markov Chains and Stochastic Stability.* London, U.K: Springer-Verlag.

MIL-HDBK-217. (1995). *Military Handbook for "Reliability Prediction of Electronic Equipment".* US Department of Defense, NY. Retrieved from http://assist.daps.dla.mil/quicksearch/basic_profile.cfm?ident_number=53939

Penczek, W., & Pólrola, A. (2006). *Advances in Verification of Time Petri Nets and Timed Automata: A Temporal Logic Approach* (1st ed.). Springer.

Pullum, L. L. (2001). *Software Fault Tolerance Techniques and Implementation.* Norwood, MA: Artech House, Inc.

Saha, G. K. (2006). Software implemented hardware - transient fault detection. *International Scientific Journal of Computing, 5*(1), 1–11.

Yu, T. J., Shen, V. Y., & Dunsmore, H. E. (1988). An Analysis of Several Software Defect Models. *IEEE Transactions on Software Engineering, 14,* 1261–1269. doi:10.1109/32.6170

ADDITIONAL READING

Avizienis, A. (1978). Fault-Tolerance: The Survival Attribute of Digital Systeme. *Proceedings of the IEEE, 66,* 1109–1115. doi:10.1109/PROC.1978.11107

Avizienis, A. (1985). The N-Version Approach to Fault-Tolerant Software. *IEEE Transactions on Software Engineering, 11*(12), 1491–1501. doi:10.1109/TSE.1985.231893

Blanke, M., Kinnaert, M., Lunze, J., & Starowiecki, M. (2003). *Diagnosis and Fault-Tolerant Control.* Berlin, DE: Springer.

Broen, R. B. (1985). New Voters for Redundant Systems. *Journal of Dynamic Systems, Measurement, and Control, 107,* 41–45.

Dugan, J. B., Bavuso, S., & Boyd, M. (1993). Fault Trees and Markov Models for Reliability Analysis of Fault Tolerant Systems. *Journal of Reliability Engineering and System Safety, 39,* 291–307. doi:10.1016/0951-8320(93)90005-J

Gersting, J. L. (1991). A Comparison of voting algorithms for N-version programming. In *Proceedings of 24th Annual Hawaii International Conference on System Sciences,* 253–262.

Gertler, J. J. (1998). *Fault Detection and Diagnosis in Engineering Systems.* New York: Marcel Dekker, Inc.

Hayes, J. P. (1985). Fault modelling. *IEEE Design & Test of Computers, 2*(2), 88–95. doi:10.1109/MDT.1985.294873

Hintze, E., & Kucera, P. (2003). Simulation of RFieldbus Networks. *5th IFAC International Conference on Fieldbus Systems and their Applications.* Aveiro: IEETA / Dept. de Electrónica e Telecomunicações, Universidade de Aveiro, p. 28-35.

Johnson, B. W. (1984). Fault-tolerant microprocessor-based system. *IEEE Micro, 4*(6), 6–21. doi:10.1109/MM.1984.291277

Latif-Shabgahi, G., Bass, J. M., & Bennett, S. (2001). History-Based Weighted Average Voter: A Novel Software Voting Algorithm for Fault-Tolerant Computer. *SystemsProc. PDP2001: 9th Euromicro Workshop on Parallel and Distributed Processing,* Mantova, Italy.

Lee, P. A., & Anderson, T. (1990). *Fault-Tolerance Principles and Practice.* London: Prentice-Hall.

Lyu, M. R. (Ed.). (1996). *Handbook of Software Reliability Engineering.* New York: McGraw-Hill.

Nelson, V. P., & Carroll, B. D. (1982). *Fault-Tolerant Computing (A Tutorial)* Fort Worth, TX. Presented at the AIAA Fault Tolerant Computing Workshop.

Pradhan, D. K. (1996). *Fault-Tolerant Computer System Design.* Upper Saddle River, NJ: Prentice Hall PTR.

Saglietti, F. (1992). The Impact of Voter Granularity in Fault-Tolerant Software on System Reliability and Availability. In Kersken, M., & Saglietti, F. (Eds.), *Software Fault Tolerance: Achievement and Assessment Strategie* (pp. 199–212). Berlin: Springer-Verlag.

Scott, R. K., Gault, J. W., & McAllister, D. F. (1987). Fault-Tolerant Reliability Modeling. *IEEE Transactions on Software Engineering, 13*(5), 582–592. doi:10.1109/TSE.1987.233463

Siewiorek, D. P., & Swarz, R. S. (1982). *The Theory and Practice of Reliable System Design.* Bedford, MA: Digital Press.

Vouk, M. A. (1988). *On Engineering of Fault-Tolerant Software.* 10th International Symposium, Computer at the University, Cavtat88, Cavtat, Croatia.

KEY TERMS AND DEFINITIONS

Failure Rate, λ: The expected number of failures per unit time.

Fault-Tolerant System: A system that can continue the correct performance of its specified task in the presence of hardware failures and several errors.

FDV: Fault Detection Voter performs not only a standard majority voting mechanism, but also includes a detection mechanism to recognise a faulty channel.

M-of-N System: A system in which M out of N components must operate correctly for the system to operate correctly.

N-Modular Redundancy: a form of passive redundancy that uses N modules and majority voting.

N-Version Programming: A technique that compares the results from N separate modules, each of which performs the same operation.

Redundancy: is the addition of information, resources, or time beyond what is needed for normal system operation.

Reliability, R: Is defined as the conditional probability that the system will perform correctly throughout the interval $<t_0, t>$, given that the system was performing correctly at time t_0.

TMR: Triple Modular Redundancy, the basic concept is to triplicate the single system and perform a majority vote to determine the correct output of the system.

Chapter 3
Application of Two-Stage Adaptive Decision Making System Based on Takagi–Sugeno Model for Scenario Selection in Rehabilitation Process

Krzysztof Brzostowski
Wrocław University of Technology, Poland

Jarosław Drapała
Wrocław University of Technology, Poland

Jerzy Świątek
Wrocław University of Technology, Poland

ABSTRACT

This chapter focuses on selected problems of complex systems identification. The first part of the chapter is devoted to identification problems in general. The tasks of determination of the plant parameters and choice of the best model are given. Then, authors describe problems of complex systems, i.e.: identification with use of limited measurements, global identification and two-stage identification. The last one is presented in details. In order to illustrate proposed methods, an adaptive system with two-stage identification and its application to biomedical problem is presented.

INTRODUCTION

In general, rehabilitation process may be described in the following way. There is a patient who suffers from disorder of some part of his body. It is possible to cure the patient using rehabilitation exercises. These exercises are applied or recommended by therapist, who designs rehabilitation plan by composing sequence of exercises. Usually, therapist makes use of predefined sequences of

DOI: 10.4018/978-1-61692-811-7.ch003

Figure 1. Identification plant with input u and output y

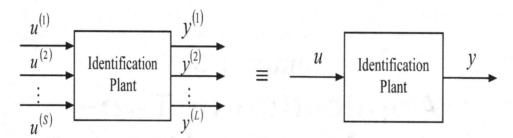

exercises that in further considerations will be called scenarios. The choice of scenario is preceded by assessment of the health state of a patient. The goal of rehabilitation process is to bring a part of a patient's body the desired state.

In this chapter rehabilitation process is treated from the system's analysis point of view. We propose input-output mathematical model for a bad part of a patient's body and parameters of this model shall reflect its health state. We also propose to model therapist's decision process and parameterized it to make adaptation possible. These two models are joined together into so called two-stage model. With use of two-stage identification procedure designed for complex systems, it is possible to employ two-stage model of rehabilitation process to the task of decision making in adaptive manner.

Due to importance of identification methods for rehabilitation process modelling, we start from introducing the idea of input-output static and dynamic systems identification. Next, we characterize the main issues of complex systems identification. Then we explain the problem of two-stage identification. The remaining part of the chapter focuses on biomedical example of application of two-stage identification to neuromuscular system rehabilitation, where Takagi-Sugeno model is proposed for the second stage.

BACKGROUND

The identification problem is to determine the model of the investigated process on the basis of measurement data collected on during the experiment. More precisely, for the identification plant (see Figure 1.) the problem is to find the relation between input values $u^{(1)}$, $u^{(2)}$, ..., $u^{(S)}$ and output values $y^{(1)}$, $y^{(2)}$, ..., $y^{(L)}$. For further consideration let us assume that input and output are S- and L-dimensional vectors, respectively. We denote them in the form:

$$u = \begin{bmatrix} u^{(1)} \\ u^{(2)} \\ \vdots \\ u^{(S)} \end{bmatrix}, \quad y = \begin{bmatrix} y^{(1)} \\ y^{(2)} \\ \vdots \\ y^{(L)} \end{bmatrix} \quad (1)$$

where: u – plant input vector, $u \in \mathsf{U} \subseteq \mathsf{R}^S$, U is a S-dimensional input space, R is the set of real numbers, y – plant output vector, $y \in \mathsf{Y} \subseteq \mathsf{R}^L$, Y is a S-dimensional output space.

It is assumed that there exists plant characteristic:

$$y = F(u), \quad (2)$$

but it is not known. The problem is to determine relation between input u and output y on the basis of experimental data. Denote by y_n – result of n-th output measurement for the given input u_n, n=1,

Figure 2. Identification system

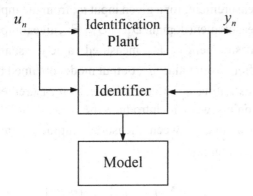

2,..., N where N is the number of the measurements. Results of measurements are collected in the following matrices:

$$U_N = \begin{bmatrix} u_1 & u_2 & \cdots & u_N \end{bmatrix},$$
$$Y_N = \begin{bmatrix} y_1 & y_2 & \cdots & y_N \end{bmatrix} \tag{3}$$

where: U_N, Y_N are matrices of input and output measurements, respectively. The identification problem is to find (see Figure 2.) the identification algorithm which allows getting the plant characteristic (plant model). The identification algorithm depends on the knowledge about investigated plant.

There are two possible cases. The first one is that we know the plant characteristic with accuracy to parameters. In this case the problem is reduced to determination of the plant parameters. The second one is to find the best approximation of the plan characteristic on the basis of the experiment.

Determination of the Plant Parameters

Now let us assume that plant characteristic is known with accuracy to parameters, i.e. the static plant characteristic (2) has the form (Bubnicki, 1974; Świątek, 2009):

$$y = F(u, \theta) \tag{4}$$

where: F – known function and θ is R – dimensional unknown vector of the plant characteristic parameters, i.e.:

$$\theta = \begin{bmatrix} \theta^{(1)} \\ \theta^{(2)} \\ \vdots \\ \theta^{(R)} \end{bmatrix} \tag{5}$$

where: θ – unknown vector parameters, $\theta \in \Theta \subseteq \mathsf{R}^R$, Θ – parameter space. It means that during the experiment we measured points from plant characteristic.

It means that each measurement point must fulfill the relation (4), i.e.:

$$y_n = F(u_n, \theta), \quad n = 1, 2, ..., N. \tag{6}$$

Consequently, we have the following system of equations:

$$\begin{bmatrix} y_1 & y_2 & \cdots & y_N \end{bmatrix} = \\ \begin{bmatrix} F(u_1, \theta) & F(u_2, \theta) & \cdots & F(u_N, \theta) \end{bmatrix} \tag{7}$$

And in comprehensive form:

$$Y_N = \bar{F}(U_N, \theta) \tag{8}$$

where:

$$\begin{bmatrix} F(u_1, \theta) & F(u_2, \theta) & \cdots & F(u_N, \theta) \end{bmatrix} \stackrel{df}{=} \bar{F}(U_N, \theta) \tag{9}$$

The solution of the system of equations (8) with respect to θ gives the identification algorithm, i.e.:

$$\theta = \overline{F}^{-1}\left(U_N, Y_N\right) \overset{df}{=} \Psi_N\left(U_N, Y_N\right) \qquad (10)$$

where: $\overline{F}^{-1}$ – inverse function, Ψ_N – identification algorithm. The required number of measurements N must fulfil the following condition:

$$N \times L \geq R. \qquad (11)$$

That solution (10) depends on the plant characteristic (4) and the results of measurements (3). Notice that sometimes it is impossible to uniquely determine plant parameters. It depends on plant prosperities called *identifiability*.

Definition 1. *The system is identifiable if there exists such a sequence* $U_N = \begin{bmatrix} u_1 & u_2 & \cdots & u_N \end{bmatrix}$ *which together with corresponding results of output measurements* $Y_N = \begin{bmatrix} y_1 & y_2 & \cdots & y_N \end{bmatrix}$ *uniquely determines plant characteristic parameters.*

Practically, it means that there exists such an input sequence U_N, for which the system of equation (8) has the unique solution (10).

Choice of the Best Model

Now let us assume that plant characteristic (2) is not known (Bubnicki, 1974; Świątek, 2009). We propose the model of the form:

$$\overline{y} = \Phi(u, \theta) \qquad (12)$$

where: Φ is a proposed, arbitrary given function describing the relation between model output $\overline{y}$ and input u, and θ is a vector of parameters of the proposed description. The values u, $\overline{y}$ and θ are elements of the respective spacer, i.e:

$$u \in \mathbf{U} \subseteq \mathbf{R}^S, \overline{y} \in \overline{\mathbf{Y}} \subseteq \mathbf{R}^L \text{ and } \theta \in \Theta \subseteq \mathbf{R}^R.$$

The result of the experiment in n-th point of measurement, for a given input u_n, from the input measurement domain $\mathbf{D}_u \subseteq \mathbf{U} \subseteq \mathbf{R}^S$, gives output measurement y_n. The measured value y_n usually differs from value $\overline{y}_n$, output model obtained by substituting u_n into (12). For each measurement n points we will introduce the measure of the difference between measured output y_n and model output $\overline{y}_n$, i.e.:

$$\forall n = 1, 2, \ldots, N \quad q\left(y_n, \overline{y}_n\right) = q\left(y_n, \Phi\left(u_n, \theta\right)\right), \qquad (13)$$

where q is a function which fulfils measure function requirements. For example q has the form:

$$q\left(y, \overline{y}\right) = \sum_{l=1}^{L} \left(y^{(l)} - \overline{y}^{(l)}\right)^2 \qquad (14)$$

or

$$q\left(y, \overline{y}\right) = \sum_{l=1}^{L} \left|y^{(l)} - \overline{y}^{(l)}\right|, \qquad (15)$$

For the whole input sequence U_N the performance index

$$Q_N\left(\theta\right) = \left\|Y_N - \overline{Y}_N\left(\theta\right)\right\|_{U_N}, \qquad (16)$$

shows the difference between experiment and proposed model (see Figure 3.), where:

$$\overline{Y}_N\left(\theta\right) \overset{df}{=} \begin{bmatrix} \Phi\left(u_1, \theta\right) & \Phi\left(u_2, \theta\right) & \cdots & \Phi\left(u_N, \theta\right) \end{bmatrix}. \qquad (17)$$

Examples of $Q_N\left(\theta\right)$ have the form of:

Figure 3. Choice of the best model

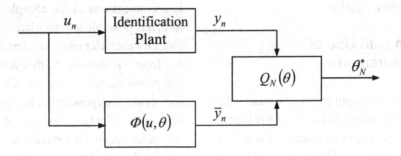

$$Q_N(\theta) = \sum_{n=1}^{N} q(y_n, \overline{y}_n) = \sum_{n=1}^{N} q(y_n, \Phi(u_n, \theta)) \tag{18}$$

or

$$Q_N(\theta) = \max_{1 \le n \le N} \{ q(y_n, \overline{y}_n) \} = \max_{1 \le n \le N} \{ q(y_n, \Phi(u_n, \theta)) \}. \tag{19}$$

For the function q of the (15) and the performance index (18) for one dimensional case ($L=1$) shows sum of difference between measured plant output and model output, i.e.:

$$Q_N(\theta) = \sum_{n=1}^{N} |y_n - \overline{y}_n| = \sum_{n=1}^{N} |y_n - \Phi(u_n, \theta)|, \tag{20}$$

and performance index (19):

$$Q_N(\theta) = \max_{1 \le n \le N} \{ |y_n - \overline{y}_n| \} = \max_{1 \le n \le N} \{ |y_n - \Phi(u_n, \theta)| \}, \tag{21}$$

shows the worst case of the difference between measured plant output and evaluated model output. We obtained the optimal value of vector model parameters by minimization of the performance index (16) with respect to θ, i.e.:

$$\theta_N^* \rightarrow \quad Q_N(\theta_N^*) = \min_{\theta \in \Theta} Q_N(\theta) \tag{22}$$

where: θ_N^* is the optimal vector of model parameters and the relation (12) with parameters θ_N^*, i.e.:

$$\overline{y} = \Phi(u, \theta_N^*), \tag{23}$$

gives us the optimal model. The obtained model (23) is the optimal one for:

- given measurement sequence (3),
- proposed model (12),
- performance index (13) and (16).

By changing any of the above elements we obtain another model not comparable with the previous one. It may have the consequence in the complex system identification. The model (12) and respective performance index (16) depends on the local or global approach.

COMPLEX SYSTEMS IDENTIFICATION PROBLEMS

In the problem of complex system identification it is possible to distinguish few concepts:

a) identification with use of limited measurements,

b)   global identification,
c)   two-stage identification.

Identification with Use of Limited Measurements

Identification of input-output complex system with use of limited measurements is related to objects which components have been distinguished. It is assumed that the structure of the system is known i.e. it means that the connections between elements are established and descriptions of all elements are known to the value of parameters. It is connected to the problem of determining object's characteristic or parameters' estimates by use of noised measurements. We are given configuration of measurements' points which means that the set of measurable inputs are known. The problem is as follows: is it possible to determine parameters' description of all elements for given measurement setup? To answer this question it is desirable to define the term of *separability* of the complex system. This term is related to the *identifiable* in the field of identification. The problem of *separability* in the complex systems is related to either complex system structure and static characteristic of its elements (Świątek, 2009).

Global Identification

Considering global identification of complex system it is assumed that the structure of the system is known e.g. interconnections between elements are fixed. In contradiction to the situation which was described in previous section here it is assumed that all inputs and outputs are measurable. It means that for fixed value of the outside inputs measurements for all outputs can be made. For each element parametric model are chosen. In the task of determining optimal model of complex system different approaches to determine quality of the model can be used. It leads to different performance indexes.

On the one hand, without taking into account interconnections in the complex system's structure, it is possible to formulate *local performance index* for each element considered as object singled out from the system. In this way we defined *local performance index* for identification task. Resolving independently, for each element, task of choosing the best model we determine models which are optimal in local sense for each elements. Having the use of structure of complex system with marked out outputs and local optimal model it is possible to build the model of complex system with outside inputs and distinguished outputs. This model is called *local optimal model*.

On the other hand, taking into account utilization of the complex system's model, in certain task, it is reasonable to pay attention to the distinguish outputs of the complex system. It leads to the problem of choosing different methods of evaluating quality of the model. Now, having the use of complex system's structure, distinguished outputs and chosen models we can determine complex system's model with outside inputs and marked outputs. Taking it into account we can formulate performance index for model as a whole system. This kind of performance index is called *global performance index*. *Global performance index* is used to estimate difference between distinguished inputs and outputs of complex system's model. As a result of resolving task of choosing the best model with global performance index we are given the model which is called global optimal model (Świątek, 2009).

Two-Stage Identification

Two-stage identification may be described as follows: for an object – which can be considered as a process, phenomena or device – the relationship between output y and input u_1 with the parameter θ_1 at the first stage can be established. *Identification task at the first stage* is to estimate the parameter θ_1 by use of the measurements of u_1 and y. Then, we pay our attention to the input

Figure 4. Proposed Two-Stage Adaptive Decision Making System

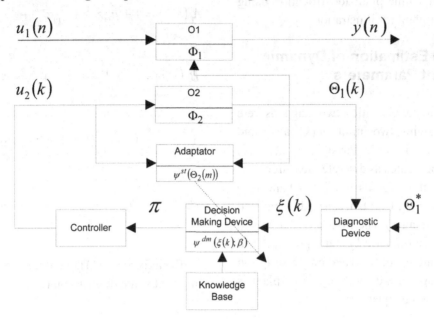

value at the second stage: u_2. The value is constant during identification task at the first stage. After changing the value of u_2 we repeat identification at the first stage and determine value of the parameter θ_1 once again. Repeating identification at the first stage for different values of the input u_2 leads to different values of θ_1. Set of values of u_2 and θ_1 can be used to describe the relationship between them and θ_2 is parameter of this relation. The task of calculating value of the parameter θ_2 using experimental data is called *identification task at the second stage*.

Let us notice that the first and the second stage may concern the same object. Moreover two-stage identification can be treated as decomposition of plant with output y and input u_1 and u_2.

The idea of two-stage identification may be generalized to multiple stages and can be called multi-stage identification.

Application of two-stage schema for an adaptive system to support making decision is given in Figure 4.

TWO-STAGE IDENTIFICATION OF DYNAMIC PLANT

The task of two-stage identification for static plants, may be also formulated for dynamic plants. In such a case, at the first stage relation between input signal $u_1(t)$ and output signal $\bar{y}(t)$ is to be established (t stands for time). Using identification procedure for input-output dynamic plants we estimate parameters of this relation. Then we take into account that these parameters at the first stage depends on another input signal $u_2(t)$. Let us denote parameters at the first stage by $\theta_1(t)$. Since $\theta_1(t)$ depends on $u_2(t)$, relation between them is taken into consideration in a two-stage identification scheme. Parameters at the second stage are denoted as $\theta_2(t)$ and are the subject of estimation procedure.

Unlike the static case, where constant value u_2 is used, identification of two-stage dynamic plant requires input time signal $u_2(t)$, for which values of parameters $\theta_1(t)$ varies for different signals $u_2(t)$ in a repetitive manner. In the remainder of this section we present the basics of two-stage approach to dynamic plant identification using discrete linear plant for illustration.

Two-Stage Estimation of Dynamic Linear Plant Parameters

Let us take into consideration two-stage discrete linear plant having two inputs $u_1(k)$, $u_2(k)$ and single output $y(k)$. In particular, signals $u_1(k)$, $u_2(k)$ and $y(k)$ can be treated as discrete measurements of continuous time signals $u_1(t_k)$, $u_1(t_k)$ and $y(t_k)$ taken at time steps t_k. The plant can be decomposed into two parts (stages). The first stage pertains to relation between output $y(k)$ and input $u_1(k)$ and $\theta_1(k)$ are parameters of this relation. Description of the first stage of a discrete dynamic plant is given by following equation:

$$y(k) + a_{11}y(k-1) + a_{12}y(k-2) + \cdots + a_{1R_{a1}}y(k-R_{a1}) =$$
$$= b_{11}u_1(k-1) + b_{12}u_1(k-2) + \cdots + u_1(k-R_{b1}), \tag{24}$$

The second stage description of this plant is given by equation:

$$a(k) + a_{21}y(k-1) + a_{22}y(k-2) + \cdots + a_{2R_{a2}}y(k-R_{a2}) =$$
$$= b_{21}u_2(k-1) + b_{22}u_2(k-2) + \cdots + u_2(k-R_{b2}). \tag{25}$$

Equations (24) and (25) may be also expressed in the form below:

$$A_1\left(z^{-1}\right)y(k) = B_1\left(z^{-1}\right)u_1(k), \tag{26}$$

$$A_2\left(z^{-1}\right)a(k) = B_2\left(z^{-1}\right)u_2(k) \tag{27}$$

where k – denotes number of time step, z^{-1} – is unit delay operator, $A_1\left(z^{-1}\right)$, $B_1\left(z^{-1}\right)$, $A_2\left(z^{-1}\right)$, $B_2\left(z^{-1}\right)$ are polynomials of delay operator and are defined as:

$$A_1\left(z^{-1}\right) = 1 + a_{11}z^{-1} + a_{12}z^{-2} + \cdots + a_{1R_{a1}}z^{-R_{a1}}, \tag{28}$$

$$B_1\left(z^{-1}\right) = b_{11}z^{-1} + b_{12}z^{-2} + \cdots + b_{1R_{b1}}z^{-R_{b1}}, \tag{29}$$

$$A_2\left(z^{-1}\right) = 1 + a_{21}z^{-1} + a_{22}z^{-2} + \cdots + a_{2R_{a2}}z^{-R_{a2}}, \tag{30}$$

$$B_2\left(z^{-1}\right) = b_{21}z^{-1} + b_{22}z^{-2} + \cdots + b_{2R_{b2}}z^{-R_{b2}}. \tag{31}$$

For a fixed k, $a(k)$ is a value of some parameter of a first stage description (24):

$$a(k) \in \left\{ a_{11},\ a_{12},\ \cdots,\ a_{1R_{a1}},\ b_{11},\ b_{12},\ \cdots,\ b_{1R_{b1}} \right\}. \tag{32}$$

In order to estimate parameters of both the first (26) and the second (27) stages, appropriate experiment should be performed. Its goal is to deliver data to two-stage estimation/identification procedure. Input at the first stage is fed up with discrete time signals $u_{1n}(k)$, $k = 1,2,\ldots,K$ (K stands for signal length), while input time signal $u_2(k)$, $k = 1,2,\ldots,K$ at the second stage remains unchanged. Response $y_n(k)$, $k = 1,2,\ldots,K$ of the plant is measured in the presence of noise. We assume that measurements of output signal $y_n(k)$ are affected by additive disturbances z_{nk} which are independent random values of variable $\underline{z}$ having zero expected value and finite variance:

$$E_{\underline{z}}[\underline{z}] = 0, \quad Var_{\underline{z}}[\underline{z}] < \infty. \tag{33}$$

Thus, the result of our experiment can be described as:

$$w_n(k) = y_n(k) + z_{nk} \tag{34}$$

where $w_n(k)$ denotes value of measured output.

Experiment described above is to be performed several times, with use of different excitation signals $u_{1n}(k)$, $n = 1,2,\ldots,N$ at the first stage and with signal $u_2(k)$ at the second stage kept unchanged. N stands for the number of experiments at the first stage.

Eventually, following measurements are gathered:

$$\left\{ u_{1n}\left(k\right)\right\}_{k=1}^{K}, n = 1,\ 2,\ \ldots,\ N, \tag{35}$$

$$\left\{ w_{n}\left(k\right)\right\}_{k=1}^{K}, n = 1,\ 2,\ \ldots,\ N, \tag{36}$$

$$\left\{ u_{2}\left(k\right)\right\}_{k=1}^{K}, \tag{37}$$

We aim at finding the best model in the parameters space. The best model minimizes sum of squared errors at the first stage:

$$Q_{1NK}\left(\theta_1, a\left(k\right)\right) =$$
$$\sum_{n=1}^{N}\sum_{k=1}^{K}\left[y_n\left(k\right) - Z_{1n}^{T}\left(k\right)\theta_1 - z_{1n}\left(k\right)a\left(k\right)\right]^2, \tag{38}$$

with respect parameters θ_1 of the first stage description and series $a(k)$, $k = 1,2,\ldots,K$, and at the second stage sum of squared estimation errors:

$$Q_{2K}\left(\theta_2\right) = \sum_{k=1}^{K}\left[a_N\left(k\right) - Z_2^{T}\left(k\right)\theta_2\right]^2, \tag{39}$$

is minimized with respect θ_2.

APPLICATION OF TWO-STAGE IDENTIFICATION: BIOMEDICAL PROBLEM

Motivation

Muscle health disorders caused by e.g. spinal cord injury may lead to significant problems with normal movement activities. Decreasing movement ability usually causes fatigue, weakness or loss of dexterity in common activities.

Paralysis of limbs is an example of complex medical disorder. In medical practice various methods are used to get patients better (Barnes, 2008):

- surgical or pharmacology treatment,
- rehabilitation through physical exercises,
- electric pulses stimulation (it is known as FES method - Functional Electrical Stimulation).

In general, rehabilitation of patients suffering from neuromuscular system disorder is based on subjective assessment of muscles' state and methods of treatment. It is performed by therapist who carries out rehabilitation process relying on his/her knowledge and experience. It is the first part of the rehabilitation process. The second part is to plan rehabilitation's schedule taking into account current health state of patients. In medical practice physicians and therapists have number of methods that can be used to restore neuromuscular system abilities. Among available methods physician has to propose the best possible one and then to plan details of it.

There are two different approaches that can be used to plan rehabilitation. The first is model-based method with use of mathematical description of the muscle to support selection of rehabilitation method. This approach has been studied in (Frey Law, 2006). It is worth stressing that by use of this scheme it is possible to individualize rehabilitation process. This means that it is possible to accelerate process of improvement of patients' health, because treatment process is adjusted to each patient.

On the other hand, hybrid method in which expert knowledge together with muscle model are used. This approach is considered in detail in the chapter. In this case decision is made on the basis of the current state of the object (characterized by values of models' parameters) and knowledge. This approach is suited not only to individual patient but also to his/her current health state. Here, decision is subjected to selection of scenario. By scenario we mean the set of activities which is composed of accessible actions e.g. different physical exercises or electrical pulse stimulation patterns etc.

In order to develop algorithm which rests on the second approach, model of neuromuscular system and pattern recognition methods are applied (Theodoridis, 2006). The scheme, in which classification procedures and expert knowledge are used, was considered e.g. in (Bristol, 1991; James, & Suski 1988; Saridis, 1981). By expert knowledge we mean learning set obtained from expert.

In order to make the system adaptive, two-stage identification is utilized. Adaptation means that whenever decision brings the state of the patient to undesired direction, parameters of the algorithm choosing rehabilitation scenario are changed (Bubnicki, 2000; Astrom 1989).

As it was mentioned before, two-stage scheme is proposed. The first stage is used to asses health state of the patients. This problem is not considered in the chapter. The issue of making diagnosis by use of neuromuscular system identification at the first stage is discussed in details in (Brzostowski, & Drapała, & Świątek, 2008; Brzostowski, & Drapała, & Świątek, & Moskała, 2006; Brzostowski, & Drapała, 2006).

At the second stage rehabilitation process is performed. By use of identification methods it is possible to build relationship between decision of therapist and health state of the patient. For this stage we propose neuro-fuzzy Takagi-Sugeno model (Babuska, & Verbruggen, 2003; Rutkowski, 2006; Łęski, 2008). Motivation for utilization of Takagi-Sugeno system, in considered problem, is ability to facilitate effective design of support making decision algorithms by make the most of data from different source (e.g. experts). On the other hand, the nature of the rehabilitation process can be easy describe by *if-then* rules by use of imprecise predicates. It means that the set of rules defines relationship between input (rehabilitation scenario) and response (health quality of the patients) represents by a parameter or set of parameters.

Two-Stage Identification

Let us consider two-stage identification object (Figure 4.) described by model (O1, see Figure 4.) at the first stage (Świątek, 1987):

$$y\big(n+1\big) = \Phi_1\Big(y\big(n\big), u_1\big(n\big), \Theta_1\big(k\big)\Big) \qquad (40)$$

where n denotes time step at this stage. Let us also take following model at the second stage (O2, see Figure 4.):

$$\Theta_1\big(k+1\big) = \Phi_2\Big(\Theta_1\big(k\big), R\big(\pi\big(k\big)\big), \Theta_2\big(k\big)\Big) \qquad (41)$$

where k denotes time step at this stage, $R\big(\pi\big(k\big)\big)$ is controller's algorithm that executes exercises which are the part of rehabilitation scenario. Scenario, as it was mentioned in previous section, is a composition of various activities which is produced on the basis of set of accessible actions.

Other parts of the proposed system are as follows: decision making device, controller, adaptator, diagnostic device and knowledge base.

Object at the first stage is described by the relationship parameterized with the vector of parameters Θ_1. Signals u_1 and y are input and output signals respectively and their measurements are only used to determine values of parameters Θ_1 (by identification at the first stage). Results of identification at this stage is taken into account when assessment of current health quality of the patients must be performed. To this end diagnostic device (Figure 4.) is used, where current value of the vector Θ_1 (which characterized current health quality of the patients) is compared to desired value of this vector (Θ_1^*, Figure 4.) and is denoted by ξ.

At the second stage decision support process brings values of these parameters to desired values Θ_1^*. In order to do this, algorithm to support making decision (which is meant as a selection of scenario or sequence of scenarios) is employed. Its action is denoted by π and model Φ_2 describes its influence on values of parameters Θ_1 of the model Φ_1. It was assumed that model Φ_2 (which depends on parameters Θ_2) approximates real relation between π and Θ_1. On the basis of selected scenario (by the decision making device), controller performs sequence of actions u_2. Decision about sequence of scenarios to be used is made resting on current value of difference between values of parameters Θ_1 and desired Θ_1^* (denoted by ξ) and with accordance to knowledge base. Therein suggestions (set of rules) how to act depending on different situation (characterized by value of ξ) are collected. For different current values of Θ_1 and desired Θ_1^*, different scenarios are proposed by expert as a set of fuzzy rules.

By virtue of two-stage scheme presented above, it is possible to exploit results of identification task at the second stage for adaptation of decision maker (more precisely, for correction of algorithm's parameters β utilized by decision maker).

Problem Statement

The statement of the problem is as follows: let us assume that in knowledge base finite set $\aleph$ of H scenarios π is available:

$$\aleph = \left\{ \pi_1, \pi_2, ..., \pi_H \right\}. \tag{42}$$

This set is given by an expert. Each scenario is composed of M actions u_{2l_m}:

$$\pi_h = \left\{ u_{2l_1}, u_{2l_2}, ..., u_{2l_M} \right\}, \tag{43}$$

that come from a given set U_2 of available actions:

$$U_2 = \left\{ u_{21}, u_{22}, ..., u_{2L} \right\}. \tag{44}$$

Quality of selected scenarios at k-th time step is measured by performance index:

$$Q^{dm}\left(\pi(1), \pi(2), ..., \pi(K); \xi(1), \xi(2), ..., \xi(K-1) \right) = \sum_{k=1}^{K} q^{dm}\left(\pi(k); \xi(k) \right), \tag{45}$$

where q^{dm} is a local assessment of decision for $\xi(k)$ which is defined by following formula:

$$\xi(k) = d^{dm}\left(\Theta_1^*, \hat{\Theta}_1(k) \right), \tag{46}$$

where $d^{dm}(\cdot, \cdot)$ is a distance between desired values Θ_1^* and current $\hat{\Theta}_1(k)$. The task of finding optimal sequence $\left(\pi^*(1), \pi^*(2), ..., \pi^*(K) \right)$ can be defined as optimization task:

$$Q^{dm}\left(\pi^*(1), \pi^*(2), ..., \pi^*(K); \xi(1), \xi(2), ..., \xi(K-1) \right) =$$
$$= \min_{\pi(1), \pi(2), ..., \pi(K)} Q^{dm}\left(\pi(k); \xi(k) \right) \tag{47}$$

In consequence – as a solution of optimization task (47) – decision making algorithm is obtained in general form:

$$\pi^*(k) = \psi^{dm}\left(\xi(k)\right).$$ (48)

SCENARIO SELECTION: PATTERN RECOGNITION APPROACH

Let us assume that we have a learning set composed by experts:

$$X_K = \left\{\left(\xi^{(1)}, \pi^*\right), \left(\xi^{(2)}, \pi^*\right), ..., \left(\xi^{(K)}, \pi^*\right)\right\},$$ (49)

where X_K denotes different object's states and scenarios which has to be triggered in proper moments (depending on the current value of the $\xi(k)$). Finally, the general form of algorithm for decision making is as follows:

$$\tilde{\pi}^*(k) = \psi_{PR}^{dm}\left(\xi(k), X_K; \beta\right)$$ (50)

where β is the vector of parameters. To resolve the task of decision making in step-by-step process, various pattern recognition procedures can be utilized.

Takagi-Sugeno System as Algorithm to Select Scenario

Let us define Takagi-Sugeno model containing set of R rules:

$$\mathrm{R}^{(r)}: \text{If } \xi_s(k) \text{ is } D^{(r)} \text{ then}$$

$$\tilde{y}^{(r)}(k) = \left(a^{(r)}\right)^T \xi_s(k) + b^{(r)},$$ (51)

for $r = 1, 2, ..., R$ and $s = 1, 2, ..., S$

where S is the number of inputs and R stands for rule. To calculate output of the model, following center of area formula can be used:

$$\overline{y}(k) = \frac{\sum\limits_{r}^{R} \mu^{(r)}\left(\xi_s(k)\right)\tilde{y}^{(r)}(k)}{\sum\limits_{r}^{R} \mu^{(r)}\left(\xi_s(k)\right)}.$$ (52)

In practical tasks membership function usually has following form:

$$\mu_s^{(r)}\left(\xi_s(k); c_s^{(r)}, \sigma_s^{(r)}\right) = \exp\left(-\frac{\left(\xi_s(k) - c_s^{(r)}\right)^2}{2\left(\sigma_s^{(r)}\right)^2}\right).$$ (53)

Finally, mathematical formula to determine outputs of Takagi-Sugeno model has form:

$$\overline{y}(k) = \frac{\sum\limits_{r}^{R}\prod\limits_{s}^{S}\exp\left(-\frac{\left(\xi_s(k) - c_s^{(r)}\right)^2}{2\left(\sigma_s^{(r)}\right)^2}\right)\tilde{y}^{(r)}(k)}{\sum\limits_{r}^{R}\prod\limits_{s}^{S}\exp\left(-\frac{\left(\xi_s(k) - c_s^{(r)}\right)^2}{2\left(\sigma_s^{(r)}\right)^2}\right)}.$$ (54)

SIMULATION RESULTS

At the beginning, model's equations which are used during computer experiments are presented. One of the methods which can be used in rehabilitation of patients suffering from neuromuscular disorder is FES (Functional Electrical Stimulation). In this method safe electrical pulses are used to restore movements abilities of the patients. As it was mentioned, to solve the problem of plan-

Figure 5. Example of four different stimulation scenarios used in numerical simulations

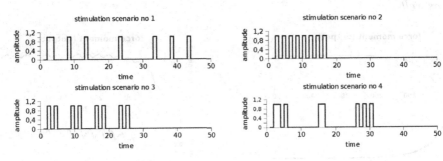

ning rehabilitation of patients, expert knowledge and neuromuscular system model is needed. In the chapter it is assumed that knowledge base has already been built on the basis of human expert. The second issue is a model. In presented studies relationship, which was utilized, is well described in literature and has the following form (Frey, 2006):

$$C(n) = \frac{1}{\tau_c} \Lambda(n-1) - \frac{C(n-1)}{\tau_c},$$

$$\bar{y}(n) = a^{(1)} \frac{C(n-1)}{1+C(n-1)} - \frac{\bar{y}(n-1)}{\tau_1 + \tau_2 \frac{C(n-1)}{1+C(n-1)}},$$

(55)

and:

$$\Lambda(n) = \sum_{w=1}^{W} \left\{ 1 + \left(\Lambda_0(n) - 1\right) \exp\left(-\frac{u(n_w) - u(n_{w-1})}{\tau_c}\right) \right\} \left[\exp\left(-\frac{n_w - u(n_w)}{\tau_c}\right) \right],$$

(56)

where:

$C(n)$: normalized amount of Ca^{2+}- troponin complex;

$\Lambda_0(n)$: characterizing the magnitude of enhancement in $C(n)$ from stimuli;

τ_c: time constant controlling rise and decay of $C(n)$;

$\Theta_1(n)$: parameter (see Figure 4.);

τ_1: time constant of force decline at the absence of strongly bound cross-bridge;

τ_2: time constant of force decline due to the extra friction between actin and myosin resulting from the presence of cross-bridge;

W: the number of electrical pulses;

w: current number of electrical pulses.

To restore patients movement abilities, functional electrical stimulation can be used. To this end set of different scenarios containing different stimulation patterns must be prepared. Stimulation pattern is characterized by number of pulses, their width and amplitude. In Figure 5. four different scenarios used in computer simulations are shown.

Functional electrical stimulation is very effective rehabilitation method but the way of stimulation of impaired muscles is unnatural. This means that fatigue ratio of the muscles is higher than stimulation from nervous system lasting the same time. Process of rehabilitation by FES is effective when fatigue rate has desired and possibly low level. It is a condition of rehabilitation process to be effective (as fast as possible). Problems described above lead to the following task: find scenario for a patient to restore health quality as quick as possible.

As a illustration of described problems, two different results of simulation of rehabilitation process for two selected scenarios are shown in Figure 6. It can be seen that utilization of one

Figure 6. Results of stimulation rehabilitation process for scenario: 2 (on the left) and 3 (on the right). See Figure 5. as well

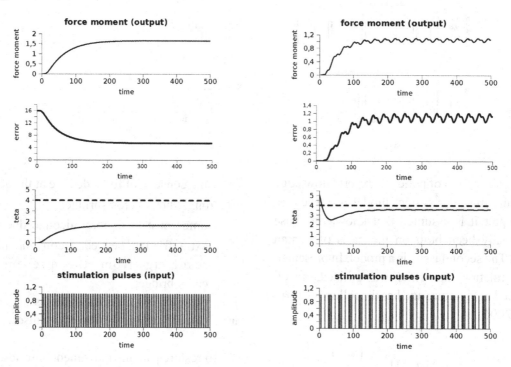

predefined scenario cannot help us to reach desired effect – keeping value of parameter Θ_1 (*teta* in Figure 6.) on desired level (rate of fatigue). It means that to solve problem of planning rehabilitation sequence of different scenarios must be applied.

Next pictures illustrate results for three different algorithms composing sequences of scenarios. First of them is Takagi-Sugeno model based algorithm which was described in details in the previous section. In order to compare obtained results for Takagi-Sugeno model based algorithm with other ones, simulating annealing and enumeration procedures are proposed as well.

In presented results number of rules for Takagi-Sugeno model is 3. In consequences part affine linear functions are applied. Membership function is Gaussian function. Defuzzification method is center of area scheme. In Figure 7. obtained results for planning rehabilitation process with utilization of algorithm based on Takagi-Sugeno model are

shown. In this figure dashed line represents desired value of parameter Θ_1 whereas curved line stands for changing of its current value. During numerical simulations it was assumed that desired value of Θ_1 equals 4. It can be seen that for chosen object it is possible to keep value of Θ_1 on the desired level. Value of the performance index is $Q=0.0088$ (see Eq. 45, where q^{dm} is Root Mean Square).

For comparison purposes, in Figure 8. results of rehabilitation planning by use of algorithms based on simulating annealing and enumeration scheme are presented.

Simulating annealing algorithm is well-known method to solve optimization problems by imitation of physical process which combines heating a material and then slowly lowering the temperature in order to decrease internal defects of the material's structure. This method is an example of random optimization algorithms.

Figure 7. Results of stimulation rehabilitation process for algorithm using Takagi-Sugeno model

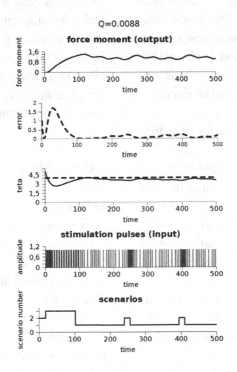

Figure 8. Results of stimulation rehabilitation process for enumeration method (on the left) and simulating annealing (on the right) based algorithms

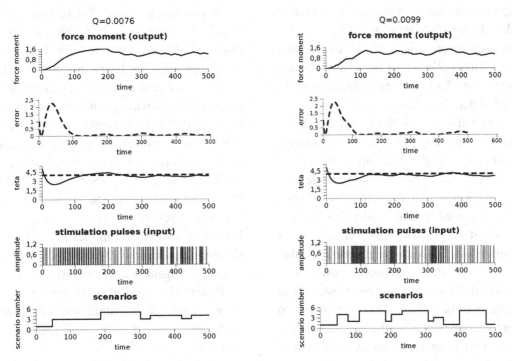

In presented studies simulating annealing procedure, to compose sequence of scenarios, with following parameters are used: initial temperature is determined experimentally and is equal 100, stopping criterion is total number of iterations and to decrement temperature exponential cooling scheme was applied.

As it can be seen, results obtained for algorithm based on enumeration scheme is considerable better ($Q = 0.0076$, see Figure 8.) than for Takagi-Sugeno base procedure. It is worth stressing that results are better but time of calculations is unacceptable long. It arises straight from algorithm scheme which rests on searching whole solution space. Takagi-Sugeno scheme is less accurate but time of calculation is shorter.

In the same figure results for simulating annealing based algorithm is shown. It is easy to see that effectiveness of this approach is considerably lower ($Q = 0.0099$ in Figure 8.).

FUTURE RESEARCH DIRECTIONS

In proposed Adaptive Decision Making System two-stage schema has been applied. It should be noted that the length of time step is usually different at each stage. This work do not concern determination of optimal time steps lengths, but it is important issue for adaptive systems and should be treated in details in further works.

We should also extend "the recognition part" of proposed adaptive system. Clustering methods may be employ to support recognition algorithm.

In this work we assumed that knowledge base is given by experts and does not change over time. The proposed system is adaptive because parameters of the second-stage relation adapt to incoming data. But knowledge base may also change. As long as the system works, new actions are performed, their result may be measured and experience may be gained. Thus, it is worth to consider two-stage system with adaptable knowledge base. This means that some facts/rules from

knowledge base may turn out useless or even false and some other rules may be proposed instead. It may also happen that few rules can be generalized by single one. This examples give motivation to allow knowledge base to change. In future works we plan to apply concepts from time varying systems identification to handle this case.

CONCLUSION

In the chapter selected problems of identification of complex systems are presented. The task of plant parameters determination and choice of the best model is described. Main issues of complex systems identification were discussed as well. One of them – two-stage identification – was presented in details.

To illustrate proposed approach, adaptive system to select scenario with utilization of two-stage scheme has been considered. In proposed system expert's set of rules collected in knowledge base was used. As it was shown during simulation studies utilization of the proposed technique usually leads to suboptimal solution.

In simulation studies Takagi-Sugeno model based algorithm to select scenario has been proposed. Results obtained for Takag-Sugeno based algorithm has been compared with results for simulated annealing and enumeration based procedures. As it was shown, using Takagi-Sugeno based algorithm helps to obtain results which are better than for simulated annealing but not as good as for enumeration scheme. It is worth stressing out that results for Takagi-Sugeno model are worst than for enumeration procedure but it is less time consuming procedure which is very important feature in real-world applications. Results for simulating annealing are the worst in comparison to Takagi-Sugeno and enumeration procedure.

Presented numerical studies prove usefulness of two-stage identification and Takagi-Sugeno model to support making decision in adaptive systems.

REFERENCES

Astrom, K. J., & Wittenmark, B. (1989). *Adaptive Control*. Reading, MA: Addison-Wesley.

Babuska, R., & Verbruggen, H. (2003). Neuro-fuzzy methods for nonlinear system identification. *Annual Reviews in Control*, *27*, 73–85. doi:10.1016/S1367-5788(03)00009-9

Barnes, M. P. (2008). *Upper Motor Neurone Syndrome and Spacticity*. Cambridge, MA: Cambridge Medicine. doi:10.1017/CBO9780511544866

Bristol, E. H. (1991). Pattern Recognition: An Alternative to Parameter Identification in Adaptive Control. *Automatica*, 197–202.

Brzostowski, K., & Drapała, J. (2006). *Analysis of Optimization Methods in Identification of Human Elbow Neuromuscular Model. Information systems architecture and technology ISAT 2006* (pp. 59–67). Wrocław, PA: Scientific Papers of Wrocław University of Technology.

Brzostowski, K., Drapała, J., & Świątek, J. (2008). *How to replace inexact expert's knowledge by precise diagnostic system - assessment of internal state of human elbow neuromuscular system. Knowledge processing and reasoning for information society*. Warszawa, Poland: Exit.

Brzostowski, K., Drapała, J., Świątek, J., & Moskała, A. (2006). Difference equations and neural networks as a diagnostic tools for human elbow neuromuscular system. *Computer systems engineering, Theory & applications, 6th & 7th Polish-British Workshop,* (pp. 128 – 137).

Bubnicki, Z. (1974). *Identification of Control Plants*. Warszawa, Poland: PWN. (In Polish)

Bubnicki, Z. (2000). Learning process in a class of knowledge-based systems. *Kybernetes*, 1016–1028. doi:10.1108/03684920010342107

Frey Law, L. A., & Shields, R. K. (2006). Predicting human chronically paralyzed muscle force: a comparison of three mathematical models. *Journal of Applied Physiology*, 1027–1036.

James, J. R., & Suski, G. J. (1988). A Survey of Some Implementations of Knowledge-Based Systems for Real-Time Control. *Proceedings of the 27th IEEE Conference on Decision and Control,* (pp. 580–585).

Łęski, J. (2008). *Neuro-Fuzzy Systems*. Warsaw, Poland: WNT.

Rutkowski, L. (2006). *Methods and Techniques of Artificial Intelligence. Computational Intelligence*. Warsaw, Poland: WNT.

Saridis, G. N. (1981). Application of Pattern Recognition Methods to Control Systems. *IEEE Transactions on Automatic Control*, 638–645. doi:10.1109/TAC.1981.1102685

Świątek, J. (1987). *Two Stage Identification and its Technical and Biomedical Applications*. Wrocław: Scientific Papers of the Institute of Control and Systems Engineering of the Wrocław Technical University.

Świątek, J. (2009). *Selected problems of static systems identification*. Wrocław: Scientific Papers of the Institute of Control and Systems Engineering of the Wrocław Technical University. (In Polish)

Theodoridis, S., & Koutroumbas, K. (2006). *Pattern Recognition*. New York: Academic Press.

ADDITIONAL READING

Abonyi, J., & Babuska, R. (2000). Local and Global Identification and Interpretation of parameters. In Takagi-Sugeno Fuzzy Models. *Proc. of IEEE Conf. Fuzzy Systems*, San Antonio, (pp. 835 – 840).

Atiya, A. F., & Parlos, A. G. (2000). New Results on Recurrent Network Training: Unifying the Algorithms and Accelerating Convergence. *IEEE Transactions on Neural Networks, 11*(3), 697–709. doi:10.1109/72.846741

Babuska, R., & Johansen, T. A. (2004). Multi-objective Identification of Takagi-Sugeno Fuzzy Models. *IEEE Transactions on Fuzzy Systems,* 847–860.

Babuska, R., Verbruggeny, H. B., & Hellendoornzy, H. (1999). Promising fuzzy modeling and control methodologies for industrial applications. *ESIT'99, Greece.*

Bazaraa, M. S., Sherali, H. D., & Shetty, C. M. (2006). *Nonlinear Programming – Theory and Algorithms.* New York: John Wiley & Sons Inc.

Billings, S. A. (1980). Identification of Nonlinear Systems – A Survey. *IEEE Proceedings, 127*(6), 272–285.

Bishop, C. M. (2005). *Neural Networks for Pattern Recognition.* New York: Oxford University Press Inc.

Brzostowski, K., & Świątek, J. (2007). On convergence an adaptive control algorithm based on pattern recognition. In *Proceedings of the 16th International Conference on Systems Science ICSS,* (pp. 341 – 350).

Brzostowski, K., & Świątek, J. (2007). On self-tuning knowledge-based controller using pattern recognition with application to non-linear biomedical object. *Information systems architecture and technology. Information models, concepts, tools and applications - 28th International Scientific School,* (pp. 175- 182).

Bubnicki, Z. (1988). Knowledge-based decision making in expert systems. *Sixth International Conference on Systems Engineering,* (pp. 629 – 635).

Cao, Y. Y., & Frank, P. M. (2000). Analysis and synthesis of nonlinear time-delay systems via fuzzy control approach. *IEEE Transactions on Fuzzy Systems,* 200–211.

Chong, E. K. P., & Zak, S. H. (2001). *An Introduction to Optimization. Wiley-Interscience series in discrete mathematics and optimization.* New York: John Wiley & Sons, Inc.

Dumont, G. A., & Huzmezan, M. (2002). Concepts, methods and techniques in adaptive control. In *Proceedings of the American Control Conference,* (pp. 1137 – 1150).

Ehrgott, M. (2005). *Multicriteria Optimization.* Berlin-Heidelberg, Germany: Springer-Verlag.

Espinosa, J., Vandewalle, J., & Wertz, V. (2004). *Fuzzy Logic, Identification and Predictive Control (Advances in Industrial Control).* New York: Springer.

Eykhoff, P. (1974). *System Identification – Parameter and State Estimation.* New York: John Wiley & Sons.

Frangu, L., Carman, B., & Ceanga, E. (2001). A pattern recognition controller applied to the bioprocess control. In *Proceedings of The 13-th International Conference on Control Systems and Computer Science CSCS13,* (pp 187 – 191).

Frangu, L., Carman, B., Ceanga, E., & Boutalis, Y. (2000). A pattern recognition approach to intelligent behaviors: Switching the strategies. *IEEE International Symposium Intelligent Systems,* (pp. 369 – 372).

Fresewinkel, T. (1984). Modelling of complex systems by sequential identification of subsystems. *Regelungstechnik,* Vol. 32, No. 2, West Germany. 51- 55.

Glass, B. J., & Wong, C. (1988). A knowledge-based approach to identification and adaptation in dynamical systems control. In *Proceedings of the 27th IEEE Conference on Decision and Control,* (pp. 881 – 886).

Goodwin, G. C., & Payne, R. L. (1977). *Dynamic System Identification: Experiment Design and Data Analysis.* New York: Academic Press Inc.

Hamrita, T. K. (2000). Pattern recognition for modeling and online diagnosis of bioprocess. *IEEE Transactions on Industry Applications, 36*(5), 1295–1299. doi:10.1109/28.871277

Ikonen, E., & Najim, K. (2002). *Advanced Process Identification and Control.* Boca Raton, FL: CRC Press LLC.

Johansen, T. A. (1994). Fuzzy model based control: stability, robustness, and performance issues. *IEEE Transactions on Fuzzy Systems, 2*(3), 221–234. doi:10.1109/91.298450

Kincaid, D., & Cheney, W. (1991). *Numerical Analysis.* Pacific Grove, CA: Brooks/Cole Publishing Company.

Krijgsman, A. J., Broeders, H. M. T., Verbruggen, H. B., & Bruijn, P. M. (1988). Knowledge based control. *Proceedings of the 27th IEEE Conference on Decision and Control,* (pp. 570 – 574).

Kukolij, D. (2004). Identification of Complex Systems Based on Neural and Takagi-Sugeno Fuzzy Model. *IEEE Trans. on Systems, Man and Cybernetics – Part B. Cybernetics, 34*(1), 272–282.

Ljung, L. (1991). Issue in System Identification. *IEEE Trans. on Control Systems, 11,* 25–29. doi:10.1109/37.103346

Ljung, L. (1998). *System Identification: Theory for the User.* Upper Saddle River, NJ: Prentice Hall PTR.

Ljung, L., & Glad, T. (1994). *Modeling of Dynamic Systems.* Englewood Cliffs, NJ: Prentice Hall PTR.

Nelles, O. (2001). *Nonlinear System Identification - From Classical Approaches to Neural Networks and Fuzzy Models.* New York: Springer.

Nocedal, J., & Wright, S. J. (2006). *Numerical Optimization.* PA: Springer Science Business Media, LLC.

Osowski, S. (2007). *Modeling and simulation of dynamical systems and processes.* Warszawa, Poland: Oficyna Wydawnicza Politechniki Warszawskiej. (In Polish)

Pingan, Z., & Renhou, L. A. (1996). New Approach to Fuzzy Identification for Complex Systems. In *Proc. of 5th IEEE International Conference on Fuzzy Systems,* Vol. 2, September. (pp. 1308 – 1313).

Poznyak, A. S., Najim, K., & Ramirez, E. G. (2000). *Self-Learning Control of Finite Markov Chains.* New York: Marcel Dekker.

Qi, R., & Brdys, M. A. (2005). Adaptive fuzzy modeling and control for discrete-time nonlinear uncertain systems. In *Proceedings of the American Control Conference,* (pp. 1108 – 1113).

Ramoni, M., Stefanelli, M., Magnani, L., & Barosi, R. (1996). An epistemological framework for medical knowledge-based systems. *IEEE Transactions on Systems, Man, and Cybernetics, 22*(6), 1361–1375. doi:10.1109/21.199462

Seif, A. A. (1992). On the adaptive pattern recognition control. In *Proceedings of Computer Systems and Software Engineering,* (pp. 706 – 709).

Shi, X. A., Zhou, X. S., Gu, J. H., & Lin, Y. (2003). Pattern recognition based adaptive real-time scheduling. *Proceeding of the second International Conference on Machine Learning and Cybernetics,* (pp. 3160 – 3166).

Snyman, J. A. (2005). *Practical Mathematical Optimization – An Introduction to Basic Optimization Theory and Classical and New Gradient-Based Algorithms.* PA: Springer Science+Business Media, Inc.

Sobajic, D. J., Pao, Y. H., & Lee, D. T. (1989). Robust control of nonlinear systems using pattern recognition. *Conference Proceedings of IEEE International Conference on Systems, Man and Cybernetics,* (pp. 315 – 320).

Spooner, J. T., Maggiore, M., Ordonez, R., & Passino, K. M. (2002). *Stable Adaptive Control and Estimation for Nonlinear Systems: Neural and Fuzzy Approximation Technique.* New York: John Wiley & Sons, Inc. doi:10.1002/0471221139

Sragovich, V. G. (2006). *Mathematical theory of adaptive control.* PA: World Scientific.

Suski, G. J. (1988). A survey of some implementations of knowledge-based systems for real-time control. In *Proceedings of the 27th IEEE Conference on Decision and Control,* (pp. 580 – 585).

Venkatesh, S. R., & Dahleh, M. A. (1996). System Identification of Complex Systems: Problem Formulation and Results. In *Proc. of 36th IEEE Conference on Decision and Control,* Vol. 3. (pp. 2441 – 2446).

Zhang, B. S., & Leigh, J. R. (1995). Learning control based on pattern recognition applied to vehicle cruise control systems. In *Proceeding of the American Control Conference,* (pp. 3101 – 3105).

KEY TERMS AND DEFINITIONS

Decision Making Systems: A systems to support the sequence of decisions or controls.

Fuzzy Systems: Systems, which are based on fuzzy logic.

Identification: Methodologies of modeling processes or systems with use of experimental data.

Neuromuscular System: The system of human skeletal muscles.

Optimization: Activities leading to find the best possible solution.

Pattern Recognition: Process of assigning the object to the predefined class.

Two-stage Identification: Identification with use of the model that is decomposed into two parts i.e., model at the first stage, which contains parameters that are outputs of the model at the second stage. Decomposition can be made respect to time, space or calculations.

Chapter 4
Probabilistic Temporal Network for Numeric and Symbolic Time Information

Malek Mouhoub
University of Regina, Canada

Jia Liu
University of Regina, Canada

ABSTRACT

We propose a probabilistic extension of Allen's Interval Algebra for managing uncertain temporal relations. Although previous work on various uncertain forms of quantitative and qualitative temporal networks have been proposed in the literature, little has been addressed to the most obvious type of uncertainty, namely the probabilistic one. More precisely, our model adapts the probabilistic Constraint Satisfaction Problem (CSP) framework in order to handle uncertain symbolic and numeric temporal constraints. In a probabilistic CSP, each constraint C is given a probability of its existence in the real world. There is thus more than one CSP to solve as opposed to the traditional CSP where no such uncertainties exist. In a probabilistic temporal CSP, since we use the Interval Algebra where a constraint is a disjunction of Allen primitives, the probability is assigned to each of these Allen primitives rather than to the temporal constraint. This means that a probabilistic temporal CSP involves many possible temporal CSPs, each with a probability of its existence. Solving a probabilistic temporal CSP consists of finding a scenario that has the highest probability to be the solution for the real world. This is an optimization problem that we solve using a branch and bound algorithm we propose and involving constraint propagation. Experimental study conducted on randomly generated temporal problems demonstrates the efficiency in time of our solving method. In the case of uncertain numeric constraints, our TemPro framework for handling numeric and symbolic temporal constraints is extended to handle uncertain domains. An algorithm for dividing domains into non-overlapping areas is proposed. This algorithm guarantees that the generated possible worlds do not intersect. Probable worlds are then constructed by combining these areas. A new branch and bound algorithm, we propose, is finally applied to find the most robust solution.

DOI: 10.4018/978-1-61692-811-7.ch004

INTRODUCTION

A Constraint Satisfaction Problem (CSP) (Dechter, 2003, Haralick, 1980, Mackworth, 1977) is a general model for many problems in the real world. A CSP is defined as a tuple $< X, D, C >$ where X is a set of variables, D their domains of values and C the set of constraints restricting the values that the variables can simultaneously take. A Temporal Constraint Satisfaction Problem (Allen, 1983, Dean 1989, Morris 2000, van Beek, 1992, Vilan 1986) is a special type of CSPs that handles temporal information. There are many applications of Temporal CSPs, such as scheduling (Baptiste, 1995), planning (Golumbic 1993, Tsamardinos 2003,Vidal 1996), natural language processing (Hwang, 1994), temporal database (Dean, 1989) and molecular biology (Golumbic 1993). These applications usually come with uncertain factors from the real world. For example, when we are trying to schedule a plan for traveling, the aircraft we take may not arrive at the destination on time. When we are allocating tasks among processors, some processors may break down. With these uncertain factors, some solutions may be better suited for the environment than others. However, all the solutions are treated equally in the traditional temporal CSPs without uncertainty. Our goal is to find the most robust solution that is associated with the highest probability to satisfy all the constraints in the uncertain temporal CSP.

Temporal information can be symbolic or numeric. In (Mouhoub, 2004), we have proposed the TemPro framework for managing discrete numeric and symbolic temporal information. The variables in TemPro are events associated with temporal intervals. The domain of each event is the discrete and finite set of the possible numeric intervals the event can take. Constraints in TemPro specify the possible temporal relationships among events. Solving a problem represented in TemPro (that we call Temporal Constraint Satisfaction Problem (TCSP)) is to find an assignment of one numeric interval to each event, in such a way that

every constraint is satisfied. In symbolic temporal CSPs, the variables are the relations between time points or time intervals. In the case of relations between time intervals, the constraint network is called Interval Algebra (IA) network (Allen, 1983). In the case of an IA network these relations are disjunctions of Allen primitives. Allen primitives are the thirteen possible relations between a pair of numeric intervals. Solving an IA network consists of finding an assignment of a possible Allen primitive to each disjunctive relation such that the entire IA network is consistent.

In order to handle the uncertainty both at the symbolic and the numeric levels, we have extended the two models above (the TCSP and the IA network). We propose a probabilistic extension of Allen's Interval Algebra for managing uncertain temporal relations. Although previous work on various uncertain forms of quantitative and qualitative temporal networks have been proposed in the literature (Baladoni, 1999, Fargier, 1996, Peintner, 2007, Ryabov 2004), little has been addressed to the most obvious type of uncertainty, namely the probabilistic one. More precisely, our model adapts the probabilistic Constraint Satisfaction Problem (CSP) framework in order to handle uncertain symbolic temporal constraints. In a probabilistic CSP, each constraint C is given a probability of its existence in the real world. There is thus more than one CSP to solve as opposed to the traditional CSP where no such uncertainties exist. In a probabilistic temporal CSP, since we use the Interval Algebra where a constraint is a disjunction of Allen primitives, the probability is assigned to each of these Allen primitives rather than to the temporal constraint itself. This means that a probabilistic temporal CSP involves many possible temporal CSPs, each with a probability of its existence. Solving a probabilistic temporal CSP consists of finding a scenario that has the highest probability to be the solution for the real world. This is an optimization problem that we solve using a branch and bound algorithm we propose and involving constraint propagation.

Based on path consistency (van Beek 1992), this propagation is used before and during the search in order to prevent earlier later failure. Note that, when path consistency is used before the search it is applied to hard (certain) constraints only. If the path consistency fails then the IA network is not consistent and there is thus no need to proceed with the search. In the case where the path consistency is successful then the hard constraints of the resulting network will have less Allen primitives which will reduce the size of the search space. After this filtering step we use a backtrack algorithm to find the first solution in order to use its robustness as a Lower Bound (LB). First, for each uncertain constraint we sort its primitives by decreasing order of their probability. We then pick a constraint (that we call current constraint) and we assign an Allen primitive to it. If this constraint is uncertain then an overestimation of the robustness of any possible solution following this decision (assignment) is computed and used as an Upper Bound (UB). If UB < LB then the current uncertain constraint is assigned another value or backtrack to the previous constraint if all the primitives have been explored. The overestimated robustness is the product of the probabilities of all the assigned primitives plus the product of the max probabilities of the uncertain constraints that are not yet assigned. The max probability of a non assigned uncertain constraint corresponds to the largest probability of its primitives. Experimental study conducted on randomly generated IA networks demonstrates the efficiency in time of our solving method.

In the case of uncertain numeric constraints, the TCSP model is extended to handle uncertain domains. An algorithm for dividing domains into non-overlapping areas is proposed. This algorithm guarantees that the generated possible worlds do not intersect. Probable worlds are then constructed by combining these areas. A new branch and bound algorithm, we propose, is finally applied to find the most robust solution. Like for IA networks, this algorithm works in two stages.

In the first one local consistency techniques are used in order to reduce the size of the problem by removing locally inconsistent values. We then calculate the probability of each area to be included in the actual domain of each uncertain event. The algorithm will then look for the first solution satisfying all the temporal constraints. The Lower Bound is then set to the probability of this solution. The next step consists of exploring the search space in a systematic manner looking for the most probable solution. During the search, each time an event is assigned a value from its domain, an overestimation of the robustness of any possible solution falling in the current assigned event is calculated and used as the upper bound UB. If UB < LB we select another interval for the current uncertain event or backtrack to the previous uncertain event if all the intervals for this current event have been explored. The overestimation of the robustness is the product of the probabilities of the already assigned events and the maximum probabilities of the domains for all the non-assigned uncertain events.

The following section is dedicated to literature review in the areas of CSPs and temporal CSPs. In section 3, we present through examples our new framework handling uncertainties at the symbolic level. Section 4 describes our branch and bound algorithm for finding the most robust solution. Section 5 is dedicated to handling uncertainties at the numeric level. In section 6 we provide a description of the experiments we conducted on randomly generated temporal problems. We conclude in section 7 and list some remarks and possible future works in section 8.

BACKGROUND

In order to solve problems in uncertain environments, many frameworks (Baladoni, 1999, Fargier, 1996, Peintner, 2007, Ryabov 2004, Vidal, 1999, Walsh, 2002) for modeling uncertain CSPs have been proposed. The uncertain factors in these frameworks include variables, domains and constraints. For example, we want to plan a working schedule for one week. In classical CSPs, working tasks are predetermined at the time of planning. However, some unexpected events may emerge from time to time in the real world. The main objectives of solving CSPs and temporal CSPs in uncertain environments include predicting future changes, reacting rapidly to these changes and finding robust solutions. The Probabilistic CSP (PCSP) (Fargier, 1996) is used to model the situation where constraints are uncertain. In a PCSP, each constraint is associated with a probability of its existence in the real world. More formally, a PCSP consists of a set of constraints $C = \{C_1, ..., C_m\}$ and a set of probabilities p_i, which are the probabilities of C_i to be existent in the real problem P_{real}. Mixed CSP (MCSP) (Fargier, 1996) is proposed to model decision problems in uncertain environments. In MCSP, variables are divided into two categories. One category is decision variables that are controllable by users and the other category is environmental variables which are uncontrollable by users. Stochastic CSP (SCSP) (Fargier, 1996, Walsh, 2002) is proposed to model uncertain worlds in a similar way as MCSPs. As in MCSPs, variables in SCSPs are divided into controllable (decision) variables and uncontrollable (stochastic) variables. The main difference between SCSPs and MCSPs is that a probability distribution is associated with the domain of each stochastic variable in SCSPs. In a one stage SCSP, the decision variables are determined before the stochastic variables are given values. A one stage SCSP is satisfiable if and only if there are values for the decision variables so that, given random values for the stochastic variables, the probability that all the constraints are satisfied equals or exceeds some threshold (Walsh, 2002). For multiple stage SCSPs, a decision policy is a tree with nodes labeled with variables, starting with the first variable labeling the root and ending with the last variable. The decision variables will have only one child for the

decision value determined by the decision policy, and the stochastic variables will have one child for each possible output. For a SCSP, the expected value of a policy (satisfaction value) is the sum of objective valuations of each leaf node weighted by their probabilities (Walsh, 2002). The goal is to find an optimal solution with a maximum satisfaction value. Forward checking has been applied to solve SCSPs (Walsh, 2002). All the variables are ordered at first. Then, values are assigned to these variables one by one. For decision variables, we will try each value in the domain and return the maximum value. For stochastic variables, we will return the weighed sum of all the answers to the sub-problems. The main goal of solving stochastic SCSPs is to make a series of decisions and maximize the degrees of satisfaction. Temporal problems, as general CSPs, are often emerging in uncertain environments. In the real world, there are many uncontrollable factors in TCSPs. In the Simple Temporal Problem with uncertainty (STPU) (Vidal, 1999), there are uncertain duration of events and uncertain temporal constraints. The usual notion of consistency is replaced by the notion of controllability (Vidal, 1999). There are three levels of controllability–strong, weak and dynamic. A strongly controllable STPU has a fully robust solution, a dynamically controllable STPU has a flexible solution, and a weakly controllable STPU has a contingent solution. In other words, strong controllability suits cases where the situation is totally unknown; weak controllability suits cases where the situation is totally known after the decisions are made; dynamic controllability suits cases where the situation is only partially known. It has been proved that the most important of these controllability levels, dynamic controllability, is tractable in polynomial time. Furthermore, the relationship among these three kinds of controllability is listed as follows (Vidal, 1999):

strong controllability ⇒ *dynamic controllability* ⇒ *weak controllability*

PROBABILISTIC SYMBOLIC TEMPORAL NETWORK

Interval Algebra (IA) Networks

An Interval Algebra Network (also called IA network) consists of a tuple $< E,$ SET $R >$ where E is a set of events 1 and SET R is the set of binary constraints between events. An event is defined here as a preposition that holds over a time interval. A relation R_{ij} represents the relative position between two events e_i and e_j and is expressed by the disjunction of some Allen primitives (Allen, 1983). Figure 1 lists all the Allen primitives. For instance the relation $R = M \vee O$ between two events E_1 and E_2 represents the fact that E_1 meets or overlaps the event E_2. Since there are 13 Allen primitives, the set SET R contains 2^{13} possible relations. One particular relation called *universal relation* (or identity relation) and denoted by I corresponds to the disjunction of the 13 primitives. This relation expresses the fact that the relation between the two involved events is completely unknown. Solving an IA network consists of assigning to each disjunctive relation one of its primitives such that all the relations are consistent together.

In order to illustrate the Interval Algebra and its related IA network, let us consider the following example taken from (Dechter, 2003).

Example 1. *Fred was reading the paper while eating his breakfast. He put the paper down and drank the last of his coffee. After breakfast he went for a walk.*

The above story can be represented by the IA network shown in Figure 2. Here each node corresponds to a given event in the story and each edge is labeled by a binary constraint between events. For example, the constraint between the events Paper (*reading paper*) and Coffee (*drinking coffee*) is expressed by the disjunctive relation DOS ($D \vee O \vee S$). This relation means that between

Figure 1. Allen primitives

Relation	Symbol	Inverse	Meaning
X precedes Y	P	P-	X Y
X equals Y	E	E	X / Y
X meets Y	M	M-	X Y
X overlaps Y	O	O-	X Y
X during Y	D	D-	X Y
X starts Y	S	S-	X Y
X finishes Y	F	F-	Y X

the events *Paper* and *Coffee* we can have one of the following three primitives: *During, Overlaps or Starts*. Note that, since there is no constraint between Coffee and Walk, we could represent the corresponding relation by the universal relation I. A possible solution for the above temporal problem is given in Figure 2 (Dechter, 2003). This solution corresponds to the following:

- *Paper O Coffee.*
- *Paper D Breakfast.*
- *Coffee D Breakfast.*
- *Breakfast B Walk*

Probabilistic Symbolic Temporal Relations (PSTR)

In probabilistic CSPs (Fargier, 1996), constraints can be certain or uncertain. Each uncertain constraint has a probability of its existence. For instance, $Pr(C) = 0.7$ means that the constraint C (involving a list of variables) has 70% chances to exist.

In the case of IA networks, we associate these types of probabilities to the Allen primitives within a given uncertain relation rather than to the relation

Figure 2. Interval Algebra (IA) Constraint Network (Dechter, 2003)

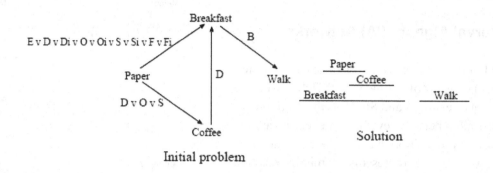

Initial problem

Solution

itself. More formally, we define a Probabilistic Symbolic Temporal Relation (PSTR) as follows.

Definition 1. Probabilistic Allen Primitive (PAP) A Probabilistic Allen Primitive (PAP) *r* is an Allen primitive that has a probability of its existence within a relation R_{ij} between two events e_i and e_j. More precisely *r* has the following probabilities where $0 \leq p \leq 1$.

- $Pr(r \in R_{ij}) = p$: the probability that r exists within R_{ij}
- $Pr(r \in / R_{ij}) = 1 - p$: the probability that r does not exist in R_{ij}

The PAP r is certain (or completely known) if and only if $Pr(r \in R_{ij}) = 1.0$. In this case we simply call it Allen Primitive (AP).

Definition 2. Probabilistic Symbolic Temporal Relation (PSTR) Given a relation R_{ij} between two events e_i and e_j; and defined by the disjunction $r_1 \vee r_2 \cdots \vee r_n$ where $r_n \leq 13$ and the r_t is Allen primitive. *R* is a Probabilistic Symbolic Temporal Relation (PSTR) if and only if at least one of its r_i's is a PAP.

The PSTR R_{ij} is certain (or completely known) if and only if all its r_i's are certain (APs). In this latter case R_{ij} is simply called Symbolic Temporal Relation (STR).

The PSTR R_{ij} can be formulated as follows. $R_{ij} = R_1 \vee \cdots \vee R_n$ where each R_k is an STR.

Let us illustrate the above definitions through the following four examples. We will consider here the cases where the PSTR involves one or two primitives. The probability of a PSTR with more than two primitives can be computed in the same manner.

Example 2. *Let us consider the story in example 1. The sentence "After breakfast he went for a walk" is certain and means that we have one primitive (B) in the relation R between the events Breakfast and Walk. B is certain (completely known) in the real world. Pr(R = B) = Pr(B V R) = 1.0. The solution to the problem including R must satisfy the relation B.*

Example 3. *Let us consider again the story in example 1 but with the last sentence being uncertain: "After breakfast he might go for a walk". Here too there is only one possible primitive (B) in R, but this time B exists in the real world with a given probability (0.6 for example).*

Pr(R) = Pr(B∈ R) = 0.6

Example 4. *In example1, let us assume that we have the following additional information: "Fred does not start drinking coffee before he starts reading his paper. Usually he starts reading the paper first."*

According to the above new information, there are now only two primitives (instead of three as shown in Figure 1) between the events Paper and Coffee. These primitives are O and S with O being the most probable one. Let us assign the following probabilities to each of these two primitives. $Pr(S) = 0.6$ and $Pr(O) = 0.8$. Using the above the PSTR R between Paper and Coffee is equal to one of three possible STRs as follows.

1. $Pr(R = S) = Pr(S) \times (1 - Pr(O)) = 0.6 \times 0.2 = 0.12$
2. $Pr(R = O) = Pr(O) \times (1 - Pr(S)) = 0.8 \times 0.4 = 0.32$
3. $Pr(R = O \vee S) = 0.6 \times 0.8 = 0.48$

The probability that R exists between *Paper* and *Coffee* is computed as follows.
$Pr(R) = Pr(R = O) + Pr(R = S) + Pr(R = O \vee S) = 0.92$

Probabilistic IA (PIA) Network

Definition 3. A Probabilistic IA (PIA) network is a IA network where some disjunctive relations are PSTRs.

Figure 3 shows the PIA network corresponding to example 1 with the additional information in examples 3 and 4. In the figure, the relations *(Paper, Coffee)* and *(Breakfast, Walk)* are PSTRs while the other two relations are STRs.

Probable Worlds and Robust Solutions

Definition 4. A probable world of a given PIA network P is a scenario (IA network) corresponding to replacing each PSTR of P by one of its possible STRs. A basic world is a probable world where all the selected STRs are APs.

Let us consider the PIA network in Figure 2 with two PSTRs: *(Paper, Coffee)* and *(Breakfast, Walk)*. A probable world (respectively basic world) can be obtained by replacing each of these two PSTRs by

Figure 3. PIA network corresponding to examples 1, 3 and 4

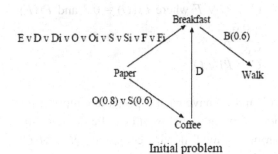

Initial problem

one of their STRs (respectively APs). Below we have the list of the three possible probable worlds where the first two are basic worlds.

1. W_1:
    ○ *Paper O Coffee.*
    ○ *Paper E $\vee D \vee D$-$\vee O \vee O$-$\vee S \vee S$-$\vee F \vee F$-Breakfast.*
    ○ *Coffee D Breakfast.*
    ○ *Breakfast B Walk.*
2. W_2:
    ○ *Paper S Coffee.*
    ○ *Paper E $\vee D \vee D$-$\vee O \vee O$-$\vee S \vee S$-$\vee F \vee F$-Breakfast.*
    ○ *Coffee D Breakfast*
    ○ *Breakfast B Walk.*
3. W_3:
    ○ *Paper OS Coffee.*
    ○ *Paper E $\vee D \vee D$-$\vee O \vee O$-$\vee S \vee S$-$\vee F \vee F$-Breakfast.*
    ○ *Coffee D Breakfast.*
    ○ *Breakfast B Walk.*

Note that, in the above, W_1 (respectively W_2) is included in W_3. Thus the set of solutions to W_1 and W_2 are included in the set of solutions to W_3.

Example 5. *Let us consider another PIA network with two PSTRs C_1 and C_2, and two STRs C_3 and C_4 defined as follows.*

- $C_1 = M \vee S$ where $Pr(M) = 0.2$ and $Pr(S) = 0.5$.
- $C_2 = O \vee F$ where $Pr(O) = 0.3$ and $Pr(F) = 0.6$.
- $C_3 = P$
- $C_4 = Pi \vee Oi$

C_1 and C_2 have each 3 possible temporal relations. One probable world can be defined, for example, by the following constraints $\{C_1 = M, C_2 = O \vee F, C_3 = P, C_4 = P_i \vee O_j\}$. The total number of probable worlds will thus be equal to 9.

Definition 5. The total number of possible worlds of a PIA network P can be computed as follows.

$$\prod_{C_i \in problem} \dim(C_i)$$

where $dim(C_i)$ is the number of different situations of C_i.

Definition 6. Let us consider a given PIA network P and WS the set of probable worlds of P that can be satisfied by a given solution S. The robustness of S is computed as follows

$$Robustness(S) = \sum_{Wi \in Ws} Pr(W_i)$$

where $Ws = \{$probable worlds satisfied *by S*

Definition 7. The most robust solution to a given problem P is the solution that has the highest degree of robustness.

In other words, the above definition means that the most robust solution is the one that has the highest probability to satisfy the real world. Solving a PIA Network is an optimization problem that consists of finding the most robust solution.

FINDING THE MOST ROBUST SOLUTION

Example 6. *Let us consider the PIA network of example 5. Here we have 4 basic worlds.*

1. $W_1 = \{C_1 = M, C_2 = O, C_3, C_4\}$
2. $W_2 = \{C_1 = M, C_2 = F, C_3, C_4\}$
3. $W_3 = \{C_1 = S, C_2 = O, C_3, C_4\}$
4. $W_4 = \{C_1 = S, C_2 = F, C_3, C_4\}$

Notice that the solutions of the above four basic worlds are all the solutions of the corresponding PIA network. Thus, in order to search for the most robust solution in a PIA network we can simply look for the most robust solution in the basic worlds only.

The probability of a basic world is the product of the probabilities of all the uncertain primitives this basic world involves. For instance, the probability of each of the above four worlds is computed as follows.

1. $Pr(W_1) = Pr(M) \times (1 - Pr(S)) \times Pr(O) \times (1 - Pr(F)) = 0.2 \times 0.5 \times 0.3 \times 0.4 = 0.012$.
2. $Pr(W_2) = Pr(M) \times (1 - Pr(S)) \times Pr(F) \times (1 - Pr(O)) = 0.2 \times 0.5 \times 0.6 \times 0.7 = 0.042$.
3. $Pr(W_3) = Pr(S) \times (1 - Pr(M)) \times Pr(O) \times (1 - Pr(F)) = 0.5 \times 0.8 \times 0.3 \times 0.4 = 0.048$.
4. $Pr(W_4) = Pr(S) \times (1 - Pr(M)) \times Pr(F) \times (1 - Pr(O)) = 0.5 \times 0.8 \times 0.6 \times 0.7 = 0.16$.

The most probable basic world is the basic world with the most probable uncertain primitives. In the above example, W_4 is the most probable world. The robustness of a solution corresponds here to the probability of the basic world it satisfies. The most robust solution is the one that satisfies the most probable consistent world.

Solving Algorithm

Solving an IA network is an NP-hard problem that requires a backtrack search algorithm of exponential time cost (Mouhoub, 2004). In order to overcome this difficulty in practice, constraint propagation based on path consistency is used before and during the search in order to prevent earlier later failure. In the case of PIA networks we will also use backtrack search with path consistency performed before and during the search.

Note that, when path consistency is used before the search it is applied to hard (certain) constraints only. If the path consistency fails then the PIA network is not consistent and there is thus no need to proceed with the search. In the case where the path consistency is successful then the hard constraints of the resulting network will have less Allen primitives which will reduce the size of the search space.

More precisely, we propose the following branch and bound algorithm for finding the most robust solution.

1. Perform path consistency (van Beek, 1992) to the sub-network containing only the hard constraints. If the sub-network is not path consistent return that the IA network is not consistent.

2. For each uncertain constraint, sort its primitives by decreasing order of their probability.

3. Following the forward check principle (Haralick, 1980), pick a constraint, assign to it one of its Allen primitives and run the path consistency algorithm on the sub-network containing the newly assigned constraint and the non assigned ones. If path consistency fails then assign another primitive to the current constraint or backtrack to the previous assigned constraint if the current constraint does not have any another primitive to assign. If the path consistency is successful, select another constraint and redo the same process until all the constraints are assigned in which case we obtain a solution otherwise return that the PIA network is not consistent. If a solution is obtained, compute its robustness (the probability of the complete assignment

it satisfies) and assign the result to the lower bound (LB).

4. The rest of the search space is then systematically explored as follows. Each time the current constraint is assigned a primitive, if this constraint is uncertain (PSTR) then an overestimation of the robustness of any possible solution following this decision is computed and used as an upper bound (UB). If $UB < LB$ then the current uncertain constraint is assigned another value or backtrack to the previous constraint if all the primitives have been explored. The overestimated robustness is the product of the probabilities of all the assigned primitives plus the product of the max probabilities of the uncertain constraints that are not yet assigned. The max probability of a non assigned uncertain constraint corresponds to the largest probability of its primitives.

PROBABILISTIC NUMERIC TEMPORAL NETWORK

In this section we show how to handle uncertain domains in the TemPro framework. An algorithm for dividing domains into non-overlapping areas is reported. We also examine the calculation of the robustness of solutions in different probable worlds. At the end, we present the branch-and-bound algorithm for searching the most robust solution in the TemPro framework with uncertainty.

TemPro Framework

TemPro (Mouhoub, 2004) transforms a temporal problem under qualitative and quantitative constraints into a binary CSP where constraints are disjunctions of Allen primitives and variables, representing temporal events, are defined on domains of time intervals. Each event domain (called also temporal window) contains the Set of Possible Occurrences (SOPO) of numeric intervals the corresponding event can take. The SOPO is the numeric constraint of the event. It is expressed by the fourfold: [earliest start, latest end, duration, step] where: earliest start is the earliest start time of the event, latest end is the latest end time of the event, duration is the duration of the event and step is the discretization step corresponding to the number of time units between the start time of two adjacent intervals. Each interval is shown as (*StartTime, EndTime*), in which *StartTime* is the actual start time of the event and *EndTime* is the actual end time which is the summation of *StartTime* and duration of the event. *StartTime* of each event should be selected based on the unary constraints it is involved in. Hence, if we consider the TemPro model, domain of *StartTime* of event *i* would be earliest *start*+(*X*×*step*) where *X* ranges in the interval of [0, (*latest end - earliest start - duration*)/step].

Extending TemPro with Uncertainty

Uncertainty of Domains

In the STPU (Peintner, 2007), the uncertainty is mainly focused on the duration of some uncertain events. In addition to duration, there could also be some other uncertainty for one event, such as the earliest start time (*INF*) and latest finish time (*SUP*). In uncertain and dynamic environment, the *INF* and *SUP* of an event are affected by some external factors. Let us consider the following example.

Example 7: Uncertain *INF* and *SUP* of an Event.

Everyday Bob takes bus to his company. Occasionally, the bus is full and he has to call a taxi. The bus arrives at the company *at 8:30 and the taxi arrives at the company at 8:20. Bob normally finishes his job in 12:00. However, his manager Tom may want to talk with him after 12:00, which will take 60 minutes. Bob doesn't know whether Tom wants to talk with him before 12:00.*

In the above example, the earliest start (*INF*) of event *workInOffice* depends on which vehicle Bob takes. Suppose 8:00 is the zero point in the time line. If Bob takes the bus, the *INF* for *workInOffice* would be 30 (corresponding to 8:30). If he takes a taxi, the *INF* for workInOffice would be 20. The latest finish (*SUP*) of event *workInOffice* is also associated with some uncertainty. If Tom does not want to talk with him, the *SUP* for *workInOffice* would be 240. Otherwise, the *SUP* of *workInOffice* would be 300. With the uncertainty in domains of events, both the *INF* and *SUP* are no longer single time points, but probability distributions of several possible time points. For example, there are three possible earliest start time points: 20, 30 and 40 for a single event E_1. These earliest start time points are caused by some external factors, as the *INF* of the event *workInOffice* in the above example. The priori probability of each earliest start can be computed by statistics or estimated by induction. Assume E_1 has a length of 15 and the step is 1 unit. The probabilities of these three *INF* are listed as follows.

$$\Pr \{E_1 = [20, SUP, 15, 1]\} = 0.2$$
$$\Pr \{E_1 = [30, SUP, 15, 1]\} = 0.3$$
$$\Pr \{E_1 = [40, SUP, 15, 1]\} = 0.5$$

The uncertainty of the latest finish (*SUP*) can be presented in a similar way. Assume that three possible latest end time points 45, 60 and 80 exist for E_1. Their probabilities can be described in a similar form.

$$\Pr \{E_1 = [INF, 45, 15, 1]\} = 0.4$$
$$\Pr \{E_1 = [INF, 60, 15, 1]\} = 0.1$$
$$\Pr \{E_1 = [INF, 45, 15, 1]\} = 0.5$$

With the addition of uncertain *INF* and *SUP*, the domain of one event is no longer a certain time frame, but rather a dynamic time window. For the previous example of event E_1, we have 3 different *INF* and 3 different *SUP*. Therefore, there are 9 (3^3) possible domains in total.

[20, 45, 15, 1], [20, 60, 15, 1], [20, 80, 15, 1]
[30, 45, 15, 1], [30, 60, 15, 1], [30, 80, 15, 1]
[40, 45, 15, 1], [40, 60, 15, 1], [40, 60, 15, 1]

More formally, the set of domains of event E can be defined as:

$$D = [INF_i, SUP_j, DUR, STEP]$$

where INF_i and SUP_j are the possible values for INF and SUP, respectively.

Continuous and Discrete Probabilities

The earliest start (*INF*) and the latest finish (*SUP*) in a SOPO define the time domain for a specific event. In the previous subsection, we assumed that the probability distribution for *INF* and *SUP* are discrete. The discrete probability distribution is applied to handle uncertainty caused by discrete external factors. For example, in the previous example, full and empty are the only two discrete possible states of the bus. The actual state of the bus affects the *INF* of the event *workInOffice*. In some real world applications, however, the determinant external factor may be a continuous variable. For example, the bus may arrive at the office within a range between 8:25 and 8:35 with a continuous probability distribution, which affects the corresponding event *workInOffice*. Since TemPro can only handle discrete time points, we have to discreterize the continuous distribution. First, the continuous distribution is divided into several areas in its range. The mid-points of each area are used as the representative values for that area. Then, cumulative probabilities are calculated for the continuous distribution in each area. Each cumulative probability will be associated with the corresponding midpoint to generate a discrete distribution.

Uncertain Domains and Probable Worlds

Calculation of Probabilities of Uncertain Constraints

Given the probabilities of uncertain *INF* and *SUP*, the probability of each possible domain (SOPO) for an event can be calculated. In the above example, we have two sets of *INF* and two sets of *SUP*. Assume the *INF* and *SUP* are caused by independent external factors, we can calculate the probabilities of the SOPO for E_I as follows.

$Pr(E_I = [20, 45, 15, 1]) = Pr(E_I = [20, SUP, 15, 1])$
$\times Pr(E_I = [INF, 45, 15, 1]) = 0.2 \times 0.4 = 0.08$
$Pr(E_I = [20, 60, 15, 1]) = Pr(E_I = [20, SUP, 15, 1])$
$\times Pr(E_I = [INF, 60, 15, 1]) = 0.02$
$Pr(E_I = [20, 80, 15, 1]) = Pr(E_I = [20, SUP, 15, 1])$
$\times Pr(E_I = [INF, 80, 15, 1]) = 0.01$
$Pr(E_I = [30, 45, 15, 1]) = Pr(E_I = [30, SUP, 15, 1])$
$\times Pr(E_I = [INF, 45, 15, 1]) = 0.12$
$Pr(E_I = [30, 60, 15, 1]) = Pr(E_I = [30, SUP, 15, 1])$
$\times Pr(E_I = [INF, 60, 15, 1]) = 0.03$
$Pr(E_I = [30, 80, 15, 1]) = Pr(E_I = [30, SUP, 15, 1])$
$\times Pr(E_I = [INF, 80, 15, 1]) = 0.15$
$Pr(E_I = [40, 45, 15, 1]) = Pr(E_I = [40, SUP, 15, 1])$
$\times Pr(E_I = [INF, 45, 15, 1]) = 0.20$
$Pr(E_I = [40, 60, 15, 1]) = Pr(E_I = [40, SUP, 15, 1])$
$\times Pr(E_I = [INF, 60, 15, 1]) = 0.05$
$Pr(E_I = [40, 80, 15, 1]) = Pr(E_I = [40, SUP, 15, 1])$
$\times Pr(E_I = [INF, 80, 15, 1]) = 0.25$

The sum of these probabilities is equal to 1. More formally, the probability of each SOPO is calculated with the following formula.

$$Pr\{E = [INF_i, SUP_j, DUR_i, STEP_i]\} = Pr\{INF = INF_i\} \times Pr\{SUP = SUP_j\}$$

$$\sum_{i,j} Pr\{E = [INF_i, SUP_j, DUR, STEP]\} = 1.0$$

Figure 4. Dividing domains into non-overlapping areas

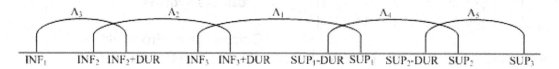

Figure 5. An incorrect way for dividing domains into non-overlapping areas

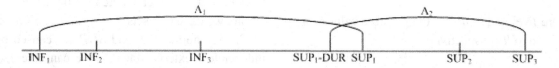

Figure 6. Another way of dividing with mixed INF and SUP

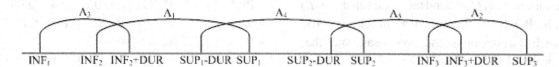

Dividing Domains into Non-Overlapping Areas

In the above example, there are nine possible domains (SOPOs) for E1. However, these domains are not separately distributed along the time line. Some of them such as [30, 60, 15, 1] and [40, 80, 15, 1] overlap each other. Actually, with three *INF* and three *SUP* for event E_1, we can order them as follows.

$$INF_1 < INF_2 < INF_3$$
$$SUP_1 < SUP_2 < SUP_3$$

We can thus divide the possible domains of E_1 into 5 non-overlapping areas.

A_1: $[INF_3, SUP_1]$
A_2: $[INF_2, INF_3 + DUR]$ A_3: $[INF_1, INF_2 + DUR]$
A_4: $[SUP_1 - DUR, SUP_2]$ A_5: $[SUP_2 - DUR, SUP_3]$

Figure 4 illustrates the above overlapping.

By dividing the entire possible domains into non-overlapping areas, a solution containing an event in one area will not be contained in any other areas. Furthermore, these non-overlapping areas cover all the possible assignments of each event in the final solution. Therefore, we can consider the assignment of events in each area. In order to calculate the probabilities of solutions, these non-overlapping areas must also not be overlapped by the original possible SOPOs. In other words, for each possible SOPO$_i$ (i=1 to 9) in the above example, A_i (*i*=1, 2, 3, 4, 5) must be either included in or excluded from SOPO$_i$.

Consider the following example (see Figure 4) for an incorrect way of dividing domains into non-overlapping areas.

In Figure 6 the domains are divided into two non-overlapping areas $[INF_1, SUP_1]$ and $[SUP_1 - DUR, SUP_1]$. Since the area $[INF_1, SUP_1]$ overlaps the original possible SOPO $[INF_2, SUP_2]$, this dividing strategy is not suitable for computing the probabilities of solutions. In the above ex-

Algorithm 1. Dividing domains into non-overlapping areas

```
Function DivideAreas (ListofSOPOs)
1. Sort INF and SUP. INF₁ < INF₂ < INFₘ, SUP₁ < SUP₂ < ... < SUPₙ
2. AreaList ← empty
3. L ← empty  // L contains minimal areas
4. for each SOPO S in ListofSOPOsdo
5.    if no other INF or SUP are in [INFₛ, SUPₛ]
6.       L ← L ∪{S}
7. end for
8. RemainList ←the combinations of [INF, SUP] except [INF₁, SUPₙ]
9. CurrentCoverage ← empty;
      // CurrentCoverage is the union of current generated areas
            // e.g. we have two areas [25,26], [22,27], then it will
            be [22,25]
10. while L is not empty do
11.    NextDomainLength ←  positive infinity
12.    NextDomain ← empty
13.    for each SOPO R in RemainListdo
14.       if R⊇ CurrentCoverageandlength(R) < NextDomainLengththen
15.          NextDomainLength = length(R)
16.          NextDomain = R
17.    end for
```

ample, *SUP* (*SUP₁*, *SUP₂*, *SUP₃*) are greater than *INF* (*INF₁*, *INF₂*, *INF₃*). In some other cases, *INF* and *SUP* may be mixed on the time line (as shown in Algorithm 1).

Probabilities of Areas

In Figure 3, we defined five non-overlapping areas. There is one begin time point and one end time point for each area ($A_i = A_i$-*begin*, A_i-*end*). For each of its possible SOPO (*INF_i*, *SUP_j*), if $INF_i < A_i$-*begin* $< A_i$-*end* $< SUP_j$, then A_i (*INF_i*, *SUP_j*), which implies that the solution in Ai is also a solution in (*INF_i*, *SUP_j*). Since A_i must be contained in either one or more SOPOs, we can use the following formula to calculate the probability of area Ai to be included in the actual domain for the corresponding uncertain event.

Pr(A_i is included in the actual domain) = $\sum$ Pr(*INF_i*, *SUP_j*) where $A_i \in$(*INF_i*, *SUP_j*)

For example, A_1 is the subset of nine possible SOPOs (see Figure 3), so the probability of A_1 to be included in the actual domain is 1.0. In other words, if we can find a solution in A_1, the probability of this solution to fall in the actual domain will be 1.0. A_2 is the subset of [*INF₂*, *SUP₁*], [*INF₂*, *SUP₂*] and [*INF₂*, *SUP₃*]. So the probability of A_2 to be included in the actual domain is 0.12 + 0.03 + 0.15 = 0.30.

Probable Worlds

Given the possible domains of each event, we can define probable worlds in numeric TCSPs as combinations of domains for each event. For events with certain *INF* and *SUP*, the domains are just the given *INF* and *SUP*. For events with uncertain *INF* and *SUP*, however, one of the possible domains will be picked up.

ProbableWorld = {D_1, D_2, . . ., D_n, {$D_{certain}$}, {C}}

where *C* is the constraint and D_i is the specific domain of each uncertain event. Let us consider the following example.

Example 8. *Probable world in the TemPro model*

We have three events E_1, E_2 and E_3. E_1 and E_2 are traditional events with certain *INF* and *SUP*. E_3 and E_4 are events with uncertain *INF* and *SUP*. Their SOPOs are given as follows.

E_1 = [20, 60, 15, 1] E_2 = [30, 70, 25, 1]
E_3 = [INF_{E3}, SUP_{E3}, 40, 1]
Pr (INF_{E3} =10) = 0.4, Pr (INF_{E3} = 20) = 0.6, Pr (SUP_{E3} = 100) = 0.3, Pr (SUP_{E3} = 120) = 0.7
E_4 = [45, SUP_{E4}, 35, 1]
Pr (SUP_{E4} =90) = 0.2, Pr (SUP_{E4} =130) = 0.8

Here we use the non-overlapping areas generated by the dividing algorithm to build probable worlds. The total number of probable worlds is the product of the number of generated non-overlapping areas of each uncertain constraint. For example, in the above example, we have three areas for E_3 and two areas for E_4. So the total number of probable worlds is 3×2 = 6. The set of these six probable worlds is called set of basic probable world. More formally, suppose the number of certain events is m while the number of uncertain events is *n*.

Set of basic probable worlds = {[*INF, SUP*]$_i$, *Area$_j$*} | 1 < i < m, 1 < j < n

[*INF, SUP*]$_i$ is one SOPO of certain events and *Area$_j$* is one area of uncertain events. One probable world *WP* in the set of basic probable worlds is E_1, E_2, E_3 = [10, 60], E_4 = [55, 80]. In this world, we use the area $Area_{E3}$ [10, 60] for E_3 and the area $Area_{E4}$ for *E4*. Their probabilities are listed below.

Pr ($Area_{E3}$ is included in the actual domain of E_3) = 0.4
Pr ($Area_{E4}$ is included in the actual domain of E_4) = 0.8

Then the probability of WP containing the real domains of E_3 and E_4 is

Pr (*WP* is included in the actual domains of both E_3 and E_4)
= Pr (Area$_{E3}$ is included in the actual domain of E_3) ×
Pr (Area$_{E4}$ is included in the actual domain of E_4)
= 0.4 × 0.8 = 0.32

Therefore, if we find a solution *Sol* to this probable world *WP*, the probability of *Sol* to fall in the real domain of E_3 and E_4 will be 0.32. Since the actual problem is determined by uncertain events, 0.32 can also be viewed as the probability of *Sol* to satisfy every constraint in the real world.

Robustness of Solutions

Given the set of basic probable worlds, our goal is to find the most robust solution. We define the robustness of a solution as the probability of this solution to satisfy every constraint in the real world. This probability can be illustrated as follows. Suppose we have a numeric TCSP *P* with uncertainty. If *P* happens *n* times and one of the solutions satisfies the problem in 0.6 × *n* times, the probability of *P* satisfying the real world is 0.6. By using non-overlapping areas to generate probable worlds, the solutions for each probable world do not overlap each other. The solution to one probable world is not the solution for any other probable world. So we can consider the solution to each probable world and calculate the robustness of each solution. More formally, it can be calculated using the following formula:

Robustness of s = Pr (W_i is included in the actual domains for all the uncertain events) where *s* satisfies W_i and W_i is in the set of probable worlds

For example, if we have four different worlds W_1, W_2, W_3, W_4 and four corresponding solutions S_1, S_2, S_3, S_4. The probability of each world is listed below.

Pr (W_1 is included in the actual domain for all the uncertain constraints) = 0.6
Pr (W_2 is included in the actual domain for all the uncertain constraints) = 0.5
Pr (W_3 is included in the actual domain for all the uncertain constraints) = 0.8
Pr (W_4 is included in the actual domain for all the uncertain constraints) = 0.2

The robustness of S_1, S_2, S_3, S_4 is 0.6, 0.5, 0.8, 0.2, respectively. S_3 is the most robust solution due to its highest probability to be the solution for the real problem. The main task of solving numeric TCSPs with uncertain events is to find the solution with the highest degree of robustness.

Solving the Problem

Removing Inconsistent Areas

We discussed earlier the algorithm for dividing domains into non-overlapping areas. However, we did not consider the validity of all the generated areas. According to the values of the lower boundary and the upper boundary, there may be some inconsistent areas. For example, we have an area of an uncertain event E_1 [A_1-begin, A_1-end] with a probability of 0.8 to be included in the actual domain. The length of the event is specified by *DURATION*. If A_1-end − A_1-begin < *DURATION*, there will be no solutions in this domain even if it is associated with a probability of 0.8. Therefore, all the probable worlds that contain this area for event E_1 should be removed from the set of basic probable worlds. By removing inconsistent areas, the number of corresponding probable worlds can be reduced exponentially, which will improve the efficiency of the solving algorithm.

Branch and Bound Algorithm

The intuitive method consists of sorting all the probable worlds by their probabilities. Then we try to find a solution to the most probable world. If a solution is found, it will be the most robust solution. If no solution is found, we switch to the next most probable world. A more effective algorithm is to use branch-and-bound through the search for the most robust solution. The different steps of the algorithm are shown below.

1. Perform path consistency check for the symbolic constraints in the problem (see Figure 3). If the problem is inconsistent, return NO SOLUTION.

2. For all the constraints involving certain events, perform the numeric to symbolic conversion we proposed in (Fargier, 1996) to remove the Allen primitives that are inconsistent with the numeric information.

3. Divide the uncertain domains of events into non-overlapping areas. For each event with uncertain domains, maintain a list of areas $L = \{A_1, A_2, \ldots, A_m\}$. Set the lower bound LB to 0.

4. Remove those areas inconsistent with the problem, i.e., $Area_{end} - Area_{begin} < DURATION$.

5. Calculate the probability of each area to be included in the actual domain of each uncertain event.

6. Pick an uncertain event and select an area from L. An overestimation of the robustness of any possible solution falling in the current assigned areas is calculated and used as the upper bound UB (see below). If UB < LB, select another area for the current uncertain event or backtrack to the previous uncertain event if all the areas for this event have been explored.

7. Perform arc-consistency check (Mackworth, 1977) for current uncertain events with assigned domains. If the arc consistency fails,

select another area for the current uncertain event or backtrack to the previous uncertain event if all the areas for this event have been explored.

8. For all the constraints related to this uncertain event, perform numeric to symbolic conversion by using the currently assigned area.

9. Repeat 6 to 8 until all the uncertain events have been assigned areas.

10. If every uncertain event has been assigned a specific area, search for a solution to the problem. Calculate the robustness of the solution. If it is larger than LB, update LB with the value. If there is no solution or the probability is less than LB, backtrack and go to step 4.

11. If all the areas of uncertain events have been tried and no solution is found, return *NO SOLUTION*.

The overestimation of the robustness is the product of probabilities of already assigned areas and the maximum probabilities of areas for all the non-assigned uncertain events. For example, there are four uncertain events E_1, E_2, E_3, E_4 and there are two assigned areas, A_1 for E_1, A_2 for E_2. The probabilities of A_1 and A_2 are

$Pr(A_1$ is included in the actual domain of $E_1) = 0.8$
$Pr(A_2$ is included in the actual domain of $E_2) = 0.6$

As shown below, we have three areas for event *E3* and two areas for event E_4.

$Pr(A_{3-1}$ is included in the actual domain of $E_3) = 0.3$
$Pr(A_{3-2}$ is included in the actual domain of $E_3) = 0.2$
$Pr(A_{3-3}$ is included in the actual domain of $E_3) = 0.9$
$Pr(A_{4-1}$ is included in the actual domain of $E_4) = 0.5$
$Pr(A_{4-2}$ is included in the actual domain of $E_4) = 0.8$

We use $Pr(A_i)$ here to simplify $Pr(A_i$ is included in the actual domain). The overestimation of the robustness of solutions in any probable worlds that contain A_1 and A_2 can be calculated as follows.

$UB = Pr(A_1) \times Pr(A_2) \times \max(Pr(A_{3-1}), Pr(A_{3-2}), Pr(A_{3-12})) \times \max(Pr(A_{4-1}), Pr(A_{4-2}))$
$= 0.8 \times 0.6 \times 0.9 \times 0.8 = 0.3456$

The pseudo code for solving symbolic TCSPs with uncertainty is shown below.

```
// Problem is the numeric TCSP
with uncertainty, FCEvtLst is
the list of fixed events
// UCEvtLst is the list of un-
certain events, Graph is the
constraint graph of the this
TCSP Function SolveUncertain-
NumericTCSP (Problem, FCEvtLst,
UCEvtLst, Graph)
1. curSol = NULL  // curSol is
the current solution
2. lowerBound = 0
3. upperBound = 0
4. oldGraph = graph
5. if DPC (oldGraph) then//
check path consistency
6. return NO_SOLUTION
7. for each ei in FCEvtLst
8. for each ej in FCEvtLst
9. Num2Sym(ei, ej) // perform
the numeric to symbolic conver-
sion
10. end for
11. areaList =
divideAreas(FCEvtLst) // divide
uncertain events into non-over-
lapping areas
12. for each area in areaList
13. if SUP(area) - INF(area) <
DURATION(area) then
14. remove(area) // remove the
area from the areaList
15. probListAreas =
calculateProbability(areaList)
16. end for
17. while
(notAllEventsExplored(Problem))
// if not all scenarios visited
```

```
18. pushScenario(oldGraph) //
save the current scenario
19. event =
removeNextEvt(UCEvtLst, new-
Graph)
20. // removing one event from
the list of uncertain events,
forming newGraph
21. if (noAreas(event)) then //
no areas left, backtrack
22. popScenario(oldGraph)
23. goto 17
24. assignNextArea (event, new-
Graph)
25. // pick one area as the
domain for this event, forming
the new graph
26. if AC3.1(newGraph) then
27. popScenario(oldGraph)
28. goto 17
29. upperBound = estimateRo-
bustness (newGraph)
30. if (upperBound < lowerBound)
then
31. popScenario(oldGraph) //
backtrack, cutting branches
32. goto 17
33. constraintList =
allRelatedConstraints(event);
34. // constraintList is the
list of all constraints related
to this event
35. for each ei in con-
straintList
36. for each ej in con-
straintList
37. Num2Sym(ei, ej) // perform
the numeric to symbolic conver-
sion
38. end for
39. if allAreasAssigned() then
// if one area is specified for
each event
40. // using backtrack search to
find a solution
41. if (BTNumericTCSP(newGraph,
curSol)) then // if one solu-
tion is found
42. newRobustness =
calculateRobustness(newGraph,
curSol)
43. if newRobustness < lower-
Bound then
44. lowerBound = newRobustness
45. else
46. popScenario(oldGraph)
47. goto 17
48. end while
```

EXPERIMENTATION

In order to evaluate the solving method we propose, we have performed several tests on randomly generated consistent PIA networks. The experiments are performed on a PC Pentium 4 computer under Windows XP system. All the procedures are coded in C++. A consistent IA network of size N (N is the number of variables) is randomly generated as follows. We first randomly generate a numeric solution (set of N numeric intervals), extract the Allen primitives that are consistent with the numeric solution and randomly add other primitives to get the set of constraints of the generated problem. To generate a PIA network having a percentage p of uncertain constraints, we randomly pick p × C constraints (where C is the total number of constraints) and randomly assign probabilities to all the primitives within each selected constraint.

Table 1 presents the results of tests conducted on randomly generated PIA networks. For each test we run the solving method on 10 instances of the same problem and we take the average running time in seconds. The generated problems are complete PIA networks (all constraints are different from the universal relation I). Thus, the number of constraints is equal to $N \times (N-1) / 2$ where N is the number of variables. The second

Table 1. Time performance of the solving method.

	PC	First Solution	10% uncertain	20% uncertain	30% uncertain
N = 40	0.05	3.204	3.495	3.675	4.689
N = 60	0.15	6.714	7.21	7.93	8.35
N = 80	0.35	15	16.5	17.2	19
N = 100	0.66	33	35	41	45
N = 120	1.11	48	52	54	57
N = 150	2.10	62	69	74	81
N = 180	3.59	187	201	231	254
N = 200	4.92	312	352	418	516

column corresponds to the time needed by the path consistency algorithm performed before the backtrack search. The third column corresponds to the time to find the first solution. The fourth, fifth and sixth columns correspond respectively to the time needed to find the most robust solution for problems where 10%, 20% and 30% of their constraints are uncertain.

As we can see from the test results, after finding the first solution, not much effort is needed to find the most robust one while there is actually a large number of probable worlds and their corresponding solutions especially in the case of large size problems. This is due to the branch and bound algorithm that prunes the search space significantly and also to the fact that the first solution obtained is of good quality which sets the lower bound of the algorithm to a good value.

CONCLUSION

In this paper we have proposed a new framework for handling uncertain symbolic and numeric temporal information. At the symbolic level, the uncertainty is represented by the probability of the existence of each Allen primitive within its uncertain constraint. A PIA network P will thus involve a list of worlds and solving P consists of finding a solution for the most probable ones. This is an optimization problem that we tackle using a branch and bound algorithm based on temporal constraint propagation. Experimental study on randomly generated uncertain temporal networks demonstrates the efficiency of our solving method. At the numeric level, our TemPro framework is extended to handle uncertain domains. An algorithm for dividing domains into non-overlapping areas is proposed. This algorithm guarantees that the generated possible worlds do not intersect. Probable worlds are then constructed by combining these areas. A new branch and bound algorithm, we propose, is finally applied to find the most robust solution.

FUTURE RESEARCH DIRECTIONS

In the near future we intend to see how handling uncertainty can be done in a dynamic environment (when temporal constraints are added and removed during the resolution of the probabilistic temporal problem). Another perspective is to consider (instead of a branch and bound based algorithm) approximation methods such as Stochastic Local Search (SLS), Genetic Algorithms (GAs) and Ant Colony Algorithms (ACAs). While these techniques do not always guarantee an optimal solution to the probabilistic temporal problem, they are very efficient in time (comparing to branch and bound) and can thus be useful if we want to trade the optimality of the solution for the time performance.

REFERENCES

Allen, J. (1983). Maintaining knowledge about temporal intervals. *CACM, 26*(11), 832–843.

Badaloni, S., & Giacomin, M. (1999). *A fuzzy extension of Allen's Interval Algebra.* In E. Lamma and P. Mello, (Eds.), *Proc. of the 6th Congress of the Italian Assoc. for Artificial Intelligence.* pp. 228–237.

Baptiste, J., & Le Pape, C. (1995). Disjunctive constraints for manufacturing scheduling: Principles and extensions. In *Third International Conference on Computer Integrated Manufacturing*, Singapore.

Dean, T. (1989). Using Temporal Hierarchies to Efficiently Maintain Large Temporal Databases. *Journal of the ACM*, 686–709.

Dechter, R. (2003). *Constraint Processing.* San Francisco: Morgan Kaufmann.

Dechter, R., Meiri, I., & Pearl, J. (1991). Temporal Constraint Networks. *Artificial Intelligence, 49,* 61–95. doi:10.1016/0004-3702(91)90006-6

Fargier, H., Lang, J., & Schiex, T. (1996). *Mixed constraint satisfaction: A framework for decision problems under incomplete knowledge.* In *the 13th National Conference on Artificial Intelligence (AAAI-96)*, pp. 175–180. New York: ACM Press.

Golumbic, & Shamir, R. (1993). Complexity and algorithms for reasoning about time: a graphic-theoretic approach. *Journal of the Association for Computing Machinery, 40*(5), 1108–1133.

Haralick, R., & Elliott, G. (1980). Increasing tree search efficiency for Constraint Satisfaction Problems. *Artificial Intelligence, 14,* 263–313. doi:10.1016/0004-3702(80)90051-X

Hwang, & Shubert, L. (1994). *Interpreting tense, aspect, and time adverbials: a compositional, unified approach.* In *Proceedings of the first International Conference on Temporal Logic, LNAI, vol 827*, pp. 237–264, Berlin.

Mackworth, A. K. (1977). Consistency in networks of relations. *Artificial Intelligence, 8,* 99–118. doi:10.1016/0004-3702(77)90007-8

Marin, R., Cardenas, M., Balsa, M., & Sanchez, J. (1997). Obtaining solutions in fuzzy constraint networks. *International Journal of Approximate Reasoning, 16,* 261–288. doi:10.1016/S0888-613X(96)00125-9

Morris, P., & Muscettola, N. (2000). Execution of temporal plans with uncertainty. *AAAI, 2000,* 491–496.

Mouhoub, M. (2004). Handling Numeric and Symbolic Time Information. *Artificial Intelligence Review, 21,* 25–56. doi:10.1023/B:AIRE.0000007179.60276.39

Peintner, B., Venable, K. B., & Yorke-Smith, N. (2007). *Strong Controllability of Disjunctive Temporal Problems with Uncertainty. CP 2007,* 856–863.

Ryabov, V., & Trudel, A. (2004). *Probabilistic temporal interval networks.* In *TIME 2004*, pp. 64–67. Tsamardinos, Vidal, T. & Pollack, M.E. (2003). *CTP: A New Constraint-Based Formalism for Conditional Temporal Planning. Constraints, 8*(4), 365–388.

van Beek, P. (1992). Reasoning about qualitative temporal information. *Artificial Intelligence, 58,* 297–326. doi:10.1016/0004-3702(92)90011-L

Vidal, T., & Fargier, H. (1999). Handling consistency in temporal constraint networks: from consistency to controllabilities. *Journal of Experimental and Theoretical AI, 11,* 23–45. doi:10.1080/095281399146607

Vidal, T., & Ghallab, M. (1996). *Dealing with uncertain durations in temporal constraint networks dedicated to planning* (pp. 48–52). ECAI.

Vilain, M., & Kautz, H. (1986). *Constraint propagation algorithms for temporal reasoning*, in *AAAI'86*, Philadelphia, PA (pp. 377–382).

Walsh, T. (2002). *Stochastic constraint programming*. In *Proceedings of the 15tʰ European Conference on Artificial Intelligence (ECAI-02)*, Lyon, France.

KEY TERMS AND DEFINITIONS

Backtracking Algorithm: A systematic search method that explores the search space in a depth first manner. In the case of a CSP, the backtracking algorithm extends a partial solution (corresponding to a partial assignment) toward a complete one.

Branch and Bound (BB): A backtracking algorithm for solving discrete optimization problems. BB explores a search space in a systematic way looking for the optimal solution. Lower and upper bounds are used to filter potential solutions that will not lead to the optimal one.

Constraint Satisfaction Problem (CSP): A problem defined with a list of variables, each taking values in discrete and finite domains and a list of relations restricting the values that the variables can simultaneously take.

Decision Problem: A problem where the solving algorithm has only two possible outputs, *yes* or *no*.

Event: A preposition that holds over a time interval.

Probabilistic Constraint Satisfaction Problem (PCSP): A CSP where each constraint has a probability to exist in the problem.

Search Space: The set of all potential solutions.

Systematic Search Method: A solving method, to a decision problem, that explores the search space in a systematic manner. The systematic search method guarantees to find a solution if it exists.

Temporal Constraint Satisfaction Problem: A CSP where the constraints or values are temporal.

Chapter 5
Object Recognition via Contour Points Reconstruction Using Hurwitz–Radon Matrices

Dariusz Jakóbczak
Technical University of Koszalin, Poland

ABSTRACT

Object recognition is one of the topics of artificial intelligence, computer vision, image processing and machine vision. The classical problem in these areas of computer science is that of determining object via characteristic features. Important feature of the object is its contour. Accurate reconstruction of contour points leads to possibility to compare the unknown object with models of specified objects. The key information about the object is the set of contour points which are treated as interpolation nodes. Classical interpolations (Lagrange or Newton polynomials) are useless for precise reconstruction of the contour. The chapter is dealing with proposed method of contour reconstruction via curves interpolation. First stage consists in computing the contour points of the object to be recognized. Then one can compare models of known objects, given by the sets of contour points, with coordinates of interpolated points of unknown object. Contour points reconstruction and curve interpolation is possible using new method of Hurwitz-Radon Matrices.

INTRODUCTION

Method of Hurwitz-Radon Matrices (MHR), invented by the author, can be applied in reconstruction and interpolation of curves in the plane. The method is based on a family of Hurwitz-Radon (HR) matrices. The matrices are skew-symmetric and possess columns composed of orthogonal vectors. The operator of Hurwitz-Radon (OHR), built from these matrices, is described. Author explains how to create the orthogonal and discrete OHR and how to use it in a process of curve interpolation and modeling. Proposed method needs suitable choice of nodes, i.e. points of the curve to be reconstructed: nodes should be settled at each extremum (minimum or maximum) of one coordinate and at least one point between two successive local extrema, and nodes should be

DOI: 10.4018/978-1-61692-811-7.ch005

monotonic in one of coordinates (for example equidistance). Created from the family of $N - 1$ HR matrices and completed with the identical matrix, system of matrices is orthogonal only for vector spaces of dimensions $N = 2$, 4 or 8. Orthogonality of columns and rows is very important and significant for stability and high precision of calculations. MHR method is modeling the curve point by point without using any formula of function. Main features of MHR method are: accuracy of curve reconstruction depending on number of nodes and method of choosing nodes, interpolation of L points of the curve is connected with the computational cost of rank $O(L)$, MHR interpolation is not a linear interpolation. The problem of curve length estimation is also considered. Algorithm of MHR method and the examples of object recognition are described.

BACKGROUND

The following question is important in mathematics and computer sciences: is it possible to find a method of curve interpolation in the plane without building the interpolation polynomials? This chapter aims at giving the positive answer to this question. Current methods of curve interpolation based on classical polynomial interpolation: Newton, Lagrange or Hermite polynomials and spline curves which are piecewise polynomials (Dahlquist & Bjoerck, 1974). Classical methods are useless to interpolate the function that fails to be differentiable at one point, for example the absolute value function $f(x) = |x|$ at $x = 0$. If point (0;0) is one of the interpolation nodes, then precise polynomial interpolation of the absolute value function is impossible. Also when the graph of interpolated function differs from the shape of polynomials considerably, for example $f(x) = 1/x$, interpolation is very hard because of existing local extrema of polynomial. We cannot forget about the Runge's phenomenon: when interpolation nodes are equidistance then high-order polyno-

mial oscillates toward the end of the interval, for example close to -1 and 1 with function $f(x) = 1/(1+25x^2)$ (Ralston, 1965). MHR method is free of these bad examples. Computational algorithm is considered and then we have to talk about time. Complexity of calculations for one unknown point in Lagrange or Newton interpolation based on n nodes is connected with the computational cost of rank $O(n^2)$.

The classical problem in machine vision, computer vision (Ballard, 1982) and image processing is that of determining whether or not the image data contains some significant and specific features or objects. Contour of the object consists of information which allows to describe many important features of the object. Analysis of the object shape has to be done in the process of image detection and recognition. There are other methods of contour reconstruction than interpolation. Digital curve (open or closed) may be represented by chain code (Freeman's code). Chain code depends on selection of the started point and transformations of the object. So Freeman's code is one of the method how to describe and to find contour of the object. Analog (continuous) version of Freeman's code is the curve $\alpha - s$. Another contour representation and reconstruction is based on Fourier coefficients calculated in Discrete Fourier Transformation (DFT). These coefficients are used to fix similarity of the contours with different sizes or directions. If we assume that contour is built from segments of a line and fragments of circles or ellipses, Hough transformation is applied to detect contour lines. Also geometrical moments of the object are used during the process of object recognition (Choraś, 2005). Edge detection is one of crucial points in shape analysis and object recognition (Pratt, 2001). MHR method requires to detect specific points of the object contour, for example in compression and reconstruction of monochromatic medical images (Jakóbczak & Kosiński, 2007). Contour is also applied in shape decomposition (Latecki & Lakaemper, 1999). Many branches of medicine, for example computed tomography

(Cierniak, 2005), need suitable and accurate methods of contour reconstruction (Soussen & Mohammad-Djafari, 2004). Also industry and manufacturing are looking for methods connected with geometry of the contour (Tang, 2005). So precise reconstruction or interpolation (Kozera, 2004) of object contour is a key factor in many applications, for example in object recognition. Also contours and curves in three dimensions (Lowe, 1991) are applied in object recognition (Kriegman & Ponce, 1990).

Problem statement: let's assume there are given some models of known objects as the sets of contour points. How the unknown object, described by its contour points, could be recognized as one of model objects?

Known methods of object recognition (Grimson, 1990) are: distance methods, statistical methods, model-based recognition (Lamdan, Schwartz & Wolfson, 1990). Classical distance method, called the Scale Invariant Feature Transform (SIFT), has been described by David Lowe (Lowe, 1999, 2004). SIFT method is based on extraction the interesting points (keypoints of objects) from a set of reference images and then the object is recognized in new image individually comparing each feature from new image to database with keypoints and finding candidate matching features based on Euclidean distance of their feature vectors. Important stages of SIFT method are: scale-invariant feature detection (minimum three features in clusters), feature matching and indexing, cluster identification by Hough transform voting, model verification by linear least squares and outlier detection. Important feature detection are: edge detection, interest point detection, corner detection, blob detection and ridge detection. Competing methods for scale invariant object recognition: RIFT (rotation-invariant generalization of SIFT), G-RIF (Generalized Robust Invariant Feature), PCA-SIFT and GLOH (Gradient Location-Orientation Histogram). SIFT version in 3D is also to analyze (Lowe, 2001). Model-based recognition (Chin & Dyer, 1986) is

working on models of unknown object (Lamdan & Wolfson, 1988) or combinations of models (Ullman & Basri, 1991). Statistical methods, depend on probabilistic models (Pope & Lowe, 2004) and statistical calculations, are nowadays loosing with SIFT and SIFT versions.

Object recognition via MHR method is a distance method together with model-based recognition. Comparing SIFT method and proposed MHR method we can say: the advantage of MHR method is connected with using only one feature of unknown object, that is contour points (SIFT depends on minimum three features), what is associated with less computational complexity of MHR method. Disadvantage of MHR method is the fact that after geometrical transformations of unknown object (translations, rotations, scaling), models of the object have to be also transformed and then MHR recognition is possible. Author hopes this disadvantage will be eliminated soon.

THE METHOD OF HURWITZ-RADON MATRICES

Issues

This chapter deals with the problem of interpolation without computing the polynomial or any fixed function. Values of nodes are used to build the orthogonal matrix operators OHR and a linear (convex) combination of OHR operators leads to calculation of curve points. Main idea of MHR method (Jakóbczak, 2006) is that the curve is interpolated point by point by computing the unknown coordinates of the points. The only significant factors in MHR method are: choosing the interpolation nodes and fixing the dimension of HR matrix ($N = 2$, 4 or 8). Other characteristic features of function or curve, such as shape or similarity to polynomials, derivative or Runge's phenomenon, are not important in the process of MHR interpolation. The curve or function in MHR method is parameterized for value $\alpha \in [0;1]$ in each range of two successive interpolation nodes. Estimation of the curve length with high precision is possible because of computing any number of curve points we want. Complexity of calculations for L unknown points in MHR interpolation, based on n nodes, is connected with the computational cost of rank $O(L)$. This is very important feature of MHR method.

The Origin of Hurwitz–Radon Matrices

Adolf Hurwitz (1859-1919) and Johann Radon (1887-1956) published the papers about specific class of matrices in 1923, working on the problem of quadratic forms. For example equation

$$(x_0^2 + x_1^2) \cdot (y_0^2 + y_1^2) = (z_0^2 + z_1^2)$$

is true when $z_0 = x_0 y_0 - x_1 y_1$, $z_1 = x_0 y_1 + x_1 y_0$. This result can be achieved from matrix equation:

$$\begin{bmatrix} x_0 & x_1 \\ -x_1 & x_0 \end{bmatrix} \cdot \begin{bmatrix} y_0 & y_1 \\ -y_1 & y_0 \end{bmatrix} = \begin{bmatrix} z_0 & z_1 \\ -z_1 & z_0 \end{bmatrix}.$$

Also equation

$$(x_0^2 + x_1^2 + x_2^2 + x_3^2) \cdot (y_0^2 + y_1^2 + y_2^2 + y_3^2) = z_0^2 + z_1^2 + z_2^2 + z_3^2$$

has solution:

$$z_0 = x_0 y_0 - x_1 y_1 - x_2 y_2 - x_3 y_3,$$

$$z_1 = x_0 y_1 + x_1 y_0 + x_2 y_3 - x_3 y_2,$$

$$z_2 = x_0 y_2 - x_1 y_3 + x_2 y_0 + x_3 y_1,$$

$$z_3 = x_0 y_3 + x_1 y_2 - x_2 y_1 + x_3 y_0.$$

This result can be achieved from matrix equation of dimension $N = 4$:

$$\begin{bmatrix} x_0 & x_1 & x_2 & x_3 \\ -x_1 & x_0 & -x_3 & x_2 \\ -x_2 & x_3 & x_0 & -x_1 \\ -x_3 & -x_2 & x_1 & x_0 \end{bmatrix} \cdot \begin{bmatrix} y_0 & y_1 & y_2 & y_3 \\ -y_1 & y_0 & -y_3 & y_2 \\ -y_2 & y_3 & y_0 & -y_1 \\ -y_3 & -y_2 & y_1 & y_0 \end{bmatrix} = \begin{bmatrix} z_0 & z_1 & z_2 & z_3 \\ -z_1 & z_0 & -z_3 & z_2 \\ -z_2 & z_3 & z_0 & -z_1 \\ -z_3 & -z_2 & z_1 & z_0 \end{bmatrix}.$$

Dimension $N = 2$, 4 and 8 are the only dimensions for these quadratic equations:

$$\left(\sum_{i=0}^{7} x_i^2\right) \cdot \left(\sum_{i=0}^{7} y_i^2\right) = \sum_{i=0}^{7} z_i^2$$

for

$$z_0 = x_0 y_0 - x_1 y_1 - x_2 y_2 - x_3 y_3 - x_4 y_4 - x_5 y_5 - x_6 y_6 - x_7 y_7,$$

$$z_1 = x_0 y_1 + x_1 y_0 - x_2 y_3 + x_3 y_2 - x_4 y_5 + x_5 y_4 + x_6 y_7 - x_7 y_6,$$

$$z_2 = x_0 y_2 + x_1 y_3 + x_2 y_0 - x_3 y_1 - x_4 y_6 - x_5 y_7 + x_6 y_4 + x_7 y_5,$$

$$z_3 = x_0 y_3 - x_1 y_2 + x_2 y_1 + x_3 y_0 - x_4 y_7 + x_5 y_6 - x_6 y_5 + x_7 y_4,$$

$$z_4 = x_0 y_4 + x_1 y_5 + x_2 y_6 + x_3 y_7 + x_4 y_0 - x_5 y_1 - x_6 y_2 - x_7 y_3,$$

$$z_5 = x_0 y_5 - x_1 y_4 + x_2 y_7 - x_3 y_6 + x_4 y_1 + x_5 y_0 + x_6 y_3 - x_7 y_2,$$

$$z_6 = x_0 y_6 - x_1 y_7 - x_2 y_4 + x_3 y_5 + x_4 y_2 - x_5 y_3 + x_6 y_0 + x_7 y_1,$$

$$z_7 = x_0 y_7 + x_1 y_6 - x_2 y_5 - x_3 y_4 + x_4 y_3 + x_5 y_2 - x_6 y_1 + x_7 y_0.$$

Matrices used to solve quadratic equations are defined: matrices A_i, $i = 1, 2, \ldots, m$ satisfying

$$A_j A_k + A_k A_j = 0,\ A_j^2 = -I,\ j \neq k,\ j,\ k = 1, 2, \ldots, m$$

are called a family of Hurwitz-Radon matrices.

A family of Hurwitz-Radon (HR) matrices has important features (Eckmann, 1999): HR matrices are skew-symmetric ($A_i^T = -A_i$) and reverse matrices are easy to find ($A_i^{-1} = -A_i$). Only for dimension $N = 2$, 4 or 8 the family of HR matrices consists of $N - 1$ matrices. For $N = 2$ we have one matrix:

$$A_1 = \begin{bmatrix} 0 & 1 \\ -1 & 0 \end{bmatrix}.$$

For $N = 4$ there are three HR matrices with integer entries:

$$A_1 = \begin{bmatrix} 0 & 1 & 0 & 0 \\ -1 & 0 & 0 & 0 \\ 0 & 0 & 0 & -1 \\ 0 & 0 & 1 & 0 \end{bmatrix},$$

$$A_2 = \begin{bmatrix} 0 & 0 & 1 & 0 \\ 0 & 0 & 0 & 1 \\ -1 & 0 & 0 & 0 \\ 0 & -1 & 0 & 0 \end{bmatrix},$$

$$A_3 = \begin{bmatrix} 0 & 0 & 0 & 1 \\ 0 & 0 & -1 & 0 \\ 0 & 1 & 0 & 0 \\ -1 & 0 & 0 & 0 \end{bmatrix}.$$

For $N = 8$ we have seven HR matrices with elements $0, \pm 1$ (Jakóbczak, 2006).

So far HR matrices are applied in electronics (Citko, Jakóbczak & Sieńko, 2005): in Space-Time Block Coding (STBC) and orthogonal design (Tarokh, Jafarkhani & Calderbank, 1999), also in signal processing (Sieńko, Citko & Wilamowski, 2002) and Hamiltonian Neural Nets (Sieńko & Citko, 2002).

The Operator of Hurwitz-Radon

Here is the beginning of proposed MHR method. Let us consider a combination of identity matrix and HR matrix of dimension $N = 2$:

$$a\begin{bmatrix} 1 & 0 \\ 0 & 1 \end{bmatrix} + b\begin{bmatrix} 0 & 1 \\ -1 & 0 \end{bmatrix} = \begin{bmatrix} a & b \\ -b & a \end{bmatrix}.$$

For any points $(x_1, y_1) \in R^2$, $(x_2, y_2) \in R^2$ matrix equation

$$\begin{bmatrix} a & b \\ -b & a \end{bmatrix} \cdot \begin{bmatrix} x_1 \\ x_2 \end{bmatrix} = \begin{bmatrix} y_1 \\ y_2 \end{bmatrix}$$

is true with

$$a = \frac{x_1 y_1 + x_2 y_2}{x_1^2 + x_2^2},$$

$$b = \frac{x_2 y_1 - x_1 y_2}{x_1^2 + x_2^2}$$

and $x_1^2 + x_2^2 > 0$.

Reverse matrix equation

$$\begin{bmatrix} a & b \\ -b & a \end{bmatrix} \cdot \begin{bmatrix} y_1 \\ y_2 \end{bmatrix} = \begin{bmatrix} x_1 \\ x_2 \end{bmatrix}$$

is true with

$$a = \frac{x_1 y_1 + x_2 y_2}{y_1^2 + y_2^2},$$

$$b = \frac{-x_2 y_1 + x_1 y_2}{y_1^2 + y_2^2}$$

and $y_1^2 + y_2^2 > 0$.

Also we can consider a combination of identity matrix and three HR matrices of dimension $N = 4$:

$$a\begin{bmatrix} 1 & 0 & 0 & 0 \\ 0 & 1 & 0 & 0 \\ 0 & 0 & 1 & 0 \\ 0 & 0 & 0 & 1 \end{bmatrix} + b\begin{bmatrix} 0 & 1 & 0 & 0 \\ -1 & 0 & 0 & 0 \\ 0 & 0 & 0 & -1 \\ 0 & 0 & 1 & 0 \end{bmatrix}$$

$$+c\begin{bmatrix} 0 & 0 & 1 & 0 \\ 0 & 0 & 0 & 1 \\ -1 & 0 & 0 & 0 \\ 0 & -1 & 0 & 0 \end{bmatrix}$$

$$+d\begin{bmatrix} 0 & 0 & 0 & 1 \\ 0 & 0 & -1 & 0 \\ 0 & 1 & 0 & 0 \\ -1 & 0 & 0 & 0 \end{bmatrix} = \begin{bmatrix} a & b & c & d \\ -b & a & -d & c \\ -c & d & a & -b \\ -d & -c & b & a \end{bmatrix}.$$

For any points $(x_1, y_1) \in \mathbf{R}^2$, $(x_2, y_2) \in \mathbf{R}^2$, $(x_3, y_3) \in \mathbf{R}^2$, $(x_4, y_4) \in \mathbf{R}^2$ matrix equation

$$\begin{bmatrix} a & b & c & d \\ -b & a & -d & c \\ -c & d & a & -b \\ -d & -c & b & a \end{bmatrix} \cdot \begin{bmatrix} x_1 \\ x_2 \\ x_3 \\ x_4 \end{bmatrix} = \begin{bmatrix} y_1 \\ y_2 \\ y_3 \\ y_4 \end{bmatrix}$$

is satisfied with

$$a = \frac{x_1 y_1 + x_2 y_2 + x_3 y_3 + x_4 y_4}{x_1^2 + x_2^2 + x_3^2 + x_4^2},$$

$$b = \frac{-x_1 y_2 + x_2 y_1 + x_3 y_4 - x_4 y_3}{x_1^2 + x_2^2 + x_3^2 + x_4^2},$$

$$c = \frac{-x_1 y_3 - x_2 y_4 + x_3 y_1 + x_4 y_2}{x_1^2 + x_2^2 + x_3^2 + x_4^2},$$

$$d = \frac{-x_1 y_4 + x_2 y_3 - x_3 y_2 + x_4 y_1}{x_1^2 + x_2^2 + x_3^2 + x_4^2}$$

and $x_1^2 + x_2^2 + x_3^2 + x_4^2 > 0$.
Reverse matrix equation

$$\begin{bmatrix} a & b & c & d \\ -b & a & -d & c \\ -c & d & a & -b \\ -d & -c & b & a \end{bmatrix} \cdot \begin{bmatrix} y_1 \\ y_2 \\ y_3 \\ y_4 \end{bmatrix} = \begin{bmatrix} x_1 \\ x_2 \\ x_3 \\ x_4 \end{bmatrix}$$

is satisfied with

$$a = \frac{x_1 y_1 + x_2 y_2 + x_3 y_3 + x_4 y_4}{y_1^2 + y_2^2 + y_3^2 + y_4^2},$$

$$b = \frac{x_1 y_2 - x_2 y_1 - x_3 y_4 + x_4 y_3}{y_1^2 + y_2^2 + y_3^2 + y_4^2},$$

$$c = \frac{x_1 y_3 + x_2 y_4 - x_3 y_1 - x_4 y_2}{y_1^2 + y_2^2 + y_3^2 + y_4^2},,$$

$$d = \frac{x_1 y_4 - x_2 y_3 + x_3 y_2 - x_4 y_1}{y_1^2 + y_2^2 + y_3^2 + y_4^2}$$

and $y_1^2 + y_2^2 + y_3^2 + y_4^2 > 0$.

A combination of identity matrix and seven HR matrices of dimension $N = 8$ looks as follows:

$$\begin{bmatrix} a_0 & a_1 & a_2 & a_3 & a_4 & a_5 & a_6 & a_7 \\ -a_1 & a_0 & a_3 & -a_2 & a_5 & -a_4 & -a_7 & a_6 \\ -a_2 & -a_3 & a_0 & a_1 & a_6 & a_7 & -a_4 & -a_5 \\ -a_3 & a_2 & -a_1 & a_0 & a_7 & -a_6 & a_5 & -a_4 \\ -a_4 & -a_5 & -a_6 & -a_7 & a_0 & a_1 & a_2 & a_3 \\ -a_5 & a_4 & -a_7 & a_6 & -a_1 & a_0 & -a_3 & a_2 \\ -a_6 & a_7 & a_4 & -a_5 & -a_2 & a_3 & a_0 & -a_1 \\ -a_7 & -a_6 & a_5 & a_4 & -a_3 & -a_2 & a_1 & a_0 \end{bmatrix}.$$

Results for matrix equations with a combination of identity matrix and seven HR matrices of dimension $N = 8$ are calculated in (3), (4) and (8). Solutions of matrix equations (Sieńko, Citko

& Jakóbczak, 2004) are used to build the matrix operator of Hurwitz-Radon.

Let's assume there is given a finite set of points of the curve, called further nodes $(x_i, y_i) \in R^2$ such as:

1. nodes (interpolation points) are settled at local extrema (maximum or minimum) of one of coordinates and at least one point between two successive local extrema;
2. each node (x_i, y_i) is monotonic in coordinates x_i or y_i (for example equidistance in one of coordinates).

Assume that the nodes belong to a curve in the plane. How the whole curve could be interpolated using this discrete set of nodes? Proposed method (Jakóbczak, 2007) is based on local, orthogonal matrix operators. Values of nodes' coordinates (x_i, y_i) are connected with HR matrices, built on N- dimensional vector space. It is important that HR matrices are skew-symmetric and only for dimensions $N = 2$, 4 or 8 columns and rows of HR matrices are orthogonal (Eckmann, 1999).

If one curve is described by a set of nodes $\{(x_i, y_i), i = 1, 2, \ldots, n\}$ monotonic (for example equidistance) in coordinates x_i, then HR matrices combined with identity matrix are used to build an orthogonal and discrete Hurwitz-Radon Operator (OHR). For nodes (x_1, y_1), (x_2, y_2) OHR of dimension $N = 2$ is constructed:

$$M = \frac{1}{x_1^2 + x_2^2} \begin{bmatrix} x_1 & x_2 \\ -x_2 & x_1 \end{bmatrix} \begin{bmatrix} y_1 & -y_2 \\ y_2 & y_1 \end{bmatrix},$$

$$M = \frac{1}{x_1^2 + x_2^2} \begin{bmatrix} x_1 y_1 + x_2 y_2 & x_2 y_1 - x_1 y_2 \\ x_1 y_2 - x_2 y_1 & x_1 y_1 + x_2 y_2 \end{bmatrix}.$$

$$(1)$$

For nodes (x_1, y_1), (x_2, y_2), (x_3, y_3), (x_4, y_4) monotonic (for example equidistance) in x_i OHR of dimension $N = 4$ is constructed:

$$M = \frac{1}{x_1^2 + x_2^2 + x_3^2 + x_4^2} \begin{bmatrix} u_0 & u_1 & u_2 & u_3 \\ -u_1 & u_0 & -u_3 & u_2 \\ -u_2 & u_3 & u_0 & -u_1 \\ -u_3 & -u_2 & u_1 & u_0 \end{bmatrix}$$

$$(2)$$

where

$$u_0 = x_1 y_1 + x_2 y_2 + x_3 y_3 + x_4 y_4,$$

$$u_1 = -x_1 y_2 + x_2 y_1 + x_3 y_4 - x_4 y_3,$$

$$u_2 = -x_1 y_3 - x_2 y_4 + x_3 y_1 + x_4 y_2,$$

$$u_3 = -x_1 y_4 + x_2 y_3 - x_3 y_2 + x_4 y_1.$$

For nodes (x_1, y_1), (x_2, y_2), ..., (x_8, y_8) monotonic in x_i OHR of dimension $N = 8$ is equal with

$$M = \frac{1}{\sum_{i=1}^{8} x_i^2} \begin{bmatrix} u_0 & u_1 & u_2 & u_3 & u_4 & u_5 & u_6 & u_7 \\ -u_1 & u_0 & u_3 & -u_2 & u_5 & -u_4 & -u_7 & u_6 \\ -u_2 & -u_3 & u_0 & u_1 & u_6 & u_7 & -u_4 & -u_5 \\ -u_3 & u_2 & -u_1 & u_0 & u_7 & -u_6 & u_5 & -u_4 \\ -u_4 & -u_5 & -u_6 & -u_7 & u_0 & u_1 & u_2 & u_3 \\ -u_5 & u_4 & -u_7 & u_6 & -u_1 & u_0 & -u_3 & u_2 \\ -u_6 & u_7 & u_4 & -u_5 & -u_2 & u_3 & u_0 & -u_1 \\ -u_7 & -u_6 & u_5 & u_4 & -u_3 & -u_2 & u_1 & u_0 \end{bmatrix}$$

$$(3)$$

where

$$u = \begin{bmatrix} y_1 & y_2 & y_3 & y_4 & y_5 & y_6 & y_7 & y_8 \\ -y_2 & y_1 & -y_4 & y_3 & -y_6 & y_5 & y_8 & -y_7 \\ -y_3 & y_4 & y_1 & -y_2 & -y_7 & -y_8 & y_5 & y_6 \\ -y_4 & -y_3 & y_2 & y_1 & -y_8 & y_7 & -y_6 & y_5 \\ -y_5 & y_6 & y_7 & y_8 & y_1 & -y_2 & -y_3 & -y_4 \\ -y_6 & -y_5 & y_8 & -y_7 & y_2 & y_1 & y_4 & -y_3 \\ -y_7 & -y_8 & -y_5 & y_6 & y_3 & -y_4 & y_1 & y_2 \\ -y_8 & y_7 & -y_6 & -y_5 & y_4 & y_3 & -y_2 & y_1 \end{bmatrix} \begin{bmatrix} x_1 \\ x_2 \\ x_3 \\ x_4 \\ x_5 \\ x_6 \\ x_7 \\ x_8 \end{bmatrix}.$$

$$(4)$$

We can see here that the components of the vector $\mathbf{u} = (u_0, u_1, \ldots, u_7)^T$, appearing in the matrix M (3) are defined by (4) in the similar way to (2) but in terms of the coordinates of the above 8 nodes. Note that OHR operators (1)-(3) satisfy the condition of interpolation

$$M \cdot \mathbf{x} = \mathbf{y} \tag{5}$$

for $\mathbf{x} = (x_1, x_2 \ldots, x_N)^T \in R^N$, $\mathbf{x} \neq 0$, $\mathbf{y} = (y_1, y_2 \ldots, y_N)^T \in R^N$, $N = 2, 4$ or 8.

If one curve is described by a set of nodes $\{(x_i, y_i), i = 1, 2, \ldots, n\}$ monotonic (for example equidistance) in coordinates y_i, then HR matrices combined with identity matrix are used to build an orthogonal and discrete reverse Hurwitz-Radon Operator (reverse OHR). For nodes (x_1, y_1), (x_2, y_2) reverse OHR of dimension $N = 2$ is constructed:

$$M^{-1} = \frac{1}{y_1^2 + y_2^2} \begin{bmatrix} x_1 & -x_2 \\ x_2 & x_1 \end{bmatrix} \begin{bmatrix} y_1 & y_2 \\ -y_2 & y_1 \end{bmatrix},$$

$$M^{-1} = \frac{1}{y_1^2 + y_2^2} \begin{bmatrix} x_1 y_1 + x_2 y_2 & -x_2 y_1 + x_1 y_2 \\ -x_1 y_2 + x_2 y_1 & x_1 y_1 + x_2 y_2 \end{bmatrix}. \tag{6}$$

For nodes (x_1, y_1), (x_2, y_2), (x_3, y_3), (x_4, y_4) monotonic in y_i the reverse OHR of dimension $N = 4$ is constructed with u_0, u_1, u_2 and u_3 from (2):

$$M^{-1} = \frac{1}{y_1^2 + y_2^2 + y_3^2 + y_4^2} \begin{bmatrix} u_0 & -u_1 & -u_2 & -u_3 \\ u_1 & u_0 & u_3 & -u_2 \\ u_2 & -u_3 & u_0 & u_1 \\ u_3 & u_2 & -u_1 & u_0 \end{bmatrix}. \tag{7}$$

For nodes (x_1, y_1), (x_2, y_2), \ldots, (x_8, y_8) monotonic in y_i the reverse OHR of dimension $N = 8$ is equal with

$$M^{-1} = \frac{1}{\sum_{i=1}^{8} y_i^2} \begin{bmatrix} u_0 & -u_1 & -u_2 & -u_3 & -u_4 & -u_5 & -u_6 & -u_7 \\ u_1 & u_0 & -u_3 & u_2 & -u_5 & u_4 & u_7 & -u_6 \\ u_2 & u_3 & u_0 & -u_1 & -u_6 & -u_7 & u_4 & u_5 \\ u_3 & -u_2 & u_1 & u_0 & -u_7 & u_6 & -u_5 & u_4 \\ u_4 & u_5 & u_6 & u_7 & u_0 & -u_1 & -u_2 & -u_3 \\ u_5 & -u_4 & u_7 & -u_6 & u_1 & u_0 & u_3 & -u_2 \\ u_6 & -u_7 & -u_4 & u_5 & u_2 & -u_3 & u_0 & u_1 \\ u_7 & u_6 & -u_5 & -u_4 & u_3 & u_2 & -u_1 & u_0 \end{bmatrix}, \tag{8}$$

where the components of the vector $\mathbf{u} = (u_0, u_1, \ldots, u_7)^T$ are defined in terms of (4). Note that reverse OHR operators (6)-(8) satisfy the condition of interpolation

$$M^{-1} \cdot \mathbf{y} = \mathbf{x} \tag{9}$$

for $\mathbf{x} = (x_1, x_2 \ldots, x_N)^T \in R^N$, $\mathbf{y} = (y_1, y_2 \ldots, y_N)^T \in R^N$, $\mathbf{y} \neq 0$, $N = 2, 4$ or 8.

THE METHOD OF HURWITZ-RADON MATRICES

Key question looks as follows: how can we compute coordinates of points settled between interpolation nodes? On a segment of a line every number "c" situated between "a" and "b" is described by a linear (convex) combination $c = \alpha \cdot a + (1-\alpha) \cdot b$ (Figure 1) for

$$\alpha = \frac{b - c}{b - a} \in [0;1]. \tag{10}$$

When the nodes are monotonic in coordinates x_i, average OHR operator M_2 of dimension $N = 2$, 4 or 8 is constructed as follows:

$$M_2 = \alpha \cdot M_0 + (1-\alpha) \cdot M_1 \tag{11}$$

Figure 1. Point "c" between "a" and "b"

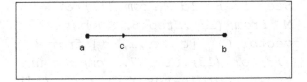

with the operator M_0 built (1)-(3) by "odd" nodes $(x_1=a,y_1), (x_3,y_3), ..., (x_{2N-1},y_{2N-1})$ and M_1 built (1)-(3) by "even" nodes $(x_2=b,y_2), (x_4,y_4), ..., (x_{2N},y_{2N})$.

When the nodes are monotonic in coordinates y_i, average reverse OHR operator M_2^{-1} of dimension $N=2, 4$ or 8 is constructed as follows:

$$M_2^{-1} = \alpha \cdot M_0^{-1} + (1-\alpha) \cdot M_1^{-1} \qquad (12)$$

with the reverse operator M_0^{-1} built (6)-(8) by nodes $(x_1,y_1=a), (x_3,y_3), ..., (x_{2N-1},y_{2N-1})$ and M_1^{-1} built (6)-(8) by nodes $(x_2,y_2=b), (x_4,y_4), ..., (x_{2N},y_{2N})$.

Notice that having the operator M_2 for coordinates $x_i < x_{i+1}$ it is possible to reconstruct the second coordinates of points (x,y) in terms of the vector C defined with

$$c_i = \alpha \cdot x_{2i-1} + (1-\alpha) \cdot x_{2i}, \ i=1, 2,..., N \qquad (13)$$

as $C = [c_1, c_2,..., c_N]^T$. The required formula is similar to (5):

$$Y(C) = M_2 \cdot C \qquad (14)$$

in which components of vector $Y(C)$ give the second coordinate of the points (x,y) corresponding to the first coordinate, given in terms of components of the vector C.

On the other hand, having the operator M_2^{-1} for coordinates $y_i < y_{i+1}$ it is possible to reconstruct the first coordinates of points (x,y) in terms of the corresponding second coordinates given by components of the new vector C defined, as previously, with

$$c_i = \alpha \cdot y_{2i-1} + (1-\alpha) \cdot y_{2i}, \ i=1, 2,..., N \qquad (15)$$

and $C = [c_1, c_2,..., c_N]^T$. The final formula is similar to (9):

$$X(C) = M_2^{-1} \cdot C \qquad (16)$$

in which components of the vector $X(C)$ give the first coordinate of the points (x,y) corresponding to the second coordinate, given in terms of components of the vector C.

After computing (14) or (16) for any $\alpha \in [0;1]$, we have a half of reconstructed points ($j=1$ in algorithm 1). Now it is necessary to find second half of unknown coordinates ($j=2$ in algorithm 1) for

$$c_i = \alpha \cdot x_{2i} + (1-\alpha) \cdot x_{2i+1}, \ i=1, 2,..., N \qquad (17)$$

or

$$c_i = \alpha \cdot y_{2i} + (1-\alpha) \cdot y_{2i+1}, \ i=1, 2,..., N \qquad (18)$$

depending on whether x_i (17) or y_i (18) is monotonic. There is no need to build the OHR for nodes $(x_2=a,y_2), (x_4,y_4), ..., (x_{2N},y_{2N})$ or the reverse OHR for nodes $(x_2,y_2=a), (x_4,y_4), ..., (x_{2N},y_{2N})$, because we have just found M_1 or M_1^{-1}. This operator will play the role as M_0 or M_0^{-1} in (11) or (12). New M_1 or M_1^{-1} must be computed for nodes $(x_3=b,y_3), ..., (x_{2N-1},y_{2N-1}), (x_{2N+1},y_{2N+1})$ or $(x_3,y_3=b), ..., (x_{2N-1},y_{2N-1}), (x_{2N+1},y_{2N+1})$.

As we see the minimum number of interpolation nodes $n = 2N+1 = 5, 9$ or 17 using OHR operators of dimension $N=2, 4$ or 8 respectively. If there is more nodes than $2N+1$, the same calculations (10)-(18) have to be done for next range(s) or last range of $2N+1$ nodes. For example, if $n = 9$ then we can use OHR operators of dimension $N=4$ or OHR operators of dimension $N=2$ for two subsets of nodes: $\{(x_1,y_1), ..., (x_5,y_5)\}$ and $\{(x_5,y_5), ...,(x_9,y_9)\}$.

Contour of the object is constructed with several number of curves. Calculation of unknown coordinates for contour points using (10)-(18) is called by author the method of Hurwitz-Radon Matrices (MHR).

ALGORITHM AND COMPLEXITY OF MHR CALCULATIONS

The algorithm of points reconstruction for $2N+1$ = 5, 9 or 17 successive nodes is presented.

Algorithm 1

Let $j = 1$. *Input: Set of interpolation nodes $\{(x_i, y_i)$, $i = 1, 2, \ldots, n; n = 5, 9$ or $17\}$ such as:*

```
a) nodes are settled at local
extrema (maximum or minimum) of
one of coordinates and at least
one point between two successive
local extrema;
b) nodes (x_i, y_i) are monotonic
in coordinates x_i or y_i.
Step 1. Determine the dimension
N of OHR operators: N = 2 if n =
5, N = 4 if n = 9, N = 8 if n =
17.
Step 2. If nodes are monoton-
ic in x_i then build M_0 for nodes
(x_1=a, y_1), (x_3, y_3), ..., (x_{2N-1}, y_{2N-1})
and M_1 for nodes (x_2=b, y_2),
(x_4, y_4), ..., (x_{2N}, y_{2N}) from (1) -
(3). If nodes are monotonic
in y_i then build M_0^{-1} for nodes
(x_1, y_1=a), (x_3, y_3), ..., (x_{2N-1}, y_{2N-1})
and M_1^{-1} for nodes (x_2, y_2=b),
(x_4, y_4), ..., (x_{2N}, y_{2N}) from (6) -
(8). Step 3. Determine the number
of points to be reconstructed
K_j > 0 between two successive
nodes, let k = 1.
Step 4. Compute α ∈ [0;1] from
```

```
(10) for c_1 = c = α·a + (1-α)·b.
Step 5. Build M_2 from (11) or
M_2^{-1} from (12). Step 6. Compute
vector C = [c_1, c_2, ..., c_N]^T from
(13) or (15). Step 7. Compute un-
known coordinates Y(C) from (14)
or X(C) from (16). Step 8. If k <
K_j, set k = k + 1 and go to Step
4. Otherwise if j = 1, set M_0 =
M_1, a = x_2, b = x_3 (if nodes are
monotonic in x_i) or M_0^{-1} = M_1^{-1}, a
= y_2, b = y_3 (if nodes are mono-
tonic in y_i), build new M_1 or
M_1^{-1} for nodes (x_3, y_3), (x_5, y_5),
..., (x_{2N+1}, y_{2N+1}), let j = 2 and go
to Step 3. Otherwise, stop.
```

The number of reconstructed points in algorithm 1 is $K = N(K_1 + K_2)$. If there are more nodes than $2N+1 = 5, 9$ or 17, algorithm 1 has to be done for next range(s) or last range of $2N + 1$ nodes. Reconstruction of curve points using algorithm 1 is called by author the method of Hurwitz-Radon Matrices (MHR). If we have n interpolation nodes, then there is $K = L - n$ points to find using algorithm 1 and MHR method. The complexity of MHR calculations has to be considered.

Lemma 1. Let $n = 5, 9$ or 17 is the number of interpolation nodes, let MHR method (algorithm 1) is done for reconstruction of the curve consists of L points. Then MHR method is connected with the computational cost of rank $O(L)$.

Proof. Using algorithm 1 we have to reconstruct $K = L - n$ points of unknown curve. Counting the number of multiplications and divisions D in algorithm 1, for example in (20) in case $n = 5$ for each c_i at first and second half of reconstructed points, here are the results:

1) $D = 4L+7$ for $n = 5$ and $L = 2i + 5$;
2) $D = 6L+21$ for $n = 9$ and $L = 4i + 9$;
3) $D = 10L+73$ for $n = 17$ and $L = 8i + 17$; $i = 2, 3, 4\ldots$

The lowest computational cost appears in MHR method with five nodes and OHR operators of dimension $N = 2$. Therefore whole set of n nodes can be divided into subsets of five nodes. Then whole curve is to be reconstructed by algorithm 1 with all subsets of five nodes: $\{(x_1,y_1), \dots, (x_5,y_5)\}$, $\{(x_5,y_5), \dots, (x_9,y_9)\}$, $\{(x_9,y_9), \dots, (x_{13},y_{13})\} \dots$ If the last node (x_n,y_n) is indexed $n \neq 4i + 1$, then we have to use last five nodes $\{(x_{n-4},y_{n-4}), \dots, (x_n,y_n)\}$ in algorithm 1.

The Formulas for a Single Point and Error Estimation

Now we present the formulas for computing one unknown coordinate of a single point. Assume there are given four nodes (x_1,y_1), (x_2,y_2), (x_3,y_3), (x_4,y_4) monotonic in x_i. OHR operators of dimension $N = 2$ are built (1) as follows:

$$M_0 = \frac{1}{x_1^2 + x_3^2}\begin{bmatrix} x_1y_1 + x_3y_3 & x_3y_1 - x_1y_3 \\ x_1y_3 - x_3y_1 & x_1y_1 + x_3y_3 \end{bmatrix},$$

$$M_1 = \frac{1}{x_2^2 + x_4^2}\begin{bmatrix} x_2y_2 + x_4y_4 & x_4y_2 - x_2y_4 \\ x_2y_4 - x_4y_2 & x_2y_2 + x_4y_4 \end{bmatrix}.$$

Let first coordinate c_1 of reconstructed point is situated between x_1 and x_2:

$$c_1 = \alpha \cdot x_1 + \beta \cdot x_2 \text{ for } 0 \leq \beta = 1 - \alpha \leq 1. \quad (19)$$

Compute second coordinate of reconstructed point $y(c_1)$ for $Y(C) = [y(c_1), y(c_2)]^T$ from (14):

$$\begin{bmatrix} y(c_1) \\ y(c_2) \end{bmatrix} = (\alpha \cdot M_0 + \beta \cdot M_1) \cdot \begin{bmatrix} \alpha \cdot x_1 + \beta \cdot x_2 \\ \alpha \cdot x_3 + \beta \cdot x_4 \end{bmatrix}. \quad (20)$$

After calculation (20):

$$y(c_1) = \alpha^2 \cdot y_1 + \beta^2 \cdot y_2 +$$
$$\frac{\alpha \cdot \beta}{x_1^2 + x_3^2}(x_1x_2y_1 + x_2x_3y_3 + x_3x_4y_1 - x_1x_4y_3) +$$

$$+ \frac{\alpha \cdot \beta}{x_2^2 + x_4^2}(x_1x_2y_2 + x_1x_4y_4 + x_3x_4y_2 - x_2x_3y_4). \quad (21)$$

So each point of the curve $P = (c_1, y(c_1))$ settled between nodes (x_1,y_1) and (x_2,y_2) is parameterized by $P(\alpha)$ for (19), (21) and $\alpha \in [0;1]$. Similar calculations are done for nodes (x_1,y_1), (x_2,y_2), (x_3,y_3), (x_4,y_4) monotonic in y_i to compute $x(c_1)$:

$$M_0^{-1} = \frac{1}{y_1^2 + y_3^2}\begin{bmatrix} x_1y_1 + x_3y_3 & -x_3y_1 + x_1y_3 \\ -x_1y_3 + x_3y_1 & x_1y_1 + x_3y_3 \end{bmatrix}$$

$$M_1^{-1} = \frac{1}{y_2^2 + y_4^2}\begin{bmatrix} x_2y_2 + x_4y_4 & -x_4y_2 + x_2y_4 \\ -x_2y_4 + x_4y_2 & x_2y_2 + x_4y_4 \end{bmatrix},$$

$$c_1 = \alpha \cdot y_1 + \beta \cdot y_2 \text{ for } 0 \leq \beta = 1 - \alpha \leq 1, \quad (22)$$

$$\begin{bmatrix} x(c_1) \\ x(c_2) \end{bmatrix} = (\alpha \cdot M_0^{-1} + \beta \cdot M_1^{-1}) \cdot \begin{bmatrix} \alpha \cdot y_1 + \beta \cdot y_2 \\ \alpha \cdot y_3 + \beta \cdot y_4 \end{bmatrix},$$

$$x(c_1) = \alpha^2 \cdot x_1 + \beta^2 \cdot x_2 + \frac{\alpha \cdot \beta}{y_1^2 + y_3^2}r_1 + \frac{\alpha \cdot \beta}{y_2^2 + y_4^2}r_2 \quad (23)$$

for $r_1 = $ const., $r_2 = $ const. depending on nodes' coordinates: see (21). If nodes are monotonic in y_i, there is parameterization of curve points P settled between nodes (x_1,y_1) and (x_2,y_2): $P(\alpha) = (x(c_1), c_1)$ for (22), (23) and $\alpha \in [0;1]$.

If nodes (x_i,y_i) are equidistance in one coordinate, then calculation of one unknown coordinate is simpler. Let four successive nodes (x_1,y_1), (x_2,y_2), (x_3,y_3), (x_4,y_4) are equidistance in coordinate x_i and $a = x_1$, $h/2 = x_{i+1} - x_i = $ const. Calculations (20)-(21) are done for c_1 (19):

$$y(c_1) = \alpha y_1 + \beta y_2 + \alpha\beta s \quad (24)$$

and

$$s = h(\frac{2ay_1 + hy_1 + hy_3}{4a^2 + 4ah + 2h^2} - \frac{2ay_2 + 2hy_2 + hy_4}{4a^2 + 8ah + 5h^2}).$$
(25)

As we can see in (21) and (23)-(25), MHR interpolation is not a linear interpolation. It is possible to estimate the interpolation error of MHR method (algorithm 1) for the class of linear function f:

$$\left| f(c_1) - y(c_1) \right| = \left| \alpha y_1 + \beta y_2 - y(c_1) \right| = \alpha\beta |s|.$$
(26)

Notice that estimation (26) has the biggest value $0.25|s|$ for $\beta = \alpha = 0.5$, when c_1 (19) is situated in the middle between x_1 and x_2.

Having four successive nodes (x_1,y_1), (x_2,y_2), (x_3,y_3), (x_4,y_4) equidistance in coordinate x_i ($a = x_1$, $h/2 = x_{i+1} - x_i$ = const.) we can compute polynomial $W_3(x) = m_3 x^3 + m_2 x^2 + m_1 x + t$ for these nodes and estimate the interpolation error of MHR method (algorithm 1) for the class of order three polynomials. After solving the system of equations:

$$y_1 = m_3 a^3 + m_2 a^2 + m_1 a + t,,$$

$$y_2 = m_3\left(a + \frac{h}{2}\right)^3 + m_2\left(a + \frac{h}{2}\right)^2 + m_1\left(a + \frac{h}{2}\right) + t,$$

$$y_3 = m_3\left(a + h\right)^3 + m_2\left(a + h\right)^2 + m_1\left(a + h\right) + t,$$

$$y_4 = m_3\left(a + \frac{3h}{2}\right)^3 + m_2\left(a + \frac{3h}{2}\right)^2 + m_1\left(a + \frac{3h}{2}\right) + t,$$

it is possible to compute m_3, m_2, m_1, t and the estimation for point c_1 (19):

$$\left| W_3(c_1) - y(c_1) \right| =$$
$$\beta\left| \frac{1}{2}h(y_2 - y_1)\frac{12\alpha\beta a + 12a\beta^2 + 2h\beta^2 - \alpha\beta ah^2 - 12a - 2h}{6ha + 12a^2 + h^2} - \alpha \cdot s \right|.$$
(27)

Notice that estimations (26)-(27) are equal with zero for $\alpha = 0$ or $\beta = 0$ (in nodes).

For eight successive nodes (x_i,y_i), $i = 1,2,\ldots,8$ equidistance in coordinate x_i, $a = x_1$, $h/2 = x_{i+1} - x_i$ == const., using OHR of dimension $N = 4$ in (14) here is a formula of second coordinate reconstruction with first coordinate c_1 (19):

$$y(c_1) = ay_1 + \beta y_2 + \frac{\beta h^2}{4a^2 + 16ah + 21h^2}[(ay_3 + \beta y_4) + 2(ay_7 + \beta y_8)] +$$
$$+ \frac{\beta h}{(4a^2 + 16ah + 21h^2)(2a^2 + 6ah + 7h^2)}[2(ay_1 + \beta y_2)(2a^3 + 10a^2 h + 19ah^2 + 14h^3) +$$
$$+ \alpha h(ay_1 + hy_7)(2a + 7h) + 3.5\alpha h^3(y_1 + y_3) +$$
$$+ 2ah(\alpha hy_3 + \alpha hy_7 + 17ay_7 - ay_4 - 2ay_8 - 3hy_4 - 6hy_8) +$$
$$- 7h^3(21y_2 + y_4 + 2y_8) - 2ay_2(2a^2 + 27ah + 19h^2)].$$
(28)

So we have another parameterization (28) of the point $P(\alpha) = (c_1, y(c_1))$ for $N = 4$ and $\beta = 1 - \alpha$. Formula (28) doesn't include values y_5 and y_6: algorithm 1 with nine successive nodes (x_i,y_i), $i = 1,2,\ldots,9$ equidistance in coordinate x_i is free of using y_5 and y_6 for computing second coordinate of the point settled between first and second node.

Algorithm 1 deals with average OHR operators (11)-(12) built with two OHR. This situation leads to parameterization of reconstructed point $P(\alpha) = (c_1, y(c_1))$ or $P(\alpha) = (x(c_1), c_1)$ settled between two successive nodes, where $\alpha \in [0;1]$ is order two in (21), (23)-(25) and (28).

Object Recognition via Contour Reconstruction

EXAMPLE 1

Models

Assume that one part of *OBJECT1* contour is described by the set of points $S_1 = \{(x_0,y_0^{(1)}), (x_1,y_1^{(1)}), \ldots, (x_M, y_M^{(1)})\}$ for $x_j < x_{j+1}$. Also one part of *OBJECT2* contour is described by the set of points $S_2 = \{(x_0,y_0^{(2)}), (x_1,y_1^{(2)}), \ldots, (x_M,y_M^{(2)})\}$. Additionally exists $k = 0,1,\ldots,M$ that $y_k^{(1)} = y_k^{(2)}$ (at least one common point of models). These sets of nodes S_1 and S_2 are models of contour fragment for *OBJECT1* and *OBJECT2*. For example $M = 4$: $S_1 = \{(0;1), (1;1), (2;1), (3;1), (4;1)\}$ and $S_2 = \{(0;0), (1;0.5), (2;1), (3;0.5), (4;0)\}$. Of course it is possible to deal with more models S_j: let there is

Figure 2. The sets of nodes S_1, S_2, S_3 and contour fragments of three objects

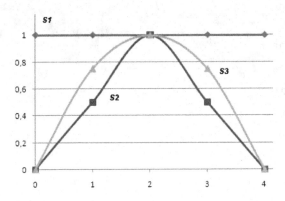

given the set $S_3 = \{(0;0), (1;0.75), (2;1), (3;0.75), (4;0)\}$ for *OBJECT3*.

The nodes from Figure 2 are monotonic in coordinates x_i. MHR method is also working with nodes monotonic in coordinates y_i. For example here are three other models of three other objects: $S_1' = \{(1;0), (1;1), (1;2), (1;3), (1;4)\}$, $S_2' = \{(3;0), (2;1), (1;2), (2;3), (3;4)\}$, $S_3' = \{(2;0), (1.1;1), (1;2), (1.1;3), (2;4)\}$.

Five nodes is the minimum number for MHR method to find points between the nodes. Curves of the contour are smooth (Figure 2) or not smooth (Figure 3). The number of nodes influences precise reconstruction of the curve.

Detection

The unknown object (one part of its contour) is described by detected interpolation nodes according to MHR method: $S = \{(x_0',y_0'), (x_1',y_1'),..., (x_m',y_m')\}$ for $x_j' < x_{j+1}'$. Also assume: exists $i = 0, 1, ..., m$ that $(x_i',y_i') \in S_1$, $(x_i',y_i') \in S_2$ (common point of models and recognized object) and $x_0' \leq x_0$, $x_m' \geq x_M$ because of using all nodes of S_1 and S_2 to recognition. Another part of the contour could be described by detected interpolation nodes monotonic in coordinates y_i: $S' = \{(\underline{x}_0',\underline{y}_0'), (\underline{x}_1',\underline{y}_1'),..., (\underline{x}_i',\underline{y}_i')\}$ for $\underline{y}_j' < \underline{y}_{j+1}'$. Number of models S_i is determined for $i = 1, 2, 3, 4...$ Let there is given

Figure 3. The set of nodes S_3' and contour fragment of the object

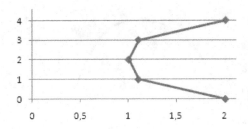

the set $S = \{(-0.1;0.2), (0.9;0.8), (2;1), (3.1;0.85), (4.1;0.1)\}$ for unknown object.

How the unknown object from Figure 4 can be recognized as *OBJECT1*, *OBJECT2* or *OBJECT3* from Figure 2?

Recognition

Contour points of unknown object have to be calculated by MHR method: (x_0,y_0), $(x_1,y_1),...,$ (x_M,y_M). Criterion of object recognition for models S_j, $j = 1,2,3...$ is given as:

$$\sum_{i=0}^{M} \left| y_i - y_i^{(j)} \right| \to \min. \qquad (29)$$

How does criterion (29) work for models S_1, S_2, S_3 and for the set of contour points S? According to (14) characteristic points (x_i,y_i) of unknown object from Figure 4 have to be computed for $x_i = 0, 1, 3, 4$. Calculations (1)-(18) are done as follows:

1)   for nodes (-0.1;0.2), (2;1) OHR operator (1)

$$M_0 = \begin{bmatrix} 0.494 & 0.125 \\ -0.125 & 0.494 \end{bmatrix},$$

for nodes (0.9;0.8), (3.1;0.85) OHR operator

$$M_1 = \begin{bmatrix} 0.322 & 0.165 \\ -0.165 & 0.322 \end{bmatrix},$$

Figure 4. The set of nodes **S** *and contour fragment of unknown object*

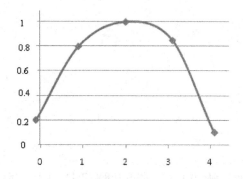

Figure 5. The set of nodes **S** *and four calculated points used in criterion (29)*

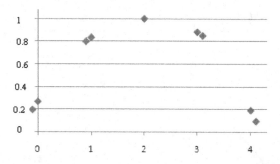

for $c_1 = 0$:

$$\alpha = \frac{0.9 - 0}{0.9 - (-0.1)} = 0.9,$$

$$c_2 = \alpha \cdot 2 + (1 - \alpha) \cdot 3.1 = 2.11,$$

$$M_2 = \alpha \cdot M_0 + (1 - \alpha) \cdot M_1 = \begin{bmatrix} 0.477 & 0.129 \\ -0.129 & 0.477 \end{bmatrix},$$

$$M_2 \cdot \begin{bmatrix} 0 \\ 2.11 \end{bmatrix} = \begin{bmatrix} 0.272 \\ 1.006 \end{bmatrix},$$

for $c_2 = 3$:

$$\alpha = \frac{3.1 - 3}{3.1 - 2} = 0.091,$$

$$c_1 = \alpha \cdot (-0.1) + (1 - \alpha) \cdot 0.9 = 0.809,$$

$$M_2 = \alpha \cdot M_0 + (1 - \alpha) \cdot M_1 = \begin{bmatrix} 0.338 & 0.161 \\ -0.161 & 0.338 \end{bmatrix},$$

$$M_2 \cdot \begin{bmatrix} 0.809 \\ 3 \end{bmatrix} = \begin{bmatrix} 0.756 \\ 0.883 \end{bmatrix};$$

2) for nodes $(0.9; 0.8), (3.1; 0.85)$ OHR operator

$$M_0 = \begin{bmatrix} 0.322 & 0.165 \\ -0.165 & 0.322 \end{bmatrix},$$

for nodes $(2; 1), (4.1; 0.1)$ OHR operator

$$M_1 = \begin{bmatrix} 0.116 & 0.187 \\ -0.187 & 0.116 \end{bmatrix},$$

for $c_1 = 1$:

$$\alpha = \frac{2 - 1}{2 - 0.9} = 0.909,$$

$$c_2 = \alpha \cdot 3.1 + (1 - \alpha) \cdot 4.1 = 3.191,$$

$$M_2 = \alpha \cdot M_0 + (1 - \alpha) \cdot M_1 = \begin{bmatrix} 0.303 & 0.167 \\ -0.167 & 0.303 \end{bmatrix},$$

$$M_2 \cdot \begin{bmatrix} 1 \\ 3.191 \end{bmatrix} = \begin{bmatrix} 0.835 \\ 0.801 \end{bmatrix},$$

Figure 6. Twenty two interpolated points of function f(x) = 1/x using MHR method (algorithm 1) together with 9 nodes

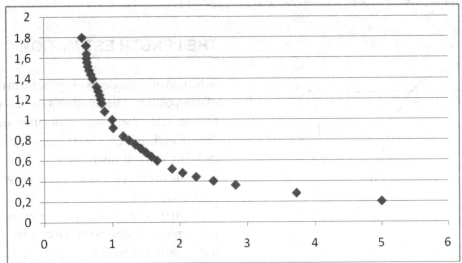

for $c_2 = 4$:

$$\alpha = \frac{4.1 - 4}{4.1 - 3.1} = 0.1,$$

$$c_1 = \alpha \cdot 0.9 + (1 - \alpha) \cdot 2 = 1.89,$$

$$M_2 = \alpha \cdot M_0 + (1 - \alpha) \cdot M_1 = \begin{bmatrix} 0.136 & 0.185 \\ -0.185 & 0.136 \end{bmatrix},$$

$$M_2 \cdot \begin{bmatrix} 1.89 \\ 4 \end{bmatrix} = \begin{bmatrix} 0.998 \\ 0.196 \end{bmatrix}.$$

So here are computed points to use in criterion (29): (0;0.272), (1;0.835), (3;0.883), (4;0.196). These coordinates could be also calculated by (20)-(21).

Criterion (29) gives the results:

1) for *OBJECT1* and set S_1:

$$\sum_{i=0}^{4} \left| y_i - y_i^{(1)} \right| = 1.814;$$

2) for *OBJECT2* and set S_2:

$$\sum_{i=0}^{4} \left| y_i - y_i^{(2)} \right| = 1.186;$$

3) for *OBJECT3* and set S_3:

$$\sum_{i=0}^{4} \left| y_i - y_i^{(3)} \right| = 0.686$$

= minimum.

It means that unknown object from Figure 4 with the set of nodes *S* is recognized as *OBJECT3* from Figure 2 with the model S_3.

EXAMPLE 2

Let's assume that one part of unknown object's contour is described by curve $f(x) = 1/x$. Function $f(x) = 1/x$ is an example when the graph of

Figure 7. Lagrange interpolation polynomial for nodes (5;0.2), (5/3;0.6), (1;1), (5/7;1.4), (5/9;1.8) differs extremely from the shape of function f(x) = 1/x

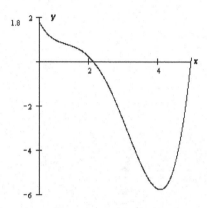

interpolated function differs from the shape of polynomials considerably. Then classical interpolation is very hard because of existing local extrema of polynomial (Figure 7). Here is the application of algorithm 1 for this function and nine nodes equidistance in second coordinate: y = 0.2, 0.4, 0.6, 0.8, 1, 1.2, 1.4, 1.6, 1.8.

Lagrange interpolation polynomial for function $f(x) = 1/x$ and nodes (5;0.2), (5/3;0.6), (1;1), (5/7;1.4), (5/9;1.8) has one extremum (minimum) and two roots. It means that Lagrange polynomial is useless.

DISCUSSION OF EXAMPLES

Each example is very simple and this chapter goes to first steps of application MHR method in object recognition. Models of known objects possess special features: appropriate contour points with characteristic (identical) one coordinate. Also unknown object must have the same one coordinate. This is very strong assumption. First version of MHR object recognition says nothing about geometrical transformations (translations, rotations, scaling): if unknown object is transformed, then

models of the object have to be also transformed and then MHR recognition is possible.

THE LENGTH ESTIMATION

Selection of the nodes is a key factor in the process of interpolation. The length of a curve is significant feature. Also the length estimation depends on the nodes. Having nodes (x_1, y_1), $(x_2, y_2), \ldots, (x_n, y_n)$ in MHR method (algorithm 1), it is possible to compute as many curve points as we want for any parameter $\alpha \in [0;1]$.

Assume that L is the number of reconstructed points plus n nodes. So curve consists of L points that could be indexed $(x_1', y_1'), (x_2', y_2'), \ldots, (x_L', y_L')$, where $(x_1', y_1') = (x_1, y_1)$ and $(x_L', y_L') = (x_n, y_n)$. The length of curve, consists of L points, is estimated:

$$d(L) = \sum_{i=1}^{L-1} \sqrt{(x_{i+1}' - x_i')^2 + (y_{i+1}' - y_i')^2}.$$

(30)

For any accuracy of length estimation $\varepsilon > 0$, it is possible to use MHR method (algorithm 1) with suitable number and location of n nodes and reconstruct curve consists of L and L_1 points, where

$$\left| d(L) - d(L_1) \right| < \varepsilon.$$

So there is no need to compute

$$\int_{x_1}^{x_n} \sqrt{1 + [f'(x)]^2} \, dx$$

(31)

as the length of curve f. Formula (30) has lower computational cost then (31).

FUTURE RESEARCH DIRECTIONS

Future works with MHR method are connected with object recognition after geometrical transformations of curve (translations, rotations, scaling)- only nodes are transformed and new curve (for example contour of the object) for new nodes is reconstructed. Also estimation of object area in the plane, using nodes of object contour, will be possible by MHR interpolation. Object area is significant feature for object recognition. Future works are dealing with smoothing the curve, parameterization of whole curve and possibility to apply MHR method to three-dimensional curves. Also case of equidistance nodes must be studied with all details. Another future research direction is to apply MHR method in artificial intelligence and computer vision, for example identification of a specific person's face or fingerprint, optical character recognition (OCR), image restoration, content-based image retrieval and pose estimation. Future works are connected with object recognition for any set of contour points. There are several specialized tasks based on recognition to consider and it is important to use the shape of whole contour for identification and detection of persons, vehicles or other objects. Other applications of MHR method will be directed to computer graphics, modeling and image processing.

CONCLUSION

The number of nodes in the model set influences precise recognition of the object. If there is need to consider another part of the object contour, the same method of object recognition must be done for another part of the contour. This chapter consists of first step to apply curve interpolation by MHR method in object recognition. Presented method needs specific sets of contour points as the models of given objects. The unknown object (one part of its contour) is described by detected interpolation nodes according to MHR method.

Computed coordinates of contour points are used in criterion of object recognition. Orthogonality of columns and rows in OHR operators is very important and significant for stability and high precision of calculations. MHR method is modeling the curve point by point without using any formula of function. Main features of MHR method are: accuracy of curve reconstruction depending on number of nodes and method of choosing nodes, interpolation of L points of the curve is connected with the computational cost of rank $O(L)$, MHR method is not a linear interpolation, MHR interpolation does not possess bad features of classical interpolations and MHR interpolation is done without polynomials or other functions.

REFERENCES

Ballard, D. H. (1982). *Computer vision*. New York: Prentice Hall.

Chin, R. T., & Dyer, C. R. (1986). Model-based recognition in robot vision. *ACM Computing Surveys, 1*(18), 67–108. doi:10.1145/6462.6464

Choraś, R. S. (2005). *Computer vision*. Warsaw, Poland: Exit.

Cierniak, R. (2005). *Computed tomography*. Warsaw, Poland: Exit.

Citko, W., Jakóbczak, D., & Sieńko, W. (2005, September). *On Hurwitz-Radon matrices based signal processing*. Paper presented at the workshop Signal Processing at Poznan University of Technology, Poznań, Poland.

Dahlquist, G., & Bjoerck, A. (1974). *Numerical methods*. Englewood Cliffs, NJ: Prentice Hall.

Eckmann, B. (1999). Topology, algebra, analysis- relations and missing links. *Notices of the American Mathematical Society, 5*(46), 520–527.

Grimson, E. (1990). *Object recognition by computer: the role of geometric constraints*. Cambridge, MA: MITPress.

Jakóbczak, D. (2006). *Application of discrete, orthogonal operator of Hurwitz-Radon in compression and reconstruction of monochromatic images' contours*. Unpublished doctoral dissertation, Polish - Japanese Institute of Information Technology, Warsaw, Poland.

Jakóbczak, D. (2007). 2D and 3D image modeling using Hurwitz-Radon matrices. *Polish Journal of Environmental Studies*, *4A*(16), 104–107.

Jakóbczak, D., & Kosiński, W. (2007). Application of Hurwitz-Radon matrices in monochromatic medical images decompression. In Kowalczuk, Z., & Wiszniewski, B. (Eds.), *Intelligent data mining in diagnostic purposes: Automatics and informatics* (pp. 389–398). Gdansk, Poland: PWNT.

Jakóbczak, D., & Kosiński, W. (2007). Hurwitz-Radon operator in monochromatic medical image reconstruction. *Journal of Medical Informatics & Technologies*, *11*, 69–78.

Kozera, R. (2004). *Curve modeling via interpolation based on multidimensional reduced data*. Gliwice, Poland: Silesian University of Technology Press.

Kriegman, D. J., & Ponce, J. (1990). On recognizing and positioning curved 3-D objects from image contours. *IEEE Transactions on Pattern Analysis and Machine Intelligence*, *12*(12), 1127–1137. doi:10.1109/34.62602

Lamdan, Y., Schwartz, J. T., & Wolfson, H. J. (1990). Affine invariant model-based object recognition. *IEEE Transactions on Robotics and Automation*, *5*(6), 578–589. doi:10.1109/70.62047

Lamdan, Y., & Wolfson, H. J. (1988, December). *Geometric hashing: a general and efficient model-based recognition scheme*. Paper presented at ICCV, Tampa, Florida.

Latecki, L. J., & Lakaemper, R. (1999). Convexity rule for shape decomposition based on Discrete Contour Evolution. *Computer Vision and Image Understanding*, *3*(73), 441–454. doi:10.1006/cviu.1998.0738

Lowe, D. G. (1991). Fitting parameterized three-dimensional models to images. *IEEE Transactions on Pattern Analysis and Machine Intelligence*, *5*(13), 441–450. doi:10.1109/34.134043

Lowe, D. G. (1999, September). *Object recognition from local scale-invariant features*. Paper presented at the International Conference on Computer Vision, Corfu, Greece.

Lowe, D. G. (2001). *Local feature view clustering for 3D object recognition*. Paper presented at the IEEE Conference on Computer Vision and Pattern Recognition, Kauai, Hawaii.

Lowe, D. G. (2004). Distinctive image features from scale-invariant keypoints. *International Journal of Computer Vision*, *2*(60), 91–110. doi:10.1023/B:VISI.0000029664.99615.94

Pope, A. R., & Lowe, D. G. (2004). Probabilistic models of appearance for 3-D object recognition. *International Journal of Computer Vision*, *2*(40), 149–167.

Pratt, W. K. (2001). *Digital image processing*. New York: John Wiley & Sons. doi:10.1002/0471221325

Ralston, A. (1965). *A first course in numerical analysis*. New York: McGraw-Hill Book Company.

Sieńko, W., & Citko, W. (2002). *Hamiltonian Neural Net based signal processing*. Paper presented at the International Conference on Signal and Electronic System ICSES, Wrocław–Świeradów Zdrój, Poland.

Sieńko, W., Citko, W., & Jakóbczak, D. (2004). Learning and system modeling via Hamiltonian Neural Networks. In Rutkowski, L., Siekmann, J., Tadeusiewicz, R., & Zadeh, A. (Eds.), *Lecture notes on artificial intelligence: Artificial intelligence and soft computing - ICAISC 2004* (pp. 266–271). Berlin - Heidelberg, Germany: Springer - Verlag.

Sieńko, W., Citko, W., & Wilamowski, B. (2002). *Hamiltonian Neural Nets as a universal signal processor*. Paper presented at the 28th Annual Conference of the IEEE Industrial Electronics Society IECON, Sevilla, Spain.

Soussen, C., & Mohammad-Djafari, A. (2004). Polygonal and polyhedral contour reconstruction in computed tomography. *IEEE Transactions on Image Processing, 11*(13), 1507–1523. doi:10.1109/TIP.2004.836159

Tang, K. (2005). Geometric optimization algorithms in manufacturing. *Computer – Aided Design & Applications, 2*(6), 747-757.

Tarokh, V., Jafarkhani, H., & Calderbank, R. (1999). Space-Time Block Codes from orthogonal designs. *IEEE Transactions on Information Theory, 5*(45), 1456–1467. doi:10.1109/18.771146

Ullman, S., & Basri, R. (1991). Recognition by linear combinations of models. *IEEE Transactions on Pattern Analysis and Machine Intelligence, 10*(13), 992–1006. doi:10.1109/34.99234

ADDITIONAL READING

Basu, S., & Bresler, Y. (2000). $O(N^2 log_2 N)$ filtered backprojection reconstruction algorithm for tomography. *IEEE Transactions on Image Processing, 9*(10), 1760–1773. doi:10.1109/83.869187

Brankov, J. G., Yang, Yongyi, & Wernick, M. N. (2004). Tomographic image reconstruction based on a Content – Adaptive Mesh Model. *IEEE Transactions on Medical Imaging, 2*(23), 202–212. doi:10.1109/TMI.2003.822822

Brasse, D., & Defrise, M. (2004). Fast fully 3-D image reconstruction in PET using planograms. *IEEE Transactions on Medical Imaging, 4*(23), 413–425. doi:10.1109/TMI.2004.824231

Cetin, M., Karl, W. C., & Willsky, A. S. (2002, September). *Edge – preserving image reconstruction for coherent imaging application*. Paper presented at the IEEE International Conference on Image Processsing, Rochester, NY.

Chlebus, E., & Cholewa, M. (1999). Rapid prototyping – rapid tooling. *CADCAM Forum, 11*, 23–28.

Cormen, T. H., Leiserson, C. E., & Rivest, R. L. (1996). *Introduction to algorithms*. Cambridge, MA: MIT Press.

Defrise, M. (2001). A short reader's guide to 3D tomographic reconstruction. *Computerized Medical Imaging and Graphics, 25*, 113–116. doi:10.1016/S0895-6111(00)00061-6

Dryja, M., Jankowska, J., & Jankowski, M. (1982). *Survey of numerical methods and algorithms. Part II*. Warsaw, Poland: WNT.

Eldar, Y. C. (2001). *Quantum Signal Processing*. (Unpublished doctoral dissertation), Massachusetts Institute of Technology, USA.

Eldar, Y. C., & Oppenheim, A. V. (2002). Quantum Signal Processing. *IEEE Signal Processing Magazine, 6*(19), 12–32. doi:10.1109/MSP.2002.1043298

Fortuna, Z., Macukow, B., & Wąsowski, J. (1982). *Numerical methods*. Warsaw, Poland: WNT.

Jakóbczak, D. (2005). Hurwitz-Radon matrices and their children. *Computer Science, 5*(8), 29–38.

Jankowska, J., & Jankowski, M. (1981). *Survey of numerical methods and algorithms. Part I.* Warsaw, Poland: WNT.

Kontaxakis, G., & Strauss, L. G. (1998). Maximum likelihood algorithms for image reconstruction in Positron Emission Tomography. *Radionuclides for Oncology – Current Status and Future Aspects, 1998,* 73-106.

Kowalczuk, Z., & Wiszniewski, B. (Eds.). (2007). *Intelligent data mining in diagnostic purposes: Automatics and informatics.* Gdansk, Poland: PWNT.

Kundur, D., & Hatzinakos, D. (1998). A novel blind deconvolution scheme for image restoration using recursive filtering. *IEEE Transactions on Signal Processing, 2*(46), 375–390. doi:10.1109/78.655423

Laine, A., & Zong, X. (1996). *Border identification of echocardiograms via multiscale edge detection and shape modeling.* Paper presented at the IEEE International Conference on Image Processsing, Lausanne, Switzerland.

Lang, S. (1970). *Algebra.* Reading, MA: Addison-Wesley Publishing Company.

Le Buhan Jordan, C., Bossen, F., & Ebrahimi, T. (1997). *Scalable shape representation for content based visual data compression.* Paper presented at the International Conference on Image Processing, Santa Barbara, CA, USA.

Marker, J., Braude, I., Museth, K., & Breen, D. (2006). Contour-based surface reconstruction using implicit curve fitting, and distance field filtering and interpolation. *Volume Graphics, 2006,* 1–9.

Meyer, Y. (1993). *Wavelets: algorithms & applications.* Philadelphia: Society for Industrial and Applied Mathematics.

Poggio, T., & Smale, S. (2003). The mathematics of learning: Dealing with data. *Notices of the American Mathematical Society, 5*(50), 537–544.

Przelaskowski, A. (2005). *Data compression.* Warsaw, Poland: BTC.

Rutkowski, L., Siekmann, J., Tadeusiewicz, R., & Zadeh, A. (Eds.). (2004). *Lecture notes on artificial intelligence: Artificial intelligence and soft computing.* Berlin - Heidelberg, Germany: Springer - Verlag.

Vakhania, N. (1993). Orthogonal random vectors and the Hurwitz – Radon - Eckmann theorem. *Proc. of the Georgian Academy of Sciences - Mathematics, 1*(1), 109-125.

Willis, M. (2000). *Algebraic reconstruction algorithms for remote sensing image enhancement.* (Unpublished doctoral dissertation), Department of Electrical and Computer Engineering, Brigham Young University.

Xu, Fang, & Mueller, K. (2005). Accelerating popular tomographic reconstruction algorithms on commodity PC graphics hardware. *IEEE Transactions on Nuclear Science, 3*(52), 654–661.

Zaletelj, J., & Tasic, J. F. (2003). *Optimization and tracking of polygon vertices for shape coding.* Berlin - Heidelberg, Germany: Springer - Verlag.

Zhang, J. K., Davidson, T., & Wong, K. M. (2004). Efficient design of orthonormal wavelet bases for signal representation. *IEEE Transactions on Signal Processing, 7*(52), 1983–1996. doi:10.1109/TSP.2004.828923

KEY TERMS AND DEFINITIONS

Artificial Intelligence: Intelligence of machines and computers, as a connection of algorithms and hardware, which makes that a man – human being can be simulated by the machines in reasoning, knowledge, planning, learning, communication, perception and the ability to move and manipulate objects.

Computer Vision: The branch of computer science that wants machines to be able to see by obtaining information from images.

Contour Reconstruction: Calculation of unknown points of the object contour having information about some points of the object contour.

Curve Interpolation: Computing new and unknown points of a curve and creating a graph of a curve using existing data points–interpolation nodes.

Hurwitz-Radon Matrices: A family of skew-symmetric and orthogonal matrices with columns and rows that create, together with identical matrix, the base in vector spaces of dimensions $N = 2$, 4 or 8.

MHR Method: A method of curve interpolation using linear (convex) combinations of OHR operators.

Object Recognition: The task of finding a given object in an image or video sequence.

OHR Operator: Matrix operator of Hurwitz-Radon built from coordinates of interpolation nodes.

Chapter 6
Fuzzy Logic Based Modeling in the Complex System Fault Diagnosis

Miroslav Pokorný
Technical University of Ostrava, Czech Republic

Pavel Fojtík
Technical University of Ostrava, Czech Republic

ABSTRACT

This chapter deals with the model-based fault diagnosis approaches that exploit the fuzzy modeling approximation abilities to obtain the appropriate model of the monitored system. This technique makes use of the Takagi-Sugeno fuzzy model to describe the non-linear dynamic system by its decomposition onto number of linear submodels, so that it is possible to overcome difficulties in conventional methods for dealing with nonlinearity. A linear residual generator formed by Kalman filters which are designed for the each of the linear subsystem is then proposed to generate diagnostic signals - residuals. Since the task is formulated on a statistical basis, the generalized likelihood ratio test is chosen as a decision-making algorithm. Finally, two practical examples are presented to demonstrate the applicability of the proposed approach.

INTRODUCTION

There is no doubt that related to safety-critical systems such as chemical plants, nuclear reactors, space shuttles and aircrafts, the issues of reliability, operating safety and environmental protection are of major importance. However, these issues together with increasing demands for availability and cost efficiency are relevant to not only mentioned safety-critical systems, but

also other industrial production facilities (power plants, paper and steel mills, oil refineries etc.), transportation vehicles and many other processes on a daily basis. In substance, this is the reason why fault diagnosis has received more and more attention in the last three decades.

In many cases, the term 'fault' is used to describe the abnormalities originate in system components (sensors, actuators, etc.) while any undesired deviations of the system parameters or variables are referred to us 'system changes'. However, in this chapter, the 'fault' is regarded as

DOI: 10.4018/978-1-61692-811-7.ch006

an undesired change in the system that leads to the inability of the system to perform the requested operations. Moreover, this change may not correspond to the failure of physical components.

The early and correct detection of the fault presence at the monitored system can help avoid the systems breakdown, performance degradation, device major damages and increase the system availability, safety while minimize their downtime. Furthermore, the prompt and precise diagnosis of the each system malfunction allow the human operator to take the corrective actions or, as a fault-tolerance system capability is needed, the automatic reconfiguration system to re-schedule the feedback control or set point parameters.

Before the measuring devices and computers were widely introduced in practical industrial applications, the only way to get the information about the system malfunctions and places of their action was by the human senses. Later with increasing availability and decreasing cost of digital hardware and software, the ideal conditions raised for the research in the field of fault detection and isolation as well as for the practical application of developed techniques. As a result, many new methods have been developed to these days.

The most frequently used method to fault detection and diagnosis is based on limit checking of a particular variables or the application of redundant sensors. It is so called physical or parallel redundancy. More advanced methods rely on the spectral analysis of properly chosen signals. This is no completed list of the existing methods. There are many others with different principles and features, but this chapter is devoted to those fault diagnosis methods, which are based on the concept of analytical redundancy. This concept uses redundant analytical relationships between various measured variables of the system to be diagnosed and thus enables the application of methods for fault diagnosis based upon the use of the quantitative or qualitative models and rule-based information. Specifically, this chapter is concerned with the family of the model-based

fault diagnosis methods that utilize an explicit mathematical model of the monitored process and that are formulated on a statistical basis. Later in this chapter, the possibility of using a Takagi-Sugeno fuzzy model to describe the non-linear dynamic system by its decomposition onto number of linear submodels will be introduced. This approach makes use of linear fault diagnosis algorithms even if the non-linear system is under the consideration. This will be followed by the application of the one of statistical hypothesis test on to the diagnostic signals along with the fuzzy regression to make a decision whether the system is subjected by the fault or not. At the end of this chapter, two case studies will be presented. The first the fault presence detection in the laboratory three tank system will be discussed and subsequently as a second example the proposed diagnostic scheme will be used for the breakout possibility detection during the steel continuous casting process.

BACKGROUND

Previously, a brief definition of the fault term has been introduced. There was posed that the fault is an undesired change in the plant or its instrumentation that leads to the inability of the system to perform the requested operations (Chen & Patton, 1999). However, there has been no mention of the types of the faults under consideration so far.

According to (Gertler, 1998) the each fault can be assigned to the one of following four categories:

- **Additive process faults**. This category covers unknown inputs that cause a change in the system outputs independent of the known inputs.
- **Multiplicative process faults**. This includes these faults, which cause changes in the system outputs that depend also on the magnitude of the known inputs.

- **Sensor faults.** These faults cause difference between real and measured system variables and may be characterized as additive or multiplicative.
- **Actuator faults.** These faults cause difference between an actuator input command and its real output.

The monitoring system that is designed to meet the fault diagnosis task is called "fault diagnostic system" and should pass through each of the following three stages:

- **Fault detection.** Making a decision either the system is subjected by the fault or not.
- **Fault isolation.** That is the determination of the location of the fault.
- **Fault identification.** The point is the estimation of the magnitude and nature of the fault.

Regardless of the relative importance of presented stages, it is clear, that the detection is essential for any practical cases and isolation is almost equally important. On the other hand, the fault identification seems to be not so necessary if no reconfiguration action is involved. It is convenient to make a remark, that fault diagnosis is very often considered as fault detection and isolation, abbreviated as FDI, in the literature. Note also that this chapter is focused only on detection stage. The isolation of the detected faults can be done in straightforward way using for example structured residual set (Gertler, 1993) or one of the others methods (Chen & Patton, 1999).

In fact, there are two major groups of the methods to handle the fault detection and diagnosis. The first group of methods uses so called physical redundancy that is the additional sensors are installed to measure the same physical value and does not utilize any a priori information about the monitored system. Other methods that belong to this group vary from special sensors through limit-checking and logical reasoning to spectrum analysis. The characteristic feature of the second group is utilization of the a priori knowledge about the relationship between the system and faults and model parameters or states. These are so called model-based methods and represent the main scope of interest of this chapter. The philosophy of these methods is that the sensor measurements are compared to analytically computed values of relevant variable. Note that there is another possibility of comparison of two analytically generated values obtained from different sets of appropriate variables.

The general structure of the model-based fault diagnosis system includes two main stages of residual generation and residual evaluation (decision making (Chow & Willsky, 1984)).

The main purposes of these two main stages are described as follows:

- **Residual generation.** The main goal of this stage is to generate a fault indicating signals – residuals. Actually, these residuals are the result of the comparison between the sensor measurements and analytically computed values as mentioned before. Ideally, if no faults occur at the system the residuals should be zero or close to zero and vise versa. It means if some fault occurs the residuals have to be markedly different from zero. However, due to modeling errors and other disturbances, this is not generally true and the demand for the robust residual generation algorithms arises (Frank & Keller, 1980). Generally, residual generation is a procedure for extracting fault symptoms from the monitored systems.
- **Residual evaluation.** During this stage, the generated residuals are subjected to examination for the likelihood of faults and some decision technique is then used to detect the potential fault. To accomplish this stage, the simple threshold test or methods of statistical decision theory can be

utilized (Willsky, 1976; Willsky & Jones, 1976; Basseville & Nikiforov, 1993). In this chapter, the generalized likelihood ratio test is then used to make a decision if the system is subjected by the fault or not.

Since the residual generation is the most important in the model-based fault diagnosis, there is the great emphasis on the method properties and its suitability. Rich variety methods are available for the residual generation. It is possible to find several, somewhat overlapping approaches to the residual generation in the literature. The observer-based approach is based on the estimation of the system outputs from the measurements by using some kind of the observers, Luenberger (Frank, 1990) or Kalman filter (Sohlberg, 1998) in the stochastic case, and then the weighted output estimation error or innovations is used as a residuals. However, there are some also widely used methods there. For example, the parity relations methods (Gertler, 1998), where the basic idea is to provide a proper consistency (parity) check of the measurements of the monitored system are included into this widely used of methods.

Note that in this chapter the Kalman filter is designed as a residual generator since the task can be always formulated on a statistical basis generally.

Now let is pointed out that there has been always possibility to obtain precise linear model of the monitored system for entire operation range so far. However, this is no generally true. The most of the industrial systems exhibit a strong non-linear behavior and only way to construct the linear model is to linearize the process model around the operating point and then robust algorithm should be applied to generate residuals (Patton & Chen, 1997). The dominant approaches in the field of robust residual generation are the disturbance de-coupling based approaches. The main idea is that the uncertain factors in the system under consideration are modeled as unknown inputs and since the distribution matrix of the unknown input

vector is assumed to be known, the unknown input vector can be de-coupled from the residual so that the residuals are not affected by the unknown disturbances (Watanabe & Himmelblau, 1982).

However, linearization does not provide a good model for the strong non-linear system and furthermore, this method only works well when the system operates close to the operating point specified. One way to deal with the non-linear systems and wide operation range is using non-linear techniques such as non-linear observer design (Hengy & Frank, 1986). The non-linear observer approach is based on the existing analytical model of the monitored system that is, unfortunately, not easy to obtain in practice, especially for the complex systems. Even in some situations the system under consideration cannot be modeled by explicit mathematical model. Moreover, mathematical models can be very time consuming to develop and there is always the risk that they rarely replicate the functions of the entire process. That is why it is convenient to find such model that can be used to represent any non-linear system approximately, but this approach can cause the large model-reality mismatch with the devastating effect on the fault diagnosis process. To solve the above mentioned problems, many approaches in the field of fault diagnosis using artificial intelligence have been proposed till these days. The formal approach is based on utilization of qualitative reasoning and qualitative modeling. By using this, it is possible to predict the behavior of the monitored system under fault free operating conditions as well as during different faulty situations and then fault diagnosis is fulfilled by comparing the actual process measurements with the predicted ones (Patton, Frank & Clark, 2000). In (Porter & Passino, 1995) authors applied of the evolutionary algorithm to the observer design. They introduced so called genetic adaptive observer, where the observer gain matrix is assigned by genetic algorithm in the real time so that the output error is minimized. The convergence conditions of such observer together with the robustness issues were discussed in (Witczak, Obuchowicz & Korbicz, 2002; Metenidis, Witczak & Korbicz, 2004) as well as novel genetic programming based approach for designing state-space models from input-output data was presented.

Another large area of fault diagnosis exploits artificial intelligence makes use of neural networks, fuzzy decision making and neuro-fuzzy methods. One of the most important advantages of the neural network application for fault diagnosis problem is that the neural networks are capable of forming an arbitrary close approximation to any continuous nonlinear function, given suitable weighting factors and network architecture. After the raining of the neural network, the relationship between the faults and their causes are identified and stored in the network weights. This trained network is then possible to use to diagnose faults by comparison the occurring malfunctions with the corresponding fault (Maki & Loparo, 1997). The application of the neural network brings undisputable advantage but on the other hand for a long time the most studies only dealt with steady-state processes and neural network was used as a fault classifier. But because of the above mentioned attractive features of neural networks, it seems to be convenient to employ neural networks as a modeling tool to obtain a dynamic model of the complex, unknown and non-linear processes and subsequently the residuals can be obtained in straightforward way.

Recently there exist many approaches to solve the dynamic system identification problem by using the neural networks, appeared in the later contributions. The simplest one is based on idea that the inputs of the multilayer feedforward network are not only the current input but also the past inputs and outputs. Such a model was used as a residual generator in (Patton, Chen & Siew, 1994) together with neural network as a classifier in decision making stage.

More sophisticated way to provide the dynamic properties of the neural network is application of locally recurrent globally feedforward network

(Patan & Parisini, 2005) composed of dynamic neuron models. Dynamics is incorporated into the neuron model structure as a linear dynamic system. In (Patan & Parisini, 2005) the considered network was trained by means of simultaneous perturbation stochastic algorithm and resulting FDI scheme was applied to the actuator fault diagnosis in the evaporation station. Modified structure of the locally recurrent network, called cascade structure was presented in (Patan, Witczak & Korbicz, 2008) where excitation of the neurons occurring in the second layer was received also form external inputs and in addition, neurons in different layers were equipped by different kind of the filter.

There is no doubt that the successful application of the fault diagnosis task largely depends on availability of the good model of the system to be diagnosed. There is a strength connection between neural network model structure and resulting quality of the model. The group method of data handling (GMDH) approach represents one way to ensure good quality of the model by the neural network structure selection (Witczak, Korbicz, Mrugalski & Patton, 2006). It is done by replacing the complex neural model by a set of hierarchically connected neurons and the parameters of each neuron are estimated so that their outputs are the best approximation of the diagnosed system output signals. Further improvement of this approach was done in (Witczak, Korbicz, Mrugalski & Patton, 2006) by application of bounded error approach (BEA) to obtain the neural network model with relatively small modeling uncertainty. BEA algorithm was used to estimate the parameter and corresponding uncertainty of the neuron as well as the uncertainty of the model output and thus the application of the adaptive threshold to ensure robust fault detection was allowed.

In (Patan, Witczak & Korbicz, 2008) the robustness of the fault diagnosis process was enabled using the model error modeling approach where the uncertainty was estimated by analyzing residuals evaluated from the input. It seems to be an alternative way to the previous one. A large spectrum of different methods to solve fault diagnosis task in this way can be found the literature. Each presented method has its own advantages and disadvantages, for example ability to detect the incipient faults and it can be said that these methods are little bit complicated, especially in the case when the robustness of the fault diagnosis process is considered. The great survey of the fault diagnosis approaches based on soft computing techniques was presented in (Korbicz, Koscielny, Kowalczuk & Cholewa, 2004; Witczak, 2006).

It follows from above that it seems to be very profitable to combine neural network with fuzzy logic to form so called neuro-fuzzy approach for non-linear dynamic system fault diagnosis and then the advantages in both methods can be entirely exploited.

In (Korbicz & Kowal, 2007) the Takagi-Sugeno neuro-fuzzy model was used for fault diagnosis. Because of the fact that the complexity and accuracy of the global model is closely associated with the suitable number of the fuzzy rules, authors developed a method that determines the number of the rules according to maximum acceptable modeling error. The method is based on input-output data analysis in order to find local linear dependencies using the BEA approach. Furthermore, authors used the BEA algorithm for the evaluation of the confidence interval of the T-S neuro-fuzzy model and then computed the adaptive threshold for the residuals to obtain the robust fault diagnosis scheme. Unfortunately, presented approach is suited only in case the consequents take the form of dynamic models without autoregressive part.

One of the recent approach uses neuro-fuzzy method is based on neuro-fuzzy multiple modeling together with robust optimal de-coupling of observers and authors called presented method as the neuro-fuzzy and de-coupling fault diagnosis scheme (Uppal, Patton & Witczak, 2006).

In this chapter the similar approach is used for the fault diagnosis but there are the some differences especially in the residual evaluation stage. It will be shown in following that to avoid the problems of fault diagnostic method applied using the linearization of the process model around the operating point or to design a non-linear observer, a set of local linear models is used, instead of a single nonlinear process model. The nonlinear process model is of fuzzy Takagi- Sugeno type (Takagi & Sugeno, 1985). This type models are not only universal approximators but also can accommodate different pieces of knowledge (e.g. qualitative knowledge) which must be integrated, in order to obtain a good process model. If little prior knowledge is available, fuzzy model can be extracted from the process measurements using various techniques such a fuzzy clustering, neuro-fuzzy learning, etc. Moreover, the local linear models can be derived from the linear rule consequences in a straightforward way.

As mentioned above the following sections of this chapter are devoted to the detailed discussion of the fault diagnosis using fuzzy non-linear modeling together with its problems, advantages as well as its disadvantages. Finally some possible future research directions will be suggested.

OBSERVER BASED DIAGNOSIS INVOLVING THE FUZZY NON-LINEAR MODELING

If the model-based approach for fault diagnosis is considered, it is logical that first step have to be the creation of the mathematical model of the system to be monitored. The model should include all possible faults that can affect on the diagnosed process. The representation of the faults effects depends more upon the detection method than upon its real nature.

Consider that the neuro-fuzzy approach, specifically the fuzzy Takagi-Sugeno type of the model that enables the decomposition of the non-linear dynamic system onto number of linear submodels is used in this chapter and further note

Figure 1. The monitored system scheme

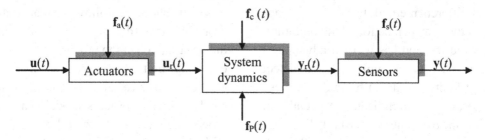

that certain kind of the observer as a residual generator is employed, state-space representation of the monitored system seems to be convenient.

Model of the Faulty System

According to (Chen & Patton, 1999) the diagnosed system together with all possible faults and their locations are depicted in Figure 1. Here the $\mathbf{f}_p(t)$ represents the parameter faults, $\mathbf{f}_c(t)$ is component faults whereas $\mathbf{f}_a(t)$ is actuator faults and sensor faults are denoted as $\mathbf{f}_s(t)$. Because this chapter is concerned with multiple input and multiple output systems, all of the variables are vectors. It can be showed that in general case the continuous state space representation of the system with all mentioned faults is formed by the following equation set:

$$
\begin{aligned}
\dot{\mathbf{x}}(t) &= \mathbf{A}\mathbf{x}(t) + \mathbf{B}\mathbf{u}(t) + \mathbf{R}_{C1}\mathbf{f}(t) \\
\mathbf{y}(t) &= \mathbf{C}\mathbf{x}(t) + \mathbf{D}\mathbf{u}(t) + \mathbf{R}_{C2}\mathbf{f}(t)
\end{aligned}
\tag{1}
$$

where $\mathbf{x}(t) \in R^n$ is the state vector, $\mathbf{u}(t) \in R^r$ is the input vector and $\mathbf{y}(t) \in R^m$ is the output vector. $\mathbf{A}$, $\mathbf{B}$, $\mathbf{C}$, $\mathbf{D}$ are known continuous system matrices with the dimensions so that the equations (1) holds true. $\mathbf{f}(k)$ is unknown function of time corresponds to a specific fault while $\mathbf{R}_{C1}$ and $\mathbf{R}_{C2}$ are the known fault distribution matrices represents the effect of the faults on the system.

Presented model of the faulty systems in the continuous time domain has been widely accepted

in the fault diagnostic literature and in this chapter this general model is only be considered.

Takagi-Sugeno Fuzzy Model Structure

As mentioned before, if the general case is assumed, i.e. the process under consideration is non-linear and linearization is not able to produce a good results, the necessity of the non-linear observer design or application of some the others non-linear analytical technique can be avoided by using the neuro-fuzzy approach to construct the model of the monitored system.

In detail, a Takagi-Sugeno fuzzy model is a way to describe a non-linear dynamic system using locally linearized linear models. Each linear model represents the local system behavior around the actual operating point. The global system is then described by a fuzzy fusion of all linear model outputs. Necessary number of fuzzy IF-THEN rules describes the global system behavior. The consequent of and particular rule represents local linear relations of the non-linear system. Suppose that the non-linear system can be described by the following general n – dimensional non-linear function:

$$
y(x) = F(x_1, x_2, \ldots, x_n)
\tag{2}
$$

where y is output of the system and x_1, x_2,..., x_n are input variables. Since equation (2) can be approximated by the piecewise liner function, it is possible to describe this non-linear function by the set of the fuzzy IF-THEN rules. The local input subspace, where the particular consequent holds true, is enclosed by the rth antecedent of the specific r^{th} rule ($r = 1,2,...,R$). TS model that approximates the non-linear function (2), has the following structure:

$$R_1 : \text{IF}(x_1 \text{is} A_{11}) \text{ and} ... \text{and } (x_n \text{is} A_{1n})$$
$$\text{THEN } y = k_{10} + k_{11}x_1 + ... + k_{1n}x_n$$
$$R_2 : \text{IF}(x_1 \text{is} A_{21}) \text{ and} ... \text{and } (x_n \text{is} A_{2n})$$
$$\text{THEN } y = k_{20} + k_{21}x_1 + ... + k_{2n}x_n$$
$$\vdots$$
$$R_R : \text{IF}(x_1 \text{is} A_{R1}) \text{ and} ... \text{and } (x_n \text{is} A_{Rn})$$
$$\text{THEN } y = k_{R0} + k_{R1}x_1 + ... + k_{Rn}x_n \quad (3)$$

where $x_1, x_2, ..., x_n$ are premise variables $A_{11}, A_{12}, ...,$ A_{Rn} are fuzzy sets and R is number of IF-THEN rules that corresponds with the number of the local linear models or else the number of the operating points. The consequents in equation (3) take the form of linear functions of input variables. Given the inputs, the global output of the system is inferred as follows:

$$y_G = \frac{\sum_{r=1}^{R} w_r y_r}{\sum_{r=1}^{R} w_r} \quad (4)$$

where w_r is the tensor product of grade memberships of the premise variables and it is given by following expression:

$$w_r = \min_i \left[\mu_{A_{ri}}(x_i^0) \right] \quad (5)$$

where $\mu_{A_{ri}}(x_i^0)$ is the grade of membership of the premise variable actual value x_i^0. The membership grade functions w_r ($r = 1,2,...,R$) satisfy the following constraints:

$$\sum_{r=1}^{R} w_r = 1, \quad (6)$$
$$0 \leq w_r \leq 1 \ \forall r = 1, 2, ..., R$$

The identification procedure of the T-S fuzzy model includes two basic stages. Those are the model structure identification and model parametrization and both are concerned with antecedents as well as consequents.

Number of the existing rules and their forms gives the primary structure of the model. Each rule defines input-output relationship inside the one single fuzzy subspace that is the part of the global, multi-dimensional space of the input variables. Structure of the model is also formed by the inner structure of the antecedents and consequents. Note that the fuzzy sets parameters and the parameters of the regression equations of the consequents act here as the T-S model parameters.

There exists many identification approaches utilizing the wide spectrum of methods (e.g. fuzzy clustering, linear programming, genetic algorithms, neural networks) (Brown & Hartus 1994). The widely used method for rules quantity identification as well as for identification of their antecedents' structure and parameters is fuzzy clustering. The regression equations coefficients can be then identified by using the least squares or linear programming method or further by application of the genetic algorithm.

Note that the number of the rules has the crucial influence on the accuracy of the resulting T-S model as well as on its complexity as mentioned in the previous section. To tackle this problem it seems to be very profitable to use for the number of the fuzzy rules determination the algorithm presented in the following contribution (Korbicz & Kowal, 2007).

T-S Fuzzy Model Modification

Now it is possible to assume that there exists the T-S fuzzy model of the system to be diagnosed. So that there is a set of the linear models represented by the regression functions and each linear model describes the behavior of the system around the particular operational point. To design the residual generator to produce the residuals for further analysis without application of the non-linear methods it seems to be useful to derive the local linear generators and each of them corresponds to particular linear model encompassed in T-S fuzzy model.

Because of the observer-based methods for residual generator design are concerned in his chapter and since the system under the consideration is supposed to be stochastic, to obtain the diagnostic signals – residuals that can be computed as a difference between the estimated and real system output, the Kalman filter can be used for construction of the output system estimate. As mentioned before, in order to compute global system estimate it is convenient to apply the Klaman filter not to the global system, but to the local linear model appeared in the consequent of each of the rule of the T-S fuzzy model. However, to do so, it is necessary to convert the linear regression functions to the corresponding state space representation. It is possible to show (Åström & Wittenmark, 1997), that if the regression equation that describes the local system behavior is given by:

$$y^r(k) = a_0^r + \sum_{j=1}^{zy} a_j^r y^r(k-j) + \sum_{j=0}^{zu_1} b_j^r u_1(k-j) + \cdots + \sum_{j=0}^{zu_S} c_j^r u_S(k-j)$$

(7)

where $y^r(k)$ is the output of the local linear model, $a_0^r, a_j^r, b_j^r, c_j^r$ are the scalar coefficients, $u_1(k),\ldots,u_S(k)$ are the input variables and $zy, zu_1, \ldots, zu_S$ represents the order of delays for the corresponding signals, the state space matrices for the particular local discrete model can be obtained in the following observable canonical form:

$$\Phi_1^r = \begin{bmatrix} -a_1^r & 1 & 0 & \cdots & 0 \\ -a_2^r & 0 & 1 & \cdots & 0 \\ \vdots & \vdots & \vdots & \ddots & \vdots \\ -a_{zy-1}^r & 0 & 0 & \cdots & 1 \\ -a_{zy}^r & 0 & 0 & \cdots & 0 \end{bmatrix}$$

$$\mathbf{C}_1^r = \begin{bmatrix} 1 & 0 & \cdots & 0 \end{bmatrix}$$

(8a)

and

$$\Gamma_1^r = \begin{bmatrix} b_1^r - a_1^r b_0^r & \cdots & c_1^r - a_1^r c_0^r & -a_1^r a_0^r \\ b_2^r - a_2^r b_0^r & \cdots & c_2^r - a_2^r c_0^r & -a_2^r a_0^r \\ \vdots & \vdots & \vdots \\ b_{zu_1-1}^r - a_{zy-1}^r b_0^r & \cdots & c_{zu_S-1}^r - a_{zy-1}^r c_0^r & -a_{zy-1}^r a_0^r \\ b_{zu_1}^r - a_{zy}^r b_0^r & \cdots & c_{zu_S}^r - a_{zy}^r c_0^r & -a_{zy}^r a_0^r \end{bmatrix}$$

$$\mathbf{D}_1^r = \begin{bmatrix} b_0^r & \cdots & c_0^r & a_0^r \end{bmatrix}$$

(8b)

and the consequent linear models take the form of the MISO discrete state space equations given by:

$$\mathbf{x}_1^r(k+1) = \Phi_1^r \mathbf{x}_1^r(k) + \Gamma_1^r \mathbf{u}(k)$$
$$y_1^r(k) = \mathbf{C}_1^r \mathbf{x}_1^r(k) + \mathbf{D}_1^r \mathbf{u}(k)$$

(9)

where $\mathbf{x}_1^r(k) \in \mathbf{R}^{zy}$ is the state vector, $y_1^r(k) \in \mathbf{R}$ is output of the local system, $\mathbf{u}(k) \in \mathbf{R}^{S+1}$ is the input vector and, $\Phi_1^r, \Gamma_1^r, \mathbf{C}_1^r$ and $\mathbf{D}_1^r$ are system matrices with appropriate dimensions.

For the MIMO systems, it is necessary to obtain the corresponding state space equations (9) for the each of existing output. So subsequently, if the dimension of the system output is m and simultaneously the identified T-S fuzzy model is consist of R rules for every single row of the system output vector then the model that corresponds to the rth rule consequent can be described by following discrete state-space equation set:

Figure 2. Modified T-S fuzzy model

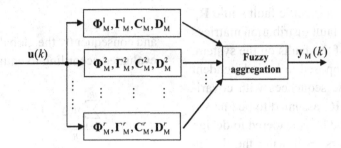

$$\mathbf{x}_{\mathrm{M}}^{r}(k+1) = \Phi_{\mathrm{M}}^{r}\mathbf{x}_{\mathrm{M}}^{r}(k) + \Gamma_{\mathrm{M}}^{r}\mathbf{u}(k)$$
$$\mathbf{y}_{\mathrm{M}}^{r}(k) = \mathbf{C}_{\mathrm{M}}^{r}\mathbf{x}_{\mathrm{M}}^{r}(k) + \mathbf{D}_{\mathrm{M}}^{r}\mathbf{u}(k) \qquad (10)$$

where $\mathbf{y}_{\mathrm{M}}{}^{r}(k) \in \mathbf{R}^{m}$, $\mathbf{x}_{\mathrm{M}}{}^{r}(k) \in \mathbf{R}^{zyxm}$ is now output and state vector of the local system respectively. The system matrices are given by:

$$\Phi_{\mathrm{M}}^{r} = \begin{bmatrix} \Phi_{1}^{r} & 0 & 0 & \cdots & 0 \\ 0 & \Phi_{2}^{r} & 0 & \cdots & 0 \\ \vdots & \vdots & \vdots & \ddots & \vdots \\ 0 & 0 & 0 & \cdots & 0 \\ 0 & 0 & 0 & \cdots & \Phi_{m}^{r} \end{bmatrix} \Phi_{\mathrm{M}}^{r} = \begin{bmatrix} \Phi_{1}^{r} \\ \Phi_{2}^{r} \\ \vdots \\ \Phi_{m}^{r} \end{bmatrix}$$

$$\mathbf{C}_{\mathrm{M}}^{r} = \begin{bmatrix} \mathbf{C}_{1}^{r} & 0 & \cdots & 0 \\ 0 & \mathbf{C}_{2}^{r} & \cdots & 0 \\ \vdots & \vdots & \ddots & \vdots \\ 0 & 0 & \cdots & \mathbf{C}_{m}^{r} \end{bmatrix} \qquad \mathbf{D}_{\mathrm{M}}^{r} = \begin{bmatrix} \mathbf{D}_{1}^{r} \\ \mathbf{D}_{2}^{r} \\ \vdots \\ \mathbf{D}_{m}^{r} \end{bmatrix}$$

$$(11)$$

and the global output vector of the system is inferred from its local versions as it is showed in Figure 2.

In accordance with equation (4) the output vector of the global model can be obtained using this expression:

$$\mathbf{y}_{\mathrm{M}} = \frac{\displaystyle\sum_{r=1}^{R} w_{r}\mathbf{y}_{\mathrm{M}}^{r}}{\displaystyle\sum_{r=1}^{R} w_{r}} \qquad (12)$$

whereas the membership grade functions w_{r} ($r = 1,2,\ldots,R$) are computed as follows:

$$w_{r} = \min\left[\mu_{A_{S,j}^{r}}(\mathbf{U}(k))\right] \qquad (13)$$

where $\mathbf{U}(k) = (u_{1}(k), u_{1}(k-1), \ldots, u_{S}(k), \ldots, u_{S}(k-j))$.

It follows from above that the all consequents related to the particular rules of the T-S fuzzy model take the form of the linear state space equations, so that it is possible to design the Klaman filter for each of the linear submodels to facilitate the residual generation problem solving based on the bank of the Kalman filters.

Residual Generation

Suppose, according to equation (1), that the local faulty stochastic system related to the particular rule of the parametrized T-S fuzzy model can be described by the linear discrete state-space equations in the following form:

$$\mathbf{x}_{\mathrm{M}}^{r}(k+1) = \Phi_{\mathrm{M}}^{r}\mathbf{x}_{\mathrm{M}}^{r}(k) + \Gamma_{\mathrm{M}}^{r}\mathbf{u}(k) + \mathbf{R}_{1}^{r}\mathbf{f}(k) + \mathbf{w}^{r}(k)$$
$$\bar{\mathbf{y}}_{\mathrm{M}}^{r}(k) = \mathbf{C}_{\mathrm{M}}^{r}\mathbf{x}_{\mathrm{M}}^{r}(k) + \mathbf{R}_{2}^{r}\mathbf{f}(k) + \mathbf{v}^{r}(k)$$

$$(14)$$

where:

$$\bar{\mathbf{y}}_{\mathrm{M}}^{r}(k) = \mathbf{y}_{\mathrm{M}}^{r}(k) - \mathbf{D}_{\mathrm{M}}^{r}\mathbf{u}(k) \qquad (15)$$

As mentioned before $\mathbf{f}(k)$ is unknown function of time corresponds to a specific fault while $\mathbf{R}_1^r$ and $\mathbf{R}_2^r$ are the known fault distribution matrices represents the effect of the faults on the system. $\mathbf{w}^r(k)$ and $\mathbf{v}^r(k)$ are supposed to be independent zero-mean white noise sequences with covariance matrices $\mathbf{Q}^r$ and $\mathbf{R}^r$, assumed to be known. A fault free case should be considered to design the local optimal filters. Following the design procedure as presented here (Grewal & Andrews, 2001) the structure of Kalman filter producing the optimal state vector estimate of the stochastic system is then:

$$\hat{\mathbf{x}}_M^r(k|k) =$$
$$\hat{\mathbf{x}}_M^r(k|k-1) + \mathbf{K}_f^r(k)(\mathbf{y}(k) - (\mathbf{C}_M^r\hat{\mathbf{x}}_M^r(k|k-1) + \mathbf{D}_M^r\mathbf{u}(k)))$$

(16)

where $\hat{\mathbf{x}}_M^r(k|k-1)$ is the state estimate extrapolation. $\mathbf{K}_f^r(k)$ is the Kalman gain matrix and it should be designed to achieve minimum variance of the estimation error. Hence, gain matrix is determined by this:

$$\mathbf{K}_f^r(k) =$$
$$\mathbf{P}^r(k|k-1)\mathbf{C}_M^{r\,T}(\mathbf{C}_M^r\mathbf{P}^r(k|k-1)\mathbf{C}_M^{r\,T} + \mathbf{R}^r)^{-1}$$

(17)

where $\mathbf{P}^r(k|k-1)$ is a priory estimation error covariance matrix and it is a function of its last a posteriori value. A posteriori covariance matrix of the estimation error is then given by:

$$\mathbf{P}^r(k|k) = \mathbf{P}^r(k|k-1) - \mathbf{K}_f^r\mathbf{C}_M^r\mathbf{P}^r(k|k-1)$$

(18)

Following all above, there is no obstruction to design the local optimal filters computing the optimal state vector estimate. Hence, to obtain the local system output estimate the following expression should be evaluate:

$$\hat{\mathbf{y}}_M^r = \mathbf{C}_M^r\hat{\mathbf{x}}_M^r(k|k-1) + \mathbf{D}_M^r\mathbf{u}(k)$$

(19)

and consequently the global system estimation is evaluated according to equation (12):

$$\hat{\mathbf{y}}_M(k) = \frac{\sum_{r=1}^{R} w_r \hat{\mathbf{y}}_M^r(k)}{\sum_{r=1}^{R} w_r}$$

(20)

Having the output vector estimation, the residual vector takes the form:

$$\mathbf{r}(k) = \mathbf{y}(k) - \hat{\mathbf{y}}_M(k) = \gamma(k)$$

(21)

Note that the equation (14) represents the general form of the rth local linear model belongs to the rth consequent. Because the successful application of the filter requires determination of the covariance matrices $\mathbf{Q}^r$ and $\mathbf{R}^r$ for each subsystem, some complication may arise. Indeed it depends on the particular practical situation but one suggestion to solve this problem is to assume that the stochastic properties of noises $\mathbf{w}^r(k)$ and $\mathbf{v}^r(k)$ are the same for all subsystems. Thus it is possible to estimate or set the instrumental matrices only from the global point of view and subsequently all local versions of these matrices are equal to each other. Some few propositions how to estimate or adjust the instrumental matrices are presented in (Kay, 1998; Witczak, 2006; Uppal, Patton & Witczak, 2006).

Residual Evaluation

Note that the residual vector given by equation (21) is, in fact, the global innovation process that can be computed from its local versions using the fuzzy fusion according to equation (4). Since the innovations $\gamma(k)$, $\gamma(k-1)$,..., $\gamma(0)$ are statistically independent of one another, the generalized likelihood ratio test (GLRT) can be performed to analyze if a fault has occurred or not. The GLR test is not only method appropriate for decision-making, however this chapter only deals with test that is mentioned below.

The hypotheses test can be expressed in terms of the innovation:

$$H_0 : \quad \gamma(k) = \gamma_0(k)$$
$$H_1 : \quad \gamma(k) = \gamma_0(k) + \rho(k, k_f) \tag{22}$$

Here $\gamma_0(k)$ is the innovation in the absence of the fault, and $\rho(k, k_f)$ is additive fault signature, which can be recursively computed (Willsky & Jones, 1976). k_f is the unknown time at which the fault occurs. Provided that innovation has the Gaussian distribution the generalized likelihood ratio for hypothesis denoted by equation (22) it can be derived in the following form (Willsky & Jones, 1976; Fojtik, 2006):

$$\lambda(k) = \max_{1 \leq k_f \leq k}(\mathbf{d}^T(k, k_f)\mathbf{S}^{-1}(k, k_f)\mathbf{d}(k, k_f)) \tag{23}$$

where $\mathbf{d}(k, k_f)$ is a least square estimate of the fault magnitude vector $\mathbf{f}(k)$ and $\mathbf{S}(k, k_f)$ is the error covariance of estimate of the vector $\mathbf{f}(k)$. $\mathbf{d}(k, k_f)$ and $\mathbf{S}(k, k_f)$ are obtained from the following expressions (Willsky & Jones, 1976; Fojtik, 2006):

$$\mathbf{d}(k, k_f) = \frac{\sum_{r=1}^{R} w_r \mathbf{d}^r(k, k_f)}{\sum_{r=1}^{R} w_r}$$
$$\mathbf{S}(k, k_f) = \frac{\sum_{r=1}^{R} w_r \mathbf{S}^r(k, k_f)}{\sum_{r=1}^{R} w_r} \tag{24}$$

where $\mathbf{d}^r(k, k_f)$, $\mathbf{S}^r(k, k_f)$ can be computed recursively (Basseville & Nikiforov, 1993) and w_r are corresponding membership grade functions.

To make a decision whether the fault has occurred, it is necessary to compare equation (23) to a properly chosen threshold. For reduction of memory and computation amount requirements, it is convenient to make the comparison at each time k inside a finite data window. Threshold selection is a trade-off between the false alarm rate and the detection time (Willsky & Jones, 1976).

Solutions and Recommendations

The best way to make majority of the advantages as well as problems obvious, is by application of the proposed fault diagnostic solution to the particular system. At first, a laboratory three-tank system model is concerned. The three-tank system, shown in Figure 3 is a non-linear system consisting of three tanks of circular cross section that are connected to each other through connecting pipes of circular cross-section.

There are two inputs to the system – the incoming flows $Q_1(t)$ and $Q_2(t)$. Assume that water levels $h_1(t)$ and $h_3(t)$ are measurable output variables while water level in the tank 2 is not available. System is parameterized as follows: $s_{13} = s_{23} = s_0 = 0,31$ cm^2, $A = 0,0707$ m^2. The task is to detect the fault occurrence represented by the leaks in the tanks using the proposed fault diagnosis scheme.

The first stage to design fault diagnosis system is to identify the three-tank system. The goal of the identification is to obtain the required form of the TS model. The three-tank system has two inputs and two outputs. A non-linear SIMULINK model is used to generate data for identification. Then the Anfis MATLAB environment has been used to identify TS model. The inputs of the TS model are $Q_1(t)$, $Q_2(t)$ and its past values up to second order together with delayed samples of output variables $h_1(t)$ and $h_3(t)$. Input signal variation is chosen from 0,0001 m^{3}s^{-1} up to 0,0005 m^{3}s^{-1} for $Q_1(t)$ and from 0,0004 m^{3}s^{-1} to 0,0008 m^{3}s^{-2} for $Q_2(t)$. For the antecedents double Gaussian membership functions are used with $Q_1(t)$ and $Q_2(t)$ being the

Figure 3. Three-tank system scheme

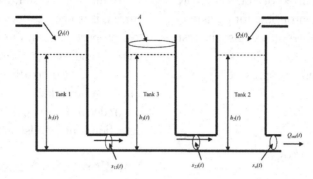

Figure 4. Likelihood ratio when leak in tank 1 is occurred

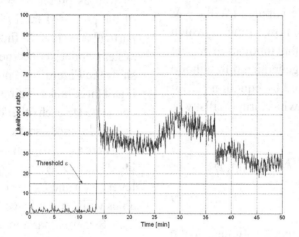

antecedent variables. The consequents are linear regression models and should be converted to its corresponding state-space representation. The mean squared errors for the two outputs are found to be $e_{r1} = 1,529.10^{-4}$ and $e_{r2} = 5,4215.10^{-5}$. The final TS model is consists of nine rules and simultaneously the consequents take the form of state-space equations.

A variety of abrupt faults (leaks) has been considered over the simulation experiments. Figure 4 shows that an abrupt leak occurs in tank 1 at 13 minutes and 20 seconds with the magnitude $0,0003$ m^3s^{-1} and this leak is correctly detected. The generalized likelihood ratio exceeds the threshold at 4 seconds and the threshold is chosen with respect to a tradeoff between the false alarm rate and the detection time and also regarding the

fact, that the residual vector has a χ^2 distribution. The threshold is find to be $\varepsilon = 14,89$.

Naturally, if no faults occur, the likelihood ratio does not exceed the chosen threshold. It follows from Figure 4 that there is some behavior changes of the likelihood ratio after the detection, mainly at 36 minutes. This effect can be observed when the change of the operation point has been realized and is caused by unequal identified model accuracy in the different operation conditions. The disadvantage, mentioned above, can be minimized by making the diagnosis system robust against the modeling uncertainty.

Another more practical application is dealing with the steel continuous casting process. This practical case has demonstrated that the detection

Figure 5. Schematic of the mould

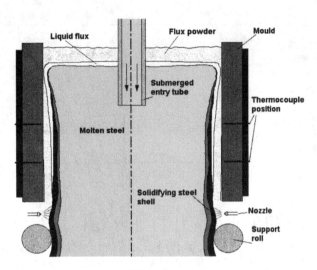

results can be used for further additional analysis to prevent the system breakout.

During the continuous casting process molten steel flows from a ladle, through a tundish into the mould, see Figure 5.

Molten steel should be protected from exposure to air by a flux powder and by ceramic entry tube between the vessels. The water-cooled walls of the mold extract heat to solidify a shell that contains the liquid pool. Drive rolls lower in the machine continuously withdraw the shell from the mould at a casting speed that matches the flow of incoming steel, so the process ideally runs in steady state. Below the mould exit, the solidifying steel shell acts as a container to support the remaining molten steel. Water and air mist sprays cool the surface of the blank between rolls to maintain its surface temperature until the molten core is solid. After the center is completely solid, the blank can be torch cut into the slabs.

To prevent the system breakdown and also to ensure the final product quality level, the presence of the certain diagnostic system seems to be necessary. One of the worst cases that can arise during the casting process is breakout. It is situation, when the molten steel bursts through the shell. One way to predict and prevent the breakouts

is to monitor the temperature fluctuations in the mould walls (Yu, 2001). To do so, there is the sets of the thermocouples installed in this walls, see Figure 5. One set is consists of two thermocouples. The first is positioned in the middle of the mould height and the second is installed in its quarter. All sets are then uniformly distributed over the whole mould perimeter.

Each presence of a surface abnormality causes a corresponding deterioration in the particular thermocouple signal. This situation can be interpreted as a presence of the fault in the system needed to be detected. In the following, the fault diagnostic scheme will be designed only for one set of thermocouples that represent the outputs of the system to be diagnosed. For the others sets the diagnostic scheme can be designed similarly.

In this case the system under consideration has three inputs and two outputs. The inputs are the level of the steel in the mould $h(t)$, casting speed $v(t)$ and flow of the cooling water through the mould $Q_c(t)$ whereas the outputs are the temperature in the middle $T_1(t)$ and in the quarter $T_2(t)$ of the mould height. The data for identification have been obtained from the real process. The Anfis MATLAB environment has been used to identify TS model again.

Figure 6. Likelihood ratio when two successive faults have occurred

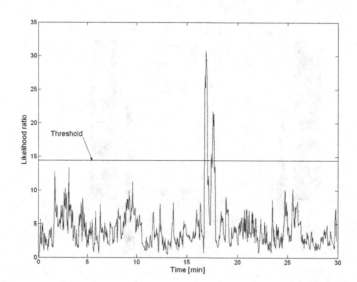

The mean squared errors for the two outputs are found to be $e_{r1} = 0,1436$ and $e_{r2} = 0,0843$. The final TS model is consists of 27 rules and the consequents take the form of state-space equations as in the previous example.

The task is to detect any unexpected temperature variations – the faults. The Figure 6 shows the situation when two successive faults have been detected.

When fault is occurred, the generalized likelihood ratio exceeds the threshold that is chosen with respect to a tradeoff between the false alarm rate and the detection time and its value is $\varepsilon = 14,89$. One way to exploit the detection results is then evaluation of the time between two successive detected faults and its shape and if they are in relation to the casting velocity, the rise of the breakout conditions is the most likely.

As previously, if no faults occur the likelihood ratio should be very close to zero value. However, it is evident from Figure 6 that the detection performance is not always so ideal. In the most cases, there are the modeling errors, which can cause false or missed alarms. Because of this phenomenon, it is convenient to make the diagnostic algorithm robust against the model-ing uncertainty. It is the same demand as in the example above. Hence, the robustness seems to be significant for the detection process. Another more simple way to tackle mentioned problem is to choose the threshold value more carefully based on the sufficient range of the experiments with regard to for example requested false or missed alarms rate.

FUTURE RESEARCH DIRECTIONS

Fault detection and isolation represents a wide field of study and there has been always combination of knowledge from many different research areas. If only observer-based approach is considered, the residual generator design producing the residual signals that are affected only by the faults occurred is essential. As it has been pointed out in the previous section, this is not generally true. No matter how good is model, there are some model uncertainties, disturbances and other perturbations usually presented here and consequently they can cause the strong fault diagnostic performance degradation. Hence, there has been a great effort to make the residuals insensitive to any disturbing influence, in other words to make the residuals robust against the disturbances. There are many methods in the literature to solve this problem. For example, the usage of the unknown input observer allows disturbance decoupling from the residuals. However, each of the methods has its own advantages and disadvantages as well. Above mentioned method assumes that the disturbance distribution matrix is known a priory. It need not be generally true. Nevertheless, the authors propose some methods for determination of this distribution matrix. It is following from above, that there is a large area for further work and research.

Note also that, the there is no universal method for threshold choice in the decision making stage. Some of the methods uses for example adaptive threshold. However, suggestion of expert system exploitation for threshold setting seems to be interesting. Finally let make a remark that at present, the robust fault isolation receives a great attention as the important part of the fault diagnosis process.

CONCLUSION

This chapter has presented the fault diagnosis scheme using the modified TS model. At the presence of the chapter, a tutorial treatment on the basic principles and terminology of observer based fault diagnosis with the emphasis on the non-linear process modeling has been presented. At the same section, other FDI methods have been discussed briefly as well.

In order to obtain an adequate model of the non-linear system to be monitored use of the Takagi-Sugeno fuzzy model has been suggested. Availability of the model is necessary as the observer-based approach is considered. Furthermore this kind of the model allows the application of the linear techniques even if the system under consideration is non-linear. In addition, it enables to overcome the difficulties in linear methods for dealing with non-linearity and

non-linear observer design as well. Note that, the Takagi-Sugeno, fuzzy model describes the non-linear dynamic system by its decomposition onto number of linear submodels. Hence regarding the monitored system is suppose to be stochastic, the Kalman filter has been designed for the each of the local linear systems to obtain the local residual vectors computed as a difference between the estimated and real system output. Subsequently the global residual vector has been constructed and with respect to the fact that the time instances of the residual vector are statistically independent of one another, the generalized likelihood ratio test has been performed to analyze if a fault has occurred or not.

The advantages, disadvantages and problems of the proposed approach have been illustrated by the two practical examples. It follows from the second example, that the fault diagnosis results can be used for further analysis to obtain the additional information included. Besides some implementation remarks such as a threshold choice, it has been showed, that the robustness of the residuals against disturbances is significant for the detection process.

Finally, some perspectives and remarks in the field of robust residual generation have been discussed as well as some suggestions for the threshold setting and further research directions have been touched.

REFERENCES

Åström, K. J., & Wittenmark, B. (1997). *Computer-controlled systems: Theory and design* (3rd ed.). Upper Saddle River, NJ: Prentice Hall.

Basseville, M., & Nikiforov, I. V. (1993). *Detection of Abrupt Changes: Theory and Application*. Upper Saddle River, NJ: Prentice Hall.

Brown, M., & Hartus, Ch. (1994). *Neurofuzzy adaptive modeling and control*. Upper Saddle River, NJ: Prentice Hall.

Chen, J., & Patton, R. J. (1999). *Robust model-based fault diagnosis for dynamic systems*. Norwell, MA: Kluwer Academic Publishers.

Chow, E. Y., & Willsky, A. S. (1984). Analytical redundancy and the design of robust detection systems. *IEEE Transactions on Automatic Control, 29*(7), 603–614. doi:10.1109/TAC.1984.1103593

Fojtik, P. (2006). *Fuzzy regression in non-linear systems diagnostics*. PhD Thesis (In Czech), Brno University of Technology, Czech Republic.

Frank, P. M. (1990). Fault diagnosis in dynamic system using analytical and knowledge based redundancy – a survey and some new results. *Automatica, 26*(3), 459–474. doi:10.1016/0005-1098(90)90018-D

Frank, P. M., & Keller, L. (1980). Sensitivity discriminating observer design for instrument failure detection. *IEEE Transactions on Aerospace and Electronic Systems, AES-16*(4), 460–467. doi:10.1109/TAES.1980.308975

Gertler, J. (1993). Analytical redundancy methods in failure detection and isolation. *Control-Theory and Advanced Technology, 9*(1), 259–285.

Gertler, J. (1998). *Fault detection and diagnosis in engineering systems*. New York: Marcel Dekker.

Grewal, M. S., & Andrews, A. P. (2001). *Kalman Filtering: Theory and Practice Using MATLAB*. New York: Wiley Interscience.

Hengy, D., & Frank, P. M. (1986). Component failure detection via nonlinear state observers. In *Proceedings of IFAC Workshop on Fault Detection and Safety in Chemical Plants* (pp. 153-157). Kyoto, Japan.

Kay, S. M. (1998). Fundamentals of statistical signal processing: *Vol. 2. Detection theory*. Upper Saddle River, NJ: Prentice Hall PTR.

Korbicz, J., Koscielny, J. M., Kowalczuk, Z., & Cholewa, W. (Eds.). (2004). *Fault Diagnosis. Models, Artificial Intelligence, Applications*. Berlin, Heidelberg: Springer-Verlag.

Korbicz, J., & Kowal, M. (2007). Neuro-fuzzy networks and their application to fault detection of dynamical systems. *Engineering Applications of Artificial Intelligence, 20*(5), 609–617. doi:10.1016/j.engappai.2006.11.009

Maki, Y., & Loparo, K. A. (1997). A neural-network approach to fault detection and diagnosis in industrial processes. *IEEE Transactions on Control Systems Technology, 5*(6), 529–541. doi:10.1109/87.641399

Metenidis, M. F., Witczak, M., & Korbicz, J. (2004). A novel genetic programming approach to non-linear system modelling: Application to the DAMADICS benchmark problem. *Engineering Applications of Artificial Intelligence, 17*(4), 363–370. doi:10.1016/j.engappai.2004.04.009

Patan, K., & Parisini, T. (2005). Identification of neural dynamic models for fault detection and isolation: the case of a real sugar evaporation process. *Journal of Process Control, 15*(1), 67–79. doi:10.1016/j.jprocont.2004.04.001

Patan, K., Witczak, K., & Korbicz, J. (2008). Toward robustness in neural network based fault diagnosis. *International Journal of Applied Mathematics and Computer Science, 18*(4), 443–454. doi:10.2478/v10006-008-0039-2

Patton, R. J., & Chen, J. (1997). Observer-based fault detection and isolation: robustness and applications. *Control Engineering Practice, 5*(5), 671–682. doi:10.1016/S0967-0661(97)00049-X

Patton, R. J., Chen, J., & Siew, T. M. (1994). Fault diagnosis in nonlinear dynamic systems via neural networks. In [Warwick, UK.]. *Proceedings of the IEE International Conference: Control, 94,* 1346–1351.

Patton, R. J., Frank, P. M., & Clark, R. N. (Eds.). (2000). *Issues of Fault Diagnosis for Dynamic Systems.* London: Springer-Verlag.

Porter, L. L., & Passino, K. M. (1995). Genetic Adaptive Observers. *Engineering Applications of Artificial Intelligence, 8*(3), 261–269. doi:10.1016/0952-1976(95)00007-N

Sohlberg, B. (1998). Monitoring and failure diagnosis of a steel strip process. *IEEE Transactions on Control Systems Technology, 6*(2), 294–303. doi:10.1109/87.664195

Takagi, T., & Sugeno, M. (1985). Fuzzy identification of systems and its application to modeling control. *IEEE Transactions on Systems, Man, and Cybernetics, 15*(1), 116–132.

Uppal, F. J., Patton, R. J., & Witczak, M. (2006). A neuro-fuzzy multiple-model observer approach to robust fault diagnosis based on the DAMADICS benchmark problem. *Control Engineering Practice, 14*(6), 699–717. doi:10.1016/j.conengprac.2005.04.015

Watanabe, K., & Himmelblau, D. M. (1982). Instrument fault detection in systems with uncertainties. *International Journal of Systems Science, 13*(2), 137–158. doi:10.1080/00207728208926337

Willsky, A. S. (1976). A survey of design methods for failure detection in dynamic systems. *Automatica, 12*(6), 601–611. doi:10.1016/0005-1098(76)90041-8

Willsky, A. S., & Jones, H. L. (1976). A generalized likelihood ratio approach to the detection and estimation of jumps in linear systems. *IEEE Transactions on Automatic Control, 21*(1), 108–112. doi:10.1109/TAC.1976.1101146

Witczak, K. (2006). Advances in model-based fault diagnosis with evolutionary algorithms and neural networks. *International Journal of Applied Mathematics and Computer Science, 16*(1), 85–99.

Witczak, M., Korbicz, J., Mrugalski, M., & Patton, R. J. (2006). A GMDH neural network-based approach to robust fault diagnosis: Application to the DAMADICS benchmark problem. *Control Engineering Practice, 14*(6), 671–683. doi:10.1016/j.conengprac.2005.04.007

Witczak, M., Obuchowicz, A., & Korbicz, J. (2002). Genetic programming based approaches to identification and fault diagnosis of non-linear dynamic systems. *International Journal of Control, 75*(13), 1012–1031. doi:10.1080/00207170210156224

Yu, K. O. (2001). *Modeling for casting and solidification processing.* Boca Raton, FL: CRC.

ADDITIONAL READING

Babuska, R. (1998). *Fuzzy Modeling for Control.* Boston: Kluwer Academic Publishers.

Bocaniala, C. D., & Sa da Costa, J. (2006). Application of a novel fuzzy classifier to fault detection and isolation of the DAMADICS benchmark problem. *Control Engineering Practice, 14*(6), 653–669. doi:10.1016/j.conengprac.2005.06.008

Chen, H. Y. (1990). Adaptive robust observers for non-linear uncertain systems. *International Journal of Systems Science, 21*(5), 803–814. doi:10.1080/00207729008910416

Chen, J., Patton, R. J., & Zhang, H. Y. (1996). Design of unknown input observers and robust fault-detection filters. *International Journal of Control, 63*(1), 85–105. doi:10.1080/00207179608921833

Chiang, L. H., Russell, E. L., & Braatz, R. D. (2001). *Fault detection and diagnosis in industrial systems.* London, UK: Springer-Verlag.

Edwards, C., Spurgeon, S. K., & Patton, R. J. (2000). Sliding mode observers for fault detection and isolation. *Automatica, 36*(4), 541–553. doi:10.1016/S0005-1098(99)00177-6

Frank, P. M. (1996). Analytical and quantitative model-based fault diagnosis: A survey and some new results. *European Journal of Control, 1*(2), 6–28.

Frank, P. M., & Ding, X. (1997). Survey of robust residual generation and evaluation methods in observer-based fault detection systems. *Journal of Process Control, 7*(6), 403–424. doi:10.1016/S0959-1524(97)00016-4

Gertler, J., & Cao, J. (2005). Design of optimal structured residuals from partial principal component models for fault diagnosis in linear systems. *Journal of Process Control, 15*(5), 585–603. doi:10.1016/j.jprocont.2004.10.005

Gertler, J., & Monajemy, R. (1995). Generating fixed direction residuals with dynamic parity equations. *Automatica, 31*(4), 627–635. doi:10.1016/0005-1098(95)98494-Q

Gustafsson, F. (2001). *Adaptive filtering and change detection*. West Sussex, UK: Wiley.

Gustafsson, F. (2006). Statistical signal processing approaches to fault detection. *6th IFAC symposium on fault detection, supervision and safety of technical processes SAFEPROCESS 2006* (pp. 24-35). Beijing, P.R. China: Elsevier Science Ltd.

Isermann, R. (1997). Supervision fault-detection and fault-diagnosis methods – an introduction. *Control Engineering Practice, 5*(5), 639–652. doi:10.1016/S0967-0661(97)00046-4

Klir, B. J., & Yuan, B. (1995). *Fuzzy Sets and Fuzzy Logic – Theory and Application*. Upper Saddle River, NJ: Prentice Hall.

Kowal, M., & Korbicz, J. (2005). Robust fault detection using neuro-fuzzy networks. In *Proceedings of the 16th IFAC World Congress* (CDROM). Prague, Czech Republic.

Kruse, R., Gebhardt, J., & Klawonn, F. (1993). *Fuzzy-Systems*. Stuttgart, Germany: Teubner.

Li, P., & Du, X. (2006). The observer design for nonlinear system with both input and output unknown disturbances. *6th IFAC symposium on fault detection, supervision and safety of technical processes SAFEPROCESS 2006* (pp. 192-197). Beijing, P.R. China: Elsevier Science Ltd.

Ljung, L. (1999). *System identification: Theory for the user* (2nd ed.). Upper Saddle River, NJ: Prentice Hall PTR.

Mandami, E. H., & Gaines, B. R. (1981). *Fuzzy Reasoning and its Application*. London, UK: Academic Press.

Mangoubi, R. S. (1998). *Robust estimation and failure detection*. London, UK: Springer-Verlag.

Novak, V. (1992). *Fuzzy Approach to Reasoning and Decision Making*. Dordrecht, The Netherlands: Prague and Kluwer Academia.

Novak, V., Perfilieva, I., & Mockor, J. (1999). *Mathematical Principles of Fuzzy Logic*. Boston, Dordrecht: Kluwer.

Patton, R. J., Frank, P. M., & Clark, R. N. (1989). *Fault Diagnosis in Dynamic Systems: Theory and Application*. Upper Saddle River, NJ: Prentice Hall.

Pedrycz, W. (1993). *Fuzzy Control and Fuzzy Systems*. Taunton, New York: Research Studies Press/Wiley.

Sugeno, M. (1985). *Industrial Application of Fuzzy Control*. Amsterdam: North-Holland.

Tanaka, H., Uejima, K., & Asahi, K. (1982). Linear Regression Analysis with Fuzzy Models. *IEEE Transactions on Systems, Man, and Cybernetics, 12*(6), 903–907. doi:10.1109/TSMC.1982.4308925

Uppal, F. J., Patton, R. J., & Witczak, M. (2003). A hybrid neuro-fuzzy and de-coupling approach applied to the DAMADICS benchmark problem. *5ᵗʰ IFAC symposium on fault detection, supervision and safety of technical processes SAFEPROCESS 2003* (pp. 1059-1064). Washington, DC: Omnipress.

White, Ch. J., & Lakany, H. (2008). A fuzzy inference system for fault detection and isolation: Application to a fluid system. *Expert Systems with Applications, 35*(3), 1021–1033. doi:10.1016/j.eswa.2007.08.029

Witczak, M., Patton, R. J., & Korbicz, J. (2003). Fault detection with observers and genetic programming: Application to the DAMADICS benchmark problem. *5ᵗʰ IFAC symposium on fault detection, supervision and safety of technical processes SAFEPROCESS 2003* (pp. 1203-1208). Washington, DC: Omnipress.

KEY TERMS AND DEFINITIONS

Analytical Redundancy: Exploitation of the at least two way to determine a real variable and simultaneously one way uses the analytical model of the system.

Disturbance: The unknown and undesirable input acting on the system.

Fault: An unpermitted deviation of at least one characteristic property or parameter of the system from the acceptable condition.

Fault Diagnosis: Involves fault detection, its isolation and identification. That is determination of the kind, size, location and starting time of the fault.

Fuzzy Logic: The form of multi-valued logic derived from fuzzy set theory to deal with reasoning that is approximate rather than precise.

Fuzzy Modeling: The part of the modeling site deals with applications of fuzzy logic to modeling, environmental assessment, and related topics.

Fuzzy Reasoning: A process of approximate solution of a system of relational assignment equations.

Fuzzy Sets: The generalize classical sets, their elements have degrees of membership taking values in the closed interval from 0 to 1.

Fuzzy T-S Model: The model described by fuzzy IF-THEN rules which represents local input-output relations of a nonlinear system in the form of the linear regression equations.

Residual: A fault indication signal, based on a difference between measurements and estimations.

Section 2
Analysis

Chapter 7
Towards Knowledge Driven Individual Integrated Indicators of Innovativeness

Tadeusz Baczko
Polish Academy of Sciences, Poland

Janusz Kacprzyk
Polish Academy of Sciences, Poland

Sławomir Zadrożny
Warsaw School of Information Technology (WIT), Poland

ABSTRACT

Innovativeness of the enterprises is a key factor for the development of a national economy and has a crucial impact on the prosperity of a country. Governments spend a lot of efforts developing, organizing and then implementing national innovation systems. Proper functioning of such a system requires a lot of information to be gathered. The situation has to be constantly monitored as the innovation is an inherently dynamic phenomenon. An important goal of information gathering is learning a profile and specifics of the most innovative enterprises, promote them and make them more visible. Due to that some non-standard data analysis techniques are needed which can provide results of data gathering in a form suitable for the specific goals of the analysis. In this paper a pioneering system for innovativeness evaluation based on integrated indicators constructed for individual enterprises in Poland is described. An evaluation methodology has been developed, incorporating both quantitative and qualitative characteristics of the enterprises. The linguistic summaries of data are shown to be a promising data analysis tool, meeting the criteria which are discussed as relevant for the task considered. Briefly, these summaries make it possible to grasp the very essence of the collected data and communicate it in an intuitive, natural language like form.

DOI: 10.4018/978-1-61692-811-7.ch007

INTRODUCTION

Innovativeness of the enterprises is a key factor for the development of a national economy and for preserving its competitiveness. Governments spend a lot of efforts in developing, organizing and then implementing national innovation systems. Proper functioning of such systems requires a lot of information to be gathered. The situation has to be constantly monitored as innovation is an inherently dynamic phenomenon. Many problems have to be addressed, both at the methodological as well as statistical level. In this paper, a Polish programme of the use of micro-data for a multi-dimensional evaluation of corporate innovativeness is shown as a base for the improvement of communication among various stakeholders of the National Innovation System. The system covers the whole spectrum of the companies in terms of, e.g., their size, ownership and scope of activities. Thus, in particular, micro-companies, SMEs, and large as well as international corporations are well represented.

Though the paper is concerned with innovativeness at the national level, along the basic lines given in, for instance, (Archibugi, Howells & Michie, 1999), many papers in (Llerena & Matt, 2004), (Malerba & Brusoni 2007) or (Malerba & Cantner, 2007), similar issues and solutions may be found in the regional context (cf. papers in Baraczyk, Cook & Heidenreich, 1996, or Howells, 2005), or in a sectoral context (cf. Malerba, 2004). Clearly, specific features of Poland have been reflected taking into account analyses given in Baczko (2007a; 2007b; 2008; 2009a). The paper is in the framework related to the future science and technology and innovation indicators, and the challenges implied (Baczko, 2009b).

A characteristic feature of the system proposed is the use of public indicators of innovativeness which have been elaborated specifically for its purposes. This means a shift in the paradigm of public statistics. Namely, a classical statistical yearbook with averages is proposed to be supplemented with a new system of public indicators which can be used at the national and international level. This is in line with the recommendations of the Frascati Manual (OECD, 2003) and the Oslo Manual (OECD, 2005), and international statistical standards according to which these indicators can be easily adjusted to specific requirements of different countries and regions. This system covers many aspects, including market and process innovativeness, research and development expenditures, and the intellectual property rights as well as networking capabilities.

The development of the system was undertaken in order to accomplish various goals. The use of publicly available indicators makes the comparison of innovativeness of the companies more fair and objective. Thus, decisions related to fund allocation in public and private organizations may be based on a more sound basis and the risk assessment cost is reduced (Baczko, 2007a; 2007b). Setting clear, verifiable criteria for the assessment of innovativeness makes it possible to produce regular rankings of companies. This stimulates social processes focused on the dissemination of innovativeness patterns, increases the public awareness of importance of this issue and motivates companies to increased efforts. In fact, the results of such annual rankings based on the developed indicators are announced during the highly visible and prestigious Public Galas of Innovativeness. These events provide a perfect opportunity for developing social and information links among stakeholders of the innovativeness process.

During the preparations for the rankings, a lot of data on the companies in operation in Poland in the years 2004-2006 has been collected. To accomplish this aim, questionnaires containing both quantitative and qualitative data as well as public statistics, patents granted, stock data, firms reports, data concerning signed contracts of EU firms and experts judgments have been used. An important goal of data gathering has been to learn profiles of the most innovative companies. Due to the very specifics of this goal, the use of some non-standard data analysis techniques should be well justified, which grasp the characteristic features of such companies and provide the results in the form suitable for a further analysis and a broad dissemination. For example, the determination of some properties shared by *most* of the highly innovative companies or their subsets may help in building such profiles. It is also important that the results of such an analysis have an intuitive form, easily understandable by a broad audience, not necessarily familiar with the "data analysis jargon". Obviously, the application of standard statistical methods is an important part of the analysis to be undertaken, but if used alone it may not reach the latter goals. Hence in this paper we propose to apply a non-standard analysis of data via verbalization through so-called *linguistic summaries of data*. They meet the aforementioned criteria, making it possible to grasp the very essence of micro data and to present the results in the form of natural language like expressions related to different types of innovative companies.

In Section 2 we present some details of the proposed system for innovativeness evaluation. We focus on the data gathering activities planned, and actually implemented in the years 2004-2006. Section 3 discusses the concept of a linguistic summary of data and puts it in a broader perspective of natural language related data processing and generation. In Section 4 we show some summaries of the data collected in the recent years, in the framework of the proposed innovation assessment system. We conclude the paper with some possible directions of further research.

BACKGROUND

The concept of the proposed innovativeness assessment system is based on some established scientific results in the area of, roughly speaking, information theory and economics. First, we refer to a famous qualitative theory of information developed by Szaniawski (1998). From this perspective information is treated not only as a technical phenomenon but also as an important component for the decision process and it is its role in the decision process which makes it possible to measure information in a meaningful way. Another inspiration for the proposed system comes from the Schumpeterian approach (Mc-Craw, 2007) which points out a crucial role of companies, entrepreneurs, and the workers in the development and implementation of innovativeness. The third foundation of the proposed system is an evolutionary theory of the company which treats the innovation process and the company as if they were the living organisms.

The development of the proposed innovativeness assessment system is conceived to reach several goals. First, it should make possible an in-depth study of the structure of business expenditures for research and development and innovativeness. This is meant as a very important component of the profile of an innovative company. This is in fact an ultimate and utmost goal of the project: to identify the factors deciding on the level of innovativeness of a company. This should help in the preparation of a diagnosis for a company innovativeness-related status and to suggest some measures to put it on the track towards obtaining a higher level. We want to identify and form fractals of an innovation system which could be copied throughout the country.

Another goal, which is indispensable for the reaching of the former, is to stimulate companies to disclose their business expenditures for research and development. Having a system of fair and objective indicators would make this task much easier. Again, it is very important that the results of the analysis of collected data be easy to comprehend and assimilate by a broad audience.

A goal closely related to the first one concerns the optimization of the allocation of public and private expenditures in science, technology and innovations. Such an optimization requires tools to identify most promising companies, branches etc. which are made available by the proposed system. The pattern ("genome") of an innovative company, emerging from the collected data analysis, makes it possible to quickly recognize the most promising companies, even at the very early stages of their development and to support them effectively. A related subgoal is to stimulate the process of increasing business expenditures for research and development. Thanks to the measures for the optimization and assessment, provided by the system, the funds spent should bring faster and better measurable effects. Thus, on a global scale, the data gathered in the framework of the system and their advanced analyses are a prerequisite for strategic planning and control of the innovation process in the economy.

The system for evaluating the innovativeness of companies based on individual integrated indicators, presented in this paper, has been developed in 2005 by the Institute of Economics, Polish Academy of Sciences. The relevant data have been collected from the companies via a special electronic questionnaire based on international and domestic standards. The data collected concern various aspects of innovativeness. For example, the market innovativeness is measured by indicators of the dynamics of a company's sales, export, and employment figures. The raw data is "normalized" with respect to the average data or with respect to the median for the population studied. Sales, export, and employment data from the period considered are compared to the previous period. The assessment of each of the elements of the integrated indicator is based on a logical dependency, involving a comparison of figures for specific companies against comparative indexes. Importantly, the evaluation made on the basis of quantitative data is supplemented by a qualitative evaluation made by experts.

This methodology yields an analysis that ranks the position of individual innovative companies and single out the most important characteristics of the innovativeness process. That makes it possible to identify types of an innovative behavior,

reference models, and characteristics of market innovativeness, process innovativeness, innovation related expenditures, patents obtained, and contracts under the 6th EU Framework Programme.

Research based on above mentioned questionnaire was continued in 2007. It was extended with the additional questionnaire developed by the Institute of Economics, Polish Academy of Sciences in the cooperation with the European University Viadrina in Frankurt (Oder) (Baczko, 2008). Moreover, Dun&Bradstreet Co. was invited to carry out a balance-sheet analysis, drawing upon data from the National Court Register that included a group of more then 25,000 companies. The research was supported by the BRE Bank (Baczko, 2007a). Another important input was provided by external experts from the National Foresight Programme "Poland 2020" who evaluated companies and their products in terms of their future potential.

An important result of the project reported was to demonstrate the viability of constructing innovativeness evaluation criteria on the microeconomic level and to advocate their practical usefulness. The indicators developed were used by representatives of companies, financial institutions, research centers, and public administration. The innovativeness of large, medium-size, small, and micro companies was evaluated, and some models of innovation were identified on the microeconomic level. All these effects of the project should result in initiating a process of boosting corporate RTD spending, implying a gradual change in the structure of RTD expenditures in Poland, and reducing development gaps on the regional and national level.

The development of the system made it possible to characterize over 2500 companies using individual integrated indicators based on micro data and experts evaluations. The ratings and rankings of those companies were published. The indicators are publicly available and contribute to the improvement of the fund allocation and to the reduction of cost of the risk assessment related to fund allocation of public and private organizations. The evaluation system aims at stimulating a social process focused on the innovativeness pattern dissemination and on the increase in fund allocation to innovation, especially among the SMEs.

INTELLIGENT DATA ANALYSIS VIA VERBALIZATION THROUGH LINGUISTIC SUMMARIES

The core element of the novel approach to the analysis of innovativeness proposed in this paper is intelligent data analysis. The recent growth of information technology (IT) has implied, on the one hand, the availability of a huge amount of data (from diverse, often remote databases). What is important is that the cost of having those data available has become low, even for small businesses and organizations due to falling prices of hardware and a rising efficiency of software products. Unfortunately, the raw data alone are often not useful and do not provide "knowledge", hence are not directly applicable per se for supporting any rational human activity, notably those related to business where requirements for speed and efficiency are particularly pronounced.

More important than data themselves are relevant, nontrivial dependencies that are encoded in those data. Unfortunately, they are usually hidden, and their discovery is a non-trivial act that requires some intelligence.

Research in broadly perceived fields of (intelligent) data analysis, data mining, knowledge discovery, etc. has been very intensive for many years, and many effective and efficient tools and techniques have been developed. Notably, statistical methods and tools have been widely used and have yielded many useful and important results. However, they can be viewed as not "human consistent" enough. One of the reasons for this is that for the human being the only fully natural means of articulation and communication is natural language which is strange to the mathematical tools and techniques.

The very essence of virtually all approaches to (intelligent) data analysis, data mining, knowledge discovery, etc. is that from a large (maybe huge) set of source data, which is incomprehensible in its original form to the humans, some smaller set of data, maybe of a different form, is derived that should subsume, or summarize, crucial elements and relations existing in the source data.

Data summarization is therefore one of basic capabilities needed in the above, as well as in many other similar "intelligent" tasks. Since for the human being the only fully natural means of communication is natural language, a linguistic summarization would be very desirable, exemplified – for a data set on employees – by a statement (linguistic summary) "almost all young and well qualified employees are well paid". We will use in this work such linguistic summaries.

Linguistic summaries, introduced by Yager (1982) and then further developed by Kacprzyk, Yager & Zadrożny (2000) are conceived as a tool to summarize the data collected in a table of a relational data base. They are exemplified, in the context considered in this paper, by a (quasi) natural language sentence:

"*Most* of the *small* companies are *highly* profitable" (1)

Such a simple, yet extremely human consistent and intuitive statement does summarize in a concise and very informative way the characteristic features of data that we may be interested in. The italicized linguistic terms "*most*", "*small*" and "*highly*" are inherently imprecise in a way typical for natural language. However, thanks to that, they abstract from unnecessary precision and make it possible to grasp and express some interesting regularities present in data. Obviously, these terms require a proper modeling which may be provided in the framework of *fuzzy logic*. The first term "*most*" is an example of a so-called *linguistic quantifier.* The remaining terms refer to the values of particular attributes of data (here: the features used to describe companies). They may be combined to form more complex expressions, using classical logical connectives ("and" and "or") or some more advanced aggregation operators.

The data set to be summarized may be denoted as follows:

Y = $\{y_1,\ldots, y_n\}$ is a set of records (rows) in a database representing some objects, e.g., companies;

A = $\{A_1,\ldots, A_m\}$ is a set of attributes characterizing objects represented by $y \in Y$, e.g., microeconomic indicators such as net profit or equity in a given year etc., in a database of companies;

Then the components of a linguistic summary of data set *Y* may be defined as follows:

1. a *summarizer S* is an attribute A_j together with a linguistic term defined on the domain of attribute A_j (e.g. "*high* net profit");
2. a linguistic quantifier *Q*, (e.g. "most") expresses in a flexible, human consistent way the size of the population described by a given summary;
3. a *truth (validity) degree T* of a summary is a number from the interval [0, 1] (e.g. 0.7) assessing the truth of a summary treated as a formula of the *calculus of linguistically quantified propositions* (Zadeh, 1983);
4. a *qualifier R* is another attribute A_k together with a linguistic term defined on its domain (e.g. "*small* company" – in terms of the number of employees), determining a fuzzy subset of *Y*, i.e., the population of records which are described by given summary; a qualifier is optional and if it is omitted then the summary concerns the whole population of records.

The concept of a linguistic summary is based on *linguistically quantified propositions*, introduced by Zadeh (Zadeh, 1983). A linguistically quantified proposition, corresponding to (1) may be written as:

$$QRy's \text{ are } S \qquad (2)$$

where *S* is a summarizer expressing a high profitability of a company, *R* is a qualifier expressing its small size, and *Q* is a quantifier expressing the fact that that most companies among those of a small size are highly profitable.

The truth degree *T* of a summary is computed as the truth of the proposition (2). In Zadeh's calculus of linguistically quantified propositions (Zadeh, 1983), a (proportional, nondecreasing) linguistic quantifier *Q* is represented by a fuzzy set in the interval [0, 1]. Each number $x \in [0, 1]$ is interpreted as a proportion of elements of the universe of discourse and its membership degree $\mu_Q(x)$ expresses how this proportion is compatible with the semantics of the quantifier *Q*. For example, for *Q* denoting "most" one may assume (subjectively) the proportion higher than 0.8 (i.e., 80%) as fully compatible with the concept of "most", while the proportion lower than 0.3 (i.e., 30%) as completely incompatible with this concept. Intermediate proportions may be treated as compatible to a degree. Thus quantifier *Q* = "most" may be, e.g., represented by a fuzzy set with the following membership function:

$$\mu_Q(x) = \begin{cases} 1 & for & x \geq 0.8 \\ 2x - 0.6 & for & 0.3 < x < 0.8 \\ 0 & for & x \leq 0.3 \end{cases} \qquad (3)$$

Due to the Zadeh's calculus, the truth value of the proposition (2) is computed as:

$$\text{truth}(QRy's \text{ are } S) = \mu_Q \left(\frac{\sum_{i=1}^{n} (\mu_R(y_i) \wedge \mu_S(y_i))}{\sum_{i=1}^{n} \mu_R(y_i)} \right) \qquad (4)$$

where ∧ denotes the minimum operator, i.e. a ∧ b = min(a, b).

Kacprzyk, Yager & Zadrożny (2000; 2001) pointed out that many aspects of linguistic summaries construction and processing are very relevant for the *fuzzy/flexible querying of databases* too. Kacprzyk & Zadrożny (1995; 2001b) designed and implemented a fuzzy querying tool FQUERY for Access making it possible to execute queries with fuzzy (linguistic) terms in the framework of the conventional Microsoft Access DBMS. This tool supports a wide range of fuzzy (linguistic) terms, including ones that may be exemplified by: "net profit is *low*", "ROA in 2005 is *much greater* than ROA in 2006", and "*most* of the *important* conditions have to be met". It is thus evident that building blocks of fuzzy queries are summarizers and qualifiers used in linguistic summaries.

One should also mention that a very convenient representation of linguistic data summaries may be through so-called *protoforms* (prototypical forms) as suggested by Kacprzyk & Zadrożny (2005) that can represent a wide array of linguistic statements of type (2) representing various concepts and relations. Moreover, a very promising direction in the derivation of linguistic data summaries, as suggested by Kacprzyk & Zadrożny (2009), may be to use tools and techniques of natural language generation (NLG), an area of modern information technology which is rapidly developing.

The fully automatic derivation of a linguistic summary is a difficult task. An interesting alternative is an interactive, semi-automatic mode using a fuzzy querying interface such as provided by the FQUERY for Access package mentioned above. In such a case a user has to propose a candidate summary and the system just checks its validity (truth degree).

Another approach to linguistic summaries starts with an observation on their similarity to (*linguistic*) *association rules* (Kacprzyk, Yager & Zadrożny, 2000; 2001). Namely, the condition and conclusion parts of an association rule (Agrawal & Srikant, 1994) may be interpreted as corresponding to the qualifier *R* and summarizer *S* of an linguistic summary, respectively, and the truth degree of the summary corresponds to the confidence measure of an association rule. This way only a subclass of linguistic summaries may be represented - namely only those with the qualifier and summarizer taking the form of a conjunction of simple conditions. This subclass is however quite rich and, what is most important, may be efficiently generated using algorithms developed for the association rules; cf., (Kacprzyk, Yager & Zadrożny, 2000; 2001) for the details. In the computational experiments reported in the next section we adopted this method for the derivation of linguistic summaries.

COMPUTATIONAL EXPERIMENTS

We have carried out a number of experiments in the use of linguistic data summaries to a human consistent analysis of data related to the innovativeness of companies. We employed a subset of the attributes, listed in Table 1, used to describe innovative companies in the framework of research on the innovativeness of the Polish economy carried out in 2007. The selection of attributes was motivated by the availability of their values for most of the companies considered. The original data on the companies has been imported to a Microsoft Access database and we employed the FQUERY for Access software (Kacprzyk & Zadrożny, 1995; 2001) to run the experiments.

The set of linguistic terms considered (a dictionary) sets the *granularity level* at which the raw data are analyzed. The choice of a proper level is not a trivial task and the decision usually requires a series of experiments to be executed. We have chosen to represent the values of each attribute by three linguistic terms: *low*, *medium* and *high*. Obviously their meaning differs in the context of various attributes and this is properly taken into account. Such a choice secures a reasonable computation time and provides a fair

Table 1. Attributes of companies used for the linguistic summarization.

Attribute name	Description
totalAssets2006	Total assets of the company in 2006
totalAssets2005	Total assets of the company in 2005
totalAssets2004	Total assets of the company in 2004
equityCapital2006	Equity of the company in 2006
equityCapital2005	Equity of the company in 2005
equityCapital2004	Equity of the company in 2004
netSales2006	Net sales of the company in 2006
netSales2005	Net sales of the company in 2005
netSales2004	Net sales of the company in 2004
grossProfit2006	Gross profit of the company in 2006
grossProfit2005	Gross profit of the company in 2005
grossProfit2004	Gross profit of the company in 2004
netProfit2006	Net profit of the company in 2006
netProfit2005	Net profit of the company in 2005
netProfit2004	Net profit of the company in 2004
salesDynamics20062005	Sales dynamics in 2005-2006
salesDynamics20052004	Sales dynamics in 2004-2005
ROA2005	Return on assets (ROA) of the company in 2005
ROADynamics20062005	ROA dynamics in 2005-2006
PointsRTDTotal2006	Total points related to RTD related activities in 2006
PointsRTDTotal2005	Total points related to RTD related activities in 2005
PointsRTDTotal20052006	Total points related to RTD related activities in 2005-2006
PointsPatentsTotal2006	Total points related to patents obtained in 2006
PointsTotal	Total points given by experts

granularity level. In the course of linguistic summaries generation the system transforms the original data to their linguistic representation (technically, it does not literally happen, but such an interpretation helps explain details of the algorithm). Thus, the original values of selected numerical attributes are replaced by their best matching linguistic terms. For example, the values of attribute "netProfit2005" will be replaced by those of new binary attributes: "netProfit-2005LOW", "netProfit2005MEDIUM" and "netProfit2005HIGH".

The definition of linguistic terms is supported by FQUERY for Access, i.e., it makes it possible to define membership functions of fuzzy sets in the domains of particular attributes which are then used to model these terms. FQUERY for Access provides two alternative ways to define linguistic terms. In the first one, the terms are defined in a universal space (an interval [-10, 10]) and are automatically adjusted to the value ranges of particular attributes. In the second approach, the linguistic terms are defined directly in the domains of the particular attributes. In the former case, an important decision concerns the determination of the ranges of attribute which have to be specified for this approach to work. They may be determined independently of a data set under consideration, referring to some general knowledge on possible values of a given attribute. Another option is to assume the limits observed in the data set. In the presented experiments we adopted the latter approach. In order to determine the supports of linguistic terms in the particular domains we applied cluster analysis.

In all our experiments the linguistic quantifier "*most*" is used in the generated summaries, and is defined as in (3).

FQUERY for Access provides the user interface as well as a proper data coding and results interpretation. The set of transformed data is processed by a well known and widely used algorithm Apriori (Agrawal & Srikant, 1994). The association rules mining is done using an external program, an implementation of the Apriori algorithm by Christian Borgelt which may be found at http://www.borgelt.net/apriori.html.

In our experiments we obtained a lot of very interesting linguistic summaries. Some of them concern the general standing of the companies analyzed. These may be exemplified by the following summary:

Most companies having *high* net revenues from sales and equivalent in 2004 had *high* total assets in 2004 which may be of interest in its own and may be useful to carry out the analysis of innovativeness.

Another class of interesting summaries shows some dependencies between particular assessments of experts evaluating innovativeness of the companies. For example:

Most of the companies having *at least a few* points for their RTD related activities in 2006 had also some points for that in 2005 indicates some persistency in the RTD related activities of the companies. It should be stressed that a vast majority of companies do not get any score (points) in this respect. The above summary suggests that the number of those which do get those points was not growing in the period analyzed. The same regularity does not directly show up in the opposite direction (i.e., when years 2005 and 2006

are compared in the reversed order). However the following summary has been obtained:

A *majority* of companies having some points related to patents registered in 2006 AND some points for their RTD related activities in 2005 had also some points for RTD related activities in 2006

Thus, in general companies being active in the RTD field in 2005 do not necessarily continue to do so in 2006. However those of them which got some patents in 2006 usually also had RTD related activities in 2006.

Due to space limitations we can show just a few of the summaries obtained. Many of them were rather trivial and were pruned out in the postprocessing phase. Most of the non-trivial summaries obtained belonged to the classes exemplified above.

FUTURE RESEARCH DIRECTIONS

The data collected give a possibility of a very interesting qualitative and quantitative research on the corporate level discovering the role of knowledge management as well as dynamic behaviors in the field of RTD and expansion on the market. The individual integrated indicators of innovativeness could be developed into a system supporting Business Process Outsourcing (BPO) services as well technology transfer applications and presented in the form of Google Maps.

The analysis of the collected data may be greatly enhanced by the use of knowledge-based techniques. The ontologies may play an important role, making it possible to formalize the domain knowledge concerning the innovation system. This may help experts in their qualitative assessment of values of some, in particular qualitative, indicators and to provide a common conceptual ground in which they may clarify and justify their positions. Moreover the reasoning capability of ontological systems may help to automatically draw some conclusions concerning the characteristics of the companies being evaluated.

The use of a domain ontology may be also very advantageous in constructing even more interesting linguistic summaries. The taxonomic part of the ontology provides a whole hierarchy of concepts that may be referred to in the summaries. For example, different levels of the hierarchy and other forms of relations among industries may be used to define the range of the companies covered by given summary. Another simple hierarchy is related to the temporal aspects of the collected data. For example, data on the number of patents registered by an enterprise in particular years naturally generalizes to a total number of patents registered over the considered period of time. Here the concept of a *generalized association rule* (Srikant & Agrawal, 1995) is relevant and related mining techniques may be applied to generating more sophisticated linguistic summaries. This is also the area of the OLAP-related techniques application.

Finally, the use of modern tools of natural language generation (NLG), as suggested by Kacprzyk & Zadrożny (2009), may provide valuable algorithmic and software tools for an effective and efficient derivation of such linguistic data summaries.

CONCLUSION

The work presented in this paper is a combination of the development of a new innovativeness assessment system coupled with an intelligent and human consistent analysis of data collected in the framework of this system implementation. This combination is hoped to provide a better insight into the data collected, and in turn, to help further develop the system and its methodological framework.

The first of the co-authors of the present paper is a leader of the team developing the system mentioned (Baczko, 2007a). Its implementation has shown that the development of a public rating of innovativeness for companies is possible and

very useful for different actors involved. The base for a further development is the social process of dissemination of innovativeness patterns and the discovery of both new innovative companies as well as innovative products of companies of a different size from the micro level to international corporations. The developed methodology is also oriented towards the enlargement of the number of innovative companies willing or being in a position to disclose their microeconomic data.

The data collected make it possible to undertake a further research on different phenomena related to innovativeness. One of very important fields concerns the RTD investments in companies in Poland. The existence of a group of over 600 companies investing in RTD has been discovered. This group includes many companies from among those quoted at the Warsaw Stock Exchange.

Small and medium companies (SMEs) have been proved to possess a high innovativeness potential thanks to the networking capabilities in the field of human resources, intellectual property and ability to get international contracts based on the EU framework programmes. The ability of developing networks of employees and supporting them in RTD activities is an important feature of innovative SMEs. Further studies related to regional factors help discover barriers of innovativeness (Baczko, 2008).

The results obtained so far show many practical applications of the public innovativeness rating not only to develop an innovation awareness of the different NIS stakeholders but also for Foresight type projects as a base for the selection of experts from companies for Delphi studies. They were applied in technological Foresight projects as well as for a national one for Poland carried out in the period of 2006-2008. The companies involved in these studies could be further coached and could be future users of results of Foresight projects for developing and improving their own strategies. We suppose that thanks to the development of ontologies it will be possible to generate processes for supplying them with data and knowledge items due to their needs and innovativeness level.

The second line of research reported in the paper concerns an intelligent analysis of data collected during this study. The modern and promising technique of verbalization through linguistic summaries seems to have a great potential for analyzing such data, communicating the findings of such a study to a broad human audience, etc. Some further research is definitely needed and in the previous section we envisage some of its possible directions.

REFERENCES

Agrawal, R., & Srikant, R. (1994). Fast algorithms for mining association rules. In J. B. Bocca, M. Jarke, & C. Zaniolo (Eds.), *20th International Conference on Very Large Databases, Santiago de Chile, Chile* (pp. 487–499). San Francisco: Morgan Kaufmann

Archibugi, D., Howells, J., & Michie, J. (1999). Innovation systems in a global economy. *Technology Analysis and Strategic Management, 11*, 527–539. doi:10.1080/095373299107311

Baczko, T. (2007b). Integrated micro indicators of innovativeness-new market and public policy institutional solution. In Jakubowska, P., Kukliński, A., & Żuber, P. (Eds.), *The Future of European Regions* (pp. 326–335). Warsaw, Poland: Ministry of Regional Development.

Baczko, T. (Ed.). (2009b). *The Future Science and Technology and Innovation Indicators and the Challenges Implied.* Warsaw, Poland: Institute of Economics, Polish Academy of Sciences.

Baczko, T. (2007a). *The Report on Innovativeness of Polish Economy in 2007.* Warsaw: Institute of Economics, Polish Academy of Sciences. (in Polish)

Baczko, T. (2008). Standortbedingungen in Ostdeutschland und Polen aus Sicht der Unternehmen. *Wochenbericht des DIW Berlin, 9*, 91–97.

Baczko, T. (2009a). *The Report on Innovativeness of Polish Economy in 2008.* Warsaw, Poland: Institute of Economics, Polish Academy of Sciences. (in Polish)

Baraczyk, H., Cook, P., & Heidenreich, R. (Eds.). (1996). *Regional Innovation Systems.* London: University of London Press.

Belton, V., & Stewart, T. J. (2001). *Multiple Criteria Decision Making.* Dordrecht, The Netherlands: Kluwer.

Biggiero, L., & Laise, D. (2003). Outranking methods. Choosing and evaluating technology policy: a multicriteria approach. *Science & Public Policy, 30*, 13–23. doi:10.3152/147154303781780641

Howells, J. (2005). Innovation and regional economic development: A matter of perspective? *Research Policy, 34*, 1220–1234. doi:10.1016/j.respol.2005.03.014

Kacprzyk, J., Yager, R. R., & Zadrożny, S. (2000). A fuzzy logic based approach to linguistic summaries of databases. *International Journal of Applied Mathematics and Computer Science, 10*, 813–834.

Kacprzyk, J., Yager, R. R., & Zadrożny, S. (2001). Fuzzy linguistic summaries of databases for an efficient business data analysis and decision support. In Abramowicz, W., & Żurada, J. (Eds.), *Knowledge Discovery for Business Information Systems* (pp. 129–152). Boston: Kluwer.

Kacprzyk, J., & Zadrożny, S. (1995). FQUERY for Access: fuzzy querying for a Windows-based DBMS. In Bosc, P., & Kacprzyk, J. (Eds.), *Fuzziness in Database Management Systems* (pp. 415–433). Heidelberg, Germany: Physica-Verlag.

Kacprzyk, J., & Zadrożny, S. (2001). Computing with words in intelligent database querying: standalone and Internet-based applications. *Information Sciences, 34,* 71–109. doi:10.1016/S0020-0255(01)00093-7

Kacprzyk, J., & Zadrożny, S. (2005). Linguistic database summaries and their protoforms: towards natural language based knowledge discovery tools. *Information Sciences, 173*(4), 281–304. doi:10.1016/j.ins.2005.03.002

Kacprzyk, J., & Zadrożny, S. (2009). Protoforms of Linguistic Database Summaries as a Human Consistent Tool for Using Natural Language in Data Mining. *International Journal of Software Science and Computational Intelligence, 1*(1), 100–111.

Llerena, P., & Matt, M. (Eds.). (2004). *Innovation Policy in a Knowledge-Based Economy Theory and Practice.* Heidelberg, Germany: Springer.

Malerba, F. (2004). *Sectoral Systems of Innovation.* Cambridge, UK: Cambridge University Press. doi:10.1017/CBO9780511493270

Malerba, F., & Brusoni, S. (2007). *Perspectives on Innovation.* Cambridge, UK: Cambridge University Press. doi:10.1017/CBO9780511618390

Malerba, F., & Cantner, U. (2007). *Innovation, Industrial Dynamics and Structural Transformation.* Heidelberg, Germany: Springer.

McCraw, Th. K. (2007). *Prophet of Innovation: Joseph Schumpeter and Creative Destruction.* Cambridge, MA: Harvard University Press.

OECD. (2003). *The Measurement of Scientific and Technological Activities. Frascati Manual 2002. Proposed Standard Practice for Surveys on Research and Experimental Development.* New York: OECD Publishing.

OECD. *(2005).* Oslo Manual: Guidelines for Collecting and Interpreting Innovation Data, 3rd Edition.

Srikant, R., & Agrawal, R. (1995). Mining generalized association rules. In *21st International Conference on Very Large Databases, Zurich, Switzerland* (pp. 407–419). Washington, DC: IEEE Press.

Szaniawski, K. (1998). *On Science, Inference, Information and Decision Making, Selected Essays in the Philosophy of Science* (Chmielewski, A., & Wolenski, J., Eds.). Dordrecht, The Netherlands: Kluwer.

Yager, R. R. (1982). A new approach to the summarization of data. *Information Sciences, 28,* 69–86. doi:10.1016/0020-0255(82)90033-0

Zadeh, L. A. (1983). A computational approach to fuzzy quantifiers in natural languages. *Computers & Mathematics with Applications (Oxford, England), 9,* 149–184. doi:10.1016/0898-1221(83)90013-5

Chapter 8
Knowledge Exchange in Collaborative Networks of Enterprises

Aleksander Moczala
University of Bielsko-Biala, Poland

ABSTRACT

The problem of information exchange in the inter-enterprise cooperation process design is presented in the chapter. Development of an innovative character of an enterprise requires facilitating the initiation, creation, and extension of cooperative links among enterprises. Collaborative design process gathers enterprises which have to achieve a common objective related to a new product – innovation by information and knowledge sharing, with a high level of activities' coordination. Development of methods and ways of data exchange in cooperation enables the creation of computer systems aiding production cooperation. System analysis of the cooperation process of enterprises, which is one of the most dynamically developing field of computer systems application in economic activity, and use of knowledge as the base of description and management described in this chapter are shown as the right approach to overcome different area specifics. Formal description of the cooperation process could be utilized also for innovation processes and links. Chapter could open new fields of application and research production engineering knowledge's application in computer systems.

INTRODUCTION

The Cooperation Phenomenon

Externalization - outsourcing is a way of strategic action which means subcontracting production

DOI: 10.4018/978-1-61692-811-7.ch008

processes and sub-processes including manufacturing of sub-assemblies by sub-suppliers, processes maintenance and failure repairing, storage, logistics, buildings security, computer service, research, training, providing services etc. outside the enterprise. If an enterprise renounces one part of added value, then mark-up, flexibility, concentration of attention, and financial outlays on the processes, which provide competitive advantage, will increase.

Tendencies to development global enterprises, creation new cooperative links are visible also in the dynamics of the need to exchange information – cooperative data. Development of cooperation requires data flow according to the elaborated standard of data exchange model of the product for cooperation at the exact time of its coming into being (Botta-Genoulaz, Millet and Grabot 2005, Rose and Girard 2007). Production cooperation process has representation and formal modeling in the literature using:

- graph theory,
- game theory,
- business processes alignment,
- petri nets,
- gaussian networks,
- social network and other.

The multidisciplinary character of cooperation phenomenon is underlined and represented in the literature review including economic theory: international economics (offshoring), theory of the firm - especially information oriented (Nonaka and Takeuchi 1995)

The problem of cooperation in production is connected with innovative activities of an enterprise. The process innovations depend in part on the variety and structure of thier links to the sources of information, knowledge, technologies, practices, human and financial resources. Linkages act as sources of knowledge and technology for an enterprise's innovation activity, ranging from passive sources of information to suppliers of embodied and disembodied knowledge and technology to co-operative partnerships – described in *Oslo Manual* (OECD 2005).

Co-operation of enterprises for innovation allows to access knowledge and technology that they would be unable to utilize on their own. There is also great potential for synergies in co-operation

as partners learn from each other. Innovation co-operation can take place along supply chains and involve customers and suppliers in the joint development of new products, processes or other innovations. The level of interaction along supply chains (i.e. whether linkages involve co-operation, or arm's-length exchanges of information or purchases of technology) may depend on the type of knowledge and technology.

BACKGROUND

The Modeling Frameworks and Organizational Structure of Production Processes in Enterprise

Modeling frameworks, methodologies and organizational structure and its rules of processes in enterprise concepts emerged in different application domains such as ARIS, CIMOSA, GRAI/GIM, GERAM, IEM, PERA, Open Group Architecture Framework (TOGAF) or the IDEF family of languages (described in FEA 2007, GERAM 2000, Lankhorst 2005, Williams, Rathwell & Li 2001).

The ARIS-architecture distinguishes Organization, Function, Information and Control views. It uses a graphic modeling system supported by software which models data movement and tasks (GERAM 2000, Lankhorst 2005). ARIS focuses on the analysis and requirements definition phase during the design of managerial information systems, not on the execution of business processes. Federal Enterprise Architecture (FEA) - an architectural description of the enterprise architecture of the U.S. federal government that includes various reference models, processes for creating organizational architectures that fit in with the federal enterprise architecture, and a methodology for measuring the success of an organization in using enterprise architectures (FEA 2007; Williams et al. 2001). The PERA model breaks the enterprise life cycle into "phases". While this is not the only possible "phase breakdown", it is one which has been proven in a large number of projects in many industries. It also breaks the investment approval process into a number of steps which works well for projects larger than a few million dollars. Smaller projects may combine phases to reduce overhead costs, but the deliverables between phases generally remain the same. GERAM defines a tool-kit of concepts for designing and maintaining enterprises for their entire life-history.

PERA, GERAM and other models are not yet-another-proposal for enterprise reference architecture, but are meant to organize existing enterprise integration knowledge.

CONDITIONING OF PRODUCTION COOPERATION

General Model Cycle of Production and Knowledge

A model of the production system, based on the macro run of the production processes, should take into account mutual interactions of the enterprises with the environment. These problems are related to the effect of world and regional economy on company's functioning. Micro-economic knowledge is also necessary and it makes possible efficient management of the possessed resources as well as allows to design systems, subsystems, and processes of production effectively – Figure 1. Collaborative design process gathers enterprises willing to achieve a common objective based on a new product, information and knowledge sharing, including a high level of activities coordination. Knowledge of the enterprise refers to all their design expertise in one or several given domains (Robin, Rose & Girard 2007) and could be defined as being at the crossroads of in-depth knowledge and collaborative knowledge.

Robin et al. (2007) proposed to structure this knowledge in four different types. So, exist possibility to define cooperation knowledge of enterprise as a set of all this knowledge:

- Popularization knowledge acquired by the enterprise, coming from the other members of the cooperation.
- Popularization knowledge distributed to the other enterprise of the cooperation project. It is a support of problem solving.
- Knowledge-being used by enterprise actor when he has to initiate communication with the other enterprise.
- Synergy knowledge, implemented to carry out and maintain the intra-group knowledge exchanges as a support of communication.

In the literature review (Nonaka and Takeuchi 1995) are proposed two types of knowledge: explicit knowledge and tacit knowledge. Explicit knowledge can be expressed in formal and systematic language and shared in the form of data, scientific formulae, specifications, manuals and the like. It can be processed, transmitted and stored relatively easily. In contrast, tacit knowledge is highly personal and hard to formalize: subjective insights, intuitions and hunches fall into this category of knowledge. Tacit knowledge is deeply rooted in action, procedures, routines, commitment, ideals, values and emotions.

Besides most of computer supported collaborative work the tools focus on communication features (messaging) and co-ordination (approval forms, workflow tools, videoconference tools) but few of them are interested in collaboration among actors. However there are relatively few studies of the role of supported collaborative work in product development and design and its effect on problem-solving activities (Moczala 2006).

Figure 1. Structure of enterprise's knowledge

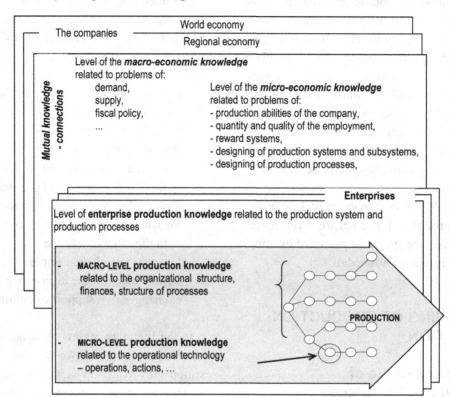

Model of Production Cooperation Management Process

The different life-cycle phases define types of activities that are pertinent during the life of the enterprise.

Life-cycle activities encompass all activities from identification to decommissioning (or end of life) of the enterprise – Figure 2a. The life-cycle diagram used in the description of the life-cycle of production is itself a model of the enterprise engineering methodology.

In particular, recognizing strategic planning, enterprise architecture of cooperation, capital planning of cooperation and investment control, as well as performance assessment and management are interconnected processes.

Modeling information architecture for the organization was described by Wang (1997). An evaluation framework for deploying Web Services in the next generation manufacturing enterprise was expanded by Estrem (2004). Parallel processes in the production life-history (from Figure 2a) and criteria of task in phase of life-cycle of production are described in Figure 2b.

Model of Cooperation Enterprise

The process-oriented concepts defined in the presented aspect include:

*   enterprise unit life-cycle and life-cycle phases,
*   life history,
*   cooperation enterprise unit types,
*   cooperation of enterprise modeling with integrated model representation and model views.

Figure 2. Life-cycle of production in enterprise: a) structure of life-cycle of production in enterprise, b) criteria of task in phase of life-cycle of production

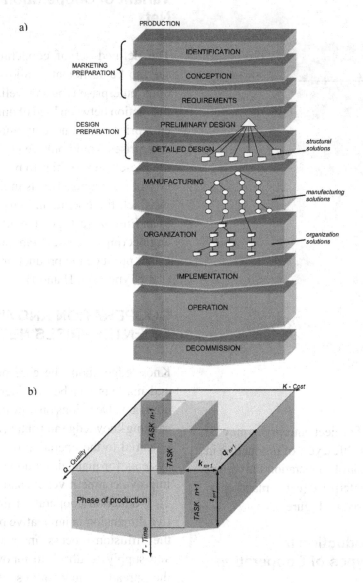

Model of enterprise architecture (EA) describes the current states of the agency without cooperation (baseline) and future based on cooperation (target), and the plan to transition from the current to the future cooperation state, with a focus on agency strategy, program performance improvements and information technology investments. Model of current EA is organized by the following segments: core mission areas (e.g., homeland security, health), business service (e.g., financial management, human resources), and enterprise services (e.g., Information Sharing).

The project enterprise is characterised by its close linkage with the life-cycle of the single product or service that it is producing. The management system of project enterprises is typically set up quickly, while the rest is created and operated in lock-step with the life-cycle activities of the product of the project.

Figure 3. Model of phase life-cycle of production in cooperation

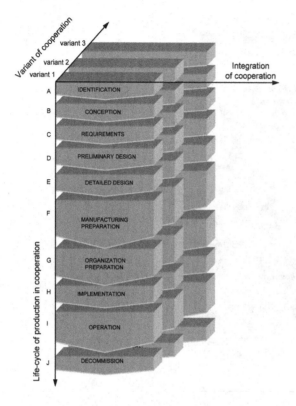

The production of project enterprises may be diverse, such as phase life-cycle of production in cooperation, integration of cooperation and variant of cooperation - an enterprise (e.g. a plant, or an infrastructure enterprise) – Figure 3.

Life-Cycle of Production in Cooperation - Types of Cooperation Enterprise

The operational relations of the different enterprise types are also shown in Figure 4 which demonstrates an example of contributions of the different enterprises to the life-cycle of a manufacturing enterprise Type I. The manufacturing enterprise itself produces the enterprise product Type E in the course of its operation phase (Figure 4a).

Integration of Cooperation and Variant of Cooperation Enterprises Net

The defined set of cooperation enterprises is seen to be sufficient to allow representation of other enterprise types as well. For example, the distinction between kind of unit or project related enterprise units and continuous operation type enterprises would only require different parts of the life-cycle activities to be used in the life history of such units. This is indicated in Figure 4b in which the operational processes could relate to an Enterprise Type I (small integration) or the engineering processes to an Enterprise Type E and F that produce the product or customer services (Unit Type F, G, H and I).

COOPERATION KNOWLEDGE OF ENTERPRISES NET

Knowledge about the core processes, products and markets can be considered to constitute a company. Decisions on how to use and exchange existing knowledge and obtain new knowledge are essential to the operation of enterprises. Proper systems for managing knowledge can therefore improve competitiveness and innovative ability.

Production cooperation links have cooperative dimension in innovative processes. Through the diffusion process, innovations may change and supply feedback to innovator. Diffusion is the spread of innovations, through market or non-market channels, from first implementation anywhere in the world to other countries and regions and to other markets and firms. The diffusion process often involves more than the mere adoption of knowledge and technology, as adopting enterprises learn from and build on the new knowledge and technology. As described in Oslo Manual - Guidelines for collecting and interpreting innovation data (OECD 2005) for use in innovation surveys, these types of linkages can be defined as:

Figure 4. Production in cooperation: a) types of cooperation enterprise, b) integration of cooperation units

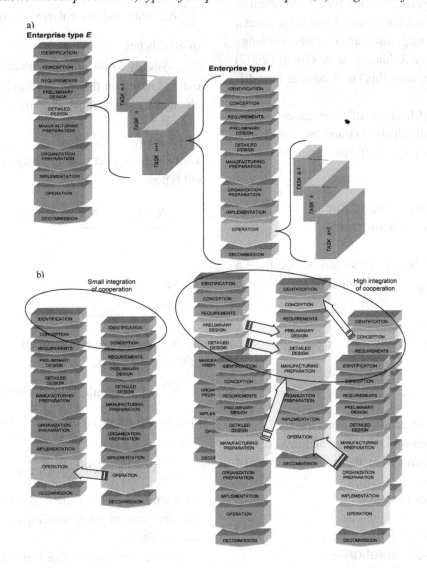

- **Open information sources:** openly available information that does not require the purchase of technology or intellectual property rights, or interaction with the source.

- **Acquisition of knowledge and technology:** purchases of external knowledge and/or knowledge and technology embodied in capital goods (machinery, equipment, software) and services, which do not involve interaction with the source.

- **Innovation co-operation:** active co-operation with other enterprises or public research institutions for innovation activities (which may include purchases of knowledge and technology).

It is recommended in Oslo Manual that data should be collected on all three types of linkages, drawing on the list of sources above.

To understand how knowledge assets are created, acquired and exploited, Nonaka I., Toyama R. and Konno N. (2000) propose to categorize knowledge assets into four types: experiential knowledge assets, conceptual knowledge assets, systemic knowledge assets and routine knowledge assets. Similarly Robin., Rose & Girard (2007) proposed to structure this knowledge in four different types.

The basic difference of cooperation design carried out individually (I) and by collaborating enterprises (N) is different range of design knowledge:

(I) Cooperative Production Design by One i-Enterprise

Knowledge of the enterprise can be define as a set of *knowledge* K_I of an enterprise:

$$K_I = K_i + \sum_n \gamma_{ni} K_{n \to i} \qquad (1)$$

where:

K_i, knowledge, enterprise's own expertise,
$K_{n \to i}$, popularization knowledge acquired by the enterprise, coming from the other members of the cooperation,
$\gamma_{ni} = 0 \div 1$ - factor reception

(N) Cooperative Production Design by Collaboration – Collaborating *n* Enterprises

Knowledge of the enterprise could be defined as a combination of in-depth knowledge and collaborative knowledge.

Cooperation knowledge K_N of enterprise net can be defined as a set of all this knowledge:

$$K_N = \sum_i^n K_i + \xi_N \qquad (2)$$

where:

$\sum_i^n K_i$, knowledge - enterprise's own expertise of all this net,
ξ_N, synergy knowledge, implemented to carry out and maintain the intra-group knowledge exchanges. It is a support of communication.

Synergy knowledge – the structure of this knowledge is a set of knowledge of four different types:

$$\xi_N = \sum_n K_{i \to n} + \sum_n K_{n \to i} + \sum_n K_{i \leftrightarrow n} + \Delta K_N$$
$$(3)$$

where:

$\sum_n K_{i \to n}$, popularization knowledge acquired by the enterprise, coming from the other members of the cooperation,

$\sum_n K_{n \to i}$, popularization knowledge distributed to the other enterprise of the cooperation project,

$\sum_n K_{i \leftrightarrow n}$, knowledge being used by enterprise actor when he has to initiate communication with the other enterprise, depending on the culture of each enterprise,

ΔK_N, new knowledge formed in the net of n enterprise

The evaluation method of synergy which links the evaluation with different criteria in one is the analysis of increase ΔU_N of innovative projects' utility of the course of production cooperation process.

$$\xi_N \cong U_N - U_n = \Delta U_N \qquad (4)$$

Knowledge K_i of enterprises is a set knowledge about designed production. In the designed object we can distinguish three groups of variables:

Figure 5. Cooperation start initiation phase: a) – data standard and flow, b) - data exchange and its analysis by initiating of cooperation

a)

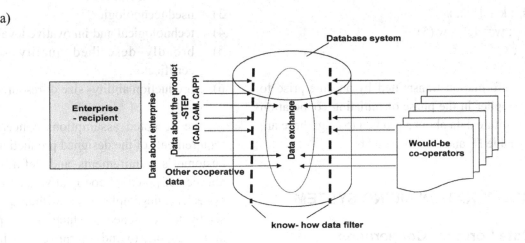

b)

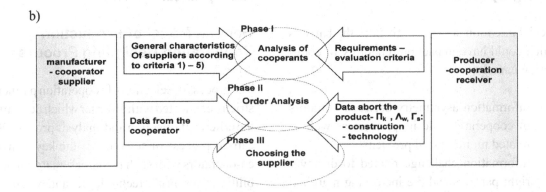

- constructional features (Π), the collection of variables explicitly describing constructions:
    ○ geometric features, dimensions and their values, parameters of the shape and location, parameters of surface geometry (within the above notion we distinguish a notion of constructional form – a record of shape without determining the dimensions),
    ○ material features, sorts and kinds of materials,
    ○ initial settings, parameters of assembly let-ups, initial tensions,

- (Λ) - minimal collection of variables determining the features of the designed object in respect of the environment, e.g. constructional qualities (durability, effectiveness, weight, dimensions, dimensions of assembly holes); qualities connected to the manufacturing process (costs of production, labour consumption), usage features (time of reaching, reliability of work).
- (Γ) technological variables – minimal collection of variables which characterize processes and phenomena of change taking place in technological processes.

This means respectively:

Π_k ; k = 1, ..., k
Λ_w ; w = 1, ..., w (5)
Γ_s ; s = 1, ..., s

Information transmitted by an enterprise to a supplier in the phase of initiating cooperation constitute data about a product (5) e.g. these are variable Π_k and Λ_w – Figure 5b.

COOPERATION AIDING SYSTEM

Data Form for Cooperation Aiding System

Special attention should be given to the barriers which could have impact on reliability of cooperation namely:

- information asymmetry between initiators of cooperation and its partners as well as related moral hazard problem.
- information challenge related to discover right partners and the increasing marginal cost of information of searching them in the global environment. Here innovative approaches are needed.

Development of cooperation requires data flow according to the elaborated standard of data exchange model of the product for cooperation at the exact time of its coming into being. Standardization should also take the need of information form determination into account, especially in the initial phases of cooperation, which is safe for know-how of the enterprise - Figure 5a.

The characteristic which describes the potential co-operator is information about the enterprise which is limited by the security of know-how of the enterprise. The fundamental features are needed in this phase are pieces of easy available information about the enterprise:

1) information which identifies the enterprise,
2) enterprise's products,
3) used technologies,
4) technological and innovative level,
5) broadly described quality - quality certificates,
6) production ability- size of resources.

The accepted assumptions concerning the requirements of the designed production specify customer's requirements and define minimal abilities of potential cooperative manufacturing system. Having implemented all the requirements, set by the designed production, the proposed system enables to find enterprises which can take part in production process.

General Model of Production Cooperation Designing Process

The process of selection of cooperation partners is strictly connected with an order which determines the criteria of selection and analysis process. Well carried process of selection is the key to match co-operators with such resources, material possibilities, appropriate technologies and well trained staff in the comparison with order-design that can guarantee gaining synergic effect and product's position on the market. Drawing on the work of Moczala (2006) and (Moller et al. 2005), we suggest that the key issues in managing strategic nets fall within four interrelated levels. Cooperation designing process in the presented aspect can be viewed in four phases as it is presented in Figure 6.

The discussed problem of cooperation designing requires production designing and its flow to be broaden through the issue of marking and optimization of organizational structures of labour run for enterprises set. Determining of the optimum production process in cooperation requires multi-criterion marking for the variant of cooperation process- production process route in the subset of enterprises. The result of the issue is regarded as NP hard problem - difficult, requiring inclining

Figure 6. Phases of designing stage of production process cooperation and searching of would-be co-operators in production

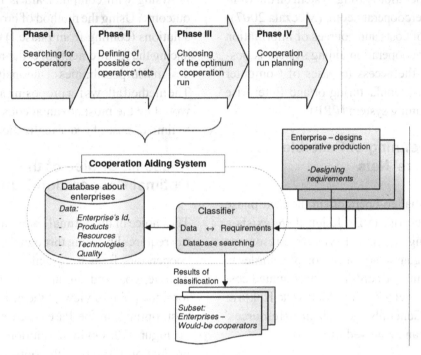

expenditures of calculations in problem size function.

To make the problem more general, it is reduced to certain answers to the given questions:

- Do the enterprises which can compete in realization of a certain project exist?
- Which of these enterprises are able to create the nets which would have free resources for order's realization?
- Which of these nets of co-operators are able to create optimum production process?
- How to organize and control the cooperative run of production in the net?

Lack of earlier information, reaction to coming information, its receiving, elaboration of the correct answer take time and as a result the total sum of these delays gives information delays in cooperative production process.

Phase I: Looking for Co-Operators

The solution of the problem will specify which subset of enterprises and which abilities guarantee keeping term-price-quality appointments with the customer. The answer to the question: *Who can cooperate in production order realization?*-requires knowledge about enterprises which exist on the market. Defining of possible co-operators set leads to the conclusion that there is a need to create a database about these enterprises where potential co-operators will be selected – Figure 6b.

The problem requires supplier- producer model creation which would describe the standard of requirements for the cooperation enterprise. The proposed solution is based on creation of a base for enterprises defined with fundamental information needed in this phase of cooperation designing, in combining with the system of base searching by the use of classifier, basing on the criterions which are specified for the designed production.

The prepared system aided of cooperation is example Cooperation Aiding System on the website: www.intercooperate.com. (Moczala 2007).

Question of costs and sources of information accessible for cooperation aiding system is possible through the access to bases of Computer Aided-Design-Manufacturing or/and Enterprise Resource Planning system (ERP).

Phase II: Defining of Possible Co-Operators' Nets

Among potential co-operators in the next phase of virtual enterprise (VE) design there exists a need of finding solutions having free resources which would guarantee realization of an order in the assumed time, according to the assumed cost and accepted level of quality (Matuszek, Kukla & Plinta 2006). Generally, the problem of resources' engagement can be proved by:

- The applied in practice simple correspondence by mail or e-mail with an answer about a possibility of order realization – the need to administer specialized technology and resources and with setting price conditions. After this the asked person analyses the order after having prepared and sent back the answer. Then potential variants of nets are created, which are composed of resources of the chosen sub-composition of enterprises. The basic disadvantage of the traditional procedure is high time consumption of the activities;
- Using the method based on the computer system of browsing the space of potential solutions, taking into account possibilities of access to production capability limited in time. The method requires knowledge of the state of resources engagement of potential co-operators in the whole planning period.

The advantage of using the procedures of browsing with computer aid is instant analysis outcome. Using the method of browsing of initial solutions (coming from phase I) consists in balancing the requirements of order realization – the design with possibilities of the analyzed enterprise. The method allows for proposing a solution which would be the most advantageous when it comes to time or cost of order realization.

Phase III: Choice of the Optimal Cooperation Run

The choice of the optimal cooperative production run requires browsing through the set of potential cooperators from the point of view of criteria of time, cost and production quality. Solutions form the point of view of the criteria of time and cost, optimal in the Pareto sense, are presented on Figure 10. Optimal solutions I1 – I3 of the production process with cooperation design by (I) i-enterprise are replaced with a new optimum solutions of cooperation (optimal in the Pareto sense) by (N) design by means of collaborating enterprises. New solutions N1 – N4, are more innovative – Figure 7.

The choice of unequivocally optimal cooperative production run is more difficult, as we are looking for a solution, which is optimal from the point of view of different criteria – multi-criterion optimization. We need such a method which would allow for carrying out a multi-criterion optimization with respect to time, cost and quality of order realization, as well as taking into account the estimated risk of failure to fulfil the requirements by a given variant of the net of cooperating enterprises.

The method which links the evaluation with different criteria in one is the analysis of utility of projects of the production cooperation process (Moczala 1996, 2006).

In respect to the basic criteria of quality, cost and time, the model of the course net of production process cooperation is subject to the proposed

Figure 7. Pareto Optimum change – increase of innovativity of cooperation solutions

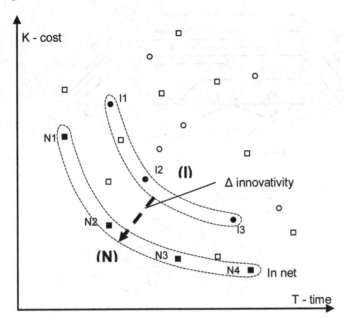

○ - solution in (I) cooperation design – by i-enterprise

□ - solution in (N) cooperation design – by collaborating enterprises

● ■ - solutions optimal in the Pareto sense

optimization activity, whose structure is described by the graph (Figure 8):

$$G_N = V_N, L_N \qquad (6)$$

where:

$V_N = \{v_i; i = 0, 1, ..., N\}$ – collection of summits, $L_N = \{l_{ij}; i = 0, 1, ..., N\text{-}1; j = 1, 2, ..., N\}$ – collection of graph's arches.

Each summit of the graph may be associated with an event which begins or ends a task of production process cooperation, and the arch represents the task itself. Each task may be attributed with:

- t_{ij} – time of realization of task i, j,

- $k_{ij}(t_{ij})$ – function interpreted as the cost of activity realization l_{ij} with time of realization t_{ij}.

Assuming that: $\{0 \leq a_{ij} \leq t_{ij} \leq b_{ij}\}$, where bij may be called normal time, and a_{ij} - emergency time, which means that realization with shorter time may cause wrong designing of the process. What is more, tij may take only values of integer numbers.

Each activity is connected with the value qij, explicitly presenting the gained quality, usually gained accuracy class, the number of shortages and even more parameters – a vector of quality.

Event which begin or end the tasks of production process, which are summits of the graph V_n may be analyzed similarly like in (Ignasiak 1996, Moczała 1996) and developing them adequately (according to their numeration) we can attribute them with collections of functions:

Figure 8. A graph of the production cooperation process

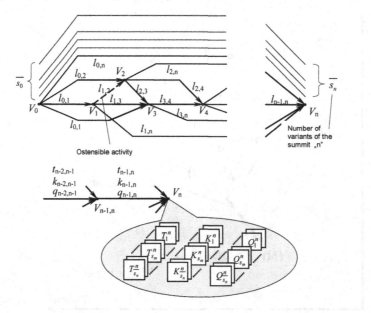

$$T^n_{s_n} = \max\left(T^{n-1}_{s_{n-1}} + t_{n-1,n}, \dots, T^1_{s_1} + t_{1n}, t_{0n}\right)$$

(7)

$$Q^n_{s_n} = \max\left(Q^{n-1}_{s_{n-1}} + q_{n-1,n}, \dots, Q^1_{s_1} + q_{1n}, q_{0n}\right)$$

(8)

$$K^n_{s_n} = \max\left(K^{n-1}_{s_{n-1}} + k_{n-1,n} + k_{n-2,n} + \dots + k_{1n}, k_{0n}\right)$$

(9)

So, the values $T^n_{s_n}, Q^n_{s_n}, K^n_{s_n}$ are the basic parameters, whose values determine the optimality of the cooperational production process, which is described by the sub-graph Gn creating the required quality determined by the admissibility condition.

The choice of the variant of the course of production cooperation process may be solved by estimating the **utility function** which links the basic criteria of cost, time and quality. In a case when one of the factors appears to be a stronger limiting one, we can introduce α, β, γ to the utility function.

Taking into account the probability w_n of non-breaking the realization of the sub-graph Gn, the utility function was formulated as follows:

$$U_N\left(\lambda^N_{s_N} \max\right) =$$
$$MAX_{\lambda^n_{s_n}} \sum_{n=1}^{N} w_n \left(T^n_{\overline{s}_n} - T^n_s\right)^\alpha \left(K^n_0 - K^n_{s_n}\right)^\beta \left(Q^n_{s_q} - Q^n_{s_n}\right)^\gamma$$

(10)

where: α + β + γ = Ω, and Ω is a constant value, for n = 0 function U0 = 0.

For the criterion of quality optimized by the admissibility condition (Moczała 1996) such defined utility function may be reduced to this form:

$$U_N\left(\lambda^N_{s_N} \max\right) =$$
$$MAX_{\lambda^n_{s_n}} \sum_{n=1}^{N} w_n \left(T^n_{\overline{s}_n} - T^n_s\right)^\alpha \left(K^n_0 - K^n_{s_n}\right)^\beta$$

(11)

In the reduced form without taking into account the probability of non-breaking the designing w_n, the form of the function is similar to the function of utility of investment projects presented in w (Ignasiak 1996), which optimizes the course of investment only in respect of two factors – the cost and time of investment. The admissible (N, s_N) process realization, which fulfils the above assumption may be called the optimal (N, s_N) project realization. As underlined in the introduction, it brings together two approaches to tasks by the optimization of production process design according to the quality criterion (or admissibility condition):

1) minimization of realization time with the assumed limit of production means,

2) minimization of total cost of project realization without exceeding the assumed date of termination.

It allows for controlling the parameters α and β depending on the preferences of the decision maker relating to the equivalent value of the cost factor and realization time of the production process. When the probability of non-breaking the cooperation w_n is the same for the tasks, the parameter w_n may be omitted. The sign of a sum results from the fact that in project practice there usually is a need to change or even to break the course of cooperation during the realization because of e.g.: lack of getting the required parameters during construction designing, conceptual assumptions or breaking the contract by the ordering person. Such a situation requires particular attention put on utility of previous bonds- which would probably be realized – it gives a sign of a sum, which causes adding of utility for preceding summits (additional considering previous summits). When there is sureness of carrying out the design according to the assumed structure up to the final summit, there exists a possibility to make the form of utility function simpler – with omitting the sign of a sum and probability w_n in the formula (11), that means taking into account only the parameters of the final summit.

Carrying out the above described method of searching for the optimal solution for production design requires access to data – bases of collaborating n enterprises - integration with Enterprise Resource Planning system.

Integration with Other Systems

Widening of information range accessible for cooperation aiding system is possible through the access to bases of Computer Aided-Design-Manufacturing systems or/and Enterprise Resource Planning systems (ERP). Main application of Classifier has 2 parts - classification according to the NACE (- European Actions Classification) and classification according to group processing – Figure 9a .

Elaboration of classifiers which divide into groups according to similarity from the point of view of different criterions creates the basis for database structures creation.

Classifier – part II – classification according to group processing enables to create the interface to Aiding System of Manufacturing Designing. Proposed Cooperation Aiding System is integrated with:

Computer Aided-Design-Manufacturing – for example Sysklass
Enterprise Resource Planning system – for example Rekord.ERP. – Figure 9b.

It is only a short description of the further parts of Cooperation Aiding System. Part of problem should be better described on the next pages - to show importance of dictionary application - proposed classification code of machining tools with semantic relations. Dictionaries translate bases of systems from different applications of various ERP systems. The represented knowledge model reflect semantic relations in cooperation aiding system - new ICT systems. The "method of dictionaries" is proposed new solution in ERP systems for integration with other system - Cooperation Aid-

Figure 9. Integration with: a) Computer Aided-Design-Manufacturing, b) Enterprise Resource Planning system

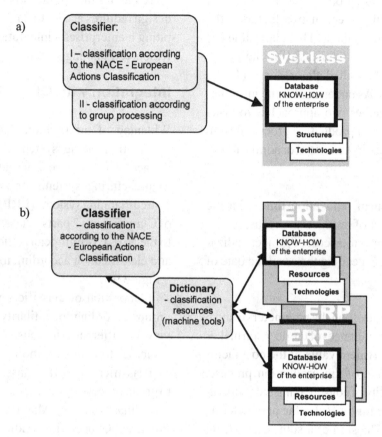

ing System. A next advantage – this method solve question of measurement of linkages in innovation process (using method of OECD Oslo Manual).

Dictionary - Proposed Classification Code of Machining Tools

The represented knowledge model of dictionaries connect numerical and semantic relations. A sample proposed classification code adopted a division of products which is determined on the same levels like in Statistical Classification of Products by Activity in the European Economic Community CPA (2002 version). The division also took five and six number symbols and names from this Classification (see Table 1). Structure of grouping according to classification code:

A fragment of proposed classification code relating to machining tools:

The proposed classification code of production means – machining tools for the designed process expands the classification code by the part which minimally describes technological possibilities. The proposed classification code of production means – machining tools for the designed process (Figure 10):

A sample code for *Manufacturing centre metal-turning lathes with continuous numerical control:*

Classification code – a ten-digit number (Figure 11):

For example the code which connect numerical and semantic relations: 29.40.21-13.12-1550-1180-9000-00-07 - Manufacturing centre metal-turning lathes with continuous numerical control,

Table 1. Structure of grouping

Symbols of Groupings	General names of groupings
A	Section
AA	Subsection
XX	Division
XX.X	Group
XX.XX	Class
XX.XX.X	Category
XX.XX.XX	Subcategory
XX.XX.XX–XX	Position
XX.XX.XX–XX.X	A nine-digit number
XX.XX.XX–XX.XX	A ten-digit number
|—.|—.|————	Classification according to NACE
|—.|—.|— |————	Classification according to CPA

diameter of turning over bed D – 1550, diameter of turning over support D – 1180, maximum length of turning – 9000, machining in 7th class of accuracy.

Dictionary - proposed classification code of machining tools enables for Cooperation Aiding System to create the interface to Enterprise Resource Planning system.

FUTURE RESEARCH DIRECTIONS

The application of Cooperation Aiding System for innovation support create new possibilities from the enterprise's perspective which uses this kind of system and for its business partners and customers as well. These are:

- enlarging the set of potential co-operators in the stage of cooperation initiation,
- widening the range of information exchange among collaborating enterprises,
- increase in innovativity of the designed production,
- time shortening of production design in cooperation,

- low costs – costs and subscribers' fees account for only 10% of costs which the enterprise would pay for realization of similar tasks by its workers,
- possibility of order creation at any time,
- cooperation with ERP systems- on –line orders registration in ERP systems,
- possibility of material management- order's registration on the basis of current stock on hand is possible,
- permanent control – monitoring of run and state of the ordered range of products among the business trade partners is possible.

The development of methods and data exchange in cooperation will allow for development and creation of new information systems of production cooperation aiding, functionally and organizationally brings closer both global enterprises and their sub-suppliers by means of taking a common type of exchanged information, normalized standard of product modelling and production process design.

CONCLUSION

A cooperation design process skillfully carried out through the three phases will allow for linking the co-operators with such possibilities relating to stock, material, possessed technologies and qualifications of staff that it will ensure the achievement of the synergic effect. In case when the values of variables ascribed to particular tasks are known, it is possible to curry out the activities.

Active net cooperation will be modern and very effective form of complex aiding of production cooperation among system users in the future. Enlarging the set of searched enterprises and the access to the chosen data bases makes it possible to find new potential co-operators, which facilitates finding innovation in production in the form of

Table 2. Fragment of proposed classification

29.40.21	Lathes for removing metal
29.40.21-13	Centre lathes, multi-tool lathes and lathes-copiers numerically controlled
29.40.21-13.1	Centre metal-turning lathes numerically controlled
29.40.21-13.11	Manufacturing centre metal-turning lathes, with partial numerical control
29.40.21-13.12	Manufacturing centre metal-turning lathes with continuous numerical control

Figure 10. Proposed classification code of production means

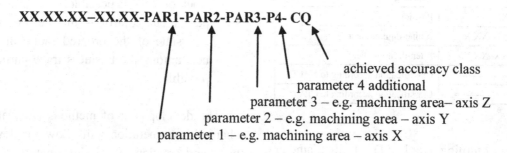

XX.XX.XX–XX.XX-PAR1-PAR2-PAR3-P4- CQ

achieved accuracy class
parameter 4 additional
parameter 3 – e.g. machining area– axis Z
parameter 2 – e.g. machining area – axis Y
parameter 1 – e.g. machining area – axis X

Figure 11. Sample code for manufacturing centre metal-turning lathes with continuous numerical control

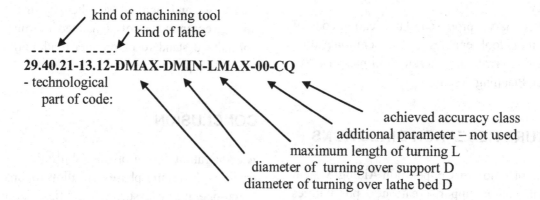

kind of machining tool
kind of lathe

29.40.21-13.12-DMAX-DMIN-LMAX-00-CQ
- technological
part of code:

achieved accuracy class
additional parameter – not used
maximum length of turning L
diameter of turning over support D
diameter of turning over lathe bed D

new quality of products and/or a new, innovative production run.

In the case when the values of variables attributed to particular tasks are known, it is possible to carry out activities aiming at analyzing and evaluation of solutions of cooperation process works by means of utility function. This method gives a deterministic evaluation of the given values of particular criteria.

Carrying out the above described method of searching for the optimal solution for production design requires access to data – bases of collaborating *n* enterprises - integration with Enterprise Resource Planning system.

Using the offered tools, which the system provides, requires setting a standard way of registration of data about the product, its production process and categorization of products and services.

All the units-enterprises introduced to the system- can be subjected to classification. It will enable to search for potential customers willing to buy certain products or services of the user and automatic matching of both units. The presented technology can be an offer for the already existing producers, virtual enterprises and many new enterprises which will exist in the future and which will offer their products for e-business and make them available as outsourcing.

REFERENCES

Botta-Genoulaz, V., Millet, P.-A., & Grabot, B. (2005). A survey on the recent research literature on ERP systems. *Computers in Industry, 56,* 510–522. doi:10.1016/j.compind.2005.02.004

FEA. (2007). *Federal Enterprise Architecture Program, FEA Practice Guidance, Management Office*, OMB US, November 2007, (http://www.whitehouse.gov/omb/egov)

GERAM (2000). *Generalised Enterprise Reference Architecture and Methodology*. Version 1.6.3 (March 1999), IFIP–IFAC Task Force on Architectures for Enterprise Integration, Permission granted to publish GERAM V1.6.3 as Annex to ISO 15704 (2000)

Ignasiak, E. (1996). *Optimization of investment projects*. Warszawa, Poland: PWE.

Jacobs, F. R., & Bendoly, E. (2003). Enterprise resource planning: developments and directions for operations management research. *European Journal of Operational Research, 146*(2). doi:10.1016/S0377-2217(02)00546-5

Lankhorst, M. (2005). *Enterprise Architecture at Work: Modelling, Communication, and Analysis*. New York: Springer.

Maber, V. A. (2007). The early road to material requirements planning. *Journal of Operations Management, 25,* 346–356. doi:10.1016/j.jom.2006.04.002

Matuszek J., Kukla S., Plinta D. (2006). *Use of modelling and simulation techniques in the management of logistic chain. Applied Computer Science, 2*(1).

Moczala, A. (1996): *Multi-criteria optimization of designing production processes*, Ph.D. thesis, Łódź Technical University, Branch of Bielsko-Biała, Poland

Moczala, A. (2006). *Designing Production Processes With Computer Aided Cooperation*. 18 International Scientific Conference in Mittweida, Germany

Moczala, A. (2007): *Computer Aided Cooperation*, EUROPEAN ICT CONFERENCE - On Research and Technology Development, Seventh Framework Program (7 FP), Organized under: European Commission, EASIER and CORDIS, Istanbul, Turkey, 29 - 30 January 2007

Moller, K., Rajala, A., & Svahn, S. (2005). Strategic business nets—their type and management. *Journal of Business Research, 58,* 1274–1284. doi:10.1016/j.jbusres.2003.05.002

Nonaka, I., & Takeuchi, H. (1995). *The Knowledge-Creating Company*. New York: Oxford University Press.

Nonaka, I., Toyama, R., & Konno, N. (2000). SECI, Ba and Leadership: a Unified Model of Dynamic Knowledge Creation. *Long Range Planning, 33,* 5–34. doi:10.1016/S0024-6301(99)00115-6

OECD. (2005). *Oslo Manual - Guidelines for collecting and interpreting innovation data*. (Third edition, 2005). A joint publication of OECD and Eurostat

Robin, V., Rose, B., & Girard, P. (2007). Modelling collaborative knowledge to support engineering design project manager. *Computers in Industry, 58,* 188–198. doi:10.1016/j.compind.2006.09.006

Wang, S. (1997). Modeling information architecture for the organization. *Information & Management, 32,* 303–315. doi:10.1016/S0378-7206(97)00025-6

Williams, T., Rathwell, G., & Li, H. (2001). *A handbook on master planning and implementation for enterprise integration programs, Purdue Enterprise Reference Architecture, Purdue Methodology, Purdue Laboratory for Applied Industrial Control.* Institute for Interdisciplinary Engineering Studies.

ADDITIONAL READING

Chituc, C. M., & Nof, S. Y. (2007). The Join/Leave/Remain (JLR) decision in collaborative networked organizations. *Computers & Industrial Engineering, 53,* 173–195. doi:10.1016/j.cie.2007.05.002

Estrem, W. A. (2003). An evaluation framework for deploying Web Services in the next generation manufacturing enterprise. *Robotics and Computer-integrated Manufacturing, 19,* 509–519. doi:10.1016/S0736-5845(03)00061-9

Hoppe, M. (2006). *A star is born.* SAP Systems Integration. Retrieved from sapinfo.net

Jacobs, F. R., & Bendoly, E. (2003). Enterprise resource planning: developments and directions for operations management research. *European Journal of Operational Research, 146*(2). doi:10.1016/S0377-2217(02)00546-5

Tan, W. A., Shen, W., & Zhao, J. (2007). A methodology for dynamic enterprise process performance evaluation. *Computers in Industry, 58,* 474–485. doi:10.1016/j.compind.2006.10.001

Ulieru, M., Norrie, D., Kremer, R., & Shen, W. (2000). A multi-resolution collaborative architecture for web-centric global manufacturing. *Information Sciences, 127,* 3–21. doi:10.1016/S0020-0255(00)00026-8

Wang, L., Shen, W., & Xie, H. (2001). Collaborative conceptual design—state of the art and future trends. *Computer Aided Design, 34,* 981–996. doi:10.1016/S0010-4485(01)00157-9

Zaidat, A., Boucher, X., & Vincent, L. (2005). A framework for organization network engineering and integration. *Robotics and Computer-integrated Manufacturing, 21,* 259–271. doi:10.1016/j.rcim.2004.10.001

KEY TERMS AND DEFINITIONS

Collaborative Design Process: Collaborative design gathers enterprises which have to achieve a common objective linked to a new product, information and knowledge sharing, with a high level of activities coordination.

Cooperation Aiding System: The use of computer technology for the design of cooperation nets of enterprises, real or virtual.

Cooperation: The process of working or acting together, in its more complicated forms, how the components of a system work together to achieve the production properties. It is the alternative to working separately in competition

Diffusion of Innovations: The way in which innovations spread, through market or non-market channels, from their very first implementation to different consumers, countries, regions, sectors, markets and firms.

Knowledge: Skills acquired by a person or organization through experience or education; the theoretical or practical understanding of a subject - what is known in enterprise field or in total; facts and roles of information. Collaborative knowledge: knowledge - enterprise's own expertise and synergy knowledge, implemented to carry out and maintain the intra-group knowledge exchanges.

Net Cooperation: Modern and very effective form of complex aiding of production cooperation among system users in the future.

Synergy Knowledge: Alliance is a cooperation or collaboration which aims for a synergy where each partner hopes that the benefits from the alliance will be greater than those from individual efforts. Set of popularization knowledge acquired by the enterprise, coming from the other members of the cooperation, popularization knowledge distributed to the other enterprise of the cooperation project, knowledge being used by enterprise actor when he has to initiate communication with the other enterprise, depending on the culture of each enterprise and new knowledge was formed in the net of n enterprise.

Utility Function: Function of prodution which links the basic criteria of cost, time and quality - method which links the evaluation with different criteria in one is the analysis of utility of projects of the course of production.

Chapter 9
A New Meta–Heuristic Multi–Objective Approach for Optimal Dispatch of Dispersed and Renewable Generating Units in Power Distribution Systems

Eleonora Riva Sanseverino
DIEET Università di Palermo, Italy

Gaetano Zizzo
DIEET Università di Palermo, Italy

Giuseppe Fileccia Scimemi
DISEG Università di Palermo, Italy

ABSTRACT

The application of stochastic methods in engineering research and optimization has been increasing over the past few decades. Ant Colony Optimization, in particular, has been attracting growing attention as a promising approach both in discrete and continuous domains. The present work proposes a multi-objective Ant Colony Optimization for continuous domains showing good convergence properties and uniform coverage of the non-dominated front. These properties have been proved both with mathematical test functions and with a complex real world problem. Besides the second part of the chapter presents the application of the new algorithm to the problem of optimal dispatch of dispersed power generation units in modern electrical distribution networks. The issue is intrinsically multi-objective and the objectives are calculated based on the solution of the power load flow problem. The performances of the algorithm have been compared to those of the Non-dominated Sorting Genetic Algorithm II on all applications. The chapter is organized as follows, in the introductory part, the relevance of multi-objective optimization problems to modern power distribution operation is outlined. Then the Non-dominated Sorting Genetic Algorithm II is described as well as the proposed Multi-objective Ant Colony Optimization algorithm in details. Both approaches are compared on a test suite of mathematical test functions. Finally, an interesting case study in the field of modern electrical distribution systems management is proposed.

DOI: 10.4018/978-1-61692-811-7.ch009

INTRODUCTION

Multi-objective optimization problems deal with more than one objective function. Evolutionary computation has often been considered as interesting option for solving these problems since most evolutionary methods are intrinsically population-based and thus provide sets of trade-off solutions. Moreover evolutionary computation methods do not explicitly use derivatives thus giving the possibility to mathematically formulate engineering problems almost without approximations. This has created a large interest in their use for real world applications.

In many engineering problems, the formulations including cost and efficiency seem obvious. Fields like electrical power distribution where market liberalization has created many interests, require multiple objectives optimization problems formulations. On the contrary, monopoles and vertically integrated market structures mostly give rise to single objective optimization problems.

Moreover, it must be taken into consideration that the electrical power distribution area in the last years has experienced an important reorganization towards active networks characterized by a high penetration of Distributed Generation Units, DGU, based on technologies such as internal combustion engines, small and micro gas turbines, fuel cells, photovoltaic and wind plants. The possibility to produce energy in a physically distributed fashion gives the idea of many interests requiring high quality and economic operation. This is why modern power distribution management problems can be formulated as multi-objective optimization problems. Complex optimal management problems can be, in particular, formulated for 'microgrids'. These are small Medium Voltage (MV) or Low Voltage (LV) distribution systems with enough local DGUs to supply entirely a local load demand.

DGUs are electric generating units (in microgrids typically in the range of 3 kW to 200 kW), parallel to the electric utility or stand-alone, located within the electric distribution system at or near the end user. DGUs also involve power electronic interfaces, as well as communications and control devices for efficient dispatch and operation of single generating units, multiple system packages, and aggregated blocks of power. Intra-system cross-supply and communal management standards differentiate a microgrid from a group of independent but physically proximate small generators.

In order to optimize the power flows in the lines, a microgrid is equipped with load controllers and microsources controllers, that are interfaces to control interruptible loads and microsources (active and reactive generation levels), and a microgrid central controller that promotes technical and economical operation and provides set points to load controllers and microsource controllers.

The scientific and economic interest in microgrids is motivated by the possibility to implement on a large scale renewable energy sources as DGUs, to limit green house gas emissions, also reducing the transmission power losses, and to delay or even prevent the construction of new energy infrastructures. The co-ordination of all these generating and loading units is a quite challenging issue also requiring distributed intelligence applications; for this reason these modern distribution systems are also referred to as 'smart grids'.

BACKGROUND

In the technical literature few articles propose operational solutions for microgrids because of the need of interdisciplinary knowledge.

As far as optimal operation is concerned, several strategies have been reported in the literature for minimizing operational costs and maximizing quality in microgrids. In (Carlos, Hernandez-Aramburo, Green & Mugniot, 2005) the optimization is aimed at reducing the fuel consumption rate of the system while constraining it to fulfil the local energy demand (both electrical and thermal) and provide a certain minimum reserve power. In this work and (Mohamed & Koivo, 2007), the problem is treated as a single objective problem by neither considering the emission nor the operation and maintenance costs as well as no sold or purchased power to or from the main grid.

In (Zeineldin, El-Saadany & Salama, 2006) a control strategy for inverter based DGUs and a protection scheme are carried out and a coordination between them is proposed to control both voltage and frequency during islanded operation. Research by Bertani, Borghetti, Bossi, De Biase, Lamquet, Massucco, Morini, Nucci, Paolone, Quaia & Silvestro (2006) proposes an efficient control system for microgrids management. The control system manages both the transient and the steady state features of the electrical system. The application is devoted to the implementation on a small Low Voltage test facility at the CESI (Centro Elettrotecnico Sperimentale Italiano, Milan, Italy)

In this chapter, the issue of optimal real and reactive power dispatching among DGUs in microgrids is faced. The problem appears to be very complicated since it is non linear and shows multiple objectives to be optimized.

Knowing the hourly upper and lower production limits of each DGU and the hourly loading level of each bus of the electrical distribution network, the objectives to be achieved are:

- the minimization of the power losses;
- the minimization of the overall production costs;
- the minimization of the voltage drops.

The unknowns of the problem are:

- the hourly power productions of the DGUs.

The problem is dealt with using two multi-objective stochastic approaches: the non-dominated sorting genetic algorithm II (Deb, Agrawal, Pratap & Meyarivan, 2000) and a multi-objective

implementation of the continuous ant colony optimization (Socha & Dorigo, 2005) proposed by the authors.

In what follows, the two approaches are described in details with reference to a general continuous multi-objective problems. Then a set of mathematical test functions are considered using a set of performance indices for comparison. The second part of the chapter is devoted to the real world power distribution engineering application already described. After a brief review on the microgrid concept and on the power dispatch problem, the multi-objective formulation is presented. Finally, application examples on a medium size test system are provided.

POPULATION-BASED ALGORITHMS FOR MULTI-OBJECTIVE OPTIMIZATION

A multi-objective optimization problem has a number of objectives that have to be maximized or minimized (Deb, 2001). Such as in single optimization problems the problem may show one or more equality and inequality constraints which any feasible solution must satisfy. The following expression gives the general statement of a multi-objective minimization problem.

$$\min_{\mathbf{x}} \ f(\mathbf{x}) \tag{1}$$

subject to

$$g_h(\mathbf{x}) \leq 0, \quad h = 1, 2, ..., p,$$
$$h_k(\mathbf{x}) = 0, \quad k = 1, 2, ..., r,$$
$$x_i^L \leq x_i \leq x_i^U$$

In this expression, $f(\mathbf{x})$, denotes a vector function composed of m local objective functions $f_j(\mathbf{x})$, $j = 1, 2, ..., m$ to be minimized, $\mathbf{x}$ is a vector of

n decision variables, i.e. $x = [x_1, x_2, ..., x_i, \;, x_n]^T$. Each variable has a range of variation between a lower and an upper bound, respectively x_i^L, x_i^U. These ranges of variation along with constraints for all decision variables given by functions g_h and h_k determine in the n-dimensional space the decision variable space D. A maximization problem can be stated analogously. The set of optimal solutions in the decision space D is in general denoted as the *Pareto set* $P \subseteq D$, and its image in the objectives space as *Pareto front*. With many multi-objective optimization problems, knowledge about this set helps the decision maker in choosing the best compromise solution.

There are different ways to deal with a multi-objective optimization problem, e.g., objectives can be aggregated into a single one, but most work in the area of multi-objective optimization has concentrated on the approximation of the Pareto set by stochastic population-based methods. Evolutionary and meta-heuristic techniques are suitable for this task, since many of these methods proceed through the modification of sets of solutions (population-based algorithms). Accordingly, the outcome of a population-based multi-objective optimization algorithm is considered to be a set of mutually non-dominated solutions, or Pareto set approximation.

The concept of non dominance is one of the basic concepts in multi-objective optimization.

For a problem having more than one objective function to minimize (say, $f_j(x)$, $j = 1, 2, ..., m$) any two multidimensional solutions $x[a]$ and $x[b]$ can have two possibilities: one dominates the other or none dominates the other. A solution $x[a]$ is said to dominate the other solution $x[b]$, if both the following conditions are true:

a.   The solution $x[a]$ is no worse than $x[b]$ in all objectives, $f_j(x[a]) \leq f_j(x[b])$, for all $j = 1, 2, ..., m$.

b.   The solution $x[a]$ is strictly better than $x[b]$ in at least one objective, or $f_{j^*}(x[a]) < f_{j^*}(x[b])$ for at least one $j^* \in 1, 2, ..., m$.

If any of the above conditions is violated, the solution $x[a]$ does *not dominate* the solution $x[b]$. If $x[a]$ dominates the solution $x[b]$, it is also customary to write $x[b]$ *is dominated* by $x[a]$, or $x[a]$ is *not dominated* by $x[b]$, or, simply, among two solutions, $x[a]$ is the *non-dominated* solution.

It is again important to underline that the concept of optimality in multi-objective optimization is related to a set of solutions, instead than to a single one. Sets of solutions can be equivalent if we aim at optimizing more than one objective. It is therefore possible to define Pareto local and global optimality for sets of solutions. P is a locally optimal Pareto set, if for every member x in P, there exist no solution y in a small neighbourhood, which dominates every member in the set P. P is a global Pareto-optimal set, if there exist no solution in the search space, which dominates every member in the set P. From the above discussion, it is possible to point out that there are primarily two goals that a multi-criterion optimization algorithm must achieve:

-    guide the search towards the global Pareto-optimal region;
-    maintain population diversity in the Pareto-optimal front (prevent crowding of solutions).

In the following sections, two population-based stochastic algorithms are described. One is the well known non-dominated sorting genetic algorithm II proposed by Deb et al. (2000). The second is an algorithm proposed by the authors that implements a multi-objective version of the continuous ant colony optimization algorithm (Socha & Dorigo, 2005). In both cases the knowledge about the problem collected by the population is used to stochastically generate a new population of individuals.

In both algorithms, the concept of non dominance is used for solutions prizing.

The algorithms described in the following only apply to unconstrained multi-objective problems. Their extension to constrained problems is possible, but is out of the scope of the chapter.

NON-DOMINATED SORTING GENETIC ALGORITHM II

The Non-dominated Sorting Genetic Algorithm II (NSGA-II) is an evolutionary optimization method, where sets of solutions are evolved by means of recombination operators such as mutation and crossover. As Non-dominated Sorting Genetic Algorithm (Srinivas & Deb, 1994), NSGAII divides the population in fronts of non-dominated solutions so that the search can be addressed towards interesting areas of the search space, where the global Pareto optimal region is presumably located.

In NSGA and NSGA-II, solutions are prized on the basis of their non-domination level, which is called solutions ranking. But basically, NSGA-II varies from the NSGA in three main things. It is more efficient computationally, since the ranking of solutions based on non-domination is performed with a $O(mN_p^2)$ algorithm, instead of $O(mN_p^3)$, where m is the number of objectives and N_p is the population size; it significantly prevents the loss of good solutions once they have been found (elitism); it does not need any parameter specification. A binary tournament selection operator is used to select the offspring population, whereas crossover and mutation operators remain as usual.

In the following subsections, the main operators of the algorithm are briefly described. Before selection is performed, the population is ranked on the basis of an individual's non-domination level and, to allow the diversification, a crowding factor is calculated for each solution.

Fast Non-Dominated Sorting

In order to sort a population of size N_p according to the level of non-domination, each solution must be compared with every other solution in the population to find if it is dominated. The fast non-dominated sorting approach will require at most $O(mN_p^2)$ computations. Further details on its implementation can be found in (Deb et al., 2000).

Density Estimation

To get an estimate of the density of solutions surrounding a particular point in the population, the average distance of the two points on either side of this point along each of the objectives is considered. In this paper, this measure has been normalized. Considering the ith solution $x[i]$, this quantity $x[i].distance$ serves as an estimate of the size of the largest cuboid enclosing the point i without including any other point in the population (crowding distance). In Figure 1, the crowding distance of the ith solution in its front (marked with solid circles) is the average side-length of the cuboid (shown with a dashed box) in the objectives space.

The following pseudo-code can be used to calculate the crowding:

```
Crowding-distance-assignment
    (solutions of front I)
Set l to the size of the set I
    to be ordered
For i=1,2,…,l {For each x ∈ I}
Set x[i].distance=0 (i=1,2,….l)
For each objective jI is sorted
    by each objective j
Set
x[1].distance = m
    (number of objectives)
and
x[l].distance = m
    (number of objectives)
```

Figure 1. Crowding distance measure. Adapted from (Deb et al., 2000)

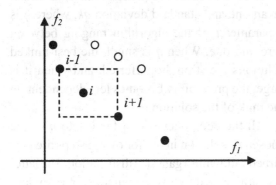

Figure 2. The NSGA-II algorithm

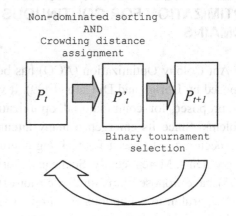

```
For each objective j
Set max_dist[j]=f_j(x[l])-f_j(x[1])
If max_dist[j]<>0 then
For i=2 to l-1 do
   x[i].distance:=x[i].
     distance+(f_j(x[i+1])-
     f_j(x[i-1]))/(max_dist[j])
```

Here $f_j(x[i])$ is the jth objective function value of the ith individual solution vector in the set *I*. It must be observed that the crowding distance is normalized along each direction of the objectives space. For the normalization, the quantity *max_dist*[j] is used; this being the maximum distance between the jth objective values along the jth direction.

Crowded Comparison Operator

The crowded comparison operator ($\geq_n$) guides the selection process at the various stages of the algorithm towards a uniformly spread out Pareto-optimal front. Every individual *x* in the population is given two attributes:

1. Non-domination rank in the objectives space directions (*x.rank*)
2. Local crowding distance in the objectives space directions (*x.distance*)

A partial order $\geq_n$ can be defined as:

```
i ≥_n j
If (x[i].rank < x[j].rank)or
  ((x[i].rank < x[j].rank)and
   (x[i].distance > x[j].distance))
```

That is, between two solutions with different non-domination ranks the point with the lower rank is preferred (the front which is closer to the axes origin). Otherwise, if both points belong to the same front then the point which is located in a region with lesser number of points (the size of the cuboid inclosing it is larger) is preferred.

Crossover and Mutation Operators

Crossover and mutation operators depend on the problem at hand. In this paper, for continuous mathematical functions, simulated binary crossover (Deb & Agrawal, 1995) and polynomial mutation (Deb & Goyal, 1996) have been applied. In the following Figure 2, one cycle of the NSGA-II procedure is represented. P_t and P_{t+1} are the populations of solutions at iteration *t* and *t*+1, while P'_t is a partially ordered ($\geq_n$) set of solutions.

MULTI-OBJECTIVE ANT COLONY OPTIMIZATION FOR CONTINUOUS DOMAINS

The Ant Colony Optimization (ACO) has been proposed by Dorigo and Di Caro (1999). It was first proposed for combinatorial optimization problems. Since its emergence many attempts have been made to use it for tackling continuous problems. More recently, Socha and Dorigo (2005), have proposed the natural extension of the ACO algorithm to continuous domains, ACOR. The idea that is central to the way ACOR works is the incremental construction of solutions based on the biased (by pheromone) probabilistic choice of solution components.

At each construction step, the ant chooses a probability density function. In what follows, the main steps of the ACOR algorithm are briefly outlined.

An archive T of k solutions, $T = \{x[1], x[2], \ldots\ldots x[k]\}$ is first created. Where $x[r] = [x_1[r], x_2[r], \ldots\ldots x_n[r]]$. The solutions of the archive T are ordered according to their objective function value. Given a decision variable x_i, $i=1,\ldots.n$, an ant constructs a solution by performing n construction steps. At construction step i, the ant chooses a value for the variable x_i. At this construction step, only the information related to the ith dimension is used. Select a base solution r from the archive T to be modified according to the following probability:

$$p_r = \frac{\omega_r}{\sum_{j=1}^{k} \omega_j} \qquad (2)$$

where

$$\omega_r = \frac{1}{qk\sqrt{2\pi}} e^{-\frac{(r-1)^2}{2q^2k^2}} \qquad (3)$$

which essentially defines the weight ω_r to be a value of the Gaussian function with argument r, mean one and standard deviation qk, where q is a parameter of the algorithm ranging between zero and one. When q is small, the best-ranked solutions are strongly preferred, and when it is large, the probability becomes less dependent on the rank of the solution.

All the components $x_i[r]$ for $i=1$ to n of the chosen r^{th} solution in the following steps are perturbed following a gaussian distribution. The latter is characterised by two parameters: the standard deviation, σ and the mean μ. The first is defined, for each component, as:

$$\sigma_i^r = \xi \sum_{e=1}^{k} \frac{|x_i[e] - x_i[r]|}{k-1} \qquad (4)$$

where ξ is a user-defined parameter ranging from 0 and 1. The higher the value of this parameter the slower the convergence speed. The second parameter, μ, is the value of the ith parameter of the chosen solution itself ($x_i[r]$). So the ith parameter is newly determined. The same procedure is repeated for all the n parameters. At the end, once the solution is entirely constructed, it is evaluated and if better than any of the solutions in T, it is included into the archive set T.

The described algorithm has been turned by the authors into multi-objective, in the following way.

In order to account for many objectives, the archive of solutions is ranked based on the non-domination level and secondarily on the crowding of solutions (namely two solutions belonging to the same non-domination rank are ordered on the basis of a crowding index, see section 'Density estimation' above). In order to preserve diversity of solutions, and differently from standard ACOR where the ants (solutions) are created and end up in the archive, in the proposed approach the ants have the chance, if certain conditions are met, to keep living for more than one iteration till when they are added to the archive or refused.

Algorithm 1. Multi-objective ACOR pseudo-code

```
Non dominance/crowding ordering (archive);
Calculation of weights (see Equation (10));
    Repeat
        Set current archive size to k
        Repeat
            If not(continue) then
                a) choose new solution from archive using (2)
            Else
                b) set current solution to new solution
Perturb the components of current solution using a Gaussian distribution having mean μ and
standard deviation σ
Evaluate new solution
Accept new solution with probability A(new solution)
for one of the following operations:
1)      Add
2)      Replace
Until archive size is >= k+nants
Non dominance/crowding ordering (archive of k+nants);
        Take the first k solutions
        Increase number of iterations
Until the number of iterations reaches a maximum number of iterations
```

The decision about saving a solution or rejecting it or even letting it run for other iterations is given to a special acceptance function *A* which is described below. The solutions that are in this way accepted can either be added to the archive or can replace one of the solution in the archive. For this reason, the archive has an adjustable size that varies between *k* and *k+nants*, where *nants* is the number of ants constructed per iteration. The algorithm pseudo-code is reported in Algorithm 1. In the pseudo-code, current solution is the solution currently processed, while new solution is the newly created solution.

As it can be observed the main differences with standard ACOR are:

- the non dominance ordering;
- the variable size archive;
- the acceptance function, *A*.

The non dominance ordering indeed is applied to the archive *T* and non dominated fronts are identified. Afterwards, within each front, solutions are ordered with respect to the crowding factor (for the generic i^{th} solution *x*[*i*] is *x*[*i*].*distance*)

calculated using the 'Crowding distance assignment' procedure already described for NSGAII.

The archive size can take values ranging from *k* to *k+nants*.

In general, the acceptance function *A* takes an exponential form similar to the one proposed for the multiobjective Simulated Annealing algorithm (Smith, Everson & Fieldsend, 2004).

In this case, it takes a different expression depending on the non domination relation between the new solution and the current solution.

If the new solution dominates the current solution then the function *A* takes the following form:

$$A = e^{-sign * \frac{\Delta dom}{n_d}} \tag{5}$$

Where n_d is the number of solutions that in the archive dominate new solution and *sign* is a variable that can take two values: -1 and 1. If the objective functions calculated in the new solution take the extreme values, it takes value -1. In this way, the exponential in (5) always gets a value that is greater than 1 and the solution is certainly accepted. See Figure 3 below:

Figure 3. Multi-objective ACOR: in this case for the new solution sign is set to -1

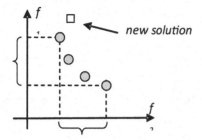

In this way, diversity is preserved. If *sign* takes the value 1, the exponential gets values ranging between 0 and 1 and thus the probability of acceptance only depends on the exponent. In equation (5), *Δdom* is the average amount of domination defined for all the points in the archive that are different from new solution as:

$$\Delta dom = \sum_{i=1}^{n_d} \prod_{j=1}^{m} \frac{\left| f_j(newsolution) - f_j(archive[i])) \right|}{R_j}$$

(6)

Where $f_j(newsolution)$ and $f_j(archive[i])$ are the values of the jth objective function respectively for the new solution and for the ith element of the archive, R_j is the range of the jth objective function in the objectives space.

If the solutions from the archive that dominate the new solution are far from it, then the amount of domination is larger and the function A gets a smaller value. Thus it is more possible that the new solution is discarded. The situation changes if the variable *sign* takes value -1, this happens if the new solution shows an extreme value in the objectives space. If the new solution also dominates the whole archive, n_d is zero and the solution is accepted and added to the archive. If the new solution is dominated by the current solution or

they are equivalent, the acceptance function takes the following form:

$$A = e^{-\Delta dom_{min}}$$

(7)

Δdom_{min} is the minimum amount of domination among the solutions in the archive dominating the new solution:

$$\Delta dom_{min} = \min_{i=1,..n_d} \prod_{j=1}^{m} \frac{\left| f_j(newsolution) - f_j(archive[i])) \right|}{R_j}$$

(8)

Then if the new solution is accepted it can either be saved into the archive (replacing the old solution or being added to the archive) and it can be used to continue the search.

The following scheme can clear out the acceptance mechanism. (see Algorithm 2)

The algorithm behaves differently in the cases shown below in Figure 4.

If *new solution* dominates *current solution* (Figure 4a)), it can be added to the archive or it can replace the current solution in the archive. The search continues with *new solution*. If *current solution* dominates *new solution* (Figure 4b)), the latter is saved into the archive and the search continue with *new solution* if and only if it shows objectives with extreme values (*sign* = -1), otherwise the search continues with *current solution*.

MATHEMATICAL TEST FUNCTIONS MINIMIZATION

Some applications have been carried out on a test suite of 5 mathematical test functions taken from the literature. In all cases, the objective functions have to be minimized.

The set of test functions is reported:

Algorithm 2. Acceptance mechanism and subsequent operations

```
If new solution is accepted then
     If new solution dominates current solution then
         It is saved into the archive
(If (continue) then add else replace)
 The search is continued with new solution
     Else
         It must be saved into the archive
But the search is continued with new solution only if
sign = -1 otherwise the search continues with current solution.
```

Figure 4. Two possible positions of the current and the new solutions with respect to the archive

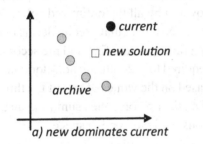

SCH is a vector of two convex functions with 1 variable ranging between $-10^3, 10^3$. Its expression is:

$$f_1(x) = x^2$$
$$f_2(x) = (x-2)^2 \tag{9}$$

FON is a vector of two non convex functions with 3 variables ranging between -4,4. Its expression is:

$$f_1(x) = 1 - \exp\left(-\sum_{i=1}^{3}\left(x_i - \frac{1}{\sqrt{3}}\right)^2\right)$$
$$f_2(x) = 1 - \exp\left(-\sum_{i=2}^{3}\left(x_i - \frac{1}{\sqrt{3}}\right)^2\right) \tag{10}$$

KUR is a vector of two non convex functions with 3 variables ranging between -5,5. Its expression is:

$$f_1(x) = \sum_{i=1}^{n-1}\left(-10\exp\left(-0.2\sqrt{x_i^2 + x_{i+1}^2}\right)\right)$$
$$f_2(x) = \sum_{i=1}^{n}\left(\left|x_i^{0.8}\right| + 5\sin x_i^3\right) \tag{11}$$

ZDT1 is a vector of two convex functions with 30 variables ranging between 0,1. Its expression is:

$$f_1(x) = x_1$$
$$f_2(x) = g(x)\left[1 - \sqrt{\frac{x_1}{g(x)}}\right] \tag{12}$$
$$g(x) = 1 + 9\frac{\sum_{i=2}^{n}x_i}{n-1}$$

ZDT6 is a vector of two non convex functions, non uniformly spaced function with 10 variables ranging between 0,1. Its expression is:

$$f_1(x) = 1 - \exp(-4x_1)\sin^6(6\pi x_1)$$

$$f_2(x) = g(x)\left[1 - \left(\frac{f_1(x)}{g(x)}\right)^2\right]$$

$$g(x) = 1 + \left(\frac{\sum_{i=2}^{n} x_i}{n-1}\right)^{0.25}$$

(13)

The algorithms have been compared on the basis of four performance measures (Tan, Lee & Khor, 2001).

The algorithm effort (*AE*) can be defined as the ratio of the total period of simulation time, T_{run}, over a number of objective function evaluations, *Neval*:

$$AE = \frac{T_{run}}{Neval}$$

(14)

As shown in equation 14, for a fixed period of T_{run}, more number of function evaluations being performed indirectly indicates that less computational effort is needed by the optimization algorithm and hence resulting in a smaller *AE*. Similarly, for a fixed value of *Neval* any optimization algorithm that requires a bigger value of T_{run} reflects the need of a larger algorithm effort, and vice versa.

For more choices of non-dominated solutions, it is always desired to have as many as possible the useful candidate solutions known as the Pareto-front from a given population size. The performance measure is denoted here as the ratio of non-dominated individuals (*RNI*) for a given population *X* and is mathematically formulated as:

$$RNI(X) = \frac{nondom - indiv}{P_X}$$

(15)

where *nondom-indiv* is the number of non-dominated individuals in population *X* while P_X is the size of population *X*. Therefore the value *RNI* = 1 means all the individuals in the population are non-dominated while the opposite, *RNI* = 0 represents the situation where none of the individuals in the population are non-dominated.

The index Size of Space Covered (*SSC*) was proposed by Zitzler and Thiele (1999). It is a quantitative measure of size of space covered to evaluate the overall size of phenotype space covered by all the optimized solutions.

It can be calculated considering two objectives at a time (i.e.: the first and the second). Then it is required to order the *nc* non-dominated solutions based on the values of one of the three objectives (i.e.: the first) and then summing up the contributions on the objective space:

$$SSC = \sum_{i=1}^{nc}\left[f_1(x[i]) - f_1(x[i-1]) * f_2(x[i])\right]$$

(16)

A measure of uniform distribution (*UD*) can be used to measure the distribution of non-dominated individuals is proposed here. Mathematically, for a given set of non-dominated individuals *X'* in a population *X*, the following expression can be calculated.

$$Sn = \sqrt{\frac{\sum_{i=1}^{nc} \dfrac{x[i].dis\tan ce}{nc} - x[i].dis\tan ce}{nc-1}}$$

(17)

Where *x[i].distance* is the crowding distance measure defined for NSGAII.

The index *UD* can be calculated as:

$$UD = \frac{1}{1+Sn}$$

(18)

Table 1. Algorithms parameters

NSGA II		MO_ACOR	
pmut	*pcross*	*q*	*csi*
0.11	0.95	0.2	0.6

The parameters chosen for the two algorithms are reported in Table I. For NSGA-II the mutation and the crossover probabilities, *pmut* and *pcross*, are reported; for MO_ACOR, the real parameters *q* and *csi*, controlling the exploration ability of the algorithm are given.

Table II shows the average values above listed performance indices calculated on a sample of 50 runs. Both algorithms have been tested on the considered set of five test functions.

The algorithm effort and size of space covered show a similar value for both algorithms. On the other hand, MO_ACOR is able to find more uniformly distributed solutions in all cases. All the runs have been carried out imposing the same number of functions evaluations for the two algorithms.

POWER DISPATCH IN MICROGRIDS

Microgrids

In this section, the authors will focus on the problem of short term power generation optimal dispatch problem in microgrids. In Figure 5, the typical layout of a MV microgrid is represented.

As Figure 5 shows, the microgrid is supplied from the main High Voltage, HV, grid through an HV/MV transformer. The MGCC, the MicroGrid Central controller, is located downstream the transformer; MC, the Microsource Controller, and LC, the Load Controller, are respectively installed close to the DGUs and the loads. In the same figure, the Photovoltaic units are identified with PV, the Combined Heat and Power generating units are indicated with CHP, while the inverter

is indicated with AC/DC (Alternating Current, Direct Current). The inverter interfaces the generating units with the electric grid. It is able to change voltage module and displacement in order to adapt to the current operating requirements. The Load Controllers and Microsource controllers are usually implemented into inverters control logic. Every generating units produces LV electric power and is connected to the grid through a MV/LV transformer.

The following Figure 6 shows the general architecture of the MicroGrid Central controller (Bertani et al., 2006). As it can be observed, in the same unit the following operations are performed:

- identification of the bus voltages all over the network, based on a set of redundant measures of electrical quantities (state estimation block);
- load and renewable energy sources renewables energy source generation potential short and long term forecasts (load and RES forecast blocks);
- short and long term power generation dispatch (Day-ahead scheduler and Intra-day scheduler blocks).

In Figure 6, 'field' indicates the power distribution system. While RES indicates Renewable energy Sources.

The 'state estimation' block takes the available measures from the power distribution system and turns them into reliable quantities to be processed for loads and renewables units output forecasts. Typically, forecasts are carried out using a Neural Networks-based approach for time series predictions. Therefore, the state estimation gives the values of loads and solar irradiation or wind velocity that are required for 24 hours and short term (15 minutes) forecasts both of loads and of renewable energy sources predictions.

The blocks termed 'short-term/24 hours forecasts' are referred to the prediction of loads and power production from renewable energy sources

Table 2. Results attained over the considered test functions

	NSGAII	MO ACOR	NSGAII	MO ACOR	NSGAII	MO ACOR	NSGAII	MO ACOR	NSGAII	MO ACOR
	SCH		FON		KUR		ZDT1		ZDT6	
AE	$3.9*10^{-4}$	$5.7*10^{-5}$	$3.5*10^{-4}$	$1.14*10^{-4}$	$2.8*10^{-4}$	$1*10^{-4}$	$4.2*10^{-4}$	$4.8*10^{-4}$	$5.6*10^{-4}$	$1*10^{-4}$
RNI	1	1	1	1	1	1	1	1	1	1
UD	0.76	0.86	0.76	0.86	0.76	0.86	0.73	0.90	0.67	0.84
SSC	2.6	2.6	0.65	0.65	26.5	26.1	0.32	0.33	0.91	0.90

Figure 5. Typical MV microgrid with its control devices

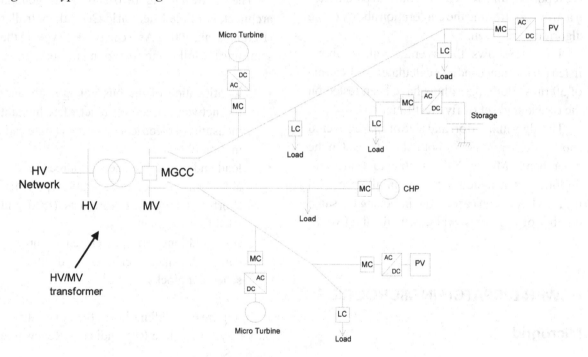

Figure 6. Scheme of MicroGrid controller and dispatcher

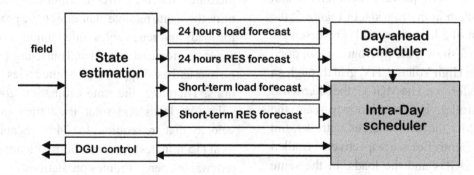

respectively in the subsequent 15 minutes or in the following 24 hours.

The 'day-ahead scheduler' calculates the active power set points during the following day in order to minimize the overall costs, it gives as outputs ranges of variation of the active power set points for the distributed energy sources. Based on the short term forecast of power production of these units and on the economically suggested optimum range of variation, the intra-day scheduler every 15 minutes updates the DGUs set points for a more precise optimization of both technical and economical objectives.

Finally the block named 'DER control' has as inputs the results of the 'Intra-day scheduler' and as outputs a set of control actions to be implemented by the Load Controllers and Microsource Controllers.

Currently, the interest in the issue of managing microgrids is quite high.

The European community indeed is supporting the research in this field with a specific platform (European Commission, 2006), and different calls within the Framework Program 7 (FP7). The latter being one of the most important EC initiatives for promoting research and playing a crucial role in reaching the goals of growth, competitiveness and employment within the European Union.

POWER DISPATCH PROBLEM DEFINITION

The technical economical power dispatching within the intra-day scheduler consists in the identification of the optimal set points of the generating units in an electrical system. Typically the objectives are connected to the minimization of the production cost of these units, although also power quality objectives can be considered within the optimization, such as power losses and voltage drops minimizations. Identifying the generated power of each unit giving the minimum production cost and the best operating indices requires

the solution of the load flow problem, based on the knowledge of:

- the short term forecasted load at the network nodes;
- the short term forecasted generating upper limits for renewable energy sources;
- results of the day-ahead scheduler;
- the units production costs and environmental data;
- the status of storage units and technical constraints.

The problem studied in this work is thus that to optimally manage the intra-day scheduler of a microgrid.

Based on the input data above listed, the scheduler elaborates a set of control signals that are sent to the DGUs. These signals are turned by suitable transducers into actions over the regulating systems that modulate the power injections at the DGUs.

Of course, it is hypothesized that renewables DGUs can store the excess of energy produced at each hour of the day. In this way, the power generated by them can be dispatched.

Consider a *n*-bus microgrid system with:

- N_{fix} load or generation nodes with fixed forecasted real and reactive power demands or injections;
- N_{DG} controllable DGU.

The problem is that to identify the $2N_{DG}$ real valued vector identifying the operating points of the DGUs in the network:

$$x = \left[P_1^g, P_2^g, \ldots P_{N_{DG}}^g, Q_1^g, Q_2^g, \ldots Q_{N_{DG}}^g \right] \quad (19)$$

where N_{DG} is the number of DGUs and

- $P_j^g, P_{j\min}^g, P_{j\max}^g, j = 1, 2, ..., N_{DG}$ respectively represent: the active production, the minimum and maximum limits of real power at the jth DGU;

- $Q_j^g, Q_{j\min}^g, Q_{j\max}^g, j = 1, 2, ..., N_{DG}$ respectively represent: the reactive production, the minimum and maximum limits of the reactive power at the jth DGU.

subject to the following constraints:

- upper and lower limits of the values of the controlled variables, namely the DGUs power outputs, taking into account the required power reserves;

$$P_{j\min}^g \leq P_j^g \leq P_{j\max}^g \quad j = 1, 2, ..., N_{DG}, \quad (20)$$

$$Q_{j\min}^g \leq Q_j^g \leq Q_{j\max}^g \quad j = 1, 2, ..., N_{DG}. \quad (21)$$

The solution must also satisfy the constraint about power transfer limits in the network lines, this constraint is usually always satisfied in well designed networks, therefore it will not be considered;

optimizing the following criteria:

- joule losses in the system, $f_1(x) = P_{loss}$
- fuel consumption cost

$$f_2(x) = \sum_{i=1}^{N_{DG}} C_{Pi} P_i^g \Delta t \quad (22)$$

where C_{Pi} is the unitary fuel consumption cost of the ith source, P_i^g the power output of the ith source, considered constant in time interval Δt;

- bus voltage deviations with respect to the rated value V_{set}

$$f_3(x) = \frac{1}{n - bus} \sum_{\substack{i=1 \\ x}}^{n-bus} |V_i - V_{set}| \quad (23)$$

Therefore, the formulated problem is that to determine the operating points of the DGUs giving rise to a technical-economical optimum as a compromise between minimum cost operation and high quality service. Minimum cost operation is ensured if the overall fuel consumption is minimum. The latter condition depends directly on the power generated by fuel-suppliedDGUs. High quality service is attained if power losses and voltage deviations, respectively connected to conductors heating and failure to meet contractual obligations are kept as limited as possible. Of course, minimum losses, minimum voltage deviations and minimum cost are not concurrent objectives, since they are normally attained with different operating points of all the DGUs in the network.

Using the general notation introduced in the section 'Population-based algorithms for multi-objective optimization', the vector of functions to be minimized has $m=3$ components and no inequality or equality constraints. Each variable has a range of variation between a lower and an upper bound, see inequalities (20) and (21).

Power losses P_{loss} and bus voltages V_i in expression (23) can be calculated if the following load flow equations are solved:

$$P_g^i = P_L^i + V_i^2 Y_{ii} \cos \vartheta_{ii} + \sum_{i \neq j}^{n-bus} V_i V_j Y_{ij} \cos(\delta_j - \delta_i + \vartheta_{ij})$$

$$Q_g^i = Q_L^i + V_i^2 Y_{ii} \sin \vartheta_{ii} + \sum_{i \neq j}^{n-bus} V_i V_j Y_{ij} \sin(\delta_j - \delta_i + \vartheta_{ij})$$

$$(24)$$

where:

n-bus is the number of buses of the network;

P_g^i and Q_g^i are, respectively, the active and reactive power generated at the ith bus;

P_L^i and Q_L^i are, respectively, the active and reactive power demand at the ith bus;

V_i is the absolute value of the voltage at the ith bus;

δ_i is the phase angle of the voltage phasor of the ith bus;

Y_{ii} is the absolute value of the sum of the admittances of all the branches connected to the ith bus;

Y_{ij} is the absolute value of the sum of the admittances of all the branches connecting the ith and the jth buses;

ϑ_{ij} is the phase angle of the admittance Y_{ij}.

The system of equations (24) expresses the equality of the generated power (both real and reactive) with the sum of the power required by the loads and the power losses in the branches of the network (the terms given as a function of V_i and Y_{ij}). Therefore, from the load flow equations the power losses in the whole system can be directly calculated as:

$$P_{loss} = \sum_{i=1,n-bus} P_g^i - P_L^i \qquad (25)$$

The solution of the load-flow problem requires that the total generated power of a network matches the total demand plus the power losses. The load-flow problem can be then solved specifying the generated active power at every generation bus (optimization variables vector expressed in (19)) except the slack one and solving the system of equations that expresses the power flows in the network. Since these equations are non-linear, iterative techniques such as the Newton–Raphson are adopted for their resolution. This explains the inherent complexity of the problem at hand.

The optimal power dispatch problem in microgrids has been solved using linear programming and sensitivity matrices (Bertani et al., 2006), but

this approach such as other methods based on a mathematical approach require the linearization of the optimization functions. Moreover, multi-objective formulations and constraints can be handled with some difficulty unless solution approaches based on evolution and meta-heuristics are adopted. These indeed allow a proper formulation of the problem and the objective functions and constraints do not need to be distorted or simplified.

OPTIMAL POWER DISPATCH

The test system for the considered power dispatch application is depicted in Figure 7. The data of the considered DGUs are reported in Table I, where P_{max} indicates the upper production capacity limits (the lower limits are zero). Each DGU has a reactive power generation unit. The unitary cost considered includes the fuel cost and the operation and maintenance (O&M) costs associated to the considered installation. The production cost of the micro-turbines is assumed to be dependant on the energy outputted by the machine. It is well known indeed that such dependency exists in terms of efficiency. Thus it is possible to translate it into monetary terms.

In Figure 7, the MV network scheme supplying the island of Lampedusa (Italy) is reported. The network has 69 nodes, of which 52 are load nodes, and is composed by a thermoelectric power plant supplying three cable lines (type RG7H1RX, Cross section: 3x95mm2) and one aerial line (Copper conductors, Cross Section: 3x35mm2). The rated voltage of the network is 10kV.

The utility that generates and distributes the electrical power is concerned with the problem of limiting the power losses that are quite high and is also interested in meeting the new environmental constraint deriving from the application of EU directives. This can be done either by substituting the existing infrastructure and changing the voltage

Figure 7. Single-line scheme of the MV system supplying the Island of Lampedusa (Italy)

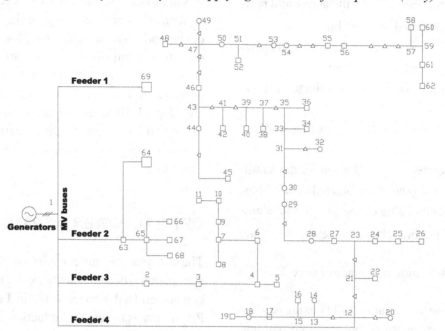

level, or by including dispersed generation units. The latter measure has a more interesting economical impact due to the governmental incentives for the installation of DGUs based on renewables. The most suitable dispersed generation unit based on renewables for the island of Lampedusa, which is at the latitude of 35°30' N, is the one based on photovoltaic generation.

Knowing:

- the hourly average insulation of the island and the real average active and reactive power profiles for each load node, differentiated between summer and winter 2008, provided by the distributor;
- the market cost of photovoltaic system;
- the energy production cost from fossil source;
- the sum of the interest and the amortization rates;

the following locations, typologies and rated powers of the DGUs have been devised (Table III):

The unitary costs in Table III refer to the fuel cost (including transportation) and the O&M costs. In the case of PV and wind units, the fuel cost is null and the O&M cost can be considered independent on the daily energy production. The fuel cost is quite high compared to other mainland thermoelectric generation units. This is due to the islanded condition of Lampedusa. Transportation costs have indeed a large incidence over the unitary cost of fuel. Some simulations have been carried out without and with the optimal control of the power injections at the DG nodes. First, the power injections in the system have been fixed to the maximum available power, considering different power factors and irradiation levels. The results reported in the Table IV below have been obtained at some hours of a typical winter day.

Of course, the control of the output power of the DGUs allows the production costs modulation along the daytime with considerable savings. Also the power losses level can be translated into monetary units. These savings are as larger as the optimization algorithm is more efficient.

Table 3. Data of the 9 DGUs connected to the distribution network (m.u. indicates a generic monetary unit)

Connection bus and DG type	Cost (m.u./kWh)	P_{max} (kW)
1-diesel	12	11000
7- photovoltaic	-	150
10- photovoltaic	-	150
20- microturbines	14	50
27- microturbines	14	50
44- microturbines	14	100
46- photovoltaic	-	100
52- photovoltaic	-	50
58- photovoltaic	-	50
63- diesel	12	400

Table 4. Evaluation of costs and production costs and voltage deviations without control

Hour	Cost*10^{-3} (mu/h)	P_{loss} (kW)	Avg.voltage deviation (p.u.)
8 a.m.	95.29	40.59	0.00679
12 a.m	108.65	45.30	0.007754
4 p.m.	119.06	70.64	0.01195
6 p.m.	115.27	64.24	0.01137

rithms can account for the load flow problem in islanded systems (Riva Sanseverino, Pecoraro, Borghetti, Bosetti & Paolone, 2007), but this is out of the scope of the present chapter.

A comparison of the algorithms described earlier is carried out on the power dispatch problem. The two algorithms have been implementing using the same parameters reported in Table I. In the application of the NSGAII algorithm, the mutation operator has been implemented as a small variation of the considered DGU injection. The crossover operator is simply the one-point crossover (Poli & Langdon, 1997) applied to the string *x* described in (19).

In the following Figure 8, it is clear the power losses and production costs reduction attainable using NSGA II and MO_ACOR for optimization at 6 p.m..

The differences are summarized in the table below.

Table V evidences how the attainable solutions are improved using MO_ACOR compared to standard NSGA-II, which in this case shows a slightly more limited search space exploration ability. Similar or even better results have been attained in the other hours of the day, thus bringing on the average a saving ranging between 1% and 2% for each objective (power losses and production cost) per hour. It must also be underlined that meta-heuristic and evolutionary algo-

FUTURE RESEARCH DIRECTIONS

This chapter tries to explore the area of modern and future power distribution systems optimal management by means of a new meta-heuristic technique for continuous multi-objective optimization problems. The proposed approach is an extension of the continuous Ant colony Optimization algorithm. In order to test the proposed algorithm, the authors have used a set of mathematical test functions and a complex power dispatch problem formulated for modern electrical distribution systems. Further research directions of this work include the extension of the considered optimization approach for the treatment of design problems in presence of constraints and parameters variations. Finally, new formulations of the optimal power dispatch problem also considering other sources types and different control modes must be considered.

CONCLUSION

This chapter provides a new multi-objective evolutionary algorithm which is an extension to multi-objective optimization of the continuous Ant colony Optimization algorithm. The algorithm

Figure 8. NSGA II and MO_ACOR for optimal power dispatch at 6 p.m.

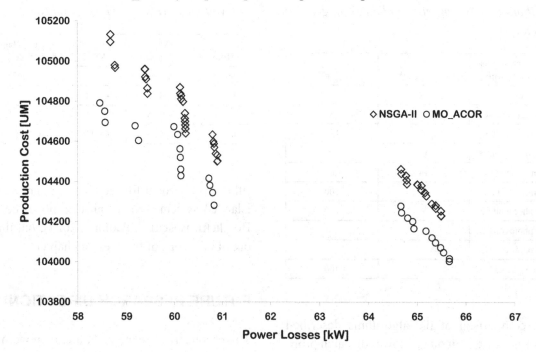

Table 5. Evaluation of costs, power losses and voltage deviations with optimization

6 p.m.	Cost*10^{-3} (mu/h)	P_{loss} (kW)	Avg.voltage deviation (p.u.)
Fixed	115.27	64.24	0.01137
NSGAII	104.22-105.13	58.67-65.49	0.0114-0.01249
MO_ACOR	104.00-104.79	58.45-65.66	0.01137-0.0125

has been tested both on a set of mathematical test functions and on a complex real world problem. Moreover its performance has been compared to the well known NSGAII algorithm. The performance measures used say that the proposed algorithm is comparable to NSGAII in terms of convergence and ability to find the Pareto front, but it finds more uniformly distributed solutions. The applications section is also devoted to a complex power dispatch issue in microgrids. These systems require, differently from the past, a lot of telecommunication and electronic facilities in order to create a reliable control system in the entire domain. Besides, efficient multi-objective optimization algorithms for optimal management purposes are of basic importance. The relevant application section shows indeed how optimization algorithms efficiency is directly related to an economical benefits for distributors.

REFERENCES

Bertani, A., Borghetti, A., Bossi, C., De Biase, L., Lamquet, O., Massucco, S., et al. (2006). Management of Low Voltage Grids with High Penetration of Distributed Generation: concepts, implementations and experiments. In CIGRE (Ed.) *Proceedings of CIGRE 2007 Session*, (paper C6-304) Paris, France.

Carlos, A., Hernandez-Aramburo, T., Green, C., & Mugniot, N. (2005). Fuel Consumption Minimization of a Microgrid. *IEEE Transactions on Industry Applications, 41*(3), 673–682. doi:10.1109/TIA.2005.847277

Deb, K. (2001). *Multi-objective Optimization using Evolutionary Algorithms*. New York: John Wiley and Sons Ltd.

Deb, K., & Agrawal, R. B. (1995). Simulated binary crossover for continuous search space. *Complex Systems, 9*, 115–148.

Deb, K., Agrawal, S., Pratap, A., & Meyarivan, T. A. (2000) Fast Elitist Non-Dominated Sorting Genetic Algorithm for Multi-Objective Optimization: NSGA-II. In Springer (Ed.) *Parallel Problem Solving from Nature VI – Lecture Notes in Computer Science* (849-858) Paris, France.

Deb, K., & Goyal, M. (1996). A combined genetic adaptive search (GeneAS) for engineering design. *Computer Science and Informatics, 26*(4), 30–45.

Dorigo, M., & Di Caro, G. (1999). The Ant Colony Optimization Meta-Heuristic. In Corne, D., Dorigo, M., & Glover, F. (Eds.), *New Ideas in Optimization* (pp. 11–32). New York: McGraw-Hill.

European Commission. (2006, April). European SmartGrids technology platform: Vision and strategy for Europe's electricity networks of the future. Retrieved from http://ec.europa.eu/research/energy/pdf/smartgrids_en.pdf.; www.smartgrids.eu

Mohamed, F., & Koivo, H. (2007) System Modelling and Online Optimal Management of MicroGrid with Battery Storage. In *Proceedings of 6th International Conference on Renewable Energies and Power Quality* Sevilla, Spain.

Poli, R., & Langdon, W. B. (1997, June) *Genetic programming with one-point crossover*. In P. K. Chawdhry, R. Roy, and R. K. Pant (Ed.) *Second On-line World Conference on Soft Computing in Engineering Design and Manufacturing*. Springer-Verlag London, 23-27.

Riva Sanseverino, E., Pecoraro, G., Borghetti, A., Bosetti, M., & Paolone, M. (2007). Optimal Operating Point Calculation for Medium Voltage Distribution Systems In *Proceedings IEEE Power Tech 2007* Lausanne, Switzerland.

Smith, K., Everson, R., & Fieldsend, J. (2004). Dominance measures for multi-objective simulated annealing. In *Proceedings IEEE Conference on Evolutionary Computation. 2004* (23–30).

Socha, K., & Dorigo, M. (2005). *Ant Colony Optimization for Continuous Domains, IRIDIA* (pp. 1–36). Technical Report Series.

Srinivas, N., & Deb, K. (1994). Multiobjective optimization using nondominated sorting in genetic algorithms. *Journal Evolutionary Computation, 2*(3), 221–248. doi:10.1162/evco.1994.2.3.221

Tan, K. C., Lee, T. H., & Khor, E. F. (2001) Evolutionary algorithms for multi-objective optimization: performance assessments and comparisons. In *Proceedings IEEE Conference on Evolutionary Computation 2001*. vol. 2 (979-986) Seoul, South Korea

Zeineldin, H. H., & El-Saadany, E. F. Salama, & M. M. A. (2006). Distributed Generation Micro-Grid Operation: Control and Protection. In *Proceedings of IEEE Power Systems Conference: Advanced Metering, Protection, Control, Communication, and Distributed Resources*, (105-111), Clemson, South Carolina.

Zitzler, E., & Thiele, L. (1999). Multiobjective evolutionary algorithms: A comparative case study and the strength Pareto approach. *IEEE Transactions on Evolutionary Computation, 3*(4), 257–271. doi:10.1109/4235.797969

Chapter 10
Output Stream of Binding Neuron with Feedback

Alexander Vidybida
Bogolyubov Institute for Theoretical Physics, Ukraine

Kseniya Kravchuk
Bogolyubov Institute for Theoretical Physics, Ukraine

ABSTRACT

The binding neuron (BN) output firing statistics is considered. The neuron is driven externally by the Poisson stream of intensity λ. *The influence of the feedback, which conveys every output impulse to the input with time delay* $\Delta \geq 0$, *on the statistics of BN's output spikes is considered. The resulting output stream is not Poissonian, and we look for its interspike intervals (ISI) distribution for the case of BN, BN with instantaneous,* $\Delta = 0$, *and delayed,* $\Delta > 0$, *feedback. For the BN with threshold 2 an exact mathematical expressions as functions of* λ, Δ *and BN's internal memory,* τ *are derived for the ISI distribution, output intensity and ISI coefficient of variation. For higher thresholds these quantities are found numerically. The distributions found for the case of instantaneous feedback include jumps and derivative discontinuities and differ essentially from those obtained for BN without feedback. Statistics of a neuron with delayed feedback has remarkable peculiarities as compared to the case of* $\Delta = 0$. *ISI distributions, found for delayed feedback, are characterized with jumps, derivative discontinuities and include singularity of Dirac's* δ *-function type. The obtained ISI coefficient of variation is a unimodal function of input intensity, with the maximum value considerably bigger than unity. It is concluded that delayed feedback presence can radically alter neuronal output firing statistics.*

DOI: 10.4018/978-1-61692-811-7.ch010

"Although a neuron requires energy, its main function is to receive signals and to send them out – that is, to handle information."

—*F. Crick, The Astonishing Hypothesis, 1994.*

INTRODUCTION

In this chapter, the main goal is to describe in mathematically exact form the output activity of a neuron, which obtains an irregular stream of impulses at its input. As the input stream we take the Poisson stream of randomly emitted impulses. As the neuronal model we take the binding neuron (BN). This model is described in detail in further sections. We consider here three cases, namely, (i) neuron without feedback, (ii) neuron with instantaneous feedback, (iii) neuron with delayed feedback. In each case we obtain exact expression for probability density function of output inter-spike interval (ISI) lengths distribution, and some other statistical characteristics derivable from the ISI distribution. In all three cases the output ISI distribution differs substantially from the input Poisson stream. In the case (iii) of delayed feedback the output ISI distribution has peculiarity of Dirac δ -function type, which suggests that, due to delayed feedback presence, seemingly structureless input Poisson stream can be transformed into a stream with a pronounced temporal structure. The expressions obtained are checked numerically for specific parameter values. Also numerically, we find the ISI distribution for leaky integrate and fire neuronal model with delayed feedback. The distribution found in this case is qualitatively similar to that for BN with delayed feddback.

BACKGROUND

The role of input spikes timing in functioning of either single neuron, or neural net has been addressed many times, as it constitutes one of the main problem in neural coding. The role of timing was observed in processes of perception (MacLeod et al., 1988), memory (Hebb, 1949), objects binding and/or segmentation (Eckhorn, 1988; Engel at al, 1991b; Llinás et al, 1994; Leonards et al, 1996). At the same time, where does the timing come from initially? In reality, some timing can be inherited from the external world during primary sensory reception. In auditory system, this happens for the evident reason that the physical signal, the air pressure time course, itself has pronounced temporal structure in the millisecond time scale, which is retained to a great extent in the inner hair cells output (Cariani, 2001). In olfaction, the physical signal is produced by means of adsorption-desorption of odor molecules, which is driven by Brownian motion. In this case, the primary sensory signal can be represented as Poisson stream, thus not having any remarkable temporal structure. Nevertheless, temporal structure can appear in the output of a neuron fed by a structureless signal. After primary reception, the output of corresponding receptor cells is further processed in primary sensory pathways, and then in higher brain areas. During this processing, statistics of poststimulus spiking activity undergoes substantial transformations, see, e.g. (Eggermont, 1991). After these transformations, the eventual pattern of activity is far away from the initial one. This process is closely related to the information condensation (König & Krüger, 2006).

We now put a question: What kind of physical mechanisms might underlie these transformations? It seems that, among others, the following features are responsible for spiking statistics of a neuron in a network: (i) several input spikes are necessary for a neuron from a higher brain area to fire an output spike (see, e.g. Andersen et al., 1990; Gerstner & Kistler, 2002); (ii) a neural net has numerous interconnections, which bring about feedback and reverberating dynamics in the net. Due to (i) a neuron must integrate over a time interval in order to gather enough input impulses to fire. As a result, in contrast to Poisson stream, the shortest ISIs between output spikes will no longer be the most probable. Due to reverberation, an individual neuron's output impulses can have some delayed influence on the input of that same neuron. This can be the source of positive feedback which results in establishing of dynamics partially independent of the stimulating input (compare with König & Krüger, 2006; Kistler & De Zeeuw, 2002), and which governs neuronal spiking statistics.

In this text, we consider a simplest possibility to test influence of (i), (ii), above on neuronal firing statistics. As neuronal model we take single binding neuron. Below, we describe the binding neuron (BN) model, as possible abstract concept of signal processing in a generic neuron. Further we obtain exact mathematical expression describing the output firing statistics when BN is fed with input Poisson stream (Vidybida, 2007). The expression obtained is then utilized for describing firing statistics of BN when each output impulse is fed back to the BN's input. Cases of instantaneous (Vidybida, 2008) and delayed feedback are considered. Exact mathematical expressions are derived if BN has threshold $N_0 = 2$. For higher thresholds, the firing statistics is calculated numerically, by means of Monte Carlo algorithm. The distributions of interspike intervals found are characterized with discontinuities of jump type, and include singularity of Dirac δ-function type. It is concluded that presence of feedback can radically alter neuronal output firing statistics.

We do all calculations mathematically rigorously, without approximations, and based on elementary probability theory. Obtaining exact mathematical expressions for statistics of neuronal activity is difficult task, mainly due to threshold-type behavior of real neurons, which must be present in any neuronal model. A substantial progress in obtaining analytical expressions for those quantities is made for diffusion models only, see (Burkitt, 2006; Gerstner & Kis-

tler, 2002; Holden, 1976; Lansky & Sato, 1999; Ricciardi, 1977; Tuckwell, 1988; Tuckwell, 1989). If input to a model neuron (usually, leaky integrate and fire one) is chosen as diffusion stochastic process, then contribution of individual input impulses is infinitesimally small, which is compensated by a possibility to have unlimited number of input impulses during a finite time interval, see (Kolmogoroff, 1931). The validity of such a situation could be approved if in reality a neuron obtains large number of inputs during short time intervals, or at least the number of inputs, which is necessary for triggering is large. This is tightly connected with the well-known spike code - rate code paradigms. In the case of rate coding, the diffusion approximation is suitable, and in the case of spike coding it does not. Available data suggest that in nervous system both paradigms coexist, see discussion in (König et al., 1996). This is also supported by experimental findings of how many synaptic impulses are necessary to trigger a neuron. This number varies from one (Miles, 1990), through fifty (Barbour, 1993), to 60-180 (Andersen, 1991), and 100-300 (Andersen, 1990). The diffusion approximation has an advantage, that it allows to obtain conclusions for a range of threshold values in a uniform manner. Considering individual input spikes as significant, requires to develop separate mathematical approach for each individual value of threshold, see (Vidybida, 2007), where output intensity is calculated for BN with $N_0 = 3$. In principle, diffusion approximation could be applied for binding neuron without feedback as well. Numerical simulations made for BN with thresholds up to 20 (unpublished data) suggest that ISIs distribution for BN stimulated with diffusion process will be qualitatively similar to that shown in Figure 3,a. But it will be difficult to preserve diffusion process paradigm while feeding back individual output spikes in BN with feedback. At the same time, consideration of individual spikes as sig-

Figure 1. Signal processing in the binding neuron model (Vidybida, 1996a)

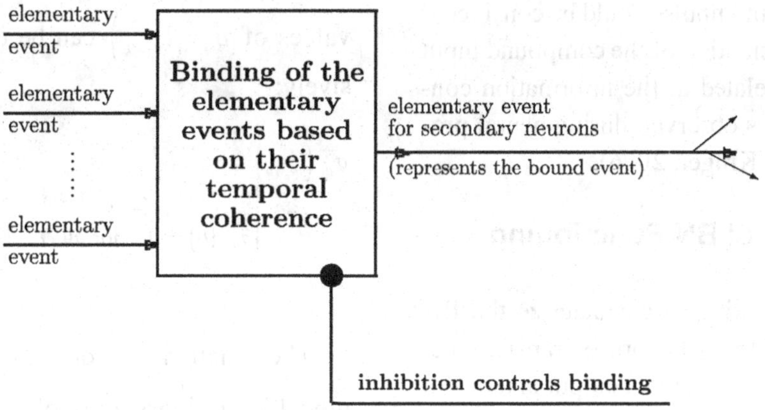

nificant, allows new behavior to appear in leaky integrate and fire neuron as well, Figure 8.

THE BINDING NEURON MODEL

The understanding of mechanisms of higher brain functions expects a continuous reduction from higher activities to lower ones, eventually, to activities in individual neurons, expressed in terms of membrane potentials and ionic currents. While this approach is correct scientifically and desirable for applications, the complete range of the reduction is unavailable to a single researcher/ engineer due to human brain limited capacity. In this connection, it would be helpful to abstract from the rules by which a neuron changes its membrane potentials to rules by which the input impulse signals are processed in the neuron. The "coincidence detector", and "temporal integrator" are the examples of such an abstraction, see discussion by König et al. (1996).

One more abstraction, the binding neuron (BN) model, is proposed as signal processing unit (Vidybida, 1996a), which can operate either as coincidence detector, or temporal integrator, depending on quantitative characteristics of stimulation applied. This conforms with behavior of real neurons, see, e.g. work by Rudolph &

Destexhe (2003). The BN model is inspired by numerical simulation of Hodgkin-Huxley-type neuron stimulated from many synaptic inputs (Vidybida, 1996b). It describes functioning of a neuron in terms of events, which are input and output impulses, and degree of temporal coherence between the input events, see Figure 1. Mathematically, this can be realized as follows. Each input impulse is stored in the BN for a fixed time, τ. The τ is similar to the "tolerance interval" discussed by MacKay (1962, p. 42).

All input lines are excitatory. Slow (potassium-type) inhibition can be introduced by decreasing the value of τ, as it controlls the degree of temporal coherence between input impulses in a compound stimulus, suitable to trigger BN (Vidybida, 1998). The neuron fires an output impulse if the number of stored impulses, Σ, is equal or higher then threshold value, N_0. It is clear, that BN is triggered when a bunch of input impulses is received in a narrow temporal interval. In this case the bunch could be considered as compound event, and the output impulse – as an abstract representation of this compound event. One could treat this mechanism as binding of individual input events into a single output event, provided the input events are coherent in time. Such interpretation is suggested by binding of features/ events in largescale neuronal circuits (Eckhorn,

1988; Damasio, 1989; Engel et al., 1991a). The idea, that the output impulse could be considered as abstract representation of the compound input event is closely related to the information condensation, which is observed during neural processing (König & Krüger, 2006).

Formalization of BN Functioning

It would be interesting to characterize the BN input-output relations in the form of transfer function, which allows to calculate output in terms of input. In our case input T_{in} is the sequence of arriving moments of standard impulses:

$$T_{in} = \left\{ l_1, l_2, l_3, l_4, \dots \right\}.$$

The output T_{out} is the sequence of firing moments of BN:

$$T_{out} = \left\{ f_1, f_2, \dots \right\}.$$

It is clear that $T_{out} \subset T_{in}$. The transfer function in our case could be the function $\sigma(l)$, $l \in T_{in}$, which equals 1 if l is the firing moment, $l \in T_{out}$, and 0 otherwise. For BN with threshold N_0 required function can be constructed as follows.

It is clear that first $N_0 - 1$ input impulses are unable to trigger firing, therefore

$$\sigma\left(l_1\right) = 0, \dots, \sigma\left(l_{N_0 - 1}\right) = 0.$$

The next input is able to trigger firing iff all N_0 inputs are coherent in time:

$$\sigma\left(l_{N_0}\right) = 1, \quad \text{iff} \quad l_{N_0} - l_1 \leq \tau.$$

In order to determine $\sigma\left(l_{N_0+k}\right)$, $k \geq 1$, one must take into acount all previous input moments,

therefore we use notation $\sigma_{T_{in}}$ instead of σ. The values of $\sigma_{T_{in}}\left(l_{N_0+k}\right)$ can be determined recursively:

$$\sigma_{T_{in}}\left(l_{N_0+k}\right) =$$
$$1, \quad \text{iff} \quad \begin{cases} l_{N_0+k} - l_{k+1} \leq \tau, \\ \sigma_{T_{in}}\left(l_i\right) = 0 \quad \text{for all} \quad i \in \left\{k+1, \dots, N_0+k-1\right\}. \end{cases}$$

The function $\sigma_{T_{in}}$ describes completely BN model for arbitrary threshold value $N_0 \geq 2$. For the trivial case $N_0 = 1$, obviously, $\sigma_{T_{in}}\left(l_i\right) = 1$ for all $i \geq 1$.

OUTPUT STREAM OF BINDING NEURON WITHOUT FEEDBACK

In this section, we consider BN, which has threshold $N_0 = 2$, internal memory duration τ and is stimulated with Poisson stream in any of its input line (Vidybida, 2007). In this case, multiple input lines shown in Figure 1 can be replaced with a single one with Poisson stream in it, which has intensity, λ, equal to the sum of intensities in all input lines. This gives schematic presentation of BN as in Figure 2 with feedback line removed.

Output Interspike Intervals (ISI) Distribution

In order to find firing statistics, one should take into account that BN with threshold 2 emits an output impulse every time when an input impulse is received not later then τ unints of time after its immediate predecessor, and the predecessor itself have not triggered emission of output impulse. The ouput stream statistics can be represented in terms of the probability density for distribution of length of interspike intervals (ISI) in the stream. For this purpose, it is enough to find the probability $P^0\left(t\right)dt$ that first output

Figure 2. Binding neuron with feedback line under Poisson stimulation. Multiple input lines with Poisson streams are joined into a single one here. Δ is the delay duration in the feedback line

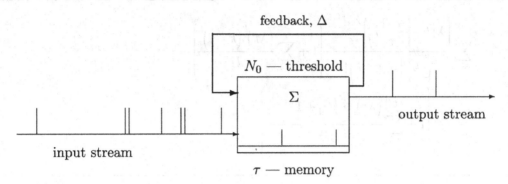

impulse appears t units of time after switching (with precision dt). This output event can be secured due to several alternative input events, which are indexed with the number k of the input impulse, which triggers the output.

It is clear that $2 \leq k \leq k_{max}$, where $k_{max} = \left[t/\tau \right] + 2$ and $[x]$ denotes integral part of x. Let $t_1, t_2, \ldots, t_{k-1}$ denote moments when input impulses are received. Then realisation of the k-th input alternative means that intervals $\left[0; t_1 \right[$, $\left] t_1; t_2 \right[, \ldots, \left] t_{k-1}; t \right[$ are free of input impulses, and each interval $dt_1, \ldots, dt_{k-1}dt$ in the vicinity of $t_1, t_2, \ldots, t_{k-1}, t$, respectively, has exactly one impulse. By the definition of Poisson process (Gnedenko, 1989), this realisation has the following probability:

$$e^{-\lambda t_1} \lambda dt_1 e^{-\lambda(t_2 - t_1)} \lambda dt_2 \ldots e^{-\lambda(t_{k-1} - t_{k-2})} \lambda dt_{k-1} e^{-\lambda(t - t_{k-1})} \lambda dt,$$

and one can calculate the probability $P_k^0 \left(t \right) dt$ of the k-th alternative by integrating the above expression over the domain of coordinates $t_1, t_2, \ldots, t_{k-1}$ defined by the following conditions:

$$t_1 \geq 0, t_1 + \tau < t_2, \ldots, t_i + \tau < t_{i+1}, \ldots, t_{k-2} + \tau < t_{k-1} < t, \tag{1}$$

and $t - t_{k-1} < \tau$. Notice that

$$e^{-\lambda t} \lambda^{k-1} \int_0^{t-(k-2)\tau} dt_1 \int_{t_1 + \tau}^{t-(k-3)\tau} dt_2 \ldots \int_{t_{k-2}+\tau}^{t} dt_{k-1} \lambda dt =$$

$$e^{-\lambda t} \lambda^{k-1} \frac{\left(t - \left(k - 2 \right) \tau \right)^{k-1}}{\left(k - 1 \right)!} \lambda dt. \tag{2}$$

If $k = k_{max}$, then condition (1) secures that $\left(k - 1 \right)$-th input impulse falls into interval $\left] t - \tau; t \right[$, and arrival of k-th impulse at moment t will trigger output impulse. Therefore, in this case

$$P_k^0 \left(t \right) dt = e^{-\lambda t} \lambda^{k-1} \frac{\left(t - \left(k - 2 \right) \tau \right)^{k-1}}{\left(k - 1 \right)!} \lambda dt, \qquad k = k_{max}.$$

If $k < k_{max}$, then integral (2) includes configurations with $t_{k-1} < t - \tau$. For those configurations, arrival of k-th input impulse at moment t will not trigger an output. The contribution of such unfavorable configurations in the integral (2) is given by the following expression:

Box 1.

$$\Pi\left(t\right) = e^{-\lambda t} \sum_{k=0}^{\left[t/\tau\right]} \frac{\left(\lambda\left(t - \left[t/\tau\right]\tau\right)\right)^{\left[t/\tau\right]+1-k}}{\left(\left[t/\tau\right]+1-k\right)!} \left[1 + \sum_{l=1}^{k} \frac{\left(\lambda\tau\right)^l \left(k-l\right)^l}{l!}\right] +$$

$$+ e^{-\lambda t} \left[1 + \sum_{l=1}^{\left[t/\tau\right]} \frac{\left(\lambda\tau\right)^l \left(\left[t/\tau\right]+1-l\right)^l}{l!}\right].$$

(7)

$$e^{-\lambda t} \lambda^{k-1} \int_{0}^{t-(k-1)\tau} dt_1 \int_{t_1+\tau}^{t-(k-2)\tau} dt_2 \ldots \int_{t_{k-2}+\tau}^{t-\tau} dt_{k-1} \lambda dt =$$

$$e^{-\lambda t} \lambda^{k-1} \frac{\left(t - \left(k-1\right)\tau\right)^{k-1}}{\left(k-1\right)!} \lambda dt,$$

which one must subtract from expression (2). Thus for $2 \leq k \leq k_{max}$ one has:

$$P_k^0\left(t\right)dt = e^{-\lambda t} \frac{\lambda^{k-1}}{\left(k-1\right)!}\left(\left(t - \left(k-2\right)\tau\right)^{k-1} - \left(t - \left(k-1\right)\tau\right)^{k-1}\right)\lambda dt.$$

The whole probability one finds as sum of probabilities of all alternatives. Notice that k_{max} is changed by 1 when the value of t crosses a point $m\tau$ with m being a whole number. Thus one can say for $m=0,1,2,\ldots$: if $m\tau \leq t < \left(m+1\right)\tau$, then

$$P^0\left(t\right)dt = e^{-\lambda t} \frac{\lambda^{m+1}}{\left(m+1\right)!}\left(t - m\tau\right)^{m+1}\lambda dt +$$

$$+ \sum_{2 \leq k \leq m+1} e^{-\lambda t} \frac{\lambda^{k-1}}{\left(k-1\right)!}\left(\left(t - \left(k-2\right)\tau\right)^{k-1} - \left(t - \left(k-1\right)\tau\right)^{k-1}\right)\lambda dt.$$

(3)

Eq. (3) can be rewritten as follows:

$$m\tau \leq t < \left(m+1\right)\tau \quad \Rightarrow \quad P^0\left(t\right) = y_m\left(t\right), \quad m = 0,1,\ldots,$$

(4)

where $y_i(t)$ are defined according to the following recurrent relation:

$$y_i\left(t\right) = y_{i-1}\left(t\right) + \frac{\lambda^{i+2}}{\left(i+1\right)!}\left(t - i\tau\right)^{i+1} e^{-\lambda t} - \frac{\lambda^{i+1}}{i!}\left(t - i\tau\right)^i e^{-\lambda t},$$

$$y_0\left(t\right) = e^{-\lambda t} \lambda^2 t, \quad i = 0,1,\ldots, \quad t > 0.$$

(5)

Let us denote with $\Pi\left(t\right)$ the probability to get an output ISI, which is longer than t:

$$\Pi\left(t\right) \equiv \int_{t}^{\infty} P^0\left(t\right)dt.$$

(6)

Taking into acconut (4) and performing integration in (6), one obtains (Vidybida, 2006) (see Box 1)

Output Intensity

One can define the BN output intensity, or firing rate, λ_o, as inversed of the mean interspike interval, W_1, in the output stream:

$$\lambda_o = \frac{1}{W_1}.$$

W_1 can be calculated based on the exact expression (3):

Figure 3. ISI distributions for BN without feedback (a) and with instantaneous feedback (b) a: $P^0(t)$ *for* $\tau = 1$ *s,* $N_0 = 2$, *calculated in accordance with (3) .Curves 1, 2, 3, 4 correspond to* $\lambda = 0.5 s^{-1}, 1$ $s^{-1}, 2 s^{-1}, 3 s^{-1}; b: P_f(t)$ *for* $\tau = 10$ *ms,* $\lambda = 10 s^{-1}$, $N_0 = 2$, *calculated in accordance with (15);.*

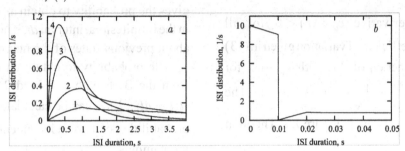

$$W_1 = \mathrm{E}(W) = \int_0^\infty t P^0(t)\,dt = \frac{1}{\lambda}\left(2 + \frac{1}{e^{\lambda\tau} - 1}\right), \tag{8}$$

which delivers for λ_o

$$\lambda_o = \frac{1 - e^{-\lambda\tau}}{2 - e^{-\lambda\tau}}\lambda. \tag{9}$$

The output intensity for thresholds 2 and 3 can be calculated without referring to exact expressions for output ISI distributions, see (Vidybida, 2007).

Properties of the ISI Distribution

By integrating expression (3) over interval $[0;\infty[$ one can check that the probability density (3) is normalized to 1, as it should be.

The ISI distribution (3) is unimodal, see Figure 3, a. It can be proven that $P^0(t)$ has maximum at point $t = \min(\tau; 1/\lambda)$. For large t, function $P^0(t)$ decreases exponentially. Namely, for any pair (λ, τ) there exist positive A, α, B, β, such, that for all t large enough the following inequality holds:

$$Be^{-\beta t} < P^0(t) < Ae^{-\alpha t}. \tag{10}$$

Theorem 1

Output ISI coefficient of variation for single BN under Poisson stimulation ranges between $1/\sqrt{2}$ *and 1 in the case* $N_0 = 2$:

$$\forall \lambda, \tau > 0 \; c_V \in \left]\frac{1}{\sqrt{2}}; 1\right[.$$

Proof.

Coefficient of variation, c_V, of distribution (3) can be found as follows. By definition

$$c_V = \sqrt{\frac{W_2}{W_1^2} - 1}, \tag{11}$$

where W_1 is given in (8), and W_2 is the second moment:

$$\int_0^\infty t^2 P^0(t)\,dt = \frac{2}{\lambda^2}\frac{3e^{2\lambda\tau} + (\lambda\tau - 3)e^{\lambda\tau} + 1}{\left(e^{\lambda\tau} - 1\right)^2}. \tag{12}$$

Substitute this into (11), which gives

$$c_V = \sqrt{\frac{2\lambda\tau e^{\lambda\tau} + 0.5}{4e^{2\lambda\tau} - 4e^{\lambda\tau} + 1} + \frac{1}{2}}. \qquad (13)$$

Since the derivative $c_V{}'\left(\lambda\tau\right) < 0$ for all $\lambda, \tau > 0$, the coefficient of variation given in (13) is decreasing function of $\lambda\tau$ with $c_V \to 1$ for $\lambda\tau \to 0$ and $c_V \to \frac{1}{\sqrt{2}}$ for $\lambda\tau \to \infty$. The graph of $c_V\left(\lambda\tau\right)$ is given in Figure 7, a. Theorem 1 is proven.

Theorem 2

Output ISI of binding neuron under Poisson stimulation are independent of eachother.
    Proof.
    Since just after firing the BN appears in the unique standard state (empty neuron), the conditional probability $P\left(t_2 \mid t_1\right)dt_2$ to obtain an output ISI of duration t_2, with precision dt_2, provided the previous one had duration t_1, equals $P^0\left(t_2\right)dt_2$. This exactly proves Theorem 2.

BINDING NEURON WITH INSTANTANEOUS FEEDBACK (BNF)

Let us assume that each output impulse of BN with Poisson stimulation is immediately fed back into BN's input. This gives BN with instantaneous feedback, Figure 2 with $\Delta = 0$ (Vidybida, 2008).
    Firing statistics of this construction can be found utilizing results obtained for BN without feedback.

Output Intensity of BNF with Threshold 2

Let us expect that the output stochastic process is stationary. This can be achived if a long period

of time has been passed after switching. In this case one can define/calculate the output intensity, λ_o, as the factor in the expression $\lambda_o dt$, which gives the probability to obtain an output impulse in the infinitesimal interval dt, if nothing is known about previous states of the neuron.

The probability to obtain an output impulse from the BNF with threshold 2 in the interval $\left[t; t + dt\right[$, $\lambda_o dt$, can be calculated as product of probabilities of two independent events: (i) an input impulse, I_1, arrives in the interval $\left[t - \tau; t\right[$; (ii) the next input impulse, I_2, arrives in the interval $\left[t; t + dt\right[$. Event (ii) has probability λdt. Event (i) has the same probability as having in Poisson stream two successive events (here I_1, I_2) separated by time interval, which is shorter than τ. This probability is $1 - e^{-\lambda\tau}$. Thus,

$$\lambda_o = \left(1 - e^{-\lambda\tau}\right)\lambda. \qquad (14)$$

Interesting, that for high input rates ($\lambda \to \infty$), the triggering rate becomes equal to the input one. This can be explained as follows. If input rate is very high, almost all input ISIs become shorter then τ. In this case, any input, stored in the BNF will eventually give rise to output spike, which is immediately used as input for empty neuron due to feedback. This effectively doubles the input rate. Namely, any input impulse triggers the BNF, and then it is applied to empty BNF through feedback. As a result, the output stream for high λ literally reproduces the input one: any input spike becomes the output one without delay. This same reasoning allows one to say that output rate of BNF with any threshold N_0 approaches $\lambda/\left(N_0 - 1\right)$ when $\lambda \to \infty$. Compare this with BN without feedback, where corresponding limit output rate is λ/N_0.

Another way to define λ_o is to use instantaneous intensity (Khinchin, 1955), $\lambda_o\left(t\right)$, which is the probability to obtain an output impulse at moment t in infinitesimal interval s divided by s:

$$\lambda_o(t) = \lim_{s \to 0} \frac{w(s,t)}{s},$$

where $w(s,t)$ denotes the probability to obtain impulse in the interval $[t; t+s[$. As λ_o one can choose the following

$$\lambda_o = \lim_{t \to \infty} \lambda_o(t).$$

It can be shown that this definition brings about the same value for λ_o as is given in Eq. (14). Calculations based on this definition can be fulfilled with the help of Theorem of §8, Part XI in (Feller, 1966).

Distribution of Output Intervals for BNF With $N_0 = 2$

Consider the ISI distribution for binding neuron with instantaneous feedback, $P_f(t)$.

Theorem 3

For binding neuron with $N_0 = 2$ and instantaneous feedback under Poisson stimulation the following holds:

$$\begin{cases} 0 \le t < \tau & \Rightarrow \quad P_f(t) = e^{-\lambda t} \lambda, \\ \tau \le t & \Rightarrow \quad P_f(t) = e^{-\lambda \tau} P^0(t - \tau). \end{cases} \quad (15)$$

Proof.

The ISI length t, where $t < \tau$, can be obtained provided the first input impulse arrives not later then τ units of time after the previous firing. In this case, the neuron still keeps impulse received from the previous firing through the feedback

line, and the input secures the threshold to be achieved and BNF to fire. There is no other way to get output interval t shorter then τ. Thus, for $t \in [0; \tau[$, the probability density distribution of ISI coincides with the distribution for the input Poisson stream:

$$P_f(t) dt = e^{-\lambda t} \lambda dt, \quad t \in [0; \tau[.$$

ISI duration t, where $t > \tau$, means that impulse from the feedback line does not contribute into firing, since it was lost at moment τ after previous firing. From that moment, the BNF works like BN without feedback and is triggered at moment t with probability $P^0(t - \tau)$. In order to obtain probability of t one should multiply this probability with the probability to have interval longer than τ in the input Poisson stream. This gives:

$$P_f(t) = e^{-\lambda \tau} P^0(t - \tau), \quad t \ge \tau.$$

Theorem 3 is proven.

Function $P_f(t)$ can also be calculated from the first principles (Vidybida, 2008).

Properties of the Distribution

The expression (15) together with the fact that $P^0(t)$ is normalized, allows one to check easily that $P_f(t)$ is normalized as well:

$$\int_0^\infty P_f(t) dt = 1.$$

It is clear from (15) that $P_f(t)$ satisfies asymptotic condition like (10), but is discontinuous at point $t = \tau$. The graph of $P_f(t)$ is shown in Figure 3, b.

Having for $P_f(t)$ representation (15), one can easily calculate mean interspike interval, W_1 (Vidybida, 2008):

$$W_1 = \int_0^\infty t P_f(t) dt = \frac{1}{\lambda(1 - e^{-\lambda\tau})}.$$

Notice, that as expected for the stationary point process, mean output ISI is reversed output intensity given in (14).

Theorem 4

Output ISI coefficient of variation for BN with instantaneous feedback under Poisson stimulation exceeds unity for any input intensity and BN's memory duration in the case $N_0 = 2$:

$$\forall \lambda, \tau > 0 \ c_V > 1.$$

Proof.

In order to prove Theorem 2 consider the second moment W_2 of distribution (15) (Vidybida, 2008):

$$W_2 = \int_0^\infty t^2 P_f(t) dt = \frac{2e^{\lambda\tau}}{\lambda^2} \frac{e^{\lambda\tau} + \lambda\tau}{\left(e^{\lambda\tau} - 1\right)^2}.$$

Substituting this into definition (11), one gets:

$$c_V = \sqrt{2\lambda\tau e^{-\lambda\tau} + 1}. \tag{16}$$

Coefficient of variation, given in (16), increases monotonically from $c_V = 1$ at $\lambda\tau = 0$ to its maximum value, $c_{V \max}$,

$$c_{V \max} = \sqrt{2e^{-1} + 1} \approx 1.32$$

at $\lambda\tau = 1$, and then gradually decreases to its asymptotic value $c_V \to 1$ when $\lambda\tau \to \infty$ (Figure 7, b). Therefore, for any finite $\lambda\tau > 0$ one obtains $c_V > 1$. Theorem 4 is proven.

Theorem 5

Output ISI of binding neuron with instantaneous feedback under Poisson stimulation are independent of eachother.

Proof.

Since just after firing the neuron starts from standard state (keeps a single impulse with time to live equal τ), the conditional probability $P(t_2 \mid t_1) dt_2$ to obtain an output ISI of duration t_2, with precision dt_2, provided the previous one had duration t_1, equals $P_f(t_2) dt_2$. This exactly proves Theorem 5.

This fact depends crucially on the immediateness of feedback.

BINDING NEURON WITH DELAYED FEEDBACK

Let us assume that each output impulse of BN with Poisson stimulation is fed back into BN's input with delay $\Delta > 0$. This gives BN with delayed feedback, Figure 2. Firing statistics of this construction can be found utilizing results obtained for BN without feedback.

Any output impulse of BN with feedback line may be produced either with impulse from the line involved, or not. We assume that, just after firing and sending output impulse, the line is never empty. This assumption is selfevident for output impulses produced without impulse from the line, or if the impulse from the line was involved, but entered empty neuron. In the letter case, the second (triggering) impulse comes from the Poisson stream, neuron fires and output impulse goes out as well as enters the empty line. On the other hand, if impulse from the line triggers BN, which already keeps one impulse from the input stream, it may be questionable if the output impulse is able to enter the line, which was just filled with the impulse. We expect it does. This means biologically that we ignore the refraction time - a short period necessary for a nervous fibre to recover from conducting previous spike before it is able to serve for the next one. Thus, at the beginning of any output ISI, the line keeps impulse with time to live s, where $s \in \left]0; \Delta\right]$.

For analytical calculations we consider threshold value $N_0 = 2$.

Calculations

In previous sections, the output stream statistics of BN (with feedback line removed, $\Delta = \infty$) and BN with instantaneous feedback ($\Delta = 0$) was considered. In both cases, at the beginning of every output ISI BN starts from the standard state, which keeps no information about previous events. On the contrary, the state of BN with delayed feedback is characterized by additional parameter, s, which gets no standard value at the beginning of output ISI and depends on previous events. In other words, in this case two sorts of random variability should be taken into account, namely, the variability of driving Poisson process and the variability in the state of the feedback line at the beginning of output ISI[1].

The main idea is to restrict ourselves first to the imaginary case of fixed s, taking into account only variability of the input Poisson stream, and then to account the variability of s. For this purpose we introduce conditional probability density $P^\Delta\left(t \mid s\right)$, corresponding to fixed s. Namely, $P^\Delta\left(t \mid s\right)dt$ gives the probability to obtain an output ISI in interval $\left[t; t + dt\right[$, if at the beginning of this ISI there was an impulse in the feedback line with time to live equal s. Once it is found, the output ISI distribution $P^\Delta\left(t\right)$ can be calculated as

$$P^\Delta\left(t\right) = \int_0^\Delta P^\Delta\left(t \mid s\right) f\left(s\right) ds, \qquad (17)$$

where $f\left(s\right)$ denotes stationary distribution for time to live $s \in \left]0; \Delta\right]$ of impulse in the feedback line at the beginning of output ISI. Function $f\left(s\right)$ keeps no information about the state of the system at the moment it was switched on.

Such stationary distribution $f\left(s\right)$ must satisfy the following balance equation:

$$\int_0^\Delta P\left(s_2 \mid s_1\right) f\left(s_1\right) ds_1 = f\left(s_2\right), \qquad (18)$$

where $P\left(s_2 \mid s_1\right)$, multiplied by ds_2, gives the probability to have at the beginning of an ISI the impulse in the feedback line with time to live equal s_2, with precision ds_2, if at the beginning of the previous ISI there was an impulse with time to live equal s_1.

So, in order to find output ISI distribution $P^\Delta\left(t\right)$ one should derive exact expressions for $P^\Delta\left(t \mid s\right)$, $P\left(s_2 \mid s_1\right)$ and $f\left(s\right)$ first.

Conditional Probability Distribution $P^\Delta\left(t \mid s\right)$

The explicit expression for conditional probability distribution $P^\Delta\left(t \mid s\right)$ depends on the domain, t belongs to. Basic domains for $P^\Delta\left(t \mid s\right)$ are shown in Figure 4, a.

Consider case C1, where $t < s$. The impulse is still passing the feedback line, thus having no influence on BN's statistics, which gives the following

$$P^\Delta\left(t \mid s\right) = P^0\left(t\right), \qquad t < s. \qquad (19)$$

Figure 4. Domains of t used for calculating conditional probability $P^\Delta\left(t\mid s\right)$ (a), ISI distribution $P^\Delta\left(t\right)$ for the cases $\Delta < \tau$ (b) and $\Delta \geq \tau$ (c)

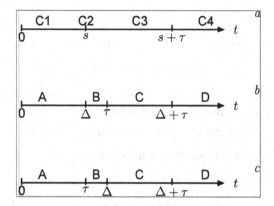

Here $P^0\left(t\right)$ denotes ISI distribution for BN without feedback, determined by Eq. (3).

Consider case C2. The probability to obtain output impulse exactly throught the time s after the last one is not infinitesimally small. This event is equivalent to the event $A_{S_1}\left(s\right)$ that BN starts empty at moment 0 and appears without triggerings in state S_1 (keeps impulse) at moment s. In order to obtain the probability $P\left\{A_{S_1}\left(s\right)\right\}$, let us take into account that $P^0\left(s\right)ds$ can be obtained as the product of $P\left\{A_{S_1}\left(s\right)\right\}$ and the probability to get input impulse in infinitesimal interval ds, which is λds. Therefore,

$$P\left\{A_{S_1}\left(s\right)\right\} = \frac{P^0\left(s\right)}{\lambda}, \qquad (20)$$

and

$$P^\Delta\left(t\mid s\right) = \frac{P^0\left(s\right)}{\lambda}\cdot\delta\left(t-s\right), \qquad t \in \left]s-\varepsilon; s+\varepsilon\right[. \qquad (21)$$

To obtain ISI from the range $s < t < s+\tau$, case C3, the following events must happen: i)

impulse from the feedback line, arriving at the moment s, doesn't trigger BN; ii) interval $\left]s;t\right[$ is free from input impulses and the first one arrives within interval $\left[t;t+dt\right[$. As the BN is driven by the Poisson stream, events i) and ii) are mutually independent.

Event i) is equivalent to event $A_{S_0}\left(s\right)$ that BN starts empty at moment 0 and appears without triggerings in state S_0 (keeps no impulses) at moment s. In order to find its probability $P\left\{A_{S_0}\left(s\right)\right\}$ one should take into account that at any moment s BN either appears without triggering in the state S_0 or S_1, or it has already fired a spike. Thus,

$$P\left\{A_{S_0}\left(s\right)\right\} =$$
$$1 - P\left\{A_{S_1}\left(s\right)\right\} - \left(1 - \Pi\left(s\right)\right) = \Pi\left(s\right) - \frac{P^0\left(s\right)}{\lambda}, \qquad (22)$$

where $\Pi\left(t\right)$ denotes the probability to obtain ISI longer then t at the output of BN without feedback, and is given in (7).

The probability of ii) is $e^{-\lambda\left(t-s\right)}\lambda dt$, which allows one to obtain

$$P^\Delta\left(t\mid s\right) =$$
$$e^{-\lambda\left(t-s\right)}\left(\lambda\Pi\left(s\right) - P^0\left(s\right)\right), \qquad t \in \left]s; s+\tau\right[. \qquad (23)$$

In the case C4, $t \geq s+\tau$. Such output ISI requires several independent events to happen: i) $A_{S_0}\left(s\right)$; ii) interval $\left]s; s+\tau\right[$ is free from input Poissonian impulses; iii) BN without feedback, which starts empty at the moment $s+\tau$, fires for the first time during interval $\left[t;t+dt\right[$. The probability of iii) is $P^0\left(t-s-\tau\right)dt$. Therefore, taking into account Eq. (22)

$$P^{\Delta}\left(t \mid s\right) =$$
$$\frac{1}{\lambda} e^{-\lambda \tau} \left(\lambda \Pi\left(s\right) - P^{0}\left(s\right)\right) P^{0}\left(t - s - \tau\right), \quad t \geq s + \tau. \tag{24}$$

Finally, taking into account Eqs. (19), (21), (23) and (24), one obtains $P^{\Delta}\left(t \mid s\right)$ as a sum of singular and regular parts:

$$P^{\Delta}\left(t \mid s\right) = P^{\text{sing}}\left(t \mid s\right) + P^{\text{reg}}\left(t \mid s\right), \text{where} \tag{25}$$

$$P^{\text{sing}}\left(t \mid s\right) = \frac{P^{0}\left(s\right)}{\lambda} \cdot \delta\left(t - s\right), \tag{26}$$

$$P^{\text{reg}}\left(t \mid s\right) = \begin{cases} P^{0}\left(t\right), & t \in \left]0;s\right], \\ e^{-\lambda\left(t-s\right)}\left(\lambda\Pi\left(s\right) - P^{0}\left(s\right)\right), & t \in \left]s;s+\tau\right], \\ \frac{1}{\lambda} e^{-\lambda\tau}\left(\lambda\Pi\left(s\right) - P^{0}\left(s\right)\right) P^{0}\left(t - s - \tau\right), & s+\tau \leq t. \end{cases} \tag{27}$$

It can be seen easily from (6) that function $P^{\Delta}\left(t \mid s\right)$ is normalized: $\int_{0}^{\infty} P^{\Delta}\left(t \mid s\right) dt = 1$.

In particular case of $\Delta < \tau$ one obtains

$$P^{\text{sing}}\left(t \mid s\right) = e^{-\lambda s} \lambda s \cdot \delta\left(t - s\right), \tag{28}$$

$$P^{\text{reg}}\left(t \mid s\right) = \begin{cases} \lambda^{2} t e^{-\lambda t}, & t \in \left]0;s\right], \\ \lambda e^{-\lambda t}, & t \in \left]s;s+\tau\right], \\ e^{-\lambda\left(s+\tau\right)} P^{0}\left(t - s - \tau\right), & s+\tau \leq t, \end{cases}$$
when $\left[\Delta \big/ \tau\right] = 0$. $\tag{29}$

Conditional Probabilities $P\left(s_{2} \mid s_{1}\right)$

In order to find conditional probabilities $P\left(s_{2} \mid s_{1}\right)$, let us first consider the case $s_{2} < s_{1}$. It means that impulse "2" was caused by external input stream,

without involvement of feedbacked impulse. Therefore, $P\left(s_{2} \mid s_{1}\right)$ coincides with $P^{0}\left(t_{1}\right)$, where $t_{1} = s_{1} - s_{2}$ denotes the first ISI duration:

$$P\left(s_{2} \mid s_{1}\right) = P^{0}\left(s_{1} - s_{2}\right), \quad s_{2} < s_{1} \in \left]0;\Delta\right]. \tag{30}$$

If the impulse leaved feedback line during first ISI, the next one will start with $s_{2} = \Delta$. Any output ISI, longer than s_{1}, will contribute to such result. So, one obtains in $P\left(s_{2} \mid s_{1}\right)$ the δ-function term with the mass $\Pi\left(s_{1}\right)$:

$$P\left(s_{2} \mid s_{1}\right) = \Pi\left(s_{1}\right) \cdot \delta\left(s_{2} - \Delta\right), \quad s_{2} \in \left]\Delta - \varepsilon;\Delta\right]. \tag{31}$$

Finally, conditional probability $P\left(s_{2} \mid s_{1}\right)$ can be written as follows:

$$P\left(s_{2} \mid s_{1}\right) = P^{\text{sing}}\left(s_{2} \mid s_{1}\right) + P^{\text{reg}}\left(s_{2} \mid s_{1}\right),$$
$$P^{\text{sing}}\left(s_{2} \mid s_{1}\right) = \Pi\left(s_{1}\right) \cdot \delta\left(s_{2} - \Delta\right),$$
$$P^{\text{reg}}\left(s_{2} \mid s_{1}\right) = \begin{cases} P^{0}\left(s_{1} - s_{2}\right), & s_{2} < s_{1} \in \left]0;\Delta\right], \\ 0, & s_{2} \geq s_{1}. \end{cases} \tag{32}$$

It is clear that function $P\left(s_{2} \mid s_{1}\right)$ is also normalized: $\int_{0}^{\Delta} P\left(s_{2} \mid s_{1}\right) ds_{2} = 1$.

In particular case $\Delta < \tau$ one obtains:

$$P^{\text{sing}}\left(s_{2} \mid s_{1}\right) = \left(\lambda s_{1} + 1\right) e^{-\lambda s_{1}} \cdot \delta\left(s_{2} - \Delta\right),$$
$$P^{\text{reg}}\left(s_{2} \mid s_{1}\right) = \begin{cases} e^{-\lambda\left(s_{1} - s_{2}\right)} \lambda^{2}\left(s_{1} - s_{2}\right), & s_{2} < s_{1} \in \left]0;\Delta\right], \\ 0, & s_{2} \geq s_{1}. \end{cases} \tag{33}$$

Delays Distribution $f\left(s\right)$

In order to find delays distribution $f\left(s\right)$, we first represent it as follows:

Box 2.

$$ae^{-\lambda\Delta}\left(\sum_{k=1}^{m_{\Delta-s_2}+1}\frac{\lambda^{k+1}}{k!}\left(\Delta-s_2-(k-1)\tau\right)^k-\sum_{k=1}^{m_{\Delta-s_2}}\frac{\lambda^{k+1}}{k!}\left(\Delta-s_2-k\tau\right)^k\right)+$$

$$+\int_{s_2}^{\Delta}\left(\sum_{k=1}^{m_{s_1-s_2}+1}\frac{\lambda^{k+1}}{k!}\left(s_1-s_2-(k-1)\tau\right)^k-\sum_{k=1}^{m_{s_1-s_2}}\frac{\lambda^{k+1}}{k!}\left(s_1-s_2-k\tau\right)^k\right)\varphi\left(s_1\right)ds_1=\varphi\left(s_2\right),\tag{36}$$

where $m_{\Delta-s_2}$, $m_{s_1-s_2}$ denote $\left[\dfrac{\Delta-s_2}{\tau}\right]$ and $\left[\dfrac{s_1-s_2}{\tau}\right]$ respectively. Obviously, $m_{s_1-s_2}$ in (36) gets integer values from the range $0,1,...,m_{\Delta-s_2}$, and $m_{\Delta-s_2}$ ranges from 0 to $m_\Delta\equiv\left[\dfrac{\Delta}{\tau}\right]$.

$$f\left(s\right)=a\delta\left(s-\Delta\right)+g\left(s\right)=a\delta\left(s-\Delta\right)+e^{\lambda s}\varphi\left(s\right),\tag{34}$$

where a is a dimentionless constant, $g\left(s\right)$ and $\varphi\left(s\right)$ – unknown functions, vanishing out of interval $]0;\Delta]$. Substituting Eqs. (32) and (34) to (18) and separating terms without δ-function, one obtains

$$aP^0\left(\Delta-s_2\right)+\int_{s_2}^{\Delta}P^0\left(s_1-s_2\right)g\left(s_1\right)ds_1=g\left(s_2\right),\tag{35}$$

or, taking into account (3), (see Box 2)

We put $m_{\Delta-s_2}$ fixed in Eq. (36). It means, that function $\varphi\left(s\right)$ and the equation it satisfies should be considered separately at different domains of s:

$$\begin{aligned}\varphi^0\left(s\right)&\equiv\varphi\left(s\right),\quad s\in\,]0;\delta[,\\\varphi^j\left(s\right)&\equiv\varphi\left(s\right),\quad s\in[\delta+(j-1)\tau;\delta+j\tau[,\quad j=1,2,...,m_\Delta,\end{aligned}$$

where

$$\delta=\Delta-m_\Delta\tau.$$

If first case is assigned with the value $j=0$, $m_{\Delta-s}$ within j-th domain can be found as

$$m_{\Delta-s}=m_\Delta-j.\tag{37}$$

In terms of $\varphi^j\left(s\right)$ equation (36) turns into equation (38). (see Box 3)

Differentiating (38) twice with respect to s_2, one obtains the second-order differential equation for $\varphi^j\left(s\right)$:

$$\frac{d^2\varphi^j\left(s\right)}{ds^2}-\lambda^2\varphi^j\left(s\right)=\Phi^j\left(s\right),\tag{39}$$

where (see Box 4.)

Curves calculated analytically fit perfectly with those found numerically for the same parameters.

So, the system of $m_\Delta+1$ second-order differential equations for $\varphi^j\left(s\right)$ was obtained: (see Box 5.)

It can be seen from Eq. (40), that system (41) of differential equations has recurrent structure. In order to solve it, one should consider domains with j decreasing from $j=m_\Delta$ to $j=0$ consequently. The solution for j-th domain is then: (see Box 6.)

Box 3.

$$ae^{-\lambda\Delta}\left(\sum_{k=1}^{m_\Delta-j+1}\frac{\lambda^{k+1}}{k!}\left(\Delta-s_2-(k-1)\tau\right)^k-\sum_{k=1}^{m_\Delta-j}\frac{\lambda^{k+1}}{k!}\left(\Delta-s_2-k\tau\right)^k\right)+$$

$$+\sum_{n=0}^{m_\Delta-j-1}\int_{\delta+(j+n)\tau}^{s_2+(n+1)\tau}\left(\sum_{k=1}^{n+1}\frac{\lambda^{k+1}}{k!}\left(s_1-s_2-(k-1)\tau\right)^k-\sum_{k=1}^{n}\frac{\lambda^{k+1}}{k!}\left(s_1-s_2-k\tau\right)^k\right)\varphi^{j+n+1}\left(s_1\right)ds_1+$$

$$+\sum_{n=0}^{m_\Delta-j-1}\int_{s_2+(n+1)\tau}^{\delta+(j+n+1)\tau}\left(\sum_{k=1}^{n+2}\frac{\lambda^{k+1}}{k!}\left(s_1-s_2-(k-1)\tau\right)^k-\sum_{k=1}^{n+1}\frac{\lambda^{k+1}}{k!}\left(s_1-s_2-k\tau\right)^k\right)\varphi^{j+n+1}\left(s_1\right)ds_1+$$

$$+\int_{s_2}^{\delta+j\tau}\lambda^2\left(s_1-s_2\right)\varphi^j\left(s_1\right)ds_1=\varphi^j\left(s_2\right).$$

(38)

Box 4.

$$\Phi^j\left(s\right)=ae^{-\lambda\Delta}\left(\sum_{k=2}^{m_\Delta-j+1}\frac{\lambda^{k+1}}{(k-2)!}\left(\Delta-s-(k-1)\tau\right)^{k-2}-\sum_{k=2}^{m_\Delta-j}\frac{\lambda^{k+1}}{k!}\left(\Delta-s-k\tau\right)^{k-2}\right)+$$

$$+\sum_{n=0}^{m_\Delta-j-1}\left(\sum_{k=2}^{n+1}\frac{\lambda^{k+1}}{(k-2)!}\int_{\delta+(j+n)\tau}^{\delta+(j+n+1)\tau}\left(s'-s-(k-1)\tau\right)^{k-2}\varphi^{j+n+1}\left(s'\right)ds'-\right.$$

$$\left.-\sum_{k=2}^{n}\frac{\lambda^{k+1}}{(k-2)!}\int_{\delta+(j+n)\tau}^{\delta+(j+n+1)\tau}\left(s'-s-k\tau\right)^{k-2}\varphi^{j+n+1}\left(s'\right)ds'+\right.$$

(40)

$$\left.+\frac{\lambda^{n+3}}{n!}\int_{s+(n+1)\tau}^{\delta+(j+n+1)\tau}\left(s'-s-(n+1)\tau\right)^n\varphi^{j+n+1}\left(s'\right)ds'\right)-\lambda^2\cdot\varphi^{j+1}\left(s+\tau\right)-$$

$$-\sum_{n=1}^{m_\Delta-j-1}\frac{\lambda^{n+2}}{(n-1)!}\int_{s+(n+1)\tau}^{\delta+(j+n+1)\tau}\left(s'-s-(n+1)\tau\right)^{n-1}\varphi^{j+n+1}\left(s'\right)ds'.$$

For example, when $j=m_\Delta$, one obtains

$$\varphi^{m_\Delta}\left(s\right)=\frac{a\lambda e^{-\lambda s}}{2}\left(1-e^{-2\lambda(\Delta-s)}\right).$$

Constant a in (34) is then found from the normalization condition:

$$a+\int_0^\Delta g\left(s\right)ds=1.$$

(43)

In particular case of $\Delta<\tau$ there exists single domain for s, namely $s\in\left]0;\delta\right]=\left]0;\Delta\right]$. For $\varphi\left(s\right)$ one obtains:

Box 5.

$$
\begin{cases}
\dfrac{d^2\varphi^{m_\Delta}(s)}{ds^2} - \lambda^2\varphi^{m_\Delta}(s) = 0, \\[4mm]
\dfrac{d^2\varphi^{m_\Delta-1}(s)}{ds^2} - \lambda^2\varphi^{m_\Delta-1}(s) = a\lambda^3 e^{-\lambda\Delta} - \lambda^2\varphi^{m_\Delta}(s+\tau) + \lambda^3 \int\limits_{s+\tau}^{\Delta} \varphi^{m_\Delta}(s')\,ds', \\[4mm]
\cdots, \\[2mm]
\dfrac{d^2\varphi^{j}(s)}{ds^2} - \lambda^2\varphi^{j}(s) = \Phi^{j}(s), \\[4mm]
\cdots, \\[2mm]
\dfrac{d^2\varphi^{0}(s)}{ds^2} - \lambda^2\varphi^{0}(s) = \Phi^{0}(s).
\end{cases}
\tag{41}
$$

Box 6.

$$
\varphi^{j}(s) = e^{\lambda s}\left(\frac{1}{2\lambda} \int\limits_{\delta+(j-1)\tau}^{s} e^{-\lambda s'}\Phi^{j}(s')\,ds' + D_1^{j} \right) + e^{-\lambda s}\left(-\frac{1}{2\lambda} \int\limits_{\delta+(j-1)\tau}^{s} e^{\lambda s'}\Phi^{j}(s')\,ds' + D_2^{j} \right),
$$
$$
s \in \left[\delta+(j-1)\tau; \delta+j\tau\right[, \quad j = 1,2,\ldots,m_\Delta,
$$
$$
\varphi^{0}(s) = e^{\lambda s}\left(\frac{1}{2\lambda} \int\limits_{0}^{s} e^{-\lambda s'}\Phi^{0}(s')\,ds' + D_1^{0} \right) + e^{-\lambda s}\left(-\frac{1}{2\lambda} \int\limits_{0}^{s} e^{\lambda s'}\Phi^{0}(s')\,ds' + D_2^{0} \right), \quad s \in \left]0;\delta\right[,
$$

$$
\tag{42}
$$

where D_1^{j} and D_2^{j} denote unknown constants of integration. In order to find D_1^{j} and D_2^{j} as functions of λ, τ, Δ, one should substitute (42) to Eq. (36) and separate terms with different power of s.

$$
\varphi(s) = \frac{a\lambda e^{-\lambda s}}{2}\left(1 - e^{-2\lambda(\Delta-s)}\right), \quad s \in \left]0;\Delta\right],
\tag{44}
$$

$$
a = \frac{4e^{2\lambda\Delta}}{\left(3+2\lambda\Delta\right)e^{2\lambda\Delta}+1}.
\tag{45}
$$

The simplest case of $\Delta > \tau$ is realized when $\Delta \in \left[\tau;2\tau\right[$. Two domains should be considered

here: $s \in \left]0;\Delta-\tau\right]$ and $s \in \left]\Delta-\tau;\Delta\right]$. Solving (41) for $m_\Delta = 1$, one obtains: (see Box 7.)

Substituting (46) to the normalization condition (43), one obtains: (see Box 8.)

Graphs of $f(s)$ corresponding to the cases $\Delta < \tau$ and $\Delta \in \left[\tau;2\tau\right[$ are shown at Figure 5, a – d.

Box 7.

$$\varphi^0(s) = \frac{a\lambda}{2} e^{-2\lambda\Delta+\lambda\tau} \left(\lambda s - \lambda(\Delta-\tau) + \frac{1}{2} - e^{-\lambda\tau}\right) \cdot e^{\lambda s} + \frac{a\lambda}{2}\left(-\frac{1}{2}e^{-\lambda\tau}+1\right) \cdot e^{-\lambda s}, \quad s \in \left]0; \Delta-\tau\right],$$

$$\varphi^1(s) = \frac{a\lambda e^{-\lambda s}}{2}\left(1 - e^{-2\lambda(\Delta-s)}\right), \quad s \in \left]\Delta-\tau; \Delta\right].$$

(46)

Box 8.

$$a = \frac{4e^{2\lambda\Delta}}{\left(3+2\lambda\tau\right)e^{2\lambda\Delta} + 1 + \lambda(\Delta-\tau)e^{\lambda\tau} - \lambda(\Delta-\tau)e^{2\lambda\Delta-\lambda\tau} + 2\lambda(\Delta-\tau)e^{2\lambda\Delta}}.$$

(47)

Figure 5. Examples of delays distribution $f(s)$, obtained analytically (a,c) in accordance withEqs. (34), (44)– (47), and found numerically by means of Monte Carlo method after 10 000 000 triggerings (b,d,e,f) a: $N_0 = 2$, $\tau = 10$ ms, $\Delta = 7$ ms, $\lambda = 50$ s^{-1}; b: same parameters as in a; c: $N_0 = 2$, $\tau = 10$ ms, $\Delta = 18$ ms, $\lambda = 50$ s^{-1}; d: same parameters as in c; e: $N_0 = 2$, $\tau = 10$ ms, $\Delta = 25$ ms, $\lambda = 50$ s^{-1}; f: $N_0 = 4$, $\tau = 10$ ms, $\Delta = 25$ ms, $\lambda = 50$ s^{-1}.

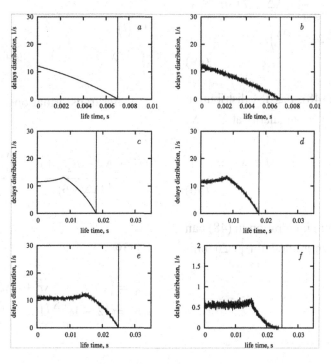

Box 9.

$$P^{\Delta}\left(t\right) = e^{-\lambda t}\lambda t \cdot a\delta\left(t - \Delta\right) + e^{-\lambda t}\lambda t g\left(t\right) + aP^{\text{reg}}\left(t \mid \Delta\right) + \int_{0}^{\Delta} P^{\text{reg}}\left(t \mid s\right) g\left(s\right) ds. \tag{48}$$

ISI Distribution for $\Delta < \tau$

For calculating $P^{\Delta}\left(t\right)$ substitute (28), (29) and (34) into Eq. (17). This gives: (see Box 9.)

Further transformation of (48) depends on the domain, t belongs to. Basic domains of t for the case $\Delta < \tau$ are shown in Figure 4, b.

Consider case A. Here integration domain, $s \in \left]0; \Delta\right]$, should be splitted into two with point $s = t$. This gives

$$P^{\Delta}\left(t\right) =$$
$$e^{-\lambda t}\lambda t g\left(t\right) + a\lambda^2 t e^{-\lambda t} + \int_{0}^{t} \lambda e^{-\lambda t} g\left(s\right) ds + \int_{t}^{\Delta} \lambda^2 t e^{-\lambda t} g\left(s\right) ds,$$

which after transformations becomes

$$P^{\Delta}\left(t\right) = \frac{\lambda e^{-\lambda t}}{\left(2\lambda\Delta + 3\right) e^{2\lambda\Delta} + 1}\left(\left(2\lambda\Delta + 7\right)\lambda t e^{2\lambda\Delta} + \right.$$
$$\left. +1 - \left(\lambda t + 1\right)e^{2\lambda t} - 2\lambda^2 t^2 e^{2\lambda\Delta}\right), \quad t < \Delta. \tag{49}$$

It can be seen from (48), that ISI distribution $P^{\Delta}\left(t\right)$ has δ-function type singularity at $t = \Delta$:

$$P^{\Delta}\left(t\right) = \frac{4\lambda\Delta e^{\lambda\Delta}}{\left(3 + 2\lambda\Delta\right)e^{2\lambda\Delta} + 1}\delta\left(t - \Delta\right), \quad t \in \left]\Delta - \varepsilon; \Delta + \varepsilon\right[. \tag{50}$$

Consider case B. Here integration in (48) can be performed over the entire domain $\left]0; \Delta\right[$ uniformly, which gives:

$$P^{\Delta}\left(t\right) = e^{-\lambda t}\lambda \int_{0}^{\Delta} f\left(s\right) ds = e^{-\lambda t}\lambda, \quad \Delta < t < \tau. \tag{51}$$

Consider case C. Here integration domain should be splitted into two with point $s = t - \tau$, and Eq. (48) turns into the following:

$$P^{\Delta}\left(t\right) =$$
$$\int_{0}^{t-\tau} e^{-\lambda\left(s+\tau\right)}P^0\left(t - s - \tau\right)g\left(s\right)ds + e^{-\lambda t}\lambda\int_{t-\tau}^{\Delta} g\left(s\right)ds + ae^{-\lambda t}\lambda.$$

Here in the first integral $\left(t - s - \tau\right) \in \left[0; t - \tau\right] \subset \left[0; \Delta\right] \subset \left[0; \tau\right]$. This allows to identify from Eqs. (4) and (5) exact expression for $P^0\left(t - s - \tau\right)$, which is

$$y_0\left(t - s - \tau\right) = e^{-\lambda\left(t-s-\tau\right)}\lambda^2\left(t - s - \tau\right):$$

$$P^{\Delta}\left(t\right) =$$
$$\int_{0}^{t-\tau} e^{-\lambda t}\lambda^2\left(t - s - \tau\right)g\left(s\right)ds + e^{-\lambda t}\lambda\int_{t-\tau}^{\Delta} g\left(s\right)ds + ae^{-\lambda t}\lambda.$$

After transformations, one obtains:

$$P^{\Delta}\left(t\right) = \frac{\left(K_0 + K_1 t + K_2 t^2 + e^{2\lambda\left(t-\tau\right)}\right)\lambda e^{-\lambda t}}{\left(4\lambda\Delta + 6\right)e^{2\lambda\Delta} + 2}, \quad \tau < t < \Delta + \tau, \tag{52}$$

where

$$K_0 = \left(2\lambda^2\tau^2 + 4\lambda\tau + 4\lambda\Delta + 6\right)e^{2\lambda\Delta} - 2\lambda\tau + 1,$$
$$K_1 = \left(2 - 4e^{2\lambda\Delta}\left(1 + \lambda\tau\right)\right)\lambda, \quad K_2 = 2\lambda^2 e^{2\lambda\Delta}.$$

Box 10.

$$P^{\Delta}(t) = ae^{-\lambda t} \cdot \sum_{k=1}^{m+1} \frac{\lambda^{k+1}}{k!} \left[(t - \Delta - k\tau)^k + \frac{\lambda}{2(k+1)} \left((t - k\tau)^{k+1} - (t - \Delta - k\tau)^{k+1} \right) + \right.$$

$$+ \frac{\lambda}{2} \sum_{j=0}^{k} \frac{k!}{(k-j)! (2\lambda)^{j+1}} \left((t - k\tau)^{k-j} e^{-2\lambda\Delta} - (t - \Delta - k\tau)^{k-j} \right) \right] -$$

$$- ae^{-\lambda t} \cdot \sum_{k=1}^{m} \frac{\lambda^{k+1}}{k!} \left[(t - \Delta - (k+1)\tau)^k + \frac{\lambda}{2(k+1)} \left((t - (k+1)\tau)^{k+1} - (t - \Delta - (k+1)\tau)^{k+1} \right) + \right.$$

$$+ \frac{\lambda}{2} \sum_{j=0}^{k} \frac{k!}{(k-j)! (2\lambda)^{j+1}} \left((t - (k+1)\tau)^{k-j} e^{-2\lambda\Delta} - (t - \Delta - (k+1)\tau)^{k-j} \right) \right],$$

$$t \in \left[(m+1)\tau + \Delta; (m+2)\tau \right].$$

$$(54)$$

Consider case D. Here Eq. (48) turns into the following:

$$P^{\Delta}(t) =$$
$$ae^{-\lambda(\Delta+\tau)} P^0(t - \Delta - \tau) + \int_0^{\Delta} e^{-\lambda(s+\tau)} P^0(t - s - \tau) g(s) ds.$$

Let us introduce a new variable of integration, $u = t - s - \tau$:

$$P^{\Delta}(t) =$$
$$ae^{-\lambda(\Delta+\tau)} P^0(t - \Delta - \tau) + \int_{t-\Delta-\tau}^{t-\tau} e^{-\lambda(t-u)} P^0(u) g(t - \tau - u) du.$$

$$(53)$$

From this expression we see, that for calculating the integral one needs to use Eq. (4) either with single, or with two consecutive values of m. Namely, if for some m: $m\tau \leq t - \Delta - \tau < t - \tau \leq (m+1)\tau$, then one should substitute $y_m(t)$ from (5), corresponding to that m, instead of $P^0(u)$ in the (53). In the opposite situation, there exist such m, that

$m\tau < t - \Delta - \tau < (m+1)\tau < t - \tau$. In this case, domain of integration in the Eq. (53) should be split with point $(m+1)\tau$, and as $P^0(u)$ one should substitute either $y_m(t)$, or $y_{m+1}(t)$. Thus, when $t \in [\Delta + \tau; \infty[$, then all possible situations are parameterized with the above mentioned number m in such a way that if $t \in \left[(m+1)\tau + \Delta; (m+2)\tau \right]$, then use $y_m(t)$ from (5), and if $t \in](m+2)\tau; \Delta + (m+2)\tau[$, then split integration domain and use both $y_m(t)$ and $y_{m+1}(t)$.

Thus, in the case when there exists such an integer m that $m\tau \leq t - \Delta - \tau < t - \tau \leq (m+1)\tau$, the integration of (53) gives: (see Box 10.)

Curves calculated analytically fit perfectly with those found numerically for the same parameters.

Consider such ISI, that $m\tau < t - \Delta - \tau < (m+1)\tau < t - \tau < (m+2)\tau$, or $t \in](m+2)\tau; \Delta + (m+2)\tau[$. Taking into

Figure 6. Examples of ISI distribution $P^{\Delta}\left(t\right)$, calculated analytically (panels a,c) in accordance with Eqs. (49)– (52), (54), (56) andEqs. (60)– (64) ; and found numerically, by means of Monte Carlo method (panels b,d,e,f) a: τ =10 ms, Δ =7 ms, λ =50 s^{-1}, N_0 = 2 ; b: same parameters as in a, 500 000 spikes were produced. c: τ =10 ms, Δ =18 ms, λ =50 s^{-1}, N_0 = 2 ; d: same parameters as in c, 500 000 spikes were produced. e: τ =10 ms, Δ =25 ms, λ =50 s^{-1}, N_0 = 2 , 10 000 000 spikes were produced. f: τ =10 ms, Δ =25 ms, λ =50 s^{-1}, N_0 = 4 , 10 000 000 spikes were produced.

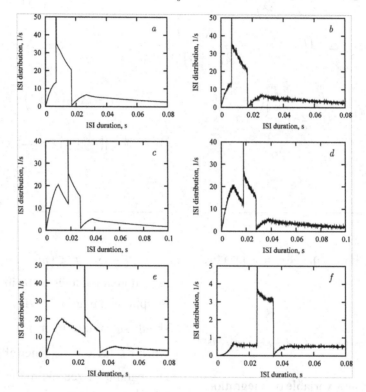

account Eqs. (4) and (5), one can rewrite (53) as follows: (see Box 11.)

Performing integration in (55) one obtains: (see Box 12.)

Note, that in the case $\Delta = 0$, ISI distribution for $t \geq \tau$ is completely defined by Eq. (54), which turns into:

$$P^{\Delta=0}\left(t\right) = e^{-\lambda\tau}P^0\left(t-\tau\right), \quad t \geq \tau. \quad (58)$$

Eq. (58) coincides with the result for BN with instantaneous feedback, obtained before (see Sec. 'Binding neuron with instantaneous feedback (BNF)' for details).

Graphs of $P^{\Delta}\left(t\right)$ for $\Delta < \tau$ are shown at the Figure 6, a,b.

ISI Distribution for $\Delta \geq \tau$

For calculating $P^{\Delta}\left(t\right)$ substitute (26) and (27) into Eq. (17). This gives

$$P^{\Delta}\left(t\right) = \frac{1}{\lambda}P^0\left(t\right)f\left(t\right) + \int_0^{\Delta} P^{\mathrm{reg}}\left(t \mid s\right)f\left(s\right)ds. \quad (59)$$

Box 11.

$$
P^\Delta(t)\Big|_{t\in\left](m+2)\tau;\Delta+(m+2)\tau\right[} = ae^{-\lambda(\Delta+\tau)}y_m\left(t-\Delta-\tau\right)+
$$

$$
+\int_0^{t-(m+2)\tau} e^{-\lambda(s+\tau)}y_{m+1}\left(t-s-\tau\right)g\left(s\right)ds + \int_{t-(m+2)\tau}^\Delta e^{-\lambda(s+\tau)}y_m\left(t-s-\tau\right)g\left(s\right)ds =
$$

$$
= ae^{-\lambda(\Delta+\tau)}y_m\left(t-\Delta-\tau\right)+\int_0^\Delta e^{-\lambda(s+\tau)}y_m\left(t-s-\tau\right)g\left(s\right)ds +
$$

$$
+\frac{\lambda^{m+3}}{(m+2)!}e^{-\lambda t}\int_0^{t-(m+2)\tau}\left(t-s-(m+2)\tau\right)^{m+2}g\left(s\right)ds -
$$

$$
-\frac{\lambda^{m+2}}{(m+1)!}e^{-\lambda t}\int_0^{t-(m+2)\tau}\left(t-s-(m+2)\tau\right)^{m+1}g\left(s\right)ds =
$$

$$
= P^\Delta(t)\Big|_{t\in\left[\Delta+(m+1)\tau;(m+2)\tau\right]} + \rho_m^\Delta\left(t\right),
$$

where

$$
\rho_m^\Delta\left(t\right) = \frac{\lambda^{m+3}}{(m+2)!}e^{-\lambda t}\int_0^{t-(m+2)\tau}\left(t-s-(m+2)\tau\right)^{m+2}g\left(s\right)ds -
$$

$$
-\frac{\lambda^{m+2}}{(m+1)!}e^{-\lambda t}\int_0^{t-(m+2)\tau}\left(t-s-(m+2)\tau\right)^{m+1}g\left(s\right)ds, \quad m=0,1,...
$$

(55)

Box 12.

$$
P^\Delta(t)\Big|_{t\in\left](m+2)\tau;\Delta+(m+2)\tau\right[} = P^\Delta(t)\Big|_{t\in\left[\Delta+(m+1)\tau;(m+2)\tau\right]} + \rho_m^\Delta\left(t\right),
$$

(56)

where

$$
\rho_m^\Delta\left(t\right) = \frac{a\lambda}{2}e^{-\lambda t}\left(\frac{x^{m+3}}{(m+3)!} - \frac{x^{m+2}}{(m+2)!} + \frac{1}{2^{m+3}}e^{-2\lambda\Delta} + \right.
$$

$$
+e^{-2\lambda\Delta}\sum_{j=0}^{m+1}\frac{x^{m+1-j}}{(m+1-j)!\,2^{j+1}}\left(\frac{x}{m+2-j}-1\right)+
$$

$$
\left.+\frac{1}{2^{m+3}}e^{-2(\lambda\Delta-x)}\right), \quad \text{where} \quad x=\lambda\left(t-(m+2)\tau\right).
$$

(57)

Further transformation of (59) depends on the domain, t belongs to. Basic domains of t for the case $\Delta > \tau$ are shown in Figure 4, c.

Consider case A, $t \in \left]0;\tau\right]$. Here integration domain, $s \in \left]0;\Delta\right]$, should be splitted into two with point $s = t$:

$$P^\Delta(t) = \int_0^t e^{-\lambda(t-s)}\left(\lambda\Pi(s) - P^0(s)\right)f(s)\,ds +$$
$$+ \frac{1}{\lambda}P^0(t)g(t) + \int_t^\Delta P^0(t)f(s)\,ds.$$
(60)

Here Eq. (34) is taken into account.

Consider case B, where $t \in \left[\tau;\Delta\right[$. Here integration in (59) should be splitted into three with points $s = t - \tau$ and $s = t$:

$$P^\Delta(t) = \int_0^{t-\tau}\frac{1}{\lambda}e^{-\lambda\tau}\left(\lambda\Pi(s) - P^0(s)\right)P^0(t-s-\tau)f(s)\,ds +$$
$$+ \int_{t-\tau}^t e^{-\lambda(t-s)}\left(\lambda\Pi(s) - P^0(s)\right)f(s)\,ds + \frac{1}{\lambda}P^0(t)g(t) + \int_t^\Delta P^0(t)f(s)\,ds.$$
(61)

It can be seen from (59), that ISI distribution $P^\Delta(t)$ has δ-function type singularity at $t = \Delta$:

$$P^\Delta(t) = \frac{a}{\lambda}P^0(\Delta)\delta(t-\Delta), \qquad t \in \left]\Delta - \varepsilon; \Delta + \varepsilon\right[.$$
(62)

Consider case C. Here integration domain should be splitted into two with point $s = t - \tau$, and Eq. (59) turns into the following:

$$P^\Delta(t) = \int_0^{t-\tau}\frac{1}{\lambda}e^{-\lambda\tau}\left(\lambda\Pi(s) - P^0(s)\right)P^0(t-s-\tau)f(s)\,ds +$$
$$+ \int_{t-\tau}^\Delta e^{-\lambda(t-s)}\left(\lambda\Pi(s) - P^0(s)\right)f(s)\,ds.$$
(63)

Consider case D. Here the intergation in Eq. (59) should be performed over the entire domain $s \in \left]0;\Delta\right]$:

$$P^\Delta(t) = \int_0^\Delta\frac{1}{\lambda}e^{-\lambda\tau}\left(\lambda\Pi(s) - P^0(s)\right)P^0(t-s-\tau)f(s)\,ds.$$
(64)

Integration in (60), (61), (63) and (64) was performed for the simplest case of $\Delta > \tau$, which is $\Delta \in \left[\tau;2\tau\right[$, and the results obtained were used to make graph of $P^\Delta(t)$, shown at the Figure 6, c.

Properties of the Distribution

We present here analytical expression and numerical results (see Sec. Numerical Simulations for details), found for statistical characteristics of output stream, namely, for its mean interspike interval, output intensity, second moment of ISI and ISI variation coefficient. Final analytical expressions are obtained for the simplest case $\Delta < \tau$ for the sake of simlicity.

Mean Interspike Interval

Let us find mean output ISI, W^Δ. Output intensity, λ_o, defined as the mean number of impulses per time unit, is inversed W^Δ. The W^Δ is defined as:

$$W^\Delta = \int_0^\infty tP^\Delta(t)\,dt.$$

Use here Eq. (17):

$$W^\Delta = \int_0^\infty t\,dt\int_0^\Delta P^\Delta(t\mid s)f(s)\,ds = \int_0^\Delta ds f(s)\int_0^\infty tP^\Delta(t\mid s)\,dt.$$

Use here representation (28), (29) and Eq. (8):

$$W^\Delta = \int_0^\Delta dsf(s)\left[\int_0^s t^2 e^{-\lambda t}\lambda^2 dt + e^{-\lambda s}\lambda s^2 + \int_s^{s+\tau} t\lambda e^{-\lambda t}dt\right] +$$
$$+ \int_0^\Delta dsf(s)e^{-\lambda(s+\tau)}\int_{s+\tau}^\infty tP^0\left(t-s-\tau\right)dt =$$
$$= \int_0^\Delta dsf(s)\frac{2-(1+\lambda s)e^{-\lambda s}-(1+\lambda\tau+\lambda s)e^{-\lambda(s+\tau)}}{\lambda} +$$
$$+ \int_0^\Delta dsf(s)e^{-\lambda(s+\tau)}\left(s+\tau+\frac{1}{\lambda}\left(2+\frac{1}{e^{\lambda\tau}-1}\right)\right).$$

Use here (34), (44), (45), which gives after transformations:

$$W^\Delta = \frac{2\left(\left(2\lambda\Delta + e^{-2\lambda\Delta}+1\right)-2\lambda\Delta e^{-\lambda\tau}\right)}{\lambda\left(2\lambda\Delta + e^{-2\lambda\Delta}+3\right)\left(1-e^{-\lambda\tau}\right)}, \quad \Delta < \tau.$$

$$(65)$$

Note, that in the case $\Delta = 0$ Eq. (65) turns into the following:

$$W^{\Delta=0} = \frac{1}{\lambda\left(1-e^{-\lambda\tau}\right)},$$

which coincides with expression obtained before for the ISI first moment of BN with instantaneous feedback (see Eq. (14)).

The output intensity is $\lambda_o^\Delta = \dfrac{1}{W^\Delta}$. At large input rates the following relation takes place

$$\lim_{\lambda\to\infty}\left(\lambda_o^\Delta - \frac{\lambda}{2}\right) = \frac{1}{2\Delta}. \quad (66)$$

Coefficient of Variation

Let's now calculate the coefficient of variation (CV) c_V^Δ of output ISI, which is defined as dimentionless dispersion:

$$c_V^\Delta \equiv \sqrt{\frac{W_2^\Delta}{\left(W^\Delta\right)^2}-1},$$

where W_2^Δ is the second moment of output ISI:

$$W_2^\Delta \equiv \int_0^\infty t^2 P^\Delta(t)dt = \int_0^\Delta dsf(s)\int_0^\infty t^2 P^\Delta(t\mid s)dt.$$

Performing such integration and taking into account Eq. (8), one obtains:

$$\left(c_V^\Delta\right)^2 = \frac{-B_1 e^{2\lambda\tau}+2B_2 e^{\lambda\tau}-B_3}{2\left(\left(2\lambda\Delta + e^{-2\lambda\Delta}+1\right)e^{\lambda\tau}-2\lambda\Delta\right)^2}-1,$$

$$(67)$$

where

$$B_1 = e^{-4\lambda\Delta}-8e^{-3\lambda\Delta}-2\left(2\lambda\Delta-3\right)e^{-2\lambda\Delta}-$$
$$-8\left(2\lambda\Delta+3\right)e^{-\lambda\Delta}-\left(12\lambda^2\Delta^2+12\lambda\Delta-9\right),$$

$$(68)$$

$$B_2 = \left(\lambda\tau+2\right)e^{-4\lambda\Delta}-8e^{-3\lambda\Delta}+2\left(\lambda^2\Delta\tau-\lambda\Delta+2\lambda\tau+6\right)e^{-2\lambda\Delta}-$$
$$-8\left(2\lambda\Delta+3\right)e^{-\lambda\Delta}-\left(12\lambda^2\Delta^2-2\lambda^2\Delta\tau+6\lambda\Delta-3\lambda\tau-18\right),$$

$$(69)$$

$$B_3 = e^{-4\lambda\Delta}-8e^{-3\lambda\Delta}-2\left(2\lambda\Delta-5\right)e^{-2\lambda\Delta}-$$
$$-8\left(2\lambda\Delta+3\right)e^{-\lambda\Delta}-\left(12\lambda^2\Delta^2+4\lambda\Delta-21\right).$$

$$(70)$$

The coefficient of variation, given by Eq. (67), depends non-monotonically on the input intensity (see Figure 7, c).

Theorem 6

For BN with delayed feedback under Poisson stimulation in the case $N_0 = 2$:

Figure 7. Coefficient of variation as the function of $x = \lambda\tau$: a: BN without feedback; b: BN with instantaneous feedback; c,d: BN with delayed feedback. c: CV is found analitically for $N_0 = 2$, $\tau = 10$ ms, $\Delta = 2$ ms (1), $\Delta = 5$ ms (2), $\Delta = 8$ ms (3); d: CV is obtained numerically for $N_0 = 10$, $\tau = 20$ ms, $\Delta = 8$ ms after 50 000 000 triggerings

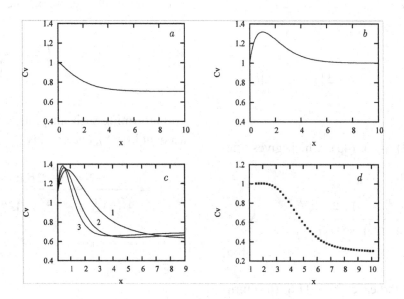

$$\forall \tau, \Delta > 0 \ \exists \tilde{\lambda} > 0 : \lambda \in \left]0; \tilde{\lambda}\right[\Rightarrow c_V^\Delta > 1 .$$

Proof.

Using Eqs. (67) one easily obtains:

$$c_V^\Delta \left(\lambda, \tau, \Delta\right)\Big|_{\lambda=0} = 1$$

and

$$\left(\frac{\partial c_V^\Delta}{\partial \lambda}\right)_{\tau,\Delta}\Bigg|_{\lambda=0} = \Delta + \tau > 0$$

for $\Delta, \tau > 0$. This, together with the fact that c_V^Δ is continuously differentiable with respect to λ, proves Theorem 6.

Note, that in the case $\Delta = 0$ Eq. (67) turns into following:

$$c_V^{\Delta=0} = \sqrt{2\lambda\tau e^{-\lambda\tau} + 1},$$

which coincides with expression obtained before for output ISI coefficient of variation of BN with instantaneous feedback (compare with Eq. (16)).

NUMERICAL SIMULATIONS

In order to check the correctness of obtained analytical expressions, as well as to get an impression of how do ISI distributions look like for higher thresholds and for the case $\Delta > 2\tau$, numerical simulations were performed. A C++ program, containing class, which models the operation manner of BN with delayed feedback, was developed. Object of this class receives the sequence of pseudorandom numbers with Poisson distribution to its input. The required distribution is achieved by using function ran_exponential() on the uniformly distributed sequence from Mersenne Twister generator from the GNU Scientific Library[2].

Figure 8. Output stream statistical characteristics for LIF neuron with delayed feedback, $C = 20$ mV, $\tau_M = 3$ ms, $y_0 = 15$ mV, $\lambda = 100$ s^{-1}, $\Delta = 4$ ms, obtained numerically after 10 000 000 triggerings: a: ISI distribution $P^\Delta(t)$; b: delays distribution $f(s)$

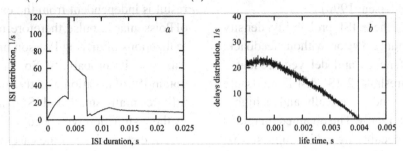

Program contains function, the time engine, which brings system to the moment just before the next input signal, bypassing moments, when neither external Poisson impulse, nor impulse from the feedback line comes. So, only the essential events are accounted. It allows one to make exact calculations faster as compared with the algorithm where time advances gradually by adding small timesteps.

The ISI probability density, $P^\Delta(t)$, is found by counting the number of output ISI of different durations and normalization (see Figure 6, b,d,e,f). In the program, distribution $f(s)$ of time to live of impulse in the feedback line (Figure 5, b,d,e,f), and the output ISI coefficient of variation, c_V^Δ (Figure 7, d), were calculated as well. Numerically obtained curves fit perfectly with the analytical expressions for $P^\Delta(t)$ given in Eqs. (49)—(52), (54), (56) and calculated from (60)—(64), for $f(s)$ given in Eqs. (34), (44), (45) and (46), (47), and for c_V^Δ given in (67) – (70).

In order to compare obtained results with those corresponding to other neuronal models, another class, modelling the operating manner of leaky integrate-and-fire (LIF) neuron (Segundo et al., 1968) with delayed feedback, was also included. Namely, the LIF neuron is characterized with the threshold voltage, C, and every input impulse

advances by y_0 the LIF membrane voltage, V. Between input impulses the V decays exponentially with time constant τ_M. The LIF neuron fires when V becomes grater or equal C, and $V=0$ just after firing. Resulting ISI and delays distributions are shown at Figure 8. Obtained curves are similar to those, found for BN with delayed feedback, see Conclusions and Discussion section for details.

CONCLUSIONS AND DISCUSSION

In this chapter, we derive statistical characteristics of the output stream for single neuron with delayed feedback and present recent results concerning single neuron (Vidybida, 2007) and single neuron with instantaneous feedback (Vidybida, 2008) for comparison. In all cases, neuron is stimulated by the Poisson stream. We use the BN model in order to mimic the operating manner of a biological neuron. This model is an abstract one as it is formulated not in terms of membrane voltage or currents, but in terms of moments when input and output elementary events, which are neuronal impulses (spikes), happen. On the other hand, it is physiologycally grounded as it was inspired by numerical simulation of Hodgkin-Huxley-type neuron (Vidybida, 1996b). The question of how many synaptic impulses in the internal memory are able to trigger the neuron, should be answered on the base of experimental data for real neurons. This number varies from one (Miles, 1990), through fifty (Barbour, 1993), to 60-180 (Andersen, 1991), and 100-300 (Andersen, 1990).

We calculated here ISI probability density functions for binding neuron without feedback, BN with instantaneous and delayed feedback. For BN with threshold 2 ISI distributions are found analytically and numerically, and for higher thresholds – numerically. The obtained functions have remarkable peculiarities which suggest what could happen with spiking statistics of individual neurons in elaborated network with delayed connections.

As we see here, signal processing in BN causes considerable changes in temporal structure of the input signal. Indeed, even in the simplest case of single neuron without feedback the output ISI distribution differs essentially from the Poisson distribution, which is the exponential one.

All ISI distributions, found for BN, BNF and BN with delayed feedback, exhibit derivative discontinuities, see Figures 3 and 6. Presence of such discontinuities, as well as derivative discontinuity in delays distribution $f(s)$ at $s = \Delta - \tau$ (Figure 5, c,d,e,f), is due to the finitness of BN's memory, τ.

In the presense of feedback, no matter is it delayed or not, ISI distributions are characterized by breaks, or jumps (see Figure 3, b and Figure 6). Such breaks are caused by the discontinuity in the number of impulses from Poisson stream needed for triggering. Namely, when the impulse from the feedback line reaches BN, such number decreases by unity, and increases again when the feedback impulse is forgotten.

In the case of delayed feedback for all considered threshold values output ISI distribution also has δ-function type peculiarity at $t = \Delta$ (see Figure 6). It can be explained as follows. If the line was empty at the moment of last output spike, impulse enters the line and after time, exactly equal to Δ, reaches BN input. If during time Δ

BN receives one impulse from Poisson stream, then the impulse from the line triggers BN exactly through the time Δ after the last spike. Such result is independent from the exact arrival time of Poissonian impulse, therefore, many alternative realizations of driving Poisson process will contribute to its probability. So, the probability to obtain ISI of duration exactly equal to Δ is not infinitesimally small, and ISI distribution exhibits the δ-function type peculiarity at $t = \Delta$.

ISI distributions in the case of delayed feedback, placed on Figure 6, are polymodal. The shape of ISI distribution and the number of its modes depends essentially on the internal BN's parameters (N_0, τ, Δ), as well as on the input Poisson stream intensity λ.

All mentioned peculiarities were also observed for ISI distributions in the case $\Delta > 2\tau$, obtained in numerical simulations.

For threshold $N_0 = 2$ we also found the mean interspike interval, which is reversed output intensity, as a function of the input one. For high input rates mean output ISI of the BN without feedback will tend to λ/N_0, because almost all input ISIs will become shorter then τ and every consequent N_0 impulses will trigger BN. For the same reasoning, mean output ISI of the BN with instantaneous feedback will tend to $\lambda/(N_0 - 1)$ as $\lambda \to \infty$.

The limiting relation (66), obtained in the case of delayed feedback for $N_0 = 2$, can be understood as follows. At high intensity, every two consecutive input impulses trigger the BN and send impulse into the feedback line, provided it is empty. Thus, output intensity should be $\lambda/2$ plus firing, caused by additional stimulation from the line. This additional stimulation has maximum rate $1/\Delta$, which explaines (66).

Another statistical characteristic of output stream, considered here, was the coefficient of variation. At Figure 7, a, graph of CV vs. $\lambda\tau$ for

$N_0 = 2$ in the case of BN without feedback is placed. It starts from the value $c_V = 1$ and drops motonically to the asymptotic value, $c_V = 1/\sqrt{2}$. It could be explained as follows. At low input rates, when $\lambda\tau \to 0$, BN output stream becomes Poisson. Indeed, the BN will generate the output spike in interval $[t; t + dt[$ if three conditions are satisfied: i) there is input spike in $[t; t + dt[$, ii) the previous input was received at $t - \tau$, or later, iii) the previous input did not trigger BN. Violation of cond. iii), with i), ii) satisfied, is improbable when $\lambda\tau \to 0$. In this case the desired probability of output is $\left(1 - e^{-\lambda\tau}\right)\lambda dt$, which describes the Poisson stream with intensity $\left(1 - e^{-\lambda\tau}\right)\lambda$. The CV of the Poisson stream equals to 1. Similar reasoning is valid for BNF and for BN with delayed feedback.

Figure 7, b contains graph of CV vs. $\lambda\tau$ for $N_0 = 2$ in the case of BN with instantaneous feedback. At lower input intensities CV increases with $\lambda\tau$, reaches its maximum at $\lambda\tau = 1$, where mean interval between input impulses from the Poisson stream equals to BN's memory duration τ, and then drops gradually to the asymptotic value, which is 1. There is nothing surprising about that. Indeed, at high input rates, the output stream of BN with instantaneous feedback literally reproduces the input one. So, its CV will coincide with the CV of input Poisson stream, which is 1.

At Figure 7, c, graphs of CV vs. $\lambda\tau$ for $N_0 = 2$ in the case of delayed feedback at different values of delay Δ are placed. All obtained curves are non-monotonic. For small delay values the maximum is observed near $\lambda\tau = 1$. For higher Δ the maximum position shifts towards lower input intensities, and the highest maximum is observed at $\Delta = \tau$, as it was found in numerical simulations. Obviously, one should expect, that for the case $\Delta \gg \tau$ obtained curve will tend to the shape of CV Graph for BN without feedback,

which is monotinically decreasing (Figure 7, a). Numerical simulations confirm that conclussion.

For high input rates, mentioned dependences stabilize and CV stops to depend on the intensity of input Poisson stream as the rate of lost input impulses tends to zero.

For higher thresholds, the maximum on the CV curve drops, but is always higher then unity. The stabilized CV value also decreases with N_0 increasing, which is crearly understood. Indeed, the variability of the time window, which encloses N_0 input impulses, is smaller for higher N_0. In the case of high input intensity there is almost no lost impulses, so every N_0 consequtive input impulses will trigger BN. If they come in regularly, the output impulsation will also be regular. In the limiting case $N_0 \to \infty$ at high input intensities one should expect output stream to be strictly regular with zero coefficient of variation.

Figure 7, d, contains CV curve for delayed feedback in the case $N_0 = 10$ for realistic input and output intensities, namely, from 10 to 1000 s^{-1} for the input and from 1 to 100 s^{-1} for the output stream.

The considerable variability of output ISI is consistent with experimental results. High CV values, ranging between 0.5 and 1, were obtained at the output of neurons from primary visual cortex and middle temporal visual area of awake behaving monkey (Softky & Koch, 1993). CV values up to 0.7 were computed from spike trains recorded during spontaneous activity in vivo from neurons in the somatosensory cortex of anesthetized rats (Nawrot et al., 2007) and from primary motor cortex of behaving monkey (Nawrot et al., 2008).

In this work we also wanted to check, wheather the results obtained for BN with feedback, are sensitive to the particular rules, accepted in neuronal model. For this purpose, we performed numerical simulation of leaky integrate-and-fire (LIF) neuron with feedback, driven by the Poisson stream (see Sec. Numerical Simulations). Obtained ISI and delays distributions are placed at the Figure 8. Obviously, there exsists remarkable similarity between results, obtained for BN and LIF neuron with delayed feedback, compare Figure 8, a with Figure 6; and Figure 8, b with Figure 5. Output ISI distributions for LIF neuron with delayed feedback exhibit δ-function type peculiarities, are polymodal, and for some parameters values contain jumps, similar to, and of the same nature as, those observed for BN with delayed feedback. This brings about the idea, that statistical characteristics of the output signal are determined mostly by the network structure (the architecture of its interconnections) and by statistics of the input signal.

On the other hand, we would like to emphasize, that all results, concerning neuron with delayed feedback, are obtained for particular (specific) rules accepted for the feedback line. Namely, at any moment, the line either contains single impulse, or is empty, and it cannot conduct two or more impulses at the same time. And, in our opinion, one should expect similar peculiarities to appear in output firing statistics for any neuronal model with feedback.

Comparing results, obtained for BN and for BN with feedback, we conclude that presence of feedback line can radically change neuronal firing statistics. Moreover, ISI distributions, found for the case $\Delta > 0$, differ essentially as compared to the case of instantaneous feedback. We also expect output ISIs of BN with delayed feedback to be correlated. Indeed, in the case of BN without feedback and BN with instantaneous feedback, at the beginning of every output ISI BN starts from the standard state, which keeps no information about previous events. But the state of BN with delayed feedback is characterized by additional parameter, s, which gets no standard value at the beginning of output ISI and depends on previous events. This, in our opinion, will cause correlations not only between neighbouring output ISI, but also between more distant ones. We

expect the output stream of BN with delayed feedback to be non-markovian. Recently, the experimental evidence of correlation between neighboring ISI from neurons in sensory periphery as well as in cortical neurons was reported (Nawrot et al., 2007; refs. in Farkhooi et al., 2009). The spike trains in electrosensory afferent fibers of the brown ghost knifefish are reported to form a Markov chain of at least fourth order (Ratnam & Nelson, 2000).

FUTURE RESEARCH DIRECTIONS

As the output stream of BN with delayed feedback is assumed to be non-renewal, its statistics cannot be completely described by the single probability distribution $P(t)$, which is in contrast to the cases of BN without feedback and BN with instantaneous feedback (see Theorems 2 and 5). We expect that due to delayed feedback the output stochastic stream should have a kind of memory and even to be non-markovian. In order to check this the exact expressions for conditional probabilities $P(t_2 \mid t_1)$ and $P(t_2 \mid t_1, t_0)$ are to be derived for BN with delayed feedback. Moreover, as the correlations between output ISIs are due to the feedback line, we expect to find the same output stream behavior for other models, which are renewal themselves (with feedback line removed). We are planning to investigate this question analytically for BN and numerically for LIF and Hodgkin-Huxley neuronal models.

We revealed here the effect of the feedback presence on the output statistics of a single neuron. However, in real neuronal systems, the feedback is usually mediated by other cells. So, it seems interesting to consider larger neuronal networks, containing more than one neuron, with feedback. In particular, the chain of two neurons, where the output of the second one is fed back to the input of the first one would be the simplest case to consider.

ACKNOWLEDGMENT

This work was supported by the Program of basic research of the National Academy of Science of Ukraine.

REFERENCES

Andersen, P. (1991). Synaptic integration in hypocampal neurons. In *Fidia Research Foundation Neuroscience Award Lectures* (pp. 51-71). New-York: Raven Press, Ltd.

Andersen, P., Raastad, M., & Storm, J. F. (1990). Excitatory synaptic integration in hippocampal pyramids and dentate granule cells. In *Cold Spring Harbor Symposia on Quantitative Biology* (pp. 81–86). Cold Spring Harbor: Cold Spring Harbor Laboratory Press.

Barbour, B. (1993). Synaptic currents evoked in Purkinje cells by stimulating individual granule cells. *Neuron, 11,* 759. doi:10.1016/0896-6273(93)90085-6

Burkitt, A. N. (2006). A review of the integrate-and-fire neuron model: I. Homogeneous synaptic input. *Biological Cybernetics, 95,* 1–19. doi:10.1007/s00422-006-0068-6

Cariani, P. (2001). Temporal codes, timing nets, and music perception. *Journal of New Music Research, 30,* 107–135. doi:10.1076/jnmr.30.2.107.7115

Damasio, A. R. (1989). The brain binds entities and events by multiregional activation from convergence zones. *Neural Computation, 1,* 123–132. doi:10.1162/neco.1989.1.1.123

Eckhorn, R., Bauer, R., Jordan, W., Brosch, M., Kruse, W., Munk, M., & Reitboeck, H. J. (1988). Coherent oscillations: a mechanism for feature linking in the visual cortex? *Biological Cybernetics, 60,* 121–130. doi:10.1007/BF00202899

Eggemont, J. J. (1991). Rate and synchronization measures of periodicity coding in cat primary auditory cortex. *Hearing Research, 56,* 153–167. doi:10.1016/0378-5955(91)90165-6

Engel, A. K., König, P., Kreiter, A. K., Gray, C. M., & Singer, W. (1991a). Temporal coding by coherent oscillations as a potential solution to the binding problem: physiological evidence. In Schuster, H.G. & Singer, W. (Ed.), *Nonlinear Dynamics and Neuronal Networks*. VCH Weinheim.

Engel, A. K., König, P., & Singer, W. (1991b). Direct physiological evidence for scene segmentation by temporal coding. *Proceedings of the National Academy of Sciences of the United States of America, 88,* 9136–9140. doi:10.1073/pnas.88.20.9136

Farkhooi, F., Strube-Bloss, M. F., & Nawrot, M. P. (2009). Serial correlation in neural spike trains: Experimental evidence, stochastic modelling, and single neuron variability. *Physical Review E: Statistical, Nonlinear, and Soft Matter Physics, 79,* 021905. doi:10.1103/PhysRevE.79.021905

Feller, W. (1966). *An introduction to probability theory and its applications (Vol. 2).* New York: John Wiley & Sons.

Gerstner, W., & Kistler, W. (2002). *Spiking Neuron Models: Single Neurons, Populations, Plasticity.* Cambridge University Press.

Gnedenko, B. (1989). *The Theory of Probability.* New York: Chelsea (Fifth Edition).

Hebb, D. O. (1949). *The Organization of Behaviour.* New York: Wiley.

Holden, A. V. (1976). Models of the stochastic activity of neurons. In *Lecture Notes in Biomathematics, 12.* Berlin: Springer.

Khinchin, A. Ya. (1955). Mathematical methods of mass-service theory. *V. A. Steklov Institute of Mathematics Trudy, 49,* 1–122.

Kistler, W. M., & De Zeeuw, C. I. (2002). Dynamical working memory and timed responses: the role of reverberating loops in the olivo-cerebellar system. *Neural Computation, 14,* 2597–2626. doi:10.1162/089976602760407991

Kolmogoroff, A. (1931). Über die analytischen Methoden in der Wahrscheinlichkeit-srechnung. *Mathematische Annalen, 104,* 415–458. doi:10.1007/BF01457949

König, P., Engel, A. K., & Singer, W. (1996). Integrator or coincidence detector? The role of the cortical neuron revisited. *Trends in Neurosciences, 19,* 130–137. doi:10.1016/S0166-2236(96)80019-1

König, P., & Krüger, N. (2006). Symbols as self-emergent entities in an optimization process of feature extraction and predictions. *Biological Cybernetics, 94,* 325–334. doi:10.1007/s00422-006-0050-3

Lánský, P., & Sato, S. (1999). The stochastic diffusion models of nerve membrane depolarization and interspike interval generation. *Journal of the Peripheral Nervous System, 4,* 27–42.

Leonards, U., Singer, W., & Fahle, M. (1996). The influence of temporal phase differences on texture segmentation. *Vision Research, 36*(17), 2689–2697. doi:10.1016/0042-6989(96)86829-5

Llinás, R., Ribary, U., Joliot, M., & Wang, X.-J. (1994). Content and Context in Temporal Thalamocortical Binding. In Buzsáki, G., Llinás, R., Singer, W., Berthoz, A., & Christen, Y. (Eds.), *Temporal Coding in the Brain* (pp. 251–272). Berlin: Springer-Verlag.

MacKay, D. M. (1962). Self-organization in the time domain. In Yovitts, M. C., Jacobi, G. T., & Goldstein, G. D. (Eds.), *Self-Organizing Systems* (pp. 37–48). Washington: Spartan Books.

MacLeod, K., Bäcker, A., & Laurent, G. (1998). Who reads temporal information contained across synchronized and oscillatory spike trains? *Nature, 395,* 693–698. doi:10.1038/27201

Miles, R. (1990). Synaptic excitation of inhibitory cells by single CA3 hyppocampal pyramidal cells of the guinea-pig *in vitro. The Journal of Physiology, 428,* 61.

Nawrot, M. P., Boucsein, C., Rodriguez-Molina, V., Aertsen, A., Grün, S., & Rotter, S. (2007). Serial interval statistics of spontaneous activity in cortical neurons *in vivo* and *in vitro. Neurocomputing, 70,* 1717–1722. doi:10.1016/j.neucom.2006.10.101

Nawrot, M. P., Boucsein, C., Rodriguez-Molina, V., Riehle, A., Aertsen, A., & Rotter, S. (2008). Measurement of variabiility dynamics in cortical spike trains. *Journal of Neuroscience Methods, 169,* 374–390. doi:10.1016/j.jneumeth.2007.10.013

Ratnam, R., & Nelson, M. E. (2000). Nonrenewal Statistics of Electrosensory Afferent Spike Trains: Implications for the Detection of Weak Sensory Signals. *The Journal of Neuroscience, 20*(17), 672–6683.

Ricciardi, L. M. (1977). Diffusion Processes and Related Topics in Biology. In *Lecture Notes in Biomathematics, 14.* Berlin: Springer.

Rudolph, M., & Destexhe, A. (2003). Tuning neocortical pyramidal neurons between integrators and coincidence detectors. *Journal of Computational Neuroscience, 14,* 239–251. doi:10.1023/A:1023245625896

Segundo, J. P., Perkel, D., Wyman, H., Hegstad, H., & Moore, G. P. (1968). Input-output relations in computer-simulated nerve cell. *Kybernetic, 4,* 157–171. doi:10.1007/BF00289038

Softky, W. R., & Koch, C. (1993). The highly irregular firing of cortical cells is inconsistent with temporal integration of random EPSPs. *The Journal of Neuroscience, 13,* 334–350.

Tuckwell, H. C. (1988). *Introduction to theoretical neurobiology*. Cambridge, UK: Cambridge University Press.

Tuckwell, H. C. (1989). *Stochastic processes in the neurosciences*. Philadelphia: Society for Industrial and Applied Mathematics.

Vidibida, A. K. (2008). Output stream of binding neuron with instantaneous feedback. *The European Physical Journal B, 65,* 577–584. doi:10.1140/epjb/e2008-00360-1

Vidybida, A. K. (1996a). Information processing in a pyramidal-type neuron. In Heinz, G. (Ed.), *BioNet'96 – Biologieorientierte Informatik und pulspropagierende Netze, 3-d Workshop* (pp. 96-99), Berlin: GFaI.

Vidybida, A. K. (1996b). Neuron as time coherence discriminator. *Biological Cybernetics, 74,* 539–544. doi:10.1007/BF00209424

Vidybida, A. K. (1998). Inhibition as binding controller at the single neuron level. *Bio Systems, 48,* 263–267. doi:10.1016/S0303-2647(98)00073-2

Vidybida, A. K. (2006). *Stochastic models*. Kyiv: NAS of Ukraine.

Vidybida, O. K. (2007). Output stream of a binding neuron. *Ukrainian Mathematical Journal, 59*(12), 1819–1839. doi:10.1007/s11253-008-0028-5

ADDITIONAL READING

Aroniadou-Anderjaska, V., Ennis, M., & Shipley, M. T. (1999). Dendrodendritic recurrent excitation in mitral cells of the rat olfactory bulb. *Journal of Neurophysiology, 82,* 489–494.

Britvina, T., & Eggermont, J. J. (2006). A Markov model for interspike interval distributions of auditory cortical neurons that do not show periodic firings. *Biological Cybernetics, 96,* 245–264. doi:10.1007/s00422-006-0115-3

Damasio, A. R. (1990). Category-related recognition defects as a clue to the neural substrates of knowledge. *Trends in Neurosciences, 13,* 95–98. doi:10.1016/0166-2236(90)90184-C

Damasio, H., Grabowski, T. J., Tranel, D., Hichwa, R. D., & Damasio, A. R. (1996). A neural basis for lexical retrieval. *Nature, 380,* 499–505. doi:10.1038/380499a0

Dayan, P., & Abbott, L. F. (2001). *Theoretical Neuroscience: computational and mathematical modelling of neural systems*. Cambridge, MA: The MIT press.

Fall, Ch. P., Marland, E. S., Wagnerand, J. M., & Tyson, J. J. (Eds.). (2002). *Computational Cell Biology*. Singapore: Springer.

Gray, C. M., König, P., Engel, A. K., & Singer, W. (1990). Synchronization of oscillatory responses in visual cortex: a plausible mechanism for scene segmentation. In Haken, H., & Stadler, M. (Eds.), *Synergetics of Cognition*. Berlin: Springer.

Haken, H. (1983). *Advanced Synergetics*. Berlin: Springer.

Haken, H. (Ed.). (1988). *Proceedings of the International Symposium of Schloß Elmau, Bavaria, June 13-17. Neural and Synergetic Computers*. Berlin: Springer-Verlag.

Haken, H. (1996). *Principles of Brain Functioning. A Synergetic Approach to Brain Activity, Behavior, and Cognition*. Berlin: Springer.

Haken, H. (2000). Effect of delay on phase locking in a pulse coupled neural network. *The European Physical Journal B, 18,* 545–550. doi:10.1007/s100510070045

Haken, H. (2008). *Brain Dynamics. An Introduction to Models and Simulations*. Berlin: Springer.

Hodgkin, A. L., & Huxley, A. F. (1952). A quantitative description of membrane current and its application to conduction and excitation in nerve. *The Journal of Physiology, 125,* 221–224.

Keener, J., & Snyde, J. (1998). *Mathematical physiology.* New York: Springer.

MacKay, D. M. (1954). On comparing the brain with machines. *American Scientist, 42,* 261–268.

MacKay, D. M. (1965). From mechanism to mind. In J. R. Smythies (ed.), *Brain and mind: Modern concepts of the nature of mind* (pp. 163-200; 129-131, etc. discussions). London: Routledge & Kegan Paul.

MacKay, D. M. (1980). Neural communication and control: Facts and theories. *Nature, 287,* 389–390. doi:10.1038/287389a0

Matsumoto, M., & Nishimura, T. (1998). Mersenne twister: a 623-dimensionally equidistributed uniform pseudorandom number generator. *ACM Transactions on Modeling and Computer Simulation, 8,* 3–30. doi:10.1145/272991.272995

Moore, B. C. J. (2003). Coding of sounds in the auditory system and its relevance to signal processing and coding in cochlear implants. *Otology & Neurotology, 24,* 243–254. doi:10.1097/00129492-200303000-00019

Nicoll, R. A., & Jahr, C. E. (1982). Self-excitation of olfactory bulb neurones. *Nature, 296,* 441–444. doi:10.1038/296441a0

Nicolls, J. G., Martin, A. R., Wallace, B. G., & Fuchs, P. A. (2001). *From Neuron to Brain* (4th ed.). Sunderland, MA: Sinauer.

Schmidt, R. (1975). *Fundamentals of Neurophysiology.* Berlin: Springer.

Scott, A. (2002). *Neuroscience: a mathematical primer.* New York: Springer-Verlag.

Smith, G. D. (2002). Modeling the Stochastic Gating of Ion Channels. In Fall, Ch. P., Marland, E. S., Wagnerand, J. M., & Tyson, J.J. (Ed.), *Computational Cell Biology* (pp. 285-319). Singapore: Springer.

Vidybida, A. K. (2007). Input-output relations in binding neuron. *Bio Systems, 89,* 160–165. doi:10.1016/j.biosystems.2006.07.015

Yovitts, M. C., Jacobi, G. T., & Goldstein, G. D. (Eds.). (1962). *Self-Organizing Systems.* Washington: Spartan Books.

KEY TERMS AND DEFINITIONS

Neuron: primary constructive unit of neural network. Neuron, either in biological network, like brain, or in tehnical/model network, has integrative function. Namely, it receives input signals from many sources through many input lines, and sends output signals through single output line. In biological neuronal cell, the input lines are named dendrites, and the output line is named axon. The difference between neuron and standard AND/OR logical units used in computers is its manner of taking decision about what output signal should be, based on received input signals. First, a logical unit operates in synchronous manner—all input signal are received simultaneously, while neuron receives signals dispersed in time. Second, a logical unit takes decision about its output based on exact content of signals received, while neuron additionally takes into account the moments the different inputs are received. For this purpose, a neuron must have an internal memory, which keeps for a period of time information about any received signal. In biological neurons, such internal memory is realized as electrochemical transient known as "excitatory postsynaptic potential", or EPSP.

Spike, or Action Potential: universal electrical signal of neural network, neural impulse.

Spikes propagate along the neuron from the place, they started, to the junction with the next neuron. Physiologically spikes are realized through the fast changes of transmembrane voltage due to the ion motion through the ion-channels.

Stochastic Process: a process of changing states by a system, in which a state at time t is not determined uniquelly, but can be any state x from some set X of states with some probability $p(x,t)$. The development in time of such a system cannot be predicted as a single trajectory $x(t)$, but can be described by a set of possible trajectories, each with its own probability.

Probability Distribution Function: Stochastic process can be characterized by a set of multidimentional probability distribution functions[3] $f\left(x_n, t_n; x_{n-1}, t_{n-1}; \ldots; x_1, t_1\right)$, which gives the probability that stochastic process has states $x_1, \ldots, x_n$ at moments $t_1, \ldots, t_n$, respectively.

Conditional Probability Distribution Function: The function $f\left(x_{n+m}, t_{n+m}; \ldots; x_{n+1}, t_{n+1} \mid x_n, t_n; x_{n-1}, t_{n-1}; \ldots; x_1, t_1\right)$, where $t_1 < t_2 < \ldots < t_n < t_{n+1} < \ldots < t_{n+m}$. This function gives the probability, that stochastic process passes states $x_{n+1}, \ldots, x_{n+m}$ at moments $t_{n+1}, \ldots, t_{n+m}$, respectively, provided that it passed states $x_1, \ldots, x_n$ at moments $t_1, \ldots, t_n$, respectively.

Markovian Stochastic Process: stochastic process, which has conditional probability distribution functions satisfying the following relation: $\forall n, m \in \mathbb{N}$,

$$t_1 < t_2 < \ldots < t_n < t_{n+1} < \ldots < t_{n+m}$$
$$f\left(x_{n+m}, t_{n+m}; \ldots; x_{n+1}, t_{n+1} \mid x_n, t_n; \ldots; x_1, t_1\right)$$
$$= f\left(x_{n+m}, t_{n+m}; \ldots; x_{n+1}, t_{n+1} \mid x_n, t_n\right).$$

Poisson Process: stochastic markovian process, which states are nonnegative integers n. The process is characterized with intensity λ, and has simplest conditional probability distribution functions of the form

$$p\left(n, t \mid n', t'\right) = e^{-\lambda(t-t')} \frac{\left(\lambda\left(t - t'\right)\right)^{n-n'}}{\left(n - n'\right)!}.$$ All

other probability distributions can be found as combinations of the simplest ones based on markovian property.

ENDNOTES

[1]   It is worth noticing, that both sorts of variability ogirinate from the variability of driving Poisson process.

[2]   http://www.gnu.org/software/gsl/.

[3]   In pure mathematical literature, the term "probability density distribution" is used.

Chapter 11
Expert Guided Autonomous Mobile Robot Learning

Gintautas Narvydas
Kaunas University of Technology, Lithuania

Vidas Raudonis
Kaunas University of Technology, Lithuania

Rimvydas Simutis
Kaunas University of Technology, Lithuania

ABSTRACT

In the control of autonomous mobile robots there exist two types of control: global control and local control. The requirement to solve global and local tasks arises respectively. This chapter concentrates on local tasks and shows that robots can learn to cope with some local tasks within minutes. The main idea of the chapter is to show that, while creating intelligent control systems for autonomous mobile robots, the beginning is most important as we have to transfer as much as possible human knowledge and human expert-operator skills into the intelligent control system. Successful transfer ensures fast and good results. One of the most advanced techniques in robotics is an autonomous mobile robot on-line learning from the experts' demonstrations. Further, the latter technique is briefly described in this chapter. As an example of local task the wall following is taken. The main goal of our experiment is to teach the autonomous mobile robot within 10 minutes to follow the wall of the maze as fast and as precisely as it is possible. This task also can be transformed to the obstacle circuit on the left or on the right. The main part of the suggested control system is a small Feed-Forward Artificial Neural Network. In some particular cases – critical situations – "If-Then" rules undertake the control, but our goal is to minimize possibility that these rules would start controlling the robot. The aim of the experiment is to implement the proposed technique on the real robot. This technique enables to reach desirable capabilities in control much faster than they would be reached using Evolutionary or Genetic Algorithms, or trying to create the control systems by hand using "If-Then" rules or Fuzzy Logic. In order to evaluate the quality of the intelligent control system to control an autonomous mobile robot we calculate objective function values and the percentage of the robot work loops when "If-Then" rules control the robot.

DOI: 10.4018/978-1-61692-811-7.ch011

INTRODUCTION

Every day in the world we have more and more robots. We already cannot imagine our lives without them. Autonomous mobile robots (AMR) have a wide range of applications. Nowadays it is produced robots toys, robots applicable in daily life needs, industry, agriculture, military, special robots, and, of course, and the ones applied in science. Robot toys become more and more sophisticated; eventually they become learning tools for children. In Japan a life-like female robot Saya can teach the fifth-graders. Robots which are applied in daily life needs relieve people of everyday cares, save a lot of their time. Robots replace people in industry. In such a way productivity and production quality are increasing, whereas expenses are decreasing. Military robots are used to complete military operations. They save troop lives. Special robots are used for cleaning polluted environments, rescuing and completing other special operations. Robots that are designed for research extend the potential boundaries of research. Scientists can use them for the research of deep water in the oceans, volcano craters, even other planets (Maimone et al., 2006). Robots for research are important for one more thing – they are used in the research of methods and algorithms applied in the intelligent robot control.

However, today AMR still cannot move, communicate, recognize and orient in the environment in the same way as the living creatures can. Intelligent control systems (ICS) are neither universal nor powerful enough to guarantee a good working of AMR in our today's environment. In the robotics it is necessary to improve both the hardware and the software as well as to pay exclusive attention to the intelligent hybrid control systems and robots learning from demonstrations. In this chapter, there will be shown that on-line learning from demonstrations technique is much faster than other (evolutionary) techniques. The objective of this chapter is to show that the AMR can learn some tasks much faster under skilled operator-expert guidance than it could learn that without guidance.

BACKGROUND

In the control of AMR there exist two types of control: global control and local control. The requirement to solve global and local tasks arises respectively. In the figure 1 the situation when an AMR – an unmanned ground vehicle must navigate from the start position to the finish position is represented. The first task is a global path planning. To solve this global task GPS tracking devices or/and GPS auto navigator should be used. It depends where a car must drive: on road or off-road terrain. For example, in the 2005 DARPA Grand Challenge project no global path planning was required (Thrun et al., 2006). The route definition data format defined the approximate route that robots would take. What concerns a local task, Sebastian Thurn et al. write: "When a faster robot overtook a slower one, the slower robot was paused by DARPA officials, allowing the second robot to pass the first as if it were a static obstacle. This eliminated the need for robots to handle the case of dynamic passing". These facts show that there still are a lot of unsolved problems in local and global control and encourage roboticists to continue their work on these tasks.

In the figure 1 it is shown that AMR must solve several local tasks: recognize moving objects, detect the pits and obstacles on the road, see road marking and signs, understand traffic-light signals, and cope with prediction of the movement of other cars, people, and even segways or horsemen.

It is obvious that one of the most important tasks in mobile robotics is a local task: obstacle detection, its avoidance and circuit. Local task can be described when the AMR is in a certain environment and via sensors gets information about this environment. Having this information the AMR must make intelligent decisions and send the commands to the motors and ac-

Figure 1. Global and local tasks and the control of an AMR

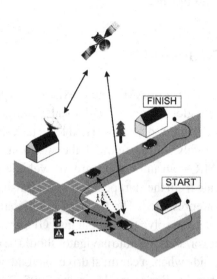

tuators in purpose to reach desirable target or some targets. Many various techniques to create intelligent control systems and implement these tasks exist (Bekey, 2005). Literature cited and our previous works also describe how to control the AMR using "If-Then" rules (Holland, 2004; Narvydas et al., 2008), Artificial Neural Networks (ANN) (Narvydas et al., 2007b), Fuzzy Logic (Narvydas et al., 2007a), Reinforcement Learning (Mahadevan & Connell, 1991; Kaelbing & Littman, 1996), Genetic Algorithm, Evolutionary Algorithm (Floreano & Mondada, 1996; Fogel, 1998; Nolfi & Floreano, 2000; Goldberg 2002), and Expert Cloning Technique (Narvydas et al., 2007b; Narvydas & Raudonis, 2008). Possibilities to combine mentioned techniques are described as well (Narvydas & Raudonis, 2008; Narvydas et al., 2007a; Narvydas et al., 2008).

When we were creating intelligent control system using "If-Then" rules we needed a lot of time to determine and set optimal parameters of the control system. Also we used only two sensors of the robot shown in figure 2. The sixth sensor was used to measure the distance from the wall on the right side and to feel the wall shape, and the fourth sensor was used to detect the obstacles

in front. Otherwise we would have needed to create many more rules and would have created a very complex system. The same we did when we created control system based on Fuzzy Logic. Moreover, using only two sensors – the robot's possibility to feel environment is rather poor. It can see only two narrow sectors. Capabilities of such a robot are very limited.

One of capabilities to find optimal parameters for various control systems is the use of the Genetic or Evolutionary Algorithms. However, it takes a lot of time to perform these algorithms in real systems. Our evolutionary experiments lasted up to three days and results (Narvydas et al., 2007a; Narvydas et al., 2008) showed that we needed up to 10 hours to establish sufficient control. If Evolutionary techniques are used to solve more sophisticated tasks, the duration of one generation can increase to up to two weeks. Such experiments we performed at EPFL with teams of Alice robots (Caprari, 2003) in the project on Evolution of Cooperation in Artificial Ants (Waibel, 2007). When Evolutionary techniques are used, the program code is longer and more error-prone. It takes more time for noticing and fixing mistakes. Also the Genetic and Evolutionary Algorithms tend to adapt the parameters of the control system to the walls shapes of the current environment. For example, if some changes of the walls shapes occur, the quality of the control drops down. If a possibility to include an expert into the learning process exists, such a possibility should be availed because that gives a big improvement in the beginning and reduces learning time significantly. After we started using the ANN for the control and the Expert Cloning technique, we got good results (Narvydas & Raudonis, 2008). However, we can see the quality of the control only after all the data are collected, filtered, and the ANN is trained. In this case there were problems with wall shapes which are not dominating in the maze. One significant lack using described techniques is that any further improvements of the control system after its

Figure 2. The miniature mobile robot Khepera II and its view from the top

 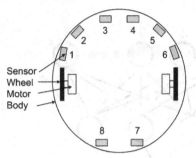

creation are not possible. For that reason we proposed and actually we implemented a new technique to create ICS for the AMR control.

This work describes an on-line learning procedure for the AMR under the guidance of the skilled operator. In the experiments, like in our previous works, we have taught AMR Khepera II to follow the walls of the maze on the right using hybrid intelligent control systems based on the ANN and "If-Then" rules. This task is universal because ability to follow the walls can be easy transformed into the ability to avoid even moving obstacles and to circuit them on the right or on the left. Finally, merits and demerits of the studied technique are emphasized. The proposed control system can be used as a frame for Behavior Based control systems (Arkin, 1998).

EXPERIMENTAL SETUP

Autonomous Mobile Robot Khepera II

All experiments were made using the miniature mobile robot Khepera II (K-team, 2002). The robot and its view from the top are shown in figure 2. The robot's diameter is 70mm, height 30mm, weight about 80g. It is designed to move on the flat surface.

It has two lateral wheels that can rotate in both directions in appointed speed. The speed is

measured in comparative measures. The possible maximum speed of the wheels is 15 and minimum speed is -15 what approximately corresponds to 12.1 and -12.1 centimeters per second respectively. Under the robot two rigid pivots in the front and in the back are installed. They do not let the robot sway forward and backward. Eight infrared proximity sensors are set around the body: six sensors in front and two sensors on the back side. Using Khepera's II sensors it is possible to detect obstacles and to estimate distances to them. Values of each sensor are integer numbers from 0 to 1023. The higher the value of the sensor, the nearer the obstacle is. The maximum sensitivity distance is about 100mm. Robot can be attached to the computer through a serial cable with rotating contacts and RS232 connector, which can be used to transfer data and to supply power.

Miniature size of the robot gives quite a few advantages using it in experiments. It is possible to build various complex environments directly on the table, for example mazes. A small working setting allows us keep a close watch on the robot behavior during experiments. One of the most important advantages of the miniature robot is its size, weight, and ability to move fast. Therefore, when the robot hits a wall or an obstacle it is neither damaged nor broken. Application possibilities of the robot are wide too. It can be used to design and to develop the movement, recognition, orientation in an environment, path planning, control, cooperation, and other algorithms.

Figure 3. The structure of the ANN used in the experiments

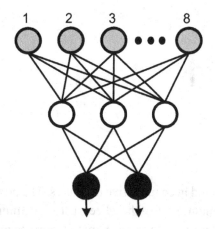

Arena for the Experiments

The arena used in the experiments is a rectangular maze 60x40 cm, shown in the figure 4. The walls of the maze are covered with white paper. That enables the robot to feel better distances up to walls via infrared proximity sensors. The surface of the arena is absolutely flat because the robot is small and it could hang on the lowest roughness. Figure 4 shows the joystick used by the expert to control the robot.

The maze is without loops. To use this particular maze in our experiments is very convenient because the robot is taught to follow the wall, to pass the internal and external angles. We can say that the walls of the arena also serve as the obstacle which is infinite and should be circuited.

EXPERT GUIDED AMR ONLINE LEARNING

The main idea of our suggested technique is inspired by real life situations. For example, when the parents teach their babies to walk they do not explain them how to walk. They simply take them by their hands and lead them. Thus they show and let feel the babies how they should walk. On the other hand, children try to remember and to learn the actions necessary for walking.

We do the same with the robot. In order the control system could learn to control the AMR, firstly, it should be trained how to do that. The skilled experts can do that. They can see the maze from above and control the robot via a joystick. The ability of the expert to control the robot reasonably is obvious. Infrared proximity sensors values and wheels speed data are collected when the robot is controlled by the expert and runs around the maze. Thus the expert experience is transferred into the database. This data is used for the training of the ANN. The intelligent control system learns what is being taught. It means that the operator has to control the robot exactly and has to avoid any unnecessary actions. It is a very difficult task to control the robot so that it could move as quickly and precisely as possible. Such control demands huge concentration that is why it wears a person out. Despite the fact that the operators have obvious competences to drive the robots they are human beings and they can get tired. This is one more argument why we need to create intelligent control systems. Also, the capability to drive the robot depends on the emotional state of the expert.

Using primary data filtering we can eliminate small operator's mistakes. In our experiments primary data processing is executed. The data records are dropped out if:

1) speed of both wheels is less than 1;
2) expert drives the robot too close to the wall or even hits on the wall;
3) expert drives the robot too far from the wall.

Usually up to 10% of the data is dropped out. Such data filtering allows teaching the control system to drive better the AMR, does not allow the robot to stop and stay still, and does not allow it to approach too close to the walls.

The Feed-Forward ANN and the Levenberg-Marquardt training algorithm are used in our experiments (Bishop, 2005). Transfer function of each artificial neuron is a log-sigmoid function. The ANN structure is depicted in the figure 3. For the AMR control and the ANN training data records of the current robot work loop is used. It means that our control system is reactive. Before the ANN training starts, we filter and normalize the obtained data. Data strings where $S_L \leq 0$ and $S_R \leq 0$ are dropped out because our goal is to teach the robot to follow the wall – move forward and avoid standing in one place. The used ANN has eight inputs, three neurons in hidden layer and two neurons in output layer. This network structure was determined experimentally and it is sufficient for a simple wall following task. The eight inputs are the data records from the AMR infrared proximity sensors (see figure 2). Two outputs are calculated wheel speed S_L and S_R.

In the figure 4 it is shown how the expert drives the AMR using a joystick. The expert watches the robot and environment from above and he uses his own senses, knowledge and skills. The trained intelligent control systems will drive the robot in a different way. It will drive the AMR only with reference to information obtained from infrared proximity sensors.

The Expert Guided AMR On-line Learning technique is very similar to the Expert Cloning technique described in (Narvydas et al., 2007b). The main difference is that the Expert Cloning technique is an off-line technique. Using the latter technique at first all the necessary data when the expert demonstrates how to control the AMR must be collected. Then the data are filtered and, finally, the training of the ANN is started. Only after these operations are performed it is possible, firstly, to observe how ICS drives the AMR and, secondly, to calculate objective function value. Whereas, in the Expert Guided AMR On-line Learning technique it is possible to collect the data, train the ANN, and calculate objective function values in on-line mode. Also, in the same way the percentage when "If-Then" rules control the robot can be calculated and the capability of the

Figure 4. The expert teaches on-line the robot Khepera II by demonstration

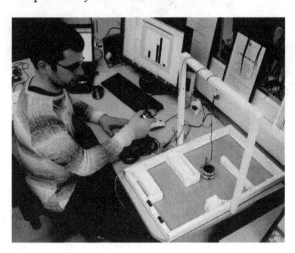

ICS to control the AMR can be estimated. One of the most convenient properties of the proposed technique is flexibility. The control system can be trained additionally after additional data collection. How this described process is implemented in a real system it will be described later.

QUALITY EVALUATION OF THE CONTROL OF THE AMR

To understand how well the intelligent control system drives the robot and how well the robot performs the task we need a way to evaluate its actions. To evaluate the quality of the AMR control an objective function presented in formula (1) is used. This technique aims to reach the maximum possible objective function value, although the objective function is not maximized directly.

To evaluate objective function from the robot work we use last 300 loops data records. In the very beginning of the experiment all up to 300 data records are used.

$$OF = 0.1a + 0.05b + 0.45c + 0.4d, \qquad (1)$$

$$a = 1 - \frac{1}{N(S_{max} - S_{min})} \sum_{i=1}^{N} \left| S_{L_i} - S_{R_i} \right|, \qquad (2)$$

$$b = 1 - \frac{1}{2N(S_{max} - S_{min})} \sum_{i=1}^{N} \left(\left| S_{L_i} - S_{L_{i-1}} \right| + \left| S_{R_i} - S_{R_{i-1}} \right| \right), \qquad (3)$$

$$c = 1 - \frac{1}{N} \sum_{i=1}^{N} \frac{\left| Sens_{6_i} - A \right|}{B}, \qquad (4)$$

$$d = \frac{1}{2} \left(\frac{1}{2N S_{max}} \sum_{i=1}^{N} \left(S_{L_i} + S_{R_i} \right) + 1 \right), \qquad (5)$$

where N is a number of measurements (data records). In our experiments N is 300 and only in the beginning of the experiment it is less. About 16 measurements per second are made (it depends on computer resources). $S_{min} = -15$ and $S_{max} = 15$ are maximum and minimum possible speed of the left and right wheels. S_{L_i} and S_{R_i} are current speed of the left and right wheels, $S_{L_0} = 0$ and $S_{R_0} = 0$. $Sens_{6_i}$ is a current value of the sixth infrared sensor (see figure 2) because it is the nearest to the wall when the robot follows it and is used to evaluate the quality of the wall following. A is a constant which shows desirable value of the sixth sensor of Khepera II – desirable average distance of the robot from the wall or obstacles. This parameter we get from the experts' drives in the previous experiments and it equals to 172. In other words, experts who know how to follow the wall, showed what the average distance must be between the robot and the wall. The result of the component c from (1, 4) is a value of the function depicted in the figure 5 where in the x axis are the values of the sixth sensor. Component c scores maximum value when the sixth sensor returns 172. There arise deviations from this value when the robot is not in good range from the wall or is not in a good position. Thus com-

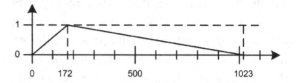

Figure 5. The penalty for the c component (4) and objective function (1) according to the sixth sensor data

ponent c decreases what means penalty and less value for the objective function.

Therefore a (1, 2) is a measure of snaking, b (1, 3) is a measure of twitch, c (1, 4) is a measure of the deviation from the regulation distance from the wall, and d (1, 5) is a measure of average speed of the AMR. It is evident that the robot must snake and twitch less, keep constant distance from the wall on the right side, and move as fast as it is possible following the wall. In our task distance from the wall and movement speed are the most important criteria, therefore, these two components in (1) have bigger weight. All the components in (1) are from interval [0, 1], thus objective function also is from interval [0, 1].

The objective function (1) would reach its maximum value 1.0 if the robot would go forward along straight wall in maximum possible speed keeping constant desirable distance from the wall. Whereas the maze wall (see figure 4) is not straight, the robot cannot always go straight ahead at full speed. It must turn according internal and external corners. Therefore objective function does not reach its maximum value.

If intelligent control system makes driving mistakes while ANN controls the AMR, "If-Then" rules undertake the control of the robot. That happens when the robot approaches too close to the wall (about 2mm), recedes far from the wall (about 50 mm) or turns with the sixth sensor from the wall. The rules "If-Then" control the robot until it regains good position for the wall following. When it happens, at once the control is returned to ANN. When the robot is driven too close to

Figure 6. "If-Then" rules undertake the control of the robot when it approaches too close to the wall (a and b) or when it goes too far or turns from the wall (c and d)

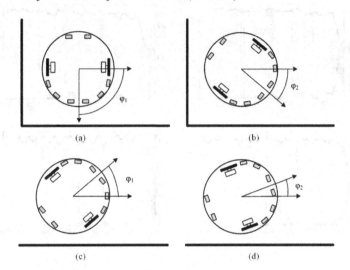

the wall the speed of the left wheel is set to -5, and speed of the right wheel is set to 5. The robot spins anticlockwise to the right position. While it is spinning, it loses time, average speed, and the quality of the movement. How long "If-Then" rules will control the robot depends on the angle in which the robot was driven too close to the wall. In the figure 6 (a) and (b) it is shown that the steeper angle between the robot and the desirable driving direction is the longer time "If-Then" rules drive it to the right position.

When intelligent control system drives the robot too far from the wall or turns the robot from the wall, speed of the left wheel is set to 4 and speed of the right wheel to 1. Such situation is depicted in figure 6 (c) and (d). How long "If-Then" rules will control the robot depends on the angle in which the robot is turned from the wall. In this case speed is reduced notably till the robot reaches right position to continue the wall following.

In both cases described above, first, the value of the objective function (1) decreases and, second, percentage when "If-Then" rules control the AMR increases.

EXPERIMENT DESCRIPTION

Our experiments are made using a miniature mobile robot Khepera II and MATLAB software. The robot always is connected to a board computer through the serial cable which was used to transfer data between a personal computer and the robot, and to supply power. The aim of the experiment is to create a very simple, flexible, and effective ICS for the AMR that it could do particular action as quickly as it is possible – to follow the wall on the right of the maze showed in figure 4. Wall following on the right and on the left are identical, but they are separate behaviors. Thus we need to teach the robot these two behaviors separately.

In our experiments at first the expert controls the AMR. Data collecting is implemented simultaneously. The first part of the collected data (AMR wheels' speed and infrared proximity sensors' values) usually is the biggest, about 80% of all collected data during the experiment. Data filtering and appending to the database is always performed right away after the data are collected. "If-Then" rules do not undertake the control and objective function values, and the percentage when "If-Then" rules control the robot are not calculated

Figure 7. Results when data filtering was (a and b) and was not (c and d) performed

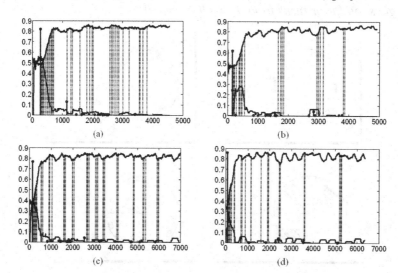

when the operator drives the AMR. After the first part of the data are collected and filtered, the expert can train the ANN by pressing the button on the joystick. One short press of the button raises an iteration of the ANN training which takes a very short time and does not interrupt the movement of the robot. The expert can see objective function values and the percentage when "If-Then" rules control the AMR on-line in the run of the entire experiment. Also, he can see how the ICS controls the AMR in the real maze. Having all this important information the expert decides either to train the ANN an additional iteration or to collect more data for the ANN training in such places of the maze where intelligent control system does not manage to control the AMR. When the expert collects additional data, straight after filtering they are added to the previously collected data. It means that the expert now will train the ANN with the entirely collected data, not only with new ones.

Human expert continues data collecting and the ANN training procedure until intelligent control system will show qualitative control: high objective function values and low percentage when "If-Then" rules control the robot. Such data collection and the ANN training allow the expert to

teach the ICS to manage difficult situations. For example in figure 4 it is shown that we placed a small white box on the right side of the maze. Khepera II can feel it only with the fourth sensor from the front sensors. The ANN is not able to learn to avoid such obstacles until more data how to circuit such obstacle are collected. This example illustrates very well that Expert Guided AMR On-line Learning technique has an advantage over Expert Cloning technique.

RESULTS

In the figure 7 four results of the experiment are shown. Results shown in the figure 7 (a) and (b) parts are obtained after the data filtering was performed and in figure 7 (c) and (d) parts when the data filtering was not performed. The results when data filtering was not performed show that the ICS learned to control the AMR with all mistakes which the operator made during data collection. Therefore "If-Then" rules controlled the robot more frequently. The objective function values in the parts (a), (b), (c), and (d) of figure

7 do not differ significantly because the rules of "If-Then" control are designed reasonably.

In the *x* axis the loops of the robot running are set. As we mentioned above, the system does 16 work loops per second. It means that 1000 loops correspond to 62.5 seconds. The experiments shown in the figure 7 last longer than we could expect seeing the figure. The time-periods when the expert controls the AMR are not shown. Nevertheless, the experiments usually last less than 10 minutes because it takes approximately three minutes to collect all data. Moreover, the good enough driving quality (objective function achieves values bigger than 0.8) is reached in approximately three minutes. Later on the objective function stops to increase and just fluctuates subject to the AMR position in the arena. The upper curve in the figures presents the objective function values calculated using 300 last robot work loops. Usually it increases up to a little bit more than 0.8. The lower curve in all parts of the figure 7 shows the percentage when "If-Then" rules controlled the robot in 300 last robot work loops. Only in the beginning it achieves higher values and after first 1000 loops it usually does not exceed 0.1 (=10%). In the experiments when data filtering is performed "If-Then" rules control AMR less, but not significantly less than in the experiments without data filtering. Vertical stems (solid lines with small circles on the top) represent time points when the expert controlled the robot and data were collected. For these periods when the ICS does not control the AMR, the objective function and the percentage values are not calculated. The values of the stems show how many percents of the data were collected in each collection moment.

For example in the figure 7 (a) we can see that during the first data collection there were more than 80% data collected, and during the second data collection – about 13%. The rest of the data were collected later in particular moments and particular places of the maze where intelligent control system had problems to control the AMR.

Vertical dotted lines show the moments when the expert pressed the button of the joystick and an iteration of the ANN training was performed. Usually up to 30 training iterations are enough to reach good control quality. Now computers are fast enough to obtain and process data, to train ANN one iteration and send a command to the actuators of the robot during one AMR control loop. If the number of collected data would increase so much or we would like to train ANN more than one iteration and the training could not be done during one control loop, we should stop the robot and objective function calculation, train ANN, then let the robot continue driving and after some time (about 1 second in our case) resume objective function calculation. Delay of objective function calculation resume is necessary that robot could run up to the right speed and the objective function value would not suffer looses during forced stops. Of course, on-line AMR learning would become slightly longer.

FUTURE RESEARCH DIRECTIONS

Future target for us is to create the technique for fast AMR learning where human expert would not perform such a big role as the presence of the expert makes the technique more expensive, especially if we have a complicated task and an advanced robot. We are planning to create an ICS based on the ANN and simple "If-Then" rules which make corrections of the AMR decisions. The "If-Then" rules would slightly correct the data of the robot wheels speed used for the ANN training. Thus the robot would perform the movements better. This ICS should learn to drive the AMR without direct expert intervention and it should seem that it learns intuitively knowing which actions are correct and which ones should be corrected.

We plan to apply described technique for other local tasks. Such tasks might include: pushing the object from start position to finish position in accordance with predefined path; grasping of the remote objects, and putting to a predetermined location with robotic arm (e.g. apple picking). Objective function for the latter task could look like this:

$$OF = 0.2a + 0.3b + 0.1c + 0.2d + 0.2e, \quad (6)$$

where a – variable, calculated using encoders values, it should show how many unwanted actions does a robotic arm, b evaluates the proportion of gripper movement distance and time needed for movement, c evaluates how smooth the movement is, d shows if the object is grasped correctly, e shows if the object is put correctly. All the components in (6) like in (1) are from interval [0, 1], thus objective function also is from interval [0, 1].

In the future for the tasks execution we plan beside infrared proximity sensors to use video camera or two cameras and stereo vision. Vision gives more information and accuracy for various tasks implementation but it also requires much more computational capacity. In addition, more complex algorithms are used.

CONCLUSION

Our created intelligent control system overcomes control systems mentioned in the beginning of the chapter and has the following main advantages:

1. It is possible to train up the AMR quite quickly (up to 10 minutes) to execute specific local tasks. Our proposed technique makes AMR training significantly faster comparing with Evolutionary techniques or techniques where parameters of ICS are found using trial and error methods.
2. If unsuspected situations emerge where created ICS does not manage control the AMR it is possible to collect additional data and to train the robot additionally for new required competences. The system is flexible.

3. All eight infrared proximity sensors are used in a very simple intelligent control system mainly based on ANN.
4. Using this technique there is no need to write dozen rules for separate infrared proximity sensors or for their combinations. Therefore, fewer things have to be done by hands.
5. As we can see in figure 7 the filtering of the data does not provide significant advantage. Neither objective function achieves higher values nor does the learning process last shorter. However, the control of the AMR is more smooth and stable when data filtering is used.
6. It is easier to analyze the programs and detect the errors in the script of this technique than in the scripts of Evolutionary techniques.
7. In the proposed technique a really big role comes to the expert. He decides when to start, when to finish, how many times to collect the data, and when and how much to train ANN.
8. To obtain better control results in static environment, reach higher objective function (1) values, and find better ICS parameters the Evolutionary Algorithms can be used.

After we did experiments using various techniques and gained experience, we can suggest the following schema, depicted in figure 8, to create quickly and effectively ICS for AMR control. Three main components should be used: data, expert and technique. The first component consists of data which will be used as entries by ICS to control the ARM, information on the used AMR and on environment where the AMR will act, and a structure of ICS which is being created. The second component consists of human expert, his knowledge and skill to control the AMR through software or directly (via joystick). The third component includes all possible techniques for the AMR control. This component is nothing else than Computational Intelligence. Evolutionary techniques, depicted in the bottom of the figure 8,

Figure 8. Schema of Intelligent Control System creation for AMR control

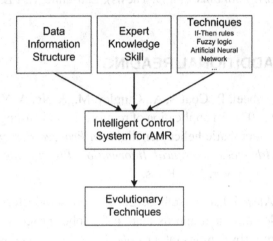

are also a part of the Computational Intelligence, but we recommend using them only for improvement of created ICS, and not in the beginning of the creation process. Expert knows the techniques, can control the robot, and having the information about the robot and environment can construct the frame of ICS and find its parameters. Such ICS should control the AMR very well, and Evolutionary techniques can be used to improve – find optimal parameters of ICS. In this way the mechanical and human resources will be saved.

The seventh item in the advantage list is that due to the presence of the expert the demerit could become as well. As we can see in the description of the technique and in figure 7, almost everything depends on the expert. The expert decides when and where to collect the data. He also decides how much data should be collected into the database for the robot learning. And eventually on the basis of his knowledge and visual information, the expert decides: to train the ANN an additional iteration or to collect more data. The possible solution how to eliminate such a big role of the expert is mentioned above in this chapter.

ACKNOWLEDGMENT

This work was partially supported by Lithuanian State Science and Studies foundation.

REFERENCES

Arkin, R. C. (1998). *Behavior-based robotics*. The MIT Press.

Bekey, G. A. (2005). *Autonomous robots: From biological inspiration to implementation and control*. Cambridge, MA: The MIT Press.

Bishop, M. C. (2005). *Neural networks for pattern recognition*. New York: Oxford University Press.

Caprari, G. (2003). *Autonomous micro-robots: Applications and limitations*. (Ph.D. Thesis), Lausanne, EPFL.

Floreano, D., & Mondada, F. (1996). Evolution of homing navigation in real mobile robot. *IEEE Transactions on Systems, Man, and Cybernetics*, 396–407.

Fogel, D. B. (1998). *Evolutionary computation: Toward a new philosophy of machine intelligence* (2nd ed.). Piscataway, NJ: IEEE Press.

Goldberg, D. E. (2002). *The design of innovation: Lessons from and for competent genetic algorithms. Genetic Algorithms and Evolutionary Computation 7*. Boston: Kluwer Academic.

Holland, M. J. (2004). *Designing autonomous mobile robots; Inside the mind of an intelligent machine*. Amsterdam: Elsevier.

K-Team. (2002). *Khepera II user manual*, EPFL, Lausanne. Retrieved March 17, 2009, from http://ftp.k-team.com/khepera/documentation/Kh2UserManual.pdf

Kaelbing, L., & Littman, M. (1996). Reinforcement learning: a survey. *Journal of Artificial Intelligence Research, 4*, 237–285.

Mahadevan, S., & Connell, J. (1991). Automatic programming of behavior-based robots using reinforcement learning. In *Proceedings of the 9th National Conference on Artificial Intelligenc* (pp. 768-773). Anaheim CA.

Maimone, M., Biesiadecki, J., Tunstel, E., Cheng, Y., & Leger, C. (2006). Surface navigation and mobility intelligence on the Mars Exploration Rovers, chapter 3, 45-69. TSI Press, San Antonio, TX.

Narvydas, G., & Raudonis, V. (2008). *Combining an expert cloning technique and evolutionary algorithm for autonomous mobile robot control. Selected papers of the 3rd international conference Electrical and Control Technologies* (pp. 23–28). Kaunas: Technologija.

Narvydas, G., Simutis, R., & Raudonis, V. (2007a). Autonomous mobile robot control using fuzzy logic and genetic algorithm. In *Proceedings of the 4th IEEE Workshop Intelligent Data Acquisition and Advanced Computing Systems* (pp. 460-464). Dortmund.

Narvydas, G., Simutis, R., & Raudonis, V. (2007b). *Learning action of skilled operator for autonomous mobile robot control. Selected papers of the 2nd international conference Electrical and Control Technologies* (pp. 78–81). Kaunas: Technologija.

Narvydas, G., Simutis, R., & Raudonis, V. (2008). Autonomous mobile robot control using "If-then" rules and genetic algorithm. *Information technology and control, 3(37)*, 193-197.

Nolfi, S., & Floreano, D. (2000). *Evolutionary robotics: The biology, intelligence, and technology of self-organizing machines*. Cambridge, MA: The MIT Press.

Thrun, S., Montemerlo, M., Dahlkamp, H., & Stavens, D. (2006). Stanley: The robot that won the DARPA Grand Challenge. *Journal of Field Robotics, 23*(9), 661–692. doi:10.1002/rob.20147

Waibel, M. (2007). *Evolution of cooperation in artificial ants.* (Ph.D. Thesis), Lausanne, EPFL.

ADDITIONAL READING

Abbeel, P., Coates, A., Quigley, M., & Ng, A. Y. (2007). An application of reinforcement learning to aerobatic helicopter flight. In *Proceedings of Advances in Neural Information Proccessing*. Vancouver: MIT Press.

Aleotti, J., & Caselli, S. (2006). Robust trajectory learning and approximation for robot programming by demonstration. *Robotics and Autonomous Systems. Special Issue on The Social Mechanisms of Robot Programming by Demonstration, 54*(5), 409–413.

Alissandrakis, A., Nehaniv, C., Dautenhahn, K., & Saunders, J. (2005). An approach for programming robots by demonstration: Generalization across different initial configurations of manipulated objects. In *Proceedings of the 6th IEEE international symposium on computational intelligence in robotics and automation* (pp. 61-66).

Amit, R., & Mataric, M. (2002). Learning movement sequences from demonstration. In *Proceedings of the 2nd International Conference on Development and Learning*.

Argall, B. D., Browning, B., & Veloso, M. (2007) Learning from demonstration with the critique of a human teacher. In *Proceedings of the 2nd ACM/IEEE International Conference on Human-Robot Interactions*.

Argall, B. D., Browning, B., & Veloso, M. (2008) Learning robot motion control with demonstration and adviceoperators. In *Proceedings of the IEEE/RSJ International Conference on Intelligent Robots and Systems*.

Argall, B. D., Chernova, S., Veloso, M., & Browning, B. (2009). *A survey of robot learning from demonstration*. Robotics and Autonomous Systems.

Atkeson, C. G., & Schaal, S. (1997). Robot learning from demonstration. In *Proceedings of the 14th International Conference on Machine Learning*, (pp. 12-20).

Bagnell, J. A., & Schneider, J. G. (2001). Autonomous helicopter control using reinforcement learning policy search methods. In *Proceedings of the IEEE International Conference on Robotics and Automation*.

Bentivegna, D. C. (2004). *Learning from Observation Using Primitives*. (PhD thesis). College of Computing, Atlanta, GA: Institute of Technology.

Billard, A., Calinon, S., & Guenter, F. (2006). Discriminative and adaptive imitation in uni-manual and bimanual tasks. *Robotics and Autonomous Systems. Special Issue on The Social Mechanisms of Robot Programming by Demonstration, 54*(5), 370–384.

Billard, A., Callinon, S., Dillmann, R., & Schaal, S. (2008). Robot programming by demonstration. In Siciliano, B., & Khatib, O. (Eds.), *Handbook of Robotics*. New York: Springer. doi:10.1007/978-3-540-30301-5_60

Billard, A., & Mataric, M. (2001). Learning human arm movements by imitation: Evaluation of biologically inspired connectionist architecture. *Robotics and Autonomous Systems, 37*(2-3), 145–160. doi:10.1016/S0921-8890(01)00155-5

Billard, A., & Siegwart, R. (2004). Special issue on robot learning from demonstration. *Robotics and Autonomous Systems, 47*(2-3), 65–67. doi:10.1016/j.robot.2004.03.001

Breazeal, C., Berlin, M., Brooks, A., Gray, J., & Thomaz, A. L. (2006). Using perspective taking to learn from ambiguous demonstrations. *Robotics and Autonomous Systems. Special Issue on The Social Mechanisms of Robot Programming by Demonstration, 54*(5), 385–393.

Breazeal, C., Brooks, A., Gray, J., Hoffman, G., Kidd, C., & Lee, H. (2004). Tutelage and collaboration for humanoid robots. *Humanoid Robots, 1*(2), 315–348. doi:10.1142/S0219843604000150

Breazeal, C., & Scassellati, B. (2002). Robots that imitate humans. *Trends in Cognitive Sciences, 6*(11), 481–487. doi:10.1016/S1364-6613(02)02016-8

Calinon, S., & Billard, A. (2007a). Incremental learning of gestures by imitation in a humanoid robot. In *Proceedings of the 2nd ACM/IEEE International Conference on Human-Robot Interactions* (pp. 255-262).

Calinon, S., & Billard, A. (2007b). What is the teacher's role in robot programming by demonstration? Toward benchmarks for improved learning. *Interaction Studies: Social Behaviour and Communication in Biological and Artificial Systems, 8*(24), 441–464.

Calinon, S., Guenter, F., & Billard, A. (2007). On learning, representing and generalizing a task in a humanoid robot. *IEEE Transactions on Systems, Man and Cybernetics, Part B. Special issue on robot learning by observation, demonstration and imitation, 37*(2).

Chen, J., & Zelinsky, A. (2003). Programing by demonstration: Coping with suboptimal teaching actions. *The International Journal of Robotics Research, 22*(5), 299–319. doi:10.1177/0278364903022005002

Delson, N., & West, H. (1996). Robot programming by human demonstration: Adaptation and inconsistency in constrained motion. In *Proceedings of the IEEE International Conference on Robotics and Automation*.

Dillmann, R., Kaiser, M., & Ude, A. (1995). Acquisition of elementary robot skills from human demonstration. In *International Symposium on Intelligent Robotic Systems*.

Guenter, F., & Billard, A. (2007). Using reinforcement learning to adapt an imitation task. In *Proceedings of the IEEE/RSJ International Conference on Intelligent Robots and Systems*.

Hawkins, J., & Blakeslee, S. (2004). *On Intelligence*. New York: Times Books.

Hovland, G., Sikka, P., & McCarragher, B. (1996). Skill acquisition from human demonstration using a hidden markov model. In *Proceedings of the IEEE International Conference on Robotics and Automation*.

Kaiser, M., Friedrich, H., & Dillmann, R. (1995). Obtaining good performance from a bad teacher. In *Programming by Demonstration vs. Learning from Examples Workshop at ML'95*.

Lieberman, J., & Breazeal, C. (2004). Improvements on action parsing and action interpolation for learning through demonstration. In *4th IEEE/RAS International Conference on Humanoid Robots*.

Nakanishi, J., Morimoto, J., Endo, G., Cheng, G., Schaal, S., & Kawato, M. (2004). Learning from demonstration and adaptation of biped locomotion. *Robotics and Autonomous Systems*, *47*, 79–91. doi:10.1016/j.robot.2004.03.003

Nicolescu, M., & Mataric, M. (2003). Natural methods for robot task learning: Instructive demonstrations, generalization and practice. In *Proceedings of the international joint conference on autonomous agents and multiagent systems* (pp. 241-248).

Pomerleau, D. (1991). Efficient training of artificial neural networks for autonomous navigation. *Neural Computation*, *3*(1), 88–97. doi:10.1162/neco.1991.3.1.88

Saunders, J., Nehaniv, C. L., & Dautenhahn, K. (2006). Teaching robots by moulding behavior and caffolding the environment. In *Proceedings of the ACM SIGCHI/SIGART conference on human-robot interaction* (pp. 118-125).

Smart, W. D. (2002). Making Reinforcement Learning Work on Real Robots. *PhD thesis*, Department of ComputerScience, Providence, RI: Brown University.

Smart, W. D., & Kaelbling, L. P. (2002). Effective reinforcement learning for mobile robots. In *Proceedings of the IEEE International Conference on Robotics and Automation*.

Thomaz, A. L., & Breazeal, C. (2006). Reinforcement learning with human teachers: Evidence of feedback and guidance with implications for learning performance. In *Proceedings of 21st National Conference on Artificial Intelligence*.

Voyles, R. M., & Khosla, P. K. (2001). A multi-agent system for programming robots by human demonstration. *Integrated Computer-Aided Engineering*, *8*(1), 59–67.

KEY TERMS AND DEFINITIONS

Artificial Neural Network: A mathematical or computational model based on biological neural networks. Artificial Neural Network can be trained up to map relations between inputs and outputs.

Autonomous Mobile Robot: A mechanical machine or device that is capable to perform a variety of complex tasks on command or by being programmed in advance. Autonomous Mobile Robot can operate independently without any human intervention.

Expert: A person with a high degree of skill to control Autonomous Mobile Robot remotely and is capable to solve a given task.

Expert Cloning Technique: A technique which allows to copy human actions and to transfer them into a real robot. After cloning operation the robot can imitate actions demonstrated by the human expert.

Expert Guided Learning: A technique when the expert trains Autonomous Mobile Robot on-line by demonstrating particular actions. The technique is similar to Expert Cloning Technique. The main difference is that there demonstrations and learning are implemented together.

Evolutionary Algorithm: A heuristic optimization algorithm. An EA uses some mechanisms inspired by biological evolution: reproduction, mutation, recombination, and selection.

"If-Then" Rules: Autonomous Mobile Robot is controlled by these rules in critical situations where created intelligent control system does not manage control the robot well enough. These rules give more rigid commands to the actuators.

Intelligent Control System: A control system, capable to control an AMR without any human being intervention.

Local Task: A task which must be solved by the robot when it obtains information only from its own sensors and can send signals to its own actuators. Any information, advices, or decisions from outside are not allowed. This task is of type: I see the environment – make decision – act.

Objective Function: This function shows how well the robot implements a given task. When there is talking about EA or GA, a term of Fitness function is used.

Chapter 12
Validation of Clustering Techniques for Student Grouping in Intelligent E–learning Systems

Danuta Zakrzewska
Technical University of Lodz, Poland

ABSTRACT

An intelligent e-learning system should be enhanced with personalization features that enable it to be tailored to different students' needs. The individual requirements of learners may depend on their characteristic traits, such as dominant learning styles. Finding groups of students with similar preferences can help when systems are being adjusted for individual requirements. The performance of personalized educational systems is dependant upon the number and quality of student clusters obtained. In this chapter the application of clustering techniques for grouping students according to their learning style preferences is considered. Such groups are evaluated by disparate validation criteria and the usage of different validation techniques is discussed. Experiments were conducted for different sets of real and artificially generated data on students' learning styles and the indices: Dunn's Index, Davies-Bouldin Index, SD Validity Index as well as the S_Dbw Validity Index are compared. From the experiment results some indications concerning the best validating criteria, as well as optimal clustering schema, are presented.

INTRODUCTION

In designing intelligent web based educational systems different student needs and preferences should be taken into consideration. Personalization of a system usually results in an increase in its effectiveness, which can be measured by the degree to which learning outcomes are achieved.

However, taking into account the individual requirements of each learner and adjusting the system to their needs may be very costly in cases of large numbers of students. Finding groups of learners with similar preferences seems to be a good solution which allows for differentiating the system in compliance with the needs of group members. Learner preferences depend on characteristic traits such as cognitive features, including dominant learning styles. Students modeled by

DOI: 10.4018/978-1-61692-811-7.ch012

learning style dimensions can be assigned into groups by using unsupervised classification. The performance of educational software depends on the quality of obtained clusters, which is connected with the degree of similarity between students who belong to the same groups. The proper choice of clustering algorithm is crucial for receiving the expected results. Evaluation of the applied clustering technique can be performed through validation of the obtained student clusters taking into account the resemblances between their members.

The aim of the chapter is to compare different validation techniques of cluster analysis for grouping students characterized by their dominant learning styles. Different validation criteria applied for disparate clustering algorithms are considered. On the basis of experiments which use real student data as well as artificially generated datasets, certain indications concerning the most appropriate validating criteria and the best clustering schema are presented.

The chapter is organized as follows. A research review concerning intelligent e-learning systems, student grouping as well as cluster analysis and validation techniques is presented in the next section. Following this, the clustering techniques and validity criteria that have been applied for student grouping are described in more detail. In the following section student models as well as problems connected with the application of unsupervised classification for finding student groups are presented. Then, on the basis of experiment results, some indications are given concerning the best validity criteria as well as the best clustering methods. Finally, future research directions and a conclusion are presented.

BACKGROUND

Related Work

Personalization features of e-learning systems enable educational processes to be differentiated

and software to be tailored to learner needs. An individual approach to student preferences can improve the performance of a system and can increase its effectiveness at achieving the assumed learning outcomes. Personalization holds great potential to improve people's ability to interact with information (Karger & Quan, 2004). The efficiency of personalized e-learning systems depends on the quality of individual student models, determined by their characteristic features. Brusilovsky (2001) called these 'individual traits', traits which are stable and usually extracted by specially designed psychological tests. However, there is little agreement on which features can and should be used in Web based learning systems (Brusilovsky, 2001). Taking the cognitive features mentioned by Brusilovsky (2001), many researchers have indicated particular personal learning styles which can determine characteristics of individual teaching paths. An overview of the research concerning building adaptive systems by using learning styles was presented by Stash, Cristea and De Bra (2004). The most frequently applied approach for student profiling consists of assigning them to previously defined groups, without the possibility of updating this assignation later (Gilbert & Han, 1999; Saarikoski et al., 2001; Triantafillou, Pomportsis & Georgiadou, 2002).

Application of cluster analysis allows student groups to be dynamically created, according to their individual characteristics, in an unsupervised way. A broad review of intelligent e-learning systems which use clustering techniques is presented by Romero and Ventura (2007). Different data mining techniques which can be applied in intelligent educational software can be also found in Romero and Ventura (2006). Methods used for student grouping that should be mentioned are descriptive statistics for building groups in collaborative learning environments, which were proposed by Alfonseca et al. (2006), or fuzzy logic for finding student models on the basis of their learning activities and interaction history (Xu, Wang & Su, 2002). Garcia et al. (2007), in turn, applied Bayesian networks for detecting student learning styles on the basis of their behaviours. The inverse approach was presented in Zakrzewska (2007), where a divisive hierarchical algorithm was used to assign students to different groups. The main disadvantage of the presented methods lies in the necessity for the determination of the number of groups of students in advance; a task which cannot be easy and requires tutor consultancy. Application of a specially built algorithm which allows the avoiding of those difficulties was proposed by Zakrzewska (2008a).

As one of the factors which decide on the effectiveness of clustering methods, the issue of the quality of obtained clusters should be mentioned. Jain et al. (1999) described several types of cluster validation technique. Jain & Koronios (2008) stated that the choice of an optimal clustering scheme, as well as compactness and cohesion, are the main criteria for cluster evaluation. To examine internal similarity and external dissimilarity of cluster members, different cluster validity indices can be used (MacQueen, 1967). The quality criteria can be divided, depending on the applied mathematical tools, into external, internal and relative. The first two approaches are based on statistical testing and are computationally complex, while the third one uses comparison of validity index values for different clustering schemas (Halkidi, Batistakis & Vazirgiannis, 2000; Theodoridis & Koutroumbas, 2006). Xu & Wunsch (2009) indicated relative criteria to be good tools, not only for comparing different clustering algorithms and their parameters, but also for determining the optimal number of clusters. They emphasized the role of relative validation indices in stopping rules, in the case of hierarchical clustering techniques. The effectiveness of some validity indices, as well as of different clustering algorithms, for both artificial and real datasets was examined by Maulik & Bandyopadhyay (2002). All the criteria, together with indices and their application for different clustering algorithms, have been broadly investigated by Halkidi, Vazirgiannis & Batistakis

(2001), Gan, Ma & Wu (2007) as well as Xu & Wunsch (2009).

Clustering Algorithms

In most applications of data mining methods the requirements concerning their features are mainly connected with their power and flexibility, whereas in e-learning systems the emphasis is placed on the simplicity of the techniques which are applied. Educators need to understand the methods they use. Most of the current data mining tools are too complex for teachers to use and their features do not meet their needs (Romero, Ventura & Garcia, 2008). Accordingly, we will limit our considerations concerning validation techniques to clusters built by the well known, simplest, algorithms; in a metric space and representing the most popular approaches such as partitioning, hierarchical, density based and statistical techniques.

K-Means

Among all partitioning methods, K-means is the most popular (Han & Kamber, 2006). The algorithm consists of assigning data into the given number of clusters, represented by their centres, which are usually randomly chosen. In each iteration objects are assigned to the closest clusters on the basis of their distance from the cluster centre. When all the objects are allocated, new cluster centres, as means of all the objects in the clusters, are determined. The process is repeated until the function, which takes the form of the square-error criterion, attains its minimum.

The main advantages of the k-means algorithm are its simplicity and effectiveness for large datasets. The main shortcoming is connected with a high dependence of obtained results on the initial assignments, which may result in the most optimal cluster allocation not being found at the end of the process. Moreover, the k-means method is noise sensitive, since even a small number of such observations may influence the results (Jain, Murty & Flynn, 1999).

Farthest First Traversal Algorithm

There are two approaches taken in hierarchical algorithms: agglomerative or divisive. The first consists of merging small clusters into the bigger ones, starting from clusters containing one element. Divisive techniques work inversely: they start from one big cluster which is step by step divided into the smaller ones. As one of the most effective of that group of methods, the Farthest First Traversal (FFT) algorithm should be mentioned. Dasgupta (2002) showed that FFT guarantees very good performance in comparison to other hierarchical techniques.

The FFT technique uses the farthest first traversal strategy, introduced by Hochman and Shmoys (1985), to number all the points. It starts with any point, the second point is the one allocated farthest from it, and the next one is the farthest from both the first and the second, and so on. Continuing the procedure all the points are numbered. First K of them will be cluster centres. All the clusters created by the technique consist of points connected in a way which guarantees maintaining the following property: any path connecting increasing node numbers has edge lengths of geometrically decreasing length. Then, a hierarchical cluster structure is obtained by dropping edges between centres at the adequate level of granularity (Dasgupta & Long, 2005). Similarly to the K-means, FFT is very simple and requires determination of the final number of clusters in advance.

DBSCAN

The third kind of clusters considered here are built using the density-based approach, as dense regions of objects, separated by regions of low density.

The most known in that group of methods: the Density-Based Spatial Clustering of Applications with Noise (DBSCAN) algorithm, allows arbitrary shape clusters to be found and detects outliers. It defines a cluster as a maximal set of so called density-connected points (Ester et al., 1996). The method uses concepts of density-reachability and density-connectivity of points. Cluster points are divided into core points (the ones inside the cluster) and border points. The algorithm is based on the following definitions (Ester et al., 1996):

Definition 1: A point, p, is directly density-reachable from a point, q, with respect to *Eps* and *MinPts* if $p \in N_{Eps}(q)$ and $|N_{Eps}(q)| \geq MinPts$, where $N_{Eps}(q)$ denotes *Eps*-neighbourhood of point q.

Point p is density-reachable from a point, q, with respect to *Eps* and *MinPts* if a chain of points $p_1, \ldots, p_n, p_1 = q, p_n = p$ exists, such that p_{i+1} is directly density-reachable from p_i.

Definition 2: A point, p, is density-connected from a point, q, with respect to *Eps* and *MinPts* if there is a point, o, such that both p and q are density reachable from o with respect to *Eps* and *MinPts*.

A density-based cluster is a set of density-connected objects that is maximal with respect to density-reachability. Every object not contained in any cluster is considered to be an outlier.

The algorithm starts with any point, p, and finds out all points density-reachable from p with respect to parameters: *Eps* and *MinPts*. If p is a core point, the new cluster is created. If it is a border point, no points are density-reachable from p. As the main advantages of DBSCAN Ester et al. (1996) mentioned the possibility it offers to discover clusters of arbitrary shape, and its outlier detection ability, as well as the minimal number of input parameters. However, the last two are strictly connected with the density of objects and difficult to determine. The approach can be very effective for multidimensional datasets containing outliers, and does not require the number of clusters as an input data.

Expectation-Maximization

The goal of the statistical model is to find the most likely set of clusters on the basis of training data and prior expectations. The Expectation-Maximization algorithm (EM) uses the finite Gaussian mixture model and it generates probabilistic descriptions of clusters in terms of means and standard deviations (Witten & Frank, 2005). Contrarily to K-means, where objects are allocated into the closest clusters, EM assigns each object to a cluster according to a weight representing the probability of membership. The algorithm consists of three steps: in the first one K objects are randomly selected to represent cluster parameters; in the second step, called 'Expectation', the probability values of cluster membership of objects for each of the clusters are calculated. During the 'Maximization' step new parameters are determined, for which likelihood of the distribution is maximized (Han & Kamber, 2006). Similarly to K-means, parameters are recomputed (last two steps are repeated) until the desired convergence value is achieved. EM converges fast but it may reach local optima (instead of global ones) depending on the initial choice of parameters.

STUDENT GROUPING IN INTELLIGENT E-LEARNING SYSTEMS

Finding Student Groups

Student Models

Students can be characterized by their dominant learning styles, which can be regarded as valuable features which indicate their preferences in the learning process (Felder & Brent, 2005). Lee (2001), as well as Lu, Yu and Liu (2003), showed that individual learning style preferences influence the effectiveness of Web based courses. Graf and

Kinshuk (2006) showed that preferred learning styles decide student needs and requirements.

There are many models of learning styles, such as those drawn up by Kolb (1984), Honey & Mumford (1986), Dunn & Dunn (1978) and Felder & Silverman (1988) to mention the most known. The last one, in particular, is often used in investigations connected with e-learning environments (Viola et al., 2007). Cha et al. (2006) applied the same model in their research concerning customisation of the interfaces of educational systems.

According to Felder & Silvermans' model (Felder, 1996; Felder & Silverman, 1988), student learning styles can be characterized by four dimensions of eight mutually excluding pairs: *active vs. reflective, sensing vs. intuitive, visual vs. verbal,* and *sequential vs. global.* Dominant learning styles characterize students as follows (Felder & Soloman, 2009):

- *Active*: those who learn by trying things out; or *reflective,* who learn by thinking things through,
- *Sensing*: those who are concrete, practical, oriented toward facts and procedures; or *intuitive,* who are conceptual, oriented toward theories and meanings,
- *Visual*: those who prefer visual representations of presented material – pictures, diagrams, flow charts; or *verbal,* who prefer written or spoken explanations,
- *Sequential*: those who are linear, orderly, and learn in small incremental steps; or *global,* who are holistic, system thinkers, and learn in large leaps.

Preferences for each dimension are represented by odd integers from the interval [-11,11]. Negative scoring is connected with *active, sensing, visual* or *sequential* dimensions, while positive values with *reflective, intuitive, verbal* or *global.* That way each student can be modelled by a vector $SL=(sl_1,sl_2,sl_3,sl_4)$ of odd integer attributes, which are based on the results of the self-scoring *Index of*

Learning Style questionnaire created by Felder and Soloman (2009). In further considerations, student *SL* vectors will be used to build student groups.

Score from the interval [-3,3] means that the student is fairly well balanced on the two dimensions of that scale. Values -5,-7 or 5,7 mean that a student learns more easily in a teaching environment which favours the considered dimension. Values -9,-11 or 9,11 mean that learner has a very strong preference for one dimension of the scale and may have real difficulty learning in an environment which does not support that preference (ILS Questionnaire, 2009).

Student Clustering

Student models represented by odd integer attributes seem to be very simple, and the application of one of the well known cluster analysis techniques to find student groups seems to be the natural choice. Zakrzewska and Ruiz-Esteban (2005) examined the performance of different clustering techniques on the test sets of real student data. The presented effects showed the high dependence of obtained clusters on the choice of input parameter values, as well as great noise sensitivity of the applied technique. Their experiment results did not allow an indication to be given of the most optimal method for guaranteeing a good quality of obtained groups. The most popular approaches and the ones examined by Zakrzewska and Ruiz-Esteban (2005) should be mentioned: partitioning methods, hierarchical techniques, density based as well as statistical approaches. All of these will be considered as possible tools for building student groups.

The partitioning approach K-means is simple and effective on large datasets but, as it was shown by Zakrzewska and Ruiz-Esteban (2005), its results depend significantly on initially selected clusters and on the number of required groups, even for small datasets which, together with its noise sensitivity, are the main disadvantages of the technique. The presence of outliers, such as

exceptional student data or errors, may result in the complete deformation of clusters. The use of validation techniques, in that case can, not only allow the optimal clustering scheme to be chosen (by selecting the optimal required number of clusters), but can also indicate clusters of wrong quality.

The EM algorithm, similarly to K-means, is noise sensitive. Experiments, described by Zakrzewska and Ruiz-Esteban (2005), showed that the presence of outliers completely changed obtained effects. Outliers were assigned into one-element clusters, with the consequence that the number of clusters decreased, resulting in building big groups of lower quality.

The hierarchical clustering algorithm has already been used for research purposes in the learning styles area (Heffler, 2001). Applied in this field, the agglomerative approach performed worse than FFT. However, it is also noise sensitive and changes cluster structures in such situations as the presence of outliers, or in the case of wrong choice of required number of groups, all of which may also result in a low quality of obtained clusters.

Density-based DBSCAN does not require the number of clusters as an input data, and can be very effective for multidimensional datasets containing outliers. In the case of learning style dimensions the range of the attribute values is limited, and that fact should simplify the choice of parameters. However, Zakrzewska and Esteban-Ruiz (2005) showed that DBSCAN did not perform well for the datasets they considered; it presented the tendency to build big clusters and indicate many outliers. The major advantage of DBSCAN consists in the minimal number of input parameters. However, on the other hand, they are strictly connected with the density of objects and difficult to determine, even in the case of data of as simple a form as learning style dimensions.

The characteristic features of the considered methods do not allow the best clustering technique to be indicated. K-means and Farthest First Traversal require number of clusters in advance. Both of them, as well as the EM algorithm, change the results in the presence of outliers. DBSCAN, in turn, strongly depends on the choice of parameters connected with the data density features. The best algorithm, as well as the optimal schema, can be chosen on the basis of the quality of obtained clusters. This may be done by evaluation of the results by asking experts (tutors) for their opinions, or by using validation techniques. The application of validity methods can also help in choosing the best clustering schema, which means indicating the best algorithm and finding optimal values of input parameters such as, for example, the required number of clusters.

Validation of Student Groups

Cluster Validity Techniques

While choosing validation techniques for student groupings, different kinds of indices should be taken into account. Since statistical testing, on which internal and external criteria are based, happens to be computationally expensive (Gan, Ma & Wu, 2007), application of relative approach is considered. Usage of relative criteria, as has been proposed by Halkidi, Batistakis and Vazirgiannis (2001), enables the inclusion of the proper index as a part of the clustering process, to choose the cluster structure of the best possible quality. Indications concerning the best validity criteria for learning style data will be determined by evaluation of the different indices on the basis of experiments done on different datasets. Our research will be focused on validating partitions – type of the evaluation (Gordon, 1996), which concern all of the considered clustering methods. From among relative criteria, the ones which do not depend on the number of clusters and clustering algorithm, and which focus on cluster compactness and separation, have been chosen. We will consider Dunn's Index, the Davies-Bouldin Index, the SD Validity Index, as well as S_Dbw

Validity Index. Other indices from the group of validating partitions require more complex operations such as, for example, RMSSTD and RS indices, which measure the degree of homogeneity between groups and, in the case of hierarchical algorithms, need to be used simultaneously with other criteria, which increases the complexity and the cost of the whole validation procedure (Gan, Ma & Wu, 2007). As a consequence, our investigations will be limited to the four, first mentioned, criteria indices. During the experimental study, how the above indicated validation techniques perform on clusters built by different clustering algorithms on datasets of student learning styles will be examined.

Let us assume that the considered clustering schema consists of K clusters C_i, $i=1,2,..,K$. Let v_i denotes the centroid of i-th cluster for $i=1,2,..,K$.

The Davies-Bouldin index (DB) was introduced by Davies and Bouldin (1979). Its aim is to maximize the between-cluster distance and to minimize the distance between the cluster centroid and the other points. The minimum DB means that clusters are compact and well separated. The Davies-Bouldin index can be defined as follows:

$$DB = \frac{1}{K} \sum_{i=1}^{K} R_i,$$ (1)

where R_i means the maximum comparison between C_i and other clusters, and is defined as:

$$R_i = \max_{j \neq i} \frac{S_i + S_j}{D_{ij}},$$ (2)

where D_{ij} is the distance between centroids v_i and v_j of clusters C_i and C_j respectively, for $i, j = 1,2,..,K$. Dispersion measure S_i of cluster C_i means its average error and is measured by the mean distance between cluster points and its centroid.

Dunn's index (VD) similarly to DB indicates compact and well separated clusters. It was introduced by Dunn (1977) and is defined as:

$$VD = \min_{i=1,...,K} \{ \max_{j=i+1,...,K} (\frac{D(C_i,C_j)}{\max\limits_{i=1,...,K} diam(C_i)}) \}, \quad (3)$$

where $D(C_i, C_j)$ is the distance between clusters C_i and C_j, measured as the minimum distance between two points belonging to C_i and C_j, respectively:

$$D(C_i,C_j) = \min_{x\in C_i, y\in C_j} D(x,y) \quad (4)$$

and the diameter of the cluster is the maximum distance between two of its members:

$$diam(C_i) = \max_{x,y\in C_i} D(x,y) \quad (5)$$

A high value of VD indicates the existence of compact and well separated clusters. Contrarily to DB, maximum value of VD indicates the optimal number of clusters. As the main disadvantages of Dunn's index, Gan, Ma & Wu, 2007 mentioned noise sensitiveness and time-consuming.

The SD validity index was introduced by Halkidi, Vazirgiannis and Batistakis (2000). It takes into account two factors: average scattering of clusters S_A and total separation between clusters S_T and is defined as:

$$SD = \alpha S_A + S_T. \quad (6)$$

The first element represents intracluster variance measures, while the second one intercluster distance measures and α is a weight coefficient. In further considerations, we will assume $\alpha =1$. The average scattering of clusters S_A is constructed as follows:

$$S_A = \frac{1}{K} \sum_{i=1}^{K} \frac{\|\sigma(C_i)\|}{\|\sigma(D)\|}, \quad (7)$$

where $\sigma(D)$ and $\sigma(C_i)$ are vectors of variances for the dataset D and the cluster $C_i, i=1,2,...K$, respectively.

Let $n = |D|$ denotes the number of objects in the set D, then $\sigma(D) = [d_1, d_2, ..., d_n]$, where $v =[v_1, v_2,..., v_n]$ is the centroid of D, $p=1,2,..,n$.

Vectors of variances for clusters are calculated similarly, by taking into account cluster objects, and cluster centroids.

$$d_p = \frac{1}{|D|} \sum_{y\in D} (y_p - \nu_p)^2, \quad (8)$$

The total separation S_t between clusters is defined by using distances between the points and cluster centroids and is defined as follows:

$$S_t = \frac{D_{max}}{D_{min}} \sum_{i=1}^{K} \left(\sum_{j=1}^{K} \|\nu_i - \nu_j\| \right)^{-1} \quad (9)$$

where $D_{max} = \max\{ \|v_i - v_j\|, 1\leq i,j\leq K\}$, and $D_{min} = \min\{ \|v_i - v_j\|, 1\leq i,j\leq K\}$.

It can be easily seen from (6), (7), (8) and (9) that minimum value of SD is obtained for optimal number of clusters.

The S_DBW validity index was defined by Halkidi and Vazirgiannis (2001). It takes into account average scattering of clusters and density of clusters:

$$S\_DBW = S_A + S_{DB}, \quad (10)$$

where S_A is defined by (7). S_{DB} means intercluster density and is constructed as:

$$S_{DB} = \frac{1}{K(K-1)} \sum_{i=1}^{K} \sum_{j=1,j\neq i} \frac{dens(C_i \cup C_j)}{\max\{dens(C_i), dens(C_j)\}}. \quad (11)$$

Function $dens(C)$ is the density function. It counts points, which distance to the cluster centroid is not greater than the average standard deviation of the cluster:

$$stdev = \frac{1}{K} \sqrt{\sum_{i=1}^{K} \|\sigma(C_i)\|}, \quad (12)$$

where $\sigma(C_i)$ is a vector of variances for the cluster $C_i, i=1,2,...K$; and

$$dens(C_i) = \sum_{j=1}^{|C_i|} f(x_j, v_i), \qquad (13)$$

where v_i is the centroid of cluster C_i, $|C_i|$ is the number of points in the cluster C_i, $i=1,2,...,K$; and for every point $x \in C_i$, $i=1,2,...,K$; $f(x,v_i)$ is calculated as follows:

$$f(x, v_i) = \begin{cases} 0 & d(x, v_i) > stdev \\ 1 & otherwise. \end{cases} \qquad (14)$$

Similarly to SDindex, the minimum of the S_DBW index means the optimal number of clusters.

Datasets and Cluster Parameters

Experiments were done for five different datasets of student learning styles: four of them containing real data, on the dominant learning styles of Polish Computer Science students, who filled in an available online ILS self-scoring questionnaire (ILS Questionnaire, 2009) The fifth dataset contains artificially generated data. To obtain the most representative test results possible, special emphasis was placed on the differentiation of the student groups that took part in the experiments.

The first two sets, which will be denoted as A and B, contain, accordingly, 71 and 123 learning style data of students who participated in international collaboration online, and used an educational environment based on Moodle http://moodle.com. The collaboration activities took place as part of a Socrates Minerva funded project: 'Collaboration Across Borders'. Data were collected during three academic years, from students attending different courses of engineering at master's level, from different years of study, also including those doing part-time and evening courses. However, all of the test participants studied Computer Science, although the ones from the second cycle of studies, and especially those who attended weekend courses, were also graduates of other programmes. Additionally, students, from

set A volunteered to take part in a simultaneous experiments concerning colour preferences that were described by Zakrzewska (2008b).

The third dataset, denoted by C, of 31 records, contains SL vectors of students all studying the same Masters programme on Information Systems in Management, in their fourth year of study. Those data were collected during one semester. The last real dataset, which will be denoted by D, contains 56 records of students, who are all studying the same MSc program in Computer Science during weekends. All of them have previously graduated with BSc degrees in different areas, including such courses as Management, Marketing, Accounting, Nursing and many others. The data for these students were also gathered during the same one semester.

Such a choice of sets suggests that it could be expected that their contents represent different student characteristics. Attribute values of A and B should be differentiated. However, students from the set A can be suspected to be more active than the ones from set B. Students whose data are contained in set C are expected to have similar profiles, as they have chosen the same programme and studied together for almost three years, whereas the ones from set D attend the same Masters course, but their origins are different.

Viola et al. (2007) showed that student learning style attributes may be correlated. To see how validity indices perform in the case of data whose attributes are not associated, the fifth artificial dataset of 100 instances is considered, each of them being a vector of four attributes which are to represent artificial student learning style values. To maintain the structure of the Felder and Silverman model (Felder & Silverman, 1988), numbers are generated randomly, as odd integers, from the interval [-11,11], of discrete uniform distribution. Let us denote this last dataset as E.

The main input parameter needed in most of the considered clustering algorithms is the number of groups required. For finding the best clustering schema it is necessary to check validity indices for different numbers of output clusters. In e-learning, student groups of similar preferences are created for the purpose of personalisation of courses, or of educational systems. In the first case, tutors have to prepare teaching materials or learning paths for each group separately. Building too many groups will entail the necessity of creating a large number of different teaching paths, as well as many versions of teaching materials and interfaces, which would prove costly or may not even be possible. The number of student groups should be limited depending on the tutors' possibilities in that area. Accordingly, in further investigations it will be assumed that output number of clusters should not exceed five. This number also seems to be reasonable, taking into account the sizes of all the considered datasets. A greater number of required clusters may result in creating one element groups of students, which would amount to changing the tutor task into creating learning paths according to individual needs, rather than those of groups. Such a situation takes place, even for the number of four clusters, in the case of the smallest set C. What is more, clustering for six groups in the pre-process phase of experiments, showed that the algorithms did not change the structure of clusters, but divided the biggest ones to build additional very small clusters. Such a situation may not be acceptable for tutors, taking into account the cost of the teaching process.

In DBSCAN algorithms, there are two crucial parameters: number of neighbours and the radius of the neighbourhood. Both of them were chosen experimentally, and will be described in the next section.

Experiment Results and Discussion

To achieve the main goal of the research, which is to check how different indices perform on students learning style datasets, and to identify the best validating index, which indicates both (i) the best clustering algorithm, and (ii) the optimal number of clusters, the experiment results will be

considered in the following. Including validation criteria into the clustering algorithm enables the quality of obtained student groups at the very early stage of the clustering process to be optimized. The validating index chosen from this experiment may be further used for finding learner clusters of good quality.

All examined validity indices were calculated for the results of four different clustering techniques: partitioning k-means, hierarchical Farthest First, statistical EM, and density based DBSCAN. In the case of the first three approaches, different clustering schemas, with numbers of clusters of from two to five, were considered. Both of the parameters of DBSCAN were experimentally chosen in the preprocessing stage. During the main part of the experiments the value of the radius of the neighborhood was constant and equal to 1, which guaranteed the smallest number of outliers indicated by the algorithm. The value of neighbouring numbers MinC was taken to be equal to 1 or 2, for which it was found that the number of clusters and outliers obtained were the least during experiments. This choice of MinC is connected with the requirement for not creating too many groups, as has been described in previous sections.

Tables 1, 2, 3 and 4 present values of all examined indices, all the datasets, and all considered algorithms, as well as different numbers of clusters. In the case of DBSCAN, only indices for optimal number of clusters, indicated by the algorithm, were calculated ('-' means that the number of clusters is not optimal for the dataset). An overview on the content of all the tables shows that the values of indices differ in indicating the best method and the optimal number of clusters for real datasets, as well as for the artificially generated data. In almost all the cases, indices are the best for DBSCAN, but the optimal number of clusters is very high and they are of a very small size. What is more, DBSCAN classified many instances as outliers, and therefore the clusters should have been of good quality. For example, in the case of

Table 1. Dunn's index values for all of the datasets

Method	No clusters	Set A	Set B	Set C	Set D	Set E
K-means	2	0.126	0.085	0.225	0.128	0.169
	3	0.262	0.154	0.273	0.138	0.113
	4	0.184	0.126	0.275	0.370	0.111
	5	0.455	0.089	0.326	0.431	0.249
Farthest First	2	0.179	0.126	0.195	0.182	0.142
	3	0.282	0.081	0.456	0.300	0.111
	4	0.454	0.164	0.928	0.352	0.202
	5	0.607	0.348	0.830	0.398	0.159
EM	2	0.121	0.081	0.225	0.197	0.162
	3	0.168	0.085	0.269	0.401	0.213
	4	0.167	0.147	0.378	0.351	0.271
	5	0.103	0.128	0.469	0.422	0.196
DBSCAN	2	-	-	-	-	2.111 (MinC=2)
	3	-	0.835 (MinC=2)	-	-	-
	4	0.408 (MinC=2)	-	-	-	-
	6	1.155 (minC=1)	-	-	-	-
	9	-	0.551 (MinC=1)	-	-	-
	14	-	-	-	-	2.796 (MinC=1)

Table 2. Davies-Bouldin's index values for all of the datasets

Method	No clusters	Set A	Set B	Set C	Set D	Set E
K-means	2	1.585	1.564	1.487	1.536	1.792
	3	1.740	1.370	1.179	1.363	1.722
	4	1.409	1.309	1.365	1.180	1.311
	5	1.632	1.463	1.222	1.254	1.295
Farthest First	2	1.141	1.607	1.235	1.161	1.821
	3	1.309	1.467	1.220	1.067	1.512
	4	1.331	1.334	1.061	1.401	1.533
	5	1.268	1.258	1.134	1.180	1.426
EM	2	1.458	1.654	1.349	1.205	1.854
	3	1.715	1.382	1.459	1.397	1.534
	4	1.633	1.494	1.189	1.695	1.514
	5	1.104	1.478	1.170	1.295	1.291
DBSCAN	2	-	-	-	-	0.316 (MinC=1)
	3	-	0.797 (MinC=2)	-	-	-
	4	0.935 (MinC=2)	-	-	-	-
	6	0.868 (MinC=1)	-	-	-	-
	9	-	0.754 (MinC=1)	-	-	-
	14	-	-	-	-	0.415 (MinC=2)

Table 3. SD Validity index values for all of the datasets

Method	No clusters	Set A	Set B	Set C	Set D	Set E
K-means	2	0.991	0.978	1.017	0.943	0.967
	3	0.963	0.787	0.738	0.774	0.865
	4	0.775	0.725	0.793	0.705	0.700
	5	0.870	0.711	0.676	0.721	0.623
Farthest First	2	0.828	1.122	0.876	0.845	0.976
	3	0.818	0.945	0.767	0.722	0.773
	4	0.741	0.802	0.646	0.796	0.720
	5	0.673	0.798	0.655	0.686	0.668
EM	2	1.098	1.008	0.929	0.931	1.010
	3	1.128	0.800	0.903	0.792	0.823
	4	1.085	0.858	0.706	0.978	0.768
	5	0.694	0.873	0.683	0.697	0.673
DBSCAN	2	-	-	-	-	0.231 (MinC=2)
	3	-	0.604 (MinC=2)	-	-	-
	4	0.592 (MinC=2)	-	-	-	-
	6	0.545 (MinC=2)	-	-	-	-
	9	-	0.406 (MinC=1)	-	-	-
	14	-	-	-	-	0.361 (MinC=1)

Table 4. S_Dbw validity index values for all the datasets

Method	No clusters	Set A	Set B	Set C	Set D	Set E
K-means	2	1.430	1.844	1.782	3.219	2.305
	3	2.545	1.837	1.561	1.907	1.891
	4	1.393	2.858	1.547	0.980	1.426
	5	2.167	1.501	1.456	1.455	1.844
Farthest First	2	1.646	2.054	0.668	3.167	1.810
	3	1.514	1.385	1.580	1.555	2.652
	4	1.610	1.866	0.919	1.349	1.761
	5	1.472	1.578	0.771	0.793	1.550
EM	2	1.885	2.099	0.710	2.421	2.844
	3	1.389	2.616	1.656	1.193	1.366
	4	1.607	0.793	1.498	1.195	1.143
	5	1.090	1.081	1.054	1.001	1.153
DBSCAN	2					0.613 (MinC=2)
	3		1.172 (MinC=2)			
	4	1.314 (MinC=2)				
	6	1.198 (MinC=1)				
	9		1.148 (MinC=1)			
	14					0.937 (MinC=1)

the dataset A, six clusters and 27 outliers were indicated. If the number of clusters is equal to 4, there were 31 outliers. For the smallest sets, C and D, the algorithm indicated only one element clusters, and for these datasets validity indices were not calculated (represented by '-' in Tables 1, 2, 3, and 4). Additionally, taking into account the fact that parameters were chosen experimentally to guarantee the least number of outliers (or one element clusters), it can be concluded that the technique needs some improvements before applying it to learning style data, otherwise it cannot be used for that kind of data at all. Moreover, from the tutors' point of view DBSCAN results cannot be accepted (tutors would have to change the approach from group teaching into individual teaching). Technically, it seems that for the sets A, B and E, the algorithm found the best clustering schemas, from among those indicated by all the other validity indices.

According to Dunn's index, in spite of all the other indices, the optimal number of clusters and the best algorithms are those with the highest index values. If we exclude results obtained for DBSCAN from the ones presented in Table 1, Dunn's index indicates that the optimal number of clusters is equal to five for datasets A, B and D, with schema built by K-means algorithm for the last dataset, and FFT for the first two ones. The same algorithm, but with four clusters, is indicated for set D. For artificially generated data four is also the optimal number of clusters, but with the structure obtained by using the EM method.

In the case of the Davies-Bouldin index values, the lowest indices point to the optimal schemas. Results are presented in Table 2. They are the same as in the case of Dunn's index for the sets B and C. For the sets A and E, the number of five clusters is optimal, but they are built, however, by EM technique in the case of the first set, and K-means for the last one. Results for set D differ significantly, as the optimal schema of two clusters built by FFT algorithm was chosen. Similarly to

Dunn's index, values of DB also indicated DBSCAN schemas as the most optimal.

For the sets A, C and E, the SD Validity index is fully consistent with Dunn's. In the case of the datasets B and D, it indicated five clusters as optimal and, respectively, FFT and K-means to be the best, as is shown in Table 3.

The S_Dbw index indicated that the EM algorithm was the optimal one for the datasets: A, B and E; and the FFT technique for the others. The main difference between S_Dbw and other indices appears, in the case of the set C (2 clusters and FFT algorithm) and the sets B and E (four clusters, EM technique). All the results for that index are presented in Table 4.

Table 5 presents all the methods together with number of clusters for all of the indices. Evaluation of the obtained results should be done, together with the analysis of number of objects in clusters of optimal schemas contained in Table 6 ('-' means that the schema was not indicated as optimal for the dataset). It can be easily noticed that different schemas were chosen by different validity indices for the same dataset. However, some of them indicate the same clustering schema. As the best choice, the ones indicated by the most of the indices can be selected. In the case of set A, indices pointed equally to EM and FFT techniques. The last algorithm was also chosen as the best for the sets B, C and D. Only for the artificial dataset E, was K-means indicated as the best. Five is the best number of clusters for all the datasets, except for the smallest one, C, for which four is indicated as being optimal.

It can be easily noticed that in most of the optimal schemas, the Farthest First Traversal algorithm built one big cluster and all the others were small, whereas K-means and EM assigned all the objects fairly regularly. Indices that indicated Farthest First as the best schemas have based their values on the scattering and compactness of smaller clusters. This fact is particularly visible for the results of Farthest First technique in the case of five clusters, and the real datasets A, B

Table 5. The best methods depending on the index

Index	Set A	Set B	Set C	Set D	Set E
Dunn	5 (FFT)	5 (FFT)	4 (FFT)	5 (k-means)	5 (k-means)
Davies-Bouldin (DB)	5 (EM)	5 (FFT)	4 (FFT)	3 (FFT)	5 (EM)
SD	5 (FFT)	5 (k-means)	4 (FFT)	5 (FFT)	5 (k-means)
S_Dbw	5 (EM)	4 (EM)	2 (FFT)	5 (FFT)	4 (EM)

Table 6. Number of objects in clusters for optimal schemas

Schema	Set A / Index	Set B / Index	Set C / Index	Set D / Index	Set E /Index
5 (FFT)	(49,3,8,7,4) / Dunn, SD	(83,9,22,5,4) / Dunn, DB	-	(17,9,3,14,3) /SD, S_Dbw	-
4 (FFT)	-	-	(23,3,4,1)/ Dunn,DB, SD	-	-
3 (FFT)	-	-	-	(44,9,3) / DB	-
2 (FFT)	-	-	(28,3) / S_Dbw	-	-
5 (k-means)	-	(18,23,21,21,40) / SD	-	(11,16,16,5,8) / Dunn	(24,18,16,21,21) / Dunn,SD
5 (EM)	(11,3,13,13,31)/ DB, S_Dbw	-	-	-	(27,18,17,17,21)/ DB
4 (EM)	-	(24,20,43,36)/ S_Dbw	-	-	(32,22,27,19)/ S_Dbw

and D, where the best schemas contain more than one cluster of less than ten objects. For the artificially generated dataset uniform distribution of attribute values was reflected in regular assignments into clusters.

From among the indices, Dunn's and SD pointed to the greater number of optimal clustering schemas. The first index usually indicated schemas built by FFT of one big cluster, and all the others small. The same characterizes the DB index. S_Dbw, in turn, indicates almost only schemas with clusters of similar sizes (the smallest set C is the exception).

Tables 5 and 6 do not take into account results for DBSCAN schemas. The large number of very small clusters (some even consisting of only one element for small datasets) generated by the algorithm should have been of the best quality. However, personalization according to them may be very costly.

FUTURE RESEARCH DIRECTIONS

As the quality of student groups can decide performance of the educational system, further research should be developed to obtain the best possible clusters. Including one of the well known validating techniques into the clustering process should be considered in the first step. To obtain the best effectiveness in that area, some other validating techniques, even those which are more costly than the considered ones, should be examined.

Another research direction can be connected with building an index which is fit to attribute characteristic features and requirements concerning student groups. For example, tutors are more interested in having students of similar characteristics inside the cluster, than they are in the dissimilarity between groups. What is more, they want to know the 'face' of each group, and may consider clusters that cannot be characterized implicitly by student preferences to be of poor quality. The possibility of finding models of groups that can represent their members' preferences should also be the subject of further investigations.

Finally, extended student models should be taken into consideration; ones which represent not only dominant learning styles, but also other preferences (such as usability), or historical behaviours which can be included in the attributes of mixed types used for student clustering. In that case, the presented validity indices could be inadequate and some other techniques should be investigated.

CONCLUSION

In the paper different validation techniques of clustering methods of student learning styles are considered. Investigations focused on the relative criteria represented by four main validating indices that are not computationally expensive: Dunn, Davies-Bouldin, SD and S_Dbw. Experiments conducted on five different datasets show that the indices considered indicated the same FFT technique and the same maximal considered number of five clusters as optimal, in most of the cases. This may mean that students should be allocated into the greatest possible number of groups that can be created. However the size of the dataset should be also taken into account.

Two of the indices: Dunn and SD, have chosen the majority of the optimal clustering schemas. Both of them prefer schemas of one big cluster and a great number of small clusters (less than ten elements). If tutors need regular assignments to clusters, then using of S_Dbw validity indices can be advised.

Consideration of the results showed that validation indices can help in choosing the optimal number of clusters, as well as the clustering algorithm for student grouping. However, further examination of indices can still be necessary.

REFERENCES

Alfonseca, E., Carro, R. M., Martin, E., Ortigosa, A., & Paredes, P. (2006). The impact of learning styles on student grouping for collaborative learning: a case study. *User Modeling and User-Adapted Interaction*, *16*(2-3), 377–401. doi:10.1007/s11257-006-9012-7

Brusilovsky, P. (2001). Adaptive hypermedia. *User Modeling and User-Adapted Interaction*, *11*(1-2), 87–110. doi:10.1023/A:1011143116306

Cha, H. J., Kim, Y. S., Park, S. H., Yoon, T. B., Jung, Y. M., & Lee, J.-H. (2006). Learning styles diagnosis based on user interface behaviors for customization of learning interfaces in an intelligent tutoring system. In M. Ikeda, K. Ashley, & T.-W. Chan (Eds.), *Proceedings of the Intelligent Tutoring Systems, 8th International Conference* (LNCS 4053, pp. 513-524). Berlin, Germany: Springer-Verlag.

Dasgupta, S. (2002). Performance guarantees for hierarchical clustering. In J. Kivinen, & R.H. Sloan (Eds), *Proceedings of COLT2002* (LNCS 2375, pp. 235-254). Berlin, Germany: Springer-Verlag.

Dasgupta, S., & Long, P. M. (2005). Performance guarantees for hierarchical clustering. *Journal of Computer and System Sciences*, *70*(4), 555–569. doi:10.1016/j.jcss.2004.10.006

Davies, D. L., & Bouldin, D. W. (1979). Cluster separation measure. *IEEE Transactions on Pattern Analysis and Machine Intelligence*, *1*(2), 224–227. doi:10.1109/TPAMI.1979.4766909

Dunn, J. C. (1977). Well separated clusters and optimal fuzzy partitions. *Journal of Cybernetics*, *4*, 95–104. doi:10.1080/01969727408546059

Dunn, R., & Dunn, K. (1978). *Teaching students through their individual learning styles: a practical approach*. Reston, VA: Reston Publishing.

Ester, M., Kriegel, H.-P., Sander, J., & Xu, X. (1996). A Density-based algorithm for discovering clusters in large spatial databases with noise. In *Proceedings of the 2nd International Conference on Knowledge Discovery and Data Mining* (pp. 226-231). Portland.

Felder, R., & Brent, R. (2005). Understanding student differences. *Journal of Engineering Education, 94*(1), 57–72.

Felder, R. M. (1996). Matters of style. *ASEE PRISM, 6*(4), 18–23.

Felder, R. M., & Silverman, L. K. (1988). Learning and teaching styles in engineering education. *English Education, 78*(7), 674–681.

Felder, R. M., & Soloman, B. A. (2009). *Index of Learning Styles*. Retrieved March 20, 2009. from http://www.ncsu.edu/felder-public/ILSpage.html

Gan, G., Ma, Ch., & Wu, J. (2007). *Data clustering: theory, algorithms and applications, ASA-SIAM Series on Statistics and Applied Probability, SIAM*. Philadelphia: ASA Alexandria.

Garcia, P., Amandi, A., Schiaffino, S., & Campo, M. (2007). Evaluating Bayesian networks' precision for detecting students' learning styles. *Computers & Education, 49*(3), 794–808. doi:10.1016/j.compedu.2005.11.017

Gilbert, J. E., & Han, C. Y. (1999). Adapting instruction in search of 'a significant difference'. *Journal of Network and Computer Applications, 22*(3), 149–160. doi:10.1006/jnca.1999.0088

Gordon, A. (1996). Hierarchical classification. In Arabie, P., Hubert, L., & Soete, G. (Eds.), *Clustering and Classification* (pp. 65–121). River Edge, NJ: World Scientific.

Graf, S. & Kinshuk. (2006). Considering learning styles in learning management systems: investigating the behavior of students in an online course. In P. Mylones, M. Wallace, & M. Angelides (Eds.), *Proceedings of the First IEEE International Workshop on Semantic Media Adaptation and Personalization, SMAP 06* (pp. 25-30). Los Alamitos, CA: IEEE Computer Society.

Halkidi, M., Batistakis, Y., & Vazirgiannis, M. (2001). On clustering validation techniques. *Journal of Intelligent Information Systems, 17*(2/3), 107–145. doi:10.1023/A:1012801612483

Halkidi, M., & Vazirgiannis, M. (2001). Clustering validity assessment: finding the optimal partitioning of a data set. In *Proceedings of 2001 International Conference on Data Mining* (pp. 187-194). San Jose, CA.

Halkidi, M., Vazirgiannis, M., & Batistakis, Y. (2000). Quality scheme assessment in the clustering process. In *Proceedings of the 4th European Conference on Principles of Data Mining and Knowledge Discovery* (pp. 265-276). Lyon, France.

Han, J., & Kamber, M. (2006). *Data mining. Concepts and techniques* (2nd ed.). San Francisco, CA: Morgan Kaufmann Publishers.

Heffler, B. (2001). Individual learning style and the learning style inventory. *Educational Studies, 27*(3), 307–316. doi:10.1080/03055690120076583

Hochbaum, S. D., & Shmoys, B. D. (1985). A best possible heuristic for the k-center problem. *Mathematics of Operations Research, 10*(2), 180–184. doi:10.1287/moor.10.2.180

Honey, P., & Mumford, A. (1986). *The manual of learning styles*. Maidenhead, UK: Peter Honey.

Jain, A. K., Murty, M. N., & Flynn, P. J. (1999). Data clustering: a review. *ACM Computing Surveys, 31*(3), 264–323. doi:10.1145/331499.331504

Jain, R., & Koronios, A. (2008). Innovation in the cluster validating techniques. *Fuzzy Optimization and Decision Making, 7*(3), 233–241. doi:10.1007/s10700-008-9033-2

Karger, D. R., & Quan, D. (2004, January). *Prerequisites for a personalizable user interfa*ce. Paper presented at the Workshop on Bahavior- Based User Interface Customization at the Intelligent User Interface 2004 Conference, Island of Madeira, Portugal.

Kolb, D. A. (1984). *Experiental learning: Experience as a source of learning and development.* Englewood Cliffs, NJ: Prentice-Hall.

Lee, M. (2001). Profiling students adaptation styles in web-based learning. *Computers & Education, 36*(2), 121–132. doi:10.1016/S0360-1315(00)00046-4

Lu, J., Yu, C. S., & Liu, C. (2003). Learning style, learning patterns, and learning performance in a WebCT-based MIS course. *Information & Management, 40*(6), 497–507. doi:10.1016/S0378-7206(02)00064-2

MacQueen, J. B. (1967). Some methods for classification and analysis of multivariate observations. In *Proceedings of 5-th Berkeley Symposium on Mathematical Statistics and Probability* (Vol. 1, pp. 281-297). Berkeley, CA: University of California Press.

Maulik, U., & Bandyopadhyay, S. (2002). Performance evaluation of some clustering algorithms and validity indices. *IEEE Transactions on Pattern Analysis and Machine Intelligence, 24*(12), 1650–1654. doi:10.1109/TPAMI.2002.1114856

Questionnaire, I. L. S. (2009). *ILS Questionnaire.* Retrieved March 20, 2009 from http://www.engr.ncsu.edu/learningstyles/ilsweb.html

Romero, C., & Ventura, S. (Eds.). (2006). *Data mining in e-learning.* Boston, MA: WIT Press. doi:10.2495/1-84564-152-3

Romero, C., & Ventura, S. (2007). Educational data mining: a survey from 1995 to 2005. *Expert Systems with Applications, 33*(1), 135–146. doi:10.1016/j.eswa.2006.04.005

Romero, C., Ventura, S., & Garcia, E. (2008). Data mining in course management systems: Moodle case study and tutorial. *Computers & Education, 51*(1), 368–384. doi:10.1016/j.compedu.2007.05.016

Saarikoski, L., Salojärvi, S., Del Corso, D., & Ovein, E. (2001). The 3DE: an environment for the development of learner-oriented customized educational packages. In *Proceedings of ITHET01.* Kumamoto, Japan.

Stash, N., Cristea, A., & De Bra, P. (2004). Authoring of learning styles in adaptive hypermedia: Problems and solutions. In *Proceedings of the Thirteenth International World Wide Web Conference* (pp. 114-123). New York: ACM Press.

Theodoridis, S., & Koutroumbas, K. (2006). *Pattern recognition* (3rd ed.). London: Academic Press.

Triantafillou, E., Pomportsis, A., & Georgiadou, E. (2002). AES-CES: Adaptive Educational System based on cognitive styles. In *Proceedings of AH Workshop* (pp. 10-20) Malaga, Spain.

Viola, S. R., & Graf, S. Kinshuk., & Leo, T. (2007). Investigating relationships within the Index of Learning Styles: a data driven approach. *Interactive Technology & Smart Education, 4*(1), 7-18.

Witten, I. H., & Frank, E. (2005). *Data Mining: Practical machine learning tools and techniques* (2nd ed.). San Francisco: Morgan Kaufmann Publishers.

Xu, D., Wang, H., & Su, K. (2002). Intelligent student profiling with fuzzy models. In *Proceedings of HICSS'02*, Hawaii.

Xu, R., & Wunsch, D. II. (2009). *Clustering.* Piscataway, NJ: IEEE Press & Wiley.

Zakrzewska, D. (2007). Cluster analysis for building personalised e-learning system. *Polish Journal of Environmental Studies, 16*(5B), 330–334.

Zakrzewska, D. (2008a). Cluster analysis for users' modeling in intelligent e-learning systems. In N.T. Nguyen, L. Borzemski, A. Grzech, M., & Ali (Eds.), *New Frontiers in applied artificial intelligence IEA/AIE 2008* (LNAI 5027, pp. 209-214). Berlin, Germany: Springer-Verlag.

Zakrzewska, D. (2008b). Using clustering technique for students' grouping in intelligent e-learning systems. In Holzinger A. (Ed.), *HCI and Usability for Education and Work USAB 2008* (LNCS 5298, pp. 403-410). Berlin, Germany: Springer-Verlag.

Zakrzewska, D., & Ruiz-Esteban, C. (2005) Cluster analysis for students profiling. In *Proceedings of the 11ᵗʰ International Conference on "System Modelling Control"* (pp. 333-338). Warsaw, Poland: AOW EXIT.

ADDITIONAL READING

Beaudoin, M. F. (2002). Learning or lurking? Tracking the "invisible" online student. *The Internet and Higher Education, 5*(2), 147–155. doi:10.1016/S1096-7516(02)00086-6

Berry, M. J., & Linoff, G. (1996). *Data Mining Techniques for Marketing, Sales and Customer Support*. New York: John Wiley, & Sons, Inc.

Brusilovsky, P., & Peylo, C. (2003). Adaptive and intelligent web-based educational systems. *International Journal of Artificial Intelligence in Education, 13*, 156–169.

Gonzalez-Rodriguez, M., Manrubia, J., Vidau, A., & Gonzalez-Gallego, M. (2009). Improving accessibility with user-tailored interfaces. *Applied Intelligence, 30*(1), 65–71. doi:10.1007/s10489-007-0098-3

Halkidi, M., Batistakis, Y., & Vazirgiannis, M. (2002). Cluster validity methods: Part 1. *SIGMOD Record, 31*(2), 40–45. doi:10.1145/565117.565124

Halkidi, M., Batistakis, Y., & Vazirgiannis, M. (2002). Cluster validity methods: Part 2. *SIGMOD Record, 31*(3), 19–27. doi:10.1145/601858.601862

Hodge, V. J., & Austin, J. (2004). A survey of outlier detection methodologies. *Artificial Intelligence Review, 22*(2), 85–126. doi:10.1023/B:AIRE.0000045502.10941.a9

Jiang, M. F., Tseng, S. S., & Su, M. M. (2001). Two-phase clustering process in outliers detection. *Pattern Recognition Letters, 22*(6-7), 691–700. doi:10.1016/S0167-8655(00)00131-8

Larose, D. T. (2006). *Data Mining Methods and Models*. New York: John Wiley, & Sons, Inc.

Li, Z., Sun, Y., & Liu, M. (2005). A web-based intelligent tutoring system. In *Proceedings of Artificial Intelligence and Innovations AIAI2005*, (IFIP International Federation for Information Processing 187, pp. 583-591). New York: Springer.

Liegle, J. O., & Janicki, T. N. (2006). The effect of learning styles on the navigation needs of Web-based learners. *Computers in Human Behavior, 22*(5), 885–898. doi:10.1016/j.chb.2004.03.024

Lu, F., Li, X., Liu, Q., Yang, Z., Tan, G., & He, T. (2007). Research on personalized e-learning system using fuzzy set based clustering algorithm. In Y. Shi, G.D. van Albada, J. Dongarra, & P.M.A. Sloot (Eds.), *Proceedings of ICCS 2007 Part III*, (LNCS 4489, pp. 587-590). Berlin, Germany: Springer-Verlag.

Merceron, A., & Yacef, K. (2005). Clustering students to help evaluate learning. In J.-P. Courtiat, C. Davarakis, & T. Villemur (Eds.), *Technology Enchanced Learning*, (171, pp. 31-42). New York: Springer.

Perera, D., Kay, J., Koprinska, I., Yacef, K., & Zaïane, O. R. (2009). Clustering and sequential pattern mining of online collaborative learning data. *IEEE Transactions on Knowledge and Data Engineering, 21*(6), 759–772. doi:10.1109/TKDE.2008.138

Rousseuw, P. J. (1990). *Finding Groups in Data: An Introduction to Cluster Analysis.* New York: Wiley.

Rovai, A. P. (2003). The relationships of communicator style, personality-based learning style, and classroom community among online graduate students. *The Internet and Higher Education, 6*(4), 347–363. doi:10.1016/j.iheduc.2003.07.004

Santally, M. I., & Alain, S. (2006). Personalisation in web-based learning environments. *International Journal of Distance Education Technologies, 4,* 15–35.

Shen, R., Han, P., Yang, F., Yang, Q., & Huang, J. (2003). Data mining and case-based reasoning for distance learning. *Journal of Distance Education Technologies, 1,* 46–58.

Stein, B., Meyer, S., & Wissbrock, F. (2003). On cluster validity and the information need of users. In *Proceedings of 3rd IASTED International Conference on Artificial Intelligence and Applications,* (pp. 216-221). Spain.

Talavera, L., & Gaudioso, E. (2004). Mining student data to characterize similar behavior groups in unstructured collaboration spaces. In *Proceedings of the Workshop on Artificial Intelligence in CSCL. 16th European Conference on Artificial Intelligence,* (pp. 17-23).

Tang, C., Yin, H., Li, T., Lau, R., Li, Q., & Kilis, D. (2000). Personalised courseware construction based on web data mining. In *Proceedings of the First International Conference on Web Information Systems Engineering* (pp. 204-211). Washington, DC.

Tang, J., Chen, Z., Fu, A. W., & Cheung, D. W. (2002). Enhancing effectiveness of outlier detections for low density patterns. In M.-S. Cheng, P.S. Yu, B. Liu (Eds.), *Advances in Knowledge Discovery and Data Mining: PAKDD 2002,* (LNCS 2336, pp. 535-548). Berlin, Germany: Springer-Verlag.

Zakrzewska, D., & Wojciechowski, A. (2008). Identifying students usability needs in collaborative learning environments. In *Proceedings of 2008 Conference on Human System Interaction* (pp. 862-867). Cracow, Poland.

KEY TERMS AND DEFINITIONS

E-Learning: It is an approach to facilitate and enhance learning through based on both: computer and communications technology. It may also be used to support distance learning

Intelligent Learning System: It is any computer system that provides direct customized instruction or feedback to students. An ILS may use a range of different technologies.

Learning Styles: They are various approaches or ways of learning. They involve educating methods, particular to an individual, that are presumed to allow that individual to learn best. It is commonly believed that most people favor some particular method of interacting with information

Student Profile: It is a collection of personal data associated to a specific student. A profile refers to the explicit digital representation of a student's identity. A student profile can also be considered as the computer representation of a student model. Profiles can be used by adaptive hypermedia systems that personalise the human computer interaction.

Personalization: It involves using technology to accommodate the differences between individuals. Once confined mainly to the Web, it is increasingly becoming a significant factor in distance education.

Cluster Analysis: Cluster analysis or clustering is the assignment of a set of physical or abstract objects into subsets of similar objects. A cluster is a collection of data objects that are similar to one another within the same cluster and are dissimilar to the objects in other clusters.

Cluster Validation: It is the process of objectively and quantitatively evaluating the resulting clusters or checking whether the clustering structure derived is meaningful.

Chapter 13
Knowledge Redundancy, Environmental Shocks, and Agents' Opportunism

Lucio Biggiero
University of L'Aquila, Italy

ABSTRACT

Notwithstanding the warning of myopic view, when giving too much emphasis to the short run and stable environments, efficiency is usually claimed by standard economics as the main goal of competitive firms. This is challenged by management and organization scholars, who argue that, in presence of strong uncertainty due to environmental turbulence, slack resources can be a competitive advantage. In order to put some sound block in this debate through, this paper tests four groups of hypotheses on an agent-based model of industry competitiveness based on suppliers' quality. It innovates current literature in two ways: first, it considers redundancy in terms of organizational knowledge, and not in terms of personnel or financial assets or other types of resources, which are usually taken as object of study. Secondly, it compares the effects of two forms of perturbations: environmental shock and opportunism. The results show that these two forms impact differently on industry profitability and that knowledge redundancy can (limitedly) compensate the effects of environmental shocks but not of opportunism. Moreover, it demonstrates that, as agents exchange (and accumulate) more information, knowledge efficiency declines, but less than proportionally to the increase of knowledge exchange.

INTRODUCTION

The aim of this contribution is to understand the relationships between profitability and knowledge at industry and segment level. In particular, by considering knowledge as a resource, the rela-

tive (dis)advantages of knowledge redundancy is discussed in different competitive environments, with a special focus on the effects of environmental shocks and opportunistic behaviors.

Redundancy indicates an excess of some resource respect to its minimum requirement, and thus, by definition it is the reverse of efficiency. Most phenomena can be analyzed in terms of

DOI: 10.4018/978-1-61692-811-7.ch013

redundancy, which can be measured in many ways. In information theory it can be measured and conceptualized in terms of signals in excess to what would be required by the receiver in order to run a certain operation. In cybernetics it could be also referred to variety in excess to that required for systems survival or to excess "copies" of the qualitative types constituting the requisite variety. In network analysis it measures the number of links over the minimum. Just to mention a few examples.

Since the traditional -and still dominant view in economics- considers firms as (almost exclusively) short run profit maximizers in a rather stable or predictable environment, redundancy should be prevented because it reduces profit margins. According to that view, efficiency and the maximum exploitation of resources is always a must. Conversely, alternative approaches argue that, in the long run with a turbulent environment, redundancy can be a competitive advantage.

Of course efficiency is a multi-dimensional phenomenon, because there are different types of resources. The same amount of total cost can be given by different combinations of resources, whose actual use can be individually more or less efficient. In other words, efficiency should be always specified in reference to a certain type of resource. In this work, the focus is put on knowledge, and hence it is questioned whether knowledge efficiency is always preferable. This choice is mainly due to the fact that, according to the knowledge based view of the firm (Conner, 1991; Conner & Prahalad, 1996; Kogut & Zander, 1992, 1996), in current and future evolution of economy, knowledge is regarded as a crucial factor of competitiveness.

However, among the many ways to categorize organizational knowledge (Amin & Cohendet, 2004; Nonaka & Nishiguchi, 2001; Nonaka & Takeuchi, 1995; Tsoukas, 1996, 2005; von Krogh and Roos, 1996; von Krogh *et al.*, 1998; Yolles, 2006), there is one particularly pertinent for the purposes of this paper: the distinction concerning the origin of knowledge, whether from external and internal sources. In fact, the effects of the acquisition of external knowledge suffer of the lack of precision or, much worst, of scarce reliability. The first failure is mainly due to cognitive distance (Fiol, 2002; Lant, 2002) and information equivocality (March, 1997; Weick, 1995), while the latter to the combination of information asymmetry (Akerlof, 1970; Mas-Colell *et al.*, 1995; Shapiro and Varian, 1999; Stigler, 1961) and opportunism (Child, 2001; Gambetta, 1988; Hall, 1992; Humphrey, 1998; Kramer & Tyler, 1996; Lane, 1995, 2001; Lane & Bachmann, 1996, 1998; Williamson, 1975, 1981, 1985, 1994, 1996). Indeed, even the internal sources of knowledge are not completely free from these two failures, but it is reasonably to assume –as most literature does- that they markedly differ in intensity, especially in the case of small-medium size organizations. These two defects play also in regard of our issue of knowledge redundancy, which here is referred only to the acquisition of external knowledge.

The role played by various forms of opportunistic behavior between firms has been extensively investigated by transaction cost economics (Williamson, 1975, 1985, 1993), according to which if only few firms do exchange and/or its products are complex, then transaction costs raise respectively, because of opportunistic behaviors and idiosyncrasy. If this latter is kept constant, the crucial variable becomes opportunism and the attention is shifted to the methods to reduce it. One of them is by increasing the ability to distinguish between opportunist and correct agents through the acquisition (and use) of information on their behaviors. Such information can come either from direct experience or from accessing others' knowledge. However, the knowledge tool is weakened if opportunism assumes the form of cheating, because such information can be false. This eventuality is receiving growing attention by most theoretical and empirical studies, because in the past opportunism was depicted by all the other variables but cheating, as transactions' specificity, frequency or uncertainty, the number of exchanging parties, and eventually their perceived effects on economic outcomes.

This study exploits the architecture of CIOPS model (Biggiero & Sevi, 2009), which is a network of agents representing firms that interact through structural and cognitive links. Through an agent-based simulation model of a three-segment industry some structural and cognitive characteristics of agents' searching, choosing and basic learning have been operationalized. The structural network is a productive system constituted by agents connected each other by (vertical) economic relationships, and interacting through orders and products. Conversely, information flows horizontally among agents of the same filiere segment. Industry is taken in a medium (200 firms) size, and sales and profits of final producers (FPs) depend on the quality of first tiers (FTs), which in turn depends on that of their suppliers (the segment of raw materials). It is supposed that clients always can sell products on the final market, and select subcontractors but not vice versa.

Cognitive variables are: type and amount of information available to agents, their rationality (computational capacity and levels of aspiration), their types of decision making processes, and attitude to cheat. Agents' decision making process is constituted by three types of choices that are compared each other in each step: random choice (RND), direct (DEBT) and indirect (INDEBT) experience-based. Clients ask each other information concerning supplier's quality, and compare it with that existing in their memory. This way they move within the information space, while their rationality is bounded by the limited number of information they can ask. In essence, there are two dynamic networks, a structural and a cognitive one, which overlap and interact in multiple ways, and each agent develops his own cognitive representation of the structural network.

Turbulence is given by two types of mechanisms: i) behavioural uncertainty due to competitors' opportunism by cheating (Biggiero & Sevi, 2009); ii) environmental changes due to a new distribution of quality among suppliers, which can approximate the rapid diffusion of a radical innovation among suppliers (Corso & Pellegrini, 2007; Li *et al.*, 2008). The analysis is run at both industry and segment level, taken as a whole.

This paper innovates current literature in two ways: firstly, it considers redundancy in terms of organizational knowledge, and not in terms of personnel or financial assets or other types of resources, which are usually taken as object of study. Secondly, it compares the effects of two forms of perturbations: environmental shock and opportunism. The results show that these two forms impact differently on industry profitability and that knowledge redundancy can (limitedly) compensate the effects of environmental shocks but not of opportunism. Moreover, it demonstrates that, as agents exchange (and accumulate) more information, knowledge efficiency declines, but less than proportionally to the increase of knowledge exchange. Finally, it shows that the two segments of final and intermediary producers perform and react to perturbations quite differently

The paper proceeds as follows. In next section theoretical background is revisited especially concerning the fields of economics and management. According to the literature review four groups of hypotheses are advanced, and referred to the effects of environmental shocks and opportunism on the level and stability of industry competitiveness. This latter is measured in terms of average quality, mean and total cumulated profit, knowledge production and its employment. In section three the characteristics of the simulation model and the parameters of virtual experiments are summarized. Then, in the next section results are discussed and analyzed in terms of final outcomes after 400 simulation steps, and in terms of dynamic patterns. Finally, these results are confronted with those of the revised literature.

THEORETICAL BACKGROUND

In economics and management redundancy is usually indicated with the concept of slack resources, which can refer to production (Leibenstein, 1966, 1987), human resource (Williamson, 1974, 1985), finance (George, 2005), power (Bourgeois and Singh, 1983), and labour (Love & Nohria, 2005; Nohria & Gulati, 1997). Indeed, the major attention has been focused on the financial and personnel sources of redundancy, also because it is relatively easier to be measured and to gather data. For the same reason most studies look for the effects of personnel redundancy in terms of downsizing and behavioural consequences.

At a closer sight it appears that, given the extension and rather chronic existence of redundancy, both its theoretical and empirical analysis has been really scarce. A good explanation of this surprising lack of studies lies into the deep core of mainstream economics, because its focus on general economic equilibrium and on the perfect rationality of agents made the case for redundancy definitely implausible. Even when industrial and managerial economics (Leibenstein, 1966, 1987; Williamson, 1974), agency cost theory (Jensen & Meckling, 1976; Jensen, 1993), and transaction cost economics (Williamson, 1975, 1985) deal deeply with the inner structure and functioning of firms, the most important imperative for economics remained efficiency. Hence, redundancy was (and is) always considered as a handicap for firms performance and competitiveness.

A different story can be told for management and organization theory. Starting from Cyert and March (1963) seminal book on the behavioural theory of the firm, slack resources have been recognized as a normal state. Further research developed their analysis showing that redundancy comes from agents' bounded rationality and the ambiguity of information they exchange and, especially in large organizations, from the power games of coalition groups (Pfeffer and Salancick, 1978; Sharfman *et al.*, 1988).

Another way to look at the issue has been developed by management science and operations research, and in particular by the approaches to total quality management (Ahire *et al.*, 1996; Anderson *et al.*, 1995; Flynn *et al.*, 1995; Ishikawa, 1985; Kekre *et al.*, 1995; Martinez-Lorente *et al.*, 1998; Ohno, 1988; Womack and Jones, 1990). It refers to the optimum size of inventory stocks either within different organizational functions and departments or between organizations. Developing American early theorization by Juran (Juran & Blanton Godfrey, 2000) and Deming (Anderson *et al.*, 1995; Deming, 1986), Japanese management approaches proposed to put zero-stock as one of the main goals (Carter & Narasimhan, 1994; Gonzales-Benito, 2003; Ishikawa, 1985; Krafcik, 1988), because stocks sharply reduce efficiency (Narasimhan and Mendez, 2001; Roy & Guin, 1999). The supplier-buyer relationship becomes a crucial issue (Bessant *et al.*, 1994; Lascelles and Dale, 1989), which leads to the fundamental action of selecting the best supplier in terms of purchasing quality, and hence to the core of the present simulation model (see the next section).

Finally, the question of redundancy clearly relates to the exploitation-exploration trade-off (March, 1991), because in order to explore it is necessary to have slack resources and so to reduce efficiency gains obtainable by exploitation strategies. However, as March and others underlie (Levinthal & March, 1993; March, 1991), a pure exploitative strategy likely brings into competency traps, because organizations become unable to perceive and to react to environmental changes. Actually, the link between redundancy and innovation capacity has been highlighted too (Damanpour, 1991; Nohria & Gulati, 1997; Richtner & Åhlström, 2006).

However, these scholars are as well concerned that firms should be efficient to be competitive, and so Nohria and Gulati (1997) argued for a curvilinear relationship between redundancy and performance: the optimum is supposed to be at an intermediate level. This hypothesis has been

255

confirmed also by other recent studies (Geiger & Cashen, 2002; Tan, 2003; Tan & Peng, 2003). Besides explaining its rationale, scholars argued also for the existence of its positive effects, especially for enhancing innovation (Geiger & Cashen, 2002; Geiger & Makri, 2006), for managing risk (Hambrick & Snow, 1977; Richtner & Åhlström, 2006; Singh, 1986), and to face with long term environmental uncertainty (Sharfman *et al.*, 1988; Van der Stede, 2000).

The latter is the main focus of this paper. Drawing from Thompson's (1967) suggestion that efficiency would the primer only if the world were quite predictable and stable, the idea here developed is that long run competitiveness in a turbulent environment requires slack resources. In fact, if the environment is likely to change, then it is necessary to perceive it and promptly react, especially if changes are radical and jolt (Meyer, 1982). Since both perceptions and reactions consume resources, in order to survive and face with radical environmental changes it is necessary to have a certain amount of slack resources.

This idea is consistent also with the theoretical perspective of the population ecology of organizations, which highlights that large organizations are characterized by longer survival rates respect to small ones (Hannan & Carroll, 1992). This is due to the huge resources they can employ to explore and experiment and adapt to changing environments. Among the many types of resources they can dedicate there is certainly knowledge, which is developed to a larger extent and it is based on a larger amount of information. Indeed, according to the knowledge-based view of the firm (Conner, 1991; Conner & Prahalad, 1996; Kogut & Zander, 1992, 1996), competitiveness is mostly due to knowledge acquisition and management, and to learning processes and abilities. That is why the key concept of this paper is on knowledge efficiency, which here is measured by the profit gained per knowledge units (information).

Other studies have recently underlined the relationships between knowledge and slack resources (Richtner & Åhlström, 2006; Van der Stede, 2001), but they have investigated the extent to which slack resources enhance knowledge creation in terms of innovation: the causal relationship is from personnel or budget resources to knowledge. Conversely, here knowledge is the resource of which the efficiency should be analyzed: the causal relationship goes from knowledge to profitability through the capacity to face with environmental uncertainty.

This latter is modelled in two ways. Firstly, it is related to agents' opportunistic behaviours, which concretely is operationalized as their attitude to give false information. If informers can be unreliable the environment becomes more uncertain than the case of honest informers, because it is necessary to discern between true and false information. Secondly, the occurrence of environmental shocks can vanish the effectiveness of current knowledge and require a prompt adaptation. In this specific model, it is supposed that a new radical innovation changed the distribution of quality among industry suppliers. The effects of the two types of uncertainty are investigated separately, and then combined, so to distinguish its specific contributions to profit losses and knowledge redundancy.

Since uncertainty is a way to look at complexity (Biggiero, 2001), this model allows to understand the relationships between knowledge and complexity in an industry setting. According to Ashby's (1956) law of requisite variety, the more complex is the environment the more complex should be system's behaviour in order to assure its survival. So, we expect that, in order to get the same performance, in more complex contexts firms should employ larger amounts of knowledge.

RESEARCH HYPOTHESES

The literature review just discussed can lead to formulate some research hypotheses with two main warnings, which limit the possibility to derive the latter from the former. The first limit is that previous literature dealt with redundancy in the form of personnel or financial slack resources. Notwithstanding cybernetics had always emphasized the role of information and knowledge, this type of redundancy has been neglected. The knowledge-based view of the firm has focused its attention on the role of competence for firms' competitiveness and innovation. There is a plenty o0f literature on competence mix and the relevance of accessing new knowledge, but nothing about the essentiality or minimum level of knowledge. On the other side most modern approaches of cybernetics to organizational knowledge are entrapped on the rather sterile dispute on the distinction between data, information and knowledge. Influenced by the applications of autopoiesis theory to social systems, they completely overlook the issue of knowledge redundancy, which indeed in their perspective would be probably acknowledged only as information redundancy.

The second problem that makes the following research hypotheses not so directly derivable from the current literature is that most studies considered only internal and not external knowledge. The main consequence is that, being external knowledge less precise and trustworthy than the internal one, some of the expected results could be easily unfulfilled. In other words, the lack of precision and trustworthiness characterizing external knowledge could produce more noise and distortion than benefits.

Besides these aspects, the need to keep distinguished the provenience of knowledge comes from the fact that that external and internal knowledge growth have marked differentiated effects on industry profitability Biggiero (2010). Such differences are not sensitive to agents' opportunism if not for the intensity of the effects. Moreover, industry segments react differently to the growth of external and internal knowledge.

As a methodological and expositional choice, instead of make a descriptive paper assuming and discounting these two limits from the beginning,

I preferred to formulate the hypotheses as if these two peculiar aspects wouldn't play, and to leave them eventually emerging from results in the attempt to test the hypotheses.

According to previous literature some authors consider knowledge redundancy as a competitive advantage and not as a failure. If this were true, then in a competitive context without information circulation, that is where agents make their choices only according to their own experience, the damage of an environmental shock would be heavier, because they could not achieve any redundancy (of external knowledge).

As we have seen reviewing the theoretical background, most authors argue that opportunism has a negative impact on industry performance. This is confirmed also by Biggiero and Sevi (2009), who demonstrate that opportunism by cheating severely reduces industry profitability, and that the corresponding profit loss is sensitive to scale effects. Hence, the first group of hypotheses sounds as follows:

Hypothesis H1a: *with less information circulation the damage of an environmental shock is superior.*
Hypothesis H1b: *in facing with damages due to an environmental shock, agents' dishonesty is relatively less disadvantageous than in the case of not trust at all –that is, no information circulation at all.*
Hypothesis H1c: *ceteris paribus, respect to a context of non-perturbed honest agents, the damage produced by an environmental shock is superior to that of an eventual dishonesty.*

Though this paper focuses on the effects of varying external knowledge, agents accumulate anyway internal knowledge too because of capitalizing direct experience. Of course, by asking more questions each other the amount of external knowledge tends to grow, even though such a tendency is limited by the amount and effectiveness of internal knowledge. In fact, the more valid and satisfying is internal knowledge, the less they ask. However, the interesting problem is to understand how the external knowledge is employed. Plausibly, it is absorbed by discovering wrong information, false informers and bad suppliers, and hence its accumulation grows in a context of dishonesty. The other rationale to employ knowledge is just to face with environmental shocks, which could vanish previous knowledge by suddenly changing the distribution of quality among suppliers. Presumably, the two conditions of dishonesty and shock had to reinforce each other by inducing more knowledge accumulation. Thus, the following hypotheses can be advanced:

Hypothesis H2a: *at industry level an environmental shock determines the accumulation of more knowledge.*

Hypothesis H2b: *at industry level with dishonest agents more knowledge is accumulated in order to discover wrong information, informers and bad suppliers.*

Hypothesis H2c: *at industry level profit loss due to environmental shock is lower when more knowledge is accumulated.*

Random choice and its consequent direct experience produces internal knowledge. If agents rely only on this source of knowledge, even supposing that suppliers' quality remains invariant, they would need more than 80 steps[1] to know all suppliers and to discover their quality. If they would access and trust others' experience they would explore the decision space (see next section) much earlier, and of course they would avoid buying satisfying products only in the 50% of cases[2].

However, such a faster and effective exploration strategy has a price. Firstly, if the trusted competitors-informers are dishonest, agents receive damage from false information and need time and information to discover false informers. Secondly, agents collect much more knowledge than what would be done using only their direct knowledge. In fact, it is unlikely that answers will fill exactly the reciprocal knowledge gaps, because agents do not know "who knows who" nor how many competitors and suppliers there are[3].

Likely, the more questions are raised the more both advantages and disadvantages increase, but in a context of environmental shock the former are lesser than the latter, because most information would reveal false. Consequently, agents should "reset" their internal and external knowledge, and this effort will likely be emphasized facing with dishonest agents. Therefore, it can be reasonably supposed that:

Hypothesis H3a: *at industry level if more questions are asked to competitors, then knowledge efficiency declines.*

Hypothesis H3b: *at industry level when more questions are asked to competitors and there has been an environmental shock, then knowledge efficiency declines relatively less or not at all.*

Hypothesis H3c: *at industry level with dishonest agents and an environmental shock profit loss is relatively less.*

Though submitted to the same general rules and number of potential suppliers, FPs and FTs differ in terms of the size of their information space (IS) (see next section). FTs have and initial IS double than that of FPs, even if over time half of them tend to switch to an inactivated state. However, it happens only in the stable regime -when all clients know all suppliers- that the inactivated suppliers are the same, and in this simple and efficient version of the CIOPS model, they are just the bad suppliers. Until that moment, in each step a certain share of activated FTs is always changing, albeit decreasing over time. Hence, new information can be exchanged and accumulated. Hence, plausibly the following hypotheses can be advanced:

Hypothesis H4a: *FPs and FTs react differently to environmental shocks.*

Hypothesis H4b: *FTs accumulate more knowledge.*

Hypothesis H4c: *FTs can better answer to the environmental shock.*

THE MODEL STRUCTURE

Agent based models are rapidly assuming a great relevance in management as well as in social sciences (Gilbert, 2008). Its advantages are really enormous, because they are the laboratory where the social scientist can test and develop theories. Moreover, virtual experiments can explore situations not yet evidenced by field or pure speculative research. Finally, the formalization forced by modeling helps inter-theoretical comparisons by making explicit hypotheses, methods and the operationalization of variables, and by allowing the replication of experiments.

The present model is a specific development of a model built by Biggiero and Sevi (2009). It allows combining cognitive and structural characteristics of agents, which here are representing firms. Cognitive characteristics enable agents to explore their competitive environment, and are based on their computational capacity, which consists: i) in gathering and comparing various amounts of information required to select the best quality suppliers; ii) in building and updating their memory, which notwithstanding is affected by various types of forgetfulness effects. Structural characteristics consist in different segments and levels of quality suppliers. Their behaviour is path dependent and they learn in a basic, substantial though not sophisticated sense.

Virtual experiments examine also agents' cheating attitude at the opposite extremes of full honesty or dishonesty. Since it is supposed that in this industry competitiveness is strictly related to product quality and this latter to suppliers' quality, agents' main goal is selecting the best suppliers. A set of virtual experiments is run distinguishing the cases of honest and opportunistic agents, who always lie when consulted by their competitors about suppliers' quality. Performance parameters

Figure 1. The general model structure

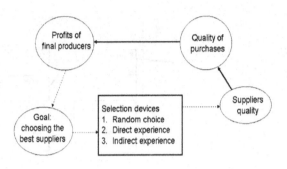

are average quality and total profit at segment and industry level.

A general view of the model (Figure 1) shows its logical structure: profits of final producers depend on the quality of their purchases, which in turn depends on supplier's quality. Thus, the goal of final producers is to choose the best suppliers. Since final producers don't know suppliers' quality, they have to select them through one of three selection mechanisms: random choice, direct and indirect experience. The latter implies information transfer between FPs, who play the role of reciprocal informers. In this model it is supposed that there are 200 agents distributed as follows: 40 FPs, 80 FTs, and 80 second tiers (suppliers of row materials). Moreover, it is supposed only an exclusive (one-to-one) relationship between a client and a supplier[4].

Some of the major points of interest of this model are in the characteristics of agents and in the ways in which they affect their selection mechanisms. Agents are trustworthy or opportunistic, and they perform this latter behavior by cheating, and not by betraying previous agreements, as it is usually supposed in most studies. This represent the main threaten to the individuation of the best suppliers, and consequently to the achievement of high profits. Moreover agents are boundedly rational, in that they can ask only a limited number of questions. Finally, they are satisfiers and not maximizers, and exchange information only among them and not with FTs.

Figure 2. The Industry structure

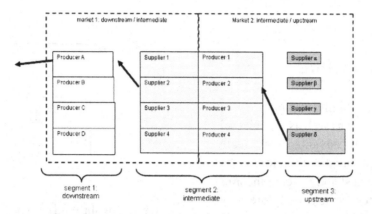

Technology (filiere structure). A final product requires more than one phase of production, each one composed by a set of specialized firms (Figure 2): FPs (downstream firms) get its intermediate product from first tiers (FTs), that is, intermediate firms that in turn are supplied by second (or source) tiers (upstream firms). Production orders flow obviously in the opposite direction. Technology defines also the number of production phases and therefore the length of the filiere, which in this model is built by three specialized filiere segments. Thus, all agents are producers and suppliers except downstream (final producer), which are merely producers, and upstream (suppliers of row materials), which are pure subcontractors. A one-to-one relationship holds between suppliers and clients, that is, in each step and in each market a client orders products to just one supplier, and vice versa. Consequently, orders and goods are exchanged within two markets: a market among downstream and intermediate firms, and another among intermediate and upstream firms. In Figure 2, the arrows indicate the movements of goods, although the orders follow the counter way. Orders start from external market, which is supposed to demand one product per each final producer. Therefore, FPs order components to one intermediate supplier who in turn, orders its products to one upstream supplier of row material. Hence, intermediate tiers are clients with

respect to upstream tiers. Agents' behavior in the downstream and in the intermediate segment is modeled alike, that is, the way they manage and use cognitive and structural variables is the same.

Suppliers are selected according to their quality. However, actual suppliers' quality is verified only after transactions, because clients either could not know it in advance or they could have incorrect information. In this model information reliability is not evaluated as such, but instead it depends on informers' reliability. Actual suppliers' selection depends on clients' experience and cognition: knowledge, computational capacity, expectations, and decision making processes. In order to choose their subcontractors clients: i) scan their own memory on past direct and indirect experience with suppliers; ii) ask other agents as informers. Notice that questioners are allowed to ask information only to members of their segment.

Sales are supposed to be a linear function of the degree of quality according to the following expression:

$$S = 1.2 \, Q_s$$

Where S = sales value and Q_s = supplier's quality. Since clients buy from suppliers at the fixed cost C, profits depend on quality as well, and are given by:

Table 1. Some paradigmatic situations of cost structure

Quality of suppliers' product (Q_s)	Clients' sales (S)	Costs of purchases (C_p)	Profits (P)
0.5	600	750	-150
0.6	720	750	-30
0.7	840	750	10
0.8	960	750	210
0.9	1,080	750	330
1.0	1,200	750	450

$$P = S - C = 1.2\, Q_s - C$$

By putting $C = 0.75$, there are some paradigmatic situations shown in Table 1. FTs have the same cost-profit structure, so that average and agent's quality is transferred from one to other segments only through its effects on agents' profits. Moreover, a ratio of 2/1 is supposed between suppliers in each segment and FPs, so that they always find some supplier. This assumption corresponds to a demand-driven industry. Things could be very different in a supply-driven industry, where competition between clients would be increased by competing for a smaller or equal number of suppliers.

Questioners' analysis of informers' trustworthiness leads to set up a list including only full reliable informers. If the number of informers entering the list is minor than the number of questions that the questioner is able to raise, the questioner asks also some unknown informer randomly chosen. The number of questions that the questioner is able to ask represents his exploration capacity

Informers' trustworthiness depends on the truth of information that that informer passed previously to the specific questioner. If, in the past, a given questioner followed the indication of a given informer, then the questioner could verify informer's reliability. Specifically, reliability is defined as the absolute value of the difference between suggested quality and actual quality of a specific supplier.

Unknown informers are assigned maximum trustworthiness value, as it is also for the required level of informers' reliability. Informers can tell truth or falseness depending on their inclination toward cheating. True informers indicate the best supplier among the ones directly experienced. False informers indicate the worst supplier as if it were their best. That is, cheaters say that the worst has the quality of their best. There is no answer when informers have no information.

Agents have an inclination towards cheating, as the probability that in each interval is given false information, and it is kept constant during the virtual experiment. If the attitude is zero, then agents pass always true information, and vice versa. It is crucial to underline that cheating concerns only the content and not the type of information. In other words, informers can indicate their worst bad experience as if they were the best, but they cannot say, for instance, that they have direct experience if they don't, or any other kind of falsity concerning the source of the information they pass.

It should also be highlighted that in this model it is supposed that all informers are available to give information; that is, they can lie about information content but not about the type of information and neither reject to give information.

Agents build their own cognitive network by coping with a number of direct experiences and

Figure 3. The nested complexity of decision-making patterns (DMP)

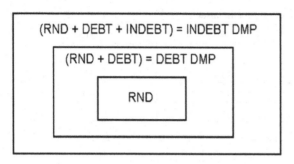

Figure 4. Decision and information space

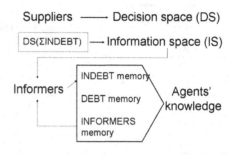

getting information from others. Through their direct experience agents get information on suppliers' actual quality and informers' reliability by interacting with the given supplier. Indirect experience-based information originates from informers' direct experience.

Agents collect and verify a set of INDEBT information, which are stored in their cognitive network in order to build and update their memory. If confirmed by direct experience, that part of memory made of INDEBT information becomes DEBT. Experimentation concerning INDEBT information and memory gives a feedback on the reliability of the agents who gave it, and of course on the corresponding supplier's quality.

Further, it should be noted that the three decision making processes are in a nested reciprocal relationship (Figure 3), because the DEBT decision making *pattern* (DMP), besides the DEBT decision making process includes also the RND option, and analogously INDEBT DMP, besides the INDEBT decision making process includes also the DEBT and the RND options. Hence, in virtual experiments DMP and not single decision making processes are confronted[5].

Agents are all equal in cognitive terms, and respect to goal seeking and expectations. In each virtual experiment they are facing the same environment and are provided with the same opportunities. They are equal also under structural respects, with the exception that first and second

(source) tiers are randomly assigned a given quality, and that to FP and FT certain initial opportunities are randomly offered.

Agents differ on which type, how much and how reliable is their knowledge. Knowledge at industry level is just the sum of agents' knowledge, but not all knowledge circulates. For instance, in those configurations in which direct experience is prevalent, and especially in which indirect experience is inhibited, transferred knowledge is only a small portion. Noticeably, though their simplicity agents store and transfer different types and amount of knowledge. Moreover, they develop different images of the others, and so they enact different cognitive networks.

Information space and agents' knowledge. The decision space (DS) is represented by the suppliers' number (Figure 4), because they constitute the alternatives among which clients should choose. Within this space, questioners move looking for the best choice. Conversely, the information space (IS) refers to indirectly gathered information that can be referred to suppliers, and hence it is composed by:

$$IS = (DS)*(\Sigma INDEBT)$$

The total knowledge (TK) residing into the industry and unevenly distributed among its agents is given by the three forms of memories about DEBT, INDEBT, and INFORMERS. This latter also help to choose reliable informers to be asked, and their answers feed the types of knowledge. It is noteworthy that, whereas decision space grows linearly with the number of suppliers, information space grows squarely with the number of informers. In fact, though not all potential informers are activated and consequently not all information are gathered in each step, potential informers are equal to $n(n-1)$ at each step, where n is the number of informers. Moreover, this information cumulates and in each step it is integrated by the information concerning DEBT, and informers' memory.

It is noteworthy that agents do not know industry size and the number of suppliers, and so they cannot decide to stop searching for better suppliers. This option could be introduced in another version of the model, when agents could be differentiated in terms of strategy: some could be more oriented to optimization and so they will always continue exploring the decision space, while others could be more oriented to satisfying behaviors, and thus, they will stop exploration once a certain level is reached. Of course, both strategies depend on other variables concerning exploration costs and advantages.

As concerning trust and opportunistic behaviors, agents' attitude could be defined as "prudent trust" in the sense that they trust others but check their information and keep track of the corresponding result. Though they do not necessarily react through pure forms of retaliation, once an informer has been recognized as unreliable, they cancel him from the list of future potential informers. Hence, even if their reactions to cheating are "soft" and only passive, agents are not "blind trustees", because they check information and learn consequently. Moreover, it should be noticed that agents acquire free information, because it has no price and informers cannot refuse to give it. Finally, it should be taken into account that in this model all these cognitive operations are costless. In short, there are no direct costs of misplacing trust or checking information coming from indirect experience.

However, though there are no such direct costs, "prudent trust" has an indirect cost, that turns to produce effects on performance: at least in consequence of the first lie received from a cheating informer, the questioner is addressed to a bad supplier, and thus, his own performance is damaged. Being industry performance simply the sum of that of individual agents, industry profitability is negatively affected.

THE METHODOLOGY AND THE CONFIGURATION OF VIRTUAL EXPERIMENTS

Parameters and initial conditions used in these virtual experiments[6] are shown in Table 2. In each step a whole cycle choice/order/production/payment takes place. Supposing that it can represent a reality in which it lasts 5 working days, 400 steps describe 10 years of industry evolution from the very beginning. This could approximate a simple-product industry, whose production cycle is very short and can be realized completely in one week, but whose quality represents a competitive advantage. Medium-high quality segments of some consumer goods markets like clothing, footwear, leather, etc. could satisfy these characteristics. The time span consideration is very important to give sense results of dynamic patterns, because while in some cases performance stabilizes already before 50 steps, in many other situations it still remains uncertain after 400 steps. Sometimes performance becomes definitely unpredictable in the short run, while in the long run keeping stable around a mean value.

Indeed, complex products would better match the crucial role assigned suppliers' quality, as it is characteristic of biotechnology, aerospace, biomedicals, and most high-tech industries. However, they have production cycles extending far beyond two or even six months, and they require even long time to define product and contractual characteristics. If such a real correspondence is

Table 2. Virtual experiments parameters

Structural parameters with constant values	
Filiere segments	3
Industry size	200 firms
Ratio FP/FT = 1/2	40 downstream firms, 80 suppliers in intermediate segment and 80 suppliers in upstream segment.
Quality	Randomly uniform distribution between 0.5 and 1
Outsourcing degree	1 subcontractor for each client
Cognitive parameters with constant and uniform values	
Decision making processes	RND, DEBT, INDEBT.
Number of questions agents can ask to explore the environment	0, 1, 4, 8, 16
Quality threshold	0.75
Varied structural parameters	
Environmental shock	At 201st interval suppliers' quality is randomly uniformly re-distributed
Varied but uniform (among agents) cognitive parameters	
Inclination to cheat	0 or 1

given each step, it is clear that even 50 intervals addresses to a very significant time span.

Experiments are executed varying: i) the presence or absence of an environmental shock; and ii) agents' inclination to cheat (0 or 1), while keeping constant other parameters. Due to the high number of variables and the value that each variable may assume for each agent, within each virtual experiment suppliers differ only in quality while keeping constant other parameters, agents have the same quality threshold, employ the same decision making *patterns*.

Other parameters not specifically discussed before are the following:

- quality threshold: this refers to agents' aspiration levels (March, 1988; Simon, 1982, 1991, 1997), who consider a supplier satisfying only if his quality is not lower than 0.75;
- clients' requirement of informers' reliability, which here it is supposed to be full reliability. In other words, an informer is supposed to be credible only if he is completely reliable.

Results are expressed in terms of:

- average quality (AQ), which is the mean quality of all agents calculated over the 400 simulation steps[7];
- total profit, total cumulated profit and profit loss, which all are calculated in absolute values;
- total knowledge, distinguished in terms of internal and external knowledge and measured in terms of number of information;
- number of informers and suppliers activated in average by all agents;
- average knowledge units per profit (TP/K), which is a measure of mean cognitive efficiency;
- average knowledge units per informer or per supplier;
- neutralization time (NT), which is the number of steps required to reach (almost) the profitability level right before the shock.

As for many agent-based models, this one is deterministic, except for the quality distribution among suppliers at the beginning (step 1) and after the environmental shock (step 201). The results discussed in next section are the mean of 10 runs for each virtual experiment. In order to interpret the results it is useful to bear in mind that an agent's knowledge is efficient when s/he has exactly 80 information, which correspond to one per each of the suppliers. Hence, in the segment of FPs knowledge is redundant when it exceeds 3200 units, while in the segment of FTs at 3600, and at industry level at 6800 units of information.

It does not matter the way in which such information have been achieved, whether by random choice, direct or indirect experience. Of course, the most parsimonious (efficient) way is through random choice accompanied by indirect experience, both steering direct experience. However, it is definitely unlikely that the lack of knowledge left by random choice were precisely covered by achieving information through indirect experience. Usually there will be a certain degree of redundant –and eventually even contradictory, in the context of dishonest agents- knowledge also in efficient cases. Clearly, the more questions are asked per each agent, the more redundancy will be created.

MAIN RESULTS

Before testing the hypotheses it is useful to see the effects of the environmental shock in contexts of honest and dishonest agents, who can ask each other different amounts of questions about suppliers' quality. As shown by Figures 5a and b, the effects are quite pronounced, because the average profit drops down, and the more questions they ask the heavier is the loss. It is also evident that the crash is much more accentuated with dishonest agents, because the "seductive" effect played by false information –competitors give their worst supplier as if it were the best- prevents for long time not only to accumulate direct knowledge, but also to cast dices through random choices. An analogous divertive role played by false informa-

tion explains the different behaviors of the two graphics during the early 100 steps. In order to well understand the meaning of this phenomenon, it should be clear that, if one step would correspond to one working week, dishonesty determines years of low profits before reaching a stable regime of high profits.

The first hypothesis (H1a) states that with less information circulation the damage of an environmental shock is superior. Data shown in Table 3 confirms this hypothesis, with the only exception of the lowest rationality in which agents ask just one question. It seems that by increasing rationality both profit loss and neutralization time decrease because agents access more knowledge: they re-build previous profitability sooner and with lower losses.

The second hypothesis (H1b) suggests that, in facing with damages due to an environmental shock, agents' dishonesty is relatively less disadvantageous than in the case of not trust at all –that is, no information circulation at all. This hypothesis should be rejected (Table 3), because, even though by increasing rationality losses decrease, losses due to dishonesty are systematically superior to those occurring with honest agents. Apparently, the unreliability of information is more disruptive than knowledge redundancy. Even though over time agents learn who lie, the damage of false informers produces serious damages, which cannot be compensated by the knowledge of suppliers.

NT = neutralization time

LOSS = profit loss (in absolute value and referred merely to the neutralization time) due to environmental shock

The third hypothesis (H1c) argues that respect to a context of non-perturbed honest agents, the damage produced by an environmental shock is superior to that of an eventual dishonesty. This hypothesis should be rejected (Table 4), because the losses due to dishonesty are systematically superior to those of the shock.

The hypothesis 2a states that at industry level an environmental shock determines the accumu-

Figure 5. A) Total profit at industry level with honest agents; B) Total profit at industry level with dishonest agents

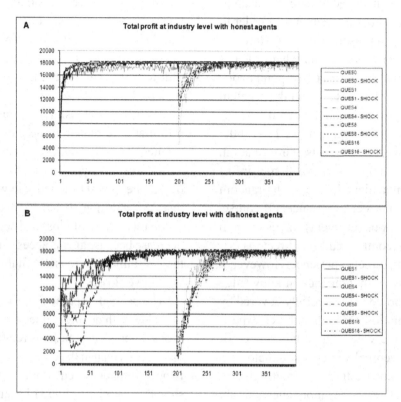

Table 3. Effects of environmental shock

QUES	0		1		4	
	NT	LOSS	NT	LOSS	NT	LOSS
honest	15	10110	113	13725	115	6810
dishonest			60	16463	67	16778
Var. honest/dishonest			-46,90%	19,95%	-41,74%	146,37%
QUES			8		16	
			NT	LOSS	NT	LOSS
honest			65	7253	61	5978
dishonest			77	14580	104	9690
Var. honest/dishonest			18,46%	101,02%	70,49%	62,09%

lation of more knowledge. This hypothesis is fully confirmed, because in every configuration the amount of knowledge sharply increases right after the shock (Figure 6). In particular, Figures 6a, b and c show that such an increase grows with the number of questions agents can ask: with just one question the gap is around the double, while with 16 questions it is about 7 times. The reason is that more knowledge is required to discover

Table 4. Cumulated profits

questions	0				1				4			
regime	STA	SHO	LOSS	LOSS %	STA	SHO	LOSS	LOSS %	STA	SHO	LOSS	LOSS %
honest	6882	6801	81	1,18%	7110	6874	236	3,32%	7220	7033	187	2,59%
dishonest					6831	6490	341	4,99%	6732	6272	460	6,83%
Var. honest-dishonest					-3,93%	-5,60%	44,47%		-6,76%	-10,82%	145,99%	
questions					8				16			
regime					STA	SHO	LOSS	LOSS %	STA	SHO	LOSS	LOSS %
honest					7198	7006	192	2,67%	7248	7055	192	2,65%
dishonest					6620	6117	503	7,59%	6387	5853	534	8,37%
Var. honest-dishonest					-8,03%	-12,69%	161,91%		-11,88%	-17,05%	177,69%	

Figure 6. A) Knowledge growth at industry level with environmental shock; B) Knowledge growth at industry level with honest agents; C) Knowledge growth at industry level with dishonest agents; D) Knowledge growth at industry level with only one question; E) Knowledge growth at industry level with 16 questions

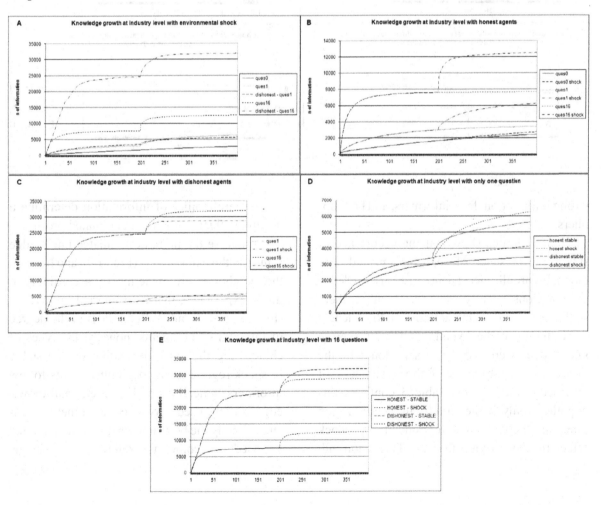

Figure 7. A) The growth of the two types of knowledge with honest agents; B) The growth of the two types of knowledge with dishonest agents; C) Choice types of honest agents at industry level with 16 questions without shock; D) The growth of the two types of knowledge with dishonest agents; E) Choice types of dishonest agents at industry level with 16 questions without shock; F) Choice types of dishonest agents at industry level with 16 questions with shock

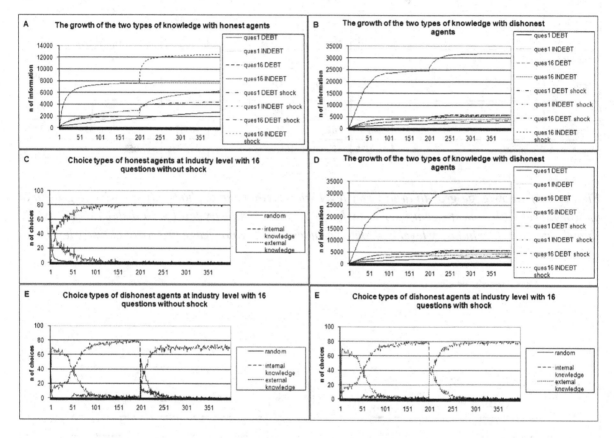

wrong information, false informers, and bad suppliers.

Hence, figures show that the occurrence of shock, the presence of opportunism, and high rationality are all independent causes of knowledge growth. Consequently, when they combine there is the maximum accumulation of knowledge. Accordingly to the hypothesis H2c, the more knowledge is created the lesser should be the profit loss just because of the advantages of knowledge redundancy. Table 3 confirms this hypothesis only for the period of the neutralization time, and therefore with reference to the shock effect. In all other cases the lack of precision and/

or the unreliability of information determine a negative effect on the total cumulated profit.

Of course the more accumulated knowledge is mostly the external one (Figure 7a and b), even though choices are made mostly accordingly to direct experience, that is to internal knowledge (Figure 7c, d, e and f). Regardless of the degree of rationality and agents' honesty, the types of choices are the same depending on the stable or shock regime: at the beginning agents follow informers' indications, and hence external knowledge is more used. However, soon they experience directly the best suppliers, and thus, internal knowledge becomes the reference knowledge.

Figure 8. A) Total cumulated profit per knowledge at industry level; B) Knowledge per informer at industry level; C) Suppliers at industry level; D) Knowledge per supplier at industry level

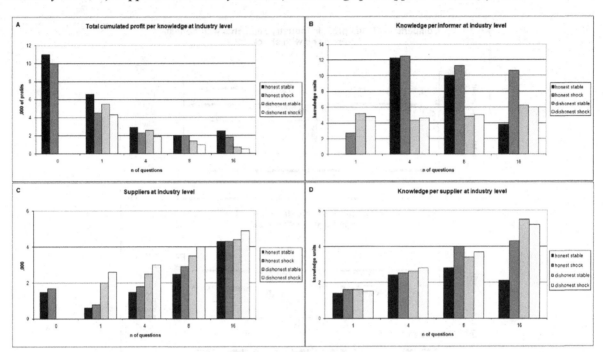

External knowledge is recalled again right after the shock, because agents understand that their memory does not give good indications any more. But then it is replicated the same situation as at the beginning, with internal knowledge rapidly and constantly replacing external knowledge as the source of choices. The difference between a context of opportunism and a context of honest agents is that in presence of false information the process of replacement of choices based on indirect experience with those based in direct experience is longer, especially at the beginning.

The hypothesis 3a suggests that when more questions are asked to competitors, then knowledge efficiency declines. This hypothesis is perfectly confirmed, because total cumulated profit per knowledge unit declines from 11 to 2.2 while giving agents the possibility to ask no questions at all up to 16 questions (Figure 8). Conversely, the hypotheses 3b and 3c should be rejected because, excepted for the case of just one available

question, the configurations in which there is a shock and/or agents are dishonest score systematically lower knowledge efficiency.

Apparently, the lack of precision and reliability of external knowledge prevail on the advantages of having more information. Hence, more and more knowledge is employed to discover false informers and bad suppliers, as it is shown by Figures 10a and b. However, these figures suggest also that, despite the large increase in the amount of informers and suppliers that are known with the additional questions and that are solicited by the environmental shock and informers' falsity, the amount of knowledge employed to know them is less then proportional respect to its increment. In other words, external knowledge is employed efficiently in terms of the exploration of the information and the decision space.

The last group of hypotheses concerns the supposedly different reaction of industry segments to environmental shock. This supposition is fully

Figure 9. A) Comparison of total profit in industry segemtns with honest agents and with shock; B) Comparison of total profit in industry segments with dishonest agents and with shock

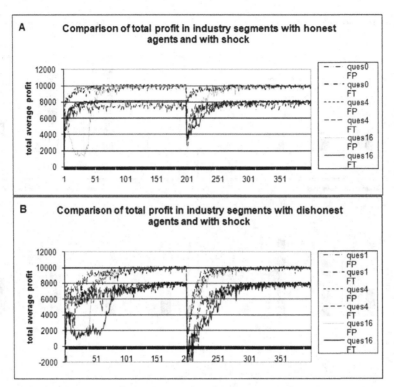

Figure 10. Comparison of knowledge production in industry segments with honest agents with shock; B) Comparison of knowledge production in industry segments with dishonest agents with shock

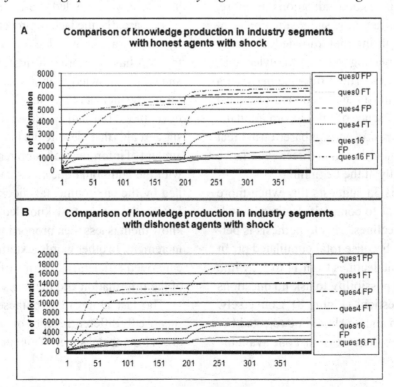

Table 5. Comparison FP-FT in terms of TP, K, and TP/K

	Honest					
	1		4		16	
	FP	FT	FP	FT	FP	FT
mean TP	9648	7500	9829	7753	8713	7685
mean K	2400	1400	5355	2191	5741	3723
TP/K	4.02	5.36	1.84	3.54	1.52	2.06
	Dishonest					
mean TP	9276	6952	8973	6708	8713	5919
mean K	1736	2033	4686	3586	12561	13108
TP/K	5.34	3.42	1.91	1.87	0.69	0.45

confirmed, as it can be seen with the Tables 6-8 in the Appendix and the two following figures. They show that FTs perform systematically worst than FPs, regardless of opportunistic or correct behaviours. The only difference is that with dishonest agents the impact of shock is so hard that FTs record even mean negative profits in absolute values.

The hypothesis H4b suggests that FTs accumulate more knowledge than FPs, because they have to face with a larger information space. The results (Figures 10a and 8, and Table 5) are not clear, and should be distinguished between honest and dishonest agents, and the steps before and after the shock. With dishonest agents and before the shock FTs employ a lower amount of knowledge respect to FPs, but after the break the relationship reverses. The final hypothesis (H4c) states that, thank to knowledge redundancy, FTs can answer to the environmental shock better than FPs. The data of Table 4 indicates that this is true only for the context with honest agents, because knowledge efficiency in terms of profits per knowledge units is higher. However, with dishonest agents there is the opposite result, and thus, the test of this hypothesis is not conclusive.

FUTURE RESEARCH DIRECTIONS

All these results do not contrast with current literature, but indeed they are hardly comparable, because the other studies do not consider the knowledge as a slack resource, and do not suppose any form of opportunism by cheating. And unfortunately this lack of researches concerns both theoretical and empirical studies, as well as simulation models.

This work can be developed in a number of ways by removing its current limitations. Some of them are relatively easy and some more complex to do. Among the former there is the re-configuration of the virtual experiments, because results are sensitive to the length of simulation runs. Since in most experiments industry performance stabilizes far sooner than the 200th step and a stable regime is re-built far sooner than the 400th step, the effects of the environmental shock are not so marked. The best configuration would be that in which the shock is introduced right after the achievement of the stable regime and the simulation is stopped right after its re-establishment.

Moreover, the effects would be much more emphasized if the firms hit by the environmental shock failed and exited out the industry. This way the unsuccessful suppliers could not be chosen again by the clients. Other relatively easy improvements concern the introduction of information and overhead costs, and of initial capital assets. Further, in order to study whether external knowledge redundancy impact differently among different agents, they could be distinguished in groups of honest and dishonest or small vs. large firms. Finally, it could be very interesting to test these same hypotheses with reference to internal knowledge redundancy and to compare the corresponding results with the present ones.

The limitations inherent to the inner structure of the CIOPS model concern its major assumptions: i) agents are all equal in terms of size, cognitive capacity and boundaries, selection devices (decision making patterns and processes); ii) their cheating attitude is invariant; iii) the sole form of product differentiation is between industry segments, that is between raw materials, intermediate goods, and final products; and finally iv) there is no firms' turn over, and therefore failed or inadequately profitable firms do not exit and new ones do not entry.

It is indeed impossible to outline the implications of these assumptions for the possibility to generalize the results here discussed, because complex phenomena hide quite surprising outcomes, which hardly could be intuited without running specific virtual experiments as those realized in this work. At the best, just some conjectures could be raised and offered for future tests. Bearing this warning in mind, here we attempt to draw some of them, at least trying to figure out the direction to which each of these assumptions points out. The invariance of agents' behavior in terms of cheating attitude could help them being very efficient in selecting suppliers, because otherwise their strategies would be subjected to much more uncertainty. Likely, this could keep industry profitability higher than what we found in these experiments. The same holds for the fact that the only form of product differentiation is that between segments, because this simplifies suppliers' selection. On the opposite direction plays the absence of firms' turn over and evolutionary mechanisms, because the permanence of unprofitable firms depresses

industry profitability. However, without making the appropriate experiments it is impossible to confirm these conjectures and neither to say whether these effects compensate each other or how they could combine in some unexpected way. Moreover, removing the assumption of agents' uniformity and introducing a retaliation strategy and a more sophisticated learning process than the one implemented here would likely undermine the stability of dynamic patterns and hinder the achievement of high average profits.

The list of minor assumptions is much longer than that of the major ones, and so we mention just a few of them: i) the technology is only sequential, and so we don't know what could happen whether segments were connected through parallel or reciprocal interdependencies; ii) opportunism is meant only in terms of cheating and not in terms of betraying previous (formal or informal) agreements; iii) information is costless; iv) there are no stocks and no fixed capital goods; v) agents ask only their competitors and not also suppliers or customers; vi) there are no inter-firm alliances; vi) there is no pure gossip, that is (individual) de-responsible information, else than (collective) reputation; vii) agents lie only in relation to information content (true or false, the worst for the best advice) and not to its nature (existing for non-existing) or type (direct for indirect experience or reputation). As evident, it is definitely impossible to draw any kind of conjecture about the possible effects of removing these assumptions. The only way is to methodically run the appropriate virtual experiments, and actually this is the strength and incomparable value of the simulation model methodology, because it would be as well impossible to find enough and clear and methodologically comparable case studies able to understand and isolate the effects of each assumption.

The same problem concerns parameters' setting, because it is well known that a property of complex systems is being sensitive to its (even small) variations. For instance, what could happen whether the reputation threshold or the informers' reliability threshold would change? And what about variations in the aspiration levels, that here have been fixed at 0.75%, or in the forgetfulness time or mix? Here something more precise can be said just concerning the ratio 1/2 between FPs and FTs, and the one-to-one relationship between each pair of supplier-buyer, just because recently CIOPS model was developed in that direction. Biggiero (2010) found that, by varying the ratio of transactions between the suppliers and the buyers –which actually is the key parameter for measuring the competitive balance between the agents of the two segments-, the increase of the number of subcontractors activated by each client impacts very differently on FPs and FTs. The former gain a lot, while the latter lose considerably both in terms of profitability and number of firms. On the contrary, accessing more others' experience by means of asking more informers helps more FTs than FPs. However, in both cases the marginal benefit decreases, and the net effects at industry level strictly depends on the combination of the two factors. Moreover, uncertainty and instability sharply grow because of the consequent higher competitive pressure among a small number of clients respect to that of suppliers.

CONCLUSION

This paper shows that if purchasing quality were a key factor of industry competitiveness, an event that radically changed the distribution of quality among suppliers would significantly hit profitability, and its damage would be much heavier if agents were opportunist. On the other hand, if honest agents exchanged each other much more information about their own previous experience, profit losses would be more limited and the conditions preceding the shock would be sooner re-established. However, if agents were fully dishonest the exchange of false information would not help at all to compensate the uncertainty generated by the environmental shock.

The virtual experiments also demonstrated that in presence of uncertainty due to either environmental shock and agents' opportunism, agents require more information. Further, the more information they can exchange, the more knowledge is accumulated. Thus, under these respects the two forms of uncertainty do not differ. They do, instead, in another aspect: knowledge redundancy is (at least partially) able to limit the damages of environmental perturbations, while it is not effective in facing with opportunism. Therefore, this characteristic is more dangerous for industry profitability, and ultimately for industry competitiveness.

Another interesting finding is that knowledge efficiency declines with redundancy, but less than proportionally to the increase of information exchange. Moreover, first tiers perform systematically worst than final producers, regardless of opportunistic or correct behaviours. They require different amounts of knowledge either before or after the environmental shock.

REFERENCES

Ahire, S. L., Golhar, D. Y., & Waller, M. A. (1996). Development and validation of TQM implementation constructs. *Decision Sciences*, *27*, 23–56. doi:10.1111/j.1540-5915.1996.tb00842.x

Akerlof, G. A. (1970). The Market for 'Lemons': Quality Uncertainty and the Market Mechanism. *The Quarterly Journal of Economics*, *84*(3), 488–500. doi:10.2307/1879431

Amin, A., & Cohendet, P. (2004). *Architectures of knowledge: firms, capabilities, and communities.* Oxford, UK: Oxford UP.

Anderson, J. C., Rungtusanatham, M., Schroeder, M. G., & Devaraj, S. (1995). A path analytic model of a theory of quality management underlying the Deming management method: preliminary empirical findings. *Decision Sciences*, *26*, 637–658. doi:10.1111/j.1540-5915.1995.tb01444.x

Bessant, J., Levy, P., Sang, B., & Lamming, R. (1994). Managing successful total quality relationships in the supply chain. *European Journal of Purchasing and Supply Management, 1*, 7–17. doi:10.1016/0969-7012(94)90038-8

Biggiero, L. (2001). Sources of complexity in human systems. *Nonlinear Dynamics and Chaos in Life Sciences, 5*, 3–19. doi:10.1023/A:1009515211632

Biggiero, L. (2010). Exploration modes and its impact on industry profitability. The differentiated effects of internal and external ways to access market knowledge. In Faggini, M., & Vinci, P. (Eds.), *Decision theory and choice: a complexity approach*. Berlin: Springer.

Biggiero, L., & Sevi, E. (2009). Opportunism by cheating and its effects on industry profitability. *Computational & Mathematical Organization Theory, 15*, 191–236. doi:10.1007/s10588-009-9057-3

Bourgeois, L. J. (1981). On the Measurement of Organizational Slack. *Academy of Management Review, 6*(1), 29–39. doi:10.2307/257138

Bourgeois, L. J., & Singh J. V. (1983). Organizational Slack and Political Behavior Among Top Management Teams. *Academy of Management Proceedings*. 43-47.

Carter, J. R., & Narsimhan R. (1994). The role of purchasing and material management in total quality management and customer satisfaction. *International Journal of Purchasing ad Material Management, 32*, 2-12.

Child, J. (2001). Trust: the fundamental bond in global collaboration. *Organizational Dynamics, 29*(4), 274–288. doi:10.1016/S0090-2616(01)00033-X

Conner, K. R. (1991). A historical comparison of resource-based theory and five schools of thought within industrial organization economics: do we have a new theory of the firm? *Journal of Management, 17*(1), 121–154. doi:10.1177/014920639101700109

Conner, K. R., & Prahalad, C. K. (1996). A resource-based theory of the firm: knowledge versus opportunism. *Organization Science, 7*(5), 477–501. doi:10.1287/orsc.7.5.477

Corso, M., & Pellegrini, L. (2007). Continuous and discontinuous innovation: overcoming the innovator dilemma. *Creativity and Innovation Management, 16*, 333–347. doi:10.1111/j.1467-8691.2007.00459.x

Cyert, R., & March, J. G. (1963). *A behavioral theory of the firm*. Englewood Cliffs, NJ: Prentice Hall.

Damanpour, F. (1991). Organizational innovation: a meta-analysis of the effects of determinants and moderators. *Academy of Management Journal, 14*(3), 555–590. doi:10.2307/256406

Deming, W. E. (1986). *Out of the crisis*. Cambridge, MA: MIT Press.

Fiol, C. M. (2002). Intraorganizational cognition and interpretation. In Baum, J. A. C. (Ed.), *Companion to organizations* (pp. 119–137). Oxford, UK: Blackwell.

Flynn, B. F., Schroeder, R. G., & Sakakibara, S. (1995). The impact of quality management practices on performance and competitive advantage. *Decision Sciences, 26*, 659–691. doi:10.1111/j.1540-5915.1995.tb01445.x

Gambetta, D. (Ed.). (1988). *Trust: making and breaking co-operative relations*. Oxford, UK: Blackwell.

Geiger, S. W., & Cashen, L. H. (2002). A Multidimensional Examination of Slack and its Impact on Innovation. *Journal of Managerial Issues*, *15*(1), 68–84.

Geiger, S. W., & Makri, M. (2006). Exploration and exploitation innovation processes: The role of organizational slack in R&D intensive firms. *The Journal of High Technology Management Research*, *17*, 97–108. doi:10.1016/j.hitech.2006.05.007

George, G. (2005). *Slack resources and the performance of privately held firms*. Academy of Management Journal.

Gonzales-Benito, J., Martinez-Lorente, A. R., & Dale, B. G. (2003). A study of the purchasing management system with respect to total quality management. *Industrial Marketing Management, 32*, 443–454. doi:10.1016/S0019-8501(02)00231-6

Hall, R. (1992). The strategic analysis of intangible resources. *Strategic Management Journal, 13*(2), 135–144. doi:10.1002/smj.4250130205

Hambrick, D. C., & Snow, C. C. (1977). *A Contextual Model of Strategic Decision Making in Organizations* (pp. 109–112). Academy of Management Proceedings.

Hannan, M. T., & Carroll, G. R. (1992). *Dynamics of organizational populations*. Oxford, UK: Oxford UP.

Humphrey, J. (1998). Trust and the transformation of supplier relations in Indian industry. In Lane, C., & Bachmann, R. (Eds.), *Trust within and between organizations* (pp. 214–240). Oxford: Oxford UP.

Ishikawa, K. (1985). *What is total quality control? The Japanese way*. Upper Saddle River, NJ: Prentice-Hall.

Jensen, M. C. (1993). The Modern Industrial Revolution, Exit, and the Failure of Internal Control Systems. *The Journal of Finance, 48*(3), 831–880. doi:10.2307/2329018

Jensen, M. C., & Meckling, W. (1976). Theory of the firm: managerial behavior, agency costs and ownership structure. *Journal of Financial Economics, 3*, 305–360. doi:10.1016/0304-405X(76)90026-X

Juran, J. M., & Blanton Godfrey, A. (2000). *Juran's Quality Handbook*. New York: McGraw-Hill Professional.

Kekre, S., Murthi, B. P. S., & Srinivasan, K. (1995). Operating decisions, supplier availability and quality: an empirical study. *Journal of Operations Management, 12*, 387–396. doi:10.1016/0272-6963(95)00002-A

Kogut, B., & Zander, U. (1992). Knowledge of the firm, combinative capabilities and the replication of technology. *Organization Science, 3*, 383–397. doi:10.1287/orsc.3.3.383

Kogut, B., & Zander, U. (1996). What firms do? Coordination, identity, and learning. *Organization Science, 7*(5), 502–518. doi:10.1287/orsc.7.5.502

Krafcik, J. F. (1988). Triumph of the lean production system. *Sloan Management Review, 30*, 41–52.

Kramer, R. M., & Tyler, T. R. (Eds.). (1996). *Trust in organizations: frontiers of theory and research*. London: Sage.

Lane, C. (1995). The social constitution of supplier relations in Britain and Germany. In Withley, R., & Kristensen, P. H. (Eds.), *The changing European firm* (pp. 271–304). London: Routledge.

Lane, C. (2001). Organizational learning in supplier networks. In Dierkes, M., Antal, A. B., Child, J., & Nonaka, I. (Eds.), *Handbook of organizational learning and knowledge* (pp. 699–715). Oxford: Oxford UP.

Lane, C., & Bachmann, R. (1996). The social constitution of trust: supplier relations in Britain and Germany. *Organization Studies, 17*(3), 365–395. doi:10.1177/017084069601700302

Lane, C., & Bachmann, R. (Eds.). (1998). *Trust within and between organizations*. Oxford, UK: Oxford UP.

Lant, T. K. (2002). Organizational cognition and interpretation. In Baum, J. A. C. (Ed.), *Companion to organizations* (pp. 344–362). Oxford: Blackwell.

Lascelles, D. M., & Dale, B. G. (1989). The buyer-supplier relationship in total quality management. *Journal of Purchasing Material Management, 25*, 10–19.

Lawson, M. B. (2001). In praise of slack: time is the essence. *The Academy of Management Executive, 15*(3), 125–135.

Leibenstein, H. (1966). Allocative Efficiency vs. "X-Efficiency. *The American Economic Review, 56*(3), 392–416.

Leibenstein, H. (1987). *Inside the firm: the inefficiencies of hierarchy*. Cambridge, MA: Harvard UP.

Levinthal, D., & March, J. G. (1993). The myopia of learning. *Strategic Management Journal, 14*, 95–112. doi:10.1002/smj.4250141009

Li, Y., Vanhaverbeke, W., & Schoenmakers, W. (2008). Exploration and exploitation in innovation: reframing the interpretation. *Creativity and Innovation Management, 17*(2), 107–126. doi:10.1111/j.1467-8691.2008.00477.x

Love, G. E., & Nohria, N. (2005). Reducing Slack: The Performance Consequences of Downsizing by Large Industrial Firms, 1977-93. *Strategic Management Journal, 26*(12), 1087–1108. doi:10.1002/smj.487

March, J. G. (1988). *Decisions and organizations*. Oxford, UK: Basil Blackwell.

March, J. G. (1991). Exploration and Exploitation in organizational learning. *Organization Science, 2*, 71–87. doi:10.1287/orsc.2.1.71

March, J. G. (1997). Understanding How Decisions Happens in Organizations. In Shapira, Z. (Ed.), *Organizational Decision Making* (pp. 9–34). Cambridge, MA: Cambridge UP.

Martinez-Lorente, A. R., Galliego-Rodriguez, A., & Dale, B. G. (1998). Total quality management and company characteristics: an examination. *Quality Management Journal, 5*, 59–71.

Mas-Colell, A., Whinston, M. D., & Green, J. R. (1995). *Microeconomic Theory*. New York: Oxford University Press.

Meyer, A. D. (1982). Adapting to environmental jolts. *Administrative Science Quarterly, 27*(4), 515–537. doi:10.2307/2392528

Narasimhan, R., & Mendez, D. (2001). Strategic aspects of quality: a theoretical analysis. *Production and Operations Management, 10*, 514–526.

Nohria, N., & Gulati, R. (1997). What is the Optimum Amount of Organizational Slack? A Study of the Relationship between Slack and Innovation in Multinational Firms. *European Management Journal, 15*(6), 603–611. doi:10.1016/S0263-2373(97)00044-3

Nonaka, I., & Nishiguchi, T. (Eds.). (2001). *Knowledge emergence: social, technical, and evolutionary dimensions of knowledge creation*. Oxford, UK: Oxford UP.

Nonaka, I., & Takeuchi, H. (1995). *The Knowledge-creating company*. New York: Oxford UP.

Ohno, T. (1988). *Toyota production system: beyond large-scale production*. New York: Productivity Press.

Richtner, A., & Åhlström, P. (2006). Influences on organizational slack in new product development. *International Journal of Innovation Management, 10*(4), 375–406. doi:10.1142/S1363919606001570

Roy, R. V., & Guin, K. K. (1999). A 'proposed model of JIT purchasing in an integrated steel plant. *International Journal of Production Economics*, *59*, 179–187. doi:10.1016/S0925-5273(98)00099-1

Shapiro, C., & Varian, H. (1999). *Information rules: a strategic guide to the network economy*. Boston: Harvard Business School Press.

Sharfman, M. P., Wolf, G., Chase, R. B., & Tansik, D. A. (1988). Antecedents of Organizational Slack. *Academy of Management Review*, *13*(4), 601–614. doi:10.2307/258378

Simon, H. A. (1982). Models of Bounded Rationality: *Vol. 1. 2: Empirically Grounded Economic Reason*. Cambridge, MA: The MIT Press.

Simon, H. A. (1991). Bounded rationality and organizational learning. *Organization Science*, *2*(1), 125–134. doi:10.1287/orsc.2.1.125

Simon, H. A. (1997). Models of Bounded Rationality: *Vol. 3. Empirically Grounded Economic Reason*. Cambridge, MA: The MIT Press.

Singh, J. V. (1986). Performance, Slack, and Risk Taking in Organizational Decision Making. *Academy of Management Journal*, *29*(3), 562–565. doi:10.2307/256224

Stigler, G. J. (1961). The Economics of Information. *The Journal of Political Economy*, *69*(3), 213–225. doi:10.1086/258464

Tan, J. (2003). Curvilinear relationship between organizational slack and firm performance: evidence from Chinese state enterprise. *European Management Journal*, *21*(6), 740–749. doi:10.1016/j.emj.2003.09.010

Tan, J., & Peng, M. W. (2003). Organizational slack and firm performance during economic transition: two studies from and emerging economy. *Strategic Management Journal*, *24*(13), 1249–1263. doi:10.1002/smj.351

Thompson, J. D. (1967). *Organizations in action*. New York: McGraw Hill.

Tsoukas, H. (1996). The firm as a distributed knowledge system: a constructionist approach. *Strategic Management Journal*, *17*, 11–25.

Tsoukas, H. (2005). *Complex knowledge. Studies in organizational epistemology*. Oxford, UK: Oxford UP.

Van der Stede, W. A. (2000). The relationship between two consequences of budgetary controls: budgetary slack creation and managerial short-term orientation. *Accounting, Organizations and Society*, *25*, 609–622. doi:10.1016/S0361-3682(99)00058-6

Von Krogh, G., & Roos, J. (Eds.). (1996). *Managing knowledge. Perspectives on cooperation and competition*. London: Sage.

Von Krogh, G., Roos, J., & Kline, D. (Eds.). (1998). *Knowing in firms: understanding, managing and measuring knowledge*. London: Sage.

Weick, K. E. (1995). *Sensemaking in organizations*. London: Sage.

Williamson, O. E. (1974). *The economics of discretionary behaviour. Managerial objectives in a theory of the firm*. London: Kershaw Publ. Comp.

Williamson, O. E. (1975). *Markets and hierarchy: analysis and antitrust implications*. New York: The Free Press.

Williamson, O. E. (1981). The Economics of Organization: The Transaction Costs Approach. *American Journal of Sociology*, *87*, 548–577. doi:10.1086/227496

Williamson, O. E. (1985). *The economic institutions of capitalism*. New York: The Free Press.

Williamson, O. E. (1994). Transaction cost economics and organization theory. In Smelser, N. J., & Swedberg, R. (Eds.), *The handbook of economic sociology* (pp. 77–107). Princeton, NJ: Princeton UP.

Williamson, O. E. (1996). *The Mechanisms of Governance*. New York: Oxford UP.

Womack, J. P., Jones, D. T., & Roos, D. (1990). *The machine that changed the world: the triumph of lean production*. New York: Macmillan.

Yolles, M. (2006). *Organizations as Complex Systems. An Introduction to Knowledge Cybernetics*. Greenwich, CT: IAP.

ENDNOTES

[1] Indeed, likely they would need not just 80 steps as the number of suppliers, because sometimes it will happen that the contacted supplier were already engaged with another client, and thus, be unavailable.

[2] Let's note that agents' levels of aspiration for purchases quality is set up at 0.75 and that suppliers' quality is randomly uniformly distributed between 0.5 and 1 (see next two sections).

[3] Actually, they also don't know how quality is distributed among suppliers and neither if quality keeps constant.

[4] For different scientific purposes the former condition is made varying in Biggiero and Sevi (2009), while the latter in Biggiero (2010).

[5] Of course, the RND DMP concerns only the RND decision making process.

[6] The program running the model will be available on the URL of Knownetlab Research Center (www.knownetlab.it). To run the program is needed the platform and language LSD (Laboratory on Simulation Development), placed at www.business.auc.dk/lsd.

[7] The maximum average profit is 0.88, which is he middle value between 0.75 and 100%. It depends on the distribution of suppliers quality between 0.5 and 100%, on agents' aspiration level of 0.75 and on the ratio between the number of clients and suppliers, which is 1 to 2. For more details, see Biggiero and Sevi (2009).

APPENDIX

Table 6. Reactions at industry level

Questions	Honest agents														
	0			1			4			8			16		
Regime	Sta	Sho	Var. (%)	Sta	Sho	Var. (%)	Sta	Sho	Var. (%)	Sta	Sho	Var. (%)	Sta	Sho	Var. (%)
AQ	0,87	0,86	-1,1	0,87	0,87	0,0	0,87	0,87	0,0	0,87	0,87	0,0	0,88	0,87	-1,1
TP	17,2	17,0	-1,2	17,7	17,2	-2,8	18,0	17,6	-2,2	18,0	17,5	-2,8	18,1	17,6	-2,8
Choice	32,0	32,0	0,0	32,0	32,0	0,0	32,0	32,0	0,0	32,0	32,0	0,0	32,0	32,0	0,0
RND	2,4	2,5	4,2	1,2	1,5	25,0	0,5	0,7	40,0	0,5	0,7	40,0	0,4	0,5	25,0
Debt	29,6	29,5	-0,3	29,9	28,8	-3,7	29,9	28,7	-4,0	29,8	28,6	-4,0	30,0	28,7	-4,3
Indebt				0,9	1,7	88,9	1,6	2,6	62,5	1,7	2,7	58,8	1,6	2,8	75,0
Know	1,5	1,7	13,3	2,7	3,8	40,7	6,1	7,5	23,0	9,0	8,9	-1,1	7,2	9,5	31,9
Debt	1,5	1,7	13,3	1,6	2,1	31,3	1,9	2,5	31,6	2,0	2,9	45,0	1,8	2,9	61,1
Indebt				1,1	1,7	54,5	4,2	5,0	19,0	7,0	6,0	-14,3	5,4	6,6	22,2
TP/K	11,5	10,0	-12,8	6,6	4,5	-31,0	3,0	2,3	-20,5	2,0	2,0	-1,7	2,5	1,9	-26,3
Informers				1,4			0,5	0,6	20,0	0,9	1,2	33,3	1,9	2,5	31,6
Suppliers	1,5	1,7	13,3	1,9	2,4	26,3	2,5	3,0	20,0	3,2	3,8	18,8	3,4	4,2	23,5
K/Informers				2,7			12,2	12,5	2,5	10,0	11,2	12,0	3,8	10,6	178,5
K/Suppliers	1,0	1,0	0,0	1,4	1,6	11,4	2,4	2,5	2,5	2,8	4,0	42,2	2,1	4,3	103,9
Questions	Dishonest agents														
				1			4			8			16		
Regime				Sta	Sho	Var. (%)	Sta	Sho	Var. (%)	Sta	Sho	Var. (%)	Sta	Sho	Var. (%)
AQ				0,87	0,86	-1,1	0,86	0,85	-1,2	0,86	0,85	-1,2	0,85	0,84	-1,2
TP				17,1	16,2	-5,3	16,8	15,7	-6,5	16,5	15,3	-7,3	16,0	14,6	-8,8
Choice				32,0	32,0	0,0	32,0	32,0	0,0	32,0	32,0	0,0	32,0	32,0	0,0
RND				1,9	2,0	5,3	1,2	1,2	0,0	1,0	0,9	-10,0	0,7	0,7	0,0
Debt				29,3	28,8	-1,7	29,2	28,1	-3,8	28,3	27,2	-3,9	27,5	26,4	-4,0
Indebt				0,8	1,2	50,0	1,6	2,7	68,8	2,7	3,9	44,4	3,8	4,9	28,9
Know				3,1	3,8	22,6	6,5	8,3	27,7	11,9	14,6	22,7	24,3	25,7	5,8
Debt				1,9	2,1	10,5	2,3	2,8	21,7	3,1	3,6	16,1	3,9	4,5	15,4
Indebt				1,2	1,7	41,7	4,2	5,5	31,0	8,8	10,9	23,9	18,5	21,2	14,6
TP/K				5,5	4,3	-22,7	2,6	1,9	-26,8	1,4	1,0	-24,4	0,7	0,6	-13,7
Informers				0,6	0,8	33,3	1,5	1,8	20,0	2,5	2,9	16,0	3,9	4,3	10,3
Suppliers				2,0	2,6	30,0	2,5	3,0	20,0	3,5	4,0	14,3	4,4	4,9	11,4
K/Informers				5,2	4,8	-8,1	4,3	4,6	6,4	4,8	5,0	5,8	6,2	6,0	-4,1
K/Suppliers				1,6	1,5	-5,7	2,6	2,8	6,4	3,4	3,7	7,4	5,5	5,2	-5,0

Table 7. Reactions of final producers

	Honest agents														
Questions	0			1			4			8			16		
Regime	Sta	Sho	Var.(%)	Sta	Sho	Var.(%)	Sta	Sho	Va.(%)	Sta	Sho	Va.(%)	Sta	Sho	Va.(%)
AQ	0,87	0,87	0,0	0,87	0,87	0,0	0,87	0,87	0,2	0,87	0,87	0,0	0,88	0,87	-1,1
TP	9,7	9,6	-1,0	9,9	9,7	-2,0	10,0	9,8	-2,0	10,0	9,8	-2,0	10,1	9,9	-2,0
Choice	16,0	16,0	0,0	16,0	16,0	0,0	16,0	16,0	0,0	16,0	16,0	0,0	16,0	16,0	0,0
RND	1,1	1,2	9,1	0,5	0,5	0,0	0,2	0,4	100,0	0,2	0,4	100,0	0,2	0,3	50,0
Debt	14,9	14,8	-0,7	14,7	14,2	-3,4	14,4	14,0	-2,8	14,4	14,1	-2,1	14,4	14,2	-1,4
Indebt				0,8	1,3	62,5	1,4	1,6	14,3	1,4	1,5	7,1	1,4	1,5	7,1
Know	0,7	0,7	0,0	1,7	2,4	41,2	5,0	5,3	6,0	5,4	5,8	7,4	5,1	5,7	11,8
Debt	0,7	0,7	0,0	1,0	1,2	20,0	1,4	1,6	14,3	1,5	1,8	20,0	1,4	1,7	21,4
Indebt				0,7	1,2	71,4	3,6	3,7	2,8	3,9	4,0	2,6	3,7	4,0	8,1
TP/K	13,9	13,7	-1,0	5,8	4,0	-30,6	2,0	1,8	-7,5	1,9	1,7	-8,8	2,0	1,7	-12,3
Informers				0,1			0,2	0,2	0,0	0,3	0,4	33,3	0,6	0,7	16,7
Suppliers	0,7	0,7	0,0	1,1	1,3	18,2	1,7	1,8	5,9	2,0	2,0	0,0	2,0	2,0	0,0
K/Informers						17,1	7,0	8,0	14,3	5,0	4,5	-10,0	2,3	2,4	4,1
K/Suppliers	1,0	1,0	0,0	0,9	0,9	1,5	0,8	0,9	7,9	0,8	0,9	20,0	0,7	0,9	21,4

	Dishonest agents														
Questions				1			4			8			16		
Regime				Sta	Sho	Var.(%)	Sta	Sho	Var.(%)	Sta	Sho	Va.(%)	Sta	Sho	Va.(%)
AQ				0,87	0,86	-1,1	0,86	0,85	-1,2	0,86	0,85	-1,2	0,86	0,85	-1,2
TP				9,6	9,3	-3,1	9,4	9,0	-4,3	9,2	8,8	-4,3	9,1	8,7	-4,4
Choice				16,0	16,0	0,0	16,0	16,0	0,0	16,0	16,0	0,0	16,0	16,0	0,0
RND				0,9	0,9	0,0	0,4	0,4	0,0	0,5	0,4	-20,0	0,4	0,4	0,0
Debt				14,7	14,6	-0,7	14,5	14,3	-1,4	14,1	13,9	-1,4	13,7	13,7	0,0
Indebt				0,4	0,5	25,0	1,1	1,3	18,2	1,4	1,7	21,4	1,9	1,9	0,0
Know				1,5	1,7	13,3	4,2	4,7	11,9	6,9	7,6	10,1	12,5	12,5	0,0
Debt				0,9	0,9	0,0	1,3	1,4	7,7	1,6	1,7	6,2	2,0	2,0	0,0
Indebt				0,6	0,8	33,3	2,9	3,3	13,8	5,3	5,9	11,3	10,1	10,5	4,0
TP/K				6,4	5,5	-14,5	2,2	1,9	-14,4	1,3	1,2	-13,2	0,7	0,7	-4,4
Informers				0,3	0,3	0,0	0,8	0,9	12,5	1,1	1,2	9,1	1,5	1,5	0,0
Suppliers				0,9	1,0	11,1	1,3	1,4	7,7	1,7	1,8	5,9	2,1	2,1	0,0
K/Informers				3,0	3,0	0,0	1,6	1,6	-4,3	1,5	1,4	-2,6	1,3	1,3	0,0
K/Suppliers				1,0	0,9	-10,0	1,0	1,0	0,0	0,9	0,9	0,3	1,0	1,0	0,0

Table 8. Reactions of first tiers

	Honest agents														
Questions	**0**			**1**			**4**			**8**			**16**		
Regime	Sta	Sho	Var. (%)	Sta	Sho	Var. (%)	Sta	Sho	Va. (%)	Sta	Sho	Va. (%)	Sta	Sho	Va. (%)
AQ	0,86	0,86	0,0	0,87	0,87	0,0	0,87	0,87	0,0	0,87	0,87	0,0	0,88	0,87	-1,1
TP	7,5	7,4	-1,3	7,9	7,5	-5,1	8,0	7,6	-5,0	8,0	7,7	-3,8	8,0	7,7	-3,8
Choice	16,0	16,0	0,0	16,0	16,0	0,0	16,0	16,0	0,0	16,0	16,0	0,0	16,0	16,0	0,0
RND	1,3	1,7	30,8	0,7	0,9	28,6	0,3	0,3	0,0	0,3	0,3	0,0	0,2	0,2	0,0
Debt	14,7	14,3	-2,7	15,1	14,7	-2,6	15,5	14,7	-5,2	15,4	14,5	-5,8	15,5	14,5	-6,5
Indebt				0,2	0,4	100,0	0,2	1,0	400,0	0,3	1,2	300,0	0,3	1,3	333,3
Know	0,8	1,0	25,0	1,0	1,4	40,0	1,0	2,2	120,0	1,6	3,1	93,8	2,1	3,7	76,2
Debt	0,8	1,0	25,0	0,7	0,9	28,6	0,4	0,9	125,0	0,5	1,2	140,0	0,4	1,2	200,0
Indebt				0,3	1,5	400,0	0,6	1,3	116,7	1,1	1,9	72,7	1,7	2,5	47,1
TP/K	9,4	7,4	-21,1	7,9	5,4	-32,2	8,0	3,5	-56,8	5,0	2,5	-50,3	3,8	2,1	-45,4
Informers				0,0	0,1		0,3	0,4	33,3	0,6	0,8	33,3	1,3	1,5	15,4
Suppliers	0,8	1,0	25,0	0,8	1,0	25,0	0,8	1,3	62,5	1,2	1,7	41,7	1,5	2,1	40,0
K/Informers					12,9		1,3	2,3	68,8	0,8	1,5	80,0	0,3	0,8	160,0
K/Suppliers	1,0	1,0	0,0	0,9	0,9	2,9	0,5	0,7	38,5	0,4	0,7	69,4	0,3	0,6	114,3
	Dishonest agents														
Questions				**1**			**4**			**8**			**16**		
Regime				Sta	Sho	Var. (%)	Sta	Sho	Var. (%)	Sta	Sho	Va. (%)	Sta	Sho	Va. (%)
AQ				0,86	0,85	-1,2	0,86	0,85	-1,2	0,87	0,84	-3,4	0,85	0,83	-2,4
TP				7,5	6,9	-8,0	7,5	6,7	-10,7	7,3	6,5	-11,0	6,8	5,9	-13,2
Choice				16,0	16,0	0,0	16,0	16,0	0,0	16,0	16,0	0,0	16,0	16,0	0,0
RND				1,0	1,1	10,0	0,8	0,7	-12,5	0,5	0,4	-20,0	0,3	0,2	-33,3
Debt				14,6	14,2	-2,7	14,6	13,9	-4,8	14,3	13,4	-6,3	13,7	12,9	-5,8
Indebt				0,4	0,7	75,0	0,6	1,4	133,3	1,2	2,2	83,3	2,0	2,9	45,0
Know				1,6	2,0	25,0	2,3	3,6	56,5	5,6	7,0	25,0	11,8	13,1	11,0
Debt				1,0	1,2	20,0	1,0	1,4	40,0	1,4	1,9	35,7	1,9	2,4	26,3
Indebt				0,6	1,8	200,0	1,3	2,2	69,2	3,6	5,1	41,7	8,4	10,7	27,4
TP/K				4,7	3,5	-26,4	3,3	1,9	-42,9	1,3	0,9	-28,8	0,6	0,5	-21,8
Informers				0,3	0,4	33,3	0,7	1,0	42,9	1,4	1,7	21,4	2,7	2,4	-11,1
Suppliers				1,1	1,3	18,2	1,2	1,6	33,3	1,8	2,1	16,7	2,7	2,4	-11,1
K/Informers				3,3	3,0	-10,0	1,4	1,4	-2,0	1,0	1,1	11,8	0,7	1,0	42,1
K/Suppliers				0,9	0,9	1,5	0,8	0,9	5,0	0,8	0,9	16,3	0,7	1,0	42,1

Section 3
Decision Making

Chapter 14
Perspectives of Multivariable Fuzzy Control

Pedro Albertos
Universidad Politécnica de Valencia, Spain

Antonio Sala
Universidad Politécnica de Valencia, Spain

Mercedes Ramírez
Universidad de Oriente, Cuba

ABSTRACT

In this work, the situation and trends in the application of fuzzy logic control to multivariable systems are analyzed. The basic steps in designing a control system are considered. The discussion is carried out first on heuristic and reasoning approaches and, later, on function-approximation fuzzy paradigms. In both cases, apart from general considerations, some specific issues arising when considering multivariable setups are considered.

INTRODUCTION

The situation and trends in the application of fuzzy logic to control multi-input/multi-output (MIMO) systems are analyzed. The basic steps in designing a control system are considered. Fuzzy control applications are either knowledge-based or model-based.

In model-based approaches, the first step is process modeling: Usually, interpolation and universal approximation are the two main features to be used in fuzzy MIMO systems in order to obtain a fuzzy function approximator which represents

the controlled plant to a desired accuracy. For instance, the well known Takagi-Sugeno (T-S) model of the plant can be obtained. This leads to an integrated model which incorporates one "local behavior" in each fuzzy rule.

Another alternative is following a reasoning approach. In this case, a MIMO plant is treated as a whole, with as many variables as required, leading to a complex set of rules and knowledge. In this case, also an integral model of the plant is obtained.

The structure of the plant can be captured if the modeling approach deals with single input-output relationships and interactions among individual variables. In this case, a particular model can be

DOI: 10.4018/978-1-61692-811-7.ch014

attached to any single relationship, being fuzzy or not. In many cases, if a suitable structural decomposition is found for a complex plant, control becomes much easier both in fuzzy and conventional approaches.

To design the control two main approaches can be considered:

(a) The mimicking approach, trying to implement the control as explained by the experts. In this case, the MIMO structure implies a complex reasoning process with multiple antecedents and, probably, disconnected output requirements. In the same direction, the fuzzy approximation of standard MIMO control laws can be considered;

(b) Alternatively, a model based control design can be considered. For integrated models, like the T-S or global models, some recent (but now standard) control design techniques can be used: Lyapunov, LMIs,...

Another alternative is the combination of classical control laws with fuzzy interpolation and refinement. This can be used for MIMO plants with multiple operational modes as well as those with well defined single-loop controls. Fuzzy techniques allow the smooth interpolation in the transfer between operational modes and to cope with uncertain interactions, leaving the "hard" control to standard controllers. Obviously, these controllers can be also approximated by fuzzy controllers if a unique fuzzy control environment is foreseen.

In the rest of the chapter, the available techniques are reviewed, keeping in mind the specific features of MIMO systems.

The chapter structure can be outlined as follows: next section provides some background, definitions and characteristics of intelligent and, particularly, fuzzy approaches to process control. Also, issues arising in an integral plant-wide control project and where fuzzy systems may be helpful are discussed. The main focus of the chapter is split into the four next sections. First, the basic ideas behind reasoning approaches to fuzzy control (direct model-free controllers and fuzzy expert systems) are reported and a case study of a heuristic approach to control a reduction furnace is outlined. Next, an account of the function-approximation approach to fuzzy modeling and control and some universal approximation ideas are discussed. Then, the popular Takagi-Sugeno approach to model nonlinear systems, including the recently proposed fuzzy polynomial systems, is presented. Last, control design techniques for this class of systems are briefly outlined, pointing out controversies and problems. All these problems and advantages, as well as future research directions are summarized in the next section. Finally, some concluding remarks close the chapter.

BACKGROUND

Given a plant and a general knowledge about its operation, and some goals and constraints, a control problem can be defined, in the more general setting, as how to design and tune the control subsystem to be connected to the plant in such a way that the whole system achieves the goals without violating the constraints. Within this general framework, a control problem can be formulated as the regulation or tracking of some signals, the monitoring and supervision of the controlled plant operation, the optimization of some criteria, to guarantee the operation under faulty conditions or with many other different objectives.

In control research, the statement of the control problem is frequently limited to a particular issue, assuming the perfect operation of the rest of activities. For instance, to compute an optimal control, abnormal disturbances or failures, the start-up, as well as the shutting down of the plant are not considered. Also, the goals and constraints are assumed to be well defined. Under those not-too-realistic settings, specific techniques have been developed to obtain the best solutions under some set of assumptions (optimal, robust, adaptive, etc.).

However, solutions in practice do not meet all the assumptions. They usually need the integration of control structures acting under different conditions, each one being implemented using a different approach or problem-solving paradigm. A key issue is the ambiguousness prevalent in many practical control problems, when compared with the precision of the assumptions in theoretical ones.

Ambiguousness. In control engineering, two fundamental sources of ambiguousness have to be tackled:

- *Plant model ambiguousness*: as a consequence of noise, time variability, nonlinearity and lack of knowledge about process details, in most practical cases only an intuitive model of the plant to be controlled is available, approximately describing *low-order* dynamics, in long time scales.

- *Control specification ambiguousness*: the "cost index" (control specifications) to be optimized, directly related to final quality and production cost, is often expressed in a qualitative, vague form. In practice, experience and "intelligence" of human operators are used to compute *setpoints* for the actual, hierarchically subordinate, regulators. Hence, there might be no noticeable final quality improvement by enhancing the performance capabilities of the low-level regulators if the setpoints from a supervisory system are suboptimal.

Intelligent control. Other than well-established solutions based on the classical control theory, artificial intelligence techniques are also becoming a common practice to develop control systems for local and global control, adaptation, learning, supervision and coordination, optimization, planning and even system management.

For the last thirty years, several new techniques have come out trying to endow controllers with facilities so far considered as belonging to the human domain. Learning, symbolic reasoning and pattern recognition are the most representative. Most of these techniques come from the *Artificial Intelligence* (AI) field, opening the so-called *Intelligent Control* research line, where fuzzy, neural, expert-systems, genetic *etc.* techniques have been tried (Gupta & Sinha, 1996).

The use of these methodologies also reaches the lower levels due to the need of controlling systems with increasing complexity. Basically, in process control one can find three main causes for difficulties: inherent complexity of the system, nonlinearities and uncertainty. To design systems with a high degree of autonomy the traditional concept of control should be enlarged so as to include features such as decision-making, plan generation, learning, etc.

The fuzzy approach. In this chapter the current situation and perspectives of the fuzzy control design approach (Zadeh, 1965) are discussed. In fact, there have been passionate discussions on whether it is better or worse than other approaches (The well-known plenary by M. Athans debating Zadeh's positions in IEEE-CDC'98 is an example).

There are two main lines in which fuzzy systems are used in control: those based on a so-called "reasoning" paradigm and the "universal function approximator" (UFA) one. The main issue is regarding fuzzy systems either as *conceptual* or *numeric* processors. On the one hand, the conceptual (logic) processing is more important in diagnosis and supervision modules, and on the other, the numeric framework allows obtaining stability results, linear parameterizations, etc. In fact, contributions in the fuzzy area stemmed from the first approach in the early days but, nowadays, most results are dominated by the numeric one, in such a way that some (or most) of the initial spirit of "computing with words" has been lost.

The Integral Control Problem

The control design problem can be stated at local, supervisory or even plant-wide level.

Local control. Dealing with process measurements and generating the control actions directly connected to the related process variables.

Supervisory control. Updating the control structures and parameters, to adapt to changing operating conditions.

Plant-wide control. Coordinating and defining the control goals of each process, usually to optimise the global behavior of a complex plant.

If we consider the local level, the usual steps in designing the control are:

1. Define which are the components of the process to be controlled, which equipment parts are manipulable and which are fixed. Also define which are the variables of interest.
2. Define the user control goals.
3. Get a draft model of the process and the attached signals.
4. Select which will be the manipulated and measured variables.
5. Choose a suitable *control structure*.
6. Translate into a control language (also appropriate for the selected control structure) the user requirements.
7. Apply the controller design methodology based on the decisions taken in the previous steps (variables, models, goals).
8. Validate (by simulation or experimentally) the design, and tune the controller parameters.
9. Define the controller implementation. In the case of digital controllers, select the hardware and software to fulfill the control requirements.
10. Install the control in the process.
11. Evaluate the controlled system performances.

Control goals. From a set of usually ambiguous "user" control goals, mainly based on qualitative and economical requirements as well as operational constraints, the desirable controlled plant performances for "control design" should be derived. They may concern different properties, such as:

- reference tracking, to follow changes in the set-points or references,
- control decoupling, to better understand and tune the different subprocesses or control variables,
- disturbance rejection, to cope with non-manipulated external variables which affect key process variables,
- measurement noise rejection, to be able to use "imperfect" sensor and transmission systems,
- robustness against changes in the plant (model) or expected disturbances.

Some of these goals may be contradictory so this is a multi-criteria decision problem. A suitable trade-off is the most we can achieve.

Control structures. The selection of the variables to be used as control variables as well as the information used to generate the control actions will determine the control system structure for a MIMO system. We must consider, at least, the following structures:

Open-loop *vs.* closed-loop. In an open-loop control structure, the control actions are generated based on external information: set-points or objectives, initial conditions, disturbances, operator data, and so on. A good model of the process is required and there is no option to cope with unexpected changes in the plant (either disturbances or plant changes). On the other hand, closed-loop control uses the information from the plant to generate the control. There are many options for dealing with disturbances, reference tracking and uncertainties, but the big issue is the controlled plant stability (and performances). Other than the closed-loop stability, obvious drawbacks of closed-loop control are the requirement of additional measurement instrumentation as well as the existence of errors to act. Thus, a combination of both structures may allow better results.

Centralized/multiple loops. In feedback controlled MIMO systems, the vector of input actions may be computed altogether from the full set of measurements and available data or, alternatively, the information is split into blocks to determine each one of the control actions. In this case, for each input, the remaining blocks of information can be considered as disturbances. This structure could be also denoted as centralized/decentralized control.

Two degree of freedom. The control action may be computed in two phases. First, the control error is evaluated and the control is based on the error. This is a feedback control action. Afterwards, an additional control action is computed based on the external inputs. There are two degrees of freedom to design the controller, and the design can be split to achieve tracking (references) and regulation (output feedback) performances.

Hierarchical, multilevel control. Groups of input (output) variables can be treated jointly to control a process variable. They will act locally, receiving commands (set-points) from higher decision levels and sending information back to these upper coordination levels.

In the context of intelligent control, the above structures may be modified, incorporating adaptation and learning, supervision and mode switching.

Hierarchical Structure

In this general framework the following common control levels can be approached by fuzzy techniques:

- Local control, by means of fuzzy direct controllers.

- Adaptive control: adaptation of the current control option, so that only decisions at parameter level are taken.
- Supervised adaptive control: extending the previous approach by including a set of fixed evaluation indices, so that structural decisions over adaptive algorithm or supervisory backup regulators are present in the option set.
- Local control switching: fixed clusters denote different operating modes, so the options are the selection of different local models and regulators based on measurements.
- Pattern classification to determine current conditions in which previous tasks operate.

A smart decomposition of a complex control problem into several easier (but coordinated) subproblems is, indeed, a key task in devising a good control solution for a particular application. The above ideas sometimes belong to the "art" of experts in a particular type of processes (distillation, electrical generation, etc.). The overall control structure selection is usually carried out prior to actually deciding whether a particular controller for a particular subsystem will be fuzzy or not and, hence, it will be developed no further in this chapter.

The above topics are discussed (albeit with some generality, given the large differences between plants to which control applies) in control engineering texts such as (Albertos & Sala, 2004; Skogestad & Postlethwaite, 2005; Tatjewski, 2007; Hori & Skogestad, 2007; Huang, Lin, & Jeng, 2007).

MIMO FUZZY CONTROL DESIGN: THE REASONING APPROACH

The early days in fuzzy control sought the replication of the reasoning processes human operators carry out when controlling complex plants. Fuzzy logic successfully captured the "continuous" nature of those decision processes as a key improvement over binary-logic based results. Interpolation is also a viable paradigm to generalize partial results to intermediate points (fuzzy logic might be considered as an *interpolative extension* to binary logic). The difference between fuzzy logic-based controllers and mere interpolation must rest on their linguistic interpretation and its parallelism to a "reasoning" processes.

When using fuzzy systems as a reasoning tool, one of the main issues was to convey a suitable interpretation of "fuzziness". There are alternatives in the interpretation of membership values (probabilistic, possibilistic, metric, ordinality, utility, *etc.*). The reader is referred to (Dubois & Prade, 1997), for example, for discussion on these issues. The key idea here is that membership assignment and its interpretation can be one of the drawbacks of the fuzzy approach, as operations appearing as reasonable under a particular interpretation may not be so under a different one.

DIRECT (MODEL-FREE) FUZZY CONTROLLERS

Direct control using fuzzy controllers implementing "control rules" from operators had a significant success in application areas such as cement kilns (Morant, Albertos, Martinez, Crespo, & Navarro, 1992; Holmblad & Ostergaard, 1982), waste-water treatment (Tong, M.B., & Latten, 1980), *etc.* These implementations did not make use of a specific plant model but mimicked operator actions. However, a striking fact was soon to be realized: many of the operator actions when controlling a vaguely-known process were markedly similar

Table 1. A Usual Fuzzy-PD Controller

u		**Error** (e)				
		$--$	$-$	0	$+$	$++$
$\frac{de}{dt}$	$--$	-4	-3	-2	-1	0
	$-$	-3	-2	-1	0	1
	0	-2	-1	0	1	2
	$+$	-1	0	1	2	3
	$++$	0	1	2	3	4

to the basic proportional, integral and derivative control actions. In fact, the so-called fuzzy PD or fuzzy PI rulebases such as those described in Table 1 were appearing almost everywhere in applications.

These rulebases, especially when designed to keeping a constant operating point, have no important difference with respect to a PID regulator (if some saturation and rate-saturation code is added to the latter). Hence, PID's can be designed as fuzzy regulators but no fundamental difference between such fuzzy-PID and a well-tuned plain-old PID exists.

But, if the process to be controlled is significantly nonlinear and a setpoint tracking task is to be successfully accomplished, then a third setpoint variable must be included in the control rules, as the same "error" may require different control actions in one operation point than in other ones. The third linguistic variable complicates the rule base. Applications with such an implementation are scarce, if any, but, at least, the fuzzy language allows this implementation. A gain-scheduling approach (Zhao, Tomizuka, & Isaka, 1993; Apkarian & Adams, 1998) can also be implemented by changing the input/output scaling factors or the width of the membership functions as a function of the setpoint. In fact, the result may be more readable than the fuzzy rules on 3 variables. Again, there would be little difference with a classic gain-scheduled PID configuration.

This hints one of the main drawbacks: the number of rules usually increases exponentially with the number of variables (the *curse of dimensionality*). A compromise solution is to define most rulebases with just two membership functions. Some flexibility in the *shape* of the membership functions remains but, however, operators in complex processes often express their "vague" knowledge as *monotonic functions*: the more a variable is high, the more intense a particular effect is. Hence, if confronted with the task of mimicking that kind of vague knowledge, a linear functional might be as good as a fuzzy one.

Another source of trouble is the *multiplicity of inference-defuzzification algorithms*. Generalization of key binary operators presents a multitude of variants for implication, defuzzification or rule chaining, based on formal or intuitive grounds. Some of them give rise to severe problems in case of nonconvex consequents or "fat shape" subsets. The choice of operators in industrial practice is usually based in ease of implementation and end-user understanding.

MIMO systems. The above curse-of-dimensionality issue basically forbids approaching the control of a multivariable system via a set of rules that cover the operating space of a process via a partition on each individual variable. The following alternatives might apply:

- Decompose the problem in a multi-level, cascade structure, and apply rule-based ideas to each of the resulting loops. This is, in fact, parallel to the cascade-control ideas in classic PID regulators: directly tuning basic control actions depending on the values, the derivatives and the integrals of a set of variables is a hard task. Dividing into subsystems (preferably with clearly separated time constants) is perhaps the only approach to set up simple enough rules that can be readable. For details, the reader is referred to (Albertos & Sala, 2004, Chapter 5).

Figure 1. Fuzzy control structure

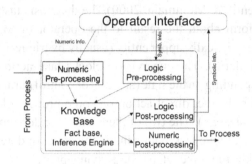

- Create supervision rules detecting high-level modes of operation and design simpler controllers for each of the modes (perhaps also decomposing in subsystems as in the previous paragraph). With fuzzy logic, the switching can be gradual.
- Design simpler controllers whose rules depend on a reduced set of variables, possibly resulting from pre-processing the original ones either with black-box approaches (say, principal components) or generating relevant expressions from physical insight or first-principle models.
- Design decoupling controllers preceded by local controllers for each one of the subprocesses with a reduced number of variables.

Fuzzy Expert Systems

The evolution of the above controllers led to the development of fuzzy expert control systems (FECS (Albertos & Sala, 2002)), where a larger set of rules and variables (possibly not covering *all* conceivable situations) was specified in the framework of Figure 1.

Usually, fuzzy expert systems are used not only for direct control but for other tasks higher in the hierarchy described in previous sections (in many practical cases, direct control may be left to conventional regulators). Supervision and diagnosis are the most successful applications implementing fuzzy reasoning strategies, for example (Carrasco & Rodriguez, 2004; Evsukoff, Gentil, & Montmain, 2000). The diagnosis tasks inform about the result to the operator or to a hierarchically upper entity (usually by triggering an alarm). The supervision blocks take actions depending on the state (stepoint or control parameter change, direct action on some process elements, *etc.*). The two of them can be understood as a unique task with a main objective: to determine the state of the underlying process, in a mostly qualitative level.

The main advantage of the fuzzy approach is that intermediate situations can be flagged (for instance, detection of *incipient* faults) and thus, corrective actions may be taken. In this way, the operation may be made much more efficient than binary-logic based counterparts (such as implementations in programmable logic controllers).

The core of an FECS (Figure 1) is its Knowledge Base, (KB). To build up a good KB some activities should be considered: *knowledge extraction, structuring and validation*.

The knowledge is extracted either by encoding the expertise of the skilled users (questionnaires) or from successful experimental operation data. The second option is more related to the UFA paradigm (next Section). Anyway, in control applications there is always a need of a substantial trial-and-error adjustment.

For the sake of simplicity, as well as to improve the maintenance, validation and upgrading capabilities a KB should be modular, with a well defined *structure*. Two main approaches can be followed: bottom-up (aggregation of simpler units solving partial aspects of the problem) or top-down. The top-down strategy is more suitable for totally new applications. In real-time control, the depth (longer tree to be explored in the reasoning) and the maximum evaluation time are important issues.

From the qualitative point of view, the KB must fulfill logic *validation* requirements, and not only

about the quality (in terms of performance) of the proposed action. For instance, compatibility problems may arise when several modules and rules operate on the same set of variables (for example, if control and diagnosis tasks are carried out simultaneously on the same subsystem). If a complex rule base is present it would be useful to detect abnormalities such as contradiction between rules, redundancies, incompleteness (missing rules), etc. In a similar context, if linguistic information comes in from different sources, mechanisms of verification of their agreement and fusion strategies should be devised.

Knowledge improvement. The structure and organization of the KB will determine its updating facilities. In any case, some of the rules should be related to the performance evaluation of the FECS leading to suggested, or automatically incorporated, new rules to deal with the detected operating conditions or to improve the results obtained with the current KB.

Bayesian Networks have arisen in the last decade as a probabilistic alternative to reasoning, being superior in some cases (see (Russell & Norvig, 2003) and references therein). A fuzzification of some of the involved variables would lead to the so-called *hybrid* network case. However, inference on this paradigm may be intractable in a general case (NP-hard).

Other paradigms. A problem arising from large rulebases where lots of variables are involved is that the lack of one measurement may stop a certain key rule from firing and, then, vague or erroneous conclusions can occur. In the same way, one outlier measurement may give rise to inconsistent solutions. Logic inference can be, in some cases, recast as an optimization problem. Then, available information (process measurements) is translated to constraints to the optimization problem. Conclusions are drafted via optimization software with no reasoning involved. For details, see (Sala, 2008).

A Case Study of Heuristic-Control of a Multivariable System

In order to illustrate pros and cons of the reasoning approach, the design of a fuzzy control of a multiple hearth furnace at the Nicaro plant in Cuba, is described. The objective of process control in a reduction furnace is to optimize nickel recovery, while minimizing fuel consumption and environmental contamination. This entails the exact control of temperature and gas composition in the furnace. Controlling the temperature of a multiple hearth furnace is a difficult task. Fast and extensive changes in operating conditions occur, complicated by non-linear and time-varying behavior of the process and interaction between the different variables. Failing to solve the control problem with simple classical solutions, such as a normal PID controller, may lead to develop a knowledge-based fuzzy controller, which keeps the temperature as close to the set profile as possible.

The dried ore is blended with fuel oil as a reductant, before being fed to the roaster, where it is roasted under reducing conditions at 700-800 ºC with a retention time of 5400 s. The ore, mainly containing nickel, cobalt and iron, is heated also by the hot reducing gas $(CO + H_2)$ formed by the combustion of the fuel oil in a deficiency of air in nine combustion chambers located along each roaster. The reduction potential of the gas phase and the temperature should be regulated, so that most of the nickel and cobalt in the ore are reduced to the metallic state, whilst the reduction of the iron is minimized. Good control of the roasting conditions is therefore essential for optimal nickel recovery in the process (Habashi, 1997).

To recover most of the chemical heat value of the reducing gases, before they are vented out to the atmosphere, both CO and H_2 are burned up by the addition of air at the hearths 4 and 6. This is known as post-combustion. The post-combustion reduces the fuel consumption by 50%. A furnace consumes about 10 million kilograms of

Figure 2. Reduction furnace

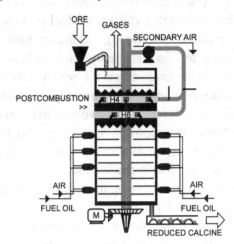

fuel oil per year. Obviously, an appropriate control of this process should lead to an important saving of fuel. Experiments (Ramírez, Haber, Peña, & Rodríguez, 2004) have demonstrated that the temperature stability in hearth 4 significantly influences the thermal stability of the roaster. The existence of temperature values below certain given limits may cause a shift of the thermal zones of the furnace, resulting in a decrease in the yield of nickel and cobalt. On the other hand, the control of temperature in the mentioned hearths contributes to a decrease in environmental contamination that takes place due to the release out to the ecosystem of polluting compounds CO and H_2.

The relationship between the temperature in the hearth 4 and the air flow at steady state is severely nonlinear; furthermore, two different regions of operation actually do exist, where the process gain sign changes. Temperature in zones 4 and 6 interact when the total air flow in these zones is manipulated, resulting in a MIMO system. Moreover, more reduction in zone 6 implies less material to reduce in zone 4, being also influenced by the air flows. The process was approached as a multivariable system, keeping in mind the output variables of interest and those that can be used for the control (action variables). We take as action variables the air flow to hearth 4 (faH4), the air flow to hearth 6 (faH6), the fuel oil flow to combustion chambers (fp), and the ore flow fed to the roaster (fm). The temperature of hearth 4 (TH4) and the temperature of hearth 6 (TH6) are taken as output variables. A non-squared MIMO process model (four inputs-two outputs) resulted from this system approach. The decoupling of this type of systems, even if they are considered linear models, is not totally resolved so far.

It is also widely recognized that this kind of process is hard to control, because it is time-varying, multivariable with interactive influences, non-linear and also stochastic. The application of any control technology to this process is thus a real challenge, and certainly a lot of energy and effort was required to develop and successfully test new control approaches in this "real world" plant.

Developing a Fuzzy Control System

To design and tune a fuzzy controller it was necessary to make a detailed study of the process and the way it was operated, based fundamentally on the observation of the operators' work as well as interviews with them and the process engineers. Finally, numerous historical records of the operation were analyzed. As a result of this study, we settled on the technological requirements to be considered during the design of the control system. After elaborating several proposals we arrived at the general structure of the control system presented in Figure 3. Besides the controller, other modules complement the implementation of the control system, which will be described later on.

The basic controller. A multivariable fuzzy logic controller was designed, see (Ramírez et al., 2004), using a Mamdani- type inference system. The controller has five input variables: the error (e) and change of the error (ce) of temperatures, **TH4** and **TH6**, and the specific fuel consumption, **fp**. Those variables were defined respectively as

Figure 3. Structure of the furnace fuzzy controller

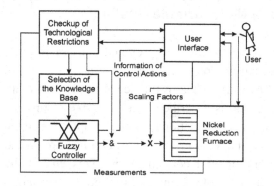

$$e(k) = y_r(k) - y(k) \qquad (1)$$

$$ce(k) = e(k) - e(k-1) \qquad (2)$$

where y_r is the reference signal, y is the output and k the discrete time. The specific fuel consumption is given by the weight in kilograms of petroleum per 1 ton of nickel fed to the furnace. The output variables (action variables, u) are the change in air flow to hearth 4 and 6, fuel oil flow to combustion chambers (fp), and ore flow fed to the roaster (fm); so that the final control signal sent to the process is calculated as

$$u(k) = u(k-1) + \Delta u(k) \qquad (3)$$

i.e., incorporating integral action.

For the partition of the universes of discourse in most of the variables, trapezoidal membership functions were used, while singletons were used for the fuel oil flow and the ore flow. The membership functions of input and output variables are shown respectively in Figures 4 and 5. The units of the variables are not expressed in the IS, because they were taken according to the actual current practice in the plant environment. The MIMO fuzzy controller can be described by a fuzzy inference system containing rules of the general form

Figure 4. Membership functions of input variables

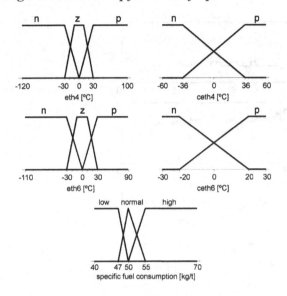

Figure 5. Membership functions of output variables

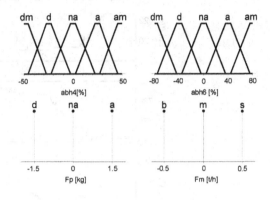

Ri: If x1 is A1i and x2 is A2i and ...and xp is Api then y1 is B1i; ...; yq is Bqi; for i = 1,2,...,k

where x1,...xp are the state (process output and its changes) variables of the process; y1, ...yq are the control (process input) variables; A1i, ...B1i are the fuzzy sets for rule i. Also resulting from the above mentioned careful study, 60 rule bases were progressively elaborated, one for each region of operation and/or technological restriction of the process, taking into account the sign of the gain and keeping in mind the different situations that can be presented. Each base has 108 rules. So, the system was divided into different local domains, each one described by its own rule base (sub-base).

The compositional operator sup-product and the centre-of-gravity methods, for the defuzzification, were used (see (Tanaka & Wang, 2001)). The knowledge bases were created, as explained, from the process's experienced operators and control engineering knowledge, i.e., using the so called verbalization technique.

Module for check-up of technological restrictions: the meta-rule approach. This module is the basis of a meta-rule switching device.

Since the 1980s, the meta-rule approach has been used in several applications to tune fuzzy logic controllers. In this case the meta-rule approach is used to dynamically commute the active rule base. During the operation of the roaster, different situations can be presented which lead to changes in the control strategy, for example: deficiencies in the addition of fuel oil to the ore; saturation of control valves; changes in the ore composition feed and/or in the characteristics of the fuel used and, alterations of the pressure inside the furnace. In these cases, changes can take place in the region of operation of the process, in the temperature profile, and/or in the composition of the atmosphere in the furnace as well as restrictions in control action capabilities arise. Meta-rules of classical non-fuzzy inference provide dynamical switching (firing) of the most suitable sub-base among the whole set of sub-bases. Therefore the algorithm possesses an adaptive character. The distinctive feature among the sub-bases is given by the fact that for equal antecedent conditions (state), each one has a different consequence (control action). Other aspects taken into account in this module are the time delays present in the system when acting on the mineral flow and the fuel oil flow. For its operation this module receives information regarding several variables of the process besides those that the controller uses as inputs.

Figure 6. Step response in the ore flow

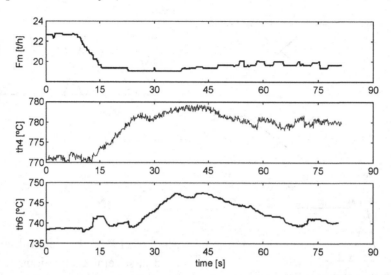

User interface. As usual in industrial processes, implementation and tuning should not disturb normal operation of the process. Therefore, our program has two kinds of user interfaces: the developer's interface and the operator's interface. The developer's interface contains information that is needed for tuning the fuzzy control system, where controller's parameters (e.g., scaling factors, knowledge bases, etc.) are accessible for changes. In the operator's interface only basic information is presented. Operators can switch the control system on or off, and change the settings (e.g., set point, limit values of technological restrictions, etc.).

Implementation of the Control System and Experimental Results

There are many tools to practically develop a fuzzy controller. Our controller was constructed and installed over the EROS supervisory system using the Object Pascal language (Delphi). EROS is a Window's application that was developed by the group of Automation of the Cuban Nickel Industry. It is a computer package that provides high reliability and functionality for instrumentation and control purposes. The basic control algorithm called Fuzzy-Reg is formed by a group of modules with easy maintainability and makes an efficient use of memory due to its dynamic data structure. It is also very friendly and the knowledge bases can be created with ease; it also contains a syntactic analyzer to detect errors that could be committed by the user.

To carry out the field tests of the control algorithm, our computer was connected in a network jointly with the computers of the existing higher level supervisory system installed in the plant. Therefore, both real time and historical information about the behavior of the operation are available. Our PC is serially connected with a Programmable Logic Controller (PLC), which acts as interface with the final control elements of the air flow to H-4 and H-6, respectively. The necessary hardware for fuel oil flow and mineral flow automatic control action is not so far implemented. The algorithm generates suitable messages displayed to the operator so that he/she can perform corrective actions over those variables. The sampling period is 30 s. During the tests the process was subjected to different disturbances and in all the cases, the controller maintained the temperature of the hearths H-4 and H-6 into the prescribed range. In Figure 6 one can observe

Figure 7. System behavior during a change toward the negative gain zone

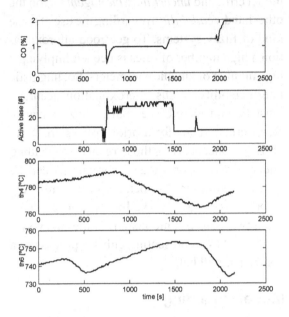

the behavior of the process during a time interval where a change of 2 t/h (8% of maximum flow) is made in the mineral flow fed to the roaster.

Another experience consisted in leading the process to the negative gain zone. To that end ore with low content of carbon was fed to the roaster, what implies shortage of reductants. In this case the controller continued working, now using the rule bases created for this zone, also showing a satisfactory behavior. This change occurred in the interval between the 700 and 1500s as shown in Figure 7. Here the success of the control system is evidenced by impeling the process operation toward the positive gain zone, as a typical example of the controller's "intelligence".

The analysis of the system stability is rather complex. It should be carried out starting from the general stability theory of non-linear systems, but a general solution does not exist for the case of Mamdani-type fuzzy controllers so far. In fact, this is an open research topic. For that reason, other approaches are foreseen to design the control, as described in the next sections.

Fuzzy adaptive PID control. In (Ramírez & Albertos, 2008), a combined solution was implemented. First, based on experimental data, a decoupling control is designed. Then a set of simple PID controllers were tuned for each one of the load operating conditions. A fuzzy adaptation system allows to smoothly transfer between operating modes.

This combination of classical control and fuzzy reasoning is one of the most practical uses of the approximation ideas so far discussed.

MIMO FUZZY CONTROL DESIGN. THE UFA PARADIGM: INTERPOLATION

This section deals with an alternative non-heuristic view of fuzzy systems. Instead of being considered reasoning tools, they are considered to act as function approximators with a particular set of properties and assumptions. Then, controllers can be designed based on the fuzzy models which are in the form of differential (difference, for discrete systems) equations. Then, a much more rigorous analysis can be undertaken and stability can be proved via Lyapunov approaches, for instance.

When fuzzy systems are conceived as function approximators, they implement a function of some input variables x with a particular structure. A widely-used choice is the one in the form (L.-X. Wang, 1994):

$$f(\mathbf{x}) = \left(\sum_r^{i=1} \phi_i(\mathbf{x}) \right)^{-1} \sum_r^{i=1} \phi_i(\mathbf{x}) f_i(\mathbf{x}) \qquad (4)$$

so that its output is a weighted sum of the so-called "local" models f_i, the weights being the membership functions $\phi_i(x)$, which fulfill $\phi_i \geq 0$, $\sum_{i=1}^{r} \phi_i \geq \bar{a} > 0$. The above expression may be interpreted as a fuzzy system with r rules in the form: IF x is ϕ_i THEN $f(x)$ is $f_i(x)$.

Such rule-based interpretation is, somehow, the link with the reasoning approach in the previous sections but in the fuzzy function approximation literature there are no logic-related considerations in most cases, with only a handful of very limited ideas on the topic, discussed in (Sala & Albertos, 1999; Sala & Albertos, 1998) and references therein. Henceforth, the rule-based interpretation of function approximators (4) will not be used any longer.

Note that expression (4) may be formally equivalent to other interpolation techniques, such as splines, radial basis neuronal nets, etc. If functions ϕ_i also have adjustable parameters, equation (4) is analogous to some multi-layer neural network configurations (Ripley, 1996; Jang, Sun, & Mizutani, 1997).

The universal-approximator paradigm has become the choice in recent developments in fuzzy control either to implement a controller model or to model a process to be controlled. The key result is the ability of fuzzy systems to be universal function approximators under mild conditions (Stone-Weierstrass theorem (L.-X. Wang, 1994)), i.e., any continuous function $\mathcal{F}$ (x) in a compact set $\mathbf{X}$ can be approximated by a fuzzy system $f(\mathbf{x})$ in the form (4) within any desired error bound ϵ, *i.e.*,

$$\forall \mathbf{x} \in \mathbf{X}, \left| \mathcal{F}(\mathbf{x}) - f(\mathbf{x}) \right| < \epsilon \qquad (5)$$

with a high enough number of rules. As just said above, this property situates fuzzy systems in the realm of interpolation instead of that of reasoning.

In fuzzy controllers, usually $\mathbf{x}$ denotes the process state and $\mathbf{X}$ is the operation domain where the controller is designed to operate. However, the approximation results above are independent on the use of the the fuzzy system as a controller, model or any other conceivable one.

There are two relevant issues (on one hand, model error and *uncertainty management*, on the other hand, *readability*) regarding the use of these kind of fuzzy systems. To get good approximation a high number of rules is needed implying a high number of tunable parameters. So, linguistic interpretability versus approximation accuracy must be considered, see (Sala, Diez, Navarro, & Albertos, 2004) for a brief discussion. Also, "fuzzy" concepts (i.e., those related to deciding under uncertain or vague information) can be lost, as controller (4) operates in a completely deterministic framework. In order to evaluate these two issues, some insight in the fuzzy system model (4) representing either a process or a controller, will help.

Model Obtaining

Based on *heuristic descriptions* expressed by rules such as:

If state-now is A_i and input is B_i, state-next will be C_i,

a system's approximate behavior may be encoded. Some difficulties arise in this task: first, the combinatorial explosion as fuzzy sets and rules must be defined over the joint (state, input) space. Second, the difficulty of encoding the process engineer knowledge if it is, as usual in practice, described as a set of descriptions of a *monotonic* function (the more the speed is, the more the position increment will be next sample). These models may be amenable to numeric analysis, but the results may be debatable.

By far, the most popular modeling paradigm is the *parameter adjustment* framework for fitting prescribed models to actual data. In fuzzy modeling, parameter adjustment can be carried out in either the antecedent membership functions or the consequent ones, *i.e.*, using the interpolating formula (4) with tunable antecedent parameters α_i and consequent ones β_i given by:

$$u(\mathbf{x}, \alpha_i, \beta_i) = \frac{\sum_{i=1}^{r} \phi_i(\mathbf{x}, \alpha_i) f_i(\mathbf{x}, \beta_i)}{\sum_{i=1}^{r} \phi_i(\mathbf{x}, \alpha_i)} \qquad (6)$$

But a number of technical issues must be solved, such as identifiability and distinguishability of the parametrization, robustness to outliers, selection of the optimisation algorithm or quality of the obtained estimates (bias-variance trade-off, parameter confidence intervals, etc.). For instance, the reader is referred to (Walter & Pronzato, 1997; Nelles, 2001) for generic and specific fuzzy identification issues. Many (neuro-)fuzzy systems are *linear in parameters* (LIP), in the sense that its output is linear in the adjustable parameters, even if nonlinear on other variables. In that case, least squares identification is straightforward.

For instance, consider a fuzzy system (6) with

$$\phi_i = e^{-\frac{\mathbf{x}-c_i}{2}}, \quad f_i = \beta_i \mathbf{x}$$

where c_i are fixed centroids. Then, it's easy to realise that the approximation is linear in β_i so $u(\mathbf{x}, \beta_i)$ may be expressed, for a suitable matrix Ξ as:

$$u(\mathbf{x}, \beta_i) = \Xi(\mathbf{x})(\beta_1, \ldots, \beta_r)^T \qquad (7)$$

hence, given a batch of experimental samples $(u_0, x_0), \ldots, (u_N, x_N)$ a standard least squares problem can be set up and easily solved with most linear algebra software.

Clustering. In order to simplify the modeling burden and to gain in interpretability, *fuzzy clustering* is gaining visibility. Each *cluster* is characterised by a prototype center and/or a prototype local model, and each data is assigned to one cluster by minimizing a cost index based on the distance to the cluster center or distance to a prototype local model. Some clustering algorithms identify only memberships and cluster centers,

and consequent parameters of a fuzzy model (6) are identified in a second step. Others include the modeling error and model parametrization into the cost index to minimise. The reader is referred to (Babuška, Mollov, & Roubos, 1998) for details.

Support vector machines are a recent pattern classification technique aimed to minimising upper bounds on generalisation error of a model. A setup in a fuzzy context appears in (Chiang & Hao, 2004).

In any case, the issue of choosing a fuzzy model instead of another black-box, grey-box or first principle one (and the number of parameters –rules– of those models) must be a tradeoff between: capability of *representation*, capability of *generalisation*, capability of *interpretation* and *computational cost* of learning and simulation (Michalski, Carbonell, & Mitchell, 1986; Hastie, Tibshirani, & Friedman, 2001).

In this way, even if in theory there is no difference between large multivariable systems and other simpler ones, the above issues may constitute practical obstacles hindering successful application of direct out-of-the-box fuzzy modeling tools to multivariable systems.

Model Domain

As previously discussed, models are usually obtained from a batch of N samples of input-output data (u_k, x_k), $k = 1, \ldots, N$. If such data come from a non-linear system to which a model (6) with several rules should be fitted, there are different interpretations of what such a "fit" could be.

Global models. An immediate approach consists in the minimization of a prediction error (based on the difference between u_k and $u(\mathbf{x}_k, \alpha, \beta)$ in (6), for all data, $\forall k$), see (Walter & Pronzato, 1997). This global approach to modeling presents a readability problem because the obtained f_i have, in general, no relationship with a "local" behavior of the overall system. Furthermore, if f_i and ϕ_i have a large number of parameters, there might be conditioning problems, as both might have capabilities to approximate the system's nonlinearities.

Local models. An alternate option for modeling non-linear systems is to partition the operating regime space into a number of subsets (either user-defined or generated in the identification process), and minimize the "local" error of a number of *local models* that represent the system in a region of its operating space (Babuška et al., 1998) and approximate the plant behavior on the given set, *i.e.*, minimizing:

$$J_i^l = \sum_{k=1}^{N} \mu_i(\mathbf{x}_k)(u_k - f_i(\mathbf{x}_k))^2, \quad i = 1,.,c$$

(8)

In this case, $f_i(\mathbf{x}_k)$ has to be fitted to the data, weighting the adjustment proportionally to membership values.

Using membership functions with a reduced support width, the f_i minimizing the index in (8) will truly approach the local models around a set of prototype points $(\mathbf{x}_i^*, u_i^*)$ which $\mu_{ik}^* = 1$. In the extreme case, if membership function support were small, linear $f_i()$ would tend to fit the Jacobian linearisation around an operating point. These models, as such, may be more readable and truly "local" in nature. They lead to a good interaction of the identified model with the user provided that intuition can be used for local design and validation work. However, its integration on a global model and controller design is not as clear as on the previous paradigms (Hunt & Johansen, 1997).

Other references discussing such global *vs.* local approaches are (Sala et al., 2004; Babuška & Verbruggen, 1996).

Specific Issues to MIMO systems

When the number of variables involved in a model increases, there are several drawbacks:

1. Curse of dimensionality, with an exponential growth on the number of regressors and adjustable parameters (if usual fuzzy partitions are used for each input, state and output variables).
2. Increment of the number of experimental data needed to fit a model within certain error bounds (bias-variance tradeoff: lots of parameters imply much larger uncertainty bounds).
3. In dynamic systems, increasing difficulty of computing input signals so that a large region of the operating space is covered with input samples. Indeed, with many independent variables, the number of data points in a gridding of the operating space increases exponentially. If initial conditions and inputs cannot be arbitrary (as it is usually the case in experimental systems), the likelihood of an arbitrary trajectory of reaching a neighborhood of a particular point sharply decreases: lack of excitation for many operating modes may be a key issue.

NON-LINEAR FUZZY SYSTEMS FROM FIRST-PRINCIPLE MODELS

So far, the UFA paradigm has been used to approximate non-linear functions. Consider an n-th order dynamic system with p manipulated inputs (denoted as u). The class of systems to be considered fulfills the following assumptions:

The dynamics of the system can be expressed as:

$$\dot{x} = f(x, u, z)$$

(9)

where $x(t)$ is the system state, $u(t)$ are input variables, and $z(t)$ is a vector of functions of time, interpreted as exogenous non-manipulated inputs or actual time-variance.

2. ($x=0$, $u=0$) is an equilibrium point for any value of z, i.e., $f(0,0,z) = 0$
3. $f(x,u,z)$, $u(t)$, $z(t)$ fulfill the required Lipschitz conditions for existence and uniqueness of the solution of (9).

The most popular modeling methodology is based on the Takagi-Sugeno fuzzy models, proposed in (Takagi & Sugeno, 1985).

The Takagi-Sugeno framework

Let us consider the basic TS model:

$$\dot{x} = \sum_{i=1}^{r} \mu_i(z)(A_i x + B_i u) \qquad (10)$$

Such models have become popular and widespread due to:

1. The sector-nonlinearity methodology (Tanaka & Wang, 2001), which is a well-established technique to obtain fuzzy models from a quite general class of nonlinear systems.
2. The resulting models are *not* approximate, so they are equivalent to the original nonlinear equations.
3. The existence of computational tools for stability analysis and control design for such a class of systems

Let us assume that there are algebraic transformations allowing express (9) in the form:

$$\dot{x}_i = \sum_{j=1}^{n} \xi_{ij}(x,z)x_j + \sum_{j=1}^{p} \xi_{i(j+n)}(x,z)u_j \quad i=1,\dots,n$$

$$(11)$$

in a region of interest Ω.

If functions $\xi_{ij}(x,z)$ are bounded in Ω, they can be expressed as an interpolation between its

minimum (say, m_{ij}) and maximum (say, M_{ij}), in the form:

$$\xi_{ij} = \mu_1(x,z) * m_{ij} + (1 - \mu_1(x,z)) * M_{ij}.$$

Doing that for all i and j, it can be shown that there exist functions $\mu_i(x,z)$, $i=1,\dots,r$ so that the system can be exactly represented (locally in Ω) as, (Tanaka & Wang, 2001):

$$\dot{x} = \sum_{i=1}^{r} \mu_i(x,z)(A_i x + B_i u) \ \forall (x,z) \in \Omega \qquad (12)$$

with the functions μ_i belonging to the standard simplex:

$$\Delta^{r-1} := \{(\mu_1,\dots,\mu_r) \in \mathbb{R}^r \mid 0 \le \mu_i \le 1, \sum_{i=1}^{r} \mu_i = 1\}$$
$$(13)$$

Such a form is denoted as Takagi-Sugeno (TS) form in fuzzy literature; functions μ_i are denoted as *membership functions* and *r* is the number of "rules" of the TS model.

It is straightforward to realize that the system may be expressed as (12), with the number of "rules" being $r=2^{n+p}$. For details, see (Tanaka & Wang, 2001; Ariño & Sala, 2007). Such a number of rules would be blatantly intractable if $n+p$ is a large number. As the decomposition (11) is usually not unique, a decomposition should be found so that the resulting model is tractable.

Note that if there are exogenous variables z which change the equilibrium point, they should be considered in the same way as u, by forming a TS model in the form:

$$\dot{x} = \sum_{i=1}^{r} \mu_i(x,z)(A_i x + B_i u + M_i z) \ \forall (x,z) \in \Omega$$
$$(14)$$

amenable to disturbance-rejection control solutions. In fact, u and z may be thought to have a very similar role regarding modeling; however, intentionally, μ_i has not been made dependent on manipulated variables u in order to avoid algebraic loops in controller implementation.

Example 1. Consider a system $\dot{x} = \sin(x)$ and $\Omega = [-3, 3]$. Define now $\xi(x) = \sin(x) / x$ for $x \neq 0$, and $\xi(0) = 1$, so $\dot{x} = \xi(x)x$. As $\min_{x \in \Omega} \xi(x) = \sin(3) / 3$ and $\max_{x \in \Omega} \xi(x) = 1$, we may write $\xi(x)$ as the interpolation between minimum and maximum, i.e., there exists $\mu_1(x)$ so

$$\xi(x) = \mu_1(x) * 1 + (1 - \mu_1(x)) * \sin(3) / 3$$

for all $x \in \Omega$ and hence, denoting $\mu_2 = 1 - \mu_1$, we may write

$$\dot{x} = \mu_1(x)x + \mu_2(x)\sin(3) / 3 * x$$

with

$$\mu_1(x) = \frac{\sin(x) / x - \sin(3) / 3}{1 - \sin(3) / 3}$$

The methodologies stemming from the previous result are nowadays classical and well-known, usually denoted as "sector-nonlinearity modeling". The reader is referred to (Tanaka & Wang, 2001) for further examples and details. Note that the resulting models have a tensor-product structure, which can be used to relax the conservativeness of some fuzzy control design techniques (Ariño & Sala, 2007).

Similar developments can be made with nonlinear output equations, $y = h(x,u)$, if any. For convenience, shorthand μ_i denoting $\mu_i(x,z)$ will be used in the sequel.

Discrete-time systems: The sector-nonlinearity modeling procedure also applies to discrete-time systems $x_{k+1} = f(x_k, u_k, z_k)$ with obvious modifications, to obtain discrete TS models $x_{k+1} = \sum_{i=1}^{r} \mu_i(x_k, z_k)(A_i x_k + B_i u_k)$. Details are omitted for brevity.

Linguistic interpretability: Non-smooth functions, those with multiple maxima and minima, might give as a result non-convex membership functions which cannot be easily interpreted linguistically as "fuzzy numbers" (Dubois & Prade, 1978). This is a possible limitation of the TS approach regarding readability of the resulting models; it is definitely not a limitation regarding accuracy or stability analysis and controller design. Nevertheless, if the function to be modeled is smooth and the region of interest is not too large, the obtained membership functions keep the linguistic interpretability (see many examples in (Tanaka & Wang, 2001)). Readability issues in TS fuzzy control (Sala et al., 2004) are, however, outside of the intended scope of this chapter.

Modeling error and uncertainty: The above methodology assumes perfect knowledge of the original nonlinear model. A simple variation allows transforming "*uncertain nonlinear models*" to "*uncertain TS models*".

Consider, for instance, $\dot{x}_i = f(x, z_1, z_2)$ where z_1 denotes known variables and z_2 are uncertain ones.

The above expression can be fuzzified to TS considering z_2 to be known (if the above outlined assumptions hold). Then, the result is a fuzzy model in the form, for instance:

$$\dot{x} = \sum_{i=1}^{r} \mu_i(z_1) \sum_{j=1}^{m} \mu_j(z_2) A_{ij} x \qquad (15)$$

i.e., a fuzzy model (using variables z_1) with polytopic uncertainty arising from the unknown z_2. If the uncertain variable z_2 changed the equilibrium point, it would appear as in (14).

Other classes of uncertain TS models in literature (see (Lee, Park, & Chen, 2001; Kruszewski, 2006; Feng, 2006)) replace A_i by $A_i + \Delta_i^A$ and B by $B + \Delta_i^B$ in (12). Some knowledge on the structure and size of Δ_i^A and Δ_i^B is usually assumed (such as $\Delta_i^A = H_i \delta E_i$, with H_i, E_i known and $\delta < 1$). Modeling issues in these literature references are usually overlooked.

Polynomial Fuzzy Systems

Recently, the advent of sum-of-squares (SOS) tools (Prajna, Papachristodoulou, Seiler, & Parrilo, 2004) has spurred some analysis and controller design techniques for (non-fuzzy) polynomial systems. Such techniques are a natural generalization of LMI-based techniques for linear systems. Fuzzy control can also benefit from this concept, by generalizing some of the polynomial system ideas to the so-called fuzzy polynomial models. Such models can also be obtained by a variation of the sector-nonlinearity technique (Sala & Ariño, 2009).

Polynomial fuzzy model of a static function.
To start with, let us consider a sufficiently smooth function of one real variable, $f(x)$, so that its Taylor expansion of degree n, $f_n(x)$, exists, i.e., there exists $\psi \in [0, x]$ so that:

$$f(x) = \sum_{n-1}^{i=0} \frac{f^{[i]}(0)}{i!} x^i + \frac{f^{[n]}(\psi)}{n!} x^n = f_n(x) + T_n(x) x^n \tag{16}$$

where $f^{[i]}$ denotes the i-th derivative of f, and f[0] is, plainly, f. Assume also that f[n] is continuous in a compact region of interest Ω. Then, an equivalent polynomial fuzzy representation exists in the form:

$$f(x) = \mu_1 p_1(x) + \mu_2 p_2(x) \quad \forall x \in \Omega \tag{17}$$

where $\mu_1 + \mu_2 = 1$ and p_1, p_2 are polynomials of degree n.

Assume that the necessary smoothness conditions for f hold so that $T_n(x)$ is bounded in the region of interest Ω, that is:

$$\psi_1 = \sup_{x \in \Omega} T_n(x), \quad \psi_2 = \inf_{x \in \Omega} T_n(x) \tag{18}$$

Thus:

$$f_n(x) + \psi_2 x^n \leq f(x) \leq f_n(x) + \psi_1 x^n \tag{19}$$

and, hence:

$$f(x) = f_n(x) + (\mu \psi_2 + (1 - \mu) \psi_1) x^n \tag{20}$$

with:

$$\mu = \frac{\dfrac{f(x) - f_n(x)}{x^n} - \psi_2}{\psi_1 - \psi_2} \tag{21}$$

so p_1 in (17) is $p_1 = f_n(x) + \psi_1 x^n$ and $p_2 = f_n(x) + \psi_2 x^n$.

Remark. If $f(0) = 0$, *setting n = 1 we obtain the usual sector-nonlinearity methodology which bounds a function as $a_1 x \leq f(x) \leq a_2 x$ and generates the fuzzy model as the interpolation between them.*

Note that, as in TS modeling, the representation (17) is *exact*, i.e., there is equality (no approximation involved) and there is no uncertainty in the membership functions, defined in (21).

Conceptually, the resulting membership functions can be thought of capturing "the nonlinearity which cannot be described by a polynomial of a prescribed degree". The idea generalizes the interpretation of classical Takagi-Sugeno memberships (they captured "all" the nonlinearity between some linear sector bounds).

Once the above result has been obtained, it can be applied to the differential equations of a nonlinear system to obtain a polynomial fuzzy system, as defined below.

Polynomial fuzzy system. By extending the above idea to a system with many (non-polynomial) nonlinearities, a polynomial fuzzy system can be defined as the system whose dynamics can be expressed as:

$$\dot{x}_i = p_i(x, u, \mu) \qquad (22)$$

with $p_i(x,u,\mu)$ being a polynomial so that $p_i(0,0,\mu) = 0$ for all μ in Δ^{r-1}.

An analogue definition would arise for discrete-time systems or those with output equations.

As memberships add one, without loss of generality, the polynomial p may be assumed to be *homogeneous* in μ, i.e., composed only of monomials whose degree in the variables μ is the same. Indeed, any monomial in p can be multiplied by $(\sum_i \mu_i)^q$ for any q in order to incorporate as many powers of μ as required to make p homogeneous.

In summary, assuming that the equations of a nonlinear system (9) may be expressed in the form:

$$\dot{x}_i = p_i(x, u, \xi_1(x, z), \dots, \xi_t(x, z)) \qquad (23)$$

where:

a. p_i are polynomials in the variables x, u, $\xi_1, \dots, \xi_t$, with real coefficients
b. $\xi_1, \dots, \xi_t$ are some known nonlinear continuous functions which depend on the state and exogenous variables;

Replacing ξ_i, $i = 1, \dots, t$ above by generic variables ϵ_i, the following equilibrium condition holds for any ϵ_i:

$$p(0, 0, \epsilon_1, \dots, \epsilon_t) = 0 \qquad (24)$$

Then, the nonlinear system can be exactly expressed as a polynomial fuzzy system in a compact region of interest Ω, see (Sala & Ariño, 2009) for details.

As a conclusion, using the Taylor-based modeling for non-polynomial nonlinearities (say, trigonometric, exponential, etc.), any nonlinear system can be exactly expressed as a fuzzy polynomial one in a compact domain Ω. Note that, as each nonlinearity results in a two-rule polynomial fuzzy description, the number of rules will still be a power of 2, keeping the tensor-product structure of the sector-nonlinearity approach (Ariño & Sala, 2007).

The reader is referred to (Sala & Ariño, 2009) for examples of the above methodology.

CONTROL DESIGN TECHNIQUES FOR THE TS APPROACH

There are many control design techniques in the fuzzy framework, apart from the direct fuzzy controllers (encoding expert knowledge) and the supervision by expert systems discussed in previous sections. cases, a *look-up-table control* is Let us discuss some alternatives, without the aim of completeness. Due to its importance, the linear matrix inequality and the polynomial approaches will be discussed in a separate subsection.

Fuzzyfication of standard control laws. As fuzzy systems are universal approximators, such fuzzy systems may be used to approximate a preexisting controller. This may improve the user interface in, say, gain scheduling control. However, the resulting controller will not be any different from the non-fuzzy one.

One of the settings in which such an idea usually appears is in sliding control with boundary-layer (Palm, 1994). Sliding control is a switching control law which switches at (theoretically) infinite frequency. In order for implementations to be realistic and avoid such a high-frequency commutation, the switching law can be softened and, instead of a discontinuous control law, a gradual interpolation can be set. Even if linear interpolation usually suffices, sometimes such a linear interpolation is presented as a two-rule fuzzy rulebase.

Applying nonlinear control to fuzzy systems. Fuzzy models may be considered as nonlinear models and apply other techniques not specially targeted to fuzzy systems, such as PID, decoupling, feedback linearisation, etc. For instance, a feedback-linearization application is discussed in (Andújar & Bravo, 2005).

Decentralised control. In the same way as nonfuzzy multivariable controllers, some fuzzy multivariable system can be modeled as a set of *p* independent systems with some "interaction terms" denoted as *Δ*

$$\dot{x}_k = \sum_{i=1}^{r_k} \mu_{i,k} A_{i,k} x_k + B_{i,k} u + \Delta_k(x_1, \ldots, x_p) \quad k = 1, \ldots, p$$

$$(25)$$

If some bounds on the interaction Δ_k are known, say $\|\Delta_k\|_\infty \leq \gamma_k$, then some stability and stabilization conditions may be set up (most of them using advanced versions of the LMI framework to be outlined in the next section).

As the details of such theories are out of the scope of the present chapter, the reader is referred to (Tseng & Chen, 2001; Akar & Ozguner, 2000; Hsiao, Hwang, Chen, & Tsai, 2005) for in-depth coverage of the topic.

Interval arithmetic. As fuzzy sets can be considered as a collection of intervals (cuts), some formal results can be obtained using interval arithmetic (Andújar, Bravo, & Peregrin, 2004; Bondia, Sala, Pico, & Sainz, 2006). Note that the interpretation of fuzzy models is, in these settings, slightly different: fuzzy sets provide possibility distributions of the parameters of a linear or non-linear model, and there is no interpolation interpretation.

Linear Matrix Inequalities (LMI)

Current fuzzy control research uses rigorous core control theory results to guarantee specifications expressed in terms of stability, performance, and robustness to modeling errors, *etc.*

The main advantage of the Takagi-Sugeno fuzzy approach when compared to generic nonlinear control is that many linear, LTV, and LPV techniques can be almost directly applied to nonlinear plants in TS form - using efficient semidefinite-programming tools (LMI (Boyd, ElGhaoui, Feron, & Balakrishnan, 1994; Boyd & Vandenberghe, 2004)) in a unified approach.

The most widely used controller for controlling TS systems (12) has membership functions equaling those of the process to be controlled, and so for a state-feedback configuration:

$$u = -\sum_{i=1}^{r} \mu_i K_i x \qquad (26)$$

This is the so-called *parallel distributed compensator* (PDC). Note that, to compute *u*, all the variables involved in μ_i must be *measurable* and μ_i should not depend on *u* (to avoid an algebraic loop). These are common assumptions in the literature. Other non-PDC control structures are mentioned later.

Linear Matrix Inequality (LMI) techniques have become the tool of choice for designing fuzzy controllers (such as (26)) when a fuzzy model of the process is available in the Takagi-Sugeno form. LMIs were introduced in linear and robust control in the late 80's and 90's (Boyd et al., 1994), and were then introduced in the late 90's (Tanaka & Wang, 2001) in the fuzzy control community – becoming widespread over the last ten years. Results are available for systems with uncertainty, delay, descriptor forms, etc. Some simple cases are shown below to illustrate the fundamentals of the approach and introduce some notation.

Joining (12) and (26) yields a closed-loop (Tanaka & Wang, 2001) given by:

$$\dot{x} = \sum_{i=1}^{r} \sum_{j=1}^{r} \mu_i \mu_j (A_i - B_i F_j) x \qquad (27)$$

A simple condition to ensure stability of (27) can be derived from a quadratic Lyapunov function (find P such that $V = x^T P x > 0$, $-\dot{V} > 0$) as shown in (H. O. Wang, Tanaka, & Griffin, 1996; Tanaka & Wang, 2001). After a standard change of variable $\psi = P^{-1}x$, stability (actually, decay rate performance $\alpha \geq 0$) is proven (Tanaka & Wang, 2001) if:

$$\sum_{i=1}^{r} \sum_{j=1}^{r} \mu_i \mu_j \psi^T Q_{ij} \psi \geq 0 \qquad (28)$$

with

$$Q_{ij} = -(A_i X + X A_i^T - B_i M_j - M_j^T B_i^T + 2\alpha X) \qquad (29)$$

for $\psi \neq 0$, where $P^{-1} = X > 0$ and $M_i = F_i X$ are LMI decision variables and α is a user-defined decay-rate parameter ($X > 0$ denotes that X should be a positive-definite matrix).

This is the simplest example of a class of widely-used conditions for stability or performance of a closed-loop fuzzy control system. These conditions may be expressed, for some matrices Q_{ij}, in the form (28), for which (29) is the simplest setup. The left-hand term of expression (28) will be denoted as *double fuzzy summation*. Note, importantly, that if Q_{ij} are linear in some matrix unknowns, then the above referenced LMI techniques (Tanaka & Wang, 2001) may be used to check condition (28) by restating it as the requirement of positive-definiteness in the matrix $\sum_{i=1}^{r} \sum_{j=1}^{r} \mu_i \mu_j Q_{ij}$.

Another example of performance-related condition uses

$$Q_{ij} = \begin{pmatrix} PA_i^T + R_j^T B_{2i}^T + A_i P + B_{2i} R_j & B_{1i} & PC_i^T + R_j^T D_{12i}^T \\ B_{1i}^T & -\gamma I & D_{11i}^T \\ C_i P + D_{12i} R_j & D_{11i} & -\gamma I \end{pmatrix} \qquad (30)$$

to prove that the H_∞ norm (i.e., H_2 to H_2 induced norm) of a TS fuzzy system given by:

$$\dot{x} = \sum_{i=1}^{r} \mu_i(z)(A_i x + B_{1i} v + B_{2i} u) \qquad (31)$$

$$y = \sum_{i=1}^{r} \mu_i(z)(C_i x + D_{11i} v + D_{12i} u) \qquad (32)$$

is lower than γ. The reader is referred to (Tuan, Apkarian, Narikiyo, & Yamamoto, 2001) for details on how (30) is obtained.

Other well-known performance and robustness requirements for fuzzy systems can also be cast as (28), as well as conditions for discrete-time TS systems $x_{n+1} = \sum_{i=1}^{r} \mu_i(A_i x_n + B_i u_n)$. The reader is referred to (Tanaka, Ikeda, & Wang, 1998; Oliveira, Bernussou, & Geromel, 1999; Tanaka & Wang, 2001), etc. for details.

As a generalisation of (28), other fuzzy control results require positiveness of a p-dimensional fuzzy summation, *i.e.*, checking $\forall x \neq 0$

$$\sum_{i_1=1}^{r} \sum_{i_2=1}^{r} \cdots \sum_{i_p=1}^{r} \mu_{i_1} \mu_{i_2} \cdots \mu_{i_p} x^T Q_{i_1 i_2 \ldots i_p} x > 0 \qquad (33)$$

The case $p = 2$ reduces to (28). Conditions requiring $p = 3$ are, for instance, the fuzzy dynamic controllers in (Li, Niemann, Wang, & Tanaka, 1999; Tanaka & Wang, 2001), using $Q_{ijk} = E_{ijk} + E_{ijk}^T$, with

$$E_{ijk} = \begin{pmatrix} A_i Q_{11} + B_i C_{jk} & A_i + B_i \mathcal{D}_j C_k \\ \mathcal{A}_{ijk} & A_i P_{11} + \mathcal{B}_{ij} C_k \end{pmatrix} < 0 \qquad (34)$$

or the output-feedback conditions in (Fang, Liu, Kau, Hong, & Lee, 2006; Chen, Chang, Su, Chung, & Lee, 2005). There are other non-PDC control laws, for instance (Guerra & Vermeiren, 2004; Kruszewski, Guerra, & Labiod, 2007), that also yield fuzzy summation conditions. Also, when the memberships of the fuzzy controller, say η_i, are not coincident with those of the process, the results are equations in the form

$$\sum_{i=1}^{r}\sum_{j=1}^{r} \mu_i \eta_j \psi^T Q_{ij} \psi \geq 0 \qquad (35)$$

In fuzzy literature, once the control requirements have been expressed as (28) or (33), some conditions to prove such positivity must be stated. As μ_i (shorthand for $\mu_i(x)$) depends on the state, the summation is a complex expression which, in a general case, is fairly difficult to handle. To avoid such issues, the dependence on x of μ_i is usually disregarded and conditions are proven for *all* possible $\mu_i > 0$ so that $\sum_i \mu_i = 1$. The set to which μ_i belongs is denoted the $(r\text{-}1)$-dimensional standard simplex.

In this way, only conservative sufficient conditions are obtained, and these are routinely used to set up a set of LMIs (see below) which, if feasible, provide a solution for the original fuzzy control problem.

Basic sufficient conditions for (28) are $Q_{ii} > 0$, $Q_{ij} + Q_{ji} > 0$ (Tanaka & Wang, 2001). Perhaps the most widely used improved conditions are those in (Liu & Zhang, 2003), and shown below:

Theorem 1. Expression (28), under fuzzy partition conditions $\sum_i \mu_i = 1$, $\mu_i \geq 0$, holds if there are matrices $X_{ij} = X_{ji}^T$ so that:

$$X_{ii} \leq Q_{ii} \qquad (36)$$

$$X_{ij} + X_{ji} \leq Q_{ij} + Q_{ji} \quad i \neq j \qquad (37)$$

$$\mathbf{X} = \begin{pmatrix} X_{11} & \dots & X_{1r} \\ \vdots & \ddots & \vdots \\ X_{r1} & \dots & X_{rr} \end{pmatrix} > 0 \qquad (38)$$

Less conservative examples appear in (Fang et al., 2006). Conditions not involving additional slack variables appear in (Tuan et al., 2001). The reader is referred to other recently published ones (Sala & Ariño, 2007; Kruszewski, Sala, Guerra, & Ariño, 2009) which are asymptotically exact (less and less conservative as computational complexity is allowed to increase), thus closing in a certain way an interesting open problem. The details are omitted in this work for brevity. An in-depth analysis of conservativeness issues in fuzzy control is carried out in (Sala, 2009).

With regard to (35) in shape-independent setups (i.e., requiring (35) to hold for all possible values of μ_i, η_i positive adding one), it holds if and only if $Q_{ij} > 0$ (usually resulting in much more conservative performance bounds than the PDC case $\mu \equiv \eta$). If some relationships between μ and η are known, then relaxations in (Ariño & Sala, 2008) may be used to overcome the above conservatism sources.

Polynomial Techniques

The results in the previous section on polynomial fuzzy systems allow obtaining polynomial fuzzy models of arbitrary degree of any smooth nonlinearity in the first-principle equations of a physical system (say, exponential, trigonometric, etc. functions). As mentioned in the introduction, some results have recently appeared dealing with stability and control design for fuzzy polynomial systems. For completeness of this chapter, those results (some by the authors) will be reviewed and briefly outlined.

Consider a polynomial fuzzy system expressed as:

$$\dot{x}_i = p_i(x, \mu) \tag{39}$$

and denote by Σ_a the set of SOS polynomials in the generic variables a, i.e., those expressed as the sum of squares of other polynomials (Prajna, Papachristodoulou, Seiler, & Parrilo, 2004).

For operational purposes (Sala, 2007), the polynomials should be made homogeneous in μ and the membership functions, positive, will be described by the change of variable $\mu_i = \sigma_i^2$.

Stability will be proved if a Lyapunov function verifying:

$$V(x) - \epsilon \in \Sigma_x \tag{40}$$

$$R(\sigma, x) = -\frac{dV}{dx} p(x, \sigma) \in \Sigma_{x,\sigma} \tag{41}$$

where ϵ is a radially unbounded positive polynomial, usually $\sum_l x_l^2$.

Indeed, setting $V(x)$ to be an arbitrary degree polynomial in the state variables (but *not* in the memberships, in order to avoid the need of its derivatives), $\dfrac{\partial V}{\partial x}$ is also a polynomial in the variables x and σ. If V is linear in some decision variables (the natural choice are the polynomial coefficients), so is $\dfrac{\partial V}{\partial x}$ and expressions (40) and (41) can be directly introduced into SOS programming packages (Prajna, Papachristodoulou, Seiler, & Parrilo, 2004) in order to get values of the decision variables fulfilling the above constraints. Examples of stability analysis of such systems appear in (Sala, 2007; Tanaka, Yoshida, Ohtake, & Wang, 2007b).

Polynomial Fuzzy Controller Design

If the fuzzy polynomial system is affine in control, the procedures in (Tanaka, Yoshida, Ohtake, & Wang, 2007a), which adapts (Prajna, Papachristo-doulou, & Wu, 2004) to the particular case of fuzzy systems, may be readily applied. Indeed, consider an *n*-th order affine in control system:

$$\dot{x} = \sum_{j=1}^{r} \mu_j (A_j(x)z + B_j(x)u) \tag{42}$$

where z is a vector composed of t known polynomials on the state variables, say $z = [x_1 \, x_2 \, x_1^2 \, x_2^2 \, x_1 x_2 \, x_1^3 \, ...]^T$. Consider now a fuzzy control law:

$$u = \sum_{j=1}^{r} \mu_j K_j(x) Q(x) z \tag{43}$$

where $K_j(x)$ and $Q(x)$ are to-be-computed polynomial matrices.

Define a $t \times n$ Jacobian matrix $M(x)$ with elements:

$$M_{ij} = \frac{\partial z_i}{\partial x_j} \qquad \dot{z} = M\dot{x} \tag{44}$$

and, also, define a candidate Lyapunov function:

$$V = z^T P^{-1}(\tilde{x}) z$$

where $\tilde{x}$ are the state variables whose time derivative does not explicitly depend on u, i.e., $\dfrac{\partial \dot{x}_i}{\partial u} = 0$ (that is, the corresponding row of B is zero) and let J denote the index set of those variables. Then, setting $P^{-1}(\tilde{x}) = Q(x)$ in (43), we have:

$$\frac{dV}{dt} = z^T \frac{dP^{-1}}{dt} z + z^T Q\dot{z} + \dot{z}^T Q z =$$
$$= z^T Q(\sum_{j \in J} \frac{dP}{dx_i} \sum_{k=1}^{r} \mu_k A_k^j z) Q z + 2z^T Q M \sum_{k=1}^{r} \mu_k (Az + Bu) \tag{45}$$

So, replacing the control action, and denoting $Qz = v$ we get:

$$\frac{dV}{dt} = \sum_{k=1}^{r} \sum_{l=1}^{r} \mu_k \mu_l v^T (\sum_{j \in J} \frac{dP}{dx_i} A_k^j z) + 2M(A_k P + B_k K_l)v$$

(46)

The reader is referred to (Tanaka et al., 2007a; Prajna, Papachristodoulou, & Wu, 2004) for details. After the change of variable $\mu_i = \sigma_i^2$, if the above expression is a SOS polynomial in (v,x,σ), a stabilising controller has been found. Of course, Polya relaxations in (Sala & Ariño, 2007; Prajna, Papachristodoulou, Seiler, & Parrilo, 2004) and triangulation conditions (Kruszewski et al., 2009) for fuzzy summations, plus other state-feedback design criteria (such as $\mathcal{H}_\infty$, etc...) in (Prajna, Papachristodoulou, & Wu, 2004) may also be adapted to the fuzzy polynomial case (details omitted for brevity).

Specific Issues to MIMO systems

The most basic aspect of the fuzzy Takagi-Sugeno modeling via the sector-nonlinearity approach is that the number of rules depends on the number of *nonlinearities*, and not on the number of *variables*. The number of nonlinearities can be reduced if some aspects of the dynamics are gathered together: for instance, an expression $f(x) = sin(x_1 x_2) + x_1^2 x_2$ may be expressed as either:

$$f(x) = (\sin(x_1 x_2) / x_1 + x_1 x_2)x_1 = f_1(x)x_1$$

(47)

$$f(x) = (\sin(x_1 x_2) / x_1)x_1 + (x_1^2)x_2 = f_2(x)x_1 + f_3(x)x_2$$

(48)

so the same function may be modeled with two (first choice) or four (second choice) rules. By trying to express the nonlinear equations of a multivariable system with a reduced number of (gathered) nonlinearities, the Takagi-Sugeno approach is a viable technique in practice for successful modeling and control of multivariable systems. In order to further reduce the number of

rules, some nonlinearities can be considered as uncertainty.

As an example of the sophistication of the models which the technique allows to use, a ten-trailer system was modeled in (Tanaka, Kosaki, Taniguchi, & Wang, 1997) with the above methodologies.

The polynomial fuzzy models also allow for reducing the number of nonlinearities to only non-polynomial ones, so it further allows obtaining fuzzy models of multivariable physical systems with a reduced number of variables.

So, in general, the TS approach seems a reasonable possibility in nonlinear fuzzy MIMO systems. However, there are some of the above control results whose computational complexity increases greatly with the number of rules and with the system order. To assess the limitations, practical applications of polynomial methods, for instance, reach a limit with a case, say, of: 6-th degree Lyapunov functions, 8 plant rules, 4th-order plant.

The number of rules, the plant order and the complexity of the Lyapunov functions are more important for applicability with limited computing resources than the number of inputs or outputs.

SUMMARY AND DISCUSSION

Some issues regarding application of fuzzy control to multivariable processes have been presented in this chapter. Some of them are well established. Some others need further research and development. Let us summarize the main issues and point out some open questions.

First, a *heuristic approach* has been presented. From direct controllers to fuzzy expert systems, the basic idea is compiling a set of rules provided by human experts or control operators in order to control a complex plant. The main advantages and drawbacks of the approach are:

- *Advantages*
  1. Unified framework applicable to all control levels (from low-level direct control to high-level supervision)
  2. Readability by humans of the resulting control strategies
  3. Model-free
  4. Successful applications reported in the last 20 years
- *Drawbacks*
  1. Need of logic validation (consistency, redundancy, checking that all conceivable situations fire at least one action rule)
  2. Most expert-provided direct-control rules are similar to PI or PD control actions.
  3. Stability proofs are cumbersome if not impossible (nothing can be done if a plant model is not available)
  4. Exponential explosion in the number of partition antecedents and the number of rules when the number of variables increases:
     - Loss of human readability
     - increased difficulty of tuning (increased interaction), increased number of rules... most rules left to default PID-like settings.
  5. In control-specific circles, the research line seems exhausted
  6. Research is nowadays addressed to find *ad hoc* solutions for given problems.

In the second half of the chapter the *function approximation* paradigm for fuzzy systems is introduced. Hence, a more formal approach to control can be achieved, closer to the core control-theory language. The main advantages and drawbacks of the approach are:

- *Advantages*
  1. Stability proofs are actually built under some assumptions. Mathematical rigor instead of heuristic speculation.
  2. It is a currently very active research line in the control engineering area.
  3. Coexistence of data-based (universal function approximation) techniques and first-principle model ones (Takagi-Sugeno, sector nonlinearity)
  4. Extension of many linear results to polynomial systems.
  5. Complexity of the results depend on system order and number of distinct nonlinearities, and not that much on the number of inputs or outputs of the systems. Multivariable systems with a low number of nonlinearities are elegantly handled.
- *Drawbacks*
  1. The techniques have not penetrated in industry applications: once formal numeric computation is needed, competition is fierce with plain old PID, predictive controllers, robust control, etc.
  2. It is unclear how many rules are needed for practical applications of identification-based universal function approximators (how to tune their antecedents is also not firmly established). Many applications do not fulfill the theoretical assumptions, particularly those needed in adaptive neuro-fuzzy control.
  3. Particularly, many of the results in this area do *not* apply to systems with non-smooth nonlinearities (switching, hystheresis, etc. which, unfortunately, are present in many industrial applications).
  4. A first-principle differential equation model is needed for Takagi-Sugeno

systems, which may be difficult or costly to obtain.

5. Most results are available only for state feedback; precise knowledge of the arguments to the membership functions is needed.

6. Although polynomial-time computation load in theory, the number of constraints and decision variables increases heavily with system order, polynomial degrees and number of rules. Hence, the limit of current solvers (Matlab, SeDuMi) is, unfortunately, reached too soon and conservative conditions are obtained.

7. It is not possible to incorporate prior knowledge on how to control a particular process.

8. The results apply only to direct control and not to supervision, fault diagnosis or control reconfiguration.

Detailed additional considerations about the conservativeness of the TS framework are discussed in (Sala, 2009).

FUTURE RESEARCH DIRECTIONS

The above section summarises the main advantages and drawbacks of the proposed methodologies. Evidently, solving or at least mitigating such drawbacks inspires the future research directions suggested below.

In the *heuristic* approach, more research is needed in

*   logic validation of control-specific rules
*   friendly user interfaces for more advanced rulebases (auto-completion, integration of different operation points, integration of fuzzy control rulebases in PLC's, Grafcet, Petri Nets, etc.)

*   Stability analysis. In particular, as some heuristic designs are model-free, research is needed on defining and capturing essential model characteristics (in fuzzy rule form) allowing such analysis.
*   Automated simplification of large rulebases to avoid the exponential explosion in the number of rules in MIMO settings.
*   Providing generic ideas and solution departing from the above-mentioned *ad hoc* solutions for given problems.

In the *function approximation* approach, some open research lines are:

*   Devising reliable software and user interfaces in order to penetrate applications.
*   Convergence between model error descriptions in functional approximation and robust-control oriented error parametrizations.
*   Extending results to fuzzy-hybrid systems to allow for non-smooth nonlinearities.
*   Direct identification of Takagi-Sugeno models from experimental data.
*   Output feedback and observers with imprecisely known antecedent variables.
*   Improving computational aspects of control-specific LMI and polynomial computations for multivariable systems.

CONCLUSION

This chapter has reviewed the possibilities of fuzzy control in multivariable cases, presenting two approaches: the heuristic one and the function-approximation one. A discussion on their main characteristics, as well as a summary of their key advantages and drawbacks has been provided.

The conclusion is that each of the two branches of fuzzy techniques has a distinctive set of advantages and drawbacks so that, when the control engineer is confronted to an actual problem, a thoughtful choice has to be made on which approach to follow and, also, whether to consider / combine the fuzzy techniques with other non-fuzzy ones. Depending on the context, issues regarding the availability/cost of obtaining a model, the existence of prior control knowledge, the need of user interpretability or the precision of the required closed-loop specifications may either favor the heuristic or the TS approach.

REFERENCES

Akar, M., & Ozguner, U. (2000). Decentralized techniques for the analysis and control of Takagi-Sugeno fuzzy systems. *IEEE Transactions on Fuzzy Systems*, 8(6), 691–704. doi:10.1109/91.890328

Albertos, P., & Sala, A. (2002). Fuzzy expert control systems: Knowledge base validation. In H. Unbehauen (Ed.), *UNESCO encyclopedia of life support systems* (p. 6.43.25.3). Oxford, UK, eolss.net: EOLSS publishers.

Albertos, P., & Sala, A. (2004). *Multivariable Control Systems: An Engineering Approach.* New York: Springer.

Andújar, J., & Bravo, J. (2005). Multivariable fuzzy control applied to the physical–chemical treatment facility of a Cellulose factory. *Fuzzy Sets and Systems*, 150(3), 475–492. doi:10.1016/j.fss.2004.03.023

Andújar, J., Bravo, J., & Peregrin, A. (2004). Stability analysis and synthesis of multivariable fuzzy systems using interval arithmetic. *Fuzzy Sets and Systems*, 148(3), 337–353. doi:10.1016/j.fss.2004.01.008

Apkarian, P., & Adams, R. (1998, January). Advanced gain-scheduling techniques for uncertain systems. *IEEE Transactions on Control Systems Technology*, 6, 21–32. doi:10.1109/87.654874

Ariño, C., & Sala, A. (2007). Relaxed LMI conditions for closed-loop fuzzy systems with tensor product structure. *Engineering Applications of Artificial Intelligence*, 8(20), 1036–1046. doi:10.1016/j.engappai.2007.02.011

Ariño, C., & Sala, A. (2008). Extensions to "stability analysis of fuzzy control systems subject to uncertain grades of membership". *IEEE Transactions on Systems, Man and Cybernetics – Part B*, 38(2), 558–563.

Babuška, R., Mollov, S., & Roubos, J. (1998, Oct). Mimo aspects in fuzzy control. In *Proceedings workshop on intelligent control systems.* Darmstadt, Germany.

Babuška, R., & Verbruggen, H. (1996). An overview of fuzzy modeling for control. *Control Engineering Practice*, 4(11), 1593–1606. doi:10.1016/0967-0661(96)00175-X

Bondia, J., Sala, A., Pico, J., & Sainz, M. (2006). Controller design under fuzzy pole-placement specifications: an interval arithmetic approach. *IEEE Transactions on Fuzzy Systems*, 14(6), 822–836. doi:10.1109/TFUZZ.2006.880002

Bouarar, T., Guelton, K., & Manamanni, N. (2007). Lmi based h_∞ controller design for uncertain takagi-sugeno descriptors subject to external disturbances. In *Proc. of ifac advanced fuzzy-neural control 2007*. France: Univ. of Valenciennes.

Boyd, S., ElGhaoui, L., Feron, E., & Balakrishnan, V. (1994). *Linear matrix inequalities in system and control theory*. Philadelphia: Ed. SIAM.

Boyd, S., & Vandenberghe, L. (2004). *Convex Optimization*. Cambridge, MA: Cambridge University Press.

Carrasco, E., & Rodriguez, J. (2004). Diagnosis of acidification states in an anaerobic wastewater treatment plant using a fuzzy-based expert system. *Control Engineering Practice*, 12(1), 59–64. doi:10.1016/S0967-0661(02)00304-0

Chen, S.-S., Chang, Y.-C., Su, S.-F., Chung, S.-L., & Lee, T.-T. (2005). Robust static output-feedback stabilization for nonlinear discrete-time systems with time delay via fuzzy control approach. *Fuzzy Systems. IEEE Transactions on, 13*(2), 263–272.

Chiang, J., & Hao, P. (2004, February). Support vector learning mechanism for fuzzy rule-based modeling: A new approach. *IEEE Transactions on Fuzzy Systems, 12*, 1–12. doi:10.1109/TFUZZ.2003.817839

Dubois, D., & Prade, H. (1978). Operations on fuzzy numbers. *International Journal of Systems Science, 9*(6), 613–626. doi:10.1080/00207727808941724

Dubois, D., & Prade, H. (1997). The three semantics of fuzzy sets. *Fuzzy Sets and Systems, 90*(2), 142–150. doi:10.1016/S0165-0114(97)00080-8

Evsukoff, A., Gentil, S., & Montmain, J. (2000). Fuzzy reasoning in co-operative supervision systems. *Control Engineering Practice, 8*(4), 389–407. doi:10.1016/S0967-0661(99)00170-7

Fang, C.-H., Liu, Y.-S., Kau, S.-W., Hong, L., & Lee, C.-H. (2006). A New LMI-Based Approach to Relaxed Quadratic Stabilization of T-S Fuzzy Control Systems. *IEEE Transactions on Fuzzy Systems, 14*, 286–397.

Feng, G. (2006, Oct.). A survey on analysis and design of model-based fuzzy control systems. *IEEE Transactions on Fuzzy Systems, 14*(5), 676–697. doi:10.1109/TFUZZ.2006.883415

Guerra, T., & Vermeiren, L. (2004). LMI-based relaxed nonquadratic stabilization conditions for nonlinear systems in the takagi-sugeno's form. *Automatica, 10*, 823–829. doi:10.1016/j.automatica.2003.12.014

Gupta, M., & Sinha, N. (Eds.). (1996). *Intelligent control systems: Concepts and applications*. IEEE press.

Habashi, F. (1997). *Handbook of Extractive Metallurgy, Vol II, Part III*. Wiley-VCH. Weinheim, Germany.

Hastie, T., Tibshirani, R., & Friedman, J. (2001). *The elements of statistical learning: data mining, inference, and prediction*. Berlin, Germany: Springer Verlag.

Holmblad, L., & Ostergaard, J. (1982). Control of a cement kiln by fuzzy logic. In Gupta, M., & Sanchez, E. (Eds.), *Fuzzy information and decision processes* (pp. 398–409). Amsterdam: North-Holland.

Hori, E., & Skogestad, S. (2007). Selection of control structure and temperature location for two-product distillation columns. *Chemical Engineering Research & Design, 85*(3), 293–306. doi:10.1205/cherd06115

Hsiao, F., Hwang, J., Chen, C., & Tsai, Z. (2005). Robust stabilization of nonlinear multiple time-delay large-scale systems via decentralized fuzzy control. *IEEE Transactions on Fuzzy Systems, 13*(1), 152–163. doi:10.1109/TFUZZ.2004.836067

Huang, H., Lin, F., & Jeng, J. (2007). Control Structure Selection and Performance Assessment for Disturbance Rejection in MIMO Processes. *Industrial & Engineering Chemistry Research, 46*(26), 9170–9178. doi:10.1021/ie070382i

Hunt, K., & Johansen, T. (1997). Design and analysis of gain-scheduled control using local controller networks. *International Journal of Control, 66*, 619–651. doi:10.1080/002071797224487

Jang, J., Sun, C., & Mizutani, E. (1997). *Neuro-fuzzy and soft computing*. Upper Saddle River, NJ: Prentice Hall.

Kruszewski, A. (2006). *Lois de commande pour une classe de modèles non linéaires sous la forme Takagi-Sugeno: Mise sous forme LMI*. Doctoral dissertation, LAMIH, Université de Valenciennes et du Hainaut-Cambresis.

Kruszewski, A., Guerra, T., & Labiod, S. (2007). Stabilization of Takagi-Sugeno discrete models: towards an unification of the results. *Fuzzy Systems Conference, 2007. FUZZ-IEEE 2007. IEEE International*, 1–6.

Kruszewski, A., Sala, A., Guerra, T., & Ariño, C. (2009). (in press). A triangulation approach to assymptotically exact conditions for fuzzy summations. *IEEE Transactions on Fuzzy Systems*. .doi:10.1109/TFUZZ.2009.2019124

Lee, H., Park, J., & Chen, G. (2001). Robust fuzzy control of nonlinear systems with parametric uncertainties. *IEEE Transactions on Fuzzy Systems*, 9(2), 369–379. doi:10.1109/91.919258

Li, J., Niemann, D., Wang, H., & Tanaka, K. (1999). Parallel distributed compensation for takagi-sugeno fuzzy models: multiobjective controller design. In *Proceedings of the 1999 American control conference*, (Vol. 3, pp. 1832–1836 vol.3).

Liu, X., & Zhang, Q. (2003, September). New approaches to H_∞ controller designs based on fuzzy observers for t-s fuzzy systems via lmi. *Automatica*, 39(9), 1571–1582. doi:10.1016/S0005-1098(03)00172-9

Michalski, R., Carbonell, J., & Mitchell, T. (1986). *Machine learning: An artificial intelligence approach (Vol. I)*. Los Altos, CA: Kaufman Publishers Inc.

Morant, F., Albertos, P., Martinez, M., Crespo, A., & Navarro, J. (1992). RIGAS: An intelligent controller for cement kiln control. In *Proc. IFAC Symp. Artif. Intelligence in Real Time Control*. Delft, The Netherlands: Elsevier.

Nelles, O. (2001). *Nonlinear system identification*. New York: Springer.

Oliveira, M. d., Bernussou, J., & Geromel, J. (1999). A new discrete-time robust stability condition. *Systems & Control Letters*, 37, 261–265. doi:10.1016/S0167-6911(99)00035-3

Palm, R. (1994). Robust control by fuzzy sliding mode. *Automatica*, 30, 1429–1429. doi:10.1016/0005-1098(94)90008-6

Prajna, S., Papachristodoulou, A., Seiler, P., & Parrilo, P. A. (2004). *SOSTOOLS: Sum of squares optimization toolbox for MATLAB*. Retrieved from http://www.cds.caltech.edu/sostools and http://www.mit.edu/~parrilo/sostools.

Prajna, S., Papachristodoulou, A., & Wu, F. (2004). Nonlinear control synthesis by sum of squares optimization: a Lyapunov-based approach. *Control Conference, 2004. 5th Asian, 1*.

Ramirez, M., & Albertos, P. (2008). Pid control with fuzzy adaptation of a metallurgical furnace. In *Granular Computing (Vol. 224). At the Junction of Rough Sets and Fuzzy Sets*. Springer.

Ramírez, M., Haber, R., Peña, V., & Rodríguez, I. (2004). Fuzzy control of a multiple hearth furnace. *IEEE Computers in Industry*, 54, 105–113. doi:10.1016/j.compind.2003.05.001

Ripley, B. D. (1996). *Pattern recognition and neural networks*. Cambridge, UK: Cambridge University Press.

Russell, S., & Norvig, P. (2003). *Artificial intelligence: a modern approach* (2nd ed.). Prentice-Hall.

Sala, A. (2007). *Reducing the gap between fuzzy and nonlinear control (invited talk). In 3rd ifac workshop on advanced fuzzy-neural control afnc'07* (pp. 1–6). Valenciennes, France.

Sala, A. (2008). Encoding fuzzy possibilistic diagnostics as a constrained optimization problem. *Information Sciences*, *178*, 4246–4263. doi:10.1016/j.ins.2008.07.017

Sala, A. (2009). On the conservativeness of fuzzy and fuzzy-polynomial control of nonlinear systems. *Annual Reviews in Control*, *33*(1), 48–58. doi:10.1016/j.arcontrol.2009.02.001

Sala, A., & Albertos, P. (1998). Fuzzy Systems Evaluation: The Inference Error Approach. *IEEE Trans. on Systems Man and Cybernetics. Part B*, *28*, 268–275.

Sala, A., & Albertos, P. (1999). Formal Validation Of Fuzzy Control Techniques. *Mathware & Soft Computing*, *6*, 305–317.

Sala, A., & Ariño, C. (2007). Assymptotically necessary and sufficient conditions for stability and performance in fuzzy control: Applications of Polya's theorem. *Fuzzy Sets and Systems*, *158*(4), 2671–2686. doi:10.1016/j.fss.2007.06.016

Sala, A., & Ariño, C. (2009). (Accepted). Polynomial fuzzy models for nonlinear control. *IEEE Transactions on Fuzzy Systems*. doi:10.1109/TFUZZ.2009.2029235

Sala, A., Diez, J., Navarro, J., & Albertos, P. (2004). Fuzzy Model Usage And Readability In Identification For Control. In *6th biannual world automation congresos wac '04* (pp. 13–18). Seville (Spain): Tsi Press.

Skogestad, S., & Postlethwaite, I. (2005). *Multivariable feedback control: analysis and design*. New York: John Wiley & Sons.

Takagi, T., & Sugeno, M. (1985). Fuzzy identification of systems and its applications to modelling and control. *IEEE Transactions on Systems, Man, and Cybernetics*, *15*(1), 116–132.

Tanaka, K., Ikeda, T., & Wang, H. (1998). Fuzzy regulators and fuzzy observers: Relaxed stability conditions and LMI-based designs. *IEEE Transactions on Fuzzy Systems*, *6*, 250–265. doi:10.1109/91.669023

Tanaka, K., Kosaki, T., Taniguchi, T., & Wang, H. (1997). An LMI Approach to Backer-Upper Control of a Truck with Ten Trailers. In *Ifsa 97 proceedings* (Vol. 3, pp. 376–381).

Tanaka, K., & Wang, H. O. (2001). *Fuzzy control systems design and analysis*. New York: John Wiley & Sons. doi:10.1002/0471224596

Tanaka, K., Yoshida, H., Ohtake, H., & Wang, H. (2007a). Stabilization of Polynomial Fuzzy Systems via a Sum of Squares Approach. *Intelligent Control, 2007. ISIC 2007. IEEE 22nd International Symposium on*, 160–165.

Tanaka, K., Yoshida, H., Ohtake, H., & Wang, H. (2007b). A Sum of Squares Approach to Stability Analysis of Polynomial Fuzzy Systems. *American Control Conference, 2007. ACC '07*, 4071–4076.

Tatjewski, P. (2007). *Advanced control of industrial processes: structures and algorithms*. Berlin, Germany: Springer Verlag.

Tong, R., M.B., B., & Latten, A. (1980). Fuzzy control of the activated sludege wastewater treatment process. *Automatica*, *16*(6), 695–701. doi:10.1016/0005-1098(80)90011-4

Tuan, H., Apkarian, P., Narikiyo, T., & Yamamoto, Y. (2001). Parameterized linear matrix inequality techniques in fuzzy control system design. *Fuzzy Systems. IEEE Transactions on*, *9*(2), 324–332.

Walter, E., & Pronzato, L. (1997). *Identification of parametric models from experimental data*. New York: Springer.

Wang, H. O., Tanaka, K., & Griffin, M. F. (1996). An approach to fuzzy control of nonlinear systems: Stability and design issues. *IEEE Transactions on Fuzzy Systems*, *4*, 14–23. doi:10.1109/91.481841

Wang, L.-X. (1994). *Adaptive fuzzy systems and control*. Englewood Cliffs, NJ: Prentice-Hall.

Zadeh, L. (1965). Fuzzy sets. *Information and Control*, *8*, 338–353. doi:10.1016/S0019-9958(65)90241-X

Zhao, Z., Tomizuka, M., & Isaka, S. (1993). Fuzzy gain scheduling of PID controllers. *IEEE Transactions on Systems, Man, and Cybernetics*, *23*(5), 1392–1398. doi:10.1109/21.260670

Chapter 15
Self–Tuning Control Systems:
A Review of Developments

Keith J. Burnham
Coventry University, UK

Ivan Zajic
Coventry University, UK

Jens G. Linden
Coventry University, UK

ABSTRACT

A concise technical overview of some of the key 'landmark' developments in self-tuning control (STC) are presented. The notion of two coupled sub-algorithms forming the basis of STC together with enhancements to produce adaptive on-line procedures is discussed as well as the potential limitations of such schemes. The techniques covered include optimal minimum variance, sub-optimal pole-placement and long range model-based predictive control. Based on the experiences of the authors in the industrial application of STC, extensions of the standard linear model-based approaches to encompass a class of bilinear model-based schemes, are proposed. Some on-going developments and future research directions in STC for bilinear systems are highlighted. These include the requirements for combined algorithms for control and fault diagnosis and the need for models of differing complexities.

INTRODUCTION

The general aim of the chapter is to provide the reader with an overview of some of the key developments in the field of linear model-based STC. It also includes an introduction to some of the definitions that allow the classification of the resulting STC forms. The definition of STC as being one form of adaptive control which requires two coupled sub-algorithms, one for on-line es-

timation of a discrete-time mathematical model of a plant and the other for control law design and implementation, is presented. The notion of repeatedly updating the model parameters via recursive estimation is introduced. Whilst reference is made to authoritative texts on the subject, a brief review of recursive least squares and Kalman filtering is given, together with extensions to enhance the adaptivity of the schemes. Then, three main categorisations of control law design are considered in the order of their historical development, namely: optimal d-step ahead control

DOI: 10.4018/978-1-61692-811-7.ch015

strategies (where *d* is defined later), sub-optimal pole-placement control strategies and long range model-based predictive control. The above developments are based on assuming a linear model representation for the system to be controlled. Various extensions and refinements have been proposed, and the chapter will provide the details of some of these developments, particularly those of the authors and their colleagues.

In particular, research conducted by the first author has shown that it is often found that the on-line parameter estimation algorithms can produce wildly varying estimations in cases when STC is applied to nonlinear systems. In such cases, the self-tuning principle may become violated, and an extension of the above STC strategies to deal with a class of bilinear systems has been considered. Adopting such a bilinear model representation potentially allows STC to be applied to a wider range of systems for which the notion of linearisation at a point is replaced by that of bilinearisation over a range. A review of some the more recent developments in the area of STC assuming a bilinear model representation is therefore included. Finally, a section containing concluding remarks is given which resumes the overall coverage of the chapter.

A discussion on future open research directions in which the notion of a combined approach for realising control and fault diagnosis and the need for different model complexities is presented in a section on additional reading.

BACKGROUND: TECHNICAL REVIEW OF SELF-TUNING CONTROL

This chapter on *'Self-tuning Control Systems: A Review of Developments'* aims to inform the reader of the major developments and historical landmarks in the topic up to the present day. The earliest reference dates back to the first International Symposium on Self-Adaptive Flight Control in 1959 which was held at what is now the Wright-Patterson Air Force Base, Dayton, Ohio, USA (Gregory, 1959), where the concept of 'self learning' control was first proposed. However, due to the lack of available technology at that time, in terms of reliable computer hardware and software, it was a decade before this concept was to re-emerge. In fact it re-emerged under the name of self-tuning control (STC) in the 1970s and was notably driven in those earlier years by Kalman (1960), Peterka (1970), and Astrom and Wittenmark (1973), who are now recognized as the early pioneers in this field. The major breakthrough by Astrom and Wittenmark (1973) with the optimal d-step ahead minimum variance (MV) self-tuning regulator/controller (STR)/STC in which convergence was proved for the simplest case was perhaps the first landmark which led to a positive resurgence and increased interest in the subject. This was followed in 1975 by the development due to Clarke and Gawthrop (1975) with the generalised minimum variance (GMV) STC in which constraints on control effort could be implemented to achieve a realizable control system. This led naturally to the incremental forms of MV and GMV STC, in which inherent integral action is automatically achieved.

The reader will be reminded that a model is only an approximation, however sophisticated it may appear, and that all models are developed and used for purpose and convenience. In fact, the notion of 'models for purpose' will feature as an underlying thread throughout the chapter, with models for the purpose of control being necessarily simpler in structure than some of their counterparts, e.g. those for fault diagnosis. The above MV and GMV schemes belong to a family of control systems which can be described as Linear Quadratic Gaussian (LQG) since the assumed plant model is linear, the cost function to be minimized is quadratic and the noise affecting the output of system is assumed to be Gaussian. The resulting MV and GMV controllers were developed initially for the auto-regressive with exogenous inputs (ARX) model representations and subsequently extended to the auto-regressive moving average with exogenous inputs (ARMAX) case. The development of the incremental forms led to proposals which made use of ARIMAX model representations, in which the assumed noise model is modified. It should be noted that model structures are normally adopted for convenience and the models commonly used in STC are outlined in the Section on *STC Model Structures*. The MV and GMV STR/C strategies are also known, as stated earlier, as optimal d-step ahead predictive schemes, since it is possible to predict the output d-steps ahead with knowledge of the system input at the current time step. Indeed, this forms the basis of the schemes, since knowing the desired output allows a quadratic cost function to be minimised in order to determine the optimal input. Unfortunately, however, to achieve this goal the resulting optimal STC cancels the process zeros, consequently rendering these approaches inadequate when dealing with non-minimum phase (NMP) systems.

Recognition of the shortfalls of the d-step ahead optimal schemes led to another landmark, namely the proposal for sub-optimal pole-placement STC strategies. These schemes are able to achieve their goals without affecting or utilizing the process zeros. Such a scheme was proposed by Wellstead et al. (1979), and developed within the ARX and ARMAX framework. The resulting controllers were demonstrated to be able to overcome the implementational problems with NMP systems, as experienced by the optimal schemes. The development led to alternative forms, and the state-space pole-placement STC was subsequently proposed by Warwick (1981). This made use of the so-called implicit delay observable canonical form within an innovations state-space setting. Whilst both control strategies are identical in the absence of output measurement noise, they differ in their behaviour in the presence of noise: the latter being due to the increased degree of filtering through the state space model structure. An interesting observation in the state-space equivalent of the ARX model is that the steady-state Kalman filter (SKF) used within the state-variable feedback (SVF) control law, is that the SKF converges to the true states in n-steps, with n being the order of the system. In the case of the equivalent ARMAX model, convergence is dependent on the locations of the zeros of the noise colouring polynomial.

Perhaps the most significant landmark in the development of control law design procedures to date has been that of long range (i.e. greater than d-steps ahead) model-based predictive control. Such an approach was proposed by Clarke et al. (1987). This approach differs from the previous proposals in that the controller not only utilises the actual measured signals, but it also utilises future predicted signals, based on knowledge of the set point in advance. The approach developed in (Clarke et al., 1987) is known as generalised predictive control (GPC) and this is formulated in the incremental control framework, i.e. it utilises the ARIMAX model structure. The basis of the approach is to assume that no further action in terms of incremental controls will take place so that the future control remains constant up to a user defined prediction horizon h-steps ahead (where h is greater than d). By separating the contributions to the future outputs which can be accounted for at the current time, due to current at previous controls, allows a deficit to be predicted, which is essentially the predicted future error that would appear if no adjustment to the control action is made. Then, by representing these future predicted errors in vector form, it is possible to design a suitable quadratic cost function, the minimisation of which will yield a vector of optimal future incremental controls. At each time step the procedure is repeated, thus leading to the notion of a receding horizon approach. Details regarding these key developments of the control law design procedures are provided in the Section on *Control Law Design Procedures*.

This historical-technical review will also consider the development of on-line parameter estimation algorithms for use in STC. Whilst only outlined briefly here, the developments are fully supported by reference material to the original works, where the reader can find detailed derivations. For example the reader will find the original development of the recursive least squares (RLS) algorithm of Plackett (1950), extensions to include extended least squares (ELS), use of forgetting factors and variable forms of forgetting (e.g. due to Fortescue et al. (1981)) to be of value. Utilisation of the Kalman filter (KF) for parameter estimation (following a brief review of its original development for linear state estimation, (Kalman, 1960)) is presented. Whilst the use of coupled KFs for joint state and parameter estimation will be briefly discussed, as well as the extended KF (EKF), e.g. (Young, 1974), for simultaneous state and parameter estimation, a detailed discussion is not given here. In parallel with developments in computer technology, the middle 1980s witnessed some important developments and enhancements in regard to the estimation algorithms used in STC. For example, for the first time it became possible to make repeated on-line use of forgetting factors (leading to variable forgetting factors), covariance matrix resetting techniques and the realisation of methods based on instrumental variables (Young, 1984). Aspects regarding the developments of the on-line parameter estimation algorithms are provided in the Section on *Parameter Estimation Procedures*.

SELF-TUNING CONTROL CONCEPT

Essentially a STC comprises two coupled sub-algorithms, one for the online estimation of the parameters of an assumed model and the other for evaluating the control action from a suitable control law design procedure. In principle any estimation algorithm can be combined with any control law design algorithm, thus the scope is wide and the final choice of this combination will depend on the particular application. In the following, the estimation and control law design algorithms will be introduced separately. Later, in the simulation study in the Section on *Bilinear GPC* the algorithms are combined when a self-tuning linear GPC scheme is applied to a nonlinear system.

In order to fully exploit the STC concept the models upon which the model-based controllers are based are required to be repeatedly updated as the system is driven over the operational range of interest. If the operating range is small then a local linear model with fixed parameters may be sufficient. If, however, the operational range is increased the assumptions on local linearity for the system to be controlled may become violated. Under such conditions the overall closed-loop performance will become reduced due to the increase in the mismatch between the system and model. Alternative approaches using controller gain scheduling, look-up tables as well as multiple switched/blended model solutions have been considered. However, the notion of STC whereby the model parameters are continually updated, as the operating range is traversed, is in effect an infinite model approach, with the advantage that as the system and/or subsystem components change over time, then so do the resulting models. This repeated updating of the model parameters exploites the notion of certainty equivalence in that the estimated values are at each time step assumed to be correct. Taking the approach one step further, it may also be possible, using the same measured input/output data, to detect the onset of a fault condition. Such a concept enables to the establishment of thresholds within which non-violation of certain inequalities allows the implementation of adaptive control via STC, and conversely would allow either a fault detection, or an active fault tolerant control scheme to be triggered. Whilst it is possible, in principle, to combine any model-based control law design procedure with any suitable estimation algorithm, there are certain classifications of STC. The first is to consider the indirect (or explicit) and direct (or implicit) STC schemes. In an indirect direct approach, or explicit scheme, the control law is obtained from the estimated model parameters; the latter are explicitly available for interrogation/ monitoring, thus allowing some degree of intervention between the two coupled algorithms. In the direct approach, on the other hand, the control law is direclty estimated from the input/output data along with the estimated model parameters; the latter being implicit within the scheme (i.e. not explicitly available). A further classification which, is possible in the case of both direct and indirect STC schemes is to make the distinction between non-dual and dual STC. In a non-dual STC the control action is required to perform the role of an ideal control signal only, whereas in the dual approach the control action is not only ideal for control, but is also an ideal signal from an estimation view point. In the remainder of the work is this chapter consideration is given to an explicit non-dual STC. In other words the control action is ideal for control only and the parameters are explicitly available from the estimation algorithm. It is also worth noting in the context of a linear STC applied to nonlinear systems that the self-tuning principle, which holds when estimated model parameters converge to steady values, may become invalidated. Thus further justifing a nonlinear, restricted here to bilinear, STC approach. A block diagram representation of a general explicit non-dual STC scheme is given in Figure 1.

STC MODEL STRUCTURES

A widely used and relatively simple model is the so-called ARX (auto regressive with exogenous inputs) model, where the additive disturbance on the output is assumed to be a white signal having zero mean value. An extension of this model structure is the so-called ARMAX (auto regressive moving average with exogenous inputs) model structure, where the noise is no longer assumed to be white, but is modelled as the output of a moving aver-

Figure 1. Block diagram representation of an explicit non-dual STC, where and θ are defined later

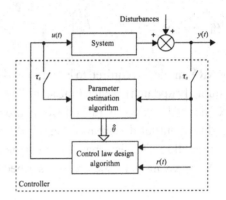

age process. A further extension is the ARIMAX (auto regressive integrated moving average with exogenous inputs) model. In order to proceed, the various model structures are briefly introduced. The ARMAX/ARIMAX model structure can be expressed in the form

$$A(q^{-1})y(t) = q^{-d}B(q^{-1})u(t) + \xi(t) \tag{1}$$

where q^{-1} denotes the backward shift operator defined such that $q^{-i}y(t) = y(t - i)$ and t is the discrete-time index. When dealing with discrete time control it is normal to assume the existence of a zero-order-hold in the input channels, such that $d \geq 1$ represents the integer valued quantity D/τ_s rounded up; D being the system time delay and τ_s the adopted sampling interval. As such, d is regarded as the normalised system time delay. The sampled discrete-time system output and input signals at time t are denoted $y(t)$ and $y(t)$, respectively, and the polynomials $A(q^{-1})$ and $B(q^{-1})$ are defined as

$$A(q^{-1}) = a_0 + a_1 q^{-1} + a_2 q^{-2} + \cdots + a_{n_a} q^{-n_a}, \ a_0 = 1, \tag{2}$$

$$B(q^{-1}) = b_0 + b_1 q^{-1} + b_2 q^{-2} + \cdots + b_{n_b} q^{-n_b}, \ b_0 \neq 0. \tag{3}$$

In STC the model parameter vector, denoted

$$\theta = \begin{bmatrix} a_1 & \cdots & a_{n_a} & b_0 & \cdots & b_{n_b} \end{bmatrix}^T \tag{4}$$

of the ARX model is required to be estimated (i.e. continuously updated) at each time step. The ARMAX and ARIMAX structures differ in the way the additive output disturbance signal, denoted $\xi(t)$, is modelled. The disturbance term in the case of the ARMAX model structure is described as a moving average process

$$\xi(t) = C(q^{-1})e(t) \tag{5}$$

where $e(t)$ is a discrete white noise signal having the variance σ_e^2 and which is coloured by the polynomial $C(q^{-1})$ defined as

$$C(q^{-1}) = c_0 + c_1 q^{-1} + c_2 q^{-2} + \cdots + c_{n_c} q^{-n_c}, \ c_0 = 1 \tag{6}$$

.

However, in many practical problems the disturbance process cannot sufficiently be described as a moving average process. Common examples for such situations are cases when the noise term contains an offset value, i.e. if $\xi(t) = C(q^{-1})e(t) + o(t)$, where $o(t)$ denotes a (potentially time-varying) offset. The disturbance term of the ARIMAX model structure can successfully deal with these cases and is defined as an integrated moving average process

$$\xi(t) = \frac{C(q^{-1})}{\Delta} e(t) \tag{7}$$

where Δ is defined such that $\Delta = 1 - q^{-1}$. The ARIMAX model structure also offers inherent integration action which is exploited for the controller design in incremental form. Finally, the ARX model structure can be considered as a subset of the ARMAX model structure for the case where

$n_c = 0$, i.e. the noise colouring polynomial $C(q^{-1}) = 1$. Note that in the case of $n_c > 0$ the parameter vector θ is extended to include the coefficients of the noise colouring polynomial, denoted c_i, $i = 1...n_c$, i.e.

$$\theta = \begin{bmatrix} a_1 & \cdots & a_{n_a} & b_0 & \cdots & b_{n_b} & c_1 & \cdots & c_{n_c} \end{bmatrix}^T, \tag{8}$$

thus requiring ELS techniques to be employed.

PARAMETER ESTIMATION PROCEDURES

Linear Least Squares

The method of linear least squares (LLS) is perhaps the most basic and yet widely used approach for estimating the parameters of an assumed model structure of a system in control engineering. LLS is used as an off-line parameter estimator, i.e. for estimating the parameter vector, denoted θ, based on a batch of past input/output data pairs. This section provides a summary of the properties of the LLS method. Assume an ARX model structure, i.e. $C(q^{-1}) = 1$, expressed in the form

$$\begin{aligned} y(t) &= -a_1 y(t-1)... - a_{n_a} y(t-n_a) \\ &+ b_0 u(t-d)... + b_{n_b} u(t-d-n_b) + e(t) \end{aligned} \tag{9}$$

or alternatively as a linear regression, i.e.

$$y(t) = \varphi^T(t)\theta + e(t), \tag{10}$$

where the vector of observations, also known as the regression vector, is given by

$$\begin{aligned} \varphi(t) = \big[-y(t-1)... - y(t-n_a) \\ u(t-d)...u(t-d-n_b) \big]^T, \end{aligned} \tag{11}$$

The regression vector comprises of $n_a + n_b + 1$ regressors, which are observed data in discrete time $t = 1, ..., N$, where N denotes the number of observations (measurements). The regression vector consists of the past values of the system output and the system input. It is interesting to note that the word 'regression' is derived from the Latin word 'regredi', which means 'to go back'.

The predicted system output, denoted $\hat{y}(t \mid \theta)$, based on the parameter vector θ can then be computed as

$$\hat{y}(t \mid \theta) = \varphi^T(t)\theta. \tag{12}$$

Thus the prediction error, or residual, between the measured and the predicted output can be expressed as

$$\varepsilon(t) = y(t) - \hat{y}(t \mid \theta). \tag{13}$$

The method of LLS estimates the parameter vector as a best fit between the measured output $y(t)$ and predicted output $\hat{y}(t \mid \theta)$ over $t = 1, ..., N$, such that the sum of squared residuals is minimised, i.e.

$$J_N(\theta) = \frac{1}{N}\sum_{t=1}^{N}\left[\varepsilon(t)\right]^2 = \frac{1}{N}\sum_{t=1}^{N}\left[y(t) - \varphi^T(t)\theta\right]^2. \tag{14}$$

The quadratic cost function eq. (14) can be solved analytically

$$\hat{\theta} = \arg\min_{\theta} J_N(\theta) \tag{15}$$

and the algorithm of LLS is then given by

$$\hat{\theta}(t) = \left[\sum_{t=1}^{N}\varphi(t)\varphi^T(t)\right]^{-1}\sum_{t=1}^{N}\varphi(t)y(t). \tag{16}$$

In order to evaluate the accuracy of the estimator consider the estimation error vector defined as

$$\tilde{\theta} = \theta - \hat{\theta}. \tag{17}$$

Since in practice the true parameter vector θ is not exactly known, it follows that the estimation error vector is also unknown. However, considering the covariance matrix corresponding to the estimation error vector, defined by

$$R = E\left[\tilde{\theta}\tilde{\theta}^T\right], \tag{18}$$

where $E[\cdot]$ denotes the mathematical expectation operator, it can be shown that

$$R = \left[\sum_{t=1}^{N}\varphi(t)\varphi^T(t)\right]^{-1}\sigma_e^2. \tag{19}$$

Commonly only the approximate scaled error covariance matrix is available, i.e.

$$P = \left[\sum_{t=1}^{N}\varphi(t)\varphi^T(t)\right]^{-1}, \tag{20}$$

which is readily observed to be related to the true covariance matrix via the unknown positive scalar σ_e^2. The scaled, matrix P can be computed together with $\hat{\theta}$ from eq. (0.16). The square roots of the diagonal elements of P correspond to the standard deviations of the individual estimated parameters. This is a useful observation which can be exploited, hence the LLS algorithm, via the error covariance matrix, automatically provides information about the accuracy of the estimates.

RECURSIVE LEAST SQUARES

In the STC framework there are practical issues, which require that it is necessary to perform on-line estimation at each time step in order to repeatedly update the estimated parameter vector $\hat{\theta}(t)$ as new observation data are obtained. For this type of problem the offline LLS method in is inefficient, because the observed data set grows larger and larger at each time step. Consequently the computation which ultimately results in the inversion of the matrix P becomes more costly and the demand on computer memory becomes higher as new observations are made. An efficient way to perform this type of on-line estimation is to make use of a RLS scheme. The general form of the RLS algorithm may be stated as

$$\begin{bmatrix}\text{New Parameter Vector}\end{bmatrix}$$
$$= \begin{bmatrix}\text{Previous Parameter Vector}\end{bmatrix} + \begin{bmatrix}\text{Correction}\end{bmatrix}$$
$$\begin{bmatrix}\text{Measured Output - Predicted Output}\end{bmatrix},$$

$$(21)$$

where the new parameter vector, denoted $\hat{\theta}(t)$, is updated based on its previous value, denoted $\hat{\theta}(t-1)$, and the latest measured output $y(t)$. The RLS algorithm originally developed by Plackett (1950), is simply stated here, see e.g. (Ljung, 1999), as:

$$L(t) = P(t-1)\varphi(t)\left[\lambda + \varphi^T(t)P(t-1)\varphi(t)\right]^{-1},$$
$$\hat{\theta}(t) = \hat{\theta}(t-1) + L(t)\left[y(t) - \varphi^T(t)\hat{\theta}(t-1)\right],$$
$$P(t) = \left[P(t-1) - L(t)\varphi^T(t)P(t-1)\right]\lambda^{-1},$$

$$(22)$$

where $0 < \lambda \leq 1$ is a forgetting factor used to repeatedly inflate elements of the covariance matrix, thus keeping the algorithm alert and assisting adaptation (Hsia, 1977). The choice of the forgetting factor is a compromise between algorithm alertness and noise sensitivity (Burnham et

al., 1985). To alleviate this problem, use may be made of a variable forgetting factor $\lambda(t)$ which is adjusted as a function of the estimation prediction error to retain the information content within the algorithm (Fortescue et al., 1981; Wellstead and Sanoff, 1981). Whilst use of a forgetting factor facilitates the tracking of slow variation in parameters, a technique that facilitates the tracking of rapid parameter variation is that of covariance matrix reset. Such a scheme, which can be operated in conjunction with forgetting factors, may trigger reset on set point change, periodically or on detection of large errors in estimation.

It should be noted that unbiased parameter estimates can only be obtained from RLS if the observation vector and the noise sequence are uncorrelated (Young, 1974); true only in the case of a white output noise sequence. Alternatively the problem of biased estimates may be alleviated using algorithms such as ELS, recursive maximum likelihood (Hsia, 1977), recursive instrumental variables (Young, 1970) or a KF configured for parameter estimation (Randall et al., 1991), which is reviewed in following section. If poor parameter estimates are obtained due to insufficient input signal excitation cautious least squares (CLS) may be employed (Burnham and James, 1986; Randall and Burnham, 1994) in which the algorithm is kept alert without disturbing the plant. CLS is also useful when attempting to constrain the estimated parameters to remain within sensible regions based on experience and knowledge of the plant. CLS has been shown to be an adaptive form of online Tikhonov regularisation (Linden, 2005).

KALMAN FILTER CONFIGURED FOR PARAMETER ESTIMATION

The KF was originally developed for estimating the unmeasurable state vector of a linear dynamic system, however the KF finds application in parameter estimation as well. This is due in part to the fact that the KF allows individual forgetting for each parameter, i.e. selective adaptivity. Consider a time varying state-space representation of an unforced discrete-time system subject to white process noise

$$x(t+1) = Ax(t) + v(t),$$
$$y(t) = Cx(t) + e(t), \tag{23}$$

where $x(t)$ is the state vector of dimension $n \times 1$, A is an $n \times n$ state transition matrix, $v(t)$ is an $n \times 1$ process noise vector, $y(t)$ is the measured system output, C is an $1 \times n$ output vector and $e(t)$ is the measurement noise. The random processes $v(t)$ and $e(t)$ have zero mean values, i.e.

$$E[v_1(t)], E[v_2(t)] \ldots E[v_n(t)] = 0, \ E[e(t)] = 0. \tag{24}$$

The covariance matrices are

$$E[v(i)v^T(j)] = V\delta_{ij},$$
$$E[e(i)e^T(j)] = R\delta_{ij}, \tag{25}$$

where δ_{ij} is the Kronecker delta function, i.e. having value of unity if $j = i$ and null if $j \neq i$. The processes are independent of each other, hence

$$E[v(t)e(t)] = 0. \tag{26}$$

The KF for state estimation comprises of two parts and is given by

Prediction (between samples based on the state equation):

The estimated state $\hat{x}(t \mid t-1)$ at time step t given information up to and including time step $t-1$ is computed as

$$\hat{x}(t \mid t-1) = A(t-1)\hat{x}(t-1 \mid t-1) \tag{27}$$

and the update of the covariance matrix is

$$P(t \mid t-1) =$$
$$A(t-1)P(t-1 \mid t-1)A^T(t-1) + V(t-1). \tag{28}$$

Correction (at the sample instants based on the output equation):

The Kalman gain vector is given by

$$K(t) = \frac{P(t \mid t-1)C^T(t)}{R(t) + C(t)P(t \mid t-1)C^T(t)} \tag{29}$$

and the new corrected state estimate is then obtained from

$$\hat{x}(t \mid t) = \hat{x}(t \mid t-1) + K(t)\big[y(t) - C(t)\hat{x}(t \mid t-1)\big]. \tag{30}$$

The updated error covariance matrix is computed as

$$P(t \mid t) = P(t \mid t-1) - K(t)C(t)P(t \mid t-1). \tag{31}$$

The KF can be also configured for parameter estimation. Consider the ARX model structure expressed in the regression form

$$y(t) = \varphi^T(t)\theta(t) + e(t), \tag{32}$$

where the parameter vector is time-varying and may be defined as

$$\theta(t) = \theta(t-1) + v(t). \tag{33}$$

The task is now to estimate the parameter vector $\theta(t)$. The similarity of the state equation in eq. (23) to eq. (33) and the output equation in eq. (23) to eq. (32) becomes obvious, hence the state-space model for the parameter estimation problem is stated

$$\theta(t) = \theta(t-1) + v(t),$$
$$y(t) = \varphi^T(t)\theta(t) + e(t), \qquad (34)$$

where the state transition matrix is simply the identity matrix and the output vector is the observation vector. The KF algorithm configured for parameter estimation is thus given by

Prediction (between samples based on the state equation and any other a prior knowledge):

$$\hat{\theta}(t \mid t-1) = \hat{\theta}(t-1 \mid t-1) \qquad (35)$$

$$P(t \mid t-1) = P(t-1 \mid t-1) + V(t-1) \qquad (36)$$

Correction (at the sampling instants based on the measurement from the output equation):

$$K(t) = \frac{P(t \mid t-1)\varphi(t)}{R(t) + \varphi^T(t)P(t \mid t-1)\varphi(t)} \qquad (37)$$

$$\hat{\theta}(t \mid t) = \hat{\theta}(t \mid t-1) + K(t)\left[y(t) - \varphi^T(t)\hat{\theta}(t \mid t-1)\right] \qquad (38)$$

$$P(t \mid t) = P(t \mid t-1) - K(t)\varphi^T(t)P(t \mid t-1) \qquad (39)$$

The main difference between RLS and the KF for parameter estimation is the way in which the algorithms are tuned to track parameter variation. Whereas the RLS algorithm uses a scalar valued forgetting factor to give equal adaptivity for all parameters, the KF, via the diagonal elements in V in the covariance matrix prediction step, utilises selective adaptivity. In other words, rather than inflating the covariance matrix by dividing by a scalar less than unity as in RLS, the inflation step in the KF is carried out by addition of the matrix V. In this way varying degrees of adaptation may be realised, thus allowing a priori knowledge to be incorporated into the algorithm. Whilst it is usual to consider only the null or positive entries on the diagonal, the off-diagonal entries may

also be exploited to build-in further knowledge on the cross-correlation between certain model parameters.

CONTROL LAW DESIGN PROCEDURES

Minimum Variance Regulator/Controller

The minimum variance (MV) regulators and controllers are considered as a class of optimal schemes, where the optimality is defined by a prescribed cost function. The aim is to minimise the variance of the system output $y(t)$ via an optimal control input $u(t)$. The optimal value of $u(t)$, in the MV sense, is fulfilled when the following assumptions hold:

Assumption 1 *The system to be controlled is linear.*
Assumption 2 *The cost function J is quadratic.*
Assumption 3 *Noise affecting the system output is Gaussian.*

Thus the MV regulators/controllers are also regarded as belonging to the family of LQG (linear, quadratic, Gaussian) regulators/controllers.

Minimum Variance Regulator

Consideration is initially restricted here to the regulator problem, i.e. the desired output or set point, denoted $r(t)$, is equal to zero. The MV regulator cost function is defined as follows

$$J_R = E\left[y^2(t+d)\right] \qquad (40)$$

where d denotes the normalised system time delay. The objective is to determine the optimum value of the current system input $u(t)$, which minimises the cost function eq. (0.40). Note that the current system input at discrete time t affects the future system output at time ($t+d$). The MV algorithm can be derived assuming different model structures. However, for ease of derivation only the ARX models are considered here.

Prior to deriving the general form of the MV algorithm for any ARX model structure it is helpful and intuitive to consider the following particular example.

Example 1. Consider the system described by an ARX model structure, i.e. $C(q^{-1}) = 1$, having $n_a = 2$, $n_b = 1$ and $d = 1$ expressed as a linear difference equation

$$(1 + a_1 q^{-1} + a_2 q^{-2})y(t) = q^{-1}(b_0 + b_1 q^{-1})u(t) + e(t). \tag{41}$$

Expanding and rearranging to a more convenient form leads to

$$y(t) = -a_1 y(t-1) - a_2 y(t-2) + b_0 u(t-1) + b_1 u(t-2) + e(t), \tag{42}$$

where $y(t)$ is a linear combination of the past outputs and past inputs with the most recent input affecting the current output being delayed by one sample step. Since the objective is to determine the current input $u(t)$, shifting forward by one step leads to

$$y(t+1) = -a_1 y(t) - a_2 y(t-1) + b_0 u(t) + b_1 u(t-1) + e(t+1). \tag{43}$$

Note that in general (i.e. for any $d \geq 1$) it is possible to predict the output values up to time ($t+d$) based on the current and past values of control actions. Consequently the MV schemes are also known as d-step ahead predictive schemes. In general, the optimal value of $u(t)$ is obtained by differentiating the cost function eq. (40) with respect to (w.r.t) the argument $u(t)$ and equating to zero for minimum, i.e.

$$u(t) = \arg \min_{u(t)} J_R(u(t)). \tag{44}$$

This procedure can be performed in four steps:

1) Expand quadratic cost function

Prior to expanding the cost function J_R a number of preliminary issues are highlighted. The output $y(t+1)$ in eq. (0.43) is unknown since the future random disturbance $e(t+1)$ is unpredictable. The quantity $y(t + 1)$ can be separated in two parts as follows

$$y(t+1) = \hat{y}(t+1 \mid t) + e(t+1),, \tag{45}$$

where $\hat{y}(t + 1 \mid t)$ denotes the best prediction of $y(t+1)$ based on information available up to and including time t (in the sense of minimising the squared prediction error) and $e(t+1)$ is the unknown noise term. The term $\hat{y}(t+1 \mid t)$ is then expressed as

$$\hat{y}(t+1 \mid t) = -a_1 y(t) - a_2 y(t-1) + b_0 u(t) + b_1 u(t-1). \tag{46}$$

The cost function eq. (40) can then be expressed in the form

$$\begin{aligned} J_R &= E\left[y^2(t+1)\right] \\ &= E\left[\hat{y}(t+1 \mid t) + e(t+1)\right]^2 \\ &= E\left[\hat{y}(t+1 \mid t)\right]^2 + 2E\left[\hat{y}(t+1 \mid t)e(t+1)\right] + E\left[e(t+1)\right]^2. \end{aligned} \tag{47}$$

Since the noise is independent of the predicted output the second term of eq. (47) vanishes. The third term, by definition, is the noise variance s_e^2. The cost function J_R can thus be expressed as

$$J_R = E\left[\hat{y}(t+1 \mid t)\right]^2 + \sigma_e^2. \tag{48}$$

Note that the minimal achievable cost of the above expression is the noise variance σ_e^2, since the term $[\hat{y}(t+1\mid t)]^2$ is forced to be null by the control action. The expansion of the cost function J_R can be carried out as follows

$$J_R = E\left[\hat{y}(t+1\mid t)\right]^2 + \sigma_e^2$$
$$= (-a_1 y(t) - a_2 y(t-1) + b_0 u(t) + b_1 u(t-1))^2 + \sigma_e^2 \tag{49}$$

by omitting terms that do not involve $u(t)$, define the modified cost function $\tilde{J}_R$, i.e.

$$\tilde{J}_R = 2b_0 u(t)(-a_1 y(t) - a_2 y(t-1) + b_1 u(t-1)) + b_0^2 u^2(t) \tag{50}$$

2)   Differentiate with respect to the argument

The expanded cost function eq. (50) is differentiated w.r.t. $u(t)$ as follows

$$\frac{\partial \tilde{J}_R}{\partial u(t)} =$$
$$2b_0(-a_1 y(t) - a_2 y(t-1) + b_1 u(t-1)) + 2b_0^2 u(t). \tag{51}$$

3)   Equate to zero for a minimum

The next step is to equate eq. (51) to zero for obtaining a minimum, hence

$$b_0(-a_1 y(t) - a_2 y(t-1) + b_1 u(t-1)) + b_0^2 u(t) = 0. \tag{52}$$

Note that since the system is linear a global minimum is obtained.

4)   Determine control action

Rearranging eq. (52) to solve for $u(t)$ gives the MV regulator algorithm

$$u(t) = \frac{a_1 y(t) + a_2 y(t-1) - b_1 u(t-1)}{b_0}. \tag{53}$$

Note that the above result reinforces the need for $b_0 \neq 0$. The MV regulator algorithm in the case of any value of n_a and n_b and for a fixed value of $d = 1$ is then given by

$$u(t) = \frac{1}{b_0}\left[\sum_{i=1}^{n_a} a_i y(t+d-i) - \sum_{i=1}^{n_b} b_i u(t-i)\right]. \tag{54}$$

The general form of the MV regulator for an ARX model structure assuming $d \geq 1$ is now cosidered. The d-step ahead prediction of the system output is required. This is accomplished through the linear predictor. The predictor of $y(t+d)$ minimises the mathematical expectation of the squared prediction error $\varepsilon(t)$, i.e.

$$\hat{y}(t+j\mid t) = \arg\min_{\hat{y}(t+j\mid t)} E\left[e^2(t+j)\right],$$
$$= \arg\min_{\hat{y}(t+j\mid t)} E\left[y(t+j) - \hat{y}(t+j\mid t)\right]^2, \tag{55}$$

where $\hat{y}(t+j\mid t)$ denotes the prediction of $y(t+j)$ based on information available up to and including time t and over the range $j = 1, \ldots, d$. Computing the prediction of the output by minimisation of eq. (55) for higher values of the delay $d > 1$ is rather impractical and a recursive form of the d-step ahead predictor is developed instead, which can be relatively straightforwardly programmed. The d-step ahead predictor of the system output for the ARX model structure is given by:

$$\hat{y}(t+j\mid t) = M_j(q^{-1})y(t) + N_j(q^{-1})u(t),, \tag{56}$$

where the polynomials $M_j(q^{-1})$ and $N_j(q^{-1})$ are, respectively, defined as:

$$M_j(q^{-1}) =$$
$$m_{j,0} + m_{j,1}q^{-1} + m_{j,2}q^{-2} + \cdots + m_{j,i}q^{-i}, \ i = n_a - 1 = n_m,$$

(57)

$$N_j(q^{-1}) =$$
$$n_{j,0} + n_{j,1}q^{-1} + n_{j,2}q^{-2} + \cdots + n_{j,i}q^{-i}, \ i = n_b + j - 1 = n_n,$$

(58)

.The individual coefficients $m_{j,i}$ and $n_{j,i}$ are generated, respectively, as follows

$$m_{j,i} = \sum_{l=1}^{j} [-a_l m_{j-l,i}] - a_{j+i}$$

(59)

and

$$n_{j,i} = b_i - \sum_{l=1}^{j} [a_l n_{j-l,i-l}],$$

(60)

where $m_{j-l,l} = 0$ if subscript $j = l$, and the term $n_{j-l,i-l} = 0$ if $j = l$ or $l \geq i$. The procedure of generating the polynomials $M_j(q^{-1})$ and $N_j(q^{-1})$ is shown in the following illustrative example.

Example 2. Generate the coefficients of the polynomials $M_j(q^{-1})$ and $N_j(q^{-1})$ for the ARX model structure having $n_a = 3$, $n_b = 2$ and $d = 2$. The model is given by

$$y(t) = -a_1 y(t-1) - a_2 y(t-2) - a_3 y(t-3)$$
$$-b_0 u(t-2) - b_1 u(t-3) - b_2 u(t-4).$$

(61)

Shifting forward by one step the prediction at time $(t+1)$ is computed as

$$\hat{y}(t+1 \mid t) = -a_1 y(t) - a_2 y(t-1) - a_3 y(t-2)$$
$$-b_0 u(t-1) - b_1 u(t-2) - b_2 u(t-3)$$

(62)

and shifting forward by one more step the prediction at time $(t+2)$ becomes

$$\hat{y}(t+2 \mid t) = -a_1 \hat{y}(t+1 \mid t) - a_2 y(t) - a_3 y(t-1)$$
$$-b_0 u(t) - b_1 u(t-1) - b_2 u(t-2).$$

(63)

Substituting eq. (62) for $\hat{y}(t+j \mid t)$ in eq. (63) leads to

$$\hat{y}(t+2 \mid t) = \left(a_1^2 - a_2\right) y(t) + \left(a_1 a_2 - a_3\right) y(t-1) + \left(a_1 a_3\right) y(t-2) + b_0 u(t)$$
$$+ \left(b_1 - a_1 b_0\right) u(t-1) + \left(b_2 - a_1 b_1\right) u(t-2) + \left(-a_1 b_2\right) u(t-3),$$

(64)

which is the desired prediction of the system output at time $(t+d)$. The same results will now be obtained utilizing the predictor eq. (56). The $M_j(q^{-1})$ and $N_j(q^{-1})$ polynomials are computed recursively for $j = 1, \ldots, d$. Starting with the prediction $j = 1$, the $M_j(q^{-1})$ polynomial has order $n_m = n_a - 1 = 2$ and, making use of eq. (59), its coefficients are computed as

$$m_{1,0} = -a_1 m_{0,0} - a_1 = -a_1,$$
$$m_{1,1} = -a_1 m_{0,1} - a_2 = -a_2,$$
$$m_{1,2} = -a_1 m_{0,2} - a_3 = -a_3.$$

(65)

The $N_j(q^{-1})$ polynomial has order $n_n = n_b + j - 1 = 2$ and, utilizing eq. (60), the individual coefficients are computed as

$$n_{1,0} = b_0 - a_1 n_{0,-1} = b_0,$$
$$n_{1,1} = b_1 - a_1 n_{0,0} = b_1,$$
$$n_{1,2} = b_2 - a_1 n_{0,1} = b_2.$$

(66)

For the prediction $j = 2$, the orders of the corresponding $M_2(q^{-1})$ and $N_2(q^{-1})$ polynomials are $n_m = n_a - 1 = 2$ and $n_n = n_b + j - 1 = 2$, respectively, so that the individual coefficients are obtained as

$$m_{2,0} = \left(-a_1 m_{1,0} - a_2 m_{0,0}\right) - a_2 = a_1 a_1 - a_2,$$
$$m_{2,1} = \left(-a_1 m_{1,1} - a_2 m_{0,1}\right) - a_3 = a_1 a_2 - a_3,$$
$$m_{2,2} = \left(-a_1 m_{1,2} - a_2 m_{0,2}\right) - a_4 = a_1 a_3,$$

$$(67)$$

and

$$n_{2,0} = b_0 - \left(a_1 n_{1,-1} + a_2 n_{0,-2}\right) = b_0,$$
$$n_{2,1} = b_1 - \left(a_1 n_{1,0} + a_2 n_{0,-1}\right) = b_1 - a_1 b_0,$$
$$n_{2,2} = b_2 - \left(a_1 n_{1,1} + a_2 n_{0,0}\right) = b_2 - a_1 b_1,$$
$$n_{2,3} = b_3 - \left(a_1 n_{1,2} + a_2 n_{0,1}\right) = -a_1 b_2,$$

$$(68)$$

respectively.

Minimising the cost function eq. (40) and utilisng the d-step ahead predictor eq. (56) leads to the general MV regulator algorithm for an ARX model structure

$$u(t) = \frac{1}{b_0}\left[-\sum_{i=0}^{n_m} m_{j,i} y(t-i) - \sum_{i=1}^{n_n} n_{j,i} u(t-i)\right],$$

$$(69)$$

Where $j = d$ and $b_0 = n_{d,0}$. Note that the recursive generation of $\hat{y}(t+j \mid t)$ from eq. (0.56) is not the only approach for developing the MV controller. A widely utilised alternative is the adoption of the so-called Diophantine equation (Clarke et al., 1987; Wellstead and Zarrop, 1991). This approach is directly applicable for any ARX, ARMAX and ARIMAX model structure.

Minimum Variance Controller

In many industrial applications the aim is not just to drive the output to a zero value, as in the regulator case, but to track a reference signal $r(t)$, which is then referred to as a servo controller. The reference signal $r(t)$ is known up to and inlcuding time t. The servo controller MV cost function is defind as

$$J_S = E\left[y(t+d) - r(t)\right]^2. \qquad (70)$$

In a similar manner to the regulator case, a derivation of the MV control algorithm is highlighted initially via a particular example which is then followed by a generalised algorithm for an ARX model structure.

Example 3. Consider a system described by an ARX model structure having $n_a = 2$, $n_b = 1$ and $d = 1$. As for the MV regulator, following the four step procedure, the first step is the expansion of the quadratic cost function, which is now defined by

$$J_S = E\left[y(t+1) - r(t)\right]^2, \qquad (71)$$

where, substituting $\hat{y}(t+1 \mid t) + e(t+1)$ for $y(t+1)$ defined in eq. (45), the cost function J_S becomes

$$J_S = E\left[\hat{y}(t+1 \mid t) + e(t+1) - r(t)\right]^2$$
$$= E\left[\hat{y}(t+1 \mid t)\right]^2 - 2E\left[\hat{y}(t+1 \mid t)r(t)\right] + E\left[r(t)\right]^2$$
$$+ E\left[e(t+1)\right]^2 - 2E\left[e(t+1)r(t)\right] + 2E\left[\hat{y}(t+1 \mid t)e(t+1)\right].$$

$$(72)$$

Since the noise $e(t+1)$ is independent of $r(t)$ and $\hat{y}(t+1 \mid t)$ the last two terms of eq. (72) vanish. Note that the variance of the reference signal $E[r(t)]^2 = \sigma_r^2$ enters the cost function and increases its reachable minimal value. Defining the modified cost function $\tilde{J}_S$, by omitting terms that do not involve $u(t)$, leads to

$$\tilde{J}_S =$$
$$2b_0 u(t)(-a_1 y(t) - a_2 y(t-1) + b_1 u(t-1) - r(t)) + b_0^2 u^2(t).$$

$$(73)$$

The minimisation of the modified cost function $\tilde{J}_S$ can be computed analytically by differentiating $\tilde{J}_S$ w.r.t. the argument and subsequently setting the derivative $\dfrac{\partial \tilde{J}_S}{\partial u(t)}$ to zero. So that differentiating gives

$$\frac{\partial \tilde{J}_s}{\partial u(t)} = 2b_0(-a_1 y(t) - a_2 y(t-1) + b_1 u(t-1) - r(t)) + 2b_0^2 u(t)$$

$$(74)$$

and setting to zero for a minimum yields

$$-a_1 y(t) - a_2 y(t-1) + b_1 u(t-1) - r(t) + b_0 u(t) = 0.$$

$$(75)$$

Rearranging to solve for $u(t)$ gives

$$u(t) = \frac{a_1 y(t) + a_2 y(t-1) - b_1 u(t-1) + r(t)}{b_0}.$$

$$(76)$$

In a similar manner to the regulator case, it is straightforward to show that the general form of the MV controller for an ARX model can be derived as

$$u(t) = \frac{1}{b_0}\left[-\sum_{i=0}^{n_m} m_{j,i} y(t-i) - \sum_{i=1}^{n_n} n_{j,i} u(t-i) + r(t)\right],$$

$$(77)$$

which may be directly compared to the regulator case given by eq. (69).

Simulation Study: MV Controller

Consider the system described by the ARX model given by

$$y(t) =$$
$$1.5y(t-1) - 0.7y(t-2) + 0.7u(t-1) + 0.3u(t-2) + e(t)$$

$$(78)$$

having the noise variance $\sigma_e^2 = 1$. The system runs in an open-loop setting during the time interval $t = \langle 1, 25 \rangle$ and in a closed-loop setting with the MV controller eq. (77) during the time interval $t = \langle 25, 100 \rangle$. The reference signal switches between ± 5 units with a period of 25 samples. In order to assess the ability of the controller to track

the reference signal the mean square error (MSE) criterion is introduced. The MSE is defined as

$$MSE = \frac{1}{N - t_0}\left[\sum_{t=t_0}^{N} (y(t) - r(t))^2\right],$$

$$(79)$$

where $N = 100$ denotes the total number of discrete time steps and t_0 denotes the start of the evaluation. The mean square control (MSC) criterion is introduced in order to evaluate the usage of control effort, e.g. energy, and this is defined as

$$MSC = \frac{1}{N - t_0}\left[\sum_{t=t_0}^{N} u^2(t)\right].$$

$$(80)$$

The results of simulation of the system together with the MV controller are shown in Figure 2. The performance in terms of MSE and MSC are *MSE* = 4.22 and *MSC* = 19.46, respectively, for $t_0 = 30$. It is evident that the MV algorithm achieves its control objectives during the closed-loop period.

GENERAL REMARKS ON THE MV CONTROLLER

The practical problems of choosing the sampling interval for the estimation of the model parameters are discussed here with connection to the MV controllers. Properties of the MV control are also discussed.

To illustrate some of the MV controller properties consider an ARX model structure having $n_a = 2$, $n_b = 1$ and $d = 1$. The discrete time transfer function for this system is

$$\frac{Y(q^{-1})}{U(q^{-1})} = \frac{q^{-1}(b_0 + b_1 q^{-1})}{1 + a_1 q^{-1} + a_2 q^{-2}}.$$

$$(81)$$

Figure 2. Simulation of the MV controller for t = ⟨1, 25⟩ in the open-loop setting and for t = ⟨25, 100⟩ in the closed loop setting

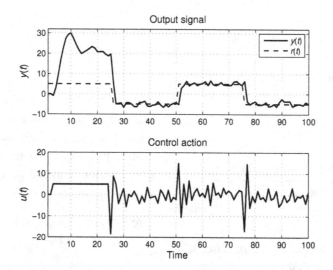

The MV control algorithm for this system is

$$u(t) = \frac{a_1 y(t) + a_2 y(t-1) - b_1 u(t-1)}{b_0} \qquad (82)$$

or in transfer function form

$$\frac{U(q^{-1})}{Y(q^{-1})} = \frac{a_1 + a_2 q^{-1}}{b_0 + b_1 q^{-1}}. \qquad (83)$$

Note that the denominator of the controller eq. (83) consists of the numerator of the system eq. (81), hence if the system zeros are outside the unit circle the controller poles become unstable. A system with the zeros outside the unit circle is known as a NMP system. This phenomenon occurs naturally or can be caused by inappropriate selection of the sampling interval τ_s; choice of τ_s is therefore crucial. It is recommended by the authors to choose τ_s such that $d \in ⟨1, 5⟩$, where 5 is considered to be high. In summary, since it is noted that MV controllers achieve their objectives by cancelling process zeros and that choice of τ_s too small can give rise to a NMP representation,

it is important when dealing with MV control in practice to consider such factors.

The closed-loop transfer function for the given system and MV controller is

$$\frac{Y(q)}{R(q)} = \frac{a_1 q + a_2}{q^2} \qquad (84)$$

hence the closed-loop poles lie at the origin and the response of such a system is as fast as possible; sometimes referred to as 'dead beat' response. This leads to excessively large demands on control action $u(t)$, which can be practically infeasible to realise.

GENERALISED MINIMUM VARIANCE CONTROLLER

The GMV controller has been proposed in order to overcome some of the issues connected with the concept of MV controllers. The issues are namely the excessive use of control effort in achieving the control objectives and the shortfall of controlling NMP systems. Introducing the cost function of the form

$$J_{GMV} = E\left[(Py(t+d) - Rr(t))^2 + (Qu(t))^2\right]$$

(85)

allows for a trade-off between tracking performance and cost of control. The scalars P, R and Q are user specified cost weighting parameters. Another formulation of the GMV cost function can be found in (Wellstead and Zarrop, 1991), where the cost weighting parameters are assumed to be polynomials. The cost weighting parameter Q is of particular importance, since for $Q > 0$ the control effort is constrained, having the effect of displacing the closed-loop poles away from the origin; i.e. no longer a deadbeat response and more practically realisable. The GMV controller is derived for the illustrative example.

Example 4. Consider a system described by an ARX model structure having $n_a = 2$, $n_b = 1$ and $d = 1$ expressed as a linear difference equation

$$y(t+1) = -a_1 y(t) - a_2 y(t-1) + b_0 u(t) + b_1 u(t-1) + e(t+1).$$

(86)

Separation of known (current and past) and unknown (future) information leads to

$$y(t+1) = \hat{y}(t+1 \mid t) + e(t+1),$$

(87)

where

$$\hat{y}(t+1 \mid t) = -a_1 y(t) - a_2 y(t-1) + b_0 u(t) + b_1 u(t-1).$$

(88)

The next step is to expand the quadratic cost function J_{GMV}, hence substituting eq. (87) into the cost function eq. (85) gives

$$\begin{aligned}
J_{GMV} &= E\left[(P\hat{y}(t+1 \mid t) + Pe(t+1) - Rr(t))^2 + (Qu(t))^2\right], \\
&= E\left[P\hat{y}(t+1 \mid t)\right]^2 - E\left[2PR\hat{y}(t+1 \mid t)r(t)\right] + E\left[Qu(t)\right]^2 \\
&\quad + E\left[Rr(t)\right]^2 + E\left[Re(t+1)\right]^2.
\end{aligned}$$

(89)

The last two terms are weighted variances of $r(t)$ and $e(t+1)$, which forms the minimum achievable cost for J_{GMV}. Omitting terms which do not involve $u(t)$ leads to the modified cost function, which takes the form

$$\begin{aligned}
\tilde{J}_{GMV} &= 2P^2 b_0 u(t)(-a_1 y(t) - a_2 y(t-2) + b_1 u(t-1)) \\
&\quad + (Pb_0 u(t))^2 - 2PRb_0 u(t)r(t) + (Qu(t))^2.
\end{aligned}$$

(90)

Differentiation of the modified cost function $\tilde{J}_{GMV}$ w.r.t. $u(t)$ is computed as

$$\begin{aligned}
\frac{\partial \tilde{J}_{GMV}}{\partial u(t)} &= 2P^2 b_0(-a_1 y(t) - a_2 y(t-2) + b_1 u(t-1)) \\
&\quad + 2(Pb_0)^2 u(t) - 2PRb_0 r(t) + 2Q^2 u(t)
\end{aligned}$$

(91)

and setting to zero for a minimum

$$\begin{aligned}
&P^2 b_0(-a_1 y(t) - a_2 y(t-2) + b_1 u(t-1)) + \\
&P^2 b_0^2 u(t) - PRb_0 r(t) + Q^2 u(t) = 0
\end{aligned}$$

(92)

leads to the GMV control algorithm

$$u(t) = \frac{Pb_0[P(a_1 y(t) + a_2 y(t-1) - b_1 u(t-1)) + Rr(t)]}{P^2 b_0^2 + Q^2}.$$

(93)

The general form of GMV controller for an ARX model structure, which holds for any value of n_a, n_b and d can be derived by adopting the d-step ahead predictor

$$\hat{y}(t+j \mid t) = M_j(q^{-1})y(t) + N_j(q^{-1})u(t),$$

(94)

where $j = 1, ..., d$ and the polynomials $M_j(q^{-1})$ and $N_j(q^{-1})$ are defined in eq. (57) and eq. (58), respectively. The same procedure for obtaining the controller for the special case of $d = 1$ is followed, but with use made of the d-step ahead predictor eq. (94). The GMV control algorithm for an ARX model structure is then given by

$$u(t) = \left[P^2 n_{j,0}^2 + Q^2 \right]^{-1} P n_{j,0} \left[Rr(t) - P\sum_{i=0}^{n_m} m_{j,i} y(t-i) - P\sum_{i=1}^{n_n} n_{j,i} u(t-i) \right] \quad (95)$$

where $j = d$ and $n_{j,0} = b_0$. The GMV controller has advantageous over the MV scheme, but choice of the controller weighting P, R and Q is not immediately straightforward. For example too large a value for Q may result in the output not achieving the set point. Whilst there are ways to overcome this via careful choice of the other weightings, alternative incremental formulations offer immediate advantages.

INCREMENTAL GMV CONTROLLER

Recognising the difficulties in achieving a satisfactory trade-off via the cost weighting parameters and the additional potential problems due to the presence of non-zero mean output disturbances with the standard GMV scheme, prompted the need for an alternative approach and the incremental form of GMV (IGMV) was proposed. Such an approach guarantees a type-1 servo mechanism performance, hence a zero steady-state error is achieved for a constant reference signal. This is due to the inherent integral action within the IGMV scheme. To realise this scheme, the IGMV cost function is defined as

$$J_{IGMV} = E\left[y(t+d) - r(t)\right]^2 + \lambda E\left[\Delta u(t)\right]^2, \quad (96)$$

in which only a single weighting parameter λ is required. The derivation of the control algorithm is illustrated via an example.

Example 5. An ARIMAX model structure is used to derive the IGMV control algorithm. The model is given by

$$A(q^{-1})y(t) = q^{-d}B(q^{-1})u(t) + \frac{C(q^{-1})}{\Delta} e(t), \quad (97)$$

where, for simplicity, the case of $C(q^{-1}) = 1$ is considered, hence yielding the ARIX model. Consideration is given to an example system in which $n_a = 2$, $n_b = 1$ and $d = 1$. The model given by eq. (97) can be expressed as

$$(1 + a_1 q^{-1} + a_2 q^{-2})\Delta y(t) = q^{-1}(b_0 + b_1 q^{-1})\Delta u(t) + e(t). \quad (98)$$

Defining the polynomial $\tilde{A}(q^{-1}) = \Delta A(q^{-1})$ an expression for eq. (98) takes the form

$$(1 + \tilde{a}_1 q^{-1} + \tilde{a}_2 q^{-2} + \tilde{a}_3 q^{-3})y(t) = q^{-1}(b_0 + b_1 q^{-1})\Delta u(t) + e(t), \quad (99)$$

where

$$\tilde{a}_i = (a_i - a_{i-1}). \quad (100)$$

The aim is to determine $u(t)$, hence shifting the output d-steps forward leads to

$$y(t+1) = -\tilde{a}_1 y(t) - \tilde{a}_2 y(t-1) - \tilde{a}_3 y(t-2) + b_0 \Delta u(t) + b_1 \Delta u(t-1) + e(t+1). \quad (101)$$

Assuming a zero mean Gaussian distributed white noise signal, the best prediction for $e(t+1)$ is zero. The predicted output at time $(t+d)$ is then expressed as

$$\hat{y}(t+1\,|\,t) =$$
$$-\tilde{a}_1 y(t) - \tilde{a}_2 y(t-1) - \tilde{a}_3 y(t-2) + b_0 \Delta u(t) + b_1 \Delta u(t-1) \tag{102}$$

and the system output at time $(t+1)$ can be re-expressed as

$$y(t+1) = \hat{y}(t+1\,|\,t) + e(t+1). . \tag{103}$$

The next step in deriving of IGMV controller is the expansion of the quadratic cost function J_{IGMV}, hence substituting eq. (103) into the cost function J_{IGMV} gives

$$J_{IGMV} = E[y(t+d) - r(t)]^2 + \lambda E[\Delta u(t)]^2,$$
$$= E[\hat{y}(t+1\,|\,t)]^2 - 2E[\hat{y}(t+1\,|\,t)r(t)] + \lambda E[\Delta u(t)]^2$$
$$+ E[r(t)]^2 + E[e(t+1)]^2. \tag{104}$$

Defining the modified cost function $\tilde{J}_{IGMV}$, (omitting terms which do not involve $\Delta u(t)$) and exapanding leads to

$$\tilde{J}_{IGMV} = 2b_0 \Delta u(t)(-\tilde{a}_1 y(t) - \tilde{a}_2 y(t-1) - \tilde{a}_3 y(t-2) + b_1 \Delta u(t-1) - r(t))$$
$$+ b_0^2 (\Delta u(t))^2 + \lambda (\Delta u(t))^2. \tag{105}$$

Differentiating w.r.t. the argument $\Delta u(t)$ and equating to zero for a minimum, leads to

$$\frac{\partial J_{IGMV}}{\partial \Delta u(t)} = 2b_0(-\tilde{a}_1 y(t) - \tilde{a}_2 y(t-1) - \tilde{a}_3 y(t-2) + b_1 \Delta u(t-1) - r(t))$$
$$+ 2b_0^2 \Delta u(t) + 2\lambda \Delta u(t) \tag{106}$$

and

$$b_0(-\tilde{a}_1 y(t) - \tilde{a}_2 y(t-1) - \tilde{a}_3 y(t-2) + b_1 \Delta u(t-1) - r(t)).$$
$$+ b_0^2 \Delta u(t) + \lambda \Delta u(t) = 0 \tag{107}$$

Rearranging the eq. (107) to solve for $\Delta u(t)$, the IGMV control algorithm is given by

$$\Delta u(t) = \frac{b_0(\tilde{a}_1 y(t) + \tilde{a}_2 y(t-1) + \tilde{a}_3 y(t-2) - b_1 \Delta u(t-1) + r(t))}{b_0^2 + \lambda}. \tag{108}$$

The applied control action to the plant is then computed as

$$u(t) = u(t-1) + \Delta u(t), \tag{109}$$

thus guaranteeing type-1 servo-mechanism performance.

The general form of the IGMV controller requires a d-step ahead predictor. In an ARIX case the predictor is derived in a similar manner to that for an ARX model structure eq. (55). The predictor for an ARIX model is given by

$$\hat{y}(t+j\,|\,t) = P_j(q^{-1})y(t) + G_j(q^{-1})\Delta u(t), \tag{110}$$

where $j = 1, \ldots, d$ and the polynomials $P_j(q^{-1})$ and $G_j(q^{-1})$ are defined as

$$P_j(q^{-1}) = p_{j,0} + p_{j,1}q^{-1} + p_{j,2}q^{-2} + \cdots + p_{j,i}q^{-i}, \ i = n_a - 1 = n_p, \tag{111}$$

$$G_j(q^{-1}) = \sum_{l=0}^{j-1}(p_{l,0}q^{-l}\sum_{i=0}^{n_b}b_i q^{-i}), \ n_g = n_b + j - 1, \tag{112}$$

respectively, where the individual coefficients $p_{j,i}$ of the successive $P_j(q^{-1})$ polynomials are evaluated as follows

$$p_{j,i} = p_{j-1,i+1} + (a_i - a_{i+1})p_{j-1,0}, \ p_{0,0} = 1. \tag{113}$$

Note that the polynomial order n_g linearly increases as the number of predictions j increases. Minimising the cost function J_{IGMV} with respect to $\Delta u(t)$, utilising the d-step ahead predictor eq.

(110) for an ARIX model structure leads to the IGMV controller

$$\Delta u(t) = [g_{j,0}^2 + \lambda]^{-1} g_{j,0} \left[r(t) - \sum_{i=1}^{n_g} g_{j,i} \Delta u(t-i) - \sum_{i=0}^{n_p} p_{j,i} y(t-i) \right]$$
(114)

where $j = d$ and $g_{j,0} = b_0$, with $u(t)$ finally being obtained as indicated in eq. (109).

General Remarks on the GMV Controller

The GMV controller is a natural extension of the MV controller. Whereby constraining the control effort of the MV controller the issues connected with NMP systems and excessive use of control action can be overcome. The choice of the cost weighting parameters is crucial and application specific. The P, R and Q parameters can be chosen either by an operator or adaptively (with some initial a priori values) within a STC framework. The former is discussed here. Setting $P = R = 1$ and $Q = 0$ results in MV control. Setting $P = R = 1$ and varying $Q > 0$ allows a trade-off between tracking ability and reduction of control effort. Hence, by over-constraining the control effort (e.g. energy) the GMV controller may not achieve the set point and steady-state errors occur. This can be overcome by retaining $P=1$ and setting $R > 1$, which results in a new 'dummy' set point aim. Note that the importance of tracking ability versus reducing control cost is governed by the ratio $P : Q$ and not by their absolute values. The steady-state offset problems can also be overcome by using IGMV control, where inherent integral action guarantees type-1 performance. In addition only one tuning parameter λ is required. Note that choice of $\lambda = 0$ results in incremental MV control.

POLE PLACEMENT CONTROL

The next chronological development in the historic-technical review is that of self-tuning pole-placement (or pole-assignment) control (Wellstead et al., 1979). The aim of pole-placement control (PPC) is to match the closed-loop transient behaviour of a feedback system to a desired user prescribed form. Often referred to as eigenvalue assignment, the effect of PPC is that of relocation of the closed-loop poles of the system. The method is suitable for controller design where the performance criteria may be expressed in terms of the classical frequency or transient response. The approach has proven to be attractive to practising engineers, due probably to its close links with classical control. For the development of the PPC the system represented by noise free ARX model is considered

$$A(q^{-1})y(t) = q^{-d}B(q^{-1})u(t).$$
(115)

The control law of the PPC is defined as

$$F(q^{-1})u(t) = G(q^{-1})y(t) + Mr(t),$$
(116)

where the controller polynomials $F(q^{-1})$ and $G(q^{-1})$ are, respectively, defined as

$$F(q^{-1}) = f_0 + f_1 q^{-1} + f_2 q^{-2} + \cdots + f_{n_f} q^{-n_f}, f_0 = 1,$$
(117)

$$G(q^{-1}) = g_0 + g_1 q^{-1} + g_2 q^{-2} + \cdots + g_{n_g} q^{-n_g}, g_0 \neq 0$$
(118)

having the corresponding recommended orders $n_f = n_b + d - 1$ and $n_g = n_a - 1$, respectively. The system configured in closed-loop with the controller is depicted in Figure 3. The closed-loop transfer function is given by

Figure 3. Pole-placement controller with compensator

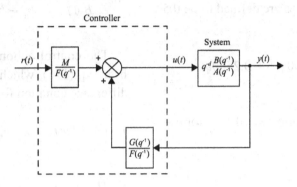

$$\frac{Y(q^{-1})}{R(q^{-1})} = \left[\frac{MB(q^{-1})}{F(q^{-1})A(q^{-1})}q^{-d}\right]\left[1 - q^{-d}\frac{G(q^{-1})B(q^{-1})}{F(q^{-1})A(q^{-1})}\right]^{-1},$$

$$= \frac{q^{-d}B(q^{-1})M}{F(q^{-1})A(q^{-1}) - q^{-d}G(q^{-1})B(q^{-1})}. \tag{119}$$

The aim is to assign the closed-loop poles to a specified location by equating the characteristic equation (denominator) of eq. (0.119) to a user specified design polynomial $\Gamma(q^{-1})$, i.e.

$$F(q^{-1})A(q^{-1}) - q^{-d}G(q^{-1})B(q^{-1}) = \Gamma(q^{-1}), \tag{120}$$

where

$$\Gamma(q^{-1}) = \gamma_0 + \gamma_1 q^{-1} + \gamma_2 q^{-2} + \cdots + \gamma_{n_\gamma} q^{-n_\gamma}, \gamma_0 = 1 \tag{121}$$

is the desired closed-loop characteristic polynomial having order $n_\gamma = n_a$. The controller polynomials $F(q^{-1})$ and $G(q^{-1})$ are related to model polynomials $A(q^{-1})$ and $B(q^{-1})$ via the Diophantine eq. (120). The desired transient response is designed through the polynomial $\Gamma(q^{-1})$, however by assigning poles for the closed-loop system the steady-state gain (SSG) will be affected. Making use of the final value theorem the closed-loop SSG is computed as

$$SSG = \left[q^{-d}\frac{B(q^{-1})M}{\Gamma(q^{-1})}\right]_{q^{-1}=1} = \frac{B(1)M}{\Gamma(1)}. \tag{122}$$

The idea is to design the gain M such that $SSG=1$, hence the compensator for such a SSG is then

$$M = \frac{G(1)}{B(1)}. \tag{123}$$

This approach, literally, cancels the offset due to $\Gamma(q^{-1})$ on the closed-loop SSG, so that, provided there is no model mismatch, the steady-state output match the reference signal $r(t)$. Such a gain compensated PPC is then able to achieve both the transient response and desired steady-state gain simultaneously. The following illustrative example shows the design approach and the implementation of PPC.

Example 6. Consider the system having $n_a = 2$, $n_b = 1$ and $d = 1$ given by

$$(1 - 1.5q^{-1} + 0.7q^{-2})y(t) = q^{-1}(0.7 + 0.3q^{-1})u(t) + e(t) \tag{124}$$

where $e(t)$ is zero mean white Gaussian distributed measurement noise with variance $\sigma_e^2 = 0.5$. The open-loop poles of the system are 0.7500 ± 0.3708, i.e. underdamped response. The aim is to achieve a critically damped response such that repeated closed-loop poles are defined to be 0.5 and 0.5, so that

$$\Gamma(q^{-1}) = 1.0000 - 1.0000q^{-1} + 0.2500q^{-2}. \tag{125}$$

The Diophantine equation eq. (0.120) for $n_f = 1$ and $n_g = 1$ becomes

$$(1 + f_1 q^{-1})(1 + a_1 q^{-1} + a_2 q^{-2}) - q^{-1}(g_0 + g_1 q^{-1})(b_0 + b_1 q^{-1}) = (1 + \gamma_1 q^{-1} + \gamma_2 q^{-2}). \tag{126}$$

By equating coefficients of like powers, the above expression may be reformulated in the convenient matrix form

$$\begin{bmatrix} 1 & -b_0 & 0 \\ a_1 & -b_0 & -b_1 \\ a_2 & 0 & -b_1 \end{bmatrix} \begin{bmatrix} f_1 \\ g_0 \\ g_1 \end{bmatrix} = \begin{bmatrix} \gamma_1 - a_1 \\ \gamma_2 - a_2 \\ 0 \end{bmatrix}. \tag{127}$$

The unknown controller parameters may be computed directly from eq. (127) via matrix inversion or using Cramer's rule

$$f_1 = b_1(b_1 s_1 - b_0 s_2)/\rho,$$
$$g_0 = ((a_1 b_1 - a_2 b_0)s_1 - b_1 s_2)/\rho, \tag{128}$$
$$g_1 = a_2(b_1 s_1 - b_0 s_2)/\rho,$$

where

$$\rho = b_1^2 + a_2 b_0^2 - a_1 b_0 b_1,$$
$$s_1 = \gamma_1 - a_1, \tag{129}$$
$$s_2 = \gamma_2 - a_2.$$

Note that ρ is the determinant of the matrix in eq. (127). In order to compensate for the steady-state error, which occurs by relocating the original open-loop poles, the compensator M is introduced, i.e.

$$M = \frac{\Gamma(1)}{B(1)} = \frac{1 + \gamma_1 + \gamma_2}{b_0 + b_1}. \tag{130}$$

The control action can then be determined from eq. (116), which may be expressed in the difference equation form as

$$u(t) = -f_1 u(t-1) + g_0 y(t) + g_1 y(t-1) + Mr(t). \tag{131}$$

The above pole placement controller has also been realised in state-space form utilising a minimal realisation representation, see (Warwick, 1981).

OUTLINE OF LONG RANGE PREDICTIVE CONTROL

The GMV and IGMV schemes are model-based d-step ahead predictive controllers. The accuracy of the prediction is closely related to the quality of the model. Not only the model parameters are required to be estimated, but also the integer valued normalised time delay of the system. If the estimated delay is less than the true system delay, then the controller attempts to generate large control action, which can destabilize the system. In the case of an overestimated delay the control is no longer optimal and the variance of the output signal may increase. The issues connected with the estimation of the delay or even a varying time delay of the system can be resolved by adopting a long range predictive control strategy. Instead of a d-step ahead prediction of the output, a prediction of the output up to a prediction horizon, denoted $H_p \geq d$, is performed, where H_p is a controller tuning parameter. Via long range prediction beyond the delay of the system and beyond the inverse response of NMP systems the control becomes stable and robust against model mismatch. One member of the class of long range predictive controllers, namely the GPC algorithm, will be covered here.

GENERALISED PREDICTIVE CONTROL

GPC has had a significant impact in terms of recent developments in control, as the currently widely adopted three term PID controller, when it become a popular choice as an industry standard. It is a popular model-based control method and is being used in industry. The approach was proposed and developed by Clarke *et al.* during the 1980's, see (Clarke et al., 1987). The idea of GPC is to minimise the variance of the future error between the output and set point by predicting the long range output of the system and separating the known contributions to future output from the unknown contributions. In this way a vector of future predicted errors can be used to generate a vector of future incremental controls. The aim is to minimise the GPC composite multi-stage quadratic cost function defined by

$$J_{GPC} = E\left[\sum_{j=d}^{H_p}\left[y(t+j) - r(t+j)\right]^2 + \sum_{j=1}^{H_c}\lambda\left[\Delta u(t+j-1)\right]^2\right]$$
(132)

with respect to current and future values of the incremental control action $\Delta u(t+j-1)$. The user specific tuning parameters are the prediction horizon, denoted $H_p \geq d$, the control horizon, denoted $H_c \geq 1$, and a cost weighting parameter λ. It is convenient here, during the derivation of the GPC algorithm, to consider the control horizon to be such that $H_c = H_p$; in practice however $H_c \leq H_p$. Note that, beyond H_c further incremental controls are assumed to be zero. The structure of the cost function for GPC can be seen as an extension of the cost function for IGMV, where the main difference is the idea of a long range receding horizon. Following this idea not only

$y(t+d)$ is required to be predicted as in IGMV, but also the predictions $y(t+j)$, $j = d, ..., H_p$; with this concept providing a basic framework for long range predictive control. In the development of the GPC algorithm the ARIMAX model structure is considered

$$A(q^{-1})y(t) = q^{-d}B(q^{-1})u(t) + \frac{C(q^{-1})}{\Delta}e(t),$$
(133)

where for simplicity $C(q^{-1}) = 1$, i.e. an ARIX model structure is assumed. The case of $C(q^{-1}) > 1$ is investigated in (Clarke and Mohtadi, 1989; Camacho and Bordons, 2004). The cost function J_{GPC} consists of future values of the reference signal $r(t+j)$, $j = d, ..., H_p$, which are assumed to be known in advance. Future values of the output are required to be predicted and future incremental values of the control action $\Delta u(t+j-1)$, $j = 1, ..., H_c$, are yet to be determined. The following example illustrates the prediction of the output up to an horizon of $H_p = H_c = 3$ steps.

Example 7. Consider a model having $n_a = 2$, $n_b = 1$ and $d = 1$ hence

$$(1 + a_1 q^{-1} + a_2 q^{-2})\Delta y(t) = q^{-1}(b_0 + b_1 q^{-1})\Delta u(t) + e(t)$$
(134)

and defining the polynomial $\tilde{A}(q^{-1}) = \Delta A(q^{-1})$ expression (134) becomes

$$(1 + \tilde{a}_1 q^{-1} + \tilde{a}_2 q^{-2} + \tilde{a}_3 q^{-3})y(t) = q^{-1}(b_0 + b_1 q^{-1})\Delta u(t) + e(t),$$
(135)

where

$$\tilde{a}_i = (a_i - a_{i-1}).$$
(136)

The output at time $(t+1)$ is then

$$y(t+1) =$$
$$-\tilde{a}_1 y(t) - \tilde{a}_2 y(t-1) - \tilde{a}_3 y(t-2). \qquad (137)$$
$$+b_0 \Delta u(t) + b_1 \Delta u(t-1) + e(t+1)$$

Assuming zero mean white noise the prediction of $e(t+1)$ is null. The best prediction of the output in the sense of minimising the squared prediction error then becomes

$$\hat{y}(t+1\,|\,t) =$$
$$-\tilde{a}_1 y(t) - \tilde{a}_2 y(t-1) - \tilde{a}_3 y(t-2) \qquad (138)$$
$$+b_0 \Delta u(t) + b_1 \Delta u(t-1).$$

The prediction at time $(t+2)$ and $(t+3)$ is computed, respectively, as

$$\hat{y}(t+2\,|\,t) = -\tilde{a}_1 \hat{y}(t+1\,|\,t) - \tilde{a}_2 y(t)$$
$$-\tilde{a}_3 y(t-1) + b_0 \Delta u(t+1) + b_1 \Delta u(t)$$
$$= -(\tilde{a}_2 - \tilde{a}_1 \tilde{a}_1) y(t) - (\tilde{a}_3 - \tilde{a}_1 \tilde{a}_2) y(t-1)$$
$$-(0 - \tilde{a}_1 \tilde{a}_3) y(t-2) + b_0 \Delta u(t+1)$$
$$+(b_1 - \tilde{a}_1 b_0) \Delta u(t) + (0 - \tilde{a}_1 b_1) \Delta u(t-1)$$

$$(139)$$

and

$$\hat{y}(t+3\,|\,t) = -\tilde{a}_1 \hat{y}(t+2\,|\,t) - \tilde{a}_2 \hat{y}(t+1\,|\,t)$$
$$-\tilde{a}_3 y(t) + b_0 \Delta u(t+2) + b_1 \Delta u(t+1)$$
$$= -(-\tilde{a}_1 (\tilde{a}_2 - \tilde{a}_1 \tilde{a}_1) - \tilde{a}_2 \tilde{a}_1 + \tilde{a}_3) y(t)$$
$$-(-\tilde{a}_1 (\tilde{a}_3 - \tilde{a}_1 \tilde{a}_2) - \tilde{a}_2 \tilde{a}_1) y(t-1)$$
$$-(-\tilde{a}_1 (0 - \tilde{a}_1 \tilde{a}_3) - \tilde{a}_2 \tilde{a}_3) y(t-2)$$
$$+b_0 \Delta u(t+2) + (b_1 - \tilde{a}_1 b_0) \Delta u(t+1)$$
$$+(-\tilde{a}_1 (b_1 - \tilde{a}_1 b_0) - \tilde{a}_2 b_0) \Delta u(t)$$
$$+(-\tilde{a}_1 (0 - \tilde{a}_1 b_1) - \tilde{a}_2 b_1) \Delta u(t-1).$$

$$(140)$$

Note that $\Delta u(t), \ldots, \Delta u(t+j-1), j = 1, \ldots,$ H_c, are unknown values of the future incremental control action, which are yet to be determined by minimisation of the multistage quadratic cost

function J_{GPC}. Note that when $H_p = d$, IGMV is a special case of GPC where the only unknown is $\Delta u(t)$.

The predictor for an ARIMAX model structure, when considering the case of $C(q^{-1}) = 1$, can be computed as follows

$$\hat{y}(t+j\,|\,t) = P_j(q^{-1}) y(t) + G_j(q^{-1}) \Delta u(t+j-1)$$
$$(141)$$

where $j = 1, \ldots, H_p$ denotes the prediction and only last $j = d, \ldots, H_p$ values are used in the development of the GPC algorithm. The polynomials $P_j(q^{-1})$ and $G_j(q^{-1})$ are defined as

$$P_j(q^{-1}) =$$
$$p_{j,0} + p_{j,1} q^{-1} + p_{j,2} q^{-2} + \ldots + p_{j,i} q^{-i}, \; i = n_p = n_a - 1,$$
$$(142)$$

and

$$G_j(q^{-1}) = \sum_{l=0}^{j-1} (p_{l,0} q^{-l} \sum_{i=0}^{n_b} b_i q^{-i}), \; n_g = n_b + j - 1,$$
$$(143)$$

respectively, and where the individual coefficients $p_{j,i}$ of successive $P_j(q^{-1})$ polynomials can be computed as follows

$$p_{j,i} = p_{j-1,i+1} + (a_i - a_{i+1}) p_{j-1,0}, P_{0,0} = 1.$$
$$(144)$$

Note, that the order of the $G_j(q^{-1})$ polynomial linearly increases as the number of the predictions j increases. The following illustrative example shows the prediction $H_p = H_c = 3$ utilising the predictor eq. (0.141).

Example 8. Consider a model having $n_a = 2$, $n_b = 2$ and $d = 1$. The prediction of the future outputs utilizing the predictor eq. (141) then becomes

$$\hat{y}(t+1\,|\,t) = p_{1,0}y(t) + p_{1,1}y(t-1)$$
$$+ p_{1,2}y(t-2) + g_{1,0}\Delta u(t) + g_{1,1}\Delta u(t-1),$$
$$\hat{y}(t+2\,|\,t) = p_{2,0}y(t) + p_{2,1}y(t-1)$$
$$+ p_{2,2}y(t-2) + g_{2,0}\Delta u(t+1) + g_{2,1}\Delta u(t)$$
$$+ g_{2,2}\Delta u(t-1),$$
$$\hat{y}(t+3\,|\,t) = p_{3,0}y(t) + p_{3,1}y(t-1) + p_{3,2}y(t-2)$$
$$+ g_{3,0}\Delta u(t+2) + g_{3,1}\Delta u(t+1) + g_{3,2}\Delta u(t)$$
$$+ g_{3,3}\Delta u(t-1).$$

$$(145)$$

The above predictions of the system output can be expressed in matrix form, where the known and unknown contributions to the predicted outputs are separated as follows

$$\begin{bmatrix} \hat{y}(t+1\,|\,t) \\ \hat{y}(t+2\,|\,t) \\ \hat{y}(t+3\,|\,t) \end{bmatrix} = \begin{bmatrix} p_{1,0} & p_{1,1} & p_{1,2} & g_{1,1} \\ p_{2,0} & p_{2,1} & p_{2,2} & g_{2,2} \\ p_{3,0} & p_{3,1} & p_{3,2} & g_{3,3} \end{bmatrix} \left.\begin{bmatrix} y(t) \\ y(t-1) \\ y(t-2) \\ \Delta u(t-1) \end{bmatrix}\right\} \text{known}$$
$$+ \begin{bmatrix} g_{1,0} & 0 & 0 \\ g_{2,1} & g_{2,0} & 0 \\ g_{3,2} & g_{3,1} & g_{3,0} \end{bmatrix} \left.\begin{bmatrix} \Delta u(t) \\ \Delta u(t+1) \\ \Delta u(t+2) \end{bmatrix}\right\} \text{unknown}$$

$$(146)$$

hence transforming the derivation of the GPC algorithm into a straightforward problem involving matrix algebra.

In general, eq. (146) can be express as

$$\hat{y} = f + Gu \tag{147}$$

where the vector of predicted outputs is given by

$$\hat{y} = [\hat{y}(t+d\,|\,t), \hat{y}(t+d+1\,|\,t), \dots, \hat{y}(t+H_p\,|\,t)]^T \tag{148}$$

and the vector of known contributions to $\hat{y}$, which forms the free response of the system (Maciejowski, 2002), assuming zero incremental controls is given by

$$f = \begin{bmatrix} P_d(q^{-1}) & \left(G_d(q^{-1}) - g_{d,0}\right)q \\ P_{d+1}(q^{-1}) & \left(G_{d+1}(q^{-1}) - g_{d+1,0} - g_{d+1,1}q^{-1}\right)q^2 \\ \vdots & \vdots \\ P_{d+H_p}(q^{-1}) & \left(G_{H_p}(q^{-1}) - g_{d+H_p,0} - \dots - g_{d+H_p,H_p-1}q^{-(H_p-1)}\right)q^{H_p} \end{bmatrix} \begin{bmatrix} y(t) \\ \Delta u(t-1) \end{bmatrix}.$$

$$(149)$$

The Toeplitz lower triangular matrix G is defined as

$$G = \begin{bmatrix} g_0 & 0 & \cdots & 0 \\ g_1 & g_0 & \cdots & 0 \\ \vdots & \vdots & \vdots & \vdots \\ g_{H_p-d} & g_{(H_p-d)-1} & \cdots & g_0 \end{bmatrix}, \tag{150}$$

where the leading j subscripts on the elements in G are omitted, since the diagonal (main and minor) elements are the same and not dependent on j. The vector of control actions, which is yet to be determined is given by

$$u = [\Delta u(t), \Delta u(t+1), \dots, \Delta u(t+H_p-d)]^T. \tag{151}$$

The cost function J_{GPC} can be expressed in the vector form as

$$J_{GPC} = (\hat{y} - r)^T(\hat{y} - r) + u^T\lambda u, \tag{152}$$

where the vector of future set points (or reference signal) is defined as

$$r = [r(t+d), r(t+d+1), \dots, r(t+H_p)]^T. \tag{153}$$

The next step of the derivation of the GPC algorithm is to differentiate the cost function eq. (152) with respect to the vector of future incremental controls, i.e.

$$\frac{\partial J_{GPC}}{\partial \mathbf{u}} = \left[(\hat{\mathbf{y}} - \mathbf{r})^T \frac{\partial}{\partial \mathbf{u}}(\hat{\mathbf{y}} - \mathbf{r})\right]^T + \left[\frac{\partial}{\partial \mathbf{u}}(\hat{\mathbf{y}} - \mathbf{r})\right]^T (\hat{\mathbf{y}} - \mathbf{r})$$
$$+ \left[\mathbf{u}^T \frac{\partial}{\partial \mathbf{u}}\lambda\mathbf{u}\right]^T + \left[\frac{\partial}{\partial \mathbf{u}}\mathbf{u}^T\right]^T \lambda\mathbf{u}$$
$$= \left[(\hat{\mathbf{y}} - \mathbf{r})^T \mathbf{G}\right]^T + \left[\mathbf{G}\right]^T (\hat{\mathbf{y}} - \mathbf{r})$$
$$+ \left[\mathbf{u}^T \lambda\right]^T + \left[\mathbf{I}\right]^T \lambda\mathbf{u}$$
$$= 2\mathbf{G}^T(\hat{\mathbf{y}} - \mathbf{r}) + 2\lambda\mathbf{u}$$

(154)

and substituting eq. (147) for the vector of predicted outputs $\hat{\mathbf{y}}$ leads to

$$\frac{\partial J_{GPC}}{\partial \mathbf{u}} = 2\mathbf{G}^T(\mathbf{f} + \mathbf{Gu} - \mathbf{r}) + 2\lambda\mathbf{u}$$
$$= 2\mathbf{G}^T(\mathbf{f} - \mathbf{r}) + 2(\mathbf{G}^T\mathbf{G} + \lambda\mathbf{I})\mathbf{u},$$

(155)

where I denotes an identity matrix of appropriate dimension. (In the case of $H_c = H_p$ it is of dimension $(H_p + 1 - d) \times (H_p + 1 - d)$.) The minimisation procedure is accomplished by setting $\frac{\partial J_{GPC}}{\partial \mathbf{u}} = 0$, hence

$$\mathbf{G}^T(\mathbf{f} - \mathbf{r}) + (\mathbf{G}^T\mathbf{G} + \lambda\mathbf{I})\mathbf{u} = 0.$$ (156)

Rearranging the expression eq. (156) to solve for vector **u** leads to the GPC algorithm

$$\mathbf{u} = \left[\mathbf{G}^T\mathbf{G} + \lambda\mathbf{I}\right]^{-1} \mathbf{G}^T \left[\mathbf{r} - \mathbf{f}\right],$$ (157)

where only the first term of the vector **u** is applied to the plant, hence

$$u(t) = u(t-1) + \Delta u(t).$$ (158)

Throughout the derivation of the GPC algorithm the control horizon has been set such that $H_c = H_p$. However, the use of $H_c \leq H_p$ is common in practice, which decreases the computational load. The control horizon is relatively simply implemented by reducing the dimension of the lower triangular matrix G by considering only the first H_c columns of G and the dimension of **u** is then $H_c \times 1$. The corresponding weighting matrix $\lambda\mathbf{I}$ is also required to be suitably truncated. The matrix inversion in eq. (0.157) for the special case of $H_c = 1$, reduces to the division by a scalar, which is often used in practice due to ease of computation.

Choice of the Control and Prediction Horizons

The choice of the control and prediction horizons H_c and H_p is a crucial issue when implementing the GPC algorithm. The horizons act as tuning or design parameters and are application specific. The choice of these is rather difficult and only a basic introduction is stated here. A detailed discussion of choosing the horizons and the cost weighting parameter λ can be found in (Clarke and Mohtadi, 1989; Clarke, 1996). The prediction horizon should be large enough to incorporate the delay and transients of the system plus any possible NMP response. It is suggested that the prediction horizon should incorporate the rise time of the plant, in order to encompass the transient effects of the plant.

Numerical Study: GPC

Consider an ARX model structure having $n_a = 2$, $n_b = 1$ and $d = 1$ given by

$$y(t) = 1.5y(t-1) - 0.7y(t-2) + 0.7u(t-1) + 0.3u(t-2) + e(t).$$ (159)

To illustrate the calculation of the $P_j(q^{-1})$ and $G_j(q^{-1})$ polynomials the first prediction for $j = 1$ is performed. Utilising the predictor eq. (141) the polynomial $P_1(q^{-1})$ for $n_p = n_a - 1 = 2$ is then

$$P_1(q^{-1}) = p_{1,0} + p_{1,1}q^{-1} + p_{1,2}q^{-1},$$ (160)

Figure 4. Simulation of the GPC controller for $t = \langle 1, 25 \rangle$ in the open-loop setting and for $t = \langle 25, 100 \rangle$ in the closed-loop setting

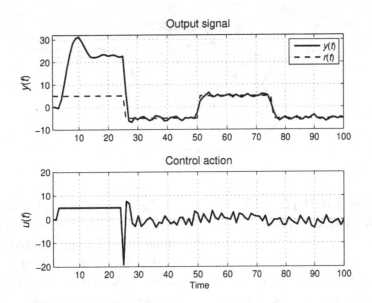

where the individual coefficients $p_{1,i}$, $i = 0 \ldots 2$, are computed utilising eq. (144) and eq. (136), hence

$$p_{1,0} = p_{0,1} + (a_0 - a_1)p_{0,0} = 0 + (1 - a_1)1 = -\tilde{a}_1,$$
$$p_{1,1} = p_{0,2} + (a_1 - a_2)p_{0,0} = 0 + (a_1 - a_2)1 = -\tilde{a}_2,$$
$$p_{1,2} = p_{0,3} + (a_2 - a_3)p_{0,0} = 0 + (a_2 - 0)1 = -\tilde{a}_3, \quad (161)$$

Utilisng eq. (143) the $G_1(q^{-1})$ polynomial is computed as

$$G_1 = b_0 + b_1 q^{-1}. \quad (162)$$

The predicted output at time $(t + 1)$ is then

$$\hat{y}(t + 1 \mid t) = -\tilde{a}_1 y(t) - \tilde{a}_2 y(t - 1)$$
$$-\tilde{a}_3 y(t - 2) + b_0 \Delta u(t) + b_1 \Delta u(t - 1), \quad (163)$$

which is exactly the same solution as in eq. (138). Following the same procedure the prediction for $j = 2$ and $j = 3$ can be computed.

The simulation setup, as previously, involves the open-loop operation during the time interval $t = \langle 1, 25 \rangle$ and closed-loop operation with the GPC controller eq. (157) during the time interval $t = \langle 25, 100 \rangle$. The reference signal switches between ±5 units with a period of 25 samples. The performance criteria are the same as used previously, see eq. (79) and eq. (80). The noise variance is assumed to be $\sigma_e^2 = 0.5$ and the start of the performance evaluation is taken to be $t_0 = 30$. The horizons are chosen as $H_p = 3$ and $H_c = 2$ and the cost weighting parameter $\lambda = 0.1$.

The results of the simulation are shown in Figure 4. The performance in terms of the MSE and MSC criteria are $MSE = 0.77$ and $MSC = 3.15$, respectively, which in comparison to the MV performance, is a superior result. Note that the first change of the system output starts before the actual reference signal changes. Indeed this is one of the advantages of GPC over alternative conventional control strategies.

Figure 5. Diagrammatic representation of bilinear systems as a subset of the wider class of nonlinear systems, and linear systems as a subclass of bilinear systems

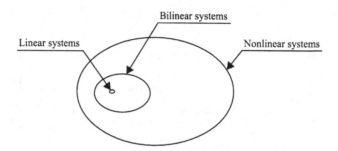

A BILINEAR APPROACH TO STC FOR NONLINEAR INDUSTRIAL SYSTEMS

Recognition that real-world nonlinear systems exhibit different behaviour over the operating range, and locally linearised models are valid only for small regions about a single operating point, has prompted the desire to extend the STC concept to encompass a wider range of nonlinear systems. Since bilinear systems represent a small, but important subset of nonlinear systems within which linear systems coexist as a special subclass, attention is focused here on extensions of STC for bilinear systems. A diagrammatic representation of linear, bilinear and nonlinear systems is shown in Figure 5. Indeed many real-world processes can be more appropriately described using bilinear models, and a good summary can be found in (Mohler, 1970; Bruni et al., 1974; Espana and Landau, 1978; Figalli et al., 1984). Bilinear systems are characterised by linear behaviour in both state and control when considered separately, with the nonlinearity arising as a product of system state and control (Mohler, 1973). These processes may be found in areas such as engineering, ecology, medicine and socioeconomics. Thus the adoption of bilinear models, hence the development of bilinear model-based control, represents a significant step towards dealing with practical real-world systems.

Based on the above observations coupled with the potential advantages of improved control, e.g. improved efficiency, reduced wastage, increased profitability and improved product quality, the need to develop bilinear model-based control strategies is justified. Indeed, this has formed the topic of much research, with potential benefits, in practical applications, see (Burnham, 1991; Goodhart, 1991; Disdell, 1995; Dunoyer, 1996; Minihan, 2001; Ziemian, 2002; Martineau, 2004). This concept of adoption of the bilinear model-based approach is demonstrated by extending the linear GPC scheme to the bilinear case. The use of bilinear GPC (BGPC) increases the operational range of the controller over the use of the linear model-based GPC when applied to systems for which a bilinear model is more appropriate. A general single-input single-output bilinear system can be modelled using a nonlinear ARMAX (NARMAX) model representation, i.e.

$$y(t) = \sum_{i=1}^{n_a} -a_i y(t-i) + \sum_{i=0}^{n_b} b_i u(t-d-i)$$
$$+ \sum_{i=0}^{n_b} \sum_{j=1}^{n_a} \eta_{i,j} y(t-i-d) u(t-i-j-d+1) + \xi(t),$$

(164)

where the a_i and b_i are assumed to correspond to the linear ARMAX model eq. (1) with the $\eta_{i,j}$ being the discrete bilinear coefficients which are required to be identified either on-line or off-line along with the a_i and b_i (Dunoyer, 1996).

BILINEAR GPC

The predictive control law is based on a bilinear model eq. (164), which for the purpose of obtaining an explicit solution to the multi stage quadratic cost function eq. (132) is interpreted as a time-step quasi-linear model such that the bilinear coefficients are combined with either the a_i or b_i parameters. The combined parameters are either given by

$$\tilde{a}_i(t) = a_i - u(t-d-i)\eta(i-1) \qquad (165)$$

or by

$$\tilde{b}_i(t) = b_i + y(t-i)\eta(i). \qquad (166)$$

For example, by recombining the bilinear terms with the a_i coefficinets the bilinear model eq. (164) can be expressed as input dependent and potentially time varying linear model, i.e.

$$y(t) = \sum_{i=1}^{n_a} -\tilde{a}_i y(t-i) + \sum_{i=0}^{n_b} b_i u(t-d-i). \qquad (167)$$

The decision to accommodate the bilinearity with the a_i or a_i coefficients depends on a particular control situation and, to some extent, user choice. Since the vector of future incremental control actions eq. (151) is computed at each time instance this knowledge can be utilised during the cost function minimisation. For example, one can obtain the predictions of the future outputs by utilising the combination approach of eq. (165) with the most recent solution for the vector of incremental controls **u**. Subsequently it may be advantageous to compute the next vector of incremental controls utilisng the combination approach of eq. (166). This latter approach of cyclic recombination of the bilinear terms has been shown to give rise to an improved overall performance (Dunoyer, 1996).

As a consequence of utilising the bilinear (bilinearised) model for the purpose of predicting the system output the prediction error decreases, hence the BGPC is more effective over the standard GPC. The BGPC algorithm retains the same structure as in the case of GPC eq. (0.157). However, since the $\tilde{a}_i(t)$ or $\tilde{b}_i(t)$ coefficients are potentially time varying and input or output dependent, respectively, the Toeplitz lower triangular matrix G and vector **f**, which comprise of these coefficients, are required to be updated at each time step. Note that some of the complexity can be overcome by taking advantage of the common factors in the case when $H_c = 1$ (Vinsonneau, 2007). In general, however, the use of the BGPC leads to a higher computational load over the standard GPC.

Numerical Study: GPC, Self-Tuning GPC, and BGPC

The system (plant) is represented by a second order single-input single-output ARX model having additional Hammerstein and bilinear nonlinearities. Similar structured nonlinear models have been assumed previously for replicating the characteristics of high temperature industrial furnaces, see (Goodhart et al., 1994; Dunoyer et al., 1997; Martineau et al., 2004), or for representing the thermodynamic processes within a heating ventilation and air conditioning system, see (Larkowski et al., 2009; Zajic et al., 2009). The nonlinear system has been chosen to show that bilinear controllers can be used to control nonlinear systems without using the adaptive control approach, leading to the use of less complex and robust controllers. The system takes the form

$$y(t) = -1.56y(t-1) + 0.607y(t-2) + 0.042u(t-1) + 0.036u(t-2)$$
$$- 0.01y(t-1)u(t-1) + 0.01u^2(t-1) + e(t). \qquad (168)$$

The coefficient of the bilinear term is $\eta_0 = -0.01$ and the coefficient of the Hammerstein term is 0.01. The negative bilinear term is indicative of a system with saturation. The noise term $e(t)$ is white normally distributed with a variance $\sigma_e^2 = 0.002$.

Three controllers are investigated and compared, which are namely: GPC, self-tuning GPC (ST-GPC) and BGPC. The GPC is based on a second order linearised ARX model of the system eq. (168) given by

$$y(t) =$$
$$-1.552y(t-1) + 0.600y(t-2) + 0.0423u(t-1) + 0.037u(t-2).$$
$$(169)$$

The linearised model eq. (169) of the system has been estimated off-line using LLS applied to recorded data obtained when the system was simulated in an open-loop seting spanning the expected working points in the operational range. The BGPC is based on the bilinearised model of the system, which is given by

$$y(t) = -1.552y(t-1) + 0.600y(t-2) + 0.0423u(t-1)$$
$$+ 0.037u(t-2) - 0.006y(t-1)u(t-1).$$
$$(170)$$

This has been similarly obtained using LLS as described for the linearised model eq. (169). The ST-GPC is based on the linear second order ARX model, where the model parameters are estimated on-line utilising the RLS method.

A Monte-Carlo simulation study with $M = 100$ runs, $N = 200$ samples and $t_0 = 30$, is performed. For all three controllers the tuning parameters are for the two horizons $H_p = 5$ and $H_c = 1$ and for the cost weighting parameter $\lambda = 0.1$. The system is subjected to a reference signal, switching between ± 1 with a period of 50 samples. The results are given in Table 1, where the mean values of MSE and MSC for each controller are presented along with a benchmark comparison expressed in normalised form with respect to the GPC (where indices are all normalised to 100%).

The results given in Table 1 show the superior performance of the BGPC over the standard

GPC for this particular case. The tracking ability improves by 11% and the control effort decreases by 19%. The ST-GPC provides moderate improvement over the GPC. It is noted, however, that for a lower demand on the tracking accuracy (slow control), e.g. $H_p = 10$, $H_c = 1$ and $\lambda = 0.2$KF was originally developed for estimating the unmeasurable , the three investigated controllers perform in an almost undistinguishable manner.

The above results highlight the benefits of adopting a bilinear model-based approach over standard linear model-based approaches. The BGPC is able to achieve its objective through the effective automatic gain scheduling via the nonlinear (bilinear) controller model structure. It is conjectured that, in the case when the set point is required to change over a wide operational range, and/or where the system may change over time, a self-tuning form of the BGPC should be beneficial.

FUTURE RESEARCH DIRECTIONS

This Section on *Future Research Directions* has been included to highlight the potential of combined algorithms for control together with fault diagnosis, condition monitoring and active fault tolerant reconfigurability. Current and future control systems will be required to handle systems of increased complexity (Bonfe et al., 2009). It is anticipated that there will be increased computer power and that it will be possible in the future to handle systems with increasingly higher bandwidths. Many of the dicrete algorithms and techniques developed up to date will be required to be extended using hybrid delta operator type models and other approximations to continuous time representations (Young, 2008), including continuous and discrete-time bilinear model approaches (Dunoyer et al., 1997). Such a future development will require parsimonious models for control and models of higher complexity for fault diagnosis for both plant and sensors.

Table 1. Mean values of MSE and MSC from a Monte-Carlo simulation together with the normalised [%] benchmark comparison between the GPC (where its values represent 100%) and the ST-GPC and BGPC.

	MSE	MSC	MSE [%]	MSC [%]
GPC	0.0586	1.0021	100.00	100.00
ST-GPC	0.0564	0.9361	96.246	93.414
BGPC	0.0523	0.8134	89.249	81.170

New methods to deal with the above complexity issues are required and whilst some recent work in this area has already been reported, see for example (Vinsonneau, 2009; Linden, 2008; Larkowski, 2009; Larkowski et al., 2009) these algorithms are still in their infancy. Consequently, much research needs to be reddressed to bring these algorithms to application readiness. It is considered that extended estimation algorithms incorporating errors-in-variables and bias elimination procedures could be beneficial for fault diagnosis in addition to the standard algorithms used for control of complex interconnected systems. This is particulary important in applications where causality is not so clearly defined and there are safety critical issues involved, e.g. hybrid-electric vehicels (Cieslar et al., 2009). Other potential future developments in the field include nonlinear model-based STC, including but not limited to bilinear models, e.g. Hammerstein, Wiener and combinations of these, together with the more general polynomial nonlinearities and state dependent representations .

CONCLUSION

By reviewing from a historic-technical perspective the chapter has provided a concise overview of some of the major developments in self-tuning control (STC). Emphasis has been placed on illuminating and demystfying the key stages in the derivation of a number of control law procedures, with a detailed account of advantages, limitations and implementational issues being given. Prior to the section on control law procedures the reader was introduced to a section on model structures for STC, where it is stressed that the models are chosen for purpose and for convenience; and a section dealing with parameter estimation schemes for STC, where standard linear least squares (LLS), recursive least squares (RLS) and the Kalman filter (KF) configured for parameter estimation were introduced.

In a chapter of limited size only a subset of the many control law design procedures could be included and these have been restricted to those which could be described using the polynomial model structures expressed as ARX (auto-regressive with exogenous inputs), and ARIX (auto-regressive integrated with exogenous inputs). The reader has been left to extend the methods to the more general case of coloured output noise, as well as to the various equivalent extensions in minimal and non-minimal realisations of the state space frame work.

The continual need for improved control systems, which are able to operate effectively on real-world nonlinear systems over wide operational ranges with a minimum of operator intevention as well as implementational simplicity, has been motivated by numerous factors. The drivers for such demands include: improved product quality, reduced energy consumption, increased efficiency, conformation to environmental regulations, and incresed profitability, to name but a few. Indeed it was in recognition of such demands from virtually all sectors of the man-made technological world, e.g. industrial, commertial and sociological, that prompted many of the early, as well as the current and future, developments in STC.

In regard to the early developments mentioned above the chapter has provided the reader with a flavour of some of this pioneering work in a attempt to re-capture the enthusiasm and to gain an in-depth insight into the details of the algorithms. The following key developments in chronological technical-historic order have been reviewed: the optimal d-step ahead predictive schemes of minimum variance (both regulator and controller), generalised minimum variance (GMV) controller, incremental GMV (IGMV) controller, the sub-optimal pole placement controller and last but not least the long range generalised predictive control (GPC) scheme.

Having informed the reader of the algorithms together with their advantages and limitations, the chapter then introduced, the scope for potential extensions to handle complex nonlinear systems. In this regard a section on bilinear systems and bilinear model-based control with particular emphasis on bilinear forms of GPC has been included. The results presented demonstrate the superiority of the bilinear GPC (BGPC) when applied to an arbitrarily chosen nonlinear system when there are high demands for accurate setpoint tracking. It has been shown in this particular example that the BGPC achieved its objectives whilst using less control effort.

Throughout the chapter the reader has been given an insight into the exciting and pioneering technical-historic developments of STC, and in this regard the authors hope that the reader will be encouraged to follow up the references herein and go further in this field of control engineering and gain deeper knowledge.

ACKNOWLEDGMENT

The authors wish to acknowledge Pawel Kret for his valuable contribution to this chapter, especially for reading and useful comments.

REFERENCES

Astrom, K. J., & Wittenmark, B. (1973). On self-tuning regulators. *Automatica*, *9*, 185–199. doi:10.1016/0005-1098(73)90073-3

Bonfe, M., Castaldi, P., Simani, S., & Beghelli, S. (2009). Integrated fault diagnosis and fault tolerant control design for an aircraft model. In *Proc. CD-ROM Int. Conf. Systems Engineering ICSE 2009* (pp. 13-18). Coventry University, UK.

Bruni, C., Di Pillo, G., & Koch, G. (1974). Bilinear systems: an appealing class of 'nearly linear' systems in theory and applications. *IEEE Transactions on Automatic Control*, *19*, 334–348. doi:10.1109/TAC.1974.1100617

Burnham, K. J. (1991). *Self-tuning control for bilinear systems*. Doctoral dissertation, Coventry Polytechnic, UK.

Burnham, K. J., & James, D. J. G. (1986). Use of cautious estimation in the self-tuning control of bilinear systems. In *Proc. RAI/IPAR, 1,* (pp. 419-432). Toulouse, France.

Burnham, K. J., James, D. J. G., & Shields, D. N. (1985). Choice of forgetting factor for self-tuning control. *J. Systems Science*, *11*, 65–73.

Camacho, E. F., & Bordons, C. (2004). *Model Predictive Control* (2nd ed.). London, UK: Springer-Verlag.

Cieslar, D., Hancock, M., & Assadian, F. (2009). A practical solution for vehicle handling stability control of a hybrid electric vehicle. In *Proc. CD-ROM Int. Conf. Systems Engineering ICSE 2009* (pp. 76-81). Coventry University, UK.

Clarke, D. W. (1996). Adaptive predictive control. *IFAC A. Rev. Control*, *20*, 83–94. doi:10.1016/S1367-5788(97)00007-2

Clarke, D. W., & Gawthrop, P. J. (1975). Self-tuning controller. In *Proc. IEE, 122,* 929-934.

Clarke, D. W., & Mohtadi, C. (1989). Properties of generalised predictive control. *Automatica, 25*(6), 859–875. doi:10.1016/0005-1098(89)90053-8

Clarke, D. W., Mohtadi, C., & Tuffs, P. S. (1987). Generalized predictive control – Parts I and II. *Automatica, 23*(2), 137-148 and 149-160.

Disdell, K. J. (1995). *Bilinear self-tuning control for multivariable high temperature furnace applications.* Doctoral dissertation, Coventry University, UK.

Dunoyer, A., Balmer, L., Burnham, K. J., & James, D. J. G. (1997). On the discretization of a single-input single-output bilinear systems. *International Journal of Control, 68*(2), 361–372. doi:10.1080/002071797223668

Dunoyer, A., Burnham, K. J., & McAlpine, T. S. (1997). Self-tuning control of an industrial pilot-scale reheating furnace: Design principles and application of a bilinear approach. In *Proc. IEE Control Theory and Applications, 144*(1), 25-31.

Dunoyer, A. P. (1996). *Bilinear self-tuning control and bilinearisation of nonlinear industrial systems.* Doctoral dissertation, Coventry University, UK.

Espana, M., & Landau, I. D. (1978). Reduced order bilinear models for distillation columns. *Automatica, 14*, 345–355. doi:10.1016/0005-1098(78)90034-1

Figalli, G., La Cava, M., & Tomasi, L. (1984). An optimal feedback control for a bilinear model of induction motor drives. *International Journal of Control, 39*, 1007–1016. doi:10.1080/00207178408933227

Fortescue, T. R., Kershenbaum, L. S., & Ydstie, B. E. (1981). Implementation of self-tuning regulators with variable forgetting factors. *Automatica, 17*, 831–835. doi:10.1016/0005-1098(81)90070-4

Goodhart, S. G. (1991). *Self-tuning control of industrial systems.* Doctoral dissertation, Coventry Polytechnic, UK.

Goodhart, S. G., Burnham, K. J., & James, D. J. G. (1994) Bilinear self-tuning control of a high temperature heat treatment plant. In *Proc. IEE Control Theory and Applications, 141(1)*, 12-18.

Gregory, P. C. (Ed.). (1959). *Proceedings of the Self-adaptive Flight Control Systems Symposium.* Dayton, OH: Wright Air Development Center.

Hsia, T. C. (1977). *System Identification.* Lexington, KY: Lexington Books.

Kalman, R. E. (1960). A new approach to linear filtering and prediction problems. *Journal of Basic Engineering, 82D*, 35–45.

Larkowski, T., Linden, J. G., Vinsonneau, B., & Burnham, K. J. (2009). Frisch scheme identification for dynamic diagonal bilinear models. *International Journal of Control, 82*(9), 1591–1604. doi:10.1080/00207170802596280

Larkowski, T., Zajic, I., Linden, J. G., Burnham, K. J., & Hill, D. (2009). Identification of a dehumidification process of the heating, ventilation and air conditioning system using bias compensated least squares approach. In *Proc. CD-ROM Int. Conf. Systems Engineering ICSE 2009* (pp. 296-305). Coventry University, UK.

Larkowski, T. M. (2009). *Extended algorithms for the errors-in-variables identification.* Doctoral dissertation, Coventry University, UK.

Linden, J. G. (2005). *Regularisation techniques and cautious least squares in parameter estimation for model based control.* (Masters dissertation), Coventry University, UK.

Linden, J. G. (2008). *Algorithms for recursive Frish scheme identification and errors-in-variables filtering.* Doctoral dissertation, Coventry University, UK.

Ljung, L. (1999). *System Identification – Theory for the user* (2nd ed.). Upper Saddle River, NJ: Prentice Hall.

Maciejowski, J. M. (2002). *Predictive Control with Constraints*. Harlow, UK: Prentice-Hall.

Martineau, S. (2004). *Nonlinear model-based control system design with application to industrial furnaces*. (Doctoral dissertation), Coventry University, UK.

Martineau, S., Burnham, K. J., Haas, O. C. L., Andrews, G., & Heely, A. (2004). Four-term bilinear PID controller applied to an industrial furnace. *Control Engineering Practice, 12*(4), 457–464. doi:10.1016/S0967-0661(03)00147-3

Minihan, J. A. (2001). *Design of bilinear controllers for industrial plant*. (Doctoral dissertation), Coventry University, UK.

Mohler, R. R. (1970). Natural bilinear control processes. *IEEE Trans. Systems Science and Cybernetics, 6*, 192–197. doi:10.1109/TSSC.1970.300341

Mohler, R. R. (1973). *Bilinear Control Processes. Mathematics in Science and Engineering 106*. New York: Academic Press.

Peterka, V. (1970). Adaptive digital regulation of noisy systems. In *Proceedings IFAC Symposium on Identification and Process Parameter Estimation*, Prague.

Plackett, R. L. (1950). Some theorems in least squares. *Biometrika, 37*, 149–157.

Randall, A., & Burnham, K. J. (1994). Cautious identification in self-tuning control – an information filtering alternative. *J. System Science, 20*(2), 55–69.

Randall, A., Burnham, K. J., & James, D. J. G. (1991). A study of Kalman filtering techniques for joint state and parameter estimation in self-tuning control. *J. Systems Science, 17*(3), 31–43.

Warwick, K. (1981). Self-tuning regulators – a state-space approach. *International Journal of Control, 33*, 839–858. doi:10.1080/00207178108922958

Wellstead, P. E., Prager, D. L., & Zanker, P. M. (1979). Pole-assignment self-tuning regulator. In *Proc. IEE, 126*, 781-787.

Wellstead, P. E., & Sanoff, S. P. (1981). Extended self-tuning algorithm. *International Journal of Control, 34*, 433–455. doi:10.1080/00207178108922541

Wellstead, P. E., & Zarrop, M. B. (1991). *Self-tuning Systems: Control and Signal Processing*. Chichester, UK: John Wiley & Sons.

Young, P. C. (1970). An instrumental variable method for real-time identification of a noisy process. *Automatica, 6*, 271–287. doi:10.1016/0005-1098(70)90098-1

Young, P. C. (1974). Recursive approaches to time series analysis. *IMA Bulletin, May/June*, 209-224.

Young, P. C. (1984). *Recursive Estimation and Time-Series Analysis*. Berlin, Germany: Springer-Verlag.

Young, P. C. (2008). Refined instrumental variable estimation for discrete and continuous-time transfer function models. In *Proc. CD-ROM IAR International Workshop on Advanced Control and Diagnosis* (pp. 1-12). Coventry University, UK.

Zajic, I., Larkowski, T., Hill, D., & Burnham, K. J. (2009). Nonlinear compensator design for HVAC systems: PI control strategy. In *Proc. CD-ROM Int. Conf. Systems Engineering ICSE 2009* (pp. 580-584). Coventry University, UK.

Ziemian, S. J. (2002). *Bilinear proportional-integral-plus control*. (Doctoral dissertation), Coventry University, UK.

KEY TERMS AND DEFINITIONS

Adaptive Control: Control is able to adapt to its environment and system changes. Many types of adaptive control available, here it is interpreted in a self-tuning context.

Bilinear Systems: Class of nonlinear systems within which linear systems coexist as a special subclass such that they are linear in state and control and nonlinear (bilinear) in products of state and control.

Control Law Design Procedures: Algorithm to realise the control action based on predefined control law, e.g. pole placement, triggered by measured data and tuned manually or automatically.

Fault Diagnosis: Utilising measured data and complex process models to identify departures from normality and distinguish from minor allowable departures.

Nonlinear Models: Real-world models, where the superposition principle does not hold. Superior models where linear model assumptions fail.

Parameter Estimation: Obtaining of coefficients of transfer function models or polynomial models based on input/output measured data.

Self-Tuning Control: Form of adaptive control based on repeatedly updated model of the plant.

Chapter 16
Active Learning in Discrete-Time Stochastic Systems

Tadeusz Banek
Lublin University of Technology, Poland

Edward Kozłowski
Lublin University of Technology, Poland

ABSTRACT

A general approach to self-learning based on the ideas of adaptive (dual) control is presented. This means that we consider the control problem for a stochastic system with uncertainty as a leading example. Some system's parameters are unknown and modeled as random variables with known a priori distribution function. To optimize an objective function, a controller has to learn the system's parameter values. The main difficulty comes from the fact that he has to optimize the objective function parallely, i.e., at the same time. Moreover, these two goals considered separately not necessarily coincide and the main problem in the adaptive control is to find the trade-off between them. Looking from the self-learning perspective the two directions are visible. The first is to extract the learning procedure from an optimal adaptive control law and to formulate it as a Cybernetic Principle of self-learning. The second is to consider a control problem with the special objective function. This function has to measure our knowledge about unknown parameters. It can be the Fisher information (Banek & Kulikowski, 2003), the joint entropy (for example Saridis, 1988; Banek & Kozłowski, 2006), or something else. This objective function in the control problem will force a controller to steer a system along trajectories that are rich in information about unknown quantities. In this chapter the authors follow the both directions. First they obtain conditions of optimality for a general adaptive control problem and resulting algorithm for computing extremal controls. The results are then applied to the simple example of the Linear Quadratic Gaussian (LQG) problem. By using analytical results and numerical simulations the authors are able to show how control actions depend on the a priori knowledge about a system. The first conclusion is that a natural, methodological candidate for the optimal self-learning strategy, the "certainty equivalence principle", fails to satisfy optimality conditions. Optimal control obtained in the case of perfect system's knowledge is not directly usable in the partial information case. The need of active learning is an essential factor. The differences between controls mentioned above are visible on a level of computations and should be

DOI: 10.4018/978-1-61692-811-7.ch016

interpreted on a higher level of cybernetic thinking in order to give a satisfactory explanation, perhaps in the form of another principle. Under absence of the perfect knowledge of parameters values, the control actions are restricted by some measurability requirement and the authors compute the Lagrange multiplier associated with this "information constraint". The multiplier is called a "dual" or "shadow" price and in the literature of the subject is interpreted as an incremental value of information. The authors compute the Lagrange multiplier and analyze its evolution to see how its value changes as the time goes on. As a second sort of conclusion the authors get the self-learning characteristic coming from the information theory point of view. In the last section the authors follow the second direction. In order to estimate the speed of self-learning they choose as an objective function, the conditional entropy. They state the optimal control problem for minimizing the conditional entropy of the system under consideration. Using general results obtained at the beginning, they get the conditions of optimality and the resulting algorithm for computing the extremal controls. Optimal evolution of the conditional entropy tells much about intensivity of self-learning and its time distribution.

INTRODUCTION

Learning is widely recognized as an important issue in modern, knowledge based societies. There is extensive literature on this subject in the areas of Management Sciences, System Sciences, Cybernetics, widely describing a need for investigations of learning processes. It is conjectured that the quality, speed and universality of these processes are crucial factors for comparison of modern and past societies.

Here is the right moment for reflection. If the self-learning processes are important and worth understanding for modern, knowledge based societies, but to difficult for studying directly, why do not try to understand them lean on the examples solved in Adaptive Control Theory? The following questions appear immediately; can these processes be described or investigated quantitatively? What means "passive" or "active" learning? There is any hope to apply the mathematical techniques helping to understand the essence of learning?

The aim of this chapter is to convince the reader that the answer could be positive and to propose an approach which is based on the ideas of adaptive control theory. To make the problem of active learning more specific we state a stochastic control problem with unknown parameters. This means we consider controlled systems having

parameters which are unknown to the controller. They are modeled as random variables with known distribution functions (a priori). The control law which has to optimize some objective function must take into account all available information, including information (posteriori) about parameters. More precise information about parameters, better results of control actions measured by the objective function. Observing system's trajectory the controller improve his knowledge about the parameters. Selecting trajectories he can choose the best one. But how to learn on line (!) the values of unknown parameters and how to do it in the most efficient way? These are the fundamental questions in the adaptive control theory. We believe in importance of this question and its universality on the general level - independently on any connections with optimal control (adaptive or not). Moreover, we hope that understanding this problem can - and must - help in much more complex and advanced problems of learning in knowledge based societies.

The chapter is organized as follows. In section 2 we state the adaptive control problem for non-linear systems which are affine with respect to controls and disturbances. Applying weak variations, a technique from Calculus of Variations, we obtain a necessary condition of optimality. Following a seminal paper by Rishel (1986), we transfer this condition into an algorithm for computing extremal controls in section 3. In sections 4 and 5 a concept of incremental value of information is introduced. Roughly speaking, it is an approximate amount of money one has to pay for the exact knowledge of the parameters value. This value can be used for several purposes, for instance, a comparison of the net profit with the extra cost of possible purchasing of this information. In the next section we apply our general results to a simple one dimensional LQG problem. This shows several surprising effects of imperfect information and consequences of learning. For instance, the certainty equivalence principle, which was widely recognized methodological candidate for finding an optimal adaptive control is not valid in this case. Numerical simulations based on Rishel's algorithm suggest an alternative candidate that is explained in Conclusions. Finally, in the last section we introduce the so-called self-learning. This is done by considering the control problems with the conditional entropy $H\left(\xi \big| y_0, ..., y_N\right)$, entering explicitly in the performance criteria. In this manner the self-learning, being the auxiliary objective, associated with the main objective in the task considered in classical automatics, became here the objective unto itself, the fundamental objective. The resulting trajectories say a lot about ξ, but, in contrast to the case analyzed in our previous paper Banek & Kozłowski (2005), where the joint entropy minimization problem was considered, now $H\left(y_0, ..., y_N\right)$ can be arbitrarily large. For non-technical systems (economical, social, etc.) such a formulation of the self-learning problem is natural. We show that this problem and its generalization can be treated as an optimal adaptive control problem, and solved by using Rishel's methodology (see e.g. Rishel, 1986; Harris & Rishel, 1986). Next, we present some results about modeling with conditional entropy and determining the optimal control for learning process without costs.

BACKGROUND

The learning process is a sealed book of its own. In Control Sciences this process has received a considerable attention in the second part of the past century. Theory of adaptive or "dual" control created by Feldbaum (1965), Bellman (1961), Kulikowski (1965) was a reaction for an increasing interest of practitioners. The subject was investigated further in hundreds of papers and books. Here we mention the monographs by Watanabe (1991) and by Isermann, Lachmann & Matko (1992), where the extensive literature are included. However, what is particular interesting in this process for us today, i.e. a "nature" of self-learning, was not recognized as important - with the exception of the early studies. In consequence the investigations were focused on finding optimal, adaptive controls for some important, mainly technological, or industrial problems. This is a case even in the most contemporary books in the subject, as is "Advances in control systems theory and applications", by Tao & Sun (ed., 2009) where the most advanced techniques and algorithms of adaptive control are presented. These include various robust techniques, performance enhancement techniques, techniques with less a-priori knowledge, nonlinear adaptive control techniques and intelligent adaptive techniques. Each technique described has been developed to provide a practical solution to a real-life problem... but a study of self-learning, the crucial factor in these solutions, is absent.

In Management Sciences a role of learning processes is recognized as well. A concept of intellectual capital is very popular and techniques of measurement and management are developed (see for example Banek & Kulikowski, 2003). However, a lack of advanced and appropriate mathematical techniques makes this goal difficult to achieve.

Box 1.

$$E\left\{\sum_{i=j}^{N-1}\nabla_{u_j}g_i\left(\xi,y_0,...,y_i,u_0^*,...,u_i^*\right)+\left[\sum_{i=j+1}^{N-1}g_i\left(\xi,y_0,...,y_i,u_0^*,...,u_i^*\right)+h\left(y_N\right)\right]\right.$$
$$\left.\times\left(y_{j+1}-f\left(\xi,y_j,u_j^*\right)\right)^T\Sigma^{-1}\left(\xi,y_j\right)\nabla_{u_j}f\left(\xi,y_j,u_j^*\right)\Big|Y_j\right\}=0 \qquad (4)$$

PROBLEM FORMULATION

Let $\left(\Omega,F,P\right)$ be a complete probability space. Suppose that $w_1,...,w_N$ are independent $n-$ dimensional random vectors (disturbances) on this space, with normal $N\left(0,I_n\right)$ distribution, let ξ be a $k-$dimensional vector. In system with complete information vector ξ is deterministic, in case with incomplete information vector ξ is random with a priori distribution $P\left(d\xi\right)$. We assume that all the above objects are stochastically independent. We will consider the adaptive control problem for a system with state equation

$$y_{i+1}=f\left(\xi,y_i,u_i\right)+\sigma\left(\xi,y_i\right)w_{i+1} \qquad (1)$$

w h e r e $i=0,...,N-1$, $y_i\in R^n$, $f:R^k\times R^n\times R^l\to R^n$ a n d $\sigma:R^k\times R^n\to R^n\times R^n$. The functions f,σ are assumed to be continuous in all their arguments. Define $\sigma-$field $Y_j=\sigma\left\{y_i:i=0,1,...,j\right\}$ and extended $\sigma-$field $F_j=\sigma\left\{\xi\right\}\vee Y_j$. A Y_j-measurable vector $u_j\in R^l$ will be called the control action and $u=\left(u_0,u_1,...,u_{N-1}\right)$ an admissible control. The set of admissible control is denoted by U. To define the purpose of control we introduce a loss function g and a heredity function h. We assume that $g_i:R^k\times R^{n\times(i+1)}\times R^{l\times(i+1)}\to R$ and $h:R^n\to R$ are continuous and bounded. The objective function has the form

$$J\left(u\right)=E\left[\sum_{i=0}^{N-1}g_i\left(\xi,y_0,...,y_i,u_0,...,u_i\right)+h\left(y_N\right)\right] \qquad (2)$$

The task is to find

$$\inf_{u\in U}J\left(u\right) \qquad (3)$$

and to determine an admissible control $u^*=\left(u_0^*,...,u_{N-1}^*\right)$ for which the infimum is attained. Our first result is included in the following

Theorem 1. *Suppose that the functions g_i and h are continuous, convex and bounded, the functions g_i and f have continuous u derivatives, the matrix valued function $\sigma\left(\xi,y\right)$ is bounded in $\left(\xi,y\right)\in R^k\times R^n$ and $\det\Sigma\left(\xi,y\right)\neq 0$ for all $\left(\xi,y\right)\in R^k\times R^n$, w h e r e $\Sigma\left(\xi,y\right)=\sigma\left(\xi,y\right)\sigma^T\left(\xi,y\right)$. Then the equality (see Box 1) for all $j\in\left\{0,1,...,N-1\right\}$ is a necessary condition for u^* to be an optimal control.*

Proof. Set:

$$\gamma\left(x-m,Q\right)=\frac{1}{\sqrt{\left(2\pi\right)^n\left|\det Q\right|}}\exp\left(-\frac{1}{2}\left[x-m\right]^T Q^{-1}\left[x-m\right]\right).$$

for density of normal $N(m,Q)$ distribution. The independence of $w_1,...,w_{N-1}$ implies that the

Box 2.

$$
\begin{aligned}
J\left(u\right) &= E\left[\sum_{i=0}^{j-1} g_i\left(\xi, y_0, ..., y_i, u_0, ..., u_i\right) + E\left[\sum_{i=j}^{N-1} g_i\left(\xi, y_0, ..., y_i, u_0, ..., u_i\right) + h\left(y_N\right)\middle| F_j\right]\right] \\
&= \int\left(\sum_{i=0}^{j-1} g_i\left(\xi, y_0, ..., y_i, u_0, ..., u_i\right)\right) P\left(d\xi, dy_0, ..., dy_{j-1}\right) + \int\left(g_j\left(\xi, y_0, ..., y_j, u_0, ..., u_j\right)\right. \\
&\quad \left. + \int\left[\sum_{i=j+1}^{N-1} g_i\left(\xi, y_0, ..., y_i, u_0, ..., u_i\right) + h\left(y_N\right)\right] P_{j+1,N}\left(dy_{j+1}, ..., dy_N\right)\right) P\left(d\xi, dy_0, ..., dy_j\right).
\end{aligned}
$$

(8)

Box 3.

$$
\begin{aligned}
\frac{\partial}{\partial \varepsilon} J\left(u_j^* + \varepsilon \nu\right) &= \int\left(\nabla_{u_j} g_j\left(\xi, y_0, ..., y_j, u_0^*, ..., u_j^*\right) + \int\left[\sum_{i=j+1}^{N-1} \nabla_{u_j} g_i\left(\xi, y_0, ..., y_i, u_0^*, ..., u_i^*\right)\right] P_{j+1,N}\left(dy_{j+1}, ..., dy_N\right)\right. \\
&\quad \left. + \int\left[\sum_{i=j+1}^{N-1} g_i\left(\xi, y_0, ..., y_i, u_0^*, ..., u_i^*\right) + h\left(y_N\right)\right] \nabla_{u_j} P_{j+1,N}\left(dy_{j+1}, ..., dy_N\right)\right) \nu_j P\left(d\xi, dy_0, ..., dy_j\right)
\end{aligned}
$$

(9)

transition probability $P\left(dy_i\middle| F_{i-1}\right)$ *for the process* $\left\{y_i : 0 \le i \le N\right\}$ *defined by (1) takes the form:*

$$
\begin{aligned}
&P\left(dy_i\middle| F_{i-1}\right) = \\
&\gamma\left(y_i - f\left(\xi, y_{i-1}, u_{i-1}\right), \Sigma\left(\xi, y_{i-1}\right)\right) dy_i.
\end{aligned}
$$

(5)

Let for $0 \le j < i \le N$

$$
P_{ji}\left(dy_j, ..., dy_i\right) = \prod_{k=j}^{i} P\left(dy_k\middle| F_{k-1}\right),
$$

(6)

$$
P\left(d\xi, dy_0, ..., dy_j\right) = P\left(d\xi\right) P\left(dy_0\right) P_{1j}\left(dy_1, ..., dy_j\right).
$$

(7)

From the properties of conditional expectation it follows that for every $j \in \left\{0, 1, ..., N-1\right\}$ the functional (2) can be represented as: (see Box 2)

Fix $j \in \left\{0, ..., N-1\right\}$. Let $u = u^* + \varepsilon\nu$, where u^* is an optimal control and ε a scalar, and let $\nu : R^{n\times(j+1)} \to R^{l\times N}$, $\nu = \left(\tilde{0}, ..., \tilde{0}, \tilde{\nu}_j, \tilde{0}, ..., \tilde{0}\right)$, $\tilde{0} = col(0, ..., 0)$ where $\tilde{\nu}_j : R^{n\times(j+1)} \to R^l$, $\tilde{\nu}_j = col\left(\nu_j, ..., \nu_j\right)$, and $\nu_j = \nu_j\left(y_0, ..., y_j\right)$ is any Borel function. From (8) we compute: (see Box 3.)

From (5), (6), (7) we have

$$
\begin{aligned}
&\nabla_{u_j} P_{j+1,N}\left(dy_{j+1}, ..., dy_N\right) = \\
&\left(y_{j+1} - f\left(\xi, y_j, u_j\right)\right)^T \Sigma^{-1}\left(\xi, y_j\right) \nabla_{u_j} f\left(\xi, y_j, u_j\right) P_{j+1,N}\left(dy_{j+1}, ..., dy_N\right)
\end{aligned}
$$

(10)

Substituting (9) to (10) and equating to zero we obtain: (see Box 4.) which proves the assertion, because condition (11) has to be satisfied by any Y_j – measurable Borel function. Q.E.D.

Box 4.

$$\int \left[\nabla_{u_j} g_j\left(\xi, y_0, ..., y_j, u_0^*, ..., u_j^*\right) + \int \left(\sum_{i=j+1}^{N-1} \nabla_{u_j} g_i\left(\xi, y_0, ..., y_i, u_0^*, ..., u_i^*\right) \right. \right.$$
$$\left. + \left[\sum_{i=j+1}^{N-1} g_i\left(\xi, y_0, ..., y_i, u_0^*, ..., u_i^*\right) + h\left(y_N\right) \right] \left(y_{j+1} - f\left(\xi, y_j, u_j\right)\right)^T \Sigma^{-1}\left(\xi, y_j\right) \right.$$
$$\left. \times \nabla_{u_j} f\left(\xi, y_j, u_j\right) \right) P_{j+1,N}\left(dy_{j+1}, ..., dy_N\right) \right] \nu_j P\left(d\xi, dy_0, ..., dy_j\right) = 0 \tag{11}$$

Box 5.

$$V_j\left(\xi, y_0, ..., y_j\right) = g\left(\xi, y_0, ..., y_j, u_0, ..., u_j\right) + E\left[V_{j+1}\left(\xi, y_0, ..., y_{j+1}\right)\middle| F_j\right]$$
$$W_j^k\left(\xi, y_0, ..., y_j\right) = \nabla_{u_k} g\left(\xi, y_0, ..., y_j, u_0, ..., u_j\right) + E\left[W_{j+1}^k\left(\xi, y_0, ..., y_{j+1}\right)\middle| F_j\right] \tag{13}$$

THE ALGORITHM OF DETERMINING THE OPTIMAL CONTROL

Following Rishel (1986), we now present a procedure for determining an optimal control u_j by applying condition (8) and the idea of dynamic programming (see Fleming & Rishel, 1975; Harris & Rishel 1986; Banek & Kozłowski 2005, 2006). We first introduce some notation. Remember that $P\left(d\xi\middle| Y_j\right)$ denotes the distribution of ξ conditioned on Y_j. For $0 \le k < j \le N-1$ set

$$V_j\left(\xi, y_0, ..., y_j\right) = E\left[\sum_{i=j}^{N-1} g_i\left(\xi, y_0, ..., y_i, u_0, ..., u_i\right) + h\left(y_N\right)\middle| F_j\right] \tag{12}$$

$$W_j^k\left(\xi, y_0, ..., y_j\right) = \nabla_{u_k} V_j\left(\xi, y_0, ..., y_j\right)$$

By the properties of conditional expectation we have: (see Box 5.) with the terminal condition

$$V_N\left(\xi, y_0, ..., y_N\right) = h\left(y_N\right).$$

From (12) and (13) the necessary condition (4) can be presented in the form: (see Box 6.)

If f is linear in ξ, and ξ is normally distributed, the conditional distribution can be determined by the Kalman - Bucy method.

1. Define $V_N\left(\xi, y_0, ..., y_N\right) = h\left(y_N\right)$ and set $j = N$.

2. Set $j = j - 1$.

3. Define

$$\tilde{V}_{j+1}\left(\xi, y_0, ..., y_j, u_j, w_{j+1}\right) =$$
$$V_{j+1}\left(\xi, y_0, ..., y_j, f\left(\xi, y_j, u_j\right) + \sigma\left(\xi, y_j\right) w_{j+1}\right),$$

$$\tilde{W}_{j+1}^j\left(\xi, y_0, ..., y_j, u_j, w_{j+1}\right) = \nabla_{u_j} \tilde{V}_{j+1}\left(\xi, y_0, ..., y_j, u_j, w_{j+1}\right).$$

4. Compute (see Box 7.)

5. Find u_j^* satisfying (4), i.e.

$$Z_j\left(y_0, ..., y_j, u_j^*\right) = 0.$$

6. Compute (see Box 8.)

7. If $j = 0$ then stop; otherwise go to step 2.

Box 6.

$$E\left\{\nabla_{u_j} g_j\left(\xi, y_0,...,y_j, u_0^*,...,u_j^*\right) + W_{j+1}^j\left(\xi, y_0,...,y_j, f\left(\xi, y_j, u_j^*\right) + \sigma\left(\xi, y_j\right) w_{j+1}\right)\right.$$
$$+V_{j+1}\left(\xi, y_0,...,y_j, f\left(\xi, y_j, u_j^*\right) + \sigma\left(\xi, y_j\right) w_{j+1}\right)\left(\sigma\left(\xi, y_j\right) w_{j+1}\right)^T \Sigma^{-1}\left(\xi, y_j\right) \nabla_{u_j} f\left(\xi, y_j, u_j^*\right)\bigg| Y_j\right\}$$
$$= \int ...\int \left(\nabla_{u_j} g_j\left(\xi, y_0,...,y_j, u_0^*,...,u_j^*\right) + W_{j+1}^j\left(\xi, y_0,...,y_j, f\left(\xi, y_j, u_j^*\right) + \sigma\left(\xi, y_j\right) x\right) + \right.$$
$$V_{j+1}\left(\xi, y_0,...,y_j, f\left(\xi, y_j, u_j^*\right) + \sigma\left(\xi, y_j\right) x\right)\left(\sigma\left(\xi, y_j\right) x\right)^T \Sigma^{-1}\left(\xi, y_j\right) \nabla_{u_j} f\left(\xi, y_j, u_j^*\right)\right) \gamma\left(x, I_n\right) dx P\left(d\xi\big| Y_j\right)$$

Box 7.

$$Z_j\left(y_0,...,y_j, u_0,...,u_j\right) = E\left\{\nabla_u g\left(\xi, y_0,...,y_j, u_0,...,u_j\right) + \tilde{W}_{j+1}^j\left(\xi, y_0,...,y_j, u_j, w_{j+1}\right)\right.$$
$$+\tilde{V}_{j+1}\left(\xi, y_0,...,y_j, u_j, w_{j+1}\right) w_{j+1}^T \sigma^T\left(\xi, y_j\right) \Sigma^{-1}\left(\xi, y_j\right) \nabla_{u_j} f\left(\xi, y_j, u_j\right)\bigg| Y_j\right\}$$
$$= \int ...\int \left\{\nabla_u g\left(\xi, y_0,...,y_j, u_0,...,u_j\right) + \tilde{W}_{j+1}^j\left(\xi, y_0,...,y_j, u_j, x\right)\right.$$
$$+\tilde{V}_{j+1}\left(\xi, y_0,...,y_j, u_j, x\right) x^T \sigma^T\left(\xi, y_j\right) \Sigma^{-1}\left(\xi, y_j\right) \nabla_{u_j} f\left(\xi, y_j, u_j\right)\right\} \gamma\left(x, I_n\right) dx P\left(d\xi\big| Y_j\right)$$

Box 8.

$$V_j\left(\xi, y_0,...,y_j\right) = g\left(\xi, y_0,...,y_j, u_0,...,u_j^*\right) + \int V_{j+1}\left(\xi, y_0,...,f\left(\xi, y_j, u_j^*\right) + \sigma\left(\xi, y_j\right) x\right) \gamma\left(x, I_n\right) dx$$

SUBSPACE CONSTRAINTS AND LAGRANGE MULTIPLERS

Let X be a Banach space with dual space X^* and let S be a linear subspace of X. We define

$$S^\perp = \left\{x^* \in X^* :< x^*, x >= 0, \forall x \in S\right\}$$

where $< x^*, x >$ denotes the pairing between $x \in X$ and $x^* \in X^*$.

Let $\varphi : X \to R$ be a Frechet differentiable functional and suppose that φ achieves its minimum over S at $x_0 \in S$. The Frechet derivative is a map $\varphi' : X \to X^*$ such that for $h, x \in X$

$$\varphi\left(x + h\right) = \varphi\left(x\right) + \left\langle\varphi'\left(x\right), h\right\rangle + o\left(\|h\|\right). \quad (14)$$

Lemma 1. *If* φ achieves its minimum over S at $x_0 \in S$, then $\varphi'\left(x_0\right) \in S^\perp$.

Proof. If $\varphi'\left(x_0\right) \notin S^\perp$ then there exist $h \in S$ such that $\left\langle\varphi'\left(x_0\right), h\right\rangle = \delta > 0$. But then $\varphi\left(x_0 - \varepsilon h\right) = \varphi\left(x_0\right) - \varepsilon\left(\delta + o\left(\varepsilon\right)/\varepsilon\right)$ so that $\varphi\left(x_0 - \varepsilon h\right) < \varphi\left(x_0\right)$ for small ε. Q.E.D.

Theorem 2. *If* $\varphi : X \to R$ is Frechet differentiable and achieves its minimum over S at $x_0 \in S$, then there exist $\lambda \in S^\perp$ such the Lagrange functional $L(x) = \varphi(x) + \langle \lambda, x \rangle$ is stationary at x_0, i.e. $L(x_0) = 0$.

Proof. We have only set $\lambda = -\varphi'(x_0)$. Q.E.D.

INCREMENTAL VALUE OF INFORMATION

In stochastic optimization problems one can meet at least two approaches for defining the value of information. First, leading to so called Incremental Value of Information was initiated by Davis, Dempster & Elliott (1991), which uses an idea of Wets (1975). Second, initiated by Banek & Kulikowski (2003) and independently by Schweizer, Becherer & Amendinger (2003) is based on the idea that the information can be the object of trade and its value for a particular agent is a consequence of its utility. In this chapter we follow the first way. By introducing the Lagrange multiplier we turn the optimization problem into a global minimization over all controls from $W \in L_p^m \left(N \times (\Omega, F, P) \right)$ which are $Z = col(z_0, z_1, ..., z_{N-1})$ - measurable, i.e., take the form $W = \left\{ W_{N-1}; w_i(Z_i), i = 0, 1, ..., N-1 \right\}$. Secondly, the Lagrange multiplier has an interpretation as a price system for small violations of the constraint, in our case, small Z_i - measurable perturbations of the controls. This is in contrast with small anticipative (allowed to know the future) perturbations considered in the paper by Davis, Dempster & Elliott (1991). Our price system perhaps may have some practical value for a controller who has an extra option, for instant he can buy the observations $Y = col(y_0, ..., y_{N-1})$, or to create a technical device, an observation system able to produce Y. The question interesting for the controller is to know, what is the right price for buying the observations $Y = col(y_0, ..., y_{N-1})$? Our price system tells only how many costs a small violation of the constraint and thus can serve as a linear approxima-

tion. To understand this approach the best way is perhaps to recall the beautiful idea of Joseph Louis de Lagrange in classical mechanics. In order to extend the Newtonian dynamics of free particles to the general case where the particles are allowed to move on some surfaces only, J.L. de Lagrange introduced a new force, a "reaction" of the surface. If there is no friction, then the reaction must be orthogonal to the surface. Thus, to determine the reaction it is enough to find its length. It appears that this can be defined uniquely such that the free particle keeps moving on the surface only, if it is affected by this reaction. Hence, the problem with constraints was reduced to the known problem with forces (but without constraints). To find analogy with our problem replace the free particles by the Z- measurable control actions, the surface of permissible movement by the linear space $V = \left\{ V_{N-1}; \left(v_0(y_0), ..., v_{N-1}(Y_{N-1}) \right) \right\}$ and the reaction by λ. Under action of λ, the Z- measurable controls (the elements of W) will stay on the space V, exactly as the particles in the Lagrange mechanics do. For economical interpretation used here one has to remember the form of the Lagrange functional. Additional term $\langle \lambda, x \rangle$, in the Lagrange functional can be viewed as an extra cost, a penalty for small violation of the constraint by the unfair control action. Due to the linearity of the term, the multiplier is a cost "per capita", i.e., the "dual" price.

To apply the results from previous section to our problem, we take Y be the space $L_p^m \left(N \times (\Omega, F, P) \right)$ of all controls

$$V = \left\{ v_i(y_i, \xi); i = 0, 1, ..., N-1 \right\},$$

i.e., anticipating controls which have access to information about the future movement of system, and S a subspace of Y of all controls $U = \left\{ u_i(y_i, \xi); i = 0, 1, ..., N-1 \right\}$. It is clear that

S is a linear subspace of Y. Then Y^* is $L_q^m\left(N\times\left(\Omega,F,P\right)\right)$ space where $q=\dfrac{p}{p-1}$ and

$$S^\perp=\left\{\lambda\in Y^*: E<\lambda,y>=0,\forall y\in S\right\}.$$

The relationship between Gateaux and Frechet derivative of φ is that, if the Gateaux derivative takes the form

$$E\sum\lambda_j v_j \tag{15}$$

for some

$$\lambda=col\left(\lambda_0,...,\lambda_{N-1}\right)\in Y^*=L_q^m\left(N\times\left(\Omega,F,P\right)\right)$$

then φ is Frechet differentiable and $\varphi'\left(u\right)=\lambda$. Hence, from (15) we obtain

Theorem 3. *Assume that* $\nabla_u g$ is bounded, then

$$\lambda_j=\nabla_u g\left(\xi,y_j,u_j^*\right) \tag{16}$$

for $j=0,1,...,N-1$.

Proof. The RHS of (16) is bounded, hence it belongs to $L_q^m\left(N\times\left(\Omega,F,P\right)\right)$ for any $q\geq 0$. Q.E.D.

From Theorem 3 follows that optimal control u_j^* is Markovian, i.e., it is in the form

$$u_j^*=v_j\left(y_j,\xi\right) \tag{17}$$

where ξ is a parameter, $\xi\in\Theta$, $v_j:R^n\times\Theta\to R^m$ is some function. Hence, from (16), (17) we obtain

$$\lambda_j=\nabla_u g\left(\xi,y_j,v_j\left(y_j,\xi\right)\right) \tag{18}$$

which shows dependence of the Incremental Value of Information on $\xi\in\Theta$ explicitly.

LQC PROBLEM FOR SYSTEMS WITH DIFFERENT INITIAL INFORMATION

In order to investigate the role initial information play in optimal control, we are going to consider a simple example of the linear quadratic control problem. A controller has to act in the circumstances; (a) all parameters are known, deterministic constants, and (b) some parameters are random variables. We shall see huge differences between the optimal controls in these cases.

Example 1. A linear stochastic system is described by the equation

$$y_{i+1}=\xi u_i+w_{i+1}$$

and the task is to find the infimum of expected joint costs and loss

$$\inf_{u\in U} E\sum_{i=0}^{N-1}u_i^2+\left(y_N-5\right)^2$$

Result 1. The optimal control action in case (a) (complete information) is

$$u_j^*=\begin{cases}0 & j=0,1,...,N-2\\[2mm]\dfrac{5\xi}{1+\xi^2} & j=N-1\end{cases}$$

Proof.

$$W_j(y_j)=\inf_{u_j}\left(u_j^2+E\left(W_{j+1}\big|Y_j\right)\right)$$

where

$$W_N(y_N)=\left(y_N-5\right)^2$$

In step $j=N-1$ we have

$$W_{N-1}(y_{N-1}) = \inf_{u_{N-1}} \left[u_{N-1}^2 + E\left((y_N - 5)^2 \Big| Y_{N-1} \right) \right]$$

$$= \inf_{u_{N-1}} \left[u_{N-1}^2 + E\left((\xi u_{N-1} + w_N - 5)^2 \Big| Y_{N-1} \right) \right]$$

$$= \inf_{u_{N-1}} u_{N-1}^2 + \xi^2 u_{N-1}^2 + 26 - 10\xi u_{N-1}$$

thus the optimal control is

$$u_{N-1}^* = \frac{5\xi}{1 + \xi^2}$$

and

$$W_{N-1}\left(y_{N-1}\right) = 26 - \frac{25\xi^2}{1 + \xi^2}$$

In step $j = N - 2$ we have

$$W_{N-2}(y_{N-2}) = \inf_{u_{N-2}} \left[u_{N-2}^2 + E\left(26 - \frac{25\xi^2}{1 + \xi^2} \Big| Y_{N-2} \right) \right]$$

and the optimal control is

$$u_{N-2}^* = 0$$

Hence, in steps $j = 0, 1 ..., N-1$ optimal controls are $u_0^* = u_1^* = ... = u_{N-2}^* = 0$ and

$$W_0\left(y_0\right) = W_1\left(y_1\right) = ... = W_{N-1}\left(y_{N-1}\right) = 26 - \frac{25\xi^2}{1 + \xi^2}$$

Q.E.D.

Remark 1. There is a well known in Cybernetics the "certainty equivalence principle", which recommend the control law

$$v_j^* = \begin{cases} 0 & j = 0, 1, ..., N-2 \\ \dfrac{5E\left(\xi | Y_j\right)}{1 + E\left(\xi^2 | Y_j\right)} & j = N-1 \end{cases}$$

as a natural candidate for optimal control for the case (b). The formula for v_j^* is obtained simply from u_j^*. It is enough to substitute ξ by $E\left(\xi | Y_j\right)$. The result below shows that this recommendation is wrong (see Conclusions in the end of the chapter).

Result 2. The optimal control action in case (b) (with partial knowledge about the system - incomplete information) is: For $j = 0, 1, ..., N-2$ is determined by the equations

$$2u_j^* + E\left\{ \left[\sum_{i=j+1}^{N-1} \left(u_i^*\right)^2 + \left(y_N - 5\right)^2 \right] \left(y_{j+1} - \xi u_j^*\right)^T \xi \Big| Y_j \right\} = 0$$

but the final step the optimal control is

$$u_{N-1}^* = \frac{5E\left(\xi | Y_{N-1}\right)}{1 + E\left(\xi^2 | Y_{N-1}\right)}$$

Incremental value of information is given by formula

$$\lambda_j = 2u_j^*$$

for $j = 0, 1, ..., N-1$.

To obtain knowledge about parameters, the simulation of the control process of the system was carried out. In the case of system with complete information, analyzing the control rules for N- time steps, we can notice that the system undertakes control only in the last time step, that is $j = N - 1$, thus in the moments $j = 0, 1, ..., N - 1$ values of control are null. The simulation and the interpretation of the above mentioned case is reduced to determine value of optimal control in the time step $j = N - 1$. Let's consider control of the system with $N = 4$ time steps. Results were introduced on the following graph, which represents dependences of the optimal control U in the step $j = N - 1$ from the parameter ξ, which is, in the case of the analysis of the system with complete information, known:

Figure 1. Values of optimal control u_{N-1} for the system with complete information (parameter ξ is known)

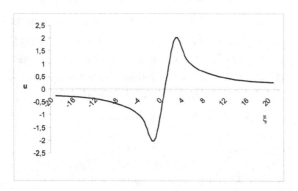

Otherwise the results of the simulation of control of the system with incomplete information are presented. Because of the large computational complexity of the algorithm, numerical techniques in the C++ object-oriented programming language with application of the MPI parallel programming library has been worked out to the simulation. Additionally, with the aim of better presentation of the results, the simulation has been conducted from the last step in the backward direction, using the method of the interpolation of the controls U in respect of the Gauss distribution parameters for random variable ξ. In every moment j, the computational process was divided on the parallel threads, where every computational unit realized simulations in respect of the parameter, describing the distribution of the random variable ξ. Afterwards, the processor steering the processes was accumulated in the information in the table, which contained the results of calculations optimum controls in respect of parameters and of the Gauss distribution of the random variable ξ and sent out the results to computational units. In the every next step, units used calculations which were realized in the previous steps, using additionally the interpolation of the secant method. To recognize the system specification, paying the attention to the self-learning and control characteristics, simulations

for $N = 4$ time steps were executed. Below we placed the graphs which represent relations U control for steps $j = 0, ..., 3$:

From simulations, we can come to the conclusion that the system described in Example 1, in the first 3 time steps, generally learns and mainly to this aim consumes energy. The conclusion indicates quantity of optimal controls, which grows up together with the next time steps and a value of optimal controls which grows up with concentration of distribution of random variable ξ. In the last time step, system works with intention of general aim realization, formulated in indicator of quality that is $E\left(y_4 - 5\right)^2$. It is proved that the graph of end optimal control has a form similar to that one from example with complete information.

CONDITIONAL ENTROPY OF LINEAR SYSTEMS

To follow the second direction of investigation mentioned at the beginning of the chapter we recall some definitions and results about filtration and entropy of stochastic systems.

Suppose that the system is described by the equation

$$y_{j+1} = f_1\left(y_j, u_j\right) + f_2\left(y_j, u_j\right)\xi + \sigma\left(y_j\right)w_{j+1} \tag{19}$$

where $j = 0, ..., N-1$, $y_j \in R^n$, $f_1 : R^n \times R^l \to R^n$, $f_2 : R^n \times R^l \to M\left(n, k\right)$, where $M(n,k)$ is the set of $n \times k$ matrices, and $\sigma : R^n \to M\left(n, m\right)$. The functions f_1, f_2, σ are assumed to be continuous in all their arguments and bounded. Additionally we assume that the square matrix $\Sigma\left(y\right) = \sigma\left(y\right)\sigma^T\left(y\right)$ is non singular. If the random vector ξ has a priori normal $N(m, Q)$ distribution, then applying the well known

Figure 2. Values of optimal control u_0^* for the system with incomplete information (random variable ξ has normal distribution $N(m,Q)$)

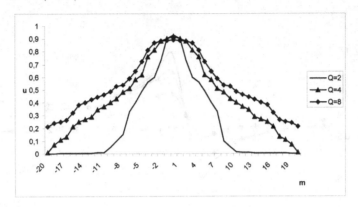

Figure 3. Values of optimal control u_1^* for the system with incomplete information (conditional distribution of parameter ξ has normal distribution $N(m,Q)$

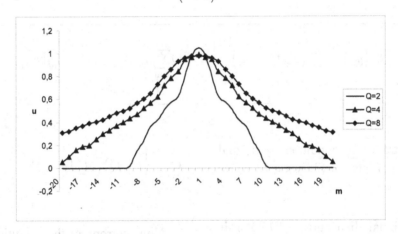

Figure 4. Values of optimal control u_2^* for the system with incomplete information (conditional distribution of parameter ξ has normal distribution $N(m,Q)$)

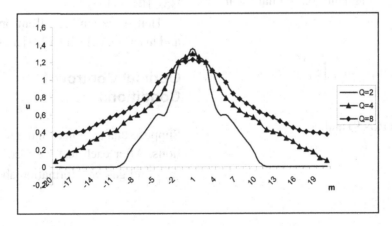

Figure 5. Values of optimal control u_3^* for the system with incomplete information (conditional distribution of parameter ξ has normal distribution $N\left(m, Q\right)$)

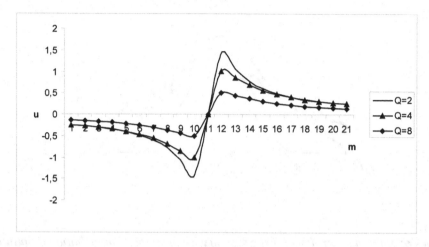

Box 9.

$$
\mathrm{m}_j = \left[I + Q\sum_{i=0}^{j-1} f_2^T\left(y_i, u_i\right)\Sigma^{-1}\left(y_i\right) f_2\left(y_i, u_i\right)\right]^{-1}\left[\mathrm{m} + Q\sum_{i=0}^{j-1} f_2^T\left(y_i, u_i\right)\Sigma^{-1}\left(y_i\right)\left(y_{i+1} - f_1\left(y_i, u_i\right)\right)\right],
$$

(20)

results about filtration of conditionally normal sequences (see e.g. Liptser & Shiryaev, 1978) we have:

1. the conditional distribution $P\left(\xi|Y_j\right)$ is normal $N\left(m_j, Q_j\right)$;

2. the best mean-square estimator of ξ, $\mathrm{m}_j = E\left(\xi|Y_j\right)$ and the conditional covariance matrix

$$
Q_j = E\left(\left[\xi - \mathrm{m}_j\right]\left[\xi - \mathrm{m}_j\right]^T \Big| Y_j\right)
$$

are given by (see Box 9) and:

$$
Q_j = \left[I + Q\sum_{i=0}^{j-1} f_2^T\left(y_i, u_i\right)\Sigma^{-1}\left(y_i\right) f_2\left(y_i, u_i\right)\right]^{-1} Q.
$$

(21)

Now, entropy of the conditional distribution of ξ in the sample $\left(y_0, ..., y_j\right)$ under control $u = \left(u_0, ..., u_{j-1}\right)$ for $0 \le j \le N$ is equal to: (see Box 10)

Hence, the conditional entropy is (see Box 11.) and inserting (21) into (22) leads to (see Box 12.)

Optimal Control of Conditional Entropy

Suppose that an object undergoes N control actions. After each test we record the state value y_{j+1} and gather information about the unknown

Box 10.

$$
H_u\left(\xi\middle|Y_j\right) = -\int\left[\ln\gamma\left(\xi - \mathrm{m}_j, \mathrm{Q}_j\right)\right]\gamma\left(\xi - \mathrm{m}_j, \mathrm{Q}_j\right)d\xi
$$
$$
= \frac{1}{2}\int\left\{\ln\left(2\pi\right)^k + \ln\det\left(\mathrm{Q}_j\right) + \left[\xi - \mathrm{m}_j\right]^T\mathrm{Q}_j^{-1}\left[\xi - \mathrm{m}_j\right]\right\}\gamma\left(\xi - \mathrm{m}_j, \mathrm{Q}_j\right)d\xi
$$
$$
= \frac{1}{2}\left\{\ln\left(2\pi\right)^k + \ln\det\left(\mathrm{Q}_j\right) + tr\left[\mathrm{Q}_j^{-\frac{1}{2}}\int\left[\xi - \mathrm{m}_j\right]\left[\xi - \mathrm{m}_j\right]^T\gamma\left(\xi - \mathrm{m}_j, \mathrm{Q}_j\right)d\xi\mathrm{Q}_j^{-\frac{1}{2}}\right]\right\}
$$
$$
= \frac{1}{2}\left\{\ln\left(2\pi\right)^k + \ln\det\left(\mathrm{Q}_j\right) + tr\left[\mathrm{Q}_j^{-\frac{1}{2}}\mathrm{Q}_j\mathrm{Q}_j^{-\frac{1}{2}}\right]\right\}
$$

Box 11.

$$
H_u\left(\xi\middle|Y_j\right) = \frac{1}{2}\ln\left[\left(2\pi e\right)^k\det\left(\mathrm{Q}_j\right)\right] = \frac{1}{2}\left\{\ln\left[\left(2\pi e\right)^k\right] + \ln\left[\det\left(\mathrm{Q}_j\right)\right]\right\}, \tag{22}
$$

Box 12.

$$
H_u\left(\xi\middle|Y_j\right) = \frac{1}{2}\left\{\ln\left[\left(2\pi e\right)^k\right] - \ln\det\left(\mathrm{Q}^{-1} + \sum_{i=0}^{j-1}f_2^T\left(y_i, u_i\right)\Sigma^{-1}\left(y_i\right)f_2\left(y_i, u_i\right)\right)\right\}.
$$

parameters ξ of the object; in this way our knowledge of the object increases. This knowledge is measured by entropy. At any time j, $j = 0, 1, ..., N-1$, we can estimate the entropy of the random variable ξ. The active learning problem is: find a control $u^* = \left(u_0^*, u_1^*, ..., u_{N-1}^*\right)$ for which the cumulative conditional entropy (sum of entropies) is smallest possible. This is modeled by

$$
\inf_{u\in U}E\sum_{j=0}^{N-1}H_u\left(\xi\middle|Y_{j+1}\right). \tag{23}
$$

By (22) we can transform the model (23) into

$$
\inf_{u\in U}E\sum_{j=0}^{N-1}h_j\left(u_0, ..., u_j, y_0, ..., y_j\right), \tag{24}
$$

where

$$
h_j\left(u_0, ..., u_j, y_0, ..., y_j\right) = \ln\det\left(\mathrm{Q}_{j+1}\right), \tag{25}
$$

and the covariance matrix Q_i, $i = 1, ..., N$, has the form (21). Let

$$
\mathrm{Q}_{j+1} = A_{j+1}^{-1}\left(u_0, ..., u_j\right)\mathrm{Q},
$$
$$
A_{j+1}\left(u_0, ..., u_j\right) = \left[I + \mathrm{Q}\sum_{i=0}^{j-1}f_2^T\left(y_i, u_i\right)\Sigma^{-1}\left(y_i\right)f_2\left(y_i, u_i\right)\right]. \tag{26}
$$

Box 13.

$$\nabla_{u_j} h_j\left(u_0^*,...,u_j^*,y_0,...,y_j\right) + E\left\{\sum_{i=j+1}^{N-1} \nabla_{u_j} h_i\left(u_0^*,...,u_i^*,y_0,...,y_i\right) + \left(\sum_{i=j+1}^{N-1} h_i\left(u_0^*,...,u_i^*,y_0,...,y_i\right)\right)\right.$$
$$\left. \times\left(y_{j+1} - f_1\left(y_j,u_j^*\right) - f_2\left(y_j,u_j^*\right)\xi\right)\Sigma^{-1}\left(y_j\right)\left(\nabla_{u_j} f_1\left(y_j,u_j^*\right) + \nabla_{u_j} f_2\left(y_j,u_j^*\right)\xi\right)\Big| Y_j\right\} = 0 \quad (28)$$

The vector $u_k \in R^l$, $u_k = col\left(u_k^1,...,u_k^l\right)$ for $0 \le k \le j \le N-1$, $1 \le i \le l$. Now, we recall from Banek & Kozłowski (2006) the formula

$$\nabla_{u_k} h_j\left(u_0,...,u_j,y_0,...,y_j\right) =$$
$$\begin{bmatrix} -2tr\left\{A_{j+1}^{-1}\left(u_0,...,u_j\right) f_2^T\left(y_k,u_k\right)\Sigma^{-1}\left(y_k\right)\dfrac{\partial}{\partial u_k^1} f_2\left(y_k,u_k\right)\right\} \\ .... \\ -2tr\left\{A_{j+1}^{-1}\left(u_0,...,u_j\right) f_2^T\left(y_k,u_k\right)\Sigma^{-1}\left(y_k\right)\dfrac{\partial}{\partial u_k^l} f_2\left(y_k,u_k\right)\right\} \end{bmatrix}.$$
$$(27)$$

Making use of Theorem 1, we obtain a necessary condition for optimal control of the self-learning process governed by equation (19).

Corollary 1. *If:*

$$tr\left\{f_2^T\left(y,u\right)\Sigma^{-1}\left(y\right) f_2\left(y,u\right)\right\} \le C < \infty$$

for all $\left(y,u\right) \in R^n \times R^l$ *and* u^* *is an optimal control, then (see Box 13.) for all*

$$j \in \left\{0,1,...,N-1\right\},$$

where $\nabla_u h_j\left(\cdot\right)$ *is given by (16)-(27).*

For the system given by (19) let us consider the problem

$$\inf_{u \in U} E\left[H_u\left(\xi|Y_N\right)\right]. \quad (29)$$

Obviously, in this case

$$h_j\left(u_0,...,u_j,y_0,...,y_j\right) = 0$$

for $j = 0,1,...,N-2$ and

$$h_{N-1}\left(u_0,...,u_{N-1},y_0,...,y_{N-1}\right) = \ln \det\left(Q_N\right). \quad (30)$$

Hence (29) can be expressed in the form

$$\inf_{u \in U} E\left[h_{N-1}\left(u_0,...,u_{N-1},y_0,...,y_{N-1}\right)\right]. \quad (31)$$

In the examples below we consider the problem (31) for some specific linear systems.

Example 2. Suppose that the system is described by the equation

$$y_{j+1} = Ay_j + Bu_j + C\xi + \sigma w_{j+1}, \quad (32)$$

where $j = 0,...,N-1$, $y_j \in R^n$, $A \in R^{n \times n}$, $B \in R^{n \times l}$, $C \in R^{n \times k}$, $\sigma \in R^{n \times m}$. Hence: (see Box 14.)

Hence (31) takes the form

$$\inf_{u \in U} E\left[\ln \det\left(\left[I + NQC^T\left(\sigma\sigma^T\right)^{-1} C\right]^{-1} Q\right)\right].$$

Since the above does not depend on control actions, we have immediately the following

Box 14.

$$H_u\left(\xi\middle|Y_N\right) = \frac{1}{2}\ln\left[\left(2\pi e\right)^k \det\left(Q_N\right)\right] = \frac{1}{2}\left\{\ln\left[\left(2\pi e\right)^k\right] + \ln\left[\det\left[\left[I + NQ\,C^T\left(\sigma\sigma^T\right)^{-1}C\right]^{-1}Q\right]\right]\right\}.$$

Box 15.

$$H_u\left(\xi\middle|Y_N\right) = \frac{1}{2}\ln\left(2\pi e Q_N\right) = \frac{1}{2}\left\{\ln\left(2\pi e\right) + \ln\left[\frac{Q}{1 + Q\sum_{i=0}^{N-1}\left(Ay_i + Bu_i\right)^T\left(\sigma\sigma^T\right)^{-1}\left(Ay_i + Bu_i\right)}\right]\right\}$$

Box 16.

$$E\left\{\frac{2Q}{1 + Q\sum_{i=0}^{N-1}\left(Ay_i + Bu_i^*\right)^T\left(\sigma\sigma^T\right)^{-1}\left(Ay_i + Bu_i^*\right)}\left(Ay_j + Bu_j^*\right)^T\left(\sigma\sigma^T\right)^{-1}B\right.$$
$$\left.-\ln\left(\frac{Q}{1 + Q\sum_{i=0}^{N-1}\left(Ay_i + Bu_i^*\right)^T\left(\sigma\sigma^T\right)^{-1}\left(Ay_i + Bu_i^*\right)}\right)\left(y_{j+1} - \left(Ay_j + Bu_j^*\right)\xi\right)^T\left(\sigma\sigma^T\right)^{-1}B\xi\,\middle|\,Y_j\right\} = 0$$

$$(35)$$

Corollary 2. *Conditional entropy is not the proper criteria for evaluation of self-learning processes appearing in linear systems in the form given by (32).*

Example 3. Suppose that the system is described by the equation

$$y_{j+1} = \left(Ay_j + Bu_j\right)\xi + \sigma w_{j+1}, \quad (33)$$

where $j = 0,...,N-1$, $y_j \in R^n$, $A \in R^{n\times n}$, $B \in R^{n\times l}$, $\sigma \in R^{n\times m}$ and random variable ξ has a priori normal $N\left(m,Q\right)$ distribution. Since (see Box 15.) thus the problem takes the form:

$$\inf_{u\in U} E\left\{\ln Q - \ln\left[1 + Q\sum_{i=0}^{N-1}\left(Ay_i + Bu_i\right)^T\left(\sigma\sigma^T\right)^{-1}\left(Ay_i + Bu_i\right)\right]\right\}$$
$$(34)$$

Using corollary 1 and (27) we get

Corollary 3 *If* u^* *is an optimal control for the problem (34), then (see Box 16.)*

for all $j \in \left\{0,1,...,N-1\right\}$.

Box 17.

$$E\left\{2h\left(u_0^*,...,u_{N-1}^*,y_0,...,y_{N-1}\right)\left(Ay_j + Bu_j^*\right)^T\left(\sigma\sigma^T\right)^{-1}B + \right.$$

$$\left. \ln h\left(u_0^*,...,u_{N-1}^*,y_0,...,y_{N-1}\right)\left(y_{j+1} - \left(Ay_j + Bu_j^*\right)\xi\right)^T\left(\sigma\sigma^T\right)^{-1}B\xi\Big|Y_j\right\} =$$

$$\int\cdots\int\left[W_{j+1}^j\left(y_0,...,y_j,\left(Ay_j + Bu_j^*\right)\xi + \sigma x\right) + V_{j+1}\left(y_0,...,y_j,\left(Ay_j + Bu_j^*\right)\xi + \sigma x\right)\right.$$

$$\times\left(\sigma x\right)^T\left(\sigma\sigma^T\right)^{-1}B\xi\right]\frac{1}{\sqrt{(2\pi)^m}}\exp\left(-\frac{x^T x}{2}\right)dx P\left(d\xi\Big|Y_j\right),$$

Below we describe a method of finding an optimal u_j by applying (35). We first introduce some necessary notation. For $0 \le k < j \le N-1$ set

$$h\left(u_0,...,u_{N-1},y_0,...,y_{N-1}\right) = \frac{Q}{1 + Q\sum_{i=0}^{N-1}\left(Ay_i + Bu_i\right)^T\left(\sigma\sigma^T\right)^{-1}\left(Ay_i + Bu_i\right)}$$

(36)

$$V_j\left(y_0,...,y_j\right) = E\left[\ln h\left(u_0,...,u_{N-1},y_0,...,y_{N-1}\right)\Big|Y_j\right],$$

(37)

$$W_j^k\left(y_0,...,y_j\right) = \nabla_{u_k}V_j\left(y_0,...,y_j\right).$$

(38)

The properties of conditional expectation imply that

$$V_j\left(y_0,...,y_j\right) = E\left[V_{j+1}\left(y_0,...,y_{j+1}\right)\Big|Y_j\right],$$

(39)

$$W_j^k\left(y_0,...,y_j\right) = E\left[2h\left(u_0,...,u_{N-1},y_0,...,y_{N-1}\right)\left(Ay_k + Bu_k\right)^T\left(\sigma\sigma^T\right)^{-1}B\Big|Y_j\right]$$

(40)

From (35) and (36)-(40) we deduce (see Box 17) where $P\left(d\xi\Big|Y_j\right)$ is the conditional probability of the random variable ξ with respect to the filtration Y_j. The conditional distribution

$P\left(d\xi\Big|Y_j\right)$ is a Gaussian $N\left(m_N, Q_N\right)$ distribution, where m_N, Q_N are defined by (20), (21).

Next we present the algorithm for determining an optimal control for the problem (34)

1. Set

$$j = N-1$$

2. Define

$$\tilde{V}_{j+1}\left(y_0,...,y_j,u_j,w_{j+1}\right) = V_{j+1}\left(y_0,...,y_j,\left(Ay_j + Bu_j\right)\xi + \sigma w_{j+1}\right),$$
$$\tilde{W}_{j+1}^j\left(y_0,...,y_j,u_j,w_{j+1}\right) = \nabla_{u_j}\tilde{V}_{j+1}\left(y_0,...,y_j,u_j,w_{j+1}\right).$$

3. Compute (see Box 18.)

4. Find an optimal control u_j^* satisfying (35),

$$Z\left(u_0,...,u_j,y_0,...,y_j\right) = 0$$

5. Make use of (37) to determine

$$V_j\left(y_0,...,y_j\right) = \int V_{j+1}\left(y_0,...,y_j,\left(Ay_j + Bu_j^*\right)\xi + \sigma x\right)\frac{\exp\left(-\frac{x^T x}{2}\right)}{\sqrt{(2\pi)^m}}dx$$

6. If $j = 0$ then stop; otherwise $j = j-1$ and go to step 2.

Box 18.

$$Z\left(u_0,...,u_j,y_0,...,y_j\right) =$$
$$\int ... \int \left[\tilde{W}_{j+1}^j\left(y_0,...,y_j,u_j,x\right) + \tilde{V}_{j+1}\left(y_0,...,y_j,u_j,x\right)\left(\sigma x\right)^T\left(\sigma\sigma^T\right)^{-1}B\xi\right]\frac{1}{\sqrt{\left(2\pi\right)^m}}\exp\left(-\frac{x^Tx}{2}\right)dxP\left(d\xi|Y_j\right)$$

FUTURE RESEARCH DIRECTIONS

As we mention in the background section, the main goal is to extract the learning procedure from an optimal adaptive control law and to formulate it as a Cybernetic Principle of self-learning. There are many reasons that makes this goal so difficult to achieve. First and most important is that optimal adaptive control laws are usually given in the form of algorithms, rather then in the form of formulae. This makes analytic investigation much more advanced and non direct. On the other hand numerical analysis of any non trivial example is time consuming and as much complex and challenging as is analytic analysis of the algorithms. However, the goal; the Cybernetic Principle of self-learning could be a very strong instrument for solving optimization problems under uncertainty giving the clear recommendation how to find the optimal rule. In order to make the guess of this principle, to find what form it could have, one has to study the process of self-learning itself. To characterize these processes quantitave, one should take into account many different criterions. Although we have tried to execute this plan, it is still much to achieve.

CONCLUSION

A general approach to self-learning based on the ideas of adaptive control is presented. We obtain the conditions of optimality for the general stochastic adaptive control problem and the resulting algorithm. These results were used next in three directions;

- Applied to simple LQG example in the previous section which shows the huge difference between control actions resulting from our knowledge about the system. Our conclusions at this point are:

1. It is evident that "the certainty equivalence principle", a methodological candidate for finding optimal adaptive control fails to satisfy optimality conditions in our example, with the exception in the final step.

2. The huge difference mentioned above visible on a level of computations should be interpreted on higher level of cybernetic thinking in order to give a satisfactory explanation, perhaps in the form of another principles.

3. Non-adaptive optimal control recommends acting only in the final step (controls in the other time instant are zero) what follows from the fact that the system does not need to learn. On the other hand, the adaptive optimal controls in the last step has the form predicted by the certainty equivalence principle, i.e. acting as in the case with perfect knowledge of parameter's value with the substitutions of estimators in the place of the parameters.

4. From the above follows that the "true" acting has the form of controls in the

final step. In the initial $N - 1$ steps the learning and only the learning is recommended by the optimal adaptive control law.

5.   Thus, the cybernetic principle based on the behavior of both systems, the principle which we are looking for could be stated as; act for the learning as long as you accumulate enough knowledge to act as the certainty equivalence principle recommend.

- Incremental value of information (IVI), a concept with a long history, introduced in decision making under uncertainty is applied here for the case of adaptive control and used next for self-learning. It appears that the Lagrange multiplier associated with information constraint (control actions can not depend on unknown parameters) can be interpreted as a "dual", or "shadow" price and consequently, can be alternatively used in definition of information value. Moreover, the way how the multiplier evolves in time shows how evolves a value of missing information, i.e., how successful is the learning strategy.

- The conditional entropy (CE) is another concept applied here. It can serve as a measure of the speed of self-learning. It appears that the CE is a very special kind of an objective function. It depends at time instant k, not on a system state value x(k) only, but on the whole previous trajectory, i.e., {x(i); for i from zero to k}. Hence, even for systems with dynamics without memory, this particular objective function introduces the memory into the control problem under consideration. Certainly, the problem becomes nonstandard, much more complex and advanced mathematically. We state the minimization problem for CE as an objective function and find the algorithm for computing the extremal controls. These controls steer the system

along some specific trajectories and these resulting trajectories give much information about this system, especially about the parameters. Uncertainty measured by the conditional entropy achieves its minimum on these trajectories. In this way the self-learning problem was posed as a optimal stochastic adaptive control problem and in the consequence, any conclusion comming from a solution of the control problem (example; the optimal control uses the whole previos trajectory and maps it into actions) is applicable and can be recommended in self-learning.

REFERENCES

Banek, T., & Kozłowski, E. (2005). Active and passive learning in control processes application of the entropy concept. *Systems Sciences*, *31*(2), 29–44.

Banek, T., & Kozłowski, E. (2006). Adaptive control of system entropy. *Control and Cybernetics*, *35*(2), 279–289.

Banek, T., & Kozłowski, E. (2006). Self- learning as a dual control problem. In Kulikowski, R., Bubnicki, Z., & Kacprzyk, J. (Eds.), *System – computer aiding of management knowledge* (pp. 157–236). Warsaw: EXIT. (in Polish)

Banek, T., & Kulikowski, R. (2003). Information pricing in portfolio optimization. *Control and Cybernetics*, *32*(4), 867–882.

Banek, T., & Kulikowski, R. (2003). Management of Intellectual Capital, *Bulletin of the Polish Academy of Sciences. Technical Sciences*, *51*(3), 205–211.

Bellman, R. (1961) *Adaptive control processes*. New York: Princeton.

Davis, M. H. A., Dempster, M. A. H., & Elliott, R. J. (1991). *On the value of information in controlled diffusion processes. Liber Amicorum for M. Zakai* (pp. 125–138). New York: Academic Press.

Feldbaum, A. A. (1965). *Optimal Control Systems.* New York: Academic Press.

Fleming, W. H., & Rishel, R. (1975). *Deterministic and stochastic optimal control.* Berlin: Springer-Verlag.

Harris, L., & Rishel, R. (1986). An algorithm for a solution of a stochastic adaptive linear quadratic optimal control problem. *IEEE Transactions on Automatic Control, 31,* 1165–1170. doi:10.1109/TAC.1986.1104200

Isermann, R., Lachmann, K. H., & Matko, D. (1992). *Adaptive control systems.* New York: Princeton Hall International.

Kulikowski, R. (1965). *Optimal and adaptive processes in control systems, Monographs of Polish Academy of Sciences, Section of Automatics.* Warsaw: PWN. (in Polish)

Liptser, R. Sh., & Shiryaev, A. N. (1978). *Statistics of Stochastic Processes.* New York: Springer-Verlag.

Rishel, R. (1986). An exact formula for a linear quadratic adaptive stochastic optimal control law. *SIAM Journal on Control and Optimization, 24*(4), 667–674. doi:10.1137/0324040

Saridis, G. N. (1988). Entropy formulation of optimal and adaptive control. *IEEE Transactions on Automatic Control, 33,* 713–721. doi:10.1109/9.1287

Schweizer, M., Becherer, D., & Amendinger, J. (2003). A monetary value for initial information in portfolio optimization. *Finance and Stochastics, 7*(1), 29–46. doi:10.1007/s007800200075

Tao, G., & Sun, J. (Eds.). (2009). *Advances in control systems theory and applications.* New York: USTC Press.

Watanabe, K. (1992). *Adaptive estimation and control. Partitioning Approach.* New York: Princeton Hall International.

Wets, R. J.-B. (1975). On the relation between stochastic and deterministic optimization in Control Theory, Numerical Methods and Computer System Modelling. In Bensoussen, A., & Lions, J. L. (Eds.), *Lecture Notes in Economcs and Math. Systems 107* (pp. 350–361). Berlin, Germany: Springer-Verlag.

ADDITIONAL READING

Aggoun, L., Bensoussan, A., Elliott, R. J., & Moore, J. B. (1995). Finite – dimensional quasi – linear risk – sensitive control. *Systems & Control Letters, 25,* 151–157. doi:10.1016/0167-6911(94)00073-5

Aoki, M. (1967). *Optimization of Stochastic Systems.* New York: Academic Press.

Astrom, K. (1970). *Introduction to Stochastic Control Theory.* New York: Academic Press.

Beneš, V. E., Karatzas, I., & Rishel, R. (1991). The separation principle for a Bayesian adaptive control problem with no strict-sense optimal law. *Stochastic Monographs, 5,* 121–156.

Bensoussan, A. (1992). *Stochastic control of partially observable systems.* Cambridge, MA: Harvard University Press. doi:10.1017/CBO9780511526503

Dai Pra, P., Rudari, C., & Runggaldier, W. J. (1997). On dynamic programming for sequential decision problems under a general form of uncertainty. *ZOR -. Mathematical Methods of Operations Research, 45,* 81–107. doi:10.1007/BF01194249

Davis, M. H. A. (1984). *Lectures on Stochastic control and nonlinear filtering*. Tata Institute of Fundamental Research, 75.

Davis, M. H. A., & Vinter, R. B. (1985). *Stochastic modeling and control*. London: Chapman and Hall.

Dorato, P., Abdallah, C., & Cerone, V. (1995). *Linear – Quadratic Control: An Introduction*. Upper Saddle River, NJ: Princeton Hall.

Feldbaum, A. A. (1960). Dual control theory. *Automation and Remote Control, 21*, 874–1033.

Feldbaum, A. A. (1961). Dual control theory. *Automation and Remote Control, 22*, 1–109.

Filatov, N. M., & Unbehauen, H. (2004). *Adaptive dual control: Theory and applications. Lecture Notes in Control and Information Sciences 302*. Berlin, Germany: Springer - Verlag.

Gao, A. J., & Pasik – Duncan, B. (1997). Stochastic linear quadratic adaptive control for continuous – time first – order systems. *Systems & Control Letters, 31*, 149–154. doi:10.1016/S0167-6911(97)00030-3

Germani, A., & Mavelli, G. (1999). Optimal quadratic solution for the non – Gaussian finite – horizon regulator problem. *Systems & Control Letters, 38*, 321–331. doi:10.1016/S0167-6911(99)00069-9

Kostyukova, O., & Kostina, E. (2006). Robust optimal feedback for terminal linear – quadratic problems under disturbances. *Mathematical Programming, 107*(2), 131–153. doi:10.1007/s10107-005-0682-4

Krylov, N. V. (1980). *Controlled diffusion processes*. Berlin, Germany: Springer-Verlag.

Liptser, R. Sh., Runggaldier, W. J., & Taksar, M. (1996). Deterministic approximation for stochastic control problems. *SIAM Journal on Control and Optimization, 34*, 161–178. doi:10.1137/S0363012993254540

Oksendal, B. (2000). *Stochastic differential equations. An introductions with applications*. Berlin, Germany: Springer - Verlag.

Pachter, M. (2009). Revisit of linear – quadratic optimal control. *Journal of Optimization Theory and Applications, 140*(2), 301–314. doi:10.1007/s10957-008-9449-4

Porosiński, Z., Szajowski, K., & Trybuła, S. (1985). Bayes control for a multidimensional stochastic system. *System Sciences, 11*, 51–64.

Rishel, R. (1985). A nonlinear discrete time stochastic adaptive control problem. *Theory and applications of nonlinear control systems*, Sel. Pap. 7th Int. Symp. Math. Theory Networks Systems, 585-592.

Runggaldier, W. J., & Zaccaria, A. (2000). A stochastic control approach to risk management under restricted information. *Mathematical Finance, 10*, 277–288. doi:10.1111/1467-9965.00094

Saridis, G. N. (1995). *Stochastic processes, estimation and control: the entropy approach*. New York: John Wiley & Sons.

Tao, G. (2003). *Adaptive control design and analysis*. New York: John Wiley & Sons. doi:10.1002/0471459100

Val, J. B. R., Geromel, J. C., & Costa, O. L. V. (1999). Solutions for the linear – quadratic control problem of Markov jump linear systems. *Journal of Optimization Theory and Applications, 103*(2), 283–311. doi:10.1023/A:1021748618305

Zabczyk, J. (1996). *Chance and decision*. Pisa: Scuola Normale Superiore.

Zwart, H. J. (1995). Linear quadratic optimal control for abstract linear systems. In Malanowski, K., Nahorski, Z., & Peszynska, M. (Eds.), *Modelling and Optimization od Distributed Parameter Systems* (pp. 175–182). Warsaw, Poland.

KEY TERMS AND DEFINITIONS

Adaptive Control: the process of modifying the control law used by a controller to cope with the fact that the parameters of the system being controlled are slowly time-varying or uncertain

Conditional Entropy: value of a remaining entropy (i.e. uncertainty) about random variable given that the value of a second random variable is known.

Dynamic Programming: the method of solving complex problems by breaking them down into simpler steps.

Gâteaux Derivative: Suppose X and Y are locally convex topological vector spaces (for example, Banach spaces), $U \in X$ is open, and $F: X \to Y$. The Gâteaux differential $dF\left(u; \psi\right)$ of F at $u \in U$ in the direction $\psi \in X$ is defined as

$$dF\left(u; \psi\right) = \lim_{\tau \to 0} \frac{F\left(u + \tau\psi\right) - F\left(u\right)}{\tau} = \frac{d}{d\tau} F\left(u + \tau\psi\right)\Big|_{\tau=0}$$

if the limit exists. If the limit exists for all $\psi \in X$, then one says that F is Gâteaux differentiable at u.

Incremental Value of Information: is defined as the Lagrange multiplier. Under partial observation the stochastic control actions are restricted by the measurability requirement and the Lagrange multiplier associated with this "information constraint" is called a "dual", or "shadow" price, and in the literature of the subject it is interpreted as an incremental value of information.

Lagrange Multiplier: a linear functional arising in constrained optimization problems as a penalty term.

Self-Learning: the process, which provides us the knowledge about functioning of system on the basis of experiences and controls.

Chapter 17
Hybrid Intelligent Diagnosis Approach Based on Neural Pattern Recognition and Fuzzy Decision–Making

Amine Chohra
Paris-East University, France

Nadia Kanaoui
Paris-East University, France

Véronique Amarger
Paris-East University, France

Kurosh Madani
Paris-East University, France

ABSTRACT

Fault diagnosis is a complex and fuzzy cognitive process, and soft computing methods and technologies based on Neural Networks (NN) and Fuzzy Logic (FL), have shown great potential in the development of Decision Support Systems (DSS). Dealing with expert (human) knowledge consideration, Computer Aided Diagnosis (CAD) dilemma is one of the most interesting, but also one of the most difficult problems. Among difficulties contributing to challenging nature of this problem, one can mention the need of fine pattern recognition (classification) and decision-making. This Chapter deals with classification and decision-making based on Artificial Intelligence using multiple model approaches under soft computing implying modular Neural Networks (NN) and Fuzzy Logic (FL) for biomedical and industrial applications. The aim of this Chapter is absolutely not to replace specialized human but to suggest decision support tools: hybrid intelligent diagnosis systems with a satisfactory reliability degree for CAD. In this Chapter, a methodology is given in order to design hybrid intelligent diagnosis systems for a large field of biomedical and industrial applications. For this purpose, first, a survey on diagnosis tasks in such applications is presented. Second, fault diagnosis systems are presented. Third, the main steps of hybrid intelligent diagnosis systems are developed, for each step emphasizing problems and suggesting

DOI: 10.4018/978-1-61692-811-7.ch017

solutions able to ensure the design of hybrid intelligent diagnosis systems with a satisfactory reliability degree. In fact, the main steps discussed are knowledge representation, classification, classifier issued information fusion, and decision-making. Then, the suggested approach is developed for a CAD in biomedicine, from Auditory Brainstem Response (ABR) test, and the prototype design and experimental results are presented. Finally, a discussion is given with regard to the reliability and large application field of the suggested approach.

INTRODUCTION

In this Chapter, the main objective is to give a methodology to design hybrid intelligent diagnosis systems for a large field of biomedical and industrial applications. From a description and analysis on diagnosis tasks and diagnosis systems in such applications, a global diagnosis system is deduced. In this global diagnosis system one can consider, in case of diagnosis of the same fault class set, the information or knowledge (from one or several sources) is represented in different knowledge representations, and independently classified (in parallel), then the decision-making of their results gives the final results (fault class set and suitable remedies or a reliability rate of the possible identified fault class).

The suggested methodology consists to develop the main steps of the global diagnosis system, for each step emphasizing problems and suggesting solutions able to ensure the design of hybrid intelligent diagnosis systems with a satisfactory reliability degree. Indeed, the main steps developed are knowledge representation (how to take advantage from image knowledge representations: global and subdivided images) from biomedical or industrial signals, classification (double neural classification: the redundancy aspect acts to the reliability benefit of overall system), classifier issued information fusion combining modular Neural Networks (NN), and decision-making using Fuzzy Systems (FS). In fact, the double classification, suggested in a hybrid intelligent diagnosis approach, is exploited in Primary Fuzzy System (PFS) to ensure a satisfactory reliability. Afterwards, this reliability is reinforced using a

Confidence Parameter (*CP*) with primary diagnosis result, exploited in Final Fuzzy System (FFS), in order to generate the appropriate diagnosis with a Confidence Index (*CI*).

For this purpose, first, a survey on diagnosis tasks in biomedical and industrial applications is presented. Second, fault diagnosis systems are presented. Third, the main steps of hybrid intelligent diagnosis systems are developed, for each step emphasizing problems and suggesting solutions able to ensure the design of hybrid intelligent diagnosis systems with a satisfactory reliability degree. In fact, the main steps discussed are knowledge representation, classification, classifier issued information fusion, and decision-making. Then, the suggested approach is developed for a Computer Aided Diagnosis (CAD) in biomedicine, from Auditory Brainstem Response (ABR) test, and the prototype design and experimental results are presented.

In fact, four Hybrid Intelligent Diagnosis Systems (HIDS) based on image representation for computer aided auditory diagnosis (in a biomedicine application: auditory diagnosis based on auditory brainstem response test), based on neural classifications (modular neural networks) and fuzzy decision-making systems has been suggested:

- Global-MLP_Global-RBF_HIDS_1,
- Subdivided-MLP_Subdivided-RBF_ HIDS_2,
- Global-MLP_Subdivided-RBF_HIDS_3,
- Global-RBF_Subdivided-MLP_HIDS_4.

Almost for all the classes, the generalization rate of FFS is higher than that of PFS for HIDS_1, HIDS_2, HIDS_3, and HIDS_4, demonstrating the pertinent rule of the Auditory Threshold (*AT*) as confidence parameter. More, from the analysis and comparison of these results, two main interesting conclusions which make the suggested approaches very promising are deduced. First, correct classifications from FFS (HIDS_1, HIDS_2, HIDS_3, and HIDS_4) are not necessarily corresponding to the same generalization example patients implying a complementary feature of FFS (HIDS_1, HIDS_2, HIDS_3, and HIDS_4). Second, FFS (HIDS_1, HIDS_2, HIDS_3, and HIDS_4) take advantage from way to process given information to classify (from global images as global indicators and from sub-divided images as local indicators as well as from different neural classifications: MultiLayer feedforward Perceptron (MLP) global approximators and Radial Basis Function (RBF) local approximators. Thus, with regard to their results, it is very important to notice that they are *complementary* rather than *competitive*.

Finally, a discussion is given with regard to the reliability and large application field of the suggested approach.

This Chapter deals with pattern recognition (classification) and decision-making based on Artificial Intelligence using soft computing methods and technologies based on modular Neural Networks (NN) and Fuzzy Logic (FL) applied to a biomedical problem. The aim of this Chapter is absolutely not to replace specialized human but to suggest Decision Support Systems (DSS): Hybrid Intelligent Diagnosis Systems (HIDS) with a satisfactory reliability degree for Computer Aided Diagnosis (CAD).

BACKGROUND

A *diagnosis system* is basically one which is capable of identifying the nature of a problem by examining the observed symptoms. The output of such a system is a diagnosis (and possibly an explanation or justification) (Balakrishnan & Honavar, 1997). In many applications of interest, it is desirable for the system to not only identify the possible causes of the problem, but also to suggest suitable remedies (systems capable of advising) or to give a reliability rate of the identification of possible causes. Recently, several Decision Support Systems (DSS) and intelligent systems have been developed (Turban & Aronson, 2001; Karray & De Silva, 2004) and the diagnosis approaches based on such intelligent systems have been developed for industrial applications (Balakrishnan & Honavar, 1997; Chohra *et al.*, 2005; Meneganti *et al.*, 1998; Palmero *et al.*, 2005), and biomedicine applications (Piater *et al.*, 1995; Vuckovic *et al.*, 2002; Wolf *et al.*, 2003; Yan *et al.*, 2005). Currently, one of the most used approaches to feature identification, classification, and decision-making problems inherent to fault detection and diagnosis, is soft computing implying mainly Neural Networks (NN) and Fuzzy Logic (FL) and exploiting their learning, generalization, and adaptation capabilities (Balakrishnan & Honavar, 1997; Chohra *et al.*, 2005; Karray & De Silva, 2004; Meneganti *et al.*, 1998; Palmero *et al.*, 2005; Piater *et al.*, 1995; Yan *et al.*, 2005).

Over the past decades, new approaches based on artificial NN have been developed aiming to solve real life problems related to optimization, modeling, decision-making, classification, data mining, and nonlinear functions (behavior) approximation. Inspired from biological nervous systems and brain structure, artificial neural networks could be seen as information processing systems, which allow elaboration of many original techniques covering a large application field based on their appealing properties such as learning and generalization capabilities (Egmont-Petersen *et al.*, 2002; Haykin, 1999; Zhang, 2000).

Another aspect of increasing importance, and strongly linked to data processing and the amount of data available concerning processes or devices (due to the high level of sensors and monitoring), is the extraction of knowledge from data to discover the information structure hidden in it. Several approaches have been developed to analyze and classify biomedicine signals: electroencephalography signals (Vuckovic *et al.*, 2002), electrocardiogram signals (Wolf *et al.*, 2003), and particularly signals based on Auditory Brainstem Response (ABR) test, which is a test for hearing and brain (neurological) functioning (Bradley & Wilson, 2004; Don *et al.*, 1997; Piater *et al.*, 1995; Vannier *et al.*, 2002). Traditionally, biomedicine signals are processed using signal processing approaches, mainly based on peak and wave identification from pattern recognition approaches, such as in (Bradley & Wilson, 2004; Don *et al.*, 1997; Piater *et al.*, 1995; Vannier *et al.*, 2002; Vuckovic *et al.*, 2002; Wolf *et al.*, 2003). The main problem is then to identify pertinent parameters. This task is not trivial, because the time (or frequency) is not always the variable that points up the studied phenomena's features leading then to a necessity of multiple knowledge representations (signal, image, …).

HYBRID INTELLIGENT DIAGNOSIS APPROACH

Diagnosis Tasks in Biomedical and Industrial Applications

Globally, diagnosis tasks consist of traducing relationship between observed symptoms (knowledge) and the consequent diagnosis. Given the observed symptoms, the diagnosis system has the tasks of ascribing symptoms to abnormal or normal functioning. Based on this basic principle, several biomedical diagnosis applications have been developed (Chohra *et al.*, 2005; Piater *et al.*, 1995; Vuckovic *et al.*, 2002; Wolf *et al.*, 2003; Yan *et al.*, 2005). For instance, the biomedical diagnosis application based on the Auditory Brainstem Response (ABR) test involves attaching electrodes to the head to record electrical activity from the

auditory nerve (the hearing nerve) and other parts of the brain (Don *et al.*, 1997). This recorded electrical activity known as Brainstem Auditory Evoked Potentials (BAEP) is the *knowledge* (records) used to the diagnosis of retro-cochlear auditory disorder's patients (abnormal), endo-cochlear auditory disorder's patients (abnormal), and healthy auditory patients (normal). In fact, such BAEP clinical test is averaged to deduce a signal: Temporal Dynamics of Cerebral trunk surface (TDC surface).

Also, based on the same basic principle, several industrial diagnosis applications have been developed (Balakrishnan & Honavar, 1997; Meneganti *et al.*, 1998; Palmero *et al.*, 2005). For instance, one can cite the industrial diagnosis application of a revolving machine of a mechatronic system. A processing chain extracts the *knowledge* (measured data from sensors) which is used to the diagnosis of unbalance defect (abnormal), chipping defect (abnormal), normal rolling (normal).

Fault Diagnosis Systems

A diagnosis system is basically one which is capable of identifying the nature of a problem by examining the observed symptoms (Balakrishnan & Honavar, 1997), as shown in Figure 1. (a). From a set of symptoms (input), the diagnosis system must be able to identify possible causes (output) and to suggest suitable remedies or to give a reliability rate of the identification of possible causes (output).

Globally, the main goals of fault diagnosis systems for Computer Aided Diagnosis (CAD) (Palmero *et al.*, 2005; Yan *et al.*, 2005) are: to detect if a fault is in progress as soon as possible, to classify the fault in progress, to be able to suggest suitable remedies (systems able of advising) or to give a reliability rate of the identified fault through a Confidence Index (*CI*).

CAD is an attractive area leading to future promising fault diagnosis applications. However, dealing with expert (human) knowledge consid-

Figure 1. (a) Fault diagnosis system. (b) Global diagnosis synopsis of the same fault classes set

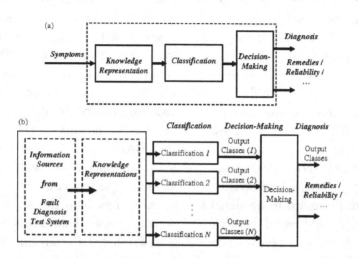

eration, the computer aided diagnosis dilemma is one of most interesting, but also one of the most difficult problems. The fault diagnosis help is often related to the classification of several information sources implying different representations. Fault diagnosis can be obtained from the classification of only one kind of information (knowledge) representation. However, experts use several knowledge representations (information) to emit their diagnosis. Then, an interesting way to build efficient fault diagnosis system can be deduced from this concept in order to take advantage from several knowledge representations (information). More, experts can use several information sources, in various forms; qualitative or quantitative data, signals, images, to emit their diagnosis. Thus, these information could be issued from different information sources and/or from different representations of a same test. For instance, in case of diagnosis of the same fault classes set, one can consider that these information are independently, in parallel, classified and after the decision-making of their results give then final results as shown in Figure 1. (b). Final results give the fault classes set and suitable remedies or a reliability rate of the possible identified fault class.

Hybrid Intelligent Diagnosis Approach

Knowledge Rrepresentations

Signal knowledge representation. The knowledge acquired as records, measured data, ... is often represented in signal knowledge representation as shown in Figure 2. (a) and Figure 2. (b), e.g., from a biomedical application and Figure 2. (d), e.g., from an industrial application.

Global Image knowledge representation. Contrary to a time or frequency (signal) based representation, the image based one, taking benefit from it's 2-D nature, offers advantage a richer representation allowing to take into account more complex features (shapes, particular information, ...). It is then interesting to represent the knowledge acquired as records, measured data, ... in image knowledge representation as shown from signals in Figure 2. (a) converted to image in Figure 2. (c), and from Wavelet transformation of signal in Figure 2. (e) converted to image in Figure 2. (f). This signal to image conversion is discussed through two main ways.

First, in the case in Figure 2. (a), BAEP clinical test which is built of a number of signals (TDC

Figure 2. Biomedical Application: (a) Brainstem Auditory Evoked Potentials (BAEP) clinical test (Temporal Dynamics of Cerebral trunk surface: TDC surface). (b) Signal knowledge representation. (c) Image knowledge representation. Industrial Application: (d) Signal knowledge representation. (e) Wavelet transformation of signal. (f) Image knowledge representation

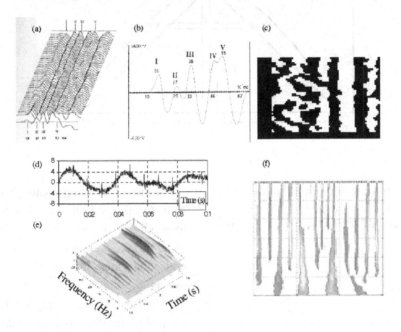

surfaces) is used to obtain its image knowledge representation from a processing based on an analytical method.

Second, in the case in Figure 2. (e), Wavelet transformation of the signal knowledge representation (from the acquired knowledge) is used to obtain its image knowledge representation from a processing based on analytical method. The used Wavelet transformation is detailed in, (Kim & Kim, 2005), see also (Graps, 1995). In both cases, the basic principle is to cut the obtained volume at a 'cut threshold', and then convert the amplitudes in grey levels in order to obtain an image (Gonzalez & Woods, 2002). However, the important point is to find this 'cut threshold' in such a way to not lose the useful information (knowledge).

Thus, the same used analytical method to find the 'cut threshold' is suggested in the following:

- X ($Xmin$, $Xmax$) denotes an index on x-axis,
- Y ($Ymax$, $Ymin$) denotes an index on y-axis,
- Z ($Zmax$, $Zmin$) denotes an index on z-axis,

- **Step 1:** a subdivision by 10 on x-axis for instance leads to for each fixed Y, ($Xmax$/10) areas are obtained (on x-axis and z-axis), then $M = (Xmax/10) Ymax$ where M represents the overall number of obtained areas.
- **Step 2:** for each area the maximal point is denoted A.
- **Step 3:** each area is then approximated by a triangle as shown in Figure 3.
- **Step 4:** for each triangle (each area) the height h of the triangle is determined.
- **Step 5:** the first equation of the following equation system, see equation (1), can be deduced geometrically and the second

Figure 3. Area approximation

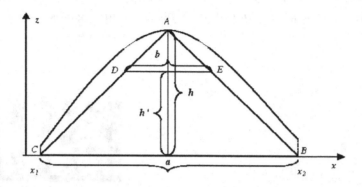

equation from the assumption that the surface of trapezoid DEBC is equal to $\dfrac{\sqrt{2}}{2}$ of the surface of triangle ABC):

$$
\begin{cases}
\dfrac{(h - h')}{h} = \dfrac{b}{a} \\[4mm]
\dfrac{h'(b + a)}{2} = \dfrac{\sqrt{2}}{2}\left(\dfrac{h \times a}{2}\right)
\end{cases}
\tag{1}
$$

- **Step 6:** the resolution of the equation system leads us to determine h' in each triangle (each area) as follows in equation (2):

$$
h' = 0.4588 \times h
\tag{2}
$$

- **Step 7:** the 'cut threshold' is then obtained such as in equation (3):

$$
H' = \min(h'_i)_{1 \le i \le M}
\tag{3}
$$

This analytical method has been used in (Chohra *et al.*, 2005) giving a satisfactory results.

It is interesting, during the classification, to exploit the global image, shown in Figure 4. (a), in order to generate a global classification indicator.

Subdivided Image knowledge representation. Another way to represent the knowledge is to subdivide the global image in sub-images in order to take advantage from both global image and subdivided image. Thus, it is interesting, during the classification, to exploit the subdivided image, shown in Figure 4. (b), in order to generate local classification indicators which are fused using a method of the classifier issued information fusion (in this case, the classifier issued information fusion is a statistical method.

How to take advantage from different knowledge representations. Traditionally, biomedicine signals are processed using signal processing approaches, mainly based on peak and wave identification from pattern recognition approaches, such as in (Balakrishnan & Honavar, 1997; Bradley & Wilson, 2004; Don *et al.*, 1997; Meneganti *et al.*, 1998; Palmero *et al.*, 2005; Piater *et al.*, 1995; Vannier *et al.*, 2002; Vuckovic *et al.*, 2002; Wolf *et al.*, 2003). The main problem is then to identify pertinent parameters. This task is not trivial, because the time (or frequency) is not always the variable that points up the studied phenomena's features leading then to a necessity of multiple knowledge representations (signal, image, …).

Thus, interesting combinations are:

Figure 4. (a) Global image knowledge representation. (b) Subdivided image knowledge representation

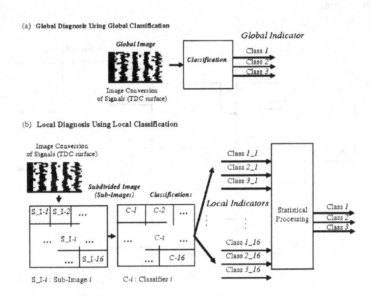

- combination of the classifications of the global image knowledge representation, in this combination several variants can be exploited using two different classifiers e.g., MultiLayer feedforward Perceptron (MLP) network classifier or Radial Basis Function (RBF) network classifier, …
- combination of the classifications of the subdivided image knowledge representation, in this combination several variants also can be exploited using two different classifiers e.g., MLP and RBF, …
- combination of the classifications of the global image knowledge representation and the one of the subdivided image knowledge representation, also in this combination several variants can be exploited using same classifier e.g., MLP or RBF for both classifications see (Chohra *et al.*, 2005), or using different classifiers e.g., MLP and RBF, …

In fact, in such combination of different classifiers the following properties are exploited: MLP are neural global approximators, whereas RBF network are neural local approximators (Haykin, 1999). The idea is to classify global images using global approximators and to classify subdivided images using local approximators.

Signal and Image Cclassification

At first, through some examples, an important problem is emphasized to illustrate the problem difficulty of the classification in diagnosis systems. In the biomedical application described in Section "Diagnosis Tasks in Biomedical and Industrial Applications" of this Chapter, three patient classes are studied: Retro-cochlear auditory disorder's patients (Retro-cochlear Class: RC), Endo-cochlear auditory disorder's patients (Endo-cochlear Class: EC), and healthy patients (Normal Class: NC). From analysis of some examples, i.e., two examples of signal knowledge representations of six patients: RC, EC, and NC, and the image (global) knowledge representations of the same six patients, it is clear that the fact that, signal or image representations could be very similar for

Figure 5. (a) Neural classification and fuzzy decision-making (from two neural classifiers). (b) Hybrid intelligent diagnosis system

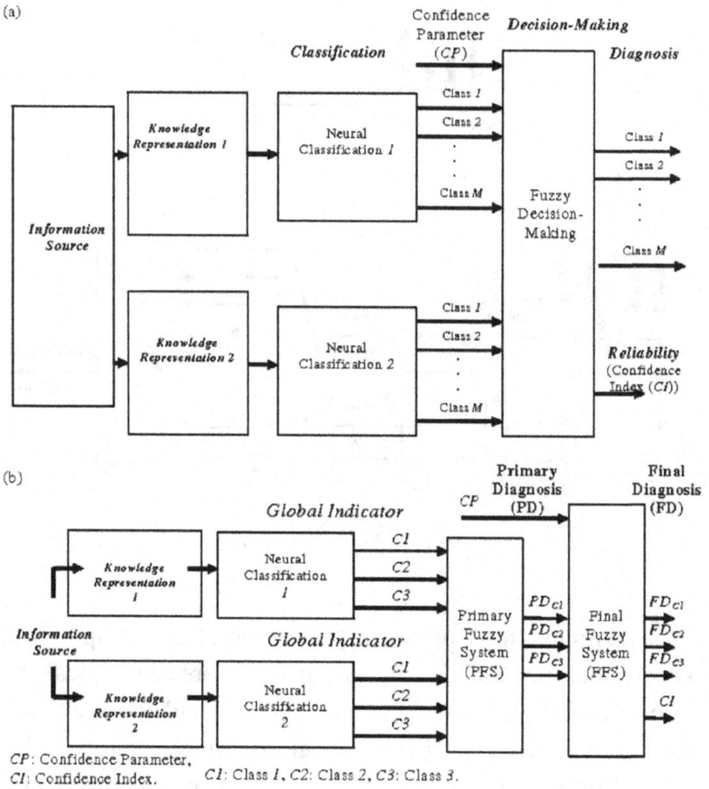

patients belonging to different classes, and they could be very different for patients belonging to a same class, demonstrating the difficulty of their classification.

Another important problem related to the classification in diagnosis systems is around the classifier issued information fusion, see also Figure 4. (b) where a Statistical processing is suggested to solve this problem. It is very interesting to exploit the classifier issued information fusion methods suggested in (Kittler *et al.*, 1998; Kuncheva *et al.*, 2003; Wanas *et al.*, 1999).

Neural Classification and Fuzzy Decision-Making (From Two Neural Classifiers)

In order to study the classification and decision-making stages of the global diagnosis system suggested in Figure 1. (b), two different knowledge representations have been considered from only one information source, as shown in Figure 5. (a). This configuration in the case of diagnosis of the same fault classes set leads to two different classifications.

More, if such classifications are handled by Neural Networks (NN), which are known to be appropriate for classification (Azouaoui & Chohra, 2002; Egmont-Petersen *et al.*, 2002; Haykin, 1999; Zhang, 2000), decision-making appears to be difficult particularly in diagnosis systems. In such cases, such systems can be useful and efficient only if results are given with a reliability parameter (e.g., a CI on each fault classes set result).

The nature of neural classification results (neural outputs) of the neural architectures used for classification are, in general, not binary values. In fact, for instance, the typical MLP used for classification with sigmoïdal outputs give output class values between [0, 1]. This makes difficult the problem of the decision-making from two neural networks. Another neural architecture is based on RBF. Analysis of neural classifier outputs shows that, in case of MLP, more the output is close to 1 and more this output will be close to be the identified fault class. Contrarily, more the output is close to 0 and more this output will be far to be the identified fault class. In case of RBF, the outputs are distances from RBF centers. In this case with a new scale of outputs it is easily to make output class values varying between [0, c], where c is a constant to be determined. Then, more the output which is a distance is close to c and more this output will be far to be identified as fault class. Contrarily, more the output is close to 0 and more this output will be close to be the identified fault class. From this purpose, one interesting way to built efficient decision-making from two NN is Fuzzy Logic (FL) (Zadeh, 1965; Zadeh, 1992).

Thus, the results of the two neural classifications, from knowledge representation 1 and knowledge representation 2, see Figure 5. (a), can be then efficiently exploited in a Fuzzy System (FS) to ensure a satisfactory reliability. The fuzzy decision-making system based on a fuzzy inference can be exploited in order to capture the expert (human) knowledge (Lee, 1990; Turban & Aronson, 2001). Then, the decision-making system allows to decide the fault classes diagnosis among: Class *1*, Class *2*, ..., and Class *M*, and its usefulness and efficiency are better traduced with the associated CI on its decision.

Thus, the Hybrid Intelligent Diagnosis System (HIDS) is suggested in Figure 5. (b), where the fuzzy decision-making stage consists of Primary Fuzzy System (PFS) and Final Fuzzy System (FFS), respectively. These systems are used to capture the decision-making behavior of a human expert while giving the appropriate diagnosis (Azouaoui & Chohra, 2002; Goonatilake & Khebbal, 1995; Turban & Aronson, 2001). Note that the two fuzzy inferences of PFS and FFS, based on Mamdani's fuzzy inference, are developed as detailed in (Azouaoui & Chohra, 2002) with the simplification detailed in (Farreny & Prade, 1985) using membership functions with three fuzzy variables.

Biomedical Application: Computer Aided Auditory Diagnosis

The ABR test involves attaching electrodes to the head to record electrical activity from the auditory nerve (the hearing nerve) and other parts of the brain. This recorded electrical activity is known as Brainstem Auditory Evoked Potentials (BAEP).

Brainstem Auditory Evoked Potentials (BAEP) Clinical Test

When a sense organ is stimulated, it generates a string of complex neurophysiology processes. BAEP are electrical response caused by the brief stimulation of a sense system. The stimulus gives rise to the start of a string of action's potentials that can be recorded on the nerve's course, or from a distance of the activated structures. BAEP are generated as follows: the patient hears clicking noise or tone bursts through earphones. The use of auditory stimuli evokes an electrical response. In fact, the stimulus triggers a number of neurophysiology responses along the auditory pathway. An action potential is conducted along the eight nerve, the brainstem, and finally to the brain. A few times after the initial stimulation, the signal evokes a response in the area of brain where sounds are interpreted.

Extraction of Image (Global and Subdivided) Knowledge Representations From Biomedical Signals

A technique of extraction (Vannier *et al.*, 2002) allows us, following 800 acquisitions such as described before, the visualization of the BAEP estimation on averages of 16 acquisitions. Thus, a surface of 50 estimations called Temporal Dynamics of Cerebral trunk (TDC) can be visualized. Average signal, which corresponds to average of 800 acquisitions, and TDC surface could be obtained. Those are then processed into a signal representation as shown in Figure 2. (a). In this figure, an example of TDC surface for a patient is shown. The average signal (named signal representation) is presented in front of TDC surface which is better shown in Figure 2. (b). The signal to image conversion (named image representation) is obtained after a processing of TDC surface signal and image processing (Chohra *et al.*, 2005; Gonzalez & Woods, 2002). Three patient classes are studied: Retro-cochlear auditory disorder's patients (Retro-cochlear Class: RC), Endo-cochlear auditory disorder's patients (Endo-cochlear Class: EC), healthy patients (Normal Class: NC).

Suggested Hybrid Intelligent Diagnosis Systems (HIDS)

The Hybrid Intelligent Diagnosis Systems (HIDS) suggested in Figure 6. (a) and Figure 6. (b) are built of data processing stage, neural classification stage, primary fuzzy decision-making stage leading to a primary diagnosis, and final fuzzy decision-making stage leading to the final diagnosis. The data processing stage consists of extracting image knowledge representations from data source (signals: TDC surface) and deducing the image data. The classification stage consists of the global

(and sub-divided) image classifications which are based on MLP and RBF networks. In fact, MLP are *neural global* approximators, whereas RBF are *neural local* approximators (Haykin, 1999).

Hybrid Intelligent Diagnosis System (Global-MLP_Global-RBF_HIDS_1). Primary and final fuzzy decision-making stages consist of the Fuzzy System 1 (FS_1) and Fuzzy System 2 (FS_2), respectively, see Figure 6. (a). These fuzzy decision-making systems are used to capture the decision-making behavior of a human expert while giving the appropriate diagnosis (Azouaoui & Chohra, 2002; Turban & Aronson, 2001). Note that the two fuzzy inferences of FS_1 and FS_2, based on Mamdani's fuzzy inference, are developed as detailed in the diagnosis approach using only image representation described in (Chohra *et al.*, 2005) with the simplification detailed in (Farreny & Prade, 1985). From this simplification, the fuzzy rule base of FS_1 which is built of $3^6 = 729$ rules will make in use only $2^6 = 64$ rules in each inference, while the fuzzy rule base of FS_2 which is built of $3^4 = 81$ rules will make in use only $2^4 = 16$ rules in each inference. Thus, the double classification, from global image representation, is exploited in FS_1 to ensure a satisfactory reliability for a computer aided auditory. Input parameters, obtained from the two neural networks, of FS_1 are RC_MLP, EC_MLP, NC_MLP, RC_RBF, EC_RBF, and NC_RBF. Thus, for each input, FS_1 is able to decide of appropriate diagnosis among Primary Diagnosis PD_{RC}, PD_{EC}, and PD_{NC}. The diagnosis reliability obtained from the FS_1 is reinforced (enhanced) using the obtained diagnosis result with an Auditory Threshold (*AT*) parameter of patients, used as a confidence parameter, exploited in FS_2 in order to generate the final diagnosis result. Input parameters, issued from FS_1, of FS_2 are *AT*, PD_{RC}, PD_{EC}, and PD_{NC}. Thus, for each input, FS_2 is able to decide of the appropriate diagnosis among Final Diagnosis: FD_{RC}, FD_{EC}, and FD_{NC} with their Confidence Index (*CI*).

Figure 6. Hybrid intelligent diagnosis systems: (a) Global-MLP_Global-RBF_HIDS_1 (MLP and RBF global images). (b) Subdivided-MLP_Subdivided-RBF_HIDS_2 (MLP sub-images and RBF sub-images)

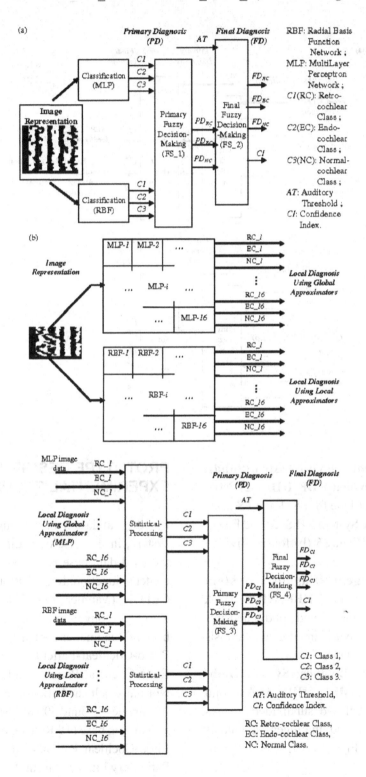

Figure 7. Hybrid intelligent diagnosis systems: (a) Global-MLP_Subdivided-RBF_HIDS_3 (MLP global image and RBF sub-images). (b) Global-RBF_Subdivided-MLP_HIDS_4 (RBF global image and MLP sub-images)

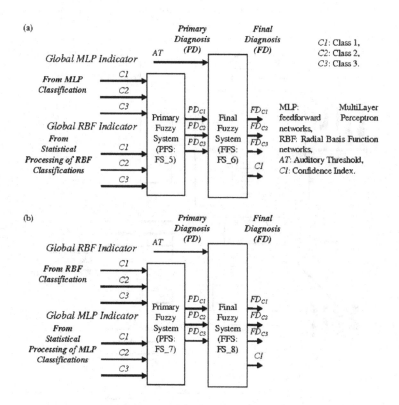

Hybrid Intelligent Diagnosis System (Subdivided-MLP_Subdivided-RBF_HIDS_2). Note that same reasoning (done for FS_1 and FS_2) is developed for Fuzzy System 3 (FS_3) and Fuzzy System 4 (FS_4), see Figure 6. (b), for sub-divided image representation.

Hybrid Intelligent Diagnosis System (Global-MLP_Subdivided-RBF_HIDS_3). A first combination of global and subdivided images leads then to the hybrid intelligent diagnosis system illustrated in Figure 7. (a).

Hybrid Intelligent Diagnosis System (Global-RBF_Subdivided-MLP_HIDS_4). A second combination of global and subdivided images leads then to the hybrid intelligent diagnosis system illustrated in Figure 7. (b).

PROTOTYPE DESIGN AND EXPERIMENTAL RESULTS

For the validation of the suggested intelligent system, in the case of auditory diagnosis help, the used data base is issued from a specialized center in functional explorations in oto-neurology CEFON[1] (Vannier *et al.*, 2002). From the signal to image conversion, the obtained database is built of 206 images such as: 38 images represent Retro-Cochlear-Patients, 77 images represent Endo-Cochlear-Patients, and 91 images represent Normal-Cochlear-Patients. From this database, 104 images (around 50% of the database) are used as learning base (19 Retro-Cochlear-Patients, 39 Endo-Cochlear-Patients, 46 Normal-Cochlear-Patients) while 102 (around 50% of the database)

Table 1. Image (global) neural classification results (MLP and RBF): Global-MLP_Global-RBF_HIDS_1

Results	Learning (MLP)	Generalization (MLP)	Learning (RBF)	Generalization (RBF)
$C1$(RC)	100%	21.05%	100%	10.52%
$C2$(EC)	97.43%	42.10%	100%	36.84%
$C3$(NC)	100%	51.11%	100%	51.11%

are used as generalization test base (19 Retro-Cochlear-Patients, 38 Endo-Cochlear-Patients, 45 Normal-Cochlear-Patients).

First suggested approach illustrated in Figure 6. (a) is mainly based on a global image knowledge representation with MLP classification and RBF classification. Learning and generalization test results of MLP and RBF networks gives the MLP global indicator see Table 1 and RBF global indicator see Table 1. Note that results of the two neural classifications, from MLP and RBF networks give RC_MLP($C1$), EC_MLP($C2$), NC_MLP($C3$) and RC_RBF($C1$), EC_RBF($C2$), NC_RBF($C3$) which are exploited in FS_1 shown in Figure 6. (a).

Second suggested approach illustrated in Figure 6. (b) is mainly based on a subdivided image knowledge representation: a subdivision of the image in several sub-images as illustrated in Figure 4. (b), in order to process each pixel in each sub-image (Piater *et al.*, 1999), avoiding thus some approximations such as mean of a set of pixels. The idea here is to process the original information (pixels), without any kind of approximation, in local sub-images (local indicators). The implemented classification strategy takes advantage from a multiple NN based structure. It includes two kind of neural classifiers operating in an independent way: MLP and RBF, as shown in Figure 6. (b). The obtained images from BAEP's signal to image conversion leaded to divide each image into 16 sub-images (12 areas of 10x20 pixels and 4 areas of 10x10 pixels). So, 16 local diagnosis (aiming to obtain 16 local indicators) are done on the 16 sub-images (S_I-*1*, ..., S_I-*i*, ..., S_I-*16*) using 16 global approximators (MLP-*1*, ..., MLP-*i*, ..., MLP-*16*), while 16 others local diagnosis (16 others local indicators) are done in the same way using 16 local approximators (RBF-*1*, ..., RBF-*i*, ..., RBF-*16*).

Indeed, MLP and RBF classifiers operate on basis of a local pattern recognition using local indicators in image, leading to a first diagnosis (local diagnosis). Learning and generalization test results after statistical processing of MLP networks and RBF networks gives two global indicators: MLP and RBF global indicators see Table 3. Note that the results of the two neural classifications, from MLP networks MLP-*1* (RC_*1*, EC_*1*, NC_*1*), ..., MLP-*16* (RC_*16*, EC_*16*, NC_*16*) and RBF networks RBF-*1* (RC_*1*, EC_*1*, NC_*1*), ..., RBF-*16* (RC_*16*, EC_*16*, NC_*16*), are processed statistically to give RC_MLP, EC_MLP, NC_MLP (i.e., $C1$, $C2$, and $C3$ from MLP) and RC_RBF, EC_RBF, NC_RBF (i.e., $C1$, $C2$, and $C3$ from RBF) and normalized between [0, 1] and exploited in FS_3 shown in Figure 6. (b).

Thus, the input vector of FS_1, see Figure 6. (a), is then **I** = [RC_MLP, EC_MLP, NC_MLP, RC_RBF, EC_RBF, NC_RBF]. The membership functions of RC_MLP, EC_MLP, NC_MLP have been defined in Figure 8. (a) and those of RC_RBF, EC_RBF, NC_RBF have been defined in Figure 8. (b). Also, input vector of FS_3, see Figure 6 (b), is then **I** = [RC_MLP, EC_MLP, NC_MLP, RC_RBF, EC_RBF, NC_RBF], i.e.,. Note that, in this case, membership functions of RC_MLP, EC_MLP, NC_MLP are the same that those of RC_RBF, EC_RBF, NC_RBF (because of statistical processing and normalization between [0, 1])

Figure 8. Membership functions of: (a) RC, EC, and NC from MLP. (b) RC, EC, and NC from RBF. (c) AT and PD$_{RC}$. (d) PD$_{EC}$ and PD$_{NC}$

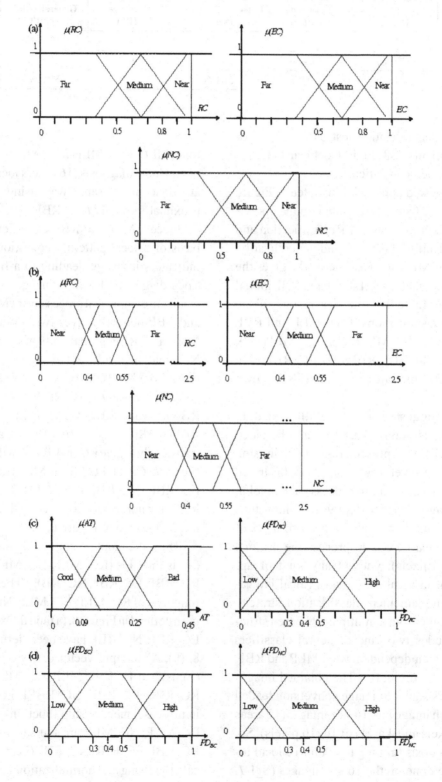

Table 2. Fuzzy decision-making system FS_1 and FS_2 results: Global-MLP_Global-RBF_HIDS_1

Results	Learning (FS_1)	Generalization (FS_1)	Learning (FS_2)	Generalization (FS_2)
C1(RC)	100%	21.05% (21.05%)	100%	15.78% (21.05%)
C2(EC)	97.43%	39.47% (52.63%)	89.74%	39.47% (47.36%)
C3(NC)	100%	46.66% (51.11%)	100%	57.77% (64.44%)

Table 3. Image (subdivided) neural classification results (MLP and RBF): Subdivided-MLP_Subdivided-RBF_HIDS_2

Results	Learning (MLP)	Generalization (MLP)	Learning (RBF)	Generalization (RBF)
C1(RC)	100%	10.52%	100%	21.05%
C2(EC)	100%	31.57%	100%	13.15%
C3(NC)	100%	66.66%	100%	88.88%

defined in Figure 8. (a). Then, for FS_2 and FS_4, the membership functions of AT and PD_{RC} have been defined in Figure 8. (c) and those of PD_{EC}, and PD_{NC} have been defined in Figure 8. (d).

Hybrid Intelligent Diagnosis System (Global-MLP_Global-RBF_HIDS_1).

Hybrid Intelligent Diagnosis System (Subdivided-MLP_ Subdivided-RBF_HIDS_2).

Results of primary FS_1 and final FS_2 are given in Table 2, while those of primary FS_3 and final FS_4 are given in Table 4. Note that the particularity of the suggested fuzzy decision system is to give for each patient the final diagnosis FDB_{RCB}, FDB_{ECB}, FDB_{NCB} and a Confidence Index (CI) on its decision, e.g., the fuzzy output result **O** = $\{\mu FDB_{RCB}, \mu FDB_{ECB}, \mu FDB_{NCB}, \mu CI\}$. Then, the final result is given by: **O** = $(\text{Max}\{\mu FDB_{RCB}, \mu FDB_{ECB}, \mu FDB_{NCB}\}, \mu CI)$. The generalization rate of NC is clearly higher for FS_1 and FS_2 (and FS_3 and FS_4) than for the two classifications. An important contribution of the final fuzzy system FS_2 (and FS_4) is that it gives each fault

diagnosis associated with a CI. More, from the analysis and comparison of these results, two main interesting conclusions which make the suggested approaches very promising are deduced. First, correct classifications from FS_2 and FS_4 are not necessarily corresponding to same generalization example patients implying a complementary feature of FS_2 and FS_4. Second, FS_2 and FS_4 take advantage from way to process given information to classify (from global images as global indicators for FS_2 and from sub-divided images as local indicators for FS_4) and from different neural classifications (MLP global approximators and RBF local approximators).

Hybrid Intelligent Diagnosis System (Global-MLP_Subdivided-RBF_HIDS_3). For HIDS_3, learning and generalization test results of the neural image classification (MLP global image and RBF subdivided image) give the MLP global indicator see Table 5 and RBF global indicator see Table 5.

Hybrid Intelligent Diagnosis System (Global-RBF_Subdivided-MLP_HIDS_4). For HIDS_4, learning and generalization test results of the neural image classification (RBF global image and MLP subdivided images) give the RBF

Table 4. Fuzzy decision-making system FS_3 and FS_4 results: Subdivided-MLP_Subdivided-RBF_HIDS_2

Results	Learning (FS_3)	Generalization (FS_3)	Learning (FS_4)	Generalization (FS_4)
C1(RC)	100%	10.52% (31.57%)	100%	21.05% (21.05%)
C2(EC)	100%	15.78% (34.21%)	94.87%	57.89% (65.78%)
C3(NC)	100%	77.77% (91.11%)	100%	82.22% (86.66%)

Table 5. Image neural classification results (MLP global image and RBF subdivided images): Global-MLP_Subdivided-RBF_HIDS_3

Results	Learning (MLP)	Generalization (MLP)	Learning (RBF)	Generalization (RBF)
C1(RC)	100%	36.84%	100%	21.05%
C2(EC)	100%	42.10%	100%	13.15%
C3(NC)	100%	66.66%	100%	88.88%

Table 6. Fuzzy decision-making system FS_5 and FS_6 results: Global-MLP_Subdivided-RBF_HIDS_3

Results	Learning (PFS)	Generalization (PFS)	Learning (FFS)	Generalization (FFS)
C1(RC)	100%	31.57% (36.84%)	100%	31.57% (31.57%)
C2(EC)	100%	31.57% (34.21%)	94.87%	26.31% (44.73%)
C3(NC)	100%	75.55% (77.77%)	100%	80.00% (86.66%

Table 7. Image neural classification results (RBF global image and MLP subdivided images): Global-RBF_Subdivided-MLP_HIDS_4

Results	Learning (RBF)	Generalization (RBF)	Learning (MLP)	Generalization (MLP)
C1(RC)	100%	36.84%	100%	10.52%
C2(EC)	94.87%	36.84%	100%	31.57%
C3(NC)	100%	55.55%	100%	66.66%

Table 8. Fuzzy decision-making system FS_7 and FS_8 results: Global-RBF_Subdivided-MLP_HIDS_4

Results	Learning (PFS)	Generalization (PFS)	Learning (FFS)	Generalization (FFS)
C1(RC)	100%	26.31% (31.57%)	100%	26.31% (26.31%)
C2(EC)	100%	28.94% (31.57%)	87.19%	36.84% (47.36%)
C3(NC)	100%	62.22% (68.88%)	100%	71.11% (77.77%)

global indicator see Table 7 and MLP global indicator see Table 7. Globally, for both HIDS_3 and HIDS_4, learning database has successfully been learnt by the two classifications, and the global correct classification rate of global image (48.53 for HIDS_3 and 43.07 for HIDS_4) is slightly better than subdivided image (41.02 for HIDS_3 and 36.25 for HIDS_4).

Then, the results of fuzzy decision-making systems: Primary diagnosis Fuzzy System (PFS) and Final diagnosis Fuzzy System (FFS) for HIDS_3 are given in Table 6 while the results of PFS and FFS for HIDS_4 are given in Table 8.

Rates written between brackets (x %) represent the generalization rates calculated taking into account the patients classified simultaneously in two classes. In majority of cases, these simultaneous classifications are obtained for $C2$(EC) and $C3$(NC). Almost for all the classes, the generalization rate of FFS is higher than that of PFS for both HIDS_3 and HIDS_4, showing the pertinent rule of the Auditory Threshold (AT) as confidence parameter.

An important contribution of the suggested FFS, for both HIDS_3 and HIDS_4, is to give for each patient the Final Diagnosis FD_{C1}, FD_{C2}, FD_{C3} with a Confidence Index (CI) on its decision, e.g., the fuzzy output result $\mathbf{O} = \{\mu FD_{RC}, \mu FD_{EC}, \mu FD_{NC}, \mu CI\}$. Then, final result is given by: $\mathbf{O} = (\text{Max}\{\mu FD_{RC}, \mu FD_{EC}, \mu FD_{NC}\}, \mu CI)$.

More, from the analysis and comparison of these results, two main interesting conclusions which make the suggested approaches very promising are deduced. First, the correct classifications from FFS(HIDS_3) and FFS(HIDS_4) are not necessarily corresponding to the same generalization example patients implying a complementary feature of FFS(HIDS_3) and FFS(HIDS_4). Second, FFS(HIDS_3) and FFS(HIDS_4) take advantage from way to process given information to classify: MLP global image as global indicator and RBF subdivided image as local indicators for FFS(HIDS_3) ; and RBF global image as global indicator and MLP subdivided image as local indicators for FFS(HIDS_4).

Solutions and Recommendations

Four hybrid intelligent diagnosis systems based on image representation for computer aided auditory diagnosis (in a biomedicine application: auditory diagnosis based on auditory brainstem response test), based on neural classifications (modular neural networks) and fuzzy decision-making systems have been suggested:

- Global-MLP_Global-RBF_HIDS_1,
- Subdivided-MLP_Subdivided-RBF_HIDS_2,
- Global-MLP_Subdivided-RBF_HIDS_3,
- Global-RBF_Subdivided-MLP_HIDS_4.

It is pertinent to notice that a large number of signal issued representations could be converted in image knowledge representations. In fact, such approaches take advantage from features which are unreachable from one-dimensional signal (time dependent waveform). More, it allows to use image-like representation and processing, which offers benefit of a richer information representation (than the signal related one), i.e., features which are unreachable from one-dimensional signal.

In fact, in each system, the double classification suggested in this work is exploited in PFS (FS_1, FS_3, FS_5, or FS_7), for a primary diagnosis, to ensure a satisfactory reliability. Second, this reliability is reinforced using a confidence parameter with the primary diagnosis result, exploited in FFS (FS_2, FS_4, FS_6, or FS_8), in order to generate the final diagnosis giving the appropriate diagnosis with a CI. Note that the double classification is of great interest for diagnosis systems, the redundancy aspect (in this double classification) acts to the reliability benefit of the overall system.

Almost for all the classes, the generalization rate of FFS is higher than that of PFS for HIDS_1,

HIDS_2, HIDS_3, and HIDS_4, demonstrating the pertinent rule of *AT* as confidence parameter. More, from the analysis and comparison of these results, two main interesting conclusions which make the suggested approaches very promising are deduced. First, correct classifications from FFS (HIDS_1, HIDS_2, HIDS_3, and HIDS_4) are not necessarily corresponding to the same generalization example patients implying a complementary feature of FFS (HIDS_1, HIDS_2, HIDS_3, and HIDS_4). Second, FFS (HIDS_1, HIDS_2, HIDS_3, and HIDS_4) take advantage from way to process given information to classify (from global images as global indicators and from sub-divided images as local indicators as well as from different neural classifications (MLP global approximators and RBF local approximators). Thus, with regard to their results, it is very important to notice that they are *complementary* rather than *competitive*. The aim is then to achieve an efficient and reliable CAD system for three classes: two auditory pathologies RC and EC and normal auditory NC. Note that the redundancy inherent in this scheme acts to the benefit of the overall system.

Another important point concerns the number of classes in the suggested approaches, i.e., only three output classes. In fact, these approaches could be generalized to many output classes exploiting concept of modular NN (Kittler *et al.*, 1998; Turban & Aronson, 2001). Such concept allows to avoid to deal with a huge number of fuzzy rules in case of a great number of output classes.

FUTURE RESEARCH DIRECTIONS

An interesting alternative for future research works could be, the investigation in aspects related to different ways to fuse neural classifiers issued information (Lai *et al.*, 2004; Wanas *et al.*, 1999), such as fuzzy neural networks or fuzzy artmap neural networks (Azouaoui & Chohra, 2002), and in generalization of the suggested approaches to a larger field of applications such as other diagnosis

problem in biomedicine, and fault detection and diagnosis in industrial plants (Balakrishnan & Honavar, 1997; Meneganti *et al.*, 1998).

However, number of current system's aspects could be enhanced with a fine tuning of fuzzy rules, and with finer statistical features which could be investigated (higher order statistical features) in statistical processing stage (Kuncheva *et al.*, 2003).

Another interesting alternative for future research works and particularly concerning sub-divided image is first to find the adequate image subdivision with regard to the number of obtained sub-images and the location of each sub-image (not necessarily regular subdivision as suggested in this Chapter); second to attribute weights (one weight to each sub-image) to sub-images to be used in the statistical processing stage. In fact, in fault diagnosis systems, from subdivided image, it is very interesting to investigate in finding which areas of image are more important than the others. That is, the faults in general and particularly the difficult faults (difficult to detect and recognize) are located in small areas of images, e.g., in image recognition of degraded locations (micro degradations) in biomedical and industrial applications. Such degraded areas arise often in approximately same areas (e.g., allowing to recognize such or such other fault). Then, if they are smartly located, they should facilitate to find the adequate image subdivision and have a higher weights (to be taken into account in the statistical processing stage). A first interesting idea to achieve such goal is to use machine learning and particularly learning from interaction, reinforcement learning, e.g., Q-learning suggested in (Watkins, 1989). Second, it is interesting also to investigate online fuzzy artmap learning suggested in (Carpenter *et al.*, 1991).

CONCLUSION

In this Chapter, the main objective was to give a methodology to design hybrid intelligent diagnosis systems for a large field of biomedicine and industrial applications. Indeed, in the suggested hybrid intelligent diagnosis system, the double classification, suggested in a hybrid intelligent diagnosis approach, is exploited in PFS to ensure a satisfactory reliability. Second, this reliability is reinforced using a confidence parameter (Auditory Threshold: *AT*) with primary diagnosis result, exploited in FFS, in order to generate the appropriate diagnosis with a Confidence Index (*CI*). In fact, the aim is then to achieve an efficient hybrid intelligent diagnosis system with a certain degree of reliability. Note that the redundancy inherent in this scheme acts to the benefit of overall system.

The image classification stage consists of the global image classification which can be based on MultiLayer feedforward Perceptron networks (MLP) or on Radial Basis Function networks (RBF) networks as well as the subdivided image classification which can be based on the same networks. These NN are chosen from their theoretical and practical features particularly the fact that MLP are *neural global* approximators, whereas RBF are *neural local* approximators (Haykin, 1999). Practically, even if RBF classifiers usually converge faster than MLP in general during training, they are almost equivalent in terms of classification performance from a same knowledge representation of an information source. The interest here is to exploit these classifiers from two different knowledge representations of an information source. In this case, it is interesting, in a double classification, to choose (between MLP and RBF) the appropriate classifier to exploit the first knowledge representation and the appropriate one to exploit the second knowledge representation.

More, this choice is motivated by the fact that such networks can be used in a double classification in such a way to take advantage from their complementary classification performances (with a confidence parameter to enhance classification rates) as well as from their competitive classification performances (with the confidence parameter, this information will contribute to enhance, for

instance, the *CI* in final decision-making in case of common classification, or inversely in case of contradictory classification) (Karray & De Silva, 2004). Indeed, in a double classification from global image and subdivided image, it is appropriated to classify the subdivided image (pixel grey level of sub-images of the subdivided image which is *more local than global*) using neural *local* approximators (RBF), while, it is appropriated to classify the global image (area mean grey level of global image which is *more global than local*) using neural *global* approximators (MLP).

An interesting way to built efficient decision-making from two neural network classifiers is fuzzy logic (Zadeh, 1965; Zadeh, 1992). In Computer Aided Diagnosis (CAD), such decision-making system should be useful and efficient giving a reliability parameter, e.g., a Confidence Index (*CI*) on each fault classes set result.

Then, in case of three output classes, a first way is to design a fuzzy system with seven (07) inputs (three inputs from first classifier, three inputs from second classifier, and one confidence parameter input) leading to a fuzzy rule base built of $3^7 = 2187$ rules which is unfortunately a huge rule number difficult and hard to implement.

In order to built useful and efficient decision making system giving a reliability parameter, Confidence Index (*CI*), an interesting way is then to design two fuzzy classifiers for the decision-making:

- the first fuzzy system for the primary decision-making from two neural classifiers with (06) inputs (three inputs from first classifier and three inputs from second classifier) leading to a fuzzy rule base built of $3^6 = 729$ rules,
- the second fuzzy system for the final decision-making from the first fuzzy system and a confidence parameter, i.e., with four (04) inputs (three inputs from first fuzzy system and one confidence parameter in-

put) leading to a fuzzy rule base built of 3^4 = 81 rules.

Thus, two fuzzy decision-making systems are necessary, avoiding a decision system with a huge rule number and associating a confidence parameter to the decision, in order to decide from two neural classifiers and to give a reliability parameter (e.g., a Confidence Index *CI*) for a useful and efficient Computer Aided Diagnosis (CAD).

REFERENCES

Azouaoui, O., & Chohra, A. (2002). Soft computing based pattern classifiers for the obstacle avoidance behavior of Intelligent Autonomous Vehicles (IAV). *International Journal of Applied Intelligence, 16*(3), Kluwer Academic Publishers, 249-271.

Balakrishnan, K., & Honavar, V. (1997). *Intelligent diagnosis systems* (pp. 50011–51040). Ames, Iowa: Technical Report, Iowa State University.

Bradley, A. P., & Wilson, W. J. (2004). On wavelet analysis of auditory evoked potentials. *Clinical Neurophysiology, 115*, 1114–1128. doi:10.1016/j.clinph.2003.11.016

Carpenter, G. A., Grossberg, S., & Rosen, D. B. (1991). Fuzzy ART: Fast stable learning and categorization of analog patterns by adaptive resonance system. *Neural Networks, 4*, 759–771. doi:10.1016/0893-6080(91)90056-B

Chohra, A., Kanaoui, N., & Amarger, V. (2005). A soft computing based approach using signal-to-image conversion for Computer Aided Medical Diagnosis (CAMD). In Saeed, K., & Pejas, J. (Eds.), *Information Processing and Security Systems* (pp. 365–374). New York: Springer. doi:10.1007/0-387-26325-X_33

Don, M., Masuda, A., Nelson, R., & Brackmann, D. (1997). Successful detection of small acoustic tumors using the stacked derived-band auditory brain stem response amplitude. *The American Journal of Otology, 18*(5), 608–621.

Egmont-Petersen, M., De Ridder, D., & Handels, H. (2002). Image processing with neural networks – a review. *Pattern Recognition, 35*, 2279–2301. doi:10.1016/S0031-3203(01)00178-9

Farreny, H., & Prade, H. (1985). Tackling uncertainty and imprecision in robotics. In *3rd International Symposium on Robotics Research*, (pp. 85-91).

Gonzalez, R. C., & Woods, R. E. (2002). *Digital image processing* (2nd ed.). Upper Saddle River, NJ: Prentice-Hall.

Goonatilake, S., & Khebbal, S. (1995). *Intelligent hybrid systems*. New York: John Wiley & Sons.

Graps, A. (1995). An introduction to wavelets. *IEEE Computational Science & Engineering, 2*(2). doi:10.1109/99.388960

Haykin, S. (1999). *Neural networks: A comprehensive foundation* (2nd ed.). Upper Saddle River, NJ: Prentice-Hall.

Karray, F. O., & De Silva, C. (2004). *Soft computing and intelligent systems design, theory, tools and applications* (Limited, I. S. B. N., Ed.). Reading, MA: Addison Wesley.

Kim, B., & Kim, S. (2005). Diagnosis of plasma processing equipment using neural network recognition of wavelet-filtered impedance matching. *Microelectronic Engineering, 82*, 44–52. doi:10.1016/j.mee.2005.05.007

Kittler, J., Hatef, M., Duin, R. P. W., & Matas, J. (1998). On combining classifiers. *IEEE Transactions on Pattern Analysis and Machine Intelligence, 20*(3), 226–239. doi:10.1109/34.667881

Kuncheva, L. I., Whitaker, C. J., & Shipp, C. A. (2003). Limits on the majority vote accuracy in classifier fusion. *Pattern Analysis & Applications, 6*, 22–31. doi:10.1007/s10044-002-0173-7

Lai, C., Tax, D. M. J., Duin, R. P. W., Pekalska, E., & Paclik, P. (2004). A study on combining image representations for image classification and retrieval. *International Journal of Pattern Recognition and Artificial Intelligence, 18*(5), World Scientific Publishing, 867-890.

Lee, C. C. (1990). Fuzzy logic in control systems: fuzzy logic controller – Part I & Part II. *IEEE Transactions on Systems, Man, and Cybernetics, 20*(2), 404–435. doi:10.1109/21.52551

Meneganti, M., Saviello, F. S., & Tagliaferri, R. (1998). Fuzzy neural networks for classification and detection of anomalies. *IEEE Transactions on Neural Networks, 9*(5), 848–861. doi:10.1109/72.712157

Palmero, G. I. S., Santamaria, J. J., de la Torre, E. J. M., & Gonzalez, J. R. P. (2005). Fault detection and fuzzy rule extraction in AC motors by a neuro-fuzzy ART-based system. [Amsterdam: Elsevier.]. *Engineering Applications of Artificial Intelligence, 18*, 867–874. doi:10.1016/j.engappai.2005.02.005

Piater, J. H., Riseman, E. M., & Utgoff, P. E. (1999). Interactively training pixel classifiers,". *International Journal of Pattern Recognition and Artificial Intelligence, 13*(2), 171–194. doi:10.1142/S0218001499000112

Piater, J. H., Stuchlik, F., von Specht, H., & Mühler, R. (1995). Fuzzy sets for feature identification in biomedical signals with self-assessment of reliability: An adaptable algorithm modeling human procedure in BAEP analysis. *Computers and Biomedical Research, an International Journal, 28*, 335–353. doi:10.1006/cbmr.1995.1023

Turban, E., & Aronson, J. E. (2001). *Decision support systems and intelligent systems.* 6th International (Ed.), Upper Saddle River, NJ: Prentice-Hall.

Vannier, E., Adam, O., & Motsch, J. F. (2002). Objective detection of brainstem auditory evoked potentials with a priori information from higher presentation levels. *Artificial Intelligence in Medicine, 25*, 283–301. doi:10.1016/S0933-3657(02)00029-5

Vuckovic, A., Radivojevic, V., Chen, A. C. N., & Popovic, D. (2002, June). Automatic recognition of alertness and drowsiness from EEG by an artificial neural network. *Medical Engineering & Physics, 24*(5), 349–360. doi:10.1016/S1350-4533(02)00030-9

Wanas, N., Kamel, M. S., Auda, G., & Karray, F. (1999). Feature-based decision aggregation in modular neural network classifiers, *Pattern Recognition Letters 20*, Elsevier, 1353-1359.

Watkins, C. J. C. H. (1989). *Learning from delayed rewards.* (Unpublished doctoral dissertation), King's College, London.

Wolf, A., Barbosa, C. H., Monteiro, E. C., & Vellasco, M. (June 2003). *Multiple MLP neural networks applied on the determination of segment limits in ECG signals. In 7th International Workshop-Conference on Artificial and Natural Neural Networks: Part II, LNCS 2687* (pp. 607–614). Berlin-Heidelberg, Germany: Springer-Verlag.

Yan, H., Jiang, Y., Zheng, J., Peng, C., & Li, Q. (2005). *A multilayer perceptron-based medical support system for heart disease diagnosis. Expert Systems with Applications.* Amsterdam: Elsevier.

Zadeh, L. A. (1965). Fuzzy sets. *Information and Control, 8*, 338–353. doi:10.1016/S0019-9958(65)90241-X

Zadeh, L. A. (1992). The calculus of fuzzy if / then rules. *AI Expert*, 23–27.

Zhang, G. P. (2000). Neural networks for classification: a survey. *IEEE Transactions on Systems, Man and Cybernetics. Part C, Applications and Reviews*, *30*(4), 451–462. doi:10.1109/5326.897072

ADDITIONAL READING

Anderson, J. A. (1995). *An Introduction to Neural Networks*. Cambridge, MA: MIT Press.

Dietterich, T. G. (2000). Hierarchical reinforcement learning with the MAXQ value function decomposition. *Journal of Artificial Intelligence Research*, *13*, 227–303.

Patterson, D. W. (1996). *Artificial Neural Networks: Theory and Applications*. Upper Saddle River, NJ: Prentice-Hall.

Pfeifer, R., & Scheier, C. (1999). *Understanding Intelligence*. Cambridge, MA: MIT press.

Sandholm, T. W. (1999). Distributed rational decision making. *MIT Press*, 201-258.

Sutton, R. S., & Barto, A. G. (1998). *Reinforcement Learning*. Cambridge, MA: MIT press.

Whitehead, S. D. (February 1992). Reinforcement learning for the adaptive control of perception and action. *Technical Report 406*, University of Rochester. Chohra, A. (June 2001) Embodied cognitive science, intelligent behavior control, machine learning, soft computing, and FPGA integration. *Technical GMD Report 136*, Germany. Langton, C. G., (Ed.). (1989). *Artificial life*. Reading, MA: Addison-Wesley Publishing Compagny.

Wooldridge, M. (2002). *An Introduction to MultiAgent Systems*. New York: John Wiley & Sons.

ENDNOTE

[1]   "Centre d'Explorations Fonctionnelles Oto-Neurologiques" (CEFON), Paris, France.

Chapter 18
Nonlinear Adaptive Ship Control Synthesis In The Case Of Model Uncertainty

Zenon Zwierzewicz
Szczecin Maritime University, Poland

ABSTRACT

This chapter covers the concerns with a problem of adaptive ship control synthesis in the case of substantially limited knowledge of the plant model. In fact we have at our disposal only its highly general structure in the form of Norrbin's-like representation with unknown nonlinearities. Two tasks of ship control are considered. The first task is concerning the ship course-keeping system design while the second refers to the path-following system. Two different approaches to the control synthesis problem are considered. One is based on an adaptive feedback linearization technique, while the second refers to the backstepping method where the tuning of unknown parameters is also taken into account. It has been demonstrated that the controllers thereby obtained enable on-line learning of unknown model characteristics, having at the same time the performance comparable to the case of fully known model parameters. The system's performance assessment for the each case has been tested via Matlab/Simulink simulations.

INTRODUCTION

A common problem of engineering practice is to cope with mathematical models of objects with only partly known structure. The model may e.g. involve some unknown (linear or nonlinear) functions that depend on the kind of object (of a given class to which the model refers) and/or of

DOI: 10.4018/978-1-61692-811-7.ch018

its operational conditions. As an example we take a general model of a single-input-single-output (SISO) system

$$y^{(n)} = f(x) + g(x)u \qquad (1)$$

that describes a wide class of objects. $x = [x, x, L, x^{(n-1)}]^T$ denotes here a system state, u is a control input, $y = x$ an output while the functions f and g are unknown or may be estimated with a considerable inaccuracy. More general classes of nonlinear control systems, not necessarily originally of the form (1) can be transformed into this structure, see e.g., Fabri & Kadrikamanathan (2001) or Spooner & Passino (1996) for details. One of the known methods of tracking control synthesis, in a case when we have a rough estimate of the above model functions, is a sliding mode control law (Slotine & Li, 1991). The alternative is to use adaptation, which offers a more subtle policy but requires a more advanced theory.

The problem of adaptive control of nonlinear systems belongs to the class of problems which suffers a lack of sufficiently general and coherent theory. In this chapter two methods of adaptive, nonlinear control synthesis are considered via examples of ship control: course-keeping as well as the path-following problem. The main feature of the presented approach is that we have very limited knowledge of the plant model that forms a basis for the control synthesis. It is assumed that nonlinear vessel dynamics is represented by Norrbin's-like ship model structure with unknown nonlinearities. The unknown model nonlinearities are assumed to be linear combinations of some known model related *basis functions* (Zwierze-wicz, 2007) i.e. some elementary knowledge of the model is assumed. Following the well-known Norrbin model structure (as a specific case of general system structure (1)) which results from experimental studies, the adopted nonlinearity approximator has a form of polynomial with unknown parameters. Generally this assumption may be substantially relaxed via applying, as the basis functions, some sort of known approxima-tors (Fabri & Kadrikamanathan, 2001; Tzirkel-Hancock & Fallside, 1992). As an example one may adopt a neuro-approximator with Gaussian radial basis functions (Sanner & Slotine, 1992). Systems of this sort are referred to as *functional adaptive* (Fabri & Kadrikamanathan, 2001) and represent a new branch of intelligent control systems.

As the model parameters are difficult for identification the proposed approach assumes a direct adaptation i.e. that without the requirement of model parameter estimation. The first of the proposed methods is based on cancellation of non-linear terms i.e. feedback linearization technique is mildly used here. The second approach uses the recently popularized method of backstepping (Krstic at al., 1995). In both cases, for the tuning of unknown model parameters, the Lyapunov function technique is exploited. The main draw-back of feedback linearization in relation to the backstepping method is that the first leads to the cancellation of all system nonlinearities irrespec-tive of their positive system influence while the backstepping is much more flexible in this respect.

The next problem one meets during the con-trol system design procedure refers to the task of tuning controller gains. In other words having a proper controller structure obtained via some of the above mentioned synthesis methods, one should find suitable parameters of the proposed controller to ensure the overall system required properties. To solve the controller parameter tuning problem we use the standard linear quadratic regulator ap-proach LQR (Ramirez, 1994). Although the LQR technique is preserved only for linear systems with quadratic performance functional we show that in the case considered here (nonlinear system) this approach may also be adequate.

It is worth emphasizing that the methods pre-sented here make it possible to realize the control synthesis not only in the case of model parametric uncertainty but also when there are some unknown elements of its structure (*functional uncertainty*) (Fabri & Kadrikamanathan, 2001). On the other hand via an example of ship path-following sys-tem control synthesis it has been shown that this concept can be extended to a more general (as compared to (1)) class of uncertain systems i.e. the class of affine-in-control systems of the form

$$x = \alpha(x) + \beta(x) \cdot u \qquad (2a)$$

Figure 1. Block diagram of identifier-based design

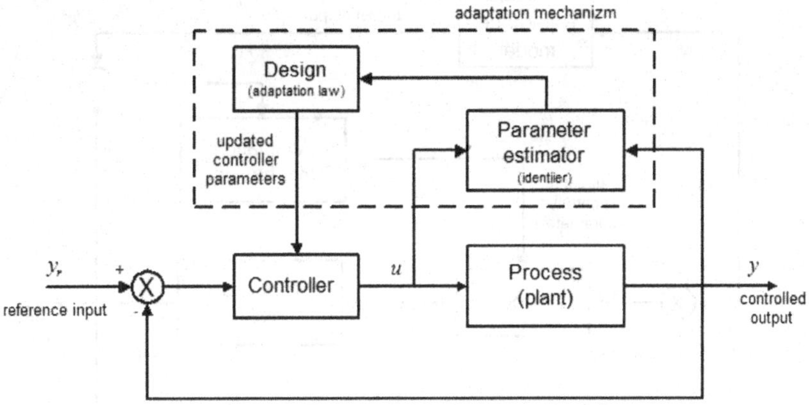

$$y = h(x) \qquad (2b)$$

where α and β are smooth vector fields on R^n and $h: R^n \rightarrow R$ a smooth function. It is assumed here also that the functions, α and β are unknown or may be estimated with a considerable inaccuracy.

In our case the model (41) belongs to this class. In addition, since some of its unknown nonlinear functions can be approximated by a sort of functional approximators we can get, as a result, an approximator-like structure (here (48)) leading to the original concept (Zwierzewicz, 2008) of *model basis functions*. As these functions contain some portion of the plant specific knowledge this approach can be effectively utilized for the synthesis of various types of partially unknown systems (of the specified-above class).

BACKGROUND

An adaptive control system is a system that is able to adapt itself to changing operating conditions, for instance, time varying characteristics of the controlled plant or process. More specifically it is a control system with adjustable parameters and mechanism for adjusting the parameters. In view of that adaptive control is the combination of a

parameter estimator, which generates parameter estimates online, with a control law in order to control classes of plants whose parameters are completely unknown and/or could change with time in unpredictable manner.

Among a variety of adaptive control schemes there are two principal i.e. identifier-based and Lyapunov-based approaches (designs) (Krstic at al., 1995). The identification based scheme (see Figure 1) contains, besides the standard feedback loop, also a second loop with adaptation mechanism which in turn consists of the plant parameter identifier and design blocks. The identifier updates an estimate of the unknown plant parameters according to which the controller parameters are tuned on line by the design block.

The example of Lyapunov-based design is illustrated in Figure 2. As compared to the former case the adaptation mechanism update law is here an error-driven algorithm that **directly** calculates controller parameter values from the discrepancy (error e_m) between plant output and the desired model output data.

In consequence, according to some alternative 'direct-indirect' classification, it is clearly a direct scheme.

The scheme depicted in Fig. 1 is, on the contrary, an indirect one. The use of the plant input/ output data in the controller parameter determina-

Figure 2. Block diagram of Lyapunov-based design

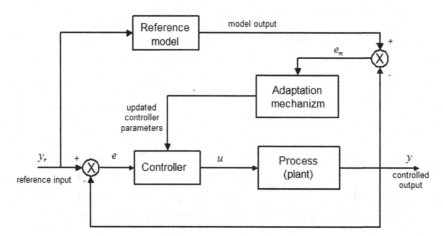

tion process, is 'indirect', since it results in only the intermediate step of plant identification. As the overall adaptive system should provide the stable operation and asymptotic tracking (stabilizability property) the proper design of controller and update law is not generally a simple task. For the case depicted e.g. in Fig.2, the key problem is to design the adaptation mechanism in such a way as to provide a stable system (i.e. bring the error e_m to zero).

In our case, based on Lyapunov approach, the adaptive versions of feedback (or exact) linearization as well as backstepping methods has been used. Roughly speaking the feedback linearization method consists in such a transformation of a given nonlinear system that results in a new, linear time-invariant one. Here, by *transformation* we mean a control law plus possibly a change of variables. Once a linear system is obtained, a secondary control law can be designed to ensure that the overall closed-loop system performs according to the specifications.

Backstepping, on the other hand, is a recursive design methodology that enables the construction of both feedback control laws and associated Lyapunov functions in a systematic way. It may be applied to the class of systems (in the so-called strict feedback form) that can be considered as a cascade connection of two (or more) subsystems. The main idea behind the backstepping can be roughly explained on the example of the following system

$$\dot{\mathbf{x}} = \mathbf{f}(\mathbf{x}) + \mathbf{g}(\mathbf{x})\xi \qquad (3a)$$

$$\dot{\xi} = u. \qquad (3b)$$

Here $x \in R^n$, $\xi \in R$ and $[x, \xi]^T \in R^{n+1}$ is the state of the system (3a)-(3b). The function $u \in R$ is the control input.

Consider the subsystem (3a). Viewing the state variable $\xi \in R$ as an independent "input" for this subsystem, we assume that there exists a stabilizing state feedback control law $\xi = \varphi(x)$ and the Lyapunov function V_1 certifying this stability. To find a state feedback law to asymptotically stabilize the system (3a)-(3b) we start by adding and subtracting $g(x)\varphi(x)$ to the subsystem (3a). We obtain the equivalent subsystem:

$$\dot{\mathbf{x}} = \mathbf{f}(\mathbf{x}) + \mathbf{g}(\mathbf{x})\varphi(\mathbf{x}) + \mathbf{g}(\mathbf{x})[\xi - \varphi(\mathbf{x})]$$

$$\dot{\xi} = u$$

Box 1.

$$\dot{V} = \frac{\partial V_1}{\partial \mathbf{x}}[\mathbf{f}(\mathbf{x}) + \mathbf{g}(\mathbf{x})\varphi(\mathbf{x}) + \mathbf{g}(\mathbf{x})z] + z\dot{z} = \frac{\partial V_1}{\partial \mathbf{x}}\mathbf{f}(\mathbf{x}) + \frac{\partial V_1}{\partial \mathbf{x}}\mathbf{g}(\mathbf{x})\varphi(\mathbf{x}) + \frac{\partial V_1}{\partial \mathbf{x}}\mathbf{g}(\mathbf{x})z + zv$$

Box 2.

$$u = u(\mathbf{x}, \xi) = v + \dot{\varphi} = \frac{\partial \varphi}{\partial \mathbf{x}}[\mathbf{f}(\mathbf{x}) + \mathbf{g}(\mathbf{x})\xi] - \frac{\partial V_1}{\partial \mathbf{x}}\mathbf{g}(\mathbf{x}) - k[\xi - \varphi(\mathbf{x})].$$

Now define $z = \xi - \varphi(x)$
$\Rightarrow \dot{z} = \dot{\xi} - \dot{\varphi}(\mathbf{x}) = u - \dot{\varphi}(\mathbf{x}) \Rightarrow \dot{z} = v.$

Whence the resulting system is

$$\dot{\mathbf{x}} = \mathbf{f}(\mathbf{x}) + \mathbf{g}(\mathbf{x})\varphi(\mathbf{x}) + \mathbf{g}(\mathbf{x})z \qquad (4a)$$

$$\dot{z} = v. \qquad (4b)$$

The system (4a)-(4b) is, once again' the cascade connection of two subsystems. However the subsystem (4a) incorporates the stabilizing state feedback law φ and is thus asymptotically stable when the input is zero. This feature can be easily exploited in the design of stabilizing control law for the overall system (4a)-(4b). To stabilize this system it is enough to consider a Lyapunov candidate of the form

$$V = V(\mathbf{x}, \xi) = V_1(\mathbf{x}) + \frac{1}{2}z^2.$$

Now from the standard, in the Lyapunov stability theory condition (see Key Terms & Definitions), of negative definiteness of its time derivative $\dot{V} < 0$ one may easily find the new asymptotically stabilizing control law $v = v(x, z)$.

We have therefore that: (see Box 1.)

We can choose

$$v = -\left(\frac{\partial V_1}{\partial \mathbf{x}}\mathbf{g}(\mathbf{x}) + kz\right), \quad k > 0$$

Thus

$$\dot{V} = -V_a(\mathbf{x}) - kz^2 < 0$$

where V_a is positive semidefinite function such that $\dot{V}_1(\mathbf{x}) \leq -V_a(\mathbf{x}) \leq 0$.

Finally the stabilizing state feedback law is given by (see Box 2.)

This idea can be of course utilized to more general classes of systems in the strict feedback form (Khalil 2002).

The most widely used ship control systems are based on simple PID controller. Modern autopilots using LQG and H_∞ control design techniques have been reported in the literature by many authors (see Fossen 2000 and the references therein). Besides, a large number of other advanced control methods such as model reference adaptive control (Amerongen, 1984), neural-network and fuzzy adaptive control (Sutton, 1996) have been tested via ship sea trials since 1980s.

As the automatically steered vessels have to face up to still more complex missions (e.g. high precision control in the case of changing dynamics), in the recent two decades a number of new nonlinear model based ship control systems design have been developed. Such design techniques like feedback linearization (Tzeng at al., 1999), backstepping (Casado 2003), output feedback control, nonlinear observer design and passivity (Fossen 2000) can be included here; also along with their adaptive or/and robust versions (Du, 2005). As the application of backstepping method, in the case of high-dimensional systems, leads to serious analytical complications, most research has focused on the simpler course-keeping problem. In this chapter, however, the method of backstepping has been successfully applied to the more complex adaptive ship path-following problem avoiding yet complicated calculations. The developed here method is also original in this respect that enables for reconstruction of unknown object nonlinearities. In this context one may classify it as *functionally adaptive*.

THE NORRBIN'S-LIKE SHIP MODEL STRUCTURE AND ITS IDENTIFICATION

Course-keeping problem is a task of designing an automatic control aid (autopilot) that is able, via appropriate rudder actions, to steer the ship motion as to maintain a pre-assigned constant heading.

In order to synthesize a course-keeping controller we apply the following Norrbin's-like (Fossen, 1994; Lisowski, 1981) ship model general structure

$$T\ddot{\psi} + F(\dot{\psi}) = k\delta \tag{5}$$

where

ψ: course (heading)
δ: rudder deflection as a control variable
T, k: unknown model parameters
$F(\cdot)$: unknown function

In the 'classical' approach to ship control the approximator structure of the function F is (according to Norrbin model) often adopted in the form of a polynomial of the third order. Generally it may be assumed as

$$F(\dot{\psi}) = a_3\dot{\psi}^3 + a_2\dot{\psi}^2 + a_1\dot{\psi} + a_0 \tag{6a}$$

or ignoring the terms of second degree we have for example

$$F(\dot{\psi}) = a_3\dot{\psi}^3 + a_1\dot{\psi} + a_0 \tag{6b}$$

Now, assuming that a structure of function F has been predetermined, the coefficients a_i are usually identified via sea trials (Lisowski, 1981). After some ship-circulation tests we apply regression analysis to the obtained data ($\dot{\psi}$ as a function of δ) for each of the mentioned structures separately and then we opt for the best fitting solution.

Since each of the tests should be performed for prescribed sailing conditions e.g. different ship load, trim and velocity it follows that the problem of sufficiently general model building is a laborious and expensive task. For this reason in practice linear models are preferred as being simpler for identification as well as we have in this case a number of linear synthesis methods at our disposal. For several control tasks however, especially for strongly nonlinear objects, the linear models are insufficient. The control algorithm obtained via such a model leads not only to the deterioration of control performance but may also produce an unpredictable system destabilization. Due to above facts we propose an approach which while dealing with nonlinear models avoids, at the same time, to cope with the demanding identification task.

Box 3.

$$\Phi(\dot{\psi}) = \frac{a_3}{T}\dot{\psi}^3 + \frac{a_2}{T}\dot{\psi}^2 + \frac{a_1}{T}\dot{\psi} + \frac{a_0}{T} = \theta_3\dot{\psi}^3 + \theta_2\dot{\psi}^2 + \theta_1\dot{\psi} + \theta_0 = \boldsymbol{\theta}^T\mathbf{w} \qquad (8)$$

Box 4.

$$\delta = -\frac{1}{c}(\hat{\theta}_3\dot{\psi}^3 + \hat{\theta}\dot{\psi}^2 + \hat{\theta}\dot{\psi} + \hat{\theta}_0 + k_P\psi + k_D\dot{\psi}) = -\frac{1}{c}(\hat{\boldsymbol{\theta}}^T\mathbf{w} + k_P\psi + k_D\dot{\psi}) \qquad (11)$$

COURSE-KEEPING VIA ADAPTIVE FEEDBACK LINEARIZATION

In this section we consider the ship course-keeping control synthesis problem based on the above presented Norrbin's model structure. It is assumed, for simplicity (but without loss of generality), that the preset (reference) course value equals to zero $\psi_d = 0$.

Rewrite the model (5) in the form

$$\ddot{\psi} = \Phi(\dot{\psi}) + c\delta \qquad (7)$$

where $\Phi = -\dfrac{F(\cdot)}{T}$; $c = k/T$.

If the function Φ and the coefficient c were fully known then the application of control law in the form $\delta = -\dfrac{1}{c}(\Phi + k_P\psi + k_D\dot{\psi})$ would result in their exact cancellation and thereby lead to the linear system $\ddot{\psi} + k_D\dot{\psi} + k_P\psi = 0$ which by virtue of the choice of coefficients k_D, k_p is asymptotically stable. One can observe that this simple system transformation is in fact the feedback linearization method mentioned in the introduction.

Now we will consider the case where the function Φ is unknown but can be parameterized in the following form (see Box 3.)

$$\theta = [\theta_0\theta_1\theta_2\theta_3]^T; \quad \mathbf{w} = \begin{bmatrix} 1 & \dot{\psi} & \dot{\psi}^2 & \dot{\psi}^3 \end{bmatrix}^T. \qquad (9)$$

The system (7) can be now written as

$$\ddot{\psi} = \boldsymbol{\theta}^T\mathbf{w} + c\delta \qquad (10)$$

and the parameters θ_i are assumed to be unknown and subject to a proper adjustment (updating). For the sake of simplicity we assume here that the parameter c is known, though one can find in the subsequent sections a more general approach.

Our aim is to design a control algorithm as well as a parameters (in fact their estimates) θ_i adaptation law as to guarantee, for the resulting feedback control system, the property of asymptotic stability. Motivated by the given above case of full system knowledge we propose the (adaptive) control law, in the simple feedback PD-like form, as follows (see Box 4)
which yields

$$\ddot{\psi} + k_D\dot{\psi} + k_P\psi = \tilde{\boldsymbol{\theta}}^T\mathbf{w} \qquad (12)$$

along with

$$\tilde{\boldsymbol{\theta}} = \boldsymbol{\theta} - \hat{\boldsymbol{\theta}} = \begin{bmatrix} (\theta_0 - \hat{\theta}_0) & (\theta_1 - \hat{\theta}_1) & (\theta_2 - \hat{\theta}_2) & (\theta_3 - \hat{\theta}_3) \end{bmatrix}^T \qquad (13)$$

Box 5.

$$\dot{V} = \mathbf{x}^T\mathbf{P}(\mathbf{A}\mathbf{x} + \mathbf{b}\tilde{\theta}^T\mathbf{w}) + (\mathbf{x}^T\mathbf{A}^T + \mathbf{w}^T\tilde{\theta}\mathbf{b}^T)\mathbf{P}\mathbf{x} + 2\tilde{\theta}^T\Gamma^{-1}\dot{\tilde{\theta}}.$$

where $\hat{\theta}_i$ denotes the parameter estimates as well as the coefficients k_p and k_D are selected so as to ensure the left side of (12) is asymptotically stable. We can e.g., (assuming perfect knowledge of the model; $\tilde{\theta} = 0$), tune k_p and k_D according to a LQR control law follows a standard reasonable criterion (see later).

Now using the Lyapunov function method we prove that after the introduction a parameter estimates update law in the form

$$\dot{\hat{\theta}} = \varepsilon \Gamma \mathbf{w} \tag{14}$$

where $\Gamma > 0$ is a diagonal weighting matrix, $\varepsilon(t) = \mu_1\psi + \mu_2\dot{\psi}$ (coefficients μ_i are defined later), the closed loop system (12) is asymptotically stable and the vector of parameters $\tilde{\theta}$ is uniformly bounded. To this end we rewrite (12) in the matrix form

$$\dot{\mathbf{x}} = \mathbf{A}\mathbf{x} + \mathbf{b}\tilde{\theta}^T\mathbf{w} \tag{15}$$

where $\mathbf{x} = [\psi, \dot{\psi}]^T$ is the system state and

$$\mathbf{A} = \begin{bmatrix} 0 & 1 \\ -k_P & -k_D \end{bmatrix}; \tag{16}$$

Since A is a stability matrix (i.e. k_p and $k_D > 0$), there exist a positive definite matrix P such that:
$A^T P + PA = -I$
where I is the identity matrix.
Let us define Lyapunov function

$$V(\mathbf{x}, \tilde{\theta}) = \mathbf{x}^T\mathbf{P}\mathbf{x} + \tilde{\theta}^T\Gamma^{-1}\tilde{\theta}. \tag{17}$$

whose time derivative along the trajectories of (12), (14) is given by (see Box 5)

Using the fact that $P = P^T$ as well as that $x^T Pb$ is a scalar yields

$$\dot{V} = -x^T x + 2\tilde{\theta}^T(x^T Pbw + \Gamma^{-1}\dot{\hat{\theta}}). \tag{18}$$

If we now apply, as parameter estimates update law, the formula

$$\dot{\hat{\theta}} = -\Gamma x^T Pbw$$

or

$$\dot{\hat{\theta}} = \Gamma x^T Pbw = \varepsilon \Gamma w \tag{19}$$

where $\varepsilon(t) = \mathbf{x}^T\mathbf{P}\mathbf{b} = \mu_1\psi + \mu_2\dot{\psi}$

we get $\dot{V} = -\mathbf{x}^T\mathbf{x} \leq 0$.

We have proved that Lyapunov function is decreasing along trajectories of (15), (19); thereby establishing bounded $x(t)$ and $\tilde{\theta}$. However, to verify that $x(t) \to 0$ as $t \to \infty$ we use Barbalat's lemma (Slotine & Li, 1991). To check the uniform continuity of $\dot{V}$ it is sufficient to prove that the second derivative of V i.e.

$$\ddot{V} = -2\mathbf{x}^T(\mathbf{A}\mathbf{x} + 2\mathbf{b}\tilde{\theta}^T\mathbf{w}) \tag{20}$$

is bounded. This in turn needs w to be bounded. Since w(see (9)) is a function of bounded state $\mathbf{x} = \begin{bmatrix} \psi & \dot{\psi} \end{bmatrix}^T$, it follows that w is also bounded.

□

COURSE-KEEPING VIA ADAPTIVE BACKSTEPPING

In order to apply the backstepping method (Krstic at al., 1995) to the control synthesis problem we rewrite equation (7) in the normal form

$$\dot{\psi} = r$$
$$\dot{r} = \boldsymbol{\theta}^{\mathrm{T}}\mathbf{w} + c\delta \tag{21}$$

where r is the ship angular velocity. Treating now the variable r as a virtual control we denote as $r = \varphi(\psi(t))$ a stabilizing synthesis with regard to the first equation (subsystem). To find it let us define the Lyapunov function in the form

$$V_1(\psi) = \frac{1}{2}\psi^2. \tag{22}$$

As its derivative should be negative definite the function φ is chosen as to satisfy the inequality

$$\dot{V}_1 = \psi \cdot r = \psi \cdot \phi(\psi) < 0 \text{ for } \psi \neq 0. \tag{23}$$

Defining now new coordinates

$$z_1 = \psi$$
$$z_2 = r - \phi \tag{24}$$

and taking into account that

$$\dot{z}_2 = \dot{r} - \dot{\phi} \tag{25}$$

the system (21) yields the following form

$$\dot{z}_1 = z_2 + \phi$$
$$\dot{z}_2 = \boldsymbol{\theta}^T w + c\delta - \dot{\phi}. \tag{26}$$

Let us take now the Lyapunov function as follows

$$V(z_1, z_2, \tilde{\boldsymbol{\theta}}) = V_1 + \frac{1}{2}z_2^2 + \frac{1}{2}\tilde{\boldsymbol{\theta}}^T\tilde{\boldsymbol{\theta}} = \frac{1}{2}z_1^2 + \frac{1}{2}z_2^2 + \frac{1}{2}\tilde{\boldsymbol{\theta}}^T\tilde{\boldsymbol{\theta}} \tag{27}$$

where $\tilde{\boldsymbol{\theta}} = \boldsymbol{\theta} - \hat{\boldsymbol{\theta}}$ and $\hat{\boldsymbol{\theta}}$ is an estimate of θ, hence

$$\dot{V} = z_1(z_2 + \phi) + z_2(\theta^T w + c\delta - \dot{\phi}) + \tilde{\theta}^T\dot{\tilde{\theta}}. \tag{28}$$

If we apply as the control δ the formula

$$\delta = -\frac{1}{c}(\hat{\theta}^T w - \dot{\phi} + z_1 + k_2 z_2), \tag{29}$$

assume that $k_2 > 0$ and take the parameters update law in the form:

$$\dot{\tilde{\theta}} = -z_2 w \text{ or } \dot{\hat{\theta}} = z_2 w \tag{30}$$

we get:

$$\dot{V} = z_1\phi - k_2 z_2^2 = \dot{V}_1 - k_2 z_2^2 \leq 0. \tag{31}$$

Now using the same arguments as in the proof of former section, (i.e. Barbalat's lemma), we can assert that $z_1, z_2 \to 0$ as $t \to \infty$ which implies (in view of (23)) that ψ, $r \to 0$ as $t \to \infty$. We have thus proven that the whole system (21),(29),(30) is globally asymptotically stable.

The function φ of (23) may be chosen however in distinct ways. If we e.g. take as the φ a formula

$$\varphi(\psi) = -k_1\psi \text{ where } k_1 > 0 \tag{32}$$

we get (see Box 6.) or

$$\delta = -\frac{1}{c}(\hat{\boldsymbol{\theta}}^T\mathbf{w} + k_P\psi + k_D r) \tag{34}$$

which, as compared to (11), is in fact the same formula. However, because of the above men-

Box 6.

$$\delta = -\frac{1}{c}(\hat{\boldsymbol{\theta}}^T\mathbf{w} + k_1 r + \psi + k_2(r + k_1\psi)) = -\frac{1}{c}(\hat{\boldsymbol{\theta}}^T\mathbf{w} + (1 + k_1 k_2)\psi + (k_1 + k_2)r) \qquad (33)$$

Box 7.

$$\delta = -\frac{1}{c}(\hat{\boldsymbol{\theta}}^T\mathbf{w} + k_1 r(1 + 3\psi^2) + \psi + k_2(r + k_1(\psi + \psi^3))) =$$
$$= -\frac{1}{c}(\hat{\boldsymbol{\theta}}^T\mathbf{w} + (1 + k_1 k_2(1 + \psi^2))\psi + (k_1(1 + 3\psi^2) + k_2)r) \qquad (36)$$

Figure 5. Exact model characteristic versus its adaptive reconstruction

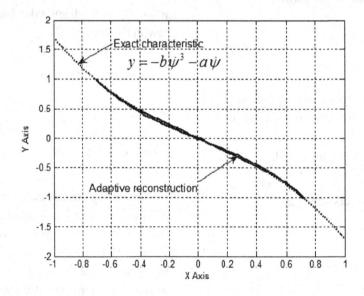

tioned flexibility of the backstepping method we have a chance to propose φ in another way. Let us take now the function

$$\varphi(\psi) = -k_1(\psi + \psi^3). \qquad (35)$$

If we substitute it to (29) we obtain (see Box 7) or finally

$$\delta = -\frac{1}{c}(\hat{\theta}^T w - k_P(\psi)\psi - k_D(\psi)r). \qquad (37)$$

The last formula is sometimes (Fossen, 1994) referred to as a nonlinear (adaptive) regulator PD algorithm. Observe that the update law (30) has now a 'stronger' form as compared to (19), where the scalar factor ε (so-called *tuning function*) is simply a linear combination of state vector components. Now we have instead, the tuning function

$$z_2 = \mathbf{r} - \varphi = r + k_1(\psi + \psi^3) \qquad (38)$$

Figure 4. Ship trajectories with two sharp turns

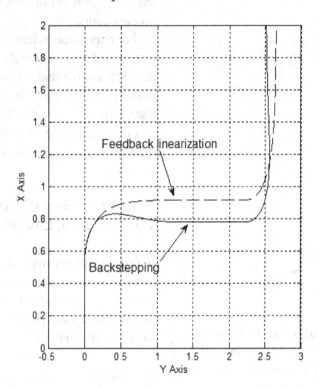

which, as compared to (19), includes a damping term ψ^3 that leads to the acceleration of the adaptation process, especially for larger values of ψ. From our simulation experience, to generate a good enough model characteristic (Fig.5) the sharp ship turns (right and left) are necessary (Fig.4). Taking also into account the fact of rudder saturation the both presented methods seem to be equivalent. The gains k_1 and k_2 can be selected via k_p and k_D of (34) which in turn can be found according to a LQR procedure given in the subsequent section.

ADAPTIVE SHIP PATH-FOLLOWING CONTROL SYNTHESIS

The method of ship course-keeping control synthesis presented above can be generalized in a straightforward way to the more complex problem of ship path following control system design. Thus, our problem is to design an auto-

matic system that is able, via appropriate rudder (or generally, set of accessible actuators) action, to see the ship along the pre-defined path at the sea surface. The designed controller has therefore to control now also the ship's position in respect to a reference track.

Prior to the introduction a model that represents further the base for controller synthesis we define some preliminary notions.

Path-following Errors Definition

Assume that a path to be followed (preset) is composed of broken line segments defined by a sequence of vertexes (turning points) $P_1(x_1, y_1)$, $P_2(x_2, y_2),...,P_i(x_i, y_i),...,P_n(x_n, y_n)$. Let us also introduce the following coordinate systems (Fig.3):

- earth-fixed coordinate system (X_g, Y_g) (these coordinates can be measured directly via *GlobalPositioningSystem* (GPS)).

Figure 3. Earth-fixed and relative coordinate systems

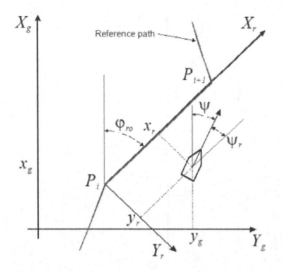

- relative (transformed) coordinate system (X_r, Y_r) whose center is located at the point $P_i(x_i, y_i)$ and with the axis OX_r directed along a segment $P_i P_{i+1}$ ($i=1,2,...,n$).

The relative ship position (x_r, y_r) as well as its relative heading ψ_r can be obtained through the following simple transformation:

$$\begin{bmatrix} x_r \\ y_r \\ \psi_r \end{bmatrix} = \begin{bmatrix} \cos\phi_{ro} & \sin\phi_{ro} & 0 \\ -\sin\phi_{ro} & \cos\phi_{ro} & 0 \\ 0 & 0 & 1 \end{bmatrix} \begin{bmatrix} x_g - x_i \\ y_g - y_i \\ \psi - \phi_{ro} \end{bmatrix}, \quad (39)$$

which expresses the successive translation and then rotation of the earth-fixed system where φ_{ro} is an angle of its rotation

$$\tan\phi_{ro} = \frac{y_{i+1} - y_i}{x_{i+1} - x_i} \quad (40)$$

Now it is reasonable to treat the coordinate y_r and the heading ψ_r as the path-following errors (corresponding to the given segment), which

should be brought to zero in the case of perfect process course.

For curvilinear reference path the local (relative) coordinate system should be tangent to the path at the point that is closest to the actual ship position. This system has to be then shifted and rotated from time step to time step in such a way, that it remains tangent to the reference path and that the *x*-coordinate represents the arc length along the path.

Path-Following Controller Synthesis via Feedback Linearization

In order to synthesize a path-following controller we apply the adaptive control concepts of the former section to the following (partially known), ship motion model presented in the form of a so-called error equation

$$\begin{cases} \dot{y}_r = u\sin\psi_r + v\cos\psi_r & (41a) \\ \dot{\psi}_r = r & (41b) \\ \dot{r} = \Phi(r) + c\delta + d & (41c) \end{cases}$$

with the output

$$y = y_r \quad (41d)$$

where

y_r – relative abscissa of the ship position (cross-track error)

ψ_r – relative heading (course-error)

r – angular velocity

u – longitudinal velocity (considered here as a constant)

v – transversal velocity

y – system output

δ – rudder deflection as a control variable

c – unknown model parameter

$\Phi(\cdot)$ – unknown function

Box 8.

$$\hat{f}(\mathbf{x}) = \sum_{i=1}^{5} \hat{\theta}_i^1 f_i + f_0 = \hat{\theta}_1^1 r^3 \cos\psi_r + \hat{\theta}_2^1 r^2 \cos\psi_r + \hat{\theta}_3^1 r \cos\psi_r + \hat{\theta}_4^1 \cos\psi_r + \hat{\theta}_5^1 r^2 \sin\psi_r + ru\cos\psi_r$$

$$(45a)$$

$$\hat{g}(\mathbf{x}) = \sum_{i=1}^{1} \hat{\theta}_i^2 g_i + g_0 = \hat{\theta}_1^2 \cos\psi_r$$

$$(45b)$$

d – unknown constant or slowly-varying parameter due to environmental disturbances and/or approximation errors

Equation (41a) is a second equation of the ship kinematical model (compare the first two equations of model (80)) while (41b) and (41c) are in fact the Norrbin ship model whose general form (5) can be transformed into the relevant equations of (41) via definition $\dot{\psi}_r = r$ and substitution of

$$\Phi = -\frac{F(\cdot)}{T} \text{ and } c = k/T \ (42)(\text{compare } (7)).$$

The first equation of kinematics, in model (41), is omitted as x_r represents movement along the path - which is irrelevant here. It is also assumed, for simplicity, that transversal velocity v is of the form $v = -r_1 r$ (compare the last equation of model (80)) where r_1 is unknown as well as that the state vector $x = [y_r \psi_r r]^T$ is accessible to measurement.

The double differentiation (which in fact represents a formalism of Lie derivatives (Isidori, 1989)) of the output y with respect to time leads to

$$\ddot{y} = f(\mathbf{x}) + g(\mathbf{x})\delta \tag{43}$$

where

$$f(x) = ru\cos\psi_r + r_1 r^2 \sin\psi_r - r_1\cos\psi_r \cdot \Phi(r) \tag{44a}$$

$$g(x) = cr_1\cos\psi_r. \tag{44b}$$

As one can observe the transformed system (43) can not be fully equivalent to the original one (41) at least because the former is only two dimensional (with respect to the new, transformed state $y = [y_1, y_2]^T$). This fact suggests that a part of the original system dynamics has been missed out. In fact we have omitted here an unobservable part of the dynamics that is called *internal dynamics* (or *zero dynamics*) (Khalil, 2002). Physical limitations as well as simple but tangled technical analysis imply however the stable system internal dynamics which means that the controller design can be based solely on the transformed system (43).

Since the system (43) has an analogical form as (5) so the controller synthesis procedure will be in fact the same as in the former section. Rewriting (44) in the form: (see Box 8.) where $\hat{f}(\mathbf{x})$ and $\hat{g}(\mathbf{x})$ denote the functions approximating $f(x)$ and $g(x)$ respectively, we can define in the same way as before (compare (8) and (9)), the vectors of parameters as well as the vectors of *model basis functions* (Zwierzewicz, 2007):

$$\theta^1 = [\theta_1^1 \ \theta_2^1 \ \theta_3^1 \ \theta_4^1 \ \theta_5^1]^T; \ \theta^2 = \theta_1^2 \tag{46}$$

$$\tilde{\theta}^1 = [\theta_1^1 - \hat{\theta}_1^1, \ \theta_2^1 - \hat{\theta}_2^1, \ \theta_3^1 - \hat{\theta}_3^1, \ \theta_4^1 - \hat{\theta}_4^1, \ \theta_5^1 - \hat{\theta}_5^1]^T;$$

$$(47)$$

$$\mathbf{w}_1 = \left[r^3 \cos\psi_r \quad r^2 \cos\psi_r \quad r\cos\psi \quad \cos\psi_r \quad r^2 \sin\psi_r \right]^T;$$

$$(48)$$

$\hat{\theta}_i$ denotes the parameter estimates.

Note that e.g. $\hat{\theta}_4^1 = (a_0 + d)r_1$, so up to three parameters are replaced by one in this case. Moreover, the disturbances in the presented method (here in the control channel) are taken into account automatically. As before the proposed controller is assumed in the PD-like form

$$\delta = \frac{-\hat{f} + v}{\hat{g}} \tag{49}$$

where $v = -k_P y - k_D \dot{y}$.

Transforming now (43)

$$\ddot{y} - v = f + g\delta - v \tag{50}$$

and substituting v obtained from (49) yields

$$\ddot{y} - v = f + g\delta - \hat{f} - \hat{g}\delta = f - \hat{f} + (g - \hat{g})\delta. \tag{51}$$

Now using (44),(45) and (47) we get a counterpart of formula (12):

$$\ddot{y} + k_D \dot{y} + k_P y = \tilde{\theta}^{1T} w_1 + \tilde{\theta}^{2T} w_2 \cdot \delta = \tilde{\theta}^T w \tag{52}$$

where

$$\tilde{\theta} = \begin{bmatrix} \tilde{\theta}^{1T} & \tilde{\theta}^{2T} \end{bmatrix}^T ; \quad \mathbf{w} = [\mathbf{w}_1^T \quad \mathbf{w}_2^T \cdot \delta]^T. \tag{53}$$

The proof of system (52) (coupled with adaptation law (19)) asymptotical stability goes on in the same way as its counterpart in the former section, it is sufficient to substitute y instead of ψ. All remaining elements apply as before. It can be seen from (45) that to implement our algorithm besides the state vector measurements the longitudinal velocity u is also required.

To sum up: the sought asymptotically stabilizing controller for the path-following problem is represented by formula (49) together with the parameter update law (19).

Note that although our controller is able to bring the output i.e. cross-track error to zero, the bringing at the same time ψ_r to zero, in presence of disturbances (e.g. transversal current), is (for the ship (80) considered here - with conventional set of actuators) not always possible (Zwierzewicz, 2003). In this way the path-following process may be, in our case, accomplished only in the presence of a course error (nonzero drift angle).

Path-following Controller Synthesis via Backstepping

In order to apply the backstepping method to the path-following control synthesis problem we rewrite equation (43) in the normal form

$$\begin{aligned} \dot{y}_1 &= y_2 \\ \dot{y}_2 &= f(\mathbf{x}) + g(\mathbf{x})\delta \end{aligned} \tag{54}$$

where $y_1 = y$ and $y_2 = \dot{y}_1 = \dot{y}$. Treating now the variable y_2 as a virtual control we denote as $y_2 = \varphi(y_1)$ a stabilizing synthesis with regard to the first equation (subsystem). To find it let us define the Lyapunov function in the form

$$V_1(y_1) = \frac{1}{2} y_1^2 \tag{55}$$

As its derivative should be negative definite the function φ is chosen as to satisfy the inequality

$$\dot{V}_1 = y_1 y_2 = y_1 \cdot \varphi(y_1) < 0 \text{ for } y_1 \neq 0. \tag{56}$$

Defining now new coordinates

$$\begin{aligned} z_1 &= y_1 \\ z_2 &= y_2 - \varphi \end{aligned} \tag{57}$$

and taking into account that

Box 9.

$$\delta = -\frac{1}{\hat{g}}(\hat{f} + k_1 y_2 + y_1 + k_2(y_2 + k_1 y_1)) = -\frac{1}{\hat{g}}(\hat{f} + (1 + k_1 k_2)y_1 + (k_1 + k_2)y_2) \tag{72}$$

$$\dot{z}_2 = \dot{y}_2 - \dot{\varphi} \tag{58}$$

the system (54) yields the following form

$$\dot{z}_1 = z_2 + \varphi - \dot{z}_2 = f(x) + g(x)\delta - \dot{\varphi} \tag{59}$$

We will prove below that applying the control δ in the form

$$\dot{z}_1 = z_2 + \varphi - \dot{z}_2 = f(x) + g(x)\delta - \dot{\varphi}, \tag{60}$$

(where the function v is defined later), together with some parameter adaptation law makes the system (59) asymptotically stable. To this end we perform the following transformations:

$$\dot{z}_2 - v = f + g \cdot \delta - \dot{\varphi} - v \tag{61}$$

and

$$\dot{z}_2 - v = f + g \cdot \delta - \dot{\varphi} - (\hat{f} + \hat{g} \cdot \delta - \dot{\varphi}) = (f - \hat{f}) + (g - \hat{g})\delta \tag{62}$$

where in the left hand side of (62) the substitution for v obtained from (60) has been used.

Now, using (44),(45),(47),(48) we have

$$f - \hat{f} = \sum_{i=1}^{5} \tilde{\theta}_i^1 f_i = \tilde{\theta}^1 w_1$$

and

$$g - \hat{g} = \sum_{i=1}^{1} \tilde{\theta}_i^2 g_i = \tilde{\theta}^2 w_2, \tag{63}$$

which yields

$$\dot{z}_2 = \tilde{\theta}^{1T} w_1 + \tilde{\theta}^{2T} w_2 \cdot \delta + v = \tilde{\theta}^T w + v. \tag{64}$$

Let us take now the Lyapunov function as follows

$$V(z_1, z_2, \tilde{\theta}) = V_1 + \frac{1}{2}z_2^2 + \frac{1}{2}\tilde{\theta}^T\tilde{\theta} = \frac{1}{2}z_1^2 + \frac{1}{2}z_2^2 + \frac{1}{2}\tilde{\theta}^T\tilde{\theta} \tag{65}$$

where $\tilde{\theta} = \theta - \hat{\theta}$ and $\hat{\theta}$ is an estimate of θ.
Hence

$$\dot{V} = z_1(z_2 + \varphi) + z_2(\tilde{\theta}^T w + v) + \tilde{\theta}^T\dot{\tilde{\theta}}. \tag{66}$$

If we apply as v the formula

$$v = -z_1 - k_2 z_2, \tag{67}$$

assume that $k_2 > 0$ and take the parameter update law in the form $\dot{\tilde{\theta}} = -z_2\mathbf{w}$ or $\dot{\hat{\theta}} = z_2\mathbf{w}$ (68) we get

$$\dot{V} = z_1\phi - k_2 z_2^2 = \dot{V}_1 - k_2 z_2^2 \leq 0. \tag{69}$$

Now using the same arguments as in the proof of the former section, (i.e. Barbalat's lemma), we can assert that $z_1, z_2 \to 0$ as $t \to \infty$ which implies (in view of (56)) that $y_1, y_2 \to 0$ as $t \to \infty$. We have thus proven that the closed loop system composed of (54), control δ in the form

$$\delta = -\frac{1}{\hat{g}}(\hat{f} - \dot{\varphi} + z_1 + k_2 z_2) \tag{70}$$

Box 10.

$$\delta = -\frac{1}{\hat{g}}(\hat{f} + k_1 y_2(1 + 3y_1^2) + y_1 + k_2(y_2 + k_1(y_1 + y_1^3))) =$$

$$= -\frac{1}{\hat{g}}(\hat{f} + (1 + k_1 k_2(1 + y_1^2))y_1 + (k_1(1 + 3y_1^2) + k_2)y_2) \qquad (75)$$

as well as the adaptation law (68) is globally asymptotically stable.

The main virtue of the backstepping method is a possibility of 'tuning' the control structure via proper choice of function ϕ. As before, at first we will take the formula $\varphi(y_1) = -k_1 y_1$ where $k_1 > 0$, (71) whence: (see Box 9.) or

$$\delta = -\frac{1}{\hat{g}}(\hat{f} + k_P y_1 + k_D y_2) \qquad (73)$$

which, as compared to (49), is in fact the same formula. However, because of the above mentioned flexibility of the backstepping method we have a chance to propose φ in another way. Let us take now the function

$$\varphi(y_1) = -k_1(y_1 + y_1^3). \qquad (74)$$

If we substitute it to (70) we obtain (see Box 10) or finally

$$\delta = -\frac{1}{\hat{g}}(\hat{f} - k_P(y_1)y_1 - k_D(y_1)y_2). \qquad (76)$$

As before, the obtained formula has the form of a nonlinear (adaptive) regulator PD algorithm. All the earlier observations as to the relation of this control algorithm to that obtained via feedback linearization hold in this case as well. Similarly we have the tuning function

$$z_2 = y_2 - \varphi = y_2 + k_1(y_1 + y_1^3) \qquad (77)$$

which, as compared to (19), includes a damping term y_1^3 that leads to the acceleration of the adaptation process, especially for larger values of y_1. The gains k_1 and k_2 can be selected via k_p and k_D of (76) which in turn can be found according to the LQR procedure as in the next section.

CONTROLLER GAIN TUNING VIA LQR PROCEDURE

The next task, after we obtained a stabilizing controller structure, is tuning of its parameters to achieve desirable properties of the overall system. To this end we will write the system canonical form (52) (see also (12)) in the matrix notation

$$\dot{\mathbf{y}} = \widehat{\mathbf{A}}\mathbf{y} + \mathbf{b}v + \mathbf{b}\tilde{\boldsymbol{\cdot}}^T \mathbf{w} \qquad (78)$$

where $y_1 = y_2$, $y_2 = \dot{y}_1 = \dot{y}$; $v = -k_p y_1 - k_D y_2$ as well as $\widehat{\mathbf{A}} = \begin{bmatrix} 0 & 1 \\ 0 & 0 \end{bmatrix}$; $\mathbf{b} = \begin{bmatrix} 0 \\ 1 \end{bmatrix}$

From the proven asymptotic stability of (12) (so also (52)) it follows that $\mathbf{b}\tilde{\boldsymbol{\theta}}^T \mathbf{w} \to 0$ as $t \to \infty$. This fact suggests that through the introduction of a proper performance criterion the problem of tuning of the feedback gains k_p and k_D may be formulated as a standard LQ regulator problem. A reasonable quadratic criterion may have a form

$$J(u) = \int_{t_0}^{\infty} (\mathbf{y}^T \mathbf{Q} \mathbf{y} + \mathbf{v}^T \mathbf{R} \mathbf{v}) dt = \int_{t_0}^{\infty} (y_1^2 + \lambda_1 y_2^2 + \lambda_2 v^2) dt \to \min$$

$$(79)$$

where, accordingly matrices Q = $diag(1, \lambda_1)$ and R = λ_2 (λ_1, λ_2 - are some constant parameters).

The problem of gain selection in the case of the backstepping method is a little more complicated because the gains k_p and k_D might not be constant (see the control structure (76) or (37)) but instead may have the form of functions $k_p(y)$ and $k_D(y)$. The values of these functions at the equilibrium point $y = 0$ are in fact the constant gains k_p and k_D found earlier via the LQR procedure, so $k_p = k_p(0)$ = $1 + k_1 k_2$ and $k_D = k_D(0) = k_1 + k_2$ are correct also in the case of the backstepping method.

To explain a practical meaning of the criterion (79) observe that the integrand is a weighting sum of squares of cross track error and its derivative plus a square of control effort. The course error is not involved in the criterion since, as it has been said before, the set of ship actuators considered here enables only tracking in the presence of nonzero course error. Obviously, for the course-keeping task, the criterion integrand would contain respectively the squares of course ψ, course derivative $\dot{\psi}$ (angular velocity) and rudder deflection δ. The criterion penalizes thereby the course error plus angular velocity versus rudder deflection whose trade-off can be designed via proper selection of parameters λ_1, λ_2. One may e.g. prefer the course-keeping (tracking) accuracy to the steering engine effort or vice versa.

The basic difference, as we compare the feedback linearization and backstepping method, lies in the fact that for the former, both the controller gains and the *tuning function* are linear combinations of the state vector components while for backstepping the coefficients of this combination are nonlinear functions of the state. Moreover the structure of these functions can be 'tuned' by the designer through their proper selection (in our case it can be done via suitable choice of the function φ). This fact makes the backstepping method much more flexible in respect of proper design of controlled system characteristics.

SHIP MODEL AND SIMULATIONS

Ship Simulation Model

As a simulation model that represents further the real ship dynamics we adopt here the following de Wit-Oppe's (W-O) ship dynamical model (Wit & Oppe, 1979-80).

$$\dot{x} = u \cos \psi - v \sin \psi$$
$$\dot{y} = u \sin \psi + v \cos \psi$$
$$\dot{\psi} = r$$
$$\dot{r} = -a\,r - br^3 + c\psi \qquad (80)$$
$$\dot{u} = -f\,u - Wr^2 + S$$
$$v = -r_1\,r - r_3 r^3$$

where:

(x, y) - Cartesian coordinates
ψ - course (heading)
r - angular velocity
u - longitudinal velocity
v - transversal velocity
δ - rudder deflection as a control variable
S - propelling force

The ship dynamics which is relevant in respect of our ship control problems (assumed constant ship velocity) is described via 4th equation of the system (80). One can see therefore that the structure of function Φ adopted here (see (7), (8)) takes the form $\Phi(\dot{\psi}) = -b\dot{\psi}^3 - a\dot{\psi}$. Note that this ship characteristic is obviously unknown to the control system designer and has to be adaptively reconstructed (see Fig.5).

As the ship model parameters the dynamic maneuvering parameters of the m.s. Compass Island model are adopted. The units of time, length and angle are respectively one minute, one nautical mile and one radian. The parameters were determined as follows $a = 1.084$ /min, $b=0.62$min, $c = 3.553$ rad/min, $r_1 = -0.0375$ nm/rad, $r_2=0, f= 0.86$ /min, $W = 0.067$ nm/rad^2, $S=0.215$ nm/min^2. The

Figure 6. Rudder deflections vs. time

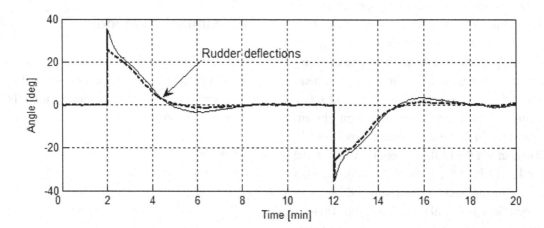

maximum speed of the rudder and rudder angle are 3.8 deg/s, and 35 deg, respectively. The ship has the following characteristics, gross register tonnage 9214 t, deadweight, 13498 t, length, 172 m, draught, 9.14 m, one propeller, and maximum speed, 20 knots. Notice that the adopted parameters make the ship directionally stable (Lisowski, 1981) and that other ship dynamic model (parameters) could be used here as well.

Simulation Results

The Simulink simulations are based on the non-linear W-O model of the ship dynamics (80) with the controllers (11), (37) or (49), including the parameter update laws (19) or (30) respectively. The adaptation mechanism is realized via tuning function ε (19) (or its counterpart (38)) and the so-called *model basis functions* (9) (or (48) in the path-following case) (Zwierzewicz, 2008). The pairs of plots depicted for the course-keeping task refer to the feedback linearization method versus backstepping, both under the assumption of un-known model functions. In the case of path-fol-lowing we use the controller obtained only via the feedback linearization method however the pairs of plots comprise those with unknown model functions versus those with fully known dynamics (exact model functions).

Each of the graphs in Figure 4, Figure 6 and Figure 7, illustrates two plots referring to feedback linearization control law (broken line) and the backstepping method (solid line) respectively. Figure 4, describes ship trajectories with two sharp turns (90° right and 90° left), and each of them is responsible for the generation of relevant half-characteristic of the ship's model (function Φ of (7); see also Figure 5). In Figure 6 and Figure 7 the rudder deflections and ship-course errors, all versus time, are depicted. In Figure 5 the exact model characteristic $\Phi(\dot{\psi}) = -b\dot{\psi}^3 - a\dot{\psi}$ versus its adaptive reconstruction is illustrated.

The graphs in Figures 8-11 refer to the path-following problem. In Figure 8 the path to be followed (preset) is a broken line defined by the *way points* (0,0); (0,10); (4,12) and (4, 20). The original ship position, its heading and angular velocity are (0,-0.5), 60° and 0 rad/min respec-tively. The adopted distance scale is 1 nm while the nominal ship velocity is 0.25 nm/min. In the simulation a transversal current has been intro-duced, as a load disturbance, (d_y=0.04 nm/min). To evaluate the accuracy of adaptive process control there is also depicted here a trajectory (broken line) driven by controller with fully known

Figure 7. Ship-course errors vs. time

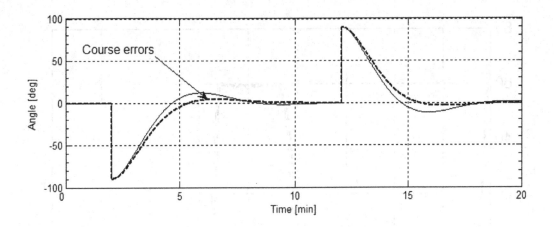

Figure 8. Ship trajectories, constant current

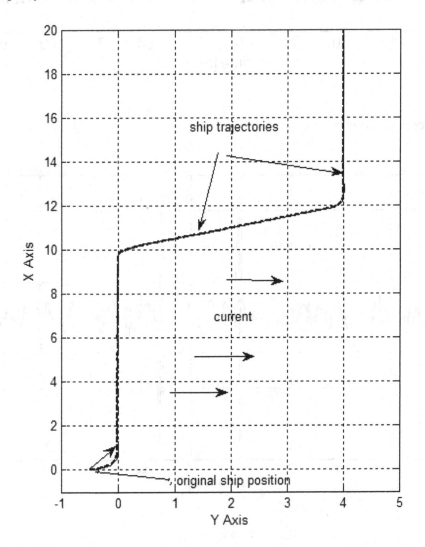

Figure 9. Ship headings vs. time

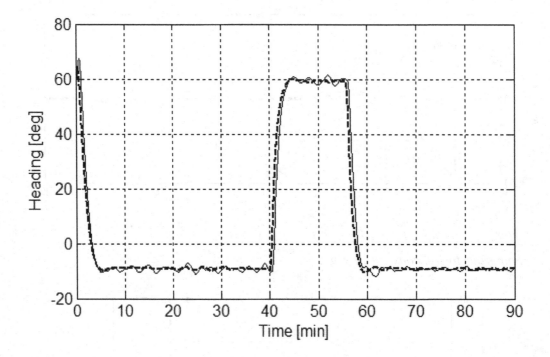

Figure 10. Rudder deflections vs. time

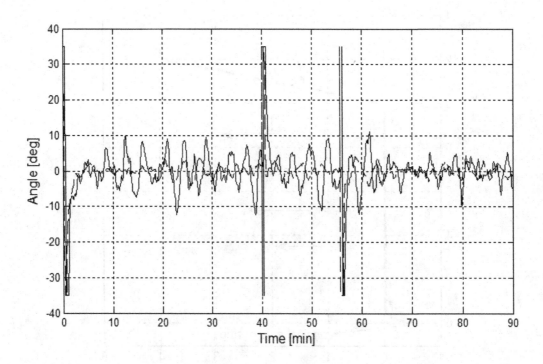

Figure 11. Cross-track errors vs. time

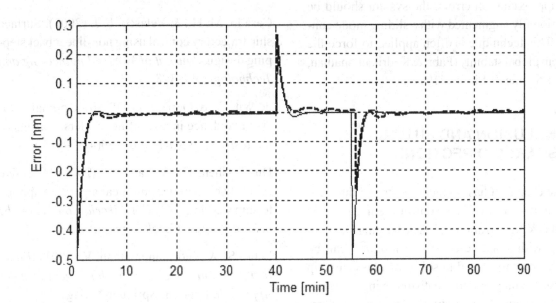

dynamics (exact model function). As we can see the differences are practically negligible.

Figure 9. describes plots of ship heading versus time. The broken line refers to the case of the fully known ship dynamic model. As one can observe, the ship heading during straight line path segments, is about -10 deg, which in fact indicates a course-error. Such a behaviour is, on the other hand, necessary to compensate an effect of disturbing currents action.

In Figure 10. it can be seen, that in the case of limited knowledge of the ship model, the rudder action is substantially more intensive (solid line), as compared to the case of full model familiarity.

Figure 11 depicts the plots of cross-track errors versus time. As before the solid line plot refers to the limited knowledge of the ship dynamics. It shows once more that the differences are relatively small.

An interesting feature of the adaptation process is that the steering process is performed without asymptotic convergence of parameters errors $\tilde{\theta} = \begin{bmatrix} \tilde{\theta}^{1T} & \tilde{\theta}^{2T} \end{bmatrix}$ to zero (we have proved, at the

most, their boundedness). This fact reflects an idea that the main goal of the adaptive system is to drive the error $e := y - y_d$ to zero, which does not necessarily imply that the model parameters approach their correct values. As have been shown above the model unknown characteristics may be (approximately) generated by the system even though the parameter errors $\tilde{\theta}$ do not converge to zero. Here the parameters play a role of slack variables rather (Zwierzewicz, 2009) on which potential errors (that otherwise would affect the state variables) cumulate.

Since a reference input comprises stepwise signals (path) changes, to fulfill the assumptions of its differentiability it has been initially prefiltered. Similarly the wave disturbances were modelled in the form of a white noise driven shaping filter (Fossen, 1994; Zwierzewicz, 2003). In the simulations carried out, the system performance turned out to be especially sensitive to the initial guess of parameter θ_1^2 that had to be chosen in some vicinity of its true value (true value 0.133; chosen value 0.5). In this respect, to ensure robustness to the disturbances that arise due, e.g., to the initial guess of parameters and thus inherent approximation errors, the system should be additionally augmented with a sliding mode control. This technique is often applied to force the system global stability (Fabri & Kadrikamanathan, 2001; Sanner & Slotine, 1992).

CONCLUSION AND FUTURE RESEARCH DIRECTIONS

In the chapter it has been demonstrated that new paradigms of nonlinear control theory, such as feedback linearization and backstepping methods along with adaptive control techniques, can be easily accommodated to solve the classical ship course-keeping as well as path following problems in a more general framework. The presented approach to control system design does not require a difficult task of ship model identification. Moreover, as it turned out, the algorithms obtained have a slightly modified form of the widely known PD control (so-called nonlinear version of PD control) and the resultant controllers thereby enable on-line learning of the unknown model characteristics.

The future, straightforward development of this research should be concerned with the extension of considered systems with the nonlinear state observer (observer backstepping design). The profound analysis should be carried out also with regard to the efficacy of the proposed methods in the case of directionally unstable ships. In this case the considered control problem is getting more complicated. This is, among other things, because of the fact that the denominator of formula (49) might be passing-through zero leading thereby to an ill-conditioned control algorithm. A more challenging problem is that of a generalization of the presented ideas to the multi-input-multi-output (MIMO) systems.

REFERENCES

Casado, M. H., & Velasco, F. J. (2003). Surface ship trajectory control using non-linear backstepping design. *Journal of Marine Engineering and Technology, A3*, 3–8.

de Wit, C., & Oppe, J. (1979-80). Optimal collision avoidance in unconfined waters. *Journal of the Institute of Navigation, 26*(4), 296–303.

Du, J. Chen, G., & Yang, C. (2005). Adaptive robust backstepping nonlinear algorithm applied to ship steering. *16th IFAC World Congress to be held in Prague, Czech Republic.*

Fabri, S., & Kadrikamanathan, V. (2001). *Functional Adaptive Control. An Intelligent Systems Approach.* London: Springer-Verlag.

Fossen, T. I. (1994). *Guidance and control of ocean vehicles.* New York: John Wiley.

Fossen, T. I. (2000). A survey on nonlinear ship control from theory to practice. In: *Proceedings of the 5th IFAC Conference on Manoeuvring and Control of Marine Craft.* (pp. 1-16). Aalborg, Denmark.

Isidori, A. (1989). *Nonlinear control systems. An introduction.* Berlin, Germany: Springer–Verlag.

Khalil, H. K. (2002). *Nonlinear Systems.* Upper Saddle River, NJ: Prentice Hall.

Krstic, M., Kanellakopoulos, I., & Kokotovic, P. (1995). *Nonlinear and adaptive control design.* New York: Wiley-Interscience.

Lisowski, J. (1981). *Ship as an object of automatic control.* Gdańsk, Poland: Wydawnictwo Morskie.

Ramirez, W. (1994). *Process control and identification.* New York: Academic Press.

Sanner, R., & Slotine, J. E. (1992). Gaussian networks for direct adaptive control. *IEEE Transactions on Neural Networks, 3*(6), 837–863. doi:10.1109/72.165588

Slotine, J. E., & Li, W. (1991). *Applied Nonlinear control*. Englewood Cliffs, NJ: Prentice Hall.

Spooner, J. T., & Passino, K. M. (1996). Stable adaptive control using fuzzy systems and neural networks. *IEEE Transactions on Fuzzy Systems*, *4*(3), 339–359. doi:10.1109/91.531775

Sutton, R., Taylor, S., & Roberts, G. (1996). Neuro-Fuzzy Techniques Applied to a Ship Autopilot Design. *Journal of Navigation*, *49*(03), 410–430. doi:10.1017/S037346330001362X

Tzeng, C. Y., Goodwin, G. C., & Crisafulli, S. (1999). Feedback linearization design of a ship steering autopilot with saturating and slew rate limiting actuator. *International Journal of Adaptive Control and Signal Processing*, *13*, 23–30. doi:10.1002/(SICI)1099-1115(199902)13:1<23::AID-ACS532>3.0.CO;2-E

Tzirkel-Hancock, E., & Fallside, F. (1992). Stable control of nonlinear systems using neural networks. *International Journal of Robust and Nonlinear Control*, *2*, 63–86. doi:10.1002/rnc.4590020105

Zwierzewicz, Z. (2003). On the ship guidance automatic system design via lqg-integral control. In: J. Battle & M. Blanke (Ed.), *6th IFAC Conference on Manoeuvring and Control of Marine Crafts* (pp. 349-353). University of Girona, Spain.

Zwierzewicz, Z. (2007). Nonlinear Adaptive Control Synthesis Using Model Basis Functions. *Int. Journal of Factory Automation. Robotics and Soft Computing*, *1*(2), 102–107.

Zwierzewicz, Z. (2008). Nonlinear adaptive tracking-control synthesis for general linearly parametrized systems. In Arreguin, J. M. R. (Ed.), *Automation and Robotics* (pp. 375–388). Vienna, Austria: I-Tech Education and Publishing.

Zwierzewicz, Z. (2009). Generalization of controller integral action in tracking and disturbances rejection problems. *Polish Journal of Environmental Studies*, *18*(2A), 223–228.

KEY TERMS AND DEFINITIONS

Lyapunov Stability Definition: Consider an autonomous nonlinear dynamical system $\dot{\mathbf{x}} = \mathbf{f}(\mathbf{x}(t))$, $\mathbf{x}(0) = \mathbf{x}_0$, (A1) where $\mathbf{x}(t) \in D \subseteq \mathbb{R}^n$ denotes the system state vector, D an open set containing the origin, and $\mathbf{f} : D \to \mathbb{R}^n$ locally Lipschitz on D. Without loss of generality, we may assume that the origin is an equilibrium. The origin of the above system is said to be: 1. Lyapunov stable if, for every $\varepsilon > 0$, there exists a $\delta = \delta(\varepsilon) > 0$ such that, if $\|\mathbf{x}(0)\| < \delta$, then $\|\mathbf{x}(t)\| < \varepsilon$, for every $t \geq 0$. 2. asymptotically stable if it is Lyapunov stable and if there exists $\delta > 0$ such that if $\|\mathbf{x}(0)\| < \delta$, then $\lim_{t \to \infty} \mathbf{x}(t) = 0$. 3. globally asymptotically stable if asymptotically stable for all $\mathbf{x}(0) \in \mathbb{R}^n$..

Theorem (Lyapunov stability of autonomous systems; Khalil (2002)): Let $x = 0$ be an equilibrium point for a system (A1) and $V : D \to \mathbb{R}$ be a continuously differentiable, positive definite function in D. 1. If $\dot{V}(\mathbf{x}) = \dfrac{\partial V}{\partial \mathbf{x}} \mathbf{f}(\mathbf{x})$ is negative semidefinite, then $x = 0$ is a stable equilibrium point. 2. If $\dot{V}(\mathbf{x})$ is negative definite, then $x = 0$ is an asymptotically stable equilibrium point. In both cases above V is called a **Lyapunov function**. Moreover, if the conditions hold for all $\mathbf{x} \in \mathbb{R}^n$ and $\|\mathbf{x}\| \to \infty$ implies that $V(x) \to \infty$, then $x = 0$ is globally stable in case 1 and globally asymptotically stable in case 2.

Stability Matrix: A square matrix A is called a Hurwitz matrix if every eigenvalue of A has strictly negative real part, A is also called a **stabil-**

ity matrix, because then the linear system $\dot{\mathbf{x}} = \mathbf{Ax}$ is stable.

PID Control: Proportional Integral Derivative control. The most common control algorithm in process control based on the process error (proportional), the integral of the error (integral) and the rate of change of the error (derivative) action.

LQR (Linear Quadratic Regulator) for a Continuous-Time: linear system described by $\dot{\mathbf{x}} = \mathbf{Ax} + \mathbf{Bu}$, with infinite-horizon cost func-

tional defined as $J = \int\limits_{0}^{\infty} \left(\mathbf{x}^T\mathbf{Qx} + \mathbf{u}^T\mathbf{Ru} \right) dt$ is the feedback control law that minimizes the value of the cost. One may prove that this control law has the form of the proportional feedback: $u = -Kx$. The gain matrix K is given by $K = R^{-1}B^TP$ where P is found by solving the continuous time algebraic Riccati equation $A^T P + PA - PBR^{-1}B^T P + Q = 0$.

Chapter 19
A Knowledge–Based Approach for Microwire Casting Plant Control

Sergiu Zaporojan
Technical University of Moldova, Republic of Moldova

Constantin Plotnic
Technical University of Moldova, Republic of Moldova

Igor Calmicov
Technical University of Moldova, Republic of Moldova

Vladimir Larin
Microfir Tehnologii Industriale Ltd, Republic of Moldova

ABSTRACT

This chapter presents the main ideas and preliminary results of an applied research project concerning the development of an intelligent plant for microwire casting. The properties of glass-coated microwires are useful for a variety of sensor applications. On the other hand, the process of casting can be one of the methods of nanotechnology and advanced materials. In microwire continuous casting, the main control problem is to maintain the optimum thermal and flow conditions of the process, in order to fabricate the microwire of a given stable diameter. Unlike a conventional casting plant, we propose to use a video camera to take the picture of the molten drop and to control the casting process by means of a knowledge based system. For this reason, a model, that is capable of taking into account the current features of the process and of describing the shape of the drop at each time, is developed. The model presented here should allow us to estimate the geometry of the metal-filled capillary and predict the diameter of microwire at each time during the casting process.

INTRODUCTION

The chapter provides the first results of an on-going applied research which deals with the

development of a knowledge based plant for the fabrication of glass-coated microwires. Glass-coated microwires are manufactured by means of the Taylor-Ulitovsky technique (Larin et al., 2002). Such microwires show magnetic proper-

DOI: 10.4018/978-1-61692-811-7.ch019

ties of great technological interest, like magnetic bistability, giant magnetoimpedance effect, soft magnetic and memory shape properties. The above properties are quite useful for a variety of sensor applications. The investigation into technology and physical properties of glass-coated microwires is presently attracting much attention because of their use in sensor devices (Cobeno et al., 2001) and fiber-based products. For example, the new generation of multi-functional ternary composite materials will be made of microwires, the bio-based polymers and paper.

Glass-coated microwires consist of an inner metallic nucleus covered by a Pyrex-like coating. The typical limits for the metallic core diameter are between 1 and 50 microns. In microwire continuous casting, the main control problem is to maintain the optimum thermal and flow conditions of the process, in order to fabricate the microwire of a given stable diameter. To control the process, the human operator uses indications of a microwire resistance meter. The typical accuracy of the resistance meter is of the order of 5% to 10% within quite narrow limits. On the one hand, it is too difficult to improve and expand the capabilities of the meter. Because of this, the operator cannot use the information from that meter in a wide range of diameters. In other words, an acceptable control of the casting process based on the measured resistance is only possible within some limits. On the other hand, a highly qualified and experienced human operator is capable of maintaining the casting process under control only by using the information captured by his eyes. That information is with respect to color, position, and shape of the molten drop during the casting. However, the quality of such a control is poor (and hence, the quality of microwire).

According to reasons stated above, in this chapter, an approach for microwire casting plant control is suggested. In order to construct a knowledge-based system for the casting plant control, we consider the concepts of machine vision and fuzzy logic control. Our goal is to develop and exploit human operator knowledge. At a first stage, the proposed approach must help (assist) the operator to cast high quality microwire of different diameters. At the same time, the operator's experience and knowledge will be accumulated on the system during continuous casting. At the second stage, we intend to provide an experimental plant capable to cast almost automatically high quality microwires in a wide range of diameters.

BACKGROUND

The aim of modeling is capturing the essence of phenomena behavior. When complete knowledge of a process eludes us, we build models in order to obtain some measure of control over that process. A model is never entirely correct but it is useful if it explains and predicts the behavior of the process within the limits of precision required for the task. It is essential that the users of the model understand well the conditions over which the model has been developed and consequently the regimes of its validity. If the phenomenon to be modeled is understood well enough to construct a model and if its mathematical formulation is suitable to be analytically or numerically solved, then the resulting model is a powerful tool as it enables us to explain and predict system behavior within the bounds of the validity of model.

The process of microwire casting is qualified with a highly elevated level of complexity. It represents a joining of interactions, such as mechanical, thermal, electrodynamical, physical, and chemical. More than that, those interactions are not just multiple but are overlapped during the time of casting. It can be supposed that a model of casting might be derived from the underlying properties of the process. However, even under various approximations, the final model will be too difficult, of high order, nonlinear and so on.

Having a high degree of complexity, the creation of a mathematical complete and proper model for the automation and optimization of the process of microwire casting represents a highly difficult problem (Berman, 1972). We believe that pure physical and mathematical evaluation of the discussed process doesn't represent a practical solution.

It is well-known that in many cases the control of a process by a human operator is more successful than any automatic control (Kickert & Van Nauta Lemke, 1976). On the other hand, a lot of human experience in the area of microwire casting has been accumulated, which can be explored in order to automate, at least partially, and optimize the control of respective process. The process put into discussion cannot be treated through the prism of some precise categories of conventional theories. The human operator doesn't supervise the casting process on the basis of sophisticated rules. The operator is largely helped by his own experience. Namely the experience and the specific accumulated knowledge enable to maintain and predict the parameters of the process checked up in the admissible limits even in conditions of uncertainty.

As the strategy, human operator uses, is vague and qualitatively described, the use of fuzzy logic control in the casting plant should be a good choice, in our opinion. Fuzzy control is a practical alternative for a variety of challenging control applications since it provides a convenient method for constructing nonlinear controllers via the use of heuristic information. Such heuristic information may come from an operator who is acting as a "human-in-the-loop" controller for a process. Since fuzzy logic is dealing with linguistic information, it can be used as a basis for knowledge-based systems. In the fuzzy control design methodology, we ask human operator to write down a set of rules on how to control the process, and then we incorporate these into a fuzzy logic-based system that emulates the decision-making process of the human (Driankov et al., 1993; Patyra et al., 1996; Passino & Yurkovich, 1998). On the other hand, a knowledge base is not a rule base (Siler & Buckley, 2005).

The fuzzy logic control represents a technology that works in conditions of uncertainty and noise. The development of systems based on the fuzzy logic started together with the appearance on the market of the sufficient performed processors and circuits. Currently, applications of this kind exist in different areas (Krause et al., 2007), especially in industrial ones (Terano, 1993; von Altrock, 2007). The explanation is very simple: fuzzy logic offers efficient and elegant solutions for diverse systems of supervision (multivariable control).

On the other hand, machine vision is successfully used today in industrial applications. This approach has become a vital component in the design of advanced systems because it provides means of maintaining control of quality during manufacture (Davies, 2004).

With above technologies, the decision-making with the aim to control the process of microwire casting shall be done on the basis of processing the captured information from different sensors, and on the basis of the accumulated human operator experience. The latter involves the knowledge acquisition phase, i.e. the acquisition of knowledge and skills of human operator.

THE CONTROL OF MICROWIRE CASTING

The Process of Microwire Casting

Currently, there are two main techniques of microwire fabrication. In the first one, microwires are made by the in-water spinning method, and then cold drawn from a diameter of about 125 microns of the as-cast microwire to diameters of 20-30 microns. The final sample undergoes annealing with a tension stress to build up a certain magnetic structure. This method requires very careful control of the annealing process to obtain repeatable magnetic parameters.

On the other hand, the Taylor-Ulitovsky technique has been employed for the fabrication of glass-coated microwires. Such microwires are manufactured by means of a modified Taylor-Ulitovsky process based on direct casting from the melt. Let us describe the process of casting. A rod of the alloy of desired composition is put into a Pyrex-like glass tube and placed within a high frequency inductor heater. The alloy is heated up to its melting point, forming a droplet. While the metal melts, the portion of the glass tube adjacent to the melting metal softens, enveloping the metal droplet. A glass capillary is then drawn from the softened glass portion and wound on a rotating bobbin. At suitable drawing conditions, the molten metal fills the glass capillary and a microwire is thus formed where the metal core is completely coated by a glass shell. The amount of glass used in the process is balanced by the continuous feeding of the glass tube through the inductor zone, whereas the formation of the metallic core is restricted by the initial quantity of the alloy droplet. The process of casting is carried out at a temperature that will melt the alloy and soften the glass tube. The final microwire structure is formed by water-cooling to obtain a metallic core in amorphous or non crystalline state.

The microstructure of a microwire (and hence, its properties) depends mainly on the cooling rate, which can be controlled by a cooling mechanism when the metal-filled capillary enters into a stream of cooling water. After passing through the cooling water of the crystallizer, the microwire comes to spool on the receiving mechanism.

The geometrical characteristics of the microwire depend on the physical properties of both the glass and alloy composition, the diameter of the initial glass tube, and the parameters of the heating inductor. The diameter of a microwire produced by Taylor-Ulitovsky method has both upper and lower limits depending on the speed of casting. Typical limits for the metallic core diameter are between 1 and 50 microns, while the thickness of the coating is in the range of 2 and 15 microns. It should be noted, that even during the stationary casting process, there is some variation in diameter

of the metallic nucleus and in the glass coating thickness along the wire length. Depending on the required diameter, the precision can vary from 5% for wires in the range between 5 and 10 microns, to 10% for wires in the range between 10 and 30 microns. On the other hand, it may be adequate to have a system that is capable of casting to a precision of rather better than 5% within quite wide limits. Currently used plants are not capable to meet the latter requirements.

Having reviewed the process of casting, let us examine more carefully the industrial plant of casting. An industrial plant is a complex technical system. Contemporary industrial systems can contain hundreds of components. How can we clearly describe them? The key is to recognize the hierarchic nature of most complex systems, including the industrial plants. The hierarchic nature of complex systems is essential to both their design and their description. The designer needs only to deal with a particular level of the system at a time. At each level, the system consists of a set of inter-related components. The behavior at each level depends only on a simplified characterization of the system at the next lower level. At each level, the designer is concerned with structure and function. Structure is the way in which the components are interrelated. Function is the operation of both the system and each individual component as part of the structure. It should be mentioned that the control function and its implementation is crucial in a system. At a time, a collision arises between old plant structure and new function requirements. Obviously, the performance of a new plant should be higher than that of the old one.

An industrial plant for the fabrication of glass-coated microwires consists of some special blocks and mechanisms. At the level of mechanisms we can distinguish three of them. Two are intended for moving down the rod alloy and the glass tube. Another mechanism is the receiving one. At this level, conventional control algorithms, such as PID controls can be used.

Figure 1. Control of the microwire casting process

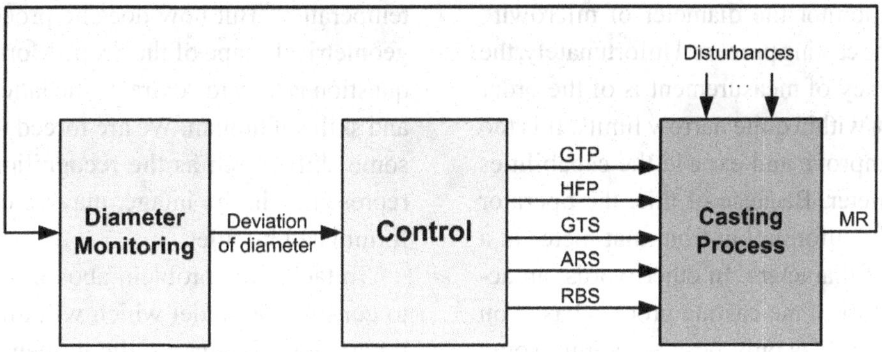

Next, the alloy of desired composition is put into the glass tube and placed within the inductive heater. To heat the alloy up to its melting point, a high frequency (HF) generator must be there. To maintain the molten drop at an optimum position over the inductive heater, it is necessary to control the pressure inside the glass tube. For this purpose the air must be pumped out from the tube.

Another level of the plant is dealing with measurement and sensor devices. The most important sensor is the meter of microwire resistance. Finally, at the top level of the plant a control block must be present.

Figure 1 shows the control of the microwire casting process. The main variables of the casting process can be listed as follows:

- the pressure inside the glass tube (GTP),
- the power of HF generator (HFP),
- glass tube speed (GTS),
- alloy rod speed (ARS),
- the speed of casting (RBS),
- the diameter of microwire,
- temperature of the molten drop.

In general, during casting, the control environment must maintain the following conditions:

- Maintenance of optimum thermal conditions in the drop.

- Maintenance of optimum flow conditions in the metal-filled capillary.
- Maintenance of optimum crystallization conditions.
- Control of the rate of casting to keep it at a constant level.

The main control problem is to maintain the optimum thermal and flow conditions of the process, in order to cast the microwire of a desired stable diameter. In other words, the main problem is to maintain the stability of geometrical characteristics of the microwire during continuous casting. As it can be seen from the Figure 1, five control variables are used: GTP and HFP, as well as GTS, ARS, and RBS. The pressure inside the glass tube and the power of HF generator must be carefully manipulated over the time. In order to monitor the diameter of microwire and control the process of casting, the operator uses a specialized meter of the microwire resistance (MR).

On the other hand, some important factors, such as microwire vibrations and defects of the quality of glass and alloy compositions may significantly disturb the casting process.

To attain the control objectives in such environment, the plant operator should be highly qualified. Moreover, in a microwire casting plant it is not possible to dispense with manual intervention because of extremely high complexity of the process.

As noted above, the meter of MR allows the operator to monitor the diameter of microwire and control the casting process. Unfortunately, the typical accuracy of measurement is of the order of 5% to 10% within quite narrow limits. It is too difficult to improve and expand the capabilities of the MR meter. Because of this, the operator cannot use the information from that meter in a large range of diameters. In other words, an acceptable control of the casting process based on the measured MR is only possible within some limits (approximately, in the range between 4 and 30 microns).

However, a highly qualified and experienced human operator is capable of maintaining the casting process under control only by using the information captured by his eyes. That information is with respect to color, position, and shape of the molten drop during the casting. It is clear, of course, that the quality of the control is poor (and hence, the quality of microwire). Therefore, in addition to a conventional casting plant, we propose to use a video camera to take the picture of the molten drop over the time of casting. Moreover, we aim to control the process by means of a fuzzy knowledge-based system.

Fuzzy logic is a technology to design solutions for complex non-linear control. As it was mentioned in the previous section, it uses human experience and experimental results rather than a mathematical model for the definition of a control strategy. On the other hand, the acquisition of knowledge and skills of human operator is required. Obviously, the operator must be highly qualified and experienced. However, this is not enough for the above purpose. It is necessary to say that the human operator can maintain the casting process under control using the information captured by his eyes. So, we may use this fact to construct a possible control strategy. To do this, we should understand how the operator proceeds with the captured image. It is clear that the operator first estimates the color and then predicts the current temperature of molten drop.

It is not a big problem to measure and control the temperature. But how does he proceed with the geometrical shape of the drop? More exactly, the question is how to "extract" the latter knowledge and skills of human. We are forced to accept that some skills, such as the recognition of what is represented in the image, may be only partially formulated by rules.

To tackle the problem above, we have to try to construct a model which will allow us to estimate the geometry of the molten drop at each time during the casting process. This goal represents a very important task in order to construct a knowledge-based control system. To solve the latter, it is necessary to start with building of a data acquisition system in order to acquire and analyze the experimental information from the casting plant.

Acquisition and Analysis of Experimental Data

According to reasons stated in the previous subsection, we have to proceed with knowledge engineering by measuring and analyzing the system behavior, because some expert skills and experience can be only partially used for the formulation of the fuzzy rules. Measurements of the values of the process and image acquisition are necessary, in order to consider system behavior.

Figure 2 presents the general scheme of data acquisition system. Essentially, it consists of a data acquisition unit based on a microcontroller unit (MCU), and a computer (PC). There are four input isolated channels and two output ones. The former ones serve to acquire a set of parameters, such as GTP, HFP, MR and RBS. All needed sensors are installed on the side of the casting plant. The outputs represent the feedback control of the pressure inside the glass tube and the power of HF generator. Obviously, all input values are measured online during casting.

The computer is designated to capture and process the image of the drop over the time of

Figure 2. The scheme of data acquisition

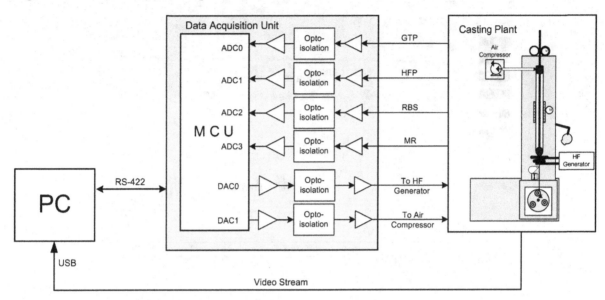

casting. The image should be processed in real-time to track the geometrical and color features of the drop.

In order to proceed with measuring of the casting parameters and acquiring of the image, an application for online capturing and processing of the above information was developed. As a result of the image processing, the molten drop features are obtained: geometrical characteristics and position of the drop during casting, the color histogram, YUV/RGB components, the color map of the drop and its color.

Figure 3 shows the application window. The image of the drop can be also visualized in that window.

After analyzing the acquired information it was established that:

- The diameter of microwire depends on the temperature and the shape of the drop. It also strongly depends on the RBS. It is important to mention, that even during the stationary casting process, there is some variation in temperature and shape of the drop. The temperature and working shape

of the drop may significantly vary over time.

- The temperature of molten drop depends on some factors, such as GTP, HFP, and the magnetic field of inductive heater.

- The shape of the drop is strongly dependent on the GTP. Especially, it should be noted that the geometry of the metal-filled capillary depends on the viscosity of the glass. Therefore, the type of glass tube influences the diameter of microwire to be obtained. Also, the shape depends on other factors, such as GTS, RBS, the temperature of molten drop and the magnetic field.

- Finally, depending on the geometry of inductive heater the working shape of the drop may vary from one plant to another.

In fact, the above conclusions confirmed the known general dependences. However, the analysis of acquired statistics showed us that the image acquisition of the drop and its analysis have a decisive importance in order to construct an intelligent high performance casting plant. Perhaps our

Figure 3. Course of casting parameters over time. A resistive alloy is used.

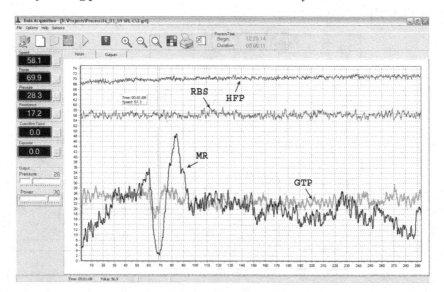

main conclusion was to concentrate our attention on the geometry of the metal-filled capillary.

Mathematical Model of the Molten Drop

First of all our purpose is to construct a model of the molten drop. The model to be developed must be useful to explain and predict behavior within the process of casting. It will be shown here that the interpolation polynomial in the Lagrange form can serve to the proposed purpose.

More precisely, we have to find a function that describes the shape of the drop. Figure 5 shows the image of the molten drop at a time when the casting process is running under working conditions. It can be observed (Figure 5) that the drop is quite symmetrical under normal working conditions. Moreover, it was established from the analysis of the above experimental data, that the upper part of the drop can be ignored. Hence, it is enough to consider the right (or left) shape of the drop due to its symmetry.

Consider the line $y = \sqrt[3]{x^2} e^x$ on the interval [0; 0.5]. It is easy to check and observe that the above line follows somewhat the shape of the drop. The

same (even better) result can be achieved using the parametrical equations of a cycloid and varying the radius. Unfortunately, this approach cannot be accepted because such a model will be static.

During casting the shape of the drop is changing. Moreover, because of both the geometry of inductive heater and some other factors the working form of the drop may vary from one plant to another. Therefore, a hydrodynamic model of the drop was developed (Chiugaevskiy, 1964). That model was an advanced one for the time but absolutely unusable for practical application.

So, we are looking for a model that will take into account current features of the process and describe the working shape at each time. On the other hand, such a model should allow us to estimate the geometry of the metal-filled capillary and predict the diameter of microwire. In order to meet these requirements, we decided to extract a given set of data points from the shape at a time. Then, the current shape must be interpolated. In this way we can obtain the function that approximates the shape at each time. Moreover, that function may offer us the information about the geometry of capillary.

For this purpose, as mentioned above, let us consider the interpolation polynomial in the Lagrange form.

Given a fixed interval $I \in R$ and a set of $(p+1)$ interpolation points $x_0 < x_1 < x_2 < ... < x_p$ on I, a function can be defined $f: I \rightarrow R$. To interpolate the function f, we define the values y_i as $y_i = f(x_i)$, for $0 \le i \le p$.

The points y_i are the values of interpolation. We must use the unique interpolation polynomial of degree $P \le p$, which verifies $P(x_i) = y_i$ for $0 \le i \le p$ and $f(x) \cong P(x)$ for any $x \in I$.

Let L_i, $0 \le i \le p$, be the Lagrange basis polynomials

$$L_j(x) = \frac{(x - x_0)...(x - x_{j-1})(x - x_{j+1})...(x - x_p)}{(x_j - x_0)...(x_j - x_{j-1})(x_j - x_{j+1})...(x_j - x_p)}. \tag{1}$$

Then, the interpolation polynomial in the Lagrange form $P(x)$, associated to the set of data points is

$$P(x) = \sum_{j=0}^{p} y_j L_j(x). \tag{2}$$

It should be noted that the Lagrange basis polynomials L_j given by formula (1) depend only on the interpolation points selected, and do not require any auxiliary restrictions (Berrut & Trefethen, 2004). This fact represents an advantage in using the interpolation polynomial in the Lagrange form (2) to approximate the shape of the molten drop.

In order to obtain the information about the optimum number of points to be used by the interpolation polynomial in the Lagrange form, a comparative experimental analysis was carried out. During this experimental study, we established that a good approximation of the working shape of the drop occurs when seven interpolation points are extracted from the shape.

Figure 4. Illustration of the geometry of capillary

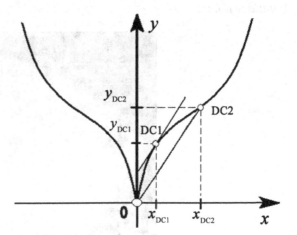

Given a set of seven ($p = 6$) data points (x_0, y_0), $(x_1, y_1),...,(x_6, y_6)$ where no two x_j are the same, the Lagrange basis polynomials can be written, according to formula (1). The resulting set of the Lagrange basis polynomials can be easily calculated by means of the recursive functions (Press, 1992). Let us compare the working shape of the drop with interpolated curve at a time of casting. The shape of the molten drop follows a curve line. The curve changes from being convex to concave (see Figure 5). The interpolated curve (on the right side of Figure 5) does the same and follows the shape of the drop. The analysis of a lot of experimental data confirms the latter. We can conclude that the approximation based on the interpolation polynomial in the Lagrange form is a satisfactory one for our purposes.

The question now is how to extract the information about the geometry of the metal-filled capillary. We decided to follow the next scheme. At first it is necessary to determine the inflection point DC2 on the interpolated curve (Figure 4).

Then, another point of the capillary should be determined. That point may be DC1 (the capillary point). The latter should be very important because it seems to be the entry point of capillary.

To calculate the coordinates (x_{DC2}, y_{DC2}) of the inflection point it is necessary to find the second

Figure 5. Comparison of the drop shape with interpolated curve. Localization of the inflection and capillary points.

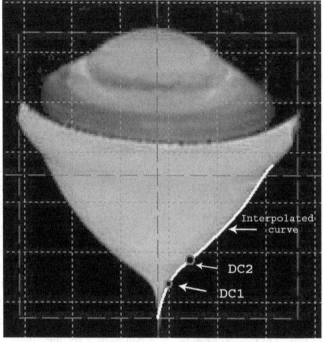

order derivative of the interpolation polynomial in the Lagrange form.

The first order derivative of the interpolation polynomial in the Lagrange form is

$$P'(x) = \sum_{j=0}^{p} \left[\frac{y_j}{\prod\limits_{\substack{i=0;i\neq j}}^{p}(x_j - x_i)} \sum_{\substack{i1=0 \\ i1\neq j}}^{p} \prod_{\substack{i=0 \\ i\neq j \\ i\neq i1}}^{p}(x - x_i) \right] \tag{3}$$

The second derivative is

$$P''(x) = \sum_{j=0}^{p} \left[\frac{y_j}{\prod\limits_{\substack{i=o;i\neq j}}^{p}(x_j - x_i)} \sum_{\substack{i1=0 \\ i1\neq j}}^{p} \sum_{\substack{i2=0 \\ i2\neq j \\ i2\neq i1}}^{p} \prod_{\substack{i=0 \\ i\neq j \\ i\neq i1 \\ i\neq i2}}^{p}(x - x_i) \right] \tag{4}$$

The second derivative (4) equals zero in the inflection point DC2. Hence, the coordinates (x_{DC2}, y_{DC2}) can be obtained at each time.

The point DC1 can be located by means of well-known Lagrange's formula:

$$f'(x_0) = \frac{f(b) - f(a)}{b - a}, \ x_0 \in (a,b). \tag{5}$$

To calculate the coordinates (x_{DC1}, y_{DC1}) of capillary point DC1, the interval [0, *DC2*] must be considered (see Figure 4). Finally, note that the model also considers the drop position (DP). This point has the coordinates (0, y_{DC1}), in the frame of developed model.

Accuracy of the Molten Drop Model

The above model should allow us to estimate the geometry of capillary at each time during casting. The validity of this model has been proved on a lot of experimental data. On the other hand, it is necessary to determine the accuracy of the developed model.

To obtain full online information about the geometry and position of the drop, its current image should be processed. The process of the geometry identification takes place in four stages:

1. Image acquisition.
2. Image segmentation and edge detection.
3. Shape approximation.
4. Calculation of the inflection and capillary points.

Obviously, we should expect that the accuracy of the geometry estimation is proportional to the resolution of the input image. Consider a molten drop image of 240×320 pixels, and a glass tube diameter of 12 mm. For that resolution the diameter equals 138 pixels. So, one pixel is equivalent to 87 microns. Note, that the image size is 230400 bytes. If the resolution is of 480×640 pixels, then the glass tube diameter equals 300 pixels. One pixel is equivalent to 40 microns, while the image size is 921600 bytes. A resolution of 600×800 pixels can be also used. In this case, the glass tube diameter equals 500 pixels. One pixel is equivalent to 24 microns, while the image size increases up to 1440000 bytes. It is obvious, that with a high resolution both the acquisition and processing time will increase. Besides this, the level of noise increases.

Segmentation involves separating the image into regions. A natural way to segment regions is through thresholding. We use thresholding to determine the region of the drop area by identifying four boundary points. Then, edge detection is performed. Edges characterize boundaries and are therefore a problem of fundamental importance in image processing. Edges are places in the image with strong intensity contrasts – a jump in intensity from one pixel to the next. There are many ways to perform edge detection. We tried different methods to detect the edge of the drop. Our experiments showed that the Canny algorithm (Canny, 1986) provides the best results. The implementation of the Canny algorithm allows us to detect the edge

of the drop with a good precision – the possible error of detection equals one pixel, while using other methods may introduce a detection error of up to three pixels.

Next stage is dealing with the approximation of the drop shape, according to the model. In order to reduce the approximation error of the model, the interpolation points are calculated as follows. At first, a lot of 25 points is extracted from the shape. Those points are integer numbers. Then, a set of five internal reference points is determined using the formula (6):

$$P_k^{ref} = P_{i-2} + 2P_{i-1} + 3P_i + 2P_{i+1} + P_{i+2},$$

$$i = 5(k\text{-}1) + 3, \qquad\qquad (6)$$

for $1 \leq k \leq 5$. It should be noted, that the coordinates of these five references are numbers in floating point format. The formula (6) was obtained experimentally. The above technique allows us to improve the precision of the coordinates of reference points – the error of calculation is about 0.25 pixels.

Given this set of five internal points (P_1^{ref}, ..., P_5^{ref}) as well as two points at the ends of the shape – P_0 and P_6, the Lagrange basis polynomials can be written and calculated. So, the stage of shape approximation is finished. After that, the coordinates of the inflection and capillary points are calculated. Figure 5 presents the calculated positions of the inflection and capillary points at a time of casting.

The Fuzzy Control System

The purpose of the proposed system is to control the process of casting in a wide range of microwire diameters. The system must process the information about the temperature of the molten drop:

- DT1 (temperature of the drop at the upper side),
- DT2 (temperature of the drop at the lower side), shape of the molten drop:
- DC1 (the capillary point) and DC2 (the inflection point), position of the drop:
- DP, and microwire resistance:
- MR.

The above linguistic variables are used as inputs. The five control variables represent the output linguistic variables. Depending on the linguistic variable, the number of terms is in the range of 3 to 5. The used linguistic terms are shown in Table 1. Taking into account the features of the casting process, we decided to use three membership functions as follows:

$$\mu_1(x, a, b, c) = \begin{cases} 0, & if \ x \le a; \\ \dfrac{x-a}{c-a}, & if \ a < x \le c; \\ \dfrac{b-x}{b-c}, & if \ c < x < b; \\ 0, & if \ x \ge b \end{cases} \quad (7)$$

$$\mu_2(x, a, b) = \exp\left[-\frac{(x-a)^2}{2b^2}\right] \quad (8)$$

$$\mu_3(x, a, b) = \{1 + \exp[-a(x-b)]\}^{-1} \quad (9)$$

As it can be seen from the equations (7-9), the commonly used shapes have been selected. The triangle shape of membership function for the critical linguistic variables GTP, and MR was chosen. The gaussian shape of membership function for the linguistic variables DT1, DT2, DC1, DC2, and DP was chosen. Finally, sigmoidal membership function is given by equation (9). This shape of membership function for all other linguistic terms was chosen.

Table 1. The set of linguistic terms

Linguistic value	Linguistic variable	Membership function
high rated low	GTP	(7)
very high high rated low very low	MR	(7)
high rated low	DT1, DT2	(8)
high rated low	DC1	(8)
over close below	DP	(8)
high rated low	HFP, GTS, ARS, RBS	(9)

The fuzzy logic-based control system is represented in Figure 6. Essentially, the proposed system consists of image processing block and fuzzy control block. The latter contains blocks of fuzzification, inference engine, and defuzzification, which are interconnected. Our intention is to construct a Mamdani fuzzy logic-based controller. The interfaces with the environment of the casting process are the fuzzification and defuzzification blocks, as well as the image processing block. Note, that the human operator is present in the loop.

The image of the molten drop must be processed in real-time to identify and track both the geometrical characteristics and the temperature of the drop. After the processing of captured image, the system obtains the information about the temperature, geometry of the metal-filled capillary, and position of the drop at each time during casting. On this basis, the fuzzy control block can take a decision with the aim to check up the process of microwire casting.

Obviously, the above information should be used by control strategies. In glass-coated microw-

Figure 6. The knowledge-based control system

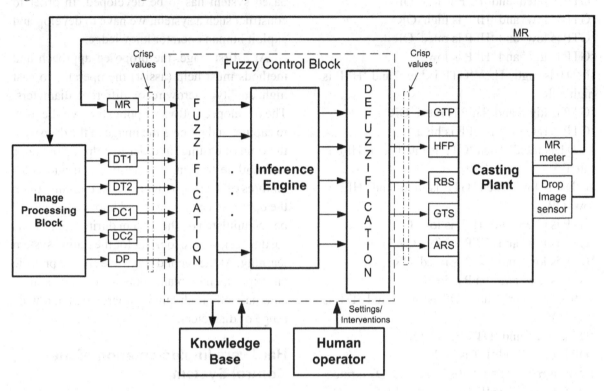

ire continuous casting two different strategies can be used to maintain a stable diameter of casting wire. The first strategy analyzes MR, while the second one considers the position and temperature (color) of the drop, as well as its form (geometry).

The basic fuzzy rules for the first strategy are defined in the following form:

If 'MR is very low' Then 'GTP is high' and 'HFP is high'
If 'MR is low' Then 'GTP is high' and 'HFP is rated' OR
'GTP is rated' and 'HFP is high'
If 'MR is rated' Then 'GTP is rated' and 'HFP is rated'
If 'MR is high' Then 'GTP is high' and 'HFP is low' OR
'GTP is rated' and 'HFP is low' OR
'GTP is low' and 'HFP is high' OR
'GTP is low' and 'HFP is rated'

If 'MR is very high' Then 'GTP is low' and 'HFP is low'

The first strategy can be used for wires in the range between 4 and 10 microns. The pressure inside the glass tube should be adjusted to maintain the MR near its rated value. If the MR meter draws a big deviation from the rated value, then both the pressure inside the glass tube and the power of HF generator should be adjusted.

The basic fuzzy rules for the second strategy are defined as follows:

If 'DP is below' Then 'GTP is high' and 'HFP is high' OR
'GTP is high' and 'HFP is rated' OR
'GTP is rated' and 'HFP is high'
If 'DP is close' Then 'GTP is rated' and 'HFP is rated'
If 'DP is over' Then 'GTP is high' and 'HFP is low' OR

'GTP is rated' and 'HFP is low' OR
'GTP is low' and 'HFP is high' OR
'GTP is low' and 'HFP is rated' OR
'GTP is low' and 'HFP is low'
If 'DT is high' Then 'GTP is high' and 'HFP is high' OR
'GTP is high' and 'HFP is rated' OR
'GTP is rated' and 'HFP is high'
If 'DT is rated' Then 'GTP is rated' and 'HFP is rated'
If 'DT is low' Then 'GTP is high' and 'HFP is low' OR
'GTP is rated' and 'HFP is low' OR
'GTP is low' and 'HFP is high' OR
'GTP is low' and 'HFP is rated' OR
'GTP is low' and 'HFP is low'
If 'DC is high' Then 'DP is over' and 'DT is high' OR
'DP is over' and 'DT is rated' OR
'DP is close' and 'DT is high'
If 'DC is rated' Then 'DP is close' and 'DT is rated'
If 'DC is low' Then 'DP is over' and 'DT is low' OR
'DP is close' and 'DT is low' OR
'DP is below' and 'DT is low' OR
'DP is below' and 'DT is high' OR
'DP is below' and 'DT is rated'

For wires in the range over 30 microns, only the second strategy can be applied. First of all, the pressure inside the glass tube should be adjusted to maintain the position and temperature of the drop near their rated values. The power of HF generator should be also adjusted, if it is the case. Note that the geometry of capillary is depending on the position and temperature of the drop. For wires in the range between 10 and 30 microns a successful combination of both strategies should be constructed.

The fuzzy logic-based controller provides a useful tool for converting the linguistic control strategy from the expert knowledge into control rules. However, as it can be seen from the above, proper control rules cannot be obtained easily for a casting plant. Hence, a self-organizing knowledge-based system has to be developed. In order to construct such a system, we have to develop and exploit human operator knowledge.

At a first stage, the proposed approach and methods must help (assist) the operator to cast high quality microwire of different diameters. The developed software application will be used to capture and process the image of the drop over the time of casting, in order to help the operator with online tracking the geometrical and color features of the drop (Figure 7). At the same time, the operator's experience and knowledge should be accumulated on the system during continuous casting. So, we are looking for the online system learning. At the second stage, we should provide an experimental plant capable to cast almost automatically high quality microwires in a wide range of diameters.

Hardware Implementation of the Control System

From the implementation point of view, any simulation results are not relevant for us. In our case simulation may only offer a general qualitative analysis. For this reason, we have started with designing software and hardware tools for the application under consideration.

At this time, data acquisition subsystem and graphic display controller (GDC) were developed and tested. A field programmable gate array (FPGA) based control processor unit (CPU) is also designed. The application uses the ability of the FPGA to provide flexibility and real-time solution for the image processing. The CPU is designated to perform online tasks of high complexity, such as the interpolation of the shape, the calculation of the geometry of metal-filled capillary and the planning of some optimal trajectories through the process. The calculation of the geometry requires computing of the first and second derivative of the interpolation polynomial in the Lagrange form. Then, the coordinates of the inflection point and capillary point are calculated. The formulas (3-5)

Figure 7. The system development

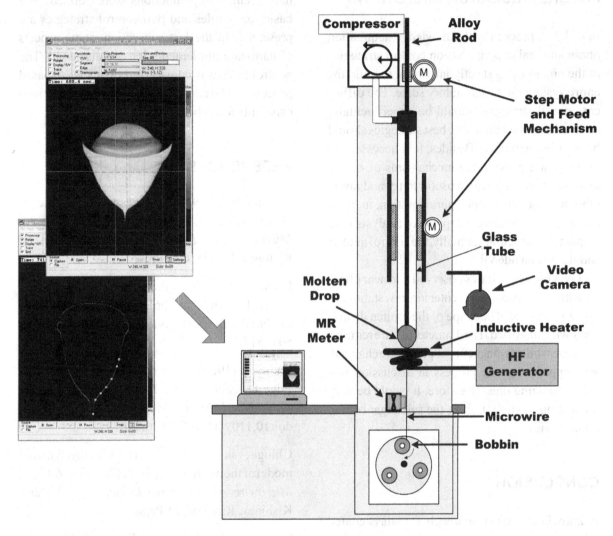

are used to do this. It is obvious that the on-board hardware can be easily configured using standard software programming tools.

The experimental board of the GDC is designed on Fujitsu MB86291A "Scarlet" controller. The MB86291 has built-in 16-Mbit SDRAM to enable high bandwidth data transfer. This permits high-speed memory access, which is the bottleneck of graphics processing. The control of GDC is provided using an ATMega128 microcontroller. The interface between these circuits is based on a complex programmable logic device from Altera MAX II family (EPM1270). The experimental

board of the CPU contains a configurable processing device (Altera ACEX EP1K50), and an ATMega16 microcontroller. There are also two external flash memory units on the board. The first one is designated to store the fuzzy rules and control strategies. Its capacity is of 64K words and is based on AT29C1024 circuit from Atmel. The second one uses two NAND01G flash memory circuits from Micron. The latter will be used to acquire and hold the knowledge information. The total size of knowledge base memory equals 256M bytes.

FUTURE RESEARCH DIRECTIONS

In order to proceed with knowledge acquisition phase and real experiments on control strategies of the process, it is strictly important to build the entire system on the laboratory scale. The different control strategies should be experimentally realized and compared. The best strategies should be then implemented. Besides, it is necessary to develop and provide the mechanisms of online learning. It would be also useful to try and apply other methods for shape approximation, in order to make a quantitative comparative analysis with respect to the accuracy. Finally, the control quality should be considered.

Over the years, it was observed that near phase transitions the process can enter in a new stationary phase of casting. The shape of the molten drop is somewhat modified. The diameter of wire remains the same while its magnetic properties are changed. We suppose that the process in discussion is a self-organizing one. Therefore, it would be very interesting to study it from the self organization point of view.

CONCLUSION

A knowledge-based approach for glass-coated microwire casting plant control is suggested in the chapter. The proposed control scheme uses the technologies of fuzzy linguistic control and machine vision. In order to construct a knowledge-based system for diameter control in microwire continuous casting, an original model was developed. This one is capable of taking into account the current features of the process and also describes the shape of the molten drop at each time. The model offers a mechanism to estimate the geometry of the metal-filled capillary. As a result, the diameter of microwire can be predicted and maintained during continuous casting.

Taking into account the features of the casting process, the input/output linguistic variables and

their membership functions were defined. The basic fuzzy rules and two control strategies are presented. In the last subsection, some aspects of hardware implementation are discussed. The control system is constructed on a FPGA-based processor. The control system is flexible and new capabilities can be introduced over the time.

REFERENCES

Berman, N. R. (1972). Some aspects of the theory of microwire casting. In Zelikowsky, Z. (Ed.), *Microwire and Resistive Devices* (pp. 3–21). Kishinev, Russia: CM Press.

Berrut, J.-P., & Trefethen, L. N. (2004). Barycentric Lagrange interpolation. *Revew of Society for Industrial and Applied Mathematics, 46*(3), 501–517.

Canny, J. (1986). A Computational Approach to Edge Detection. *IEEE Transactions on Pattern Analysis and Machine Intelligence, 8*(6), 679–714. doi:10.1109/TPAMI.1986.4767851

Chiugaevskiy, I. V. (1964). A hydrodynamic model of the molten drop. In Zelikowsky, Z. (Ed.), *Microwire and Resistive Devices* (pp. 16–26). Kishinev, Russia: CM Press.

Cobeno, A. F., Zhukov, A., Blanco, J. M., Larin, V., & Gonzalez, J. (2001). Magnetoelastic sensor based on giant magnetoimpedance of amorphous microwire. *Sensors and Actuators. A, Physical, 91*, 95–98. doi:10.1016/S0924-4247(01)00502-7

Davies, E. R. (2004). *Machine vision. Theory, algorithms, practicalities*. San Francisco: Morgan Kaufmann.

Driankov, D., Hellendorn, H., & Reinfrank, M. (1993). *An introduction to fuzzy control*. New York: Springer-Verlag.

Kickert, W. J. M., & Van Nauta Lemke, H. R. (1976). Application of a fuzzy controller in a warm water plant. *Automatica, 12*, 301–308. doi:10.1016/0005-1098(76)90050-9

Krause, B., von Altrock, C., Limper, K., & Schafers, W. (2007). Development of a fuzzy knowledge-based system for the control of a refuse incineration plant. *Fuzzy Application Library/Technical Applications.* Retrieved January 20, 2007, from http://fuzzytech.com/e/e_a_mull.html

Larin, V., Torcunov, A., Zhukov, A., González, J., Vazquez, M., & Panina, L. (2002). Preparation and properties of glass-coated microwires. *Journal of Magnetism and Magnetic Materials, 249*(1-2), 39–45. doi:10.1016/S0304-8853(02)00501-2

Passino, K. M., & Yurkovich, S. (1998). *Fuzzy control.* Reading, MA: Addison-Wesley Longman.

Patyra, M., Grantner, J., & Koster, K. (1996). Digital fuzzy logic controller. Design and implementation. *IEEE Transactions on Fuzzy Systems, 4*(4), 439–459. doi:10.1109/91.544304

Press, W. H., Teukolsky, S. A., Vetterling,, W. T., & Flannery, B. P. (1992). *Numerical recipes in C. The art of scientific computing.* Cambridge, UK: Cambridge University Press.

Siler, W., & Buckley, J. J. (2005). *Fuzzy expert systems and fuzzy reasoning.* Hoboken, NJ: John Wiley & Sons.

Terano, T., Asai, K., & Sugeno, M. (Eds.). (1993). *Applied fuzzy systems.* Moskva, Russia: Mir.

von Altrock, C., & Krause, B. (2007). Optimization of a water treatment system. *Fuzzy Application Library/Technical Applications.* Retrieved January 20, 2007, from http://fuzzytech.com/e/e_a_dek.html

ADDITIONAL READING

Akhromeeva, T., S., & Malinetskii, G., G. (2008). Synergetics and measurement problems. *Measurement Techniques, 51*(11), 1155–1159. doi:10.1007/s11018-009-9180-z

Albertos, P., & Sala, A. (2004). *Multivariable control systems. An engineering approach.* London: Springer-Verlag.

Alty, J. L., & Coombs, M., J. (1984). *Expert systems. Concepts and examples.* London: National Computing Centre.

Asadov, K., G., & Nabiev, N., A. (2008). Optimizing a data acquisition system for the nonstationary information energy state by deterministic and fuzzy methods. *Measurement Techniques, 51*(7), 706–708. doi:10.1007/s11018-008-9104-3

Babuska, R., & Mamdani, E. (2008). Fuzzy control. *Scholarpedia, 3*(2), 2103. doi:10.4249/scholarpedia.2103

Banks, W., & Hayward, G. (2002). *Fuzzy logic in embedded microcomputers and control systems.* Waterloo: Byte Craft Limited.

Barbulescu, D., & Bologea, G. (1997). Shape analysis and classifying algorithms in videoinspection. In I. Dumitrache (Ed.), *11th International Conference on Control Systems and Computer Science: Vol. 2.* (pp. 227-231). Bucharest: "Politehnica" University Press.

Boiculese, L., Teodorescu, H., & Dimitriu, G. (1996). Optimization of fuzzy controllers by exhaustive, trial & error and genetic methods. Medical applications. *Computer Science Journal of Moldova, 4*(1), 69–87.

Cesa-Bianchi, N., & Lugosi, G. (2006). *Prediction, learning, and games.* New York: Cambridge University Press. doi:10.1017/CBO9780511546921

Chen, C., & Chen, Y. (1993). Self-organizing fuzzy logic controller design. *Computers in Industry, 22*(3), 249–261. doi:10.1016/0166-3615(93)90092-F

Forsyth, D. A., & Ponce, J. (2003). *Computer vision. A modern approach.* Upper Saddle River, NJ: Prentice Hall.

Gorez, R., & Calcev, G. (1997). A survey of PID auto-tuning methods. In I. Dumitrache (Ed.), *11th International Conference on Control Systems and Computer Science: Vol. 1.* (pp. 18-27). Bucharest: "Politehnica" University Press.

Haken, H. (1983). *Advanced synergetics. Instability hierarchies of self-organizing systems and devices.* Berlin, Germany: Springer-Verlag.

Haken, H. (1988). *Information and self-organization. A macroscopic approach to complex systems.* Berlin, Germany: Springer-Verlag.

Ketata, R., De Geest, D., & Titli, A. (1995). Fuzzy controller: design, evaluation, parallel and hierarchical combination with a PID controller. *Fuzzy Sets and Systems, 71*, 113–129. doi:10.1016/0165-0114(94)00189-E

Maeda, M., & Murakami, S. (1988). A design for a fuzzy logic controller. *Information Sciences, 45*(2), 315–330. doi:10.1016/0020-0255(88)90045-X

Mastacan, L., Olah, I., & Anita, L. (1998). Fuzzy control for thermal plant. In A. Graur (Ed.), *International Conference on Development and applications systems: nr. 9.* (pp. 107-112). Suceava: "Stefan cel Mare" University Press.

Mendel, J., M., & Mouzouris, G., C. (1997). Designing fuzzy logic systems. *IEEE Transactions on Circuits and Systems-II: Analog and Digital Signal Processing, 44*(11), 885-895.

Nilsson, N. (1998). *Artificial intelligence. A new synthesis.* San Francisco: Morgan Kaufmann.

Nixon, M. S., & Aguado, A. S. (2007). *Feature extraction and image processing.* New York: Academic Press.

Paragios, N., & Deriche, R. (2002). Geodesic active regions and level set methods for supervised texture segmentation. *International Journal of Computer Vision, 46*(3), 223–247. doi:10.1023/A:1014080923068

Russel, S. J., & Norvig, P. (2003). *Artificial Intelligence. A modern approach.* Upper Saddle River, NJ: Prentice Hall.

Sorkine, O., Cohen-Or, D., Irony, D., & Toledo, S. (2005). Geometry-Aware Bases for Shape Approximation. *IEEE Transactions on Visualization and Computer Graphics, 11*(2), 171–180. doi:10.1109/TVCG.2005.33

Vatavu, R., Pentiuc, S., Grisoni, L., & Chaillou, C. (2008). Modeling Shapes for Pattern Recognition: A simple low-cost spline-based approach. *Advances in Electrical and Computer Engineering, 8*(15), 67–71. doi:10.4316/aece.2008.01012

von Altrock, C. (2008). Practical fuzzy logic design. *Fuzzy Application Library/Technical Applications.* Retrieved February 19, 2008, from http://fuzzytech.com/e/e_a_pfd.html

Weizenbaum, J. (1976). *Computer power and human reason. From judgment to calculation.* San Francisco: W. H. Freeman and Company.

Wiener, N. (1961). *Cybernetics or control and communication in the animal and the machine.* Cambridge, MA: The MIT Press.

Yager, R. R. (Ed.). (1982). *Fuzzy set and possibility theory. Recent developments.* New York: Pergamon Press.

Zaharia, M. D. (1998). Approaches for curve representation in spatial databases. In S. Holban (Ed.), *Third International Conference on Technical Informatics: Vol. 1.* (pp. 107-115). Timisoara: "Politehnica" University Press.

Zhukov, A., Garcia, C., Zhukova, V., Larin, V., Gonzalez, J., & del Val, J. J. (2007). Fabrication and magnetic properties of Cu (FeSiBC) thin microwires. *Journal of Non-Crystalline Solids, 353,* 922–924. doi:10.1016/j.jnoncrysol.2006.12.061

Zhukov, A., Sinnecker, E., Paramo, D., Guerrero, F., Larin, V., González, J., & Vazquez, M. (1999). Fabrication and magnetic properties of glass-coated microwires from immiscible elements. *Journal of Applied Physics, 85*(8), 4482–4484. doi:10.1063/1.370382

KEY TERMS AND DEFINITIONS

Control Variables: The input variables of a control system which are adjusted in such a way as to maintain a given output stable.

Data Acquisition: The automatic collection of data from sensors and peripheral devices.

Fuzzy Control: A specific type of knowledge-based control in which the control actions are described in terms of IF-THEN rules.

Glass-Coated Microwires: Thin metal-based fibers covered by a glass coating.

Knowledge-Based Control System: A system in which the goal is to capture, develop, and implement experience and knowledge available from human operators (experts).

Machine Vision: An engineering concept based on the use of sensors (video cameras) and image processing software, in order to monitor and control a manufacturing process.

Microwire Casting: A process for the fabrication of microwires which is based on continuous filling of a capillary drawn out of a vertical glass tube with liquid metal.

Shape Approximation: A method (technique) for modeling shapes in order to describe almost correct the geometry of a form.

Compilation of References

Agrawal, R., & Srikant, R. (1994). Fast algorithms for mining association rules. In J. B. Bocca, M. Jarke, & C. Zaniolo (Eds.), *20th International Conference on Very Large Databases, Santiago de Chile, Chile* (pp. 487–499). San Francisco: Morgan Kaufmann

Ahire, S. L., Golhar, D. Y., & Waller, M. A. (1996). Development and validation of TQM implementation constructs. *Decision Sciences, 27,* 23–56. doi:10.1111/j.1540-5915.1996.tb00842.x

Aidemark, J., Folkesson, P., & Karlsson, J. (2003). On the probability of detecting data errors generated by permanent faults using time redundancy. In *Proceedings of the 9th IEEE International On-Line Testing Symposium,* IOLTS'03, pp. 68-74.

Akar, M., & Ozguner, U. (2000). Decentralized techniques for the analysis and control of Takagi-Sugeno fuzzy systems. *IEEE Transactions on Fuzzy Systems, 8*(6), 691–704. doi:10.1109/91.890328

Akerlof, G. A. (1970). The Market for 'Lemons': Quality Uncertainty and the Market Mechanism. *The Quarterly Journal of Economics, 84*(3), 488–500. doi:10.2307/1879431

Albertos, P., & Sala, A. (2004). *Multivariable Control Systems: An Engineering Approach.* New York: Springer.

Albertos, P., & Sala, A. (2002). Fuzzy expert control systems: Knowledge base validation. In H. Unbehauen (Ed.), *UNESCO encyclopedia of life support systems* (p. 6.43.25.3). Oxford, UK, eolss.net: EOLSS publishers.

Alfonseca, E., Carro, R. M., Martin, E., Ortigosa, A., & Paredes, P. (2006). The impact of learning styles on student grouping for collaborative learning: a case study. *User Modeling and User-Adapted Interaction, 16*(2-3), 377–401. doi:10.1007/s11257-006-9012-7

Allen, J. (1983). Maintaining knowledge about temporal intervals. *CACM, 26*(11), 832–843.

Amin, A., & Cohendet, P. (2004). *Architectures of knowledge: firms, capabilities, and communities.* Oxford, UK: Oxford UP.

Andersen, P., Raastad, M., & Storm, J. F. (1990). Excitatory synaptic integration in hippocampal pyramids and dentate granule cells. In *Cold Spring Harbor Symposia on Quantitative Biology* (pp. 81–86). Cold Spring Harbor: Cold Spring Harbor Laboratory Press.

Andersen, P. (1991). Synaptic integration in hypocampal neurons. In *Fidia Research Foundation Neuroscience Award Lectures* (pp. 51-71). New-York: Raven Press, Ltd.

Anderson, J. C., Rungtusanatham, M., Schroeder, M. G., & Devaraj, S. (1995). A path analytic model of a theory of quality management underlying the Deming management method: preliminary empirical findings. *Decision Sciences, 26,* 637–658. doi:10.1111/j.1540-5915.1995. tb01444.x

Andújar, J., & Bravo, J. (2005). Multivariable fuzzy control applied to the physical–chemical treatment facility of a Cellulose factory. *Fuzzy Sets and Systems, 150*(3), 475–492. doi:10.1016/j.fss.2004.03.023

Andújar, J., Bravo, J., & Peregrin, A. (2004). Stability analysis and synthesis of multivariable fuzzy systems using interval arithmetic. *Fuzzy Sets and Systems, 148*(3), 337–353. doi:10.1016/j.fss.2004.01.008

Apkarian, P., & Adams, R. (1998, January). Advanced gain-scheduling techniques for uncertain systems. *IEEE Transactions on Control Systems Technology, 6*, 21–32. doi:10.1109/87.654874

Archibugi, D., Howells, J., & Michie, J. (1999). Innovation systems in a global economy. *Technology Analysis and Strategic Management, 11*, 527–539. doi:10.1080/095373299107311

Ariño, C., & Sala, A. (2007). Relaxed LMI conditions for closed-loop fuzzy systems with tensor product structure. *Engineering Applications of Artificial Intelligence, 8*(20), 1036–1046. doi:10.1016/j.engappai.2007.02.011

Ariño, C., & Sala, A. (2008). Extensions to "stability analysis of fuzzy control systems subject to uncertain grades of membership". *IEEE Transactions on Systems, Man and Cybernetics – Part B, 38*(2), 558–563.

Arkin, R. C. (1998). *Behavior-based robotics.* The MIT Press.

Astrom, K. J., & Wittenmark, B. (1989). *Adaptive Control.* Reading, MA: Addison-Wesley.

Astrom, K. J., & Wittenmark, B. (1973). On self-tuning regulators. *Automatica, 9*, 185–199. doi:10.1016/0005-1098(73)90073-3

Åström, K. J., & Wittenmark, B. (1997). *Computer-controlled systems: Theory and design* (3rd ed.). Upper Saddle River, NJ: Prentice Hall.

Azouaoui, O., & Chohra, A. (2002). Soft computing based pattern classifiers for the obstacle avoidance behavior of Intelligent Autonomous Vehicles (IAV). *International Journal of Applied Intelligence, 16*(3), Kluwer Academic Publishers, 249-271.

Babuska, R., & Verbruggen, H. (2003). Neuro-fuzzy methods for nonlinear system identification. *Annual Reviews in Control, 27*, 73–85. doi:10.1016/S1367-5788(03)00009-9

Babuška, R., & Verbruggen, H. (1996). An overview of fuzzy modeling for control. *Control Engineering Practice, 4*(11), 1593–1606. doi:10.1016/0967-0661(96)00175-X

Babuška, R., Mollov, S., & Roubos, J. (1998, Oct). Mimo aspects in fuzzy control. In *Proceedings workshop on intelligent control systems.* Darmstadt, Germany.

Baczko, T. (2008). Standortbedingungen in Ostdeutschland und Polen aus Sicht der Unternehmen. *Wochenbericht des DIW Berlin, 9*, 91–97.

Badaloni, S., & Giacomin, M. (1999). *A fuzzy extension of Allen's Interval Algebra.* In E. Lamma and P. Mello, (Eds.), *Proc. of the 6th Congress of the Italian Assoc. for Artificial Intelligence.* pp. 228–237.

Balakrishnan, K., & Honavar, V. (1997). *Intelligent diagnosis systems* (pp. 50011–51040). Ames, Iowa: Technical Report, Iowa State University.

Ballard, D. H. (1982). *Computer vision.* New York: Prentice Hall.

Banek, T., & Kozłowski, E. (2005). Active and passive learning in control processes application of the entropy concept. *Systems Sciences, 31*(2), 29–44.

Banek, T., & Kozłowski, E. (2006). Adaptive control of system entropy. *Control and Cybernetics, 35*(2), 279–289.

Banek, T., & Kulikowski, R. (2003). Information pricing in portfolio optimization. *Control and Cybernetics, 32*(4), 867–882.

Banek, T., & Kulikowski, R. (2003). Management of Intellectual Capital, *Bulletin of the Polish Academy of Sciences. Technical Sciences, 51*(3), 205–211.

Banek, T., & Kozłowski, E. (2006). Self- learning as a dual control problem. In Kulikowski, R., Bubnicki, Z., & Kacprzyk, J. (Eds.), *System – computer aiding of management knowledge* (pp. 157–236). Warsaw: EXIT. (in Polish)

Baptiste, J., & Le Pape, C. (1995). Disjunctive constraints for manufacturing scheduling: Principles and extensions. In *Third International Conference on Computer Integrated Manufacturing*, Singapore.

Baraczyk, H., Cook, P., & Heidenreich, R. (Eds.). (1996). *Regional Innovation Systems*. London: University of London Press.

Barbour, B. (1993). Synaptic currents evoked in Purkinje cells by stimulating individual granule cells. *Neuron, 11*, 759. doi:10.1016/0896-6273(93)90085-6

Barnes, M. P. (2008). *Upper Motor Neurone Syndrome and Spacticity*. Cambridge, MA: Cambridge Medicine. doi:10.1017/CBO9780511544866

Baron, M., & Grannot, N. (2003). Consistent estimation of early and frequent change points. In *Foundation of statistical inference*. Heidelberg, Germany: Springer.

Basseville, M., & Nikiforov, I. V. (1993). *Detection of Abrupt Changes: Theory and Application*. Upper Saddle River, NJ: Prentice Hall.

Bekey, G. A. (2005). *Autonomous robots: From biological inspiration to implementation and control*. Cambridge, MA: The MIT Press.

Bell, T., Cleary, J., & Witten, I. (1990). Text compression. In Bickel, P., & Doksum, K. (Eds.), *Mathematical statistics: Basic ideas and selected topics* (2nd ed., *Vol. I*). Upper Saddle River, NJ: Prentice Hall.

Bellman, R. (1961) *Adaptive control processes*. New York: Princeton.

Belton, V., & Stewart, T. J. (2001). *Multiple Criteria Decision Making*. Dordrecht, The Netherlands: Kluwer.

Berman, N. R. (1972). Some aspects of the theory of microwire casting. In Zelikowsky, Z. (Ed.), *Microwire and Resistive Devices* (pp. 3–21). Kishinev, Russia: CM Press.

Berrut, J.-P., & Trefethen, L. N. (2004). Barycentric Lagrange interpolation. *Revew of Society for Industrial and Applied Mathematics, 46*(3), 501–517.

Bertani, A., Borghetti, A., Bossi, C., De Biase, L., Lamquet, O., Massucco, S., et al. (2006). Management of Low Voltage Grids with High Penetration of Distributed Generation: concepts, implementations and experiments. In CIGRE (Ed.) *Proceedings of CIGRE 2007 Session*, (paper C6-304) Paris, France.

Bessant, J., Levy, P., Sang, B., & Lamming, R. (1994). Managing successful total quality relationships in the supply chain. *European Journal of Purchasing and Supply Management, 1*, 7–17. doi:10.1016/0969-7012(94)90038-8

Biggiero, L., & Laise, D. (2003). Outranking methods. Choosing and evaluating technology policy: a multi-criteria approach. *Science & Public Policy, 30*, 13–23. doi:10.3152/147154303781780641

Biggiero, L. (2001). Sources of complexity in human systems. *Nonlinear Dynamics and Chaos in Life Sciences, 5*, 3–19. doi:10.1023/A:1009515211632

Biggiero, L., & Sevi, E. (2009). Opportunism by cheating and its effects on industry profitability. *Computational & Mathematical Organization Theory, 15*, 191–236. doi:10.1007/s10588-009-9057-3

Biggiero, L. (2010). Exploration modes and its impact on industry profitability. The differentiated effects of internal and external ways to access market knowledge. In Faggini, M., & Vinci, P. (Eds.), *Decision theory and choice: a complexity approach*. Berlin: Springer.

Bishop, M. C. (2005). *Neural networks for pattern recognition*. New York: Oxford University Press.

Bondia, J., Sala, A., Pico, J., & Sainz, M. (2006). Controller design under fuzzy pole-placement specifications: an interval arithmetic approach. *IEEE Transactions on Fuzzy Systems, 14*(6), 822–836. doi:10.1109/TFUZZ.2006.880002

Bonfe, M., Castaldi, P., Simani, S., & Beghelli, S. (2009). Integrated fault diagnosis and fault tolerant control design for an aircraft model. In *Proc. CD-ROM Int. Conf. Systems Engineering ICSE 2009* (pp. 13-18). Coventry University, UK.

Botta-Genoulaz, V., Millet, P.-A., & Grabot, B. (2005). A survey on the recent research literature on ERP systems. *Computers in Industry, 56*, 510–522. doi:10.1016/j.compind.2005.02.004

Bouarar, T., Guelton, K., & Manamanni, N. (2007). Lmi based h_∞ controller design for uncertain takagi-sugeno descriptors subject to external disturbances. In *Proc. of ifac advanced fuzzy-neural control 2007*. France: Univ. of Valenciennes.

Bourgeois, L. J. (1981). On the Measurement of Organizational Slack. *Academy of Management Review, 6*(1), 29–39. doi:10.2307/257138

Bourgeois, L. J., & Singh J. V. (1983). Organizational Slack and Political Behavior Among Top Management Teams. *Academy of Management Proceedings*. 43-47.

Boyd, S., ElGhaoui, L., Feron, E., & Balakrishnan, V. (1994). *Linear matrix inequalities in system and control theory*. Philadelphia: Ed. SIAM.

Boyd, S., & Vandenberghe, L. (2004). *Convex Optimization*. Cambridge, MA: Cambridge University Press.

Bradley, A. P., & Wilson, W. J. (2004). On wavelet analysis of auditory evoked potentials. *Clinical Neurophysiology, 115*, 1114–1128. doi:10.1016/j.clinph.2003.11.016

Bristol, E. H. (1991). Pattern Recognition: An Alternative to Parameter Identification in Adaptive Control. *Automatica*, 197–202.

Brown, M., & Hartus, Ch. (1994). *Neurofuzzy adaptive modeling and control*. Upper Saddle River, NJ: Prentice Hall.

Bruni, C., Di Pillo, G., & Koch, G. (1974). Bilinear systems: an appealing class of 'nearly linear' systems in theory and applications. *IEEE Transactions on Automatic Control, 19*, 334–348. doi:10.1109/TAC.1974.1100617

Brusilovsky, P. (2001). Adaptive hypermedia. *User Modeling and User-Adapted Interaction, 11*(1-2), 87–110. doi:10.1023/A:1011143116306

Brzostowski, K., & Drapała, J. (2006). *Analysis of Optimization Methods in Identification of Human Elbow Neuromuscular Model. Information systems architecture and technology ISAT 2006* (pp. 59–67). Wrocław, PA: Scientific Papers of Wrocław University of Technology.

Brzostowski, K., Drapała, J., & Świątek, J. (2008). *How to replace inexact expert's knowledge by precise diagnostic system - assessment of internal state of human elbow neuromuscular system. Knowledge processing and reasoning for information society*. Warszawa, Poland: Exit.

Brzostowski, K., Drapała, J., Świątek, J., & Moskała, A. (2006). Difference equations and neural networks as a diagnostic tools for human elbow neuromuscular system. *Computer systems engineering, Theory & applications, 6th & 7th Polish-British Workshop*, (pp. 128 – 137).

Bubnicki, Z. (1974). *Identification of Control Plants*. Warszawa, Poland: PWN. (In Polish)

Bubnicki, Z. (2000). Learning process in a class of knowledge-based systems. *Kybernetes*, 1016–1028. doi:10.1108/03684920010342107

Burkitt, A. N. (2006). A review of the integrate-and-fire neuron model: I. Homogeneous synaptic input. *Biological Cybernetics, 95*, 1–19. doi:10.1007/s00422-006-0068-6

Burnham, K. J., James, D. J. G., & Shields, D. N. (1985). Choice of forgetting factor for self-tuning control. *J. Systems Science, 11*, 65–73.

Burnham, K. J. (1991). *Self-tuning control for bilinear systems*. Doctoral dissertation, Coventry Polytechnic, UK.

Burnham, K. J., & James, D. J. G. (1986). Use of cautious estimation in the self-tuning control of bilinear systems. In *Proc. RAI/IPAR, 1*,(pp. 419-432). Toulouse, France.

Camacho, E. F., & Bordons, C. (2004). *Model Predictive Control* (2nd ed.). London, UK: Springer-Verlag.

Canny, J. (1986). A Computational Approach to Edge Detection. *IEEE Transactions on Pattern Analysis and Machine Intelligence, 8*(6), 679–714. doi:10.1109/TPAMI.1986.4767851

Caprari, G. (2003). *Autonomous micro-robots: Applications and limitations*. (Ph.D. Thesis), Lausanne, EPFL.

Cariani, P. (2001). Temporal codes, timing nets, and music perception. *Journal of New Music Research, 30*, 107–135. doi:10.1076/jnmr.30.2.107.7115

Carlos, A., Hernandez-Aramburo, T., Green, C., & Mugniot, N. (2005). Fuel Consumption Minimization of a Microgrid. *IEEE Transactions on Industry Applications, 41*(3), 673–682. doi:10.1109/TIA.2005.847277

Carpenter, G. A., Grossberg, S., & Rosen, D. B. (1991). Fuzzy ART: Fast stable learning and categorization of analog patterns by adaptive resonance system. *Neural Networks, 4*, 759–771. doi:10.1016/0893-6080(91)90056-B

Carrasco, E., & Rodriguez, J. (2004). Diagnosis of acidification states in an anaerobic wastewater treatment plant using a fuzzy-based expert system. *Control Engineering Practice, 12*(1), 59–64. doi:10.1016/S0967-0661(02)00304-0

Carter, J. R., & Narsimhan R. (1994). The role of purchasing and material management in total quality management and customer satisfaction. *International Journal of Purchasing ad Material Management, 32*, 2-12.

Casado, M. H., & Velasco, F. J. (2003). Surface ship trajectory control using non-linear backstepping design. *Journal of Marine Engineering and Technology, A3*, 3–8.

Casella, G., & Berger, R. (2001). *Statistical inference* (2nd ed.). Pacific Grove, CA: Brooks/Cole Pub. Co.

Cha, H. J., Kim, Y. S., Park, S. H., Yoon, T. B., Jung, Y. M., & Lee, J.-H. (2006). Learning styles diagnosis based on user interface behaviors for customization of learning interfaces in an intelligent tutoring system. In M. Ikeda, K. Ashley, & T.-W. Chan (Eds.), *Proceedings of the Intelligent Tutoring Systems, 8th International Conference* (LNCS 4053, pp. 513-524). Berlin, Germany: Springer-Verlag.

Chen, J., & Patton, R. J. (1999). *Robust model-based fault diagnosis for dynamic systems*. Norwell, MA: Kluwer Academic Publishers.

Chen, S.-S., Chang, Y.-C., Su, S.-F., Chung, S.-L., & Lee, T.-T. (2005). Robust static output-feedback stabilization for nonlinear discrete-time systems with time delay via fuzzy control approach. *Fuzzy Systems. IEEE Transactions on, 13*(2), 263–272.

Chiang, J., & Hao, P. (2004, February). Support vector learning mechanism for fuzzy rule-based modeling: A new approach. *IEEE Transactions on Fuzzy Systems, 12*, 1–12. doi:10.1109/TFUZZ.2003.817839

Child, J. (2001). Trust: the fundamental bond in global collaboration. *Organizational Dynamics, 29*(4), 274–288. doi:10.1016/S0090-2616(01)00033-X

Chin, R. T., & Dyer, C. R. (1986). Model-based recognition in robot vision. *ACM Computing Surveys, 1*(18), 67–108. doi:10.1145/6462.6464

Chiugaevskiy, I. V. (1964). A hydrodynamic model of the molten drop. In Zelikowsky, Z. (Ed.), *Microwire and Resistive Devices* (pp. 16–26). Kishinev, Russia: CM Press.

Chohra, A., Kanaoui, N., & Amarger, V. (2005). A soft computing based approach using signal-to-image conversion for Computer Aided Medical Diagnosis (CAMD). In Saeed, K., & Pejas, J. (Eds.), *Information Processing and Security Systems* (pp. 365–374). New York: Springer. doi:10.1007/0-387-26325-X_33

Choraś, R. S. (2005). *Computer vision*. Warsaw, Poland: Exit.

Chow, E. Y., & Willsky, A. S. (1984). Analytical redundancy and the design of robust detection systems. *IEEE Transactions on Automatic Control, 29*(7), 603–614. doi:10.1109/TAC.1984.1103593

Cierniak, R. (2005). *Computed tomography*. Warsaw, Poland: Exit.

Cieslar, D., Hancock, M., & Assadian, F. (2009). A practical solution for vehicle handling stability control of a hybrid electric vehicle. In *Proc. CD-ROM Int. Conf. Systems Engineering ICSE 2009* (pp. 76-81). Coventry University, UK.

Citko, W., Jakóbczak, D., & Sieńko, W. (2005, September). *On Hurwitz - Radon matrices based signal processing*. Paper presented at the workshop Signal Processing at Poznan University of Technology, Poznań, Poland.

Clarke, D. W. (1996). Adaptive predictive control. *IFAC A. Rev. Control, 20*, 83–94. doi:10.1016/S1367-5788(97)00007-2

Clarke, D. W., & Mohtadi, C. (1989). Properties of generalised predictive control. *Automatica, 25*(6), 859–875. doi:10.1016/0005-1098(89)90053-8

Clarke, D. W., & Gawthrop, P. J. (1975). Self-tuning controller. In *Proc. IEE, 122*, 929-934.

Clarke, D. W., Mohtadi, C., & Tuffs, P. S. (1987). Generalized predictive control – Parts I and II. *Automatica, 23*(2), 137-148 and 149-160.

Cobeno, A. F., Zhukov, A., Blanco, J. M., Larin, V., & Gonzalez, J. (2001). Magnetoelastic sensor based on giant magnetoimpedance of amorphous microwire. *Sensors and Actuators. A, Physical, 91*, 95–98. doi:10.1016/S0924-4247(01)00502-7

Conner, K. R. (1991). A historical comparison of resource-based theory and five schools of thought within industrial organization economics: do we have a new theory of the firm? *Journal of Management, 17*(1), 121–154. doi:10.1177/014920639101700109

Conner, K. R., & Prahalad, C. K. (1996). A resource-based theory of the firm: knowledge versus opportunism. *Organization Science, 7*(5), 477–501. doi:10.1287/orsc.7.5.477

Cormack, G., & Horspool, R. (1984). Algorithms for Adaptive Huffman Codes. *Information Processing Letters*, 169–165.

Corso, M., & Pellegrini, L. (2007). Continuous and discontinuous innovation: overcoming the innovator dilemma. *Creativity and Innovation Management, 16*, 333–347. doi:10.1111/j.1467-8691.2007.00459.x

Cyert, R., & March, J. G. (1963). *A behavioral theory of the firm*. Englewood Cliffs, NJ: Prentice Hall.

Dahlquist, G., & Bjoerck, A. (1974). *Numerical methods*. Englewood Cliffs, NJ: Prentice Hall.

Damanpour, F. (1991). Organizational innovation: a meta-analysis of the effects of determinants and moderators. *Academy of Management Journal, 14*(3), 555–590. doi:10.2307/256406

Damasio, A. R. (1989). The brain binds entities and events by multiregional activation from convergence zones. *Neural Computation, 1*, 123–132. doi:10.1162/neco.1989.1.1.123

Dasgupta, S., & Long, P. M. (2005). Performance guarantees for hierarchical clustering. *Journal of Computer and System Sciences, 70*(4), 555–569. doi:10.1016/j.jcss.2004.10.006

Dasgupta, S. (2002). Performance guarantees for hierarchical clustering. In J. Kivinen, & R.H. Sloan (Eds), *Proceedings of COLT2002* (LNCS 2375, pp. 235-254). Berlin, Germany: Springer-Verlag.

Davies, D. L., & Bouldin, D. W. (1979). Cluster separation measure. *IEEE Transactions on Pattern Analysis and Machine Intelligence, 1*(2), 224–227. doi:10.1109/TPAMI.1979.4766909

Davies, E. R. (2004). *Machine vision. Theory, algorithms, practicalities*. San Francisco: Morgan Kaufmann.

Davis, M. H. A., Dempster, M. A. H., & Elliott, R. J. (1991). *On the value of information in controlled diffusion processes. Liber Amicorum for M. Zakai* (pp. 125–138). New York: Academic Press.

de Wit, C., & Oppe, J. (1979-80). Optimal collision avoidance in unconfined waters. *Journal of the Institute of Navigation, 26*(4), 296–303.

Dean, T. (1989). Using Temporal Hierarchies to Efficiently Maintain Large Temporal Databases. *Journal of the ACM*, 686–709.

Deb, K. (2001). *Multi-objective Optimization using Evolutionary Algorithms*. New York: John Wiley and Sons Ltd.

Deb, K., & Agrawal, R. B. (1995). Simulated binary crossover for continuous search space. *Complex Systems, 9*, 115–148.

Deb, K., & Goyal, M. (1996). A combined genetic adaptive search (GeneAS) for engineering design. *Computer Science and Informatics*, *26*(4), 30–45.

Deb, K., Agrawal, S., Pratap, A., & Meyarivan, T. A. (2000) Fast Elitist Non-Dominated Sorting Genetic Algorithm for Multi-Objective Optimization: NSGA-II. In Springer (Ed.) *Parallel Problem Solving from Nature VI – Lecture Notes in Computer Science* (849-858) Paris, France.

Dechter, R. (2003). *Constraint Processing*. San Francisco: Morgan Kaufmann.

Dechter, R., Meiri, I., & Pearl, J. (1991). Temporal Constraint Networks. *Artificial Intelligence*, *49*, 61–95. doi:10.1016/0004-3702(91)90006-6

Deming, W. E. (1986). *Out of the crisis*. Cambridge, MA: MIT Press.

Disdell, K. J. (1995). *Bilinear self-tuning control for multivariable high temperature furnace applications*. Doctoral dissertation, Coventry University, UK.

Don, M., Masuda, A., Nelson, R., & Brackmann, D. (1997). Successful detection of small acoustic tumors using the stacked derived-band auditory brain stem response amplitude. *The American Journal of Otology*, *18*(5), 608–621.

Dorigo, M., & Di Caro, G. (1999). The Ant Colony Optimization Meta-Heuristic. In Corne, D., Dorigo, M., & Glover, F. (Eds.), *New Ideas in Optimization* (pp. 11–32). New York: McGraw-Hill.

Driankov, D., Hellendorn, H., & Reinfrank, M. (1993). *An introduction to fuzzy control*. New York: Springer-Verlag.

Du, J. Chen, G., & Yang, C. (2005). Adaptive robust backstepping nonlinear algorithm applied to ship steering. *16th IFAC World Congress to be held in Prague, Czech Republic*.

Dubois, D., & Prade, H. (1978). Operations on fuzzy numbers. *International Journal of Systems Science*, *9*(6), 613–626. doi:10.1080/00207727808941724

Dubois, D., & Prade, H. (1997). The three semantics of fuzzy sets. *Fuzzy Sets and Systems*, *90*(2), 142–150. doi:10.1016/S0165-0114(97)00080-8

Duda, R., Hart, P., & Stork, D. (2000). *Pattern Classification* (2nd ed.). New York: John Wiley and Sons, Inc.

Dunn, J. C. (1977). Well separated clusters and optimal fuzzy partitions. *Journal of Cybernetics*, *4*, 95–104. doi:10.1080/01969727408546059

Dunn, R., & Dunn, K. (1978). *Teaching students through their individual learning styles: a practical approach*. Reston, VA: Reston Publishing.

Dunoyer, A., Balmer, L., Burnham, K. J., & James, D. J. G. (1997). On the discretization of a single-input single-output bilinear systems. *International Journal of Control*, *68*(2), 361–372. doi:10.1080/002071797223668

Dunoyer, A. P. (1996). *Bilinear self-tuning control and bilinearisation of nonlinear industrial systems*. Doctoral dissertation, Coventry University, UK.

Dunoyer, A., Burnham, K. J., & McAlpine, T. S. (1997). Self-tuning control of an industrial pilot-scale reheating furnace: Design principles and application of a bilinear approach. In *Proc. IEE Control Theory and Applications*, *144*(1), 25-31.

Eckhorn, R., Bauer, R., Jordan, W., Brosch, M., Kruse, W., Munk, M., & Reitboeck, H. J. (1988). Coherent oscillations: a mechanism for feature linking in the visual cortex? *Biological Cybernetics*, *60*, 121–130. doi:10.1007/BF00202899

Eckmann, B. (1999). Topology, algebra, analysis- relations and missing links. *Notices of the American Mathematical Society*, *5*(46), 520–527.

Effros, M., Visweswariah, K., Kulkarni, S., & Verdú, S. (2002). Universal Lossless Source Coding With the Burrows Wheeler Transform. *IEEE Transactions on Information Theory*, *48*(5), 1061–1081. doi:10.1109/18.995542

Eggemont, J. J. (1991). Rate and synchronization measures of periodicity coding in cat primary auditory cortex. *Hearing Research*, *56*, 153–167. doi:10.1016/0378-5955(91)90165-6

Egmont-Petersen, M., De Ridder, D., & Handels, H. (2002). Image processing with neural networks – a review. *Pattern Recognition, 35*, 2279–2301. doi:10.1016/S0031-3203(01)00178-9

Espana, M., & Landau, I. D. (1978). Reduced order bilinear models for distillation columns. *Automatica, 14*, 345–355. doi:10.1016/0005-1098(78)90034-1

Ester, M., Kriegel, H.-P., Sander, J., & Xu, X. (1996). A Density- based algorithm for discovering clusters in large spatial databases with noise. In *Proceedings of the 2nd International Conference on Knowledge Discovery and Data Mining* (pp. 226-231). Portland.

European Commission. (2006, April). European SmartGrids technology platform: Vision and strategy for Europe's electricity networks of the future. Retrieved from http://ec.europa.eu/research/energy/pdf/smartgrids_en.pdf.; www. smartgrids.eu

Evsukoff, A., Gentil, S., & Montmain, J. (2000). Fuzzy reasoning in co-operative supervision systems. *Control Engineering Practice, 8*(4), 389–407. doi:10.1016/S0967-0661(99)00170-7

Fabri, S., & Kadrikamanathan, V. (2001). *Functional Adaptive Control. An Intelligent Systems Approach*. London: Springer-Verlag.

Fang, C.-H., Liu, Y.-S., Kau, S.-W., Hong, L., & Lee, C.-H. (2006). A New LMI-Based Approach to Relaxed Quadratic Stabilization of T-S Fuzzy Control Systems. *IEEE Transactions on Fuzzy Systems, 14*, 286–397.

Fargier, H., Lang, J., & Schiex, T. (1996). *Mixed constraint satisfaction: A framework for decision problems under incomplete knowledge*. In *the 13th National Conference on Artificial Intelligence (AAAI-96)*, pp. 175–180. New York: ACM Press.

Farkhooi, F., Strube-Bloss, M. F., & Nawrot, M. P. (2009). Serial correlation in neural spike trains: Experimental evidence, stochastic modelling, and single neuron variability. *Physical Review E: Statistical, Nonlinear, and Soft Matter Physics, 79*, 021905. doi:10.1103/PhysRevE.79.021905

Farreny, H., & Prade, H. (1985). Tackling uncertainty and imprecision in robotics. In *3rd International Symposium on Robotics Research*, (pp. 85-91).

FEA. (2007). *Federal Enterprise Architecture Program, FEA Practice Guidance, Management Office*, OMB US, November 2007, (http://www.whitehouse.gov/omb/egov)

Feldbaum, A. A. (1965). *Optimal Control Systems*. New York: Academic Press.

Felder, R., & Brent, R. (2005). Understanding student differences. *Journal of Engineering Education, 94*(1), 57–72.

Felder, R. M. (1996). Matters of style. *ASEE PRISM, 6*(4), 18–23.

Felder, R. M., & Silverman, L. K. (1988). Learning and teaching styles in engineering education. *English Education, 78*(7), 674–681.

Felder, R. M., & Soloman, B. A. (2009). *Index of Learning Styles*. Retrieved March 20, 2009. from http://www.ncsu.edu/felder-public/ILSpage.html

Feller, W. (1966). *An introduction to probability theory and its applications* (*Vol. 2*). New York: John Wiley & Sons.

Feng, G. (2006, Oct.). A survey on analysis and design of model-based fuzzy control systems. *IEEE Transactions on Fuzzy Systems, 14*(5), 676–697. doi:10.1109/TFUZZ.2006.883415

Figalli, G., La Cava, M., & Tomasi, L. (1984). An optimal feedback control for a bilinear model of induction motor drives. *International Journal of Control, 39*, 1007–1016. doi:10.1080/00207178408933227

Fiol, C. M. (2002). Intraorganizational cognition and interpretation. In Baum, J. A. C. (Ed.), *Companion to organizations* (pp. 119–137). Oxford, UK: Blackwell.

Fleming, W. H., & Rishel, R. (1975). *Deterministic and stochastic optimal control*. Berlin: Springer-Verlag.

Floreano, D., & Mondada, F. (1996). Evolution of homing navigation in real mobile robot. *IEEE Transactions on Systems, Man, and Cybernetics, •••*, 396–407.

Flynn, B. F., Schroeder, R. G., & Sakakibara, S. (1995). The impact of quality management practices on performance and competitive advantage. *Decision Sciences, 26*, 659–691. doi:10.1111/j.1540-5915.1995.tb01445.x

Fogel, D. B. (1998). *Evolutionary computation: Toward a new philosophy of machine intelligence* (2nd ed.). Piscataway, NJ: IEEE Press.

Fojtik, P. (2006). *Fuzzy regression in non-linear systems diagnostics.* PhD Thesis (In Czech), Brno University of Technology, Czech Republic.

Fortescue, T. R., Kershenbaum, L. S., & Ydstie, B. E. (1981). Implementation of self-tuning regulators with variable forgetting factors. *Automatica, 17*, 831–835. doi:10.1016/0005-1098(81)90070-4

Fossen, T. I. (1994). *Guidance and control of ocean vehicles.* New York: John Wiley.

Fossen, T. I. (2000). A survey on nonlinear ship control from theory to practice. In: *Proceedings of the 5th IFAC Conference on Manoeuvring and Control of Marine Craft.* (pp. 1-16). Aalborg, Denmark.

Frank, P. M. (1990). Fault diagnosis in dynamic system using analytical and knowledge based redundancy – a survey and some new results. *Automatica, 26*(3), 459–474. doi:10.1016/0005-1098(90)90018-D

Frank, P. M., & Keller, L. (1980). Sensitivity discriminating observer design for instrument failure detection. *IEEE Transactions on Aerospace and Electronic Systems, AES-16*(4), 460–467. doi:10.1109/TAES.1980.308975

Frey Law, L. A., & Shields, R. K. (2006). Predicting human chronically paralyzed muscle force: a comparison of three mathematical models. *Journal of Applied Physiology*, 1027–1036.

Gallager, R. (1978). Variations on a Theme by Huffman. *IEEE Transactions on Information Theory, 24*(6), 668–674. doi:10.1109/TIT.1978.1055959

Gambetta, D. (Ed.). (1988). *Trust: making and breaking co-operative relations.* Oxford, UK: Blackwell.

Gan, G., Ma, Ch., & Wu, J. (2007). *Data clustering: theory, algorithms and applications, ASA-SIAM Series on Statistics and Applied Probability, SIAM.* Philadelphia: ASA Alexandria.

Garcia, P., Amandi, A., Schiaffino, S., & Campo, M. (2007). Evaluating Bayesian networks' precision for detecting students' learning styles. *Computers & Education, 49*(3), 794–808. doi:10.1016/j.compedu.2005.11.017

Geiger, S. W., & Cashen, L. H. (2002). A Multidimensional Examination of Slack and its Impact on Innovation. *Journal of Managerial Issues, 15*(1), 68–84.

Geiger, S. W., & Makri, M. (2006). Exploration and exploitation innovation processes: The role of organizational slack in R&D intensive firms. *The Journal of High Technology Management Research, 17*, 97–108. doi:10.1016/j.hitech.2006.05.007

George, G. (2005). *Slack resources and the performance of privately held firms.* Academy of Management Journal.

GERAM (2000). *Generalised Enterprise Reference Architecture and Methodology.* Version 1.6.3 (March 1999), IFIP–IFAC Task Force on Architectures for Enterprise Integration, Permission granted to publish GERAM V1.6.3 as Annex to ISO 15704 (2000)

Gerstner, W., & Kistler, W. (2002). *Spiking Neuron Models: Single Neurons, Populations, Plasticity.* Cambridge University Press.

Gertler, J. (1993). Analytical redundancy methods in failure detection and isolation. *Control-Theory and Advanced Technology, 9*(1), 259–285.

Gertler, J. (1998). *Fault detection and diagnosis in engineering systems.* New York: Marcel Dekker.

Gilbert, J. E., & Han, C. Y. (1999). Adapting instruction in search of 'a significant difference'. *Journal of Network and Computer Applications, 22*(3), 149–160. doi:10.1006/jnca.1999.0088

Gnedenko, B. (1989). *The Theory of Probability.* New York: Chelsea (Fifth Edition).

Goldberg, D. E. (2002). *The design of innovation: Lessons from and for competent genetic algorithms. Genetic Algorithms and Evolutionary Computation 7*. Boston: Kluwer Academic.

Golumbic, & Shamir, R. (1993). Complexity and algorithms for reasoning about time: a graphic-theoretic approach. *Journal of the Association for Computing Machinery, 40*(5), 1108–1133.

Gombay, E. (2003). Sequential Change-point Detection and Estimation. *Sequential Analysis, 22*, 203–222. doi:10.1081/SQA-120025028

Gonzales-Benito, J., Martinez-Lorente, A. R., & Dale, B. G. (2003). A study of the purchasing management system with respect to total quality management. *Industrial Marketing Management, 32*, 443–454. doi:10.1016/S0019-8501(02)00231-6

Gonzalez, R. C., & Woods, R. E. (2002). *Digital image processing* (2nd ed.). Upper Saddle River, NJ: Prentice-Hall.

Goodhart, S. G. (1991). *Self-tuning control of industrial systems*. Doctoral dissertation, Coventry Polytechnic, UK.

Goodhart, S. G., Burnham, K. J., & James, D. J. G. (1994) Bilinear self-tuning control of a high temperature heat treatment plant. In *Proc. IEE Control Theory and Applications, 141(1)*, 12-18.

Goonatilake, S., & Khebbal, S. (1995). *Intelligent hybrid systems*. New York: John Wiley & Sons.

Gordon, A. (1996). Hierarchical classification. In Arabie, P., Hubert, L., & Soete, G. (Eds.), *Clustering and Classification* (pp. 65–121). River Edge, NJ: World Scientific.

Graf, S. & Kinshuk. (2006). Considering learning styles in learning management systems: investigating the behavior of students in an online course. In P. Mylones, M. Wallace, & M. Angelides (Eds.), *Proceedings of the First IEEE International Workshop on Semantic Media Adaptation and Personalization, SMAP 06* (pp. 25-30). Los Alamitos, CA: IEEE Computer Society.

Graps, A. (1995). An introduction to wavelets. *IEEE Computational Science & Engineering, 2*(2). doi:10.1109/99.388960

Gregory, P. C. (Ed.). (1959). *Proceedings of the Self-adaptive Flight Control Systems Symposium*. Dayton, OH: Wright Air Development Center.

Grewal, M. S., & Andrews, A. P. (2001). *Kalman Filtering: Theory and Practice Using MATLAB*. New York: Wiley Interscience.

Grimson, E. (1990). *Object recognition by computer: the role of geometric constraints*. Cambridge, MA: MIT Press.

Guerra, T., & Vermeiren, L. (2004). LMI-based relaxed nonquadratic stabilization conditions for nonlinear systems in the takagi-sugeno's form. *Automatica, 10*, 823–829. doi:10.1016/j.automatica.2003.12.014

Gupta, M., & Sinha, N. (Eds.). (1996). *Intelligent control systems: Concepts and applications*. IEEE press.

Habashi, F. (1997). *Handbook of Extractive Metallurgy, Vol II, Part III*. Wiley-VCH. Weinheim, Germany.

Halkidi, M., Batistakis, Y., & Vazirgiannis, M. (2001). On clustering validation techniques. *Journal of Intelligent Information Systems, 17*(2/3), 107–145. doi:10.1023/A:1012801612483

Halkidi, M., & Vazirgiannis, M. (2001). Clustering validity assessment: finding the optimal partitioning of a data set. In *Proceedings of 2001 International Conference on Data Mining* (pp. 187-194). San Jose, CA.

Halkidi, M., Vazirgiannis, M., & Batistakis, Y. (2000). Quality scheme assessment in the clustering process. In *Proceedings of the 4th European Conference on Principles of Data Mining and Knowledge Discovery* (pp. 265-276). Lyon, France.

Hall, R. (1992). The strategic analysis of intangible resources. *Strategic Management Journal, 13*(2), 135–144. doi:10.1002/smj.4250130205

Hambrick, D. C., & Snow, C. C. (1977). *A Contextual Model of Strategic Decision Making in Organizations* (pp. 109–112). Academy of Management Proceedings.

Han, J., & Kamber, M. (2006). *Data mining. Concepts and techniques* (2nd ed.). San Francisco, CA: Morgan Kaufmann Publishers.

Hankerson, D., Harris, G., & Jr, P. J. (1998). *Introduction to information theory and data compression.* Boca Raton, FL: CRC Press.

Hannan, M. T., & Carroll, G. R. (1992). *Dynamics of organizational populations.* Oxford, UK: Oxford UP.

Haralick, R., & Elliott, G. (1980). Increasing tree search efficiency for Constraint Satisfaction Problems. *Artificial Intelligence, 14,* 263–313. doi:10.1016/0004-3702(80)90051-X

Harris, L., & Rishel, R. (1986). An algorithm for a solution of a stochastic adaptive linear quadratic optimal control problem. *IEEE Transactions on Automatic Control, 31,* 1165–1170. doi:10.1109/TAC.1986.1104200

Hastie, T., Tibshirani, R., & Friedman, J. (2001). *The elements of statistical learning: data mining, inference, and prediction.* Berlin, Germany: Springer Verlag.

Haykin, S. (1999). *Neural networks: A comprehensive foundation* (2nd ed.). Upper Saddle River, NJ: Prentice-Hall.

Hebb, D. O. (1949). *The Organization of Behaviour.* New York: Wiley.

Heffler, B. (2001). Individual learning style and the learning style inventory. *Educational Studies, 27*(3), 307–316. doi:10.1080/03055690120076583

Hengy, D., & Frank, P. M. (1986). Component failure detection via nonlinear state observers. In *Proceedings of IFAC Workshop on Fault Detection and Safety in Chemical Plants* (pp. 153-157). Kyoto, Japan.

Herbrich, R. (2001). *Learning Kernel Classifiers: Theory and Algorithms.* Cambridge, MA: MIT Press.

Ho, T., Stapleton, R., & Subrahmanyam, M. (1995). Multivariate Binomial Approximations for Asset Prices with Non-stationary Variance and Covariance Characteristics. *Review of Financial Studies, 8*(4), 1125–1152. doi:10.1093/rfs/8.4.1125

Hochbaum, S. D., & Shmoys, B. D. (1985). A best possible heuristic for the k-center problem. *Mathematics of Operations Research, 10*(2), 180–184. doi:10.1287/moor.10.2.180

Holden, A. V. (1976). Models of the stochastic activity of neurons. In *Lecture Notes in Biomathematics, 12.* Berlin: Springer.

Holland, M. J. (2004). *Designing autonomous mobile robots; Inside the mind of an intelligent machine.* Amsterdam: Elsevier.

Holmblad, L., & Ostergaard, J. (1982). Control of a cement kiln by fuzzy logic. In Gupta, M., & Sanchez, E. (Eds.), *Fuzzy information and decision processes* (pp. 398–409). Amsterdam: North-Holland.

Honey, P., & Mumford, A. (1986). *The manual of learning styles.* Maidenhead, UK: Peter Honey.

Hori, E., & Skogestad, S. (2007). Selection of control structure and temperature location for two-product distillation columns. *Chemical Engineering Research & Design, 85*(3), 293–306. doi:10.1205/cherd06115

Howells, J. (2005). Innovation and regional economic development: A matter of perspective? *Research Policy, 34,* 1220–1234. doi:10.1016/j.respol.2005.03.014

Hsia, T. C. (1977). *System Identification.* Lexington, KY: Lexington Books.

Hsiao, F., Hwang, J., Chen, C., & Tsai, Z. (2005). Robust stabilization of nonlinear multiple time-delay large-scale systems via decentralized fuzzy control. *IEEE Transactions on Fuzzy Systems, 13*(1), 152–163. doi:10.1109/TFUZZ.2004.836067

Huang, H., Lin, F., & Jeng, J. (2007). Control Structure Selection and Performance Assessment for Disturbance Rejection in MIMO Processes. *Industrial & Engineering Chemistry Research, 46*(26), 9170–9178. doi:10.1021/ie070382i

Humphrey, J. (1998). Trust and the transformation of supplier relations in Indian industry. In Lane, C., & Bachmann, R. (Eds.), *Trust within and between organizations* (pp. 214–240). Oxford: Oxford UP.

Hunt, K., & Johansen, T. (1997). Design and analysis of gain-scheduled control using local controller networks. *International Journal of Control, 66*, 619–651. doi:10.1080/002071797224487

Hwang, & Shubert, L. (1994). *Interpreting tense, aspect, and time adverbials: a compositional, unified approach.* In *Proceedings of the first International Conference on Temporal Logic, LNAI, vol 827*, pp. 237–264, Berlin.

Ignasiak, E. (1996). *Optimization of investment projects.* Warszawa, Poland: PWE.

Isermann, R., Lachmann, K. H., & Matko, D. (1992). *Adaptive control systems.* New York: Princeton Hall International.

Ishikawa, K. (1985). *What is total quality control? The Japanese way.* Upper Saddle River, NJ: Prentice-Hall.

Isidori, A. (1989). *Nonlinear control systems. An introduction.* Berlin, Germany: Springer –Verlag.

Jacobs, F. R., & Bendoly, E. (2003). Enterprise resource planning: developments and directions for operations management research. *European Journal of Operational Research, 146*(2). doi:10.1016/S0377-2217(02)00546-5

Jacquet, P., Szpankowski, W., & Apostol, I. (2002). A Universal Predictor Based on Stochastic Learning-based Weak Estimation of Multinomial Random Variables and Its Applications to Pattern Matching. *IEEE Transactions on Information Theory, 48*(6), 1462–1472. doi:10.1109/TIT.2002.1003834

Jain, A. K., Murty, M. N., & Flynn, P. J. (1999). Data clustering: a review. *ACM Computing Surveys, 31*(3), 264–323. doi:10.1145/331499.331504

Jain, R., & Koronios, A. (2008). Innovation in the cluster validating techniques. *Fuzzy Optimization and Decision Making, 7*(3), 233–241. doi:10.1007/s10700-008-9033-2

Jakóbczak, D. (2007). 2D and 3D image modeling using Hurwitz-Radon matrices. *Polish Journal of Environmental Studies, 4A*(16), 104–107.

Jakóbczak, D., & Kosiński, W. (2007). Hurwitz - Radon operator in monochromatic medical image reconstruction. *Journal of Medical Informatics & Technologies, 11*, 69–78.

Jakóbczak, D., & Kosiński, W. (2007). Application of Hurwitz - Radon matrices in monochromatic medical images decompression. In Kowalczuk, Z., & Wiszniewski, B. (Eds.), *Intelligent data mining in diagnostic purposes: Automatics and informatics* (pp. 389–398). Gdansk, Poland: PWNT.

Jakóbczak, D. (2006). *Application of discrete, orthogonal operator of Hurwitz - Radon in compression and reconstruction of monochromatic images' contours.* Unpublished doctoral dissertation, Polish - Japanese Institute of Information Technology, Warsaw, Poland.

James, J. R., & Suski, G. J. (1988). A Survey of Some Implementations of Knowledge-Based Systems for Real-Time Control. *Proceedings of the 27th IEEE Conference on Decision and Control*, (pp. 580–585).

Jang, Y. M. (2000). Estimation and Prediction-Based Connection Admission Control in Broadband Satellite Systems. *ETRI Journal, 22*(4), 40–50. doi:10.4218/etrij.00.0100.0405

Jang, J., Sun, C., & Mizutani, E. (1997). *Neuro-fuzzy and soft computing.* Upper Saddle River, NJ: Prentice Hall.

Jensen, M. C. (1993). The Modern Industrial Revolution, Exit, and the Failure of Internal Control Systems. *The Journal of Finance, 48*(3), 831–880. doi:10.2307/2329018

Jensen, M. C., & Meckling, W. (1976). Theory of the firm: managerial behavior, agency costs and ownership structure. *Journal of Financial Economics, 3*, 305–360. doi:10.1016/0304-405X(76)90026-X

Johnson, B. W. (1976). *Design and Analysis of Fault-Tolerant Digital Systems.* Boston, MA: Addison-Wesley Longman Publishing Co., Inc.

Jones, B., Garthwaite, P., & Jolliffe, I. (2002). *Statistical Inference* (2nd ed.). Oxford, UK: Oxford University Press.

Juran, J. M., & Blanton Godfrey, A. (2000). *Juran's Quality Handbook*. New York: McGraw-Hill Professional.

Kacprzyk, J., Yager, R. R., & Zadrożny, S. (2000). A fuzzy logic based approach to linguistic summaries of databases. *International Journal of Applied Mathematics and Computer Science*, *10*, 813–834.

Kacprzyk, J., & Zadrożny, S. (2001). Computing with words in intelligent database querying: standalone and Internet-based applications. *Information Sciences*, *34*, 71–109. doi:10.1016/S0020-0255(01)00093-7

Kacprzyk, J., & Zadrożny, S. (2005). Linguistic database summaries and their protoforms: towards natural language based knowledge discovery tools. *Information Sciences*, *173*(4), 281–304. doi:10.1016/j.ins.2005.03.002

Kacprzyk, J., & Zadrożny, S. (2009). Protoforms of Linguistic Database Summaries as a Human Consistent Tool for Using Natural Language in Data Mining. *International Journal of Software Science and Computational Intelligence*, *1*(1), 100–111.

Kacprzyk, J., Yager, R. R., & Zadrożny, S. (2001). Fuzzy linguistic summaries of databases for an efficient business data analysis and decision support. In Abramowicz, W., & Żurada, J. (Eds.), *Knowledge Discovery for Business Information Systems* (pp. 129–152). Boston: Kluwer.

Kacprzyk, J., & Zadrożny, S. (1995). FQUERY for Access: fuzzy querying for a Windows-based DBMS. In Bosc, P., & Kacprzyk, J. (Eds.), *Fuzziness in Database Management Systems* (pp. 415–433). Heidelberg, Germany: Physica-Verlag.

Kaelbing, L., & Littman, M. (1996). Reinforcement learning: a survey. *Journal of Artificial Intelligence Research*, *4*, 237–285.

Kalman, R. E. (1960). A new approach to linear filtering and prediction problems. *Journal of Basic Engineering*, *82D*, 35–45.

Karger, D. R., & Quan, D. (2004, January). *Prerequisites for a personalizable user interfa*ce. Paper presented at the Workshop on Bahavior-Based User Interface Customization at the Intelligent User Interface 2004 Conference, Island of Madeira, Portugal.

Karray, F. O., & De Silva, C. (2004). *Soft computing and intelligent systems design, theory, tools and applications* (Limited, I. S. B. N., Ed.). Reading, MA: Addison Wesley.

Kay, S. M. (1998). Fundamentals of statistical signal processing: *Vol. 2. Detection theory*. Upper Saddle River, NJ: Prentice Hall PTR.

Kekre, S., Murthi, B. P. S., & Srinivasan, K. (1995). Operating decisions, supplier availability and quality: an empirical study. *Journal of Operations Management*, *12*, 387–396. doi:10.1016/0272-6963(95)00002-A

Khalil, H. K. (2002). *Nonlinear Systems*. Upper Saddle River, NJ: Prentice Hall.

Khinchin, A. Ya. (1955). Mathematical methods of mass-service theory. *V. A. Steklov Institute of Mathematics Trudy*, *49*, 1–122.

Kickert, W. J. M., & Van Nauta Lemke, H. R. (1976). Application of a fuzzy controller in a warm water plant. *Automatica*, *12*, 301–308. doi:10.1016/0005-1098(76)90050-9

Kieffer, J. C., & Yang, E. (2000). Grammar-Based Codes: A New Class of Universal Lossless Source Codes. *IEEE Transactions on Information Theory*, *46*(3), 737–754. doi:10.1109/18.841160

Kim, B., & Kim, S. (2005). Diagnosis of plasma processing equipment using neural network recognition of wavelet-filtered impedance matching. *Microelectronic Engineering*, *82*, 44–52. doi:10.1016/j.mee.2005.05.007

Kistler, W. M., & De Zeeuw, C. I. (2002). Dynamical working memory and timed responses: the role of reverberating loops in the olivo-cerebellar system. *Neural Computation*, *14*, 2597–2626. doi:10.1162/089976602760407991

Kittler, J., Hatef, M., Duin, R. P. W., & Matas, J. (1998). On combining classifiers. *IEEE Transactions on Pattern Analysis and Machine Intelligence, 20*(3), 226–239. doi:10.1109/34.667881

Knuth, D. (1985). Dynamic Huffman Coding. *Journal of Algorithms, 6*, 163–180. doi:10.1016/0196-6774(85)90036-7

Kogut, B., & Zander, U. (1992). Knowledge of the firm, combinative capabilities and the replication of technology. *Organization Science, 3*, 383–397. doi:10.1287/orsc.3.3.383

Kogut, B., & Zander, U. (1996). What firms do? Coordination, identity, and learning. *Organization Science, 7*(5), 502–518. doi:10.1287/orsc.7.5.502

Kolb, D. A. (1984). *Experiental learning: Experience as a source of learning and development.* Englewood Cliffs, NJ: Prentice-Hall.

Kolmogoroff, A. (1931). Über die analytischen Methoden in der Wahrscheinlichkeit-srechnung. *Mathematische Annalen, 104*, 415–458. doi:10.1007/BF01457949

König, P., Engel, A. K., & Singer, W. (1996). Integrator or coincidence detector? The role of the cortical neuron revisited. *Trends in Neurosciences, 19*, 130–137. doi:10.1016/S0166-2236(96)80019-1

König, P., & Krüger, N. (2006). Symbols as self-emergent entities in an optimization process of feature extraction and predictions. *Biological Cybernetics, 94*, 325–334. doi:10.1007/s00422-006-0050-3

Korbicz, J., Koscielny, J. M., Kowalczuk, Z., & Cholewa, W. (Eds.). (2004). *Fault Diagnosis. Models, Artificial Intelligence, Applications.* Berlin, Heidelberg: Springer-Verlag.

Korbicz, J., & Kowal, M. (2007). Neuro-fuzzy networks and their application to fault detection of dynamical systems. *Engineering Applications of Artificial Intelligence, 20*(5), 609–617. doi:10.1016/j.engappai.2006.11.009

Kozera, R. (2004). *Curve modeling via interpolation based on multidimensional reduced data.* Gliwice, Poland: Silesian University of Technology Press.

Krafcik, J. F. (1988). Triumph of the lean production system. *Sloan Management Review, 30*, 41–52.

Kramer, R. M., & Tyler, T. R. (Eds.). (1996). *Trust in organizations: frontiers of theory and research.* London: Sage.

Krause, B., von Altrock, C., Limper, K., & Schafers, W. (2007). Development of a fuzzy knowledge-based system for the control of a refuse incineration plant. *Fuzzy Application Library/Technical Applications.* Retrieved January 20, 2007, from http://fuzzytech.com/e/e_a_mull.html

Kriegman, D. J., & Ponce, J. (1990). On recognizing and positioning curved 3-D objects from image contours. *IEEE Transactions on Pattern Analysis and Machine Intelligence, 12*(12), 1127–1137. doi:10.1109/34.62602

Krishnaiah, P., & Miao, B. (1988). Review about estimation of change points. In *Handbook of Statistics* (Vol. 7, pp. 375–402). Amsterdam: Elsevier.

Krstic, M., Kanellakopoulos, I., & Kokotovic, P. (1995). *Nonlinear and adaptive control design.* New York: Wiley-Interscience.

Kruszewski, A., Sala, A., Guerra, T., & Ariño, C. (2009). (in press). A triangulation approach to assymptotically exact conditions for fuzzy summations. *IEEE Transactions on Fuzzy Systems.* .doi:10.1109/TFUZZ.2009.2019124

Kruszewski, A. (2006). *Lois de commande pour une classe de modèles non linéaires sous la forme Takagi-Sugeno: Mise sous forme LMI.* Doctoral dissertation, LAMIH, Université de Valenciennes et du Hainaut-Cambresis.

Kruszewski, A., Guerra, T., & Labiod, S. (2007). Stabilization of Takagi-Sugeno discrete models: towards an unification of the results. *Fuzzy Systems Conference, 2007. FUZZ-IEEE 2007. IEEE International*, 1–6.

K-Team. (2002). *Khepera II user manual*, EPFL, Lausanne. Retrieved March 17, 2009, from http://ftp.k-team.com/khepera/documentation/Kh2UserManual.pdf

Kucera, P., & Honzik, P. (2009). Automation of Real-Time Embedded System Design. *Proceedings on The 13th World Multi-Conference on Systemics, Cybernetics and Informatics: WMSCI 2009.* [Orlando, FL.]. *Intern. Inst. of Informatics and Systemics., I,* 237–242.

Kucera, P., & Zezulka, F. (2004). *Software reliability model for PLC. Proceedings on the 8th World Multi-conference SCI'04. Intern. Inst. of Informatics and Systemics* (pp. 349–352). Orlando: Nagib Callaos.

Kucera, P. (2003). *Formal methods in industrial communication.* Unpublished Ph.D. thesis, Brno University of Technology, Czech Republic. Retrieved from http://taceo.eu

Kucera, P., & Hyncica, O. (2006). Reliability model of TMR system with fault detection. *Proceedings of IFAC WORKSHOP on Programmable Devices and Embedded Systems PDeS2006.* Brno: VUT v Brne, p. 468-472

Kucera, P., Honzik, P., Hyncica, O., & Fojtik, P. (2008). On Analogue TMR System. In *14th International Congress of Cybernetics and Systems of WOSC Proceedings.* Poland, Wroclaw: Oficyna Wydawnicza Politechniki Wroclawskiej, p. 501-510

Kucera, P., Zezulka, F., Sveda, M., & Vrba, R. (2002). Executable specifications for Process Automation and Microelectronics. *IEEE TC-ECBS and IFIP WG10.1 Joint Workshop on Formal Specifications of Computer-Based Systems.* Lund, University of Stirling, p. 91-98.

Kulikowski, R. (1965). *Optimal and adaptive processes in control systems, Monographs of Polish Academy of Sciences, Section of Automatics.* Warsaw: PWN. (in Polish)

Kuncheva, L. I., Whitaker, C. J., & Shipp, C. A. (2003). Limits on the majority vote accuracy in classifier fusion. *Pattern Analysis & Applications, 6,* 22–31. doi:10.1007/s10044-002-0173-7

Lai, C., Tax, D. M. J., Duin, R. P. W., Pekalska, E., & Paclik, P. (2004). A study on combining image representations for image classification and retrieval. *International Journal of Pattern Recognition and Artificial Intelligence, 18*(5), World Scientific Publishing, 867-890.

Lakshmivarahan, S. (1981). *Learning Algorithms Theory and Applications.* New York: Springer-Verlag.

Lakshmivarahan, S., & Thathachar, M. A. L. (1973). Absolutely Expedient Algorithms for Stochastic Automata. *IEEE Transactions on Systems, Man, and Cybernetics, SMC-3,* 281–286.

Lamdan, Y., Schwartz, J. T., & Wolfson, H. J. (1990). Affine invariant model-based object recognition. *IEEE Transactions on Robotics and Automation, 5*(6), 578–589. doi:10.1109/70.62047

Lamdan, Y., & Wolfson, H. J. (1988, December). *Geometric hashing: a general and efficient model-based recognition scheme.* Paper presented at ICCV, Tampa, Florida.

Lanctot, J. K., & Oommen, B. J. (1992). Discretized Estimator Learning Automata. *IEEE Transactions on Systems, Man, and Cybernetics, 22*(6), 1473–1483. doi:10.1109/21.199471

Lane, C., & Bachmann, R. (1996). The social constitution of trust: supplier relations in Britain and Germany. *Organization Studies, 17*(3), 365–395. doi:10.1177/017084069601700302

Lane, C., & Bachmann, R. (Eds.). (1998). *Trust within and between organizations.* Oxford, UK: Oxford UP.

Lane, C. (2001). Organizational learning in supplier networks. In Dierkes, M., Antal, A. B., Child, J., & Nonaka, I. (Eds.), *Handbook of organizational learning and knowledge* (pp. 699–715). Oxford: Oxford UP.

Lane, C. (1995). The social constitution of supplier relations in Britain and Germany. In Withley, R., & Kristensen, P. H. (Eds.), *The changing European firm* (pp. 271–304). London: Routledge.

Lankhorst, M. (2005). *Enterprise Architecture at Work: Modelling, Communication, and Analysis.* New York: Springer.

Lánský, P., & Sato, S. (1999). The stochastic diffusion models of nerve membrane depolarization and interspike interval generation. *Journal of the Peripheral Nervous System, 4,* 27–42.

Lant, T. K. (2002). Organizational cognition and interpretation. In Baum, J. A. C. (Ed.), *Companion to organizations* (pp. 344–362). Oxford: Blackwell.

Larin, V., Torcunov, A., Zhukov, A., González, J., Vazquez, M., & Panina, L. (2002). Preparation and properties of glass-coated microwires. *Journal of Magnetism and Magnetic Materials, 249*(1-2), 39–45. doi:10.1016/S0304-8853(02)00501-2

Larkowski, T., Linden, J. G., Vinsonneau, B., & Burnham, K. J. (2009). Frisch scheme identification for dynamic diagonal bilinear models. *International Journal of Control, 82*(9), 1591–1604. doi:10.1080/00207170802596280

Larkowski, T. M. (2009). *Extended algorithms for the errors-in-variables identification.* Doctoral dissertation, Coventry University, UK.

Larkowski, T., Zajic, I., Linden, J. G., Burnham, K. J., & Hill, D. (2009). Identification of a dehumidification process of the heating, ventilation and air conditioning system using bias compensated least squares approach. In *Proc. CD-ROM Int. Conf. Systems Engineering ICSE 2009* (pp. 296-305). Coventry University, UK.

Lascelles, D. M., & Dale, B. G. (1989). The buyer-supplier relationship in total quality management. *Journal of Purchasing Material Management, 25*, 10–19.

Latecki, L. J., & Lakaemper, R. (1999). Convexity rule for shape decomposition based on Discrete Contour Evolution. *Computer Vision and Image Understanding, 3*(73), 441–454. doi:10.1006/cviu.1998.0738

Lawson, M. B. (2001). In praise of slack: time is the essence. *The Academy of Management Executive, 15*(3), 125–135.

Lee, M. (2001). Profiling students adaptation styles in web-based learning. *Computers & Education, 36*(2), 121–132. doi:10.1016/S0360-1315(00)00046-4

Lee, H., Park, J., & Chen, G. (2001). Robust fuzzy control of nonlinear systems with parametric uncertainties. *IEEE Transactions on Fuzzy Systems, 9*(2), 369–379. doi:10.1109/91.919258

Lee, C. C. (1990). Fuzzy logic in control systems: fuzzy logic controller – Part I & Part II. *IEEE Transactions on Systems, Man, and Cybernetics, 20*(2), 404–435. doi:10.1109/21.52551

Leibenstein, H. (1966). Allocative Efficiency vs. "X-Efficiency. *The American Economic Review, 56*(3), 392–416.

Leibenstein, H. (1987). *Inside the firm: the inefficiencies of hierarchy.* Cambridge, MA: Harvard UP.

Leonards, U., Singer, W., & Fahle, M. (1996). The influence of temporal phase differences on texture segmentation. *Vision Research, 36*(17), 2689–2697. doi:10.1016/0042-6989(96)86829-5

Łęski, J. (2008). *Neuro-Fuzzy Systems.* Warsaw, Poland: WNT.

Levinthal, D., & March, J. G. (1993). The myopia of learning. *Strategic Management Journal, 14*, 95–112. doi:10.1002/smj.4250141009

Li, Y., Vanhaverbeke, W., & Schoenmakers, W. (2008). Exploration and exploitation in innovation: reframing the interpretation. *Creativity and Innovation Management, 17*(2), 107–126. doi:10.1111/j.1467-8691.2008.00477.x

Li, J., Niemann, D., Wang, H., & Tanaka, K. (1999). Parallel distributed compensation for takagi-sugeno fuzzy models: multiobjective controller design. In *Proceedings of the 1999 American control conference,* (Vol. 3, pp. 1832–1836 vol.3).

Linden, J. G. (2005). *Regularisation techniques and cautious least squares in parameter estimation for model based control.* (Masters dissertation), Coventry University, UK.

Linden, J. G. (2008). *Algorithms for recursive Frish scheme identification and errors-in-variables filtering.* Doctoral dissertation, Coventry University, UK.

Liptser, R. Sh., & Shiryaev, A. N. (1978). *Statistics of Stochastic Processes.* New York: Springer-Verlag.

Lisowski, J. (1981). *Ship as an object of automatic control.* Gdańsk, Poland: Wydawnictwo Morskie.

Liu, X., & Zhang, Q. (2003, September). New approaches to H_∞ controller designs based on fuzzy observers for t-s fuzzy systems via lmi. *Automatica*, *39*(9), 1571–1582. doi:10.1016/S0005-1098(03)00172-9

Ljung, L. (1999). *System Identification – Theory for the user* (2nd ed.). Upper Saddle River, NJ: Prentice Hall.

Llerena, P., & Matt, M. (Eds.). (2004). *Innovation Policy in a Knowledge-Based Economy Theory and Practice*. Heidelberg, Germany: Springer.

Llinás, R., Ribary, U., Joliot, M., & Wang, X.-J. (1994). Content and Context in Temporal Thalamocortical Binding. In Buzsáki, G., Llinás, R., Singer, W., Berthoz, A., & Christen, Y. (Eds.), *Temporal Coding in the Brain* (pp. 251–272). Berlin: Springer-Verlag.

Love, G. E., & Nohria, N. (2005). Reducing Slack: The Performance Consequences of Downsizing by Large Industrial Firms, 1977-93. *Strategic Management Journal*, *26*(12), 1087–1108. doi:10.1002/smj.487

Lowe, D. G. (1991). Fitting parameterized three-dimensional models to images. *IEEE Transactions on Pattern Analysis and Machine Intelligence*, *5*(13), 441–450. doi:10.1109/34.134043

Lowe, D. G. (2004). Distinctive image features from scale-invariant keypoints. *International Journal of Computer Vision*, *2*(60), 91–110. doi:10.1023/B:VISI.0000029664.99615.94

Lowe, D. G. (1999, September). *Object recognition from local scale-invariant features*. Paper presented at the International Conference on Computer Vision, Corfu, Greece.

Lowe, D. G. (2001). *Local feature view clustering for 3D object recognition*. Paper presented at the IEEE Conference on Computer Vision and Pattern Recognition, Kauai, Hawaii.

Lu, J., Yu, C. S., & Liu, C. (2003). Learning style, learning patterns, and learning performance in a WebCT-based MIS course. *Information & Management*, *40*(6), 497–507. doi:10.1016/S0378-7206(02)00064-2

Lyu, R. M. (Ed.). (1995). *Software fault tolerance*. Chichester, UK: John Wiley & Sons, Inc.

Maber, V. A. (2007). The early road to material requirements planning. *Journal of Operations Management*, *25*, 346–356. doi:10.1016/j.jom.2006.04.002

Maciejowski, J. M. (2002). *Predictive Control with Constraints*. Harlow, UK: Prentice-Hall.

MacKay, D. M. (1962). Self-organization in the time domain. In Yovitts, M. C., Jacobi, G. T., & Goldstein, G. D. (Eds.), *Self-Organizing Systems* (pp. 37–48). Washington: Spartan Books.

Mackworth, A. K. (1977). Consistency in networks of relations. *Artificial Intelligence*, *8*, 99–118. doi:10.1016/0004-3702(77)90007-8

MacLeod, K., Bäcker, A., & Laurent, G. (1998). Who reads temporal information contained across synchronized and oscillatory spike trains? *Nature*, *395*, 693–698. doi:10.1038/27201

MacQueen, J. B. (1967). Some methods for classification and analysis of multivariate observations. In *Proceedings of 5-th Berkeley Symposium on Mathematical Statistics and Probability* (Vol. 1, pp. 281-297). Berkeley, CA: University of California Press.

Mahadevan, S., & Connell, J. (1991). Automatic programming of behavior-based robots using reinforcement learning. In *Proceedings of the 9th National Conference on Artificial Intelligenc* (pp. 768-773). Anaheim CA.

Maimone, M., Biesiadecki, J., Tunstel, E., Cheng, Y., & Leger, C. (2006). Surface navigation and mobility intelligence on the Mars Exploration Rovers, chapter 3, 45-69. TSI Press, San Antonio, TX.

Maki, Y., & Loparo, K. A. (1997). A neural-network approach to fault detection and diagnosis in industrial processes. *IEEE Transactions on Control Systems Technology*, *5*(6), 529–541. doi:10.1109/87.641399

Malerba, F. (2004). *Sectoral Systems of Innovation*. Cambridge, UK: Cambridge University Press. doi:10.1017/CBO9780511493270

Malerba, F., & Brusoni, S. (2007). *Perspectives on Innovation*. Cambridge, UK: Cambridge University Press. doi:10.1017/CBO9780511618390

Malerba, F., & Cantner, U. (2007). *Innovation, Industrial Dynamics and Structural Transformation*. Heidelberg, Germany: Springer.

March, J. G. (1988). *Decisions and organizations*. Oxford, UK: Basil Blackwell.

March, J. G. (1991). Exploration and Exploitation in organizational learning. *Organization Science, 2*, 71–87. doi:10.1287/orsc.2.1.71

March, J. G. (1997). Understanding How Decisions Happens in Organizations. In Shapira, Z. (Ed.), *Organizational Decision Making* (pp. 9–34). Cambridge, MA: Cambridge UP.

Marin, R., Cardenas, M., Balsa, M., & Sanchez, J. (1997). Obtaining solutions in fuzzy constraint networks. *International Journal of Approximate Reasoning, 16*, 261–288. doi:10.1016/S0888-613X(96)00125-9

Martineau, S., Burnham, K. J., Haas, O. C. L., Andrews, G., & Heely, A. (2004). Four-term bilinear PID controller applied to an industrial furnace. *Control Engineering Practice, 12*(4), 457–464. doi:10.1016/S0967-0661(03)00147-3

Martineau, S. (2004). *Nonlinear model-based control system design with application to industrial furnaces*. (Doctoral dissertation), Coventry University, UK.

Martinez-Lorente, A. R., Galliego-Rodriguez, A., & Dale, B. G. (1998). Total quality management and company characteristics: an examination. *Quality Management Journal, 5*, 59–71.

Mas-Colell, A., Whinston, M. D., & Green, J. R. (1995). *Microeconomic Theory*. New York: Oxford University Press.

Matuszek J., Kukla S., Plinta D. (2006). *Use of modelling and simulation techniques in the management of logistic chain. Applied Computer Science, 2*(1).

Maulik, U., & Bandyopadhyay, S. (2002). Performance evaluation of some clustering algorithms and validity indices. *IEEE Transactions on Pattern Analysis and Machine Intelligence, 24*(12), 1650–1654. doi:10.1109/TPAMI.2002.1114856

McCraw, Th. K. (2007). *Prophet of Innovation: Joseph Schumpeter and Creative Destruction*. Cambridge, MA: Harvard University Press.

Meneganti, M., Saviello, F. S., & Tagliaferri, R. (1998). Fuzzy neural networks for classification and detection of anomalies. *IEEE Transactions on Neural Networks, 9*(5), 848–861. doi:10.1109/72.712157

Metenidis, M. F., Witczak, M., & Korbicz, J. (2004). A novel genetic programming approach to non-linear system modelling: Application to the DAMADICS benchmark problem. *Engineering Applications of Artificial Intelligence, 17*(4), 363–370. doi:10.1016/j.engappai.2004.04.009

Meyer, A. D. (1982). Adapting to environmental jolts. *Administrative Science Quarterly, 27*(4), 515–537. doi:10.2307/2392528

Meyn, S. P., & Tweedie, R. L. (1993). *Markov Chains and Stochastic Stability*. London, U.K: Springer-Verlag.

Michalski, R., Carbonell, J., & Mitchell, T. (1986). *Machine learning: An artificial intelligence approach* (*Vol. I*). Los Altos, CA: Kaufman Publishers Inc.

Miles, R. (1990). Synaptic excitation of inhibitory cells by single CA3 hyppocampal pyramidal cells of the guinea-pig in vitro. *The Journal of Physiology, 428*, 61.

MIL-HDBK-217. (1995). *Military Handbook for "Reliability Prediction of Electronic Equipment"*. US Department of Defense, NY. Retrieved from http://assist.daps.dla.mil/quicksearch/basic_profile.cfm?ident_number=53939

Minihan, J. A. (2001). *Design of bilinear controllers for industrial plant*. (Doctoral dissertation), Coventry University, UK.

Moczala, A. (1996): *Multi-criteria optimization of designing production processes*, Ph.D. thesis, Łódź Technical University, Branch of Bielsko-Biała, Poland

Moczala, A. (2006). *Designing Production Processes With Computer Aided Cooperation*. 18 International Scientific Conference in Mittweida, Germany

Moczala, A. (2007): *Computer Aided Cooperation*, EUROPEAN ICT CONFERENCE - On Research and Technology Development, Seventh Framework Program (7 FP), Organized under: European Commission, EASIER and CORDIS, Istanbul, Turkey, 29 - 30 January 2007

Mohamed, F., & Koivo, H. (2007) System Modelling and Online Optimal Management of MicroGrid with Battery Storage. In *Proceedings of 6th International Conference on Renewable Energies and Power Quality* Sevilla, Spain.

Mohler, R. R. (1970). Natural bilinear control processes. *IEEE Trans. Systems Science and Cybernetics, 6*, 192–197. doi:10.1109/TSSC.1970.300341

Mohler, R. R. (1973). *Bilinear Control Processes. Mathematics in Science and Engineering 106*. New York: Academic Press.

Moller, K., Rajala, A., & Svahn, S. (2005). Strategic business nets—their type and management. *Journal of Business Research, 58*, 1274–1284. doi:10.1016/j.jbusres.2003.05.002

Morant, F., Albertos, P., Martinez, M., Crespo, A., & Navarro, J. (1992). RIGAS: An intelligent controller for cement kiln control. In *Proc. IFAC Symp. Artif. Intelligence in Real Time Control.* Delft, The Netherlands: Elsevier.

Morris, P., & Muscettola, N. (2000). Execution of temporal plans with uncertainty. *AAAI, 2000*, 491–496.

Mouhoub, M. (2004). Handling Numeric and Symbolic Time Information. *Artificial Intelligence Review, 21*, 25–56. doi:10.1023/B:AIRE.0000007179.60276.39

Muramatsu, J. (2002). On the Performance of Recency Rank and Block Sorting Universal Lossless Data Compression Algorithms. *IEEE Transactions on Information Theory, 48*(9), 2621–2625. doi:10.1109/TIT.2002.801477

Narasimhan, R., & Mendez, D. (2001). Strategic aspects of quality: a theoretical analysis. *Production and Operations Management, 10*, 514–526.

Narendra, K., & Thathachar, M. (1989). *Learning Automata. An Introduction.* Upper Saddle River, NJ: Prentice Hall.

Narvydas, G., & Raudonis, V. (2008). *Combining an expert cloning technique and evolutionary algorithm for autonomous mobile robot control. Selected papers of the 3rd international conference Electrical and Control Technologies* (pp. 23–28). Kaunas: Technologija.

Narvydas, G., Simutis, R., & Raudonis, V. (2008). Autonomous mobile robot control using "If-then" rules and genetic algorithm. *Information technology and control, 3(37)*, 193-197.

Nawrot, M. P., Boucsein, C., Rodriguez-Molina, V., Aertsen, A., Grün, S., & Rotter, S. (2007). Serial interval statistics of spontaneous activity in cortical neurons *in vivo* and *in vitro*. *Neurocomputing, 70*, 1717–1722. doi:10.1016/j.neucom.2006.10.101

Nawrot, M. P., Boucsein, C., Rodriguez-Molina, V., Riehle, A., Aertsen, A., & Rotter, S. (2008). Measurement of variabiility dynamics in cortical spike trains. *Journal of Neuroscience Methods, 169*, 374–390. doi:10.1016/j.jneumeth.2007.10.013

Nelles, O. (2001). *Nonlinear system identification.* New York: Springer.

Nohria, N., & Gulati, R. (1997). What is the Optimum Amount of Organizational Slack? A Study of the Relationship between Slack and Innovation in Multinational Firms. *European Management Journal, 15*(6), 603–611. doi:10.1016/S0263-2373(97)00044-3

Nolfi, S., & Floreano, D. (2000). *Evolutionary robotics: The biology, intelligence, and technology of self-organizing machines.* Cambridge, MA: The MIT Press.

Nonaka, I., & Takeuchi, H. (1995). *The Knowledge-Creating Company.* New York: Oxford University Press.

Nonaka, I., Toyama, R., & Konno, N. (2000). SECI, Ba and Leadership: a Unified Model of Dynamic Knowledge Creation. *Long Range Planning, 33*, 5–34. doi:10.1016/S0024-6301(99)00115-6

Nonaka, I., & Nishiguchi, T. (Eds.). (2001). *Knowledge emergence: social, technical, and evolutionary dimensions of knowledge creation.* Oxford, UK: Oxford UP.

Nonaka, I., & Takeuchi, H. (1995). *The Knowledge-creating company.* New York: Oxford UP.

Norris, J. (1999). *Markov chains.* New York: Springer.

OECD. (2003). *The Measurement of Scientific and Technological Activities. Frascati Manual 2002. Proposed Standard Practice for Surveys on Research and Experimental Development.* New York: OECD Publishing.

OECD. (2005). *Oslo Manual - Guidelines for collecting and interpreting innovation data.* (Third edition, 2005). A joint publication of OECD and Eurostat

Ohno, T. (1988). *Toyota production system: beyond large-scale production.* New York: Productivity Press.

Oliveira, M. d., Bernussou, J., & Geromel, J. (1999). A new discrete-time robust stability condition. *Systems & Control Letters, 37*, 261–265. doi:10.1016/S0167-6911(99)00035-3

Oommen, B. (1986). Absorbing and Ergodic Discretized Two-Action Learning Automata. *IEEE Transactions on Systems, Man, and Cybernetics, SMC-16*, 282–296.

Oommen, B., & Christensen, J. R. P. (1988). Epsilon-Optimal Discretized Reward-Penalty Learning Automata. *IEEE Transactions on Systems, Man, and Cybernetics, SMC-18*, 451–458. doi:10.1109/21.7494

Oommen, B., & Lanctot, J. K. (1990). Discretized Pursuit Learning Automata. *IEEE Transactions on Systems, Man, and Cybernetics, 20*(4), 931–938. doi:10.1109/21.105092

Oommen, B. J., & Rueda, L. (2006). Stochastic Learning-based Weak Estimation of Multinomial Random Variables and Its Applications to Non-stationary Environments. *Pattern Recognition, 39*, 328–341. doi:10.1016/j.patcog.2005.09.007

Oommen, B., & Agache, M. (2001). Continuous and Discretized Pursuit Learning Stochastic Learning-based Weak Estimation of Multinomial Random Variables and Its Applications to Pattern Schemes: Various Algorithms and Their Comparison. *IEEE Trans. on Systems, Man and Cybernetics, SMC-31(B)*, 277-287.

Oommen, B., & Rueda, L. (2004). A New Family of Weak Estimators for Training in Non-stationary Distributions. In *Proceedings of the Joint IAPR International Workshops SSPR 2004 and SPR 2004* (pp. 644-652). Lisbon, Portugal.

Palm, R. (1994). Robust control by fuzzy sliding mode. *Automatica, 30*, 1429–1429. doi:10.1016/0005-1098(94)90008-6

Palmero, G. I. S., Santamaria, J. J., de la Torre, E. J. M., & Gonzalez, J. R. P. (2005). Fault detection and fuzzy rule extraction in AC motors by a neuro-fuzzy ART-based system. [Amsterdam: Elsevier.]. *Engineering Applications of Artificial Intelligence, 18*, 867–874. doi:10.1016/j.engappai.2005.02.005

Passino, K. M., & Yurkovich, S. (1998). *Fuzzy control.* Reading, MA: Addison-Wesley Longman.

Patan, K., & Parisini, T. (2005). Identification of neural dynamic models for fault detection and isolation: the case of a real sugar evaporation process. *Journal of Process Control, 15*(1), 67–79. doi:10.1016/j.jprocont.2004.04.001

Patan, K., Witczak, K., & Korbicz, J. (2008). Toward robustness in neural network based fault diagnosis. *International Journal of Applied Mathematics and Computer Science, 18*(4), 443–454. doi:10.2478/v10006-008-0039-2

Patton, R. J., & Chen, J. (1997). Observer-based fault detection and isolation: robustness and applications. *Control Engineering Practice, 5*(5), 671–682. doi:10.1016/S0967-0661(97)00049-X

Patton, R. J., Chen, J., & Siew, T. M. (1994). Fault diagnosis in nonlinear dynamic systems via neural networks. In [Warwick, UK.]. *Proceedings of the IEE International Conference: Control, 94*, 1346–1351.

Patton, R. J., Frank, P. M., & Clark, R. N. (Eds.). (2000). *Issues of Fault Diagnosis for Dynamic Systems.* London: Springer-Verlag.

Patyra, M., Grantner, J., & Koster, K. (1996). Digital fuzzy logic controller. Design and implementation. *IEEE Transactions on Fuzzy Systems, 4*(4), 439–459. doi:10.1109/91.544304

Peintner, B., Venable, K. B., & Yorke-Smith, N. (2007). *Strong Controllability of Disjunctive Temporal Problems with Uncertainty. CP 2007,* 856–863.

Penczek, W., & Pólrola, A. (2006). *Advances in Verification of Time Petri Nets and Timed Automata: A Temporal Logic Approach* (1st ed.). Springer.

Peterka, V. (1970). Adaptive digital regulation of noisy systems. In *Proceedings IFAC Symposium on Identification and Process Parameter Estimation,* Prague.

Piater, J. H., Riseman, E. M., & Utgoff, P. E. (1999). Interactively training pixel classifiers,''. *International Journal of Pattern Recognition and Artificial Intelligence, 13*(2), 171–194. doi:10.1142/S0218001499000112

Piater, J. H., Stuchlik, F., von Specht, H., & Mühler, R. (1995). Fuzzy sets for feature identification in biomedical signals with self-assessment of reliability: An adaptable algorithm modeling human procedure in BAEP analysis. *Computers and Biomedical Research, an International Journal, 28,* 335–353. doi:10.1006/cbmr.1995.1023

Plackett, R. L. (1950). Some theorems in least squares. *Biometrika, 37,* 149–157.

Poli, R., & Langdon, W. B. (1997, June) *Genetic programming with one-point crossover.* In P. K. Chawdhry, R. Roy, and R. K. Pant (Ed.) *Second On-line World Conference on Soft Computing in Engineering Design and Manufacturing.* Springer-Verlag London, 23-27.

Pope, A. R., & Lowe, D. G. (2004). Probabilistic models of appearance for 3-D object recognition. *International Journal of Computer Vision, 2*(40), 149–167.

Porter, L. L., & Passino, K. M. (1995). Genetic Adaptive Observers. *Engineering Applications of Artificial Intelligence, 8*(3), 261–269. doi:10.1016/0952-1976(95)00007-N

Prajna, S., Papachristodoulou, A., & Wu, F. (2004). Nonlinear control synthesis by sum of squares optimization: a Lyapunov-based approach. *Control Conference, 2004. 5th Asian, 1.*

Prajna, S., Papachristodoulou, A., Seiler, P., & Parrilo, P. A. (2004). *SOSTOOLS: Sum of squares optimization toolbox for MATLAB.* Retrieved from http://www.cds.caltech.edu/sostools and http://www.mit.edu/~parrilo/sostools.

Pratt, W. K. (2001). *Digital image processing.* New York: John Wiley & Sons. doi:10.1002/0471221325

Press, W. H., Teukolsky, S. A., Vetterling,, W. T., & Flannery, B. P. (1992). *Numerical recipes in C. The art of scientific computing.* Cambridge, UK: Cambridge University Press.

Pullum, L. L. (2001). *Software Fault Tolerance Techniques and Implementation.* Norwood, MA: Artech House, Inc.

Questionnaire, I. L. S. (2009). *ILS Questionnaire.* Retrieved March 20, 2009 from http://www.engr.ncsu.edu/learningstyles/ilsweb.html

Rajaraman, K., & Sastry, P. S. (1996). Finite Time Analysis of the Pursuit Algorithm for Learning Automata. *IEEE Transactions on Systems, Man, and Cybernetics, 26*(4), 590–598. doi:10.1109/3477.517033

Ralston, A. (1965). *A first course in numerical analysis.* New York: McGraw-Hill Book Company.

Ramirez, M., & Albertos, P. (2008). Pid control with fuzzy adaptation of a metallurgical furnace. In *Granular Computing* (*Vol. 224*). At the Junction of Rough Sets and Fuzzy Sets. Springer.

Ramirez, W. (1994). *Process control and identification.* New York: Academic Press.

Ramírez, M., Haber, R., Peña, V., & Rodríguez, I. (2004). Fuzzy control of a multiple hearth furnace. *IEEE Computers in Industry, 54,* 105–113. doi:10.1016/j.compind.2003.05.001

Randall, A., & Burnham, K. J. (1994). Cautious identification in self-tuning control – an information filtering alternative. *J. System Science, 20*(2), 55–69.

Randall, A., Burnham, K. J., & James, D. J. G. (1991). A study of Kalman filtering techniques for joint state and parameter estimation in self-tuning control. *J. Systems Science, 17*(3), 31–43.

Ratnam, R., & Nelson, M. E. (2000). Nonrenewal Statistics of Electrosensory Afferent Spike Trains: Implications for the Detection of Weak Sensory Signals. *The Journal of Neuroscience, 20*(17), 672–6683.

Ray, B., & Tsay, R. (2002). Bayesian Methods for Change-point Detection in Long-range Dependent Processes. *Journal of Time Series Analysis, 23*(6), 687–705. doi:10.1111/1467-9892.00286

Ricciardi, L. M. (1977). Diffusion Processes and Related Topics in Biology. In *Lecture Notes in Biomathematics, 14.* Berlin: Springer.

Richtner, A., & Åhlström, P. (2006). Influences on organizational slack in new product development. *International Journal of Innovation Management, 10*(4), 375–406. doi:10.1142/S1363919606001570

Ripley, B. D. (1996). *Pattern recognition and neural networks.* Cambridge, UK: Cambridge University Press.

Rishel, R. (1986). An exact formula for a linear quadratic adaptive stochastic optimal control law. *SIAM Journal on Control and Optimization, 24*(4), 667–674. doi:10.1137/0324040

Riva Sanseverino, E., Pecoraro, G., Borghetti, A., Bosetti, M., & Paolone, M. (2007). Optimal Operating Point Calculation for Medium Voltage Distribution Systems In *Proceedings IEEE Power Tech 2007* Lausanne, Switzerland.

Robin, V., Rose, B., & Girard, P. (2007). Modelling collaborative knowledge to support engineering design project manager. *Computers in Industry, 58,* 188–198. doi:10.1016/j.compind.2006.09.006

Romero, C., & Ventura, S. (Eds.). (2006). *Data mining in e-learning.* Boston, MA: WIT Press. doi:10.2495/1-84564-152-3

Romero, C., & Ventura, S. (2007). Educational data mining: a survey from 1995 to 2005. *Expert Systems with Applications, 33*(1), 135–146. doi:10.1016/j.eswa.2006.04.005

Romero, C., Ventura, S., & Garcia, E. (2008). Data mining in course management systems: Moodle case study and tutorial. *Computers & Education, 51*(1), 368–384. doi:10.1016/j.compedu.2007.05.016

Roy, R. V., & Guin, K. K. (1999). A 'proposed model of JIT purchasing in an integrated steel plant. *International Journal of Production Economics, 59,* 179–187. doi:10.1016/S0925-5273(98)00099-1

Rudolph, M., & Destexhe, A. (2003). Tuning neocortical pyramidal neurons between integrators and coincidence detectors. *Journal of Computational Neuroscience, 14,* 239–251. doi:10.1023/A:1023245625896

Rueda, L., & Oommen, B. J. (2004). A Nearly Optimal Fano-Based Coding Algorithm. *Information Processing & Management, 40*(2), 257–268. doi:10.1016/S0306-4573(03)00007-4

Rueda, L., & Oommen, B. J. (2006). Stochastic Automata-based Estimators fro Adaptively Compressing Files with Nonstationary Distributions. *IEEE Transactions on Systems, Man, and Cybernetics, 36*(5), 1196–1200. doi:10.1109/TSMCB.2006.872256

Rueda, L. (2002). *Advances in Data Compression and Pattern Recognition.* (PhD Thesis), School of Computer Science, Carleton University, Ottawa. Canada.

Rueda, L., & Oommen, B. J. (2002, March). Greedy Adaptive Fano Coding. In *Proceedings of the 2002 IEEE Aerospace Conference.* BigSky, MT, USA. Track 10.0407.

Russell, S., & Norvig, P. (2003). *Artificial intelligence: a modern approach* (2nd ed.). Prentice-Hall.

Rutkowski, L. (2006). *Methods and Techniques of Artificial Intelligence. Computational Intelligence.* Warsaw, Poland: WNT.

Ryabov, V., & Trudel, A. (2004). *Probabilistic temporal interval networks.* In *TIME 2004*, pp. 64–67. Tsamardinos, Vidal, T. & Pollack, M.E. (2003). *CTP: A New Constraint-Based Formalism for Conditional Temporal Planning. Constraints, 8*(4), 365–388.

Saarikoski, L., Salojärvi, S., Del Corso, D., & Ovein, E. (2001). The 3DE: an environment for the development of learner-oriented customized educational packages. In *Proceedings of ITHET01.* Kumamoto, Japan.

Saha, G. K. (2006). Software implemented hardware - transient fault detection. *International Scientific Journal of Computing, 5*(1), 1–11.

Sala, A. (2007). *Reducing the gap between fuzzy and nonlinear control (invited talk). In 3rd ifac workshop on advanced fuzzy-neural control afnc'07* (pp. 1–6). Valenciennes, France.

Sala, A. (2008). Encoding fuzzy possibilistic diagnostics as a constrained optimization problem. *Information Sciences, 178,* 4246–4263. doi:10.1016/j.ins.2008.07.017

Sala, A. (2009). On the conservativeness of fuzzy and fuzzy-polynomial control of nonlinear systems. *Annual Reviews in Control, 33*(1), 48–58. doi:10.1016/j.arcontrol.2009.02.001

Sala, A., & Albertos, P. (1998). Fuzzy Systems Evaluation: The Inference Error Approach. *IEEE Trans. on Systems Man and Cybernetics. Part B, 28,* 268–275.

Sala, A., & Albertos, P. (1999). Formal Validation Of Fuzzy Control Techniques. *Mathware & Soft Computing, 6,* 305–317.

Sala, A., & Ariño, C. (2007). Assymptotically necessary and sufficient conditions for stability and performance in fuzzy control: Applications of Polya's theorem. *Fuzzy Sets and Systems, 158*(4), 2671–2686. doi:10.1016/j.fss.2007.06.016

Sala, A., & Ariño, C. (2009). (Accepted). Polynomial fuzzy models for nonlinear control. *IEEE Transactions on Fuzzy Systems.* doi:10.1109/TFUZZ.2009.2029235

Sala, A., Diez, J., Navarro, J., & Albertos, P. (2004). Fuzzy Model Usage And Readability In Identification For Control. In *6th biannual world automation congresos wac'04* (pp. 13–18). Seville (Spain): Tsi Press.

Sanner, R., & Slotine, J. E. (1992). Gaussian networks for direct adaptive control. *IEEE Transactions on Neural Networks, 3*(6), 837–863. doi:10.1109/72.165588

Santo, M. D., Percannella, G., Sansone, C., & Vento, M. (2004). A multi-expert approach for shot classification in news videos. In *Image analysis and recognition, LNCS* (Vol. 3211, pp. 564-571). Amsterdam: Elsevier.

Saridis, G. N. (1981). Application of Pattern Recognition Methods to Control Systems. *IEEE Transactions on Automatic Control,* 638–645. doi:10.1109/TAC.1981.1102685

Saridis, G. N. (1988). Entropy formulation of optimal and adaptive control. *IEEE Transactions on Automatic Control, 33,* 713–721. doi:10.1109/9.1287

Schweizer, M., Becherer, D., & Amendinger, J. (2003). A monetary value for initial information in portfolio optimization. *Finance and Stochastics, 7*(1), 29–46. doi:10.1007/s007800200075

Segundo, J. P., Perkel, D., Wyman, H., Hegstad, H., & Moore, G. P. (1968). Input-output relations in computer-simulated nerve cell. *Kybernetic, 4,* 157–171. doi:10.1007/BF00289038

Shapiro, C., & Varian, H. (1999). *Information rules: a strategic guide to the network economy.* Boston: Harvard Business School Press.

Sharfman, M. P., Wolf, G., Chase, R. B., & Tansik, D. A. (1988). Antecedents of Organizational Slack. *Academy of Management Review, 13*(4), 601–614. doi:10.2307/258378

Sieńko, W., Citko, W., & Jakóbczak, D. (2004). Learning and system modeling via Hamiltonian Neural Networks. In Rutkowski, L., Siekmann, J., Tadeusiewicz, R., & Zadeh, A. (Eds.), *Lecture notes on artificial intelligence: Artificial intelligence and soft computing - ICAISC 2004* (pp. 266–271). Berlin - Heidelberg, Germany: Springer - Verlag.

Sieńko, W., & Citko, W. (2002). *Hamiltonian Neural Net based signal processing.* Paper presented at the International Conference on Signal and Electronic System ICSES, Wrocław – Świeradów Zdrój, Poland.

Sieńko, W., Citko, W., & Wilamowski, B. (2002). *Hamiltonian Neural Nets as a universal signal processor.* Paper presented at the 28th Annual Conference of the IEEE Industrial Electronics Society IECON, Sevilla, Spain.

Siler, W., & Buckley, J. J. (2005). *Fuzzy expert systems and fuzzy reasoning.* Hoboken, NJ: John Wiley & Sons.

Simon, H. A. (1982). Models of Bounded Rationality: *Vol. 1.2: Empirically Grounded Economic Reason.* Cambridge, MA: The MIT Press.

Simon, H. A. (1991). Bounded rationality and organizational learning. *Organization Science, 2*(1), 125–134. doi:10.1287/orsc.2.1.125

Simon, H. A. (1997). Models of Bounded Rationality: *Vol. 3. Empirically Grounded Economic Reason.* Cambridge, MA: The MIT Press.

Singh, J. V. (1986). Performance, Slack, and Risk Taking in Organizational Decision Making. *Academy of Management Journal, 29*(3), 562–565. doi:10.2307/256224

Skogestad, S., & Postlethwaite, I. (2005). *Multivariable feedback control: analysis and design.* New York: John Wiley & Sons.

Slotine, J. E., & Li, W. (1991). *Applied Nonlinear control.* Englewood Cliffs, NJ: Prentice Hall.

Smith, K., Everson, R., & Fieldsend, J. (2004). Dominance measures for multi-objective simulated annealing. In *Proceedings IEEE Conference on Evolutionary Computation. 2004* (23–30).

Socha, K., & Dorigo, M. (2005). *Ant Colony Optimization for Continuous Domains, IRIDIA* (pp. 1–36). Technical Report Series.

Softky, W. R., & Koch, C. (1993). The highly irregular firing of cortical cells is inconsistent with temporal integration of random EPSPs. *The Journal of Neuroscience, 13,* 334–350.

Sohlberg, B. (1998). Monitoring and failure diagnosis of a steel strip process. *IEEE Transactions on Control Systems Technology, 6*(2), 294–303. doi:10.1109/87.664195

Soussen, C., & Mohammad-Djafari, A. (2004). Polygonal and polyhedral contour reconstruction in computed tomography. *IEEE Transactions on Image Processing, 11*(13), 1507–1523. doi:10.1109/TIP.2004.836159

Spooner, J. T., & Passino, K. M. (1996). Stable adaptive control using fuzzy systems and neural networks. *IEEE Transactions on Fuzzy Systems, 4*(3), 339–359. doi:10.1109/91.531775

Srikant, R., & Agrawal, R. (1995). Mining generalized association rules. In *21st International Conference on Very Large Databases, Zurich, Switzerland* (pp. 407–419). Washington, DC: IEEE Press.

Srinivas, N., & Deb, K. (1994). Multiobjective optimization using nondominated sorting in genetic algorithms. *Journal Evolutionary Computation, 2*(3), 221–248. doi:10.1162/evco.1994.2.3.221

Stash, N., Cristea, A., & De Bra, P. (2004). Authoring of learning styles in adaptive hypermedia: Problems and solutions. In *Proceedings of the Thirteenth International World Wide Web Conference* (pp. 114-123). New York: ACM Press.

Stigler, G. J. (1961). The Economics of Information. *The Journal of Political Economy, 69*(3), 213–225. doi:10.1086/258464

Sutton, R., Taylor, S., & Roberts, G. (1996). Neuro-Fuzzy Techniques Applied to a Ship Autopilot Design. *Journal of Navigation*, *49*(03), 410–430. doi:10.1017/S037346330001362X

Świątek, J. (1987). *Two Stage Identification and its Technical and Biomedical Applications*. Wrocław: Scientific Papers of the Institute of Control and Systems Engineering of the Wrocław Technical University.

Świątek, J. (2009). *Selected problems of static systems identification*. Wrocław: Scientific Papers of the Institute of Control and Systems Engineering of the Wrocław Technical University. (In Polish)

Szaniawski, K. (1998). *On Science, Inference, Information and Decision Making, Selected Essays in the Philosophy of Science* (Chmielewski, A., & Wolenski, J., Eds.). Dordrecht, The Netherlands: Kluwer.

Takagi, T., & Sugeno, M. (1985). Fuzzy identification of systems and its application to modeling control. *IEEE Transactions on Systems, Man, and Cybernetics*, *15*(1), 116–132.

Tan, J. (2003). Curvilinear relationship between organizational slack and firm performance: evidence from Chinese state enterprise. *European Management Journal*, *21*(6), 740–749. doi:10.1016/j.emj.2003.09.010

Tan, J., & Peng, M. W. (2003). Organizational slack and firm performance during economic transition: two studies from and emerging economy. *Strategic Management Journal*, *24*(13), 1249–1263. doi:10.1002/smj.351

Tan, K. C., Lee, T. H., & Khor, E. F. (2001) Evolutionary algorithms for multi-objective optimization: performance assessments and comparisons. In *Proceedings IEEE Conference on Evolutionary Computation 2001*. vol. 2 (979-986) Seoul, South Korea

Tanaka, K., Ikeda, T., & Wang, H. (1998). Fuzzy regulators and fuzzy observers: Relaxed stability conditions and LMI-based designs. *IEEE Transactions on Fuzzy Systems*, *6*, 250–265. doi:10.1109/91.669023

Tanaka, K., & Wang, H. O. (2001). *Fuzzy control systems design and analysis*. New York: John Wiley & Sons. doi:10.1002/0471224596

Tanaka, K., Kosaki, T., Taniguchi, T., & Wang, H. (1997). An LMI Approach to Backer-Upper Control of a Truck with Ten Trailers. In *Ifsa 97 proceedings* (Vol. 3, pp. 376–381).

Tang, K. (2005). Geometric optimization algorithms in manufacturing. *Computer – Aided Design & Applications*, *2*(6), 747-757.

Tao, G., & Sun, J. (Eds.). (2009). *Advances in control systems theory and applications*. New York: USTC Press.

Tarokh, V., Jafarkhani, H., & Calderbank, R. (1999). Space-Time Block Codes from orthogonal designs. *IEEE Transactions on Information Theory*, *5*(45), 1456–1467. doi:10.1109/18.771146

Tatjewski, P. (2007). *Advanced control of industrial processes: structures and algorithms*. Berlin, Germany: Springer Verlag.

Terano, T., Asai, K., & Sugeno, M. (Eds.). (1993). *Applied fuzzy systems*. Moskva, Russia: Mir.

Thathachar, M. A. L., & Sastry, P. (1985). A Class of Rapidly Converging Algorithms for Learning Automata. *IEEE Transactions on Systems, Man, and Cybernetics*, *SMC-15*, 168–175.

Thathachar, M. A. L., & Oommen, B. J. (1979). Discretized Reward-Inaction Learning Automata. *Journal of Cybernetics and Information Sciences*, 24-29.

Thathachar, M. A. L., & Sastry, P. (1986, December). Estimator Algorithms for Learning Automata. In *Proc. of the platinum jubilee conference on systems and signal processing*. Bangalore, India.

Theodoridis, S., & Koutroumbas, K. (2006). *Pattern recognition* (3rd ed.). London: Academic Press.

Thompson, J. D. (1967). *Organizations in action*. New York: McGraw Hill.

Thrun, S., Montemerlo, M., Dahlkamp, H., & Stavens, D. (2006). Stanley: The robot that won the DARPA Grand Challenge. *Journal of Field Robotics, 23*(9), 661–692. doi:10.1002/rob.20147

Tong, R., M.B., B., & Latten, A. (1980). Fuzzy control of the activated sludege wastewater treatment process. *Automatica, 16*(6), 695–701. doi:10.1016/0005-1098(80)90011-4

Triantafillou, E., Pomportsis, A., & Georgiadou, E. (2002). AES-CES: Adaptive Educational System based on cognitive styles. In *Proceedings of AH Workshop* (pp. 10-20) Malaga, Spain.

Tsoukas, H. (1996). The firm as a distributed knowledge system: a constructionist approach. *Strategic Management Journal, 17*, 11–25.

Tsoukas, H. (2005). *Complex knowledge. Studies in organizational epistemology*. Oxford, UK: Oxford UP.

Tuan, H., Apkarian, P., Narikiyo, T., & Yamamoto, Y. (2001). Parameterized linear matrix inequality techniques in fuzzy control system design. *Fuzzy Systems. IEEE Transactions on, 9*(2), 324–332.

Tuckwell, H. C. (1988). *Introduction to theoretical neurobiology*. Cambridge, UK: Cambridge University Press.

Tuckwell, H. C. (1989). *Stochastic processes in the neurosciences*. Philadelphia: Society for Industrial and Applied Mathematics.

Turban, E., & Aronson, J. E. (2001). *Decision support systems and intelligent systems*. 6th International (Ed.), Upper Saddle River, NJ: Prentice-Hall.

Tzeng, C. Y., Goodwin, G. C., & Crisafulli, S. (1999). Feedback linearization design of a ship steering autopilot with saturating and slew rate limiting actuator. *International Journal of Adaptive Control and Signal Processing, 13*, 23–30. doi:10.1002/(SICI)1099-1115(199902)13:1<23::AID-ACS532>3.0.CO;2-E

Tzirkel-Hancock, E., & Fallside, F. (1992). Stable control of nonlinear systems using neural networks. *International Journal of Robust and Nonlinear Control, 2*, 63–86. doi:10.1002/rnc.4590020105

Ullman, S., & Basri, R. (1991). Recognition by linear combinations of models. *IEEE Transactions on Pattern Analysis and Machine Intelligence, 10*(13), 992–1006. doi:10.1109/34.99234

Uppal, F. J., Patton, R. J., & Witczak, M. (2006). A neuro-fuzzy multiple-model observer approach to robust fault diagnosis based on the DAMADICS benchmark problem. *Control Engineering Practice, 14*(6), 699–717. doi:10.1016/j.conengprac.2005.04.015

van Beek, P. (1992). Reasoning about qualitative temporal information. *Artificial Intelligence, 58*, 297–326. doi:10.1016/0004-3702(92)90011-L

Van der Stede, W. A. (2000). The relationship between two consequences of budgetary controls: budgetary slack creation and managerial short-term orientation. *Accounting, Organizations and Society, 25*, 609–622. doi:10.1016/S0361-3682(99)00058-6

Vannier, E., Adam, O., & Motsch, J. F. (2002). Objective detection of brainstem auditory evoked potentials with a priori information from higher presentation levels. *Artificial Intelligence in Medicine, 25*, 283–301. doi:10.1016/S0933-3657(02)00029-5

Vidal, T., & Fargier, H. (1999). Handling consistency in temporal constraint networks: from consistency to controllabilities. *Journal of Experimental and Theoretical AI, 11*, 23–45. doi:10.1080/095281399146607

Vidal, T., & Ghallab, M. (1996). *Dealing with uncertain durations in temporal constraint networks dedicated to planning* (pp. 48–52). ECAI.

Vidibida, A. K. (2008). Output stream of binding neuron with instantaneous feedback. *The European Physical Journal B, 65*, 577–584. doi:10.1140/epjb/e2008-00360-1

Vidybida, A. K. (1998). Inhibition as binding controller at the single neuron level. *Bio Systems, 48*, 263–267. doi:10.1016/S0303-2647(98)00073-2

Vidybida, A. K. (2006). *Stochastic models*. Kyiv: NAS of Ukraine.

Vilain, M., & Kautz, H. (1986). *Constraint propagation algorithms for temporal reasoning*, in *AAAI'86*, Philadelphia, PA (pp. 377–382).

Viola, S. R., & Graf, S. Kinshuk., & Leo, T. (2007). Investigating relationships within the Index of Learning Styles: a data driven approach. *Interactive Technology & Smart Education, 4*(1), 7-18.

von Altrock, C., & Krause, B. (2007). Optimization of a water treatment system. *Fuzzy Application Library/ Technical Applications.* Retrieved January 20, 2007, from http://fuzzytech.com/e/e_a_dek.html

Von Krogh, G., & Roos, J. (Eds.). (1996). *Managing knowledge. Perspectives on cooperation and competition.* London: Sage.

Von Krogh, G., Roos, J., & Kline, D. (Eds.). (1998). *Knowing in firms: understanding, managing and measuring knowledge.* London: Sage.

Vuckovic, A., Radivojevic, V., Chen, A. C. N., & Popovic, D. (2002, June). Automatic recognition of alertness and drowsiness from EEG by an artificial neural network. *Medical Engineering & Physics, 24*(5), 349–360. doi:10.1016/S1350-4533(02)00030-9

Waibel, M. (2007). *Evolution of cooperation in artificial ants.* (Ph.D. Thesis), Lausanne, EPFL.

Walsh, T. (2002). *Stochastic constraint programming.* In *Proceedings of the 15t^h European Conference on Artificial Intelligence (ECAI-02),* Lyon, France.

Walter, E., & Pronzato, L. (1997). *Identification of parametric models from experimental data.* New York: Springer.

Wanas, N., Kamel, M. S., Auda, G., & Karray, F. (1999). Feature-based decision aggregation in modular neural network classifiers, *Pattern Recognition Letters 20,* Elsevier, 1353-1359.

Wang, S. (1997). Modeling information architecture for the organization. *Information & Management, 32,* 303–315. doi:10.1016/S0378-7206(97)00025-6

Wang, H. O., Tanaka, K., & Griffin, M. F. (1996). An approach to fuzzy control of nonlinear systems: Stability and design issues. *IEEE Transactions on Fuzzy Systems, 4,* 14–23. doi:10.1109/91.481841

Wang, L.-X. (1994). *Adaptive fuzzy systems and control.* Englewood Cliffs, NJ: Prentice-Hall.

Warwick, K. (1981). Self-tuning regulators – a state-space approach. *International Journal of Control, 33,* 839–858. doi:10.1080/00207178108922958

Watanabe, K., & Himmelblau, D. M. (1982). Instrument fault detection in systems with uncertainties. *International Journal of Systems Science, 13*(2), 137–158. doi:10.1080/00207728208926337

Watanabe, K. (1992). *Adaptive estimation and control. Partitioning Approach.* New York: Princeton Hall International.

Watkins, C. J. C. H. (1989). *Learning from delayed rewards.* (Unpublished doctoral dissertation), King's College, London.

Webb, A. (2002). *Statistical Pattern Recognition* (2nd ed.). New York: John Wiley & Sons. doi:10.1002/0470854774

Weick, K. E. (1995). *Sensemaking in organizations.* London: Sage.

Weinberger, M. J., & Ordentlich, E. (2002). On Delayed Prediction of Individual Sequences. *IEEE Transactions on Information Theory, 48*(7), 1959–1976. doi:10.1109/TIT.2002.1013136

Wellstead, P. E., & Sanoff, S. P. (1981). Extended self-tuning algorithm. *International Journal of Control, 34,* 433–455. doi:10.1080/00207178108922541

Wellstead, P. E., & Zarrop, M. B. (1991). *Self-tuning Systems: Control and Signal Processing.* Chichester, UK: John Wiley & Sons.

Wellstead, P. E., Prager, D. L., & Zanker, P. M. (1979). Pole-assignment self-tuning regulator. In *Proc. IEE, 126,* 781-787.

Wets, R. J.-B. (1975). On the relation between stochastic and deterministic optimization in Control Theory, Numerical Methods and Computer System Modelling. In Bensoussen, A., & Lions, J. L. (Eds.), *Lecture Notes in Economcs and Math. Systems 107* (pp. 350–361). Berlin, Germany: Springer-Verlag.

Williams, T., Rathwell, G., & Li, H. (2001). *A handbook on master planning and implementation for enterprise integration programs, Purdue Enterprise Reference Architecture, Purdue Methodology, Purdue Laboratory for Applied Industrial Control*. Institute for Interdisciplinary Engineering Studies.

Williamson, O. E. (1974). *The economics of discretionary behaviour. Managerial objectives in a theory of the firm*. London: Kershaw Publ. Comp.

Williamson, O. E. (1975). *Markets and hierarchy: analysis and antitrust implications*. New York: The Free Press.

Williamson, O. E. (1981). The Economics of Organization: The Transaction Costs Approach. *American Journal of Sociology*, *87*, 548–577. doi:10.1086/227496

Williamson, O. E. (1985). *The economic institutions of capitalism*. New York: The Free Press.

Williamson, O. E. (1996). *The Mechanisms of Governance*. New York: Oxford UP.

Williamson, O. E. (1994). Transaction cost economics and organization theory. In Smelser, N. J., & Swedberg, R. (Eds.), *The handbook of economic sociology* (pp. 77–107). Princeton, NJ: Princeton UP.

Willsky, A. S. (1976). A survey of design methods for failure detection in dynamic systems. *Automatica*, *12*(6), 601–611. doi:10.1016/0005-1098(76)90041-8

Willsky, A. S., & Jones, H. L. (1976). A generalized likelihood ratio approach to the detection and estimation of jumps in linear systems. *IEEE Transactions on Automatic Control*, *21*(1), 108–112. doi:10.1109/TAC.1976.1101146

Witczak, K. (2006). Advances in model-based fault diagnosis with evolutionary algorithms and neural networks. *International Journal of Applied Mathematics and Computer Science*, *16*(1), 85–99.

Witczak, M., Korbicz, J., Mrugalski, M., & Patton, R. J. (2006). A GMDH neural network-based approach to robust fault diagnosis: Application to the DAMADICS benchmark problem. *Control Engineering Practice*, *14*(6), 671–683. doi:10.1016/j.conengprac.2005.04.007

Witczak, M., Obuchowicz, A., & Korbicz, J. (2002). Genetic programming based approaches to identification and fault diagnosis of non-linear dynamic systems. *International Journal of Control*, *75*(13), 1012–1031. doi:10.1080/00207170210156224

Witten, I. H., & Frank, E. (2005). *Data Mining: Practical machine learning tools and techniques* (2nd ed.). San Francisco: Morgan Kaufmann Publishers.

Wolf, A., Barbosa, C. H., Monteiro, E. C., & Vellasco, M. (June 2003). *Multiple MLP neural networks applied on the determination of segment limits in ECG signals*. In *7th International Workshop-Conference on Artificial and Natural Neural Networks: Part II, LNCS 2687* (pp. 607–614). Berlin-Heidelberg, Germany: Springer-Verlag.

Womack, J. P., Jones, D. T., & Roos, D. (1990). *The machine that changed the world: the triumph of lean production*. New York: Macmillan.

Xu, R., & Wunsch, D. II. (2009). *Clustering*. Piscataway, NJ: IEEE Press & Wiley.

Xu, D., Wang, H., & Su, K. (2002). Intelligent student profiling with fuzzy models. In *Proceedings of HICSS'02*, Hawaii.

Yager, R. R. (1982). A new approach to the summarization of data. *Information Sciences*, *28*, 69–86. doi:10.1016/0020-0255(82)90033-0

Yan, H., Jiang, Y., Zheng, J., Peng, C., & Li, Q. (2005). *A multilayer perceptron-based medical support system for heart disease diagnosis. Expert Systems with Applications*. Amsterdam: Elsevier.

Yolles, M. (2006). *Organizations as Complex Systems. An Introduction to Knowledge Cybernetics*. Greenwich, CT: IAP.

Young, P. C. (1970). An instrumental variable method for real-time identification of a noisy process. *Automatica, 6*, 271–287. doi:10.1016/0005-1098(70)90098-1

Young, P. C. (1984). *Recursive Estimation and Time-Series Analysis*. Berlin, Germany: Springer-Verlag.

Young, P. C. (1974). Recursive approaches to time series analysis. *IMA Bulletin, May/June*, 209-224.

Young, P. C. (2008). Refined instrumental variable estimation for discrete and continuous-time transfer function models. In *Proc. CD-ROM IAR International Workshop on Advanced Control and Diagnosis* (pp. 1-12). Coventry University, UK.

Yu, T. J., Shen, V. Y., & Dunsmore, H. E. (1988). An Analysis of Several Software Defect Models. *IEEE Transactions on Software Engineering, 14*, 1261–1269. doi:10.1109/32.6170

Yu, K. O. (2001). *Modeling for casting and solidification processing*. Boca Raton, FL: CRC.

Zadeh, L. A. (1983). A computational approach to fuzzy quantifiers in natural languages. *Computers & Mathematics with Applications (Oxford, England), 9*, 149–184. doi:10.1016/0898-1221(83)90013-5

Zadeh, L. (1965). Fuzzy sets. *Information and Control, 8*, 338–353. doi:10.1016/S0019-9958(65)90241-X

Zadeh, L. A. (1992). The calculus of fuzzy if / then rules. *AI Expert*, 23–27.

Zajic, I., Larkowski, T., Hill, D., & Burnham, K. J. (2009). Nonlinear compensator design for HVAC systems: PI control strategy. In *Proc. CD-ROM Int. Conf. Systems Engineering ICSE 2009* (pp. 580-584). Coventry University, UK.

Zakrzewska, D. (2007). Cluster analysis for building personalised e-learning system. *Polish Journal of Environmental Studies, 16*(5B), 330–334.

Zakrzewska, D., & Ruiz-Esteban, C. (2005) Cluster analysis for students profiling. In *Proceedings of the 11th International Conference on "System Modelling Control"* (pp. 333-338). Warsaw, Poland: AOW EXIT.

Zeineldin, H. H., & El-Saadany, E. F. Salama, & M. M. A. (2006). Distributed Generation Micro-Grid Operation: Control and Protection. In *Proceedings of IEEE Power Systems Conference: Advanced Metering, Protection, Control, Communication, and Distributed Resources*, (105-111), Clemson, South Carolina.

Zhang, G. P. (2000). Neural networks for classification: a survey. *IEEE Transactions on Systems, Man and Cybernetics. Part C, Applications and Reviews, 30*(4), 451–462. doi:10.1109/5326.897072

Zhao, Z., Tomizuka, M., & Isaka, S. (1993). Fuzzy gain scheduling of PID controllers. *IEEE Transactions on Systems, Man, and Cybernetics, 23*(5), 1392–1398. doi:10.1109/21.260670

Ziemian, S. J. (2002). *Bilinear proportional-integral-plus control*. (Doctoral dissertation), Coventry University, UK.

Zitzler, E., & Thiele, L. (1999). Multiobjective evolutionary algorithms: A comparative case study and the strength Pareto approach. *IEEE Transactions on Evolutionary Computation, 3*(4), 257–271. doi:10.1109/4235.797969

Zwierzewicz, Z. (2007). Nonlinear Adaptive Control Synthesis Using Model Basis Functions. *Int. Journal of Factory Automation. Robotics and Soft Computing, 1*(2), 102–107.

Zwierzewicz, Z. (2009). Generalization of controller integral action in tracking and disturbances rejection problems. *Polish Journal of Environmental Studies, 18*(2A), 223–228.

Zwierzewicz, Z. (2008). Nonlinear adaptive tracking-control synthesis for general linearly parametrized systems. In Arreguin, J. M. R. (Ed.), *Automation and Robotics* (pp. 375–388). Vienna, Austria: I-Tech Education and Publishing.

Zwierzewicz, Z. (2003). On the ship guidance automatic system design via lqg-integral control. In: J. Battle & M. Blanke (Ed.), *6th IFAC Conference on Manoeuvring and Control of Marine Crafts* (pp. 349-353). University of Girona, Spain.

About the Contributors

Jerzy Józefczyk graduated in automatic control systems from the Wrocław University of Technology, in 1980. He received the PhD degree in computer science from the Poznań University of Technology, in 1987, and Dr. Sc. degree in automation and robotics from the Systems Research Institute of the Polish Academy of Sciences, Warsaw, in 1996. Presently, he is a full professor in the Wroclaw University of Technology, and a head of the Department of Intelligent Decision Support Systems. His research interests include operations research, complex control systems, uncertain systems and artificial intelligence which resulted in more than 100 publications. He was a Scientific Secretary of the Committee of Automation and Robotics of the Polish Academy of Sciences in 1988–2006 and a member of this Committee from 1988. He is currently a member of a Board of Directors of the World Organisation of Systems and Cybernetics.

Donat Orski received MSc and PhD degrees in computer science from the Wrocław University of Technology (WUT), in 1995 and 2000, respectively. Currently, he is an assistant professor in the Department of Intelligent Decision Support Systems in WUT. His research interests include knowledge-based systems, expert systems, uncertain systems, neural networks, learning systems, and their applications to decision making in complex operation systems. He is an author or co-author of more than 30 conference papers, journal articles and book chapters on these topics.

* * *

Pedro Albertos, full Professor since 1975, at Systems Engineering and Control Dept. UPV, Spain, Director from 1979 to 1995 and in 1998. He has been teaching courses on Advanced Control Systems, Intelligent Control Systems and Systems Theory. Honorary Profesor at the Northwestern University, Senhyang, China and Doctor Honoris Causa at the Universities of Oulu (Finland) and Polytechnic of Bucarest (Rumania). As an Invited Professor he has delivered courses and seminars in more than 30 universities and research centres. Authored more than 300 papers, book chapters and congress communications, he is co-editor of 7 books and co-author of "Multivariable Control Systems" (Springer 2004). He has directed 18 PhD thesis, being the coordinator of the PhD Program on Automatica and Industrial Informatics, which has been implemented in Spain, Mexico, Columbia and Venezuela. Involved in many national and international research projectss. Associated editor of Control Engineering Practice and Automatica and editor in chief of the journal RIAI (Revista Iberoamericana de Automática e Informática Industrial). IFAC Fellow and Advisor, IFAC President (1999-2002), Senior Member of IEEE, and member of the Board of Governors of the Control Systems Society (1996-97).

Véronique Amarger received her PhD degree in Microelectronics and Computer Science from the University of Paris 7, France, in 1993. Since 1993, she has joined Senart Institute of Technology of Paris 12-Val de Marne University, one of two Institutes of Technology of this University, where she works as Assistant Professor. She is a Staff Member of Image, Signal and Intelligent Systems Laboratory (LISSI/ EA 3956) of Paris 12 University. Her main research interests concern the field of Bio-inspired Artificial Intelligence, Neural Networks and Computer Aided Diagnosis Systems design and applications.

Tadeusz Baczko is a professor at the Institute of Economics Polish Academy of Sciences and Warsaw School of Information Technology deals with issues of innovation standards and measurement, surveys of enterprises, R&D and innovation policy, corporate finance, theory of the firm, microeconomic foundations, future studies and applied statistics. He coordinated numerous international research projects and developed the science network "Assessment of the R&D Innovation Activity Impact on Social and Economic Development" Editor and co-author of the 4 national and 16 regional reports on the innovativeness of the Polish economy" since 2005.

Tadeusz Banek was born in Tarnów, Poland, on November 19, 1945. He graduated in the Ship Building Faculty of Gdańsk Polytechnic in1969, received a PhD degree in automatic control from Electric Eng. Department in AGH in 1975 and postdoctoral lecturing qualification (habilitacja) in 1991 again at AGH. He cooperated with Systems Research Institute of Polish Academy of Sciences and AGH through many years. In 1979 – 1981 he worked as an assistant professor in Institute of Applied Mathematics in Bonn University, Germany and in Technion Institute of Technology in Haifa, Israel. He is a head of Quantitative Methods Department at Management Faculty of Technical University in Lublin, Poland. His research interest is in the area of stochastic processes, filtering, stochastic control, chaos expansion and Malliavin calculus.

Lucio Biggiero is Full Professor of Organization Theory and Design at the Faculty of Economics of the Università dell'Aquila, and he is the director of the Knownetlab Research Center (www.knownetlab. it). He wrote papers on the following journals: Computational & Mathematical Organization Theory; Entrepreneurship & Regional Development; Human Systems Management; Industry and Higher Education; International Journal of Technology Transfer & Commercialization; International Review of Sociology; Journal of Financial Decision Making; Journal of Management and Governance; Journal of Management Studies; Journal of Technology Transfer; Nonlinear Dynamics, Psychology and Life Sciences; Science and Public Policy; Systemica. His main interests are in the following fields: industrial clusters/districts; (inter-)organisational design theory and methods; coordination theory; socio-cognitive aspects of organisational behaviour (trust, identity, norms, reputation); organisational consequences of computer-mediated communication; methodology and epistemology of organisation science. He applies the following main methodologies: outranking methods for decision making; social network analysis; data analysis; agent-based simulation models.

Krzysztof Brzostowski was born in 1978. He graduated from Electronics Department, Wrocław University of Technology, in 2003. In 2009, he received the PhD degree from Institute of Informatics, Wrocław University of Technology. His scientific fields of interest are system identification, pattern recognition, decision support systems, mathematical modeling, stochastic process and complex systems, semantic web services. Krzysztof Brzostowski is the author over twenty scientific papers which are connected with his research. Most of these works are presented at International Scientific Conferences. He is commit himself on work with students. Results of their works were numerous scientific articles which was presented at polish and international Scientific Conferences.

Keith J. Burnham has been Professor of Industrial Control Systems, and Director of the Control Theory and Applications Centre (CTAC), a multidisciplinary research centre based within the Faculty of Engineering and Computing, Coventry University, UK, since 1999. The CTAC is engaged with a number of collaborative research programmes with industrial organisations, involving the design and implementation of adaptive control systems. Keith Burnham obtained his BSc (Mathematics), MSc (Control Engineering) and PhD (Adaptive Control) at Coventry University in 1981, 1984 and 1991, respectively. He is regularly consulted by industrial organisations to provide advice in areas of advanced algorithm development for control and condition monitoring. He serves on the Editorial Board of the Transactions of the Institute of Measurement and Control (InstMC), and is currently Chair of the InstMC Systems Control Technology Panel, and a member of the Informatics and Control Working Group of the Institution of Mechanical Engineers (IMechE). He is currently General Conference Chair for the UKACC International Conference on CONTROL 2010. He is a Chartered Mathematician (CMath) and a corporate member of the InstMC, the Institute of Mathematics and its Applications (IMA) and the Institution of Engineering and Technology (IET).

Igor Calmicov received the MSc degree in Computer Science from Technical University of Moldova, Republic of Moldova, in 2007. His applied research interests include digital system design based on microcontrollers and FPGA, intelligent control systems, signal and image processing. Currently, he works as a Senior Lecturer at the Department of Computer Science, Technical University of Moldova, Republic of Moldova.

Amine Chohra received his Doctorate es-sciences in 1999 from ENP (Ecole Nationale Polytechnique), Algiers (Algeria). He was member of Artificial Intelligence and Robotics Laboratory (LRIA) of CDTA from July 1991 to November 1999. He had an ERCIM (European Research Consortium for Informatics and Mathematics) post doctoral position from December 1999 to July 2001, with Behavior Engineering team of AiS-GMD, Sankt Augustin (Germany), and with Dependable Computing Group team of IEI-CNR, Pisa (Italy). From September 2001 to August 2003, he was teacher/researcher at Orleans University, ENSI de Bourges (France), and a member of Vision and Robotics Laboratory (LVR / UPRES EA 2078). He is teacher/researcher at Senart Institute of Tehnology, Lieusaint (France) and member of Images, Signals, and Intelligent Systems Laboratory (LISSI / EA 3956) of Paris-East University (France). His research interests are complex systems, decision-making, negotiation, diagnosis, knowledge based systems, behavior based cybernetics, hybrid intelligent systems, soft computing, machine learning.

Jarosław Drapała was born in 1979. He graduated from Department of Computer Science and Management, Wrocław University of Technology, in 2004. In 2009, he received the PhD degree from Institute of Informatics, Wrocław University of Technology. His scientific fields of interest are mathematical modeling of complex systems, neural networks, optimization, genetic algorithms, knowledge processing, clustering, multidimensional data visualization, pattern recognition, statistical analysis of biomedical data, ontology driven web services, service oriented architecture. He organizes meetings of student's scientific circle "Estimator". Jarosław Drapała is the author of over twenty scientific papers, most of which were presented at International Scientific Conferences. He has four-months-old baby.

Pavel Fojtík was born in Ostrava, Czech Republic, in 1976. He received his MSc degree in Measurement and Automatic Control from the Brno University of Technology in 1999 and PhD degree in Cybernetics, Control and Measurements from the Brno University of Technology in 2006. In 2004 he joined the Center of Advanced Innovation Technologies at the Technical University of Ostrava where he was a research assistant until 2006. Currently he has a research position at the Faculty of Metallurgy and Materials Engineering of the Technical University of Ostrava and his main research interests include fault detection and diagnosis, estimation and control problems, modeling and system identification and statistical signal processing.

Dariusz Jakóbczak was born in Koszalin, Poland, on December 30, 1965. He graduated in mathematics (numerical methods and programming) from the University of Gdansk, Poland in 1990. He received the Ph.D. degree in 2007 in computer science from the Polish – Japanese Institute of Information Technology, Warsaw, Poland. From 1991 to 1994 he was a civilian programmer in the High Military School in Koszalin. He was a teacher of mathematics and computer science in the Private Economic School in Koszalin from 1995 to 1999. Since March 1998 he has worked in the Department of Electronics and Computer Science, Technical University of Koszalin, Poland and since October 2007 he has been an Assistant Professor in the Chair of Computer Science and Management in this department. His research interests include computer vision, shape representation, curve interpolation, contour reconstruction and geometric modeling, probabilistic methods and discrete mathematics.

Janusz Kacprzyk is Professor of CS at the Systems Research Institute, Polish Academy of Sciences, WIT – Warsaw School of Information Technology, and PIAP – Industrial Institute of Automation and Measurements, in Warsaw, Poland. He is Member of the Polish Academy of Sciences and of Spanish Royal Academy of Economic and Financial Sciences. He is Fellow of IEEE and of IFSA. He was a visiting professor in the USA, Italy, China. His research includes: soft computing, fuzzy logic and computing with words, in decisions and optimization, control, database querying, information retrieval. He is the author of 5 books, (co)editor of 30 volumes, (co)author of 300 papers. He is the editor in chief of 4 book series at Springer, and of 2 journals. He received many awards, notably: 2005 IEEE CIS Pioneer Award in Fuzzy Systems, The Sixth Kaufmann Prize and Gold Medal for pioneering works on soft computing in economics. Currently he is President of the Polish Society for Operational and Systems Research and Immediate Past President of IFSA.

Nadia Kanaoui received her PhD in Computer Sciences at Images, Signals, and Intelligent Systems Laboratory (LISSI / EA 3956) of Paris-East University (France) in December 2007, the Engineer degree in IEEA (Informatique Electronique Electrotechnique Automatique) in January 2000 from Electrical Engineering Department of FST (Faculté des Sciences et des Techniques de Settat), Settat (Morocco). She received DEA (Diplôme d'Etudes Approfondies) in September 2002 in Computer Sciences (option: Architecture Logicielle) from Ecole Polytechnique, Nantes (France). Her research interests are computer aided diagnosis, image processing, pattern recognition, classification, decision-making, neural networks, fuzzy logic.

Edward Kozłowski was born in Nowaya Mysh, Belarus, on January 6, 1973. He educated at the Maria Curie-Skłodowska University in Lublin on the Faculty of Mathematics. He received a MS degree in mathematic from Maria Curie-Skłodowska University in 1996, a Ph.D. degree in automatic control from Systems Research Institute Polish Academy of Sciences in 2002. In 1996 – 2003 he worked as an assistant in the Department of Operational Research and from 2003 as an adjunct in the Department of Quantitative Methods in Management, Lublin University of Technology, Poland. His research interest is in the area of optimal control linear and nonlinear systems with deterministic and random horizons, problems connected with costs of learning and information, stochastic processes and filtering.

Kseniya G. Kravchuk was graduated with honors from the Physics Department of Taras Shevchenko National University of Kyiv in 2006 with degree in Medical Physics. Same year she received the Mykchaylo Bily annual reward for her study of critical phenomena in liquid systems. Since 2008 K. Kravchuk collaborates with Dr. Vidybida in a field of signal processing in neural systems. In 2009 she takes up a junior engineer post at the Department of Synergetics of Bogolyubov Institute for Theoretical Physics, Kyiv. Since 2009 she is a member of ESMTB (European Society for Mathematical and Theoretical Biology).

Pavel Kucera is a Research Worker at the Centre of Applied Cybernetics, Brno University of Technology in Czech Republic. His research activities are focused on the area of formal methods and fault-tolerant systems. Results of the research are used in application of reliability modelling of the turbine control systems and real-time diagnostic systems for steel continuous casting processes. Pavel Kucera graduated from the Brno University of Technology in 2000 with a MSc in Cybernetics, Automation and Measurement. In 2003, he earned PhD in Cybernetics, Control and Measurement from the same university. In 2001 he joined research team in University of Huddersfield where he worked on the project of the Tiny Home Automation System. Between 2002 and 2003 he worked as a research worker in the Institut für Automation und Kommunikation e.V. Magdeburg where he developed formal model of the industrial communication bus.

Vladimir Larin received the MSc degree (1979) in Mathematics from the Tiraspol State Pedagogical Institute, Republic of Moldova. Graduated (1989) of special courses on "Amorphous Alloys", Moscow State Institute of Alloys, Russia. In 1979-1992 he was as researcher with the Institute of Research in the field of glass-coated microwires, Republic of Moldova. In 1992 he joined the Institute of Applied Physics of Academy of Sciences, Republic of Moldova. From 1993 to 2002 he was with "AmoTec" Ltd Company, Republic of Moldova. Since 2002, he joined as director the MFTI Ltd R&D Company, Republic of Moldova. His specialist research and technological experience is in the field of glass-coated microwire casting, wire-based technologies and products.

Jens G. Linden was born in Dueren, Germany, in 1980. In 2005 he received the Diploma in Technical Mathematics from Aachen University of Applied Sciences, Germany as well as the MSc Degree (with Distinction) in Control Engineering from Coventry University, United Kingdom. In 2005 he became a full-time PhD student within the Control Theory and Applications Centre (CTAC) at Coventry University. He received the PhD Degree in the field of system identification from Coventry University in 2008. From 2007 to 2009 he held the position of Senior Lecturer within the CTAC, where he was responsible for coordinating the system identification research group. Currently, he is working for ista International GmbH in Essen, Germany, where he is developing concepts for energy saving products for domestic heating systems.

Jia Liu received his MSc degree in Computer Science in 2008, from the University of Regina in Canada. His research interests include probabilistic reasoning, temporal reasoning and constraint satisfaction. Jia is currently a Quantitative Investment Analyst at Harrow Partners, Winnipeg Canada.

Kurosh Madani graduated in fundamental physics in 1985 from PARIS 7 – Jussieu University, he received his MSc. in Microelectronics and chip architecture (in1986) and his Ph.D. in Electrical Engineering and Computer Sciences (in 1990), from University PARIS-SUD, Orsay, France. In 1995, he received the DHDR Doctor-Hab. degree from University PARIS-EST / PARIS 12, where he works as Chair Professor at Senart-FB Institute of Technology of this University. Co-creator of LISSI laboratory in 2005, he is director of SCTIC division, one of the two research components of this laboratory. Author and coauthor of more than 250 publications, he is regularly invited as key-note by international conferences and symposiums. His current research interests include: complex structures and behaviors modeling, self-organizing modular hybrid processing systems, humanoid and collective robotics and intelligent fault detection and diagnosis systems. He is elected Academician of International Informatization Academy (since 1996) and of International Academy of Technological Cybernetics (since 1997).

Aleksander Moczala - doctor of science, is a worker of the Department for Production Engineering at University of Bielsko-Biala. His scientific work object is problem of system aiding of inter-enterprise cooperation process. He was coordinator of European projects e.g. Coordinator of project "Development of trans-boarder economic cooperation - virtual center of small and medium-size enterprises cooperation …", within the frames of Program of Trans-boarder Cooperation Program Phare WFMP PL-SL 2002/2003 of the European Union. He is editor of a magazine *Productivity and Innovation* and a certified lecturer of REFA in the field of work organization, cost calculation and production steering. He had a practical training in: 1995 in CFDF in Lilie, 1999 in Audi AG in Ingolstadt, 2001 in Siemens Schaltanlagenwerk in Frankfurt/M and collaborates with Fiat-GM Powertrain in Bielsko-Biala. He is author of more than 60 publications and works.

Malek Mouhoub received his PhD degree in Computer Science in 1996, from the University of Nancy (France). He is currently Professor of Computer Science at the University of Regina, Canada. His research interests are in artificial intelligence and include knowledge representation, temporal reasoning, constraint satisfaction, search techniques, scheduling, planning and optimization methods. Federal and provincial grants of Canada support Dr. Mouhoub's research program.

Gintautas Narvydas received the Bachelor and Master degrees in applied mathematics from Kaunas University of Technology, Lithuania in 2001 and 2003 respectively. He is currently working toward the PhD degree in Informatics at Kaunas University of Technology. Also he is lecturer at Department of Mathematical Research in Systems and at Department of Control Technologies. His research interests include control of autonomous mobile robots, fast and/or on-line machine learning, artificial and computational intelligence, application of artificial neural networks, fuzzy logic, evolutionary and other learning techniques. G. Narvydas published over 15 scientific publications in this field. Together with colleagues from Lithuania and Ukraine he is participating in various research projects on the control of autonomous mobile robots.

John Oommen was born in Coonoor, India on September 9, 1953. He obtained his B.Tech. degree from the Indian Institute of Technology, Madras, India in 1975. He obtained his M.E. from the Indian Institute of Science in Bangalore, India in 1977. He then went on for his M.S. and Ph. D. which he obtained from Purdue University, in West Lafayette, Indiana in 1979 and 1982 respectively. He joined the School of Computer Science at Carleton University in Ottawa, Canada, in the 1981-82 academic year. He is still at Carleton and holds the rank of a Full Professor. Since July 2006, he has been awarded the honorary rank of *Chancellor's Professor*, which is a lifetime award from Carleton University. His research interests include Automata Learning, Adaptive Data Structures, Statistical and Syntactic Pattern Recognition, Stochastic Algorithms and Partitioning Algorithms. He is the author of more than 320 refereed journal and conference publications, and is a *Fellow of the IEEE* and a *Fellow of the IAPR*. Dr. Oommen has been on the Editorial Board of the *IEEE Transactions on Systems, Man and Cybernetics*, and *Pattern Recognition*.

Constantin Plotnic received the MSc degree (1974) in Mathematics and Cybernetics from the State University of Moldova, Republic of Moldova. In 1977-1991 he worked as Analytical and System Programming Engineer, and Director of Computer Center of the Department of Construction, Republic of Moldova. From 1991 to 2002 he was with the Department of Computer Science, Republican College of Microelectronics and Computer Engineering, Republic of Moldova. In 2002 he joined the Technical University of Moldova, Republic of Moldova. Currently, he works as Senior Lecturer at the Department of Computer Science. His main research interests include three-dimensional modeling, and industrial applications based on fuzzy logic.

Miroslav Pokorný was born in Zlín, Czech Republic, in 1941. He graduated from the Brno University of Technology, 1963 and received the M.Sc. degree in Radio-communication Technology. The PhD degree he received from Brno University of Technology, 1994 in Control and Informatics. From 1964 to 1992 he was a research worker at the Iron and Metallurgy Research Institute, Dobrá. In 1993 he joined the VŠB – Technical University Ostrava as an Associate Professor. He is currently a Professor in Control and Measurement Technology. His research interests include artificial intelligence, fuzzy modelling, fuzzy control and signal processing.

Mercedes Ramírez graduated in automatic control from the University of Oriente (UO, Santiago de Cuba, Cuba) in 1983, and obtained a PhD from the Cuban National Permanent Commission for PhD degrees granting in automatics and computers science, in 2002. Since 1983, she is professor at the Automatic Control Department, Electrical Engineering Faculty, UO. She representing his faculty in Ibero-American Network under Program CYTED. His main research area is fuzzy control.

Vidas Raudonis, PhD student at Faculty of Electrical and Control Engineering from Kaunas University of Technology, Lithuania. He obtained Master degree in electrical and control technologies. His research interest is application of computation intelligence in human-computer interaction, computer vision, assistive technology and robotics. V. Raudonis published over 20 scientific papers in this field. He is currently working as the assistant at Department of Control Technologies and as the engineer at Institute for Automation and Control Systems. He is the chairman of the Students Science Society. Together with colleagues from Lithuania he is participating in various research projects with industrial companies like Siemens, Beijer Electronics.

Luis Rueda obtained his Bachelor's in computer science from the National University of San Juan, Argentina, in 1993, and his Master's and Ph.D. degrees in computer science from Carleton University, Canada, in 1998 and 2002, respectively. He was an assistant professor in the School of Computer Science, Univesity of Windsor Canada, from 2002 to 2005. He spent two years at the University of Concepcion, Chile, as an associate professor in the Department of Computer Science and as an associate researcher in the Center for Biotechnology. Luis Rueda is currently an associate professor in the School of Computer Science, University of Windsor, Canada. His research interests are in pattern recognition, image processing, bioinformatics and DNA microarray data analysis. He holds one patent and more than 50 publications in prestigious journals and conferences. He is a Senior Member of the IEEE, and member of the IAPR.

Antonio Sala was born in Valencia, Spain, in 1968. He received the B.Eng. (honors) degree in combined engineering from Coventry University, Coventry, U.K., in 1990, M.Sc. degree in electrical engineering in 1993 and the Ph.D. degree in control engineering in 1998 both from Valencia Technical University (UPV), Valencia, Spain. Prof. Sala was awarded the Second Spanish National Prize for University Graduation in 1993. Since 1993, he has been with the Systems and Control Engineering Department, UPV, where he is currently full professor, teaching in a wide range of subjects in areas such as linear systems theory, multivariable process control, and intelligent control, and has supervised four Ph.D. theses. He has taken part in research and mobility projects funded by local industries, government, and European community. He is the coauthor of 22 papers in middle or top Journal Citation Report (JCR) impact journals, eight plenaries or invited panel talks in Spanish and international conferences, and the book Multivariable Feeback Control (Springer-Verlag), and co-editor of Iterative Identification and Control (Springer-Verlag). In the triennium 2002-05, he was member of IFAC Publications committee. His current research interests include fuzzy control, fuzzy fault diagnosis, system identification, multirate and networked control systems, and process control applications.

Eleonora Riva Sanseverino was born in 1971 in Palermo, Italy. She graduated at the University of Palermo in Electrical Engineering in 1995 and received the PhD in February 2000 in Electrical Engineering at the same University. From December 2001 to October 2002 she's been working at the National Council of Research, CNR, as a full-time researcher in the field of Computer Science. Since October 2002, she's Associate Professor in Power Systems. Her main research interest is in the field of optimization methods on electrical distribution system's design, operation and planning; distribution systems fault diagnosis and service restoration strategies; theory and applications of soft-computing techniques.

Giuseppe Fileccia Scimemi was born in 1971 in Palermo, Italy. He graduated at the University of Palermo in Civil Engineering in 1998 and received the PhD in February 2004 in Structural Engineering at the same University. Since January 2005 he is assistant professor of structural engineering at the University of Palermo. He teaches basic Finite Element course for undergraduate civil engineering students. His main research interest is in the field of computational mechanics, constitutive modeling and structural optimization.

Rimvydas Simutis, professor at Kaunas University of Technology, Lithuania, head of Institute for Automation and Control Systems. He obtained PhD degree in technical cybernetics (1983) and habil. dr. degree in informatics-engineering (1998) at Kaunas University of Technology. His research interest is application of computation intelligence in technical, biological and financial systems. R. Simutis published over 150 scientific papers in this field. 1991-1993 he was granted Alexander von Humboldt research fellowship and has investigated application of intelligent measurement and control systems in biotechnology. Together with colleagues from Germany and other countries he is participating in various research projects with industrial companies like Siemens, Roche, Novartis, Sanofi-Aventis.

Jerzy Świątek was born in 1953. He graduated from Electronics Department, Wrocław University of Technology, in 1977. In 1979, he received the Ph.D degree from Cybernetics Institute, Wrocław University of Technology. Degree of Doctor of Sciences Jerzy Świątek received from University of Mining and Metallurgy, Krakow, in 1987. His research concerning system identification, pattern recognition and support decision systems. He is a member of Polish Academy of Science and Wrocław Scientific Society. He is the author of numerous scientific publications and two monographs. For his achievements in the fields of his research and organizations activities he was awarded many prestigious honors.

Alexander K. Vidybida received his PhD in Mathematical and Theoretical Physics (Kandidat of Physics and Mathematics) in 1975 at the Institute for Theoretical Physics, Kyiv, for his study of the BBGKY hierarchy of equations in nonequilibrium statistical mechanics. He received his DrHab degree in Theoretical Physics (Doktor of Physics and Mathematics) in 2000 at the Institute for Theoretical Physics, Kyiv, for his study of interaction of periodic electromagnetic fields with macromolecular and cooperative systems, including interaction of microwaves with living objects. At present time he works as Principal Scientist in the Institute for Theoretical Physics. Dr. A.K. Vidybida, in varioys periods of time, is a Member of Euroscience, IBRO (International Brain Research Organization), EBEA (European Bioelectromagnetic Association), AMS (America Mathematical Society), ESMTB (European Society for Mathematical and Theoretical Biology). His current research interests are devoted to neurophysics, including formation of high discriminating ability in natural sensory systems and neural coding, as well as to implementation of basic ideas in technical devices.

Sławomir Zadrożny is Associate Professor (PhD 1994, DSc 2006) at the Warsaw School of Information Technology. His current scientific interests include applications of fuzzy logic in database management systems, data mining, information retrieval and decision support. He is the author and co-author of ca. 150 journal and conference papers. He has been involved in the design and implementation of several prototype software packages. He is also Associate Professor at the Systems Research Institute of the Polish Academy of Sciences.

Ivan Zajic was born in Prague, Czech Republic, in 1985. In 2004 he started his undergraduate bachelor studies at the Czech Technical University in Prague, Czech Republic, and completed at Coventry University, United Kingdom, in 2008, where he obtained his BEng (Hons) Degree in European Engineering Studies. He has been member of the Control Theory and Applications Centre (CTAC) since 2008. He received the MSc Degree (with Distinction) in Control Engineering from Coventry University in 2009. Currently he is a PhD student within the CTAC with main focus on identification and control of state dependent dynamical systems with application to heating ventilation and air conditioning systems.

Danuta Zakrzewska is an Assistant Professor at the Institute of Information Technology, Technical University of Lodz, Poland. She received her PhD in Mathematics in 1987. Her current research interests focus on intelligent e-learning systems especially taking into account personalization according to cognitive styles and usability needs. In her investigations, she considers application of such techniques as data warehousing and data mining, to build student models and to identify their requirements. For several years, she has been involved in organizing international students' collaborative activities, with emphasis on peer review and discussions. She has published more than 40 articles in conferences, journals, and books.

Sergiu Zaporojan received the MSc degree (1984) in Computer Science from the Polytechnical Institute of Ulyanovsk, Russia. In 1986-1990 he was with the Department of Computer Science and Engineering of the Electrotechnical Institute of Sanct-Petersburg, Russia. In 1991 he joined the Department of Computer Science of the Technical University of Moldova, Republic of Moldova. He received the PhD degree from the Technical University of Moldova (1995). His specialist research and engineering experience is in the field of Computer Science and Electrical Engineering. He has been actively involved with design of digital and specialized microprocessor systems since 1984. His current research interests include knowledge-based systems and their application to complex industrial processes. To date, he is head of the Department of R&D, Technical University of Moldova.

Gaetano Zizzo was born in 1976 in Palermo, Italy. He graduated at the University of Palermo in Electrical Engineering in 2002 and received the PhD in February 2006 in Electrical Engineering at the same University. Since March 2002 he is been working as Post-doc Fellow with the Power System group at the Department of Electrical, Electronic and Telecommunications Engineering of the University of Palermo. His main research interest is in the field of optimization methods on electrical distribution system's design, operation and planning; distribution systems fault diagnosis; electrical safety and grounding systems; renewable energy sources-based systems.

Zenon Zwierzewicz received the MSc degree in mathematics from the University of Szczecin, Poland in 1978. The PhD and DSc degrees (doctor and doctor habilitatus), all in automatic control, he received from the Electrical Engineering Faculty (of the Technical University of Szczecin) and the University of Rostock, Germany in 1986 and 1993 respectively. From 1978 to 1994 he was a lecturer in applied mathematics at the Szczecin Maritime Academy where since 1994 he has occupied a professor position. In 2001 he also joined the Computer Science Faculty of the Szczecin Technical University. His research interests include control and systems theory: nonlinear and optimal control, adaptive and intelligent as well as autonomous systems control techniques with applications (mainly in marine systems).

Index